HUMBER COLLEGE LIBRARY

D1544780

HUMBER COLLEGE LIBRARY
205 HUMBER COLLEGE BLVD.
P.O. BOX 1900
REXDALE, ONTARIO, CANADA
M9W 5L7

Handbook of Virtual Humans

Handbook of Virtual Humans

Edited by

N. Magnenat-Thalmann
*MIRALab, University of Geneva,
Switzerland*

D. Thalmann
VRlab, EPFL, Switzerland

160101

John Wiley & Sons, Ltd

Copyright © 2004   John Wiley & Sons Ltd, The Atrium, Southern Gate, Chichester,
West Sussex PO19 8SQ, England

Telephone   (+44) 1243 779777

Email (for orders and customer service enquiries): cs-books@wiley.co.uk
Visit our Home Page on www.wileyeurope.com or www.wiley.com

All Rights Reserved. No part of this publication may be reproduced, stored in a retrieval system or
transmitted in any form or by any means, electronic, mechanical, photocopying, recording, scanning or
otherwise, except under the terms of the Copyright, Designs and Patents Act 1988 or under the terms of
a licence issued by the Copyright Licensing Agency Ltd, 90 Tottenham Court Road, London W1T 4LP,
UK, without the permission in writing of the Publisher. Requests to the Publisher should be addressed
to the Permissions Department, John Wiley & Sons Ltd, The Atrium, Southern Gate, Chichester, West
Sussex PO19 8SQ, England, or emailed to permreq@wiley.co.uk, or faxed to (+44) 1243 770571.

This publication is designed to provide accurate and authoritative information in regard to the subject
matter covered. It is sold on the understanding that the Publisher is not engaged in rendering
professional services. If professional advice or other expert assistance is required, the services of a
competent professional should be sought.

Other Wiley Editorial Offices

John Wiley & Sons Inc., 111 River Street, Hoboken, NJ 07030, USA

Jossey-Bass, 989 Market Street, San Francisco, CA 94103-1741, USA

Wiley-VCH Verlag GmbH, Boschstr. 12, D-69469 Weinheim, Germany

John Wiley & Sons Australia Ltd, 33 Park Road, Milton, Queensland 4064, Australia

John Wiley & Sons (Asia) Pte Ltd, 2 Clementi Loop #02-01, Jin Xing Distripark, Singapore 129809

John Wiley & Sons Canada Ltd, 22 Worcester Road, Etobicoke, Ontario, Canada M9W 1L1

British Library Cataloguing in Publication Data

A catalogue record for this book is available from the British Library

ISBN 0-470-02316-3

Typeset in 10/12pt Times by Integra Software Services Pvt. Ltd, Pondicherry, India
Printed and bound in Great Britain by TJ International Ltd, Padstow, Cornwall
This book is printed on acid-free paper responsibly manufactured from sustainable forestry
in which at least two trees are planted for each one used for paper production.

Contents

Preface   xiv

List of Contributors   xv

List of Figures   xvi

List of Tables   xxiv

1 An Overview of Virtual Humans   **1**
Nadia Magnenat-Thalmann and Daniel Thalmann
1.1   Why Virtual Humans?   1
1.2   History of Virtual Humans   3
    1.2.1   Early Models   3
    1.2.2   Short Films and Demos   5
    1.2.3   The Evolution towards Real-Time   7
1.3   The Applications of Virtual Humans   8
    1.3.1   Numerous Applications   8
    1.3.2   Virtual Presenters for TV and the Web   8
    1.3.3   Virtual Assistants for Training in Case of Emergency   9
    1.3.4   Virtual Ancient People in Inhabited Virtual Cultural Heritage   11
    1.3.5   Virtual Audience for Treatment of Social Phobia   12
    1.3.6   Virtual Mannequins for Clothing   13
    1.3.7   Virtual Workers in Industrial Applications   14
    1.3.8   Virtual Actors in Computer-Generated Movies   16
    1.3.9   Virtual Characters in Video Games   18
1.4   The Challenges in Virtual Humans   20
    1.4.1   A Good Representation of Faces and Bodies   20
    1.4.2   A Flexible Motion Control   20
    1.4.3   A High-Level Behavior   21
    1.4.4   Emotional Behavior   22
    1.4.5   A Realistic Appearance   22

	1.4.6	Interacting with the Virtual World	23
	1.4.7	Interacting with the Real World	24
1.5	Conclusion		24

2 Face Cloning and Face Motion Capture   **26**
Wonsook Lee, Taro Goto, Sumedha Kshirsagar, Tom Molet
2.1	Introduction		26
2.2	Feature-Based Facial Modeling		27
	2.2.1	Facial Modeling Review and Analysis	27
	2.2.2	Generic Human Face Structure	31
	2.2.3	Photo-Cloning	32
	2.2.4	Feature Location and Shape Extraction	33
	2.2.5	Shape Modification	38
	2.2.6	Texture Mapping	39
	2.2.7	Face Cloning from Range Data	41
	2.2.8	Validation of the Face Cloning Results	41
2.3	Facial Motion Capture		46
	2.3.1	Motion Capture for Facial Animation	46
	2.3.2	MPEG-4-Based Face Capture	47
	2.3.3	Generation of Static Expressions or Key-Frames	49
	2.3.4	Analysis of Facial Capture Data to Improve Facial Animation	50

3 Body Cloning and Body Motion Capture   **52**
Pascal Fua, Ralf Plaenkers, WonSook Lee, Tom Molet
3.1	Introduction		52
3.2	Body Models for Fitting Purposes		53
	3.2.1	Stick Figure	53
	3.2.2	Simple Volumetric Primitives	53
	3.2.3	Multi-Layered Models	54
	3.2.4	Anatomically Correct Models	55
3.3	Static Shape Reconstruction		55
	3.3.1	3-D Scanners	55
	3.3.2	Finding Structure in Scattered 3-D Data	56
	3.3.3	Conforming Animatable Models to 3-D Scanned Data	57
	3.3.4	Photo-Based Shape Reconstruction	58
	3.3.5	Video-Based Shape Reconstruction	60
3.4	Dynamic Motion Capture		60
	3.4.1	Early Motion Analysis	61
	3.4.2	Electro-Magnetic and Optical Motion Capture Systems	62
	3.4.3	Video-Based Motion Capture	64
3.5	Articulated Soft Objects for Shape and Motion Estimation		67
	3.5.1	State Vector	67
	3.5.2	Metaballs and Quadratic Distance Function	68
	3.5.3	Optimization Framework	68
	3.5.4	Implementation and Results	70
3.6	Conclusion		71

4 Anthropometric Body Modeling **75**
Hyewon Seo
4.1 Introduction 75
4.2 Background 77
  4.2.1 Anthropometry 77
  4.2.2 Anthropometric Human Models in CG 81
  4.2.3 Motivating Applications 84
  4.2.4 Challenging Problems 85
4.3 Our Approaches to Anthropometric Models 86
  4.3.1 Overview 87
  4.3.2 Data Acquisition 87
  4.3.3 Pre-Processing 89
  4.3.4 Interpolator Construction 94
  4.3.5 Results and Implementation 96
4.4 Conclusion 98

5 Body Motion Control **99**
Ronan Boulic, Paolo Baerlocher
5.1 Introduction 99
5.2 State of the Art in 3-D Character Animation 101
  5.2.1 The Levels of Abstraction of the Musculo-Skeletal System 101
  5.2.2 Techniques for the Animation and the Control of the Multi-Body
    System 103
  5.2.3 What Is Motion? 104
  5.2.4 Background to Inverse Kinematics 107
  5.2.5 Review of Inverse Kinematics Resolution Methods 109
  5.2.6 Other Issues in the Production of 3-D Character Animation 112
5.3 The Multiple Priority Levels IK (MPL-IK) 113
  5.3.1 Background to Numeric IK 113
  5.3.2 Handling Two Conflicting Constraints 115
  5.3.3 Generalizing to p Priority Levels 116
5.4 MPL-IK Results 116
5.5 Conclusion 117

6 Facial Deformation Models **119**
Prem Kalra, Stephane Garchery, Sumedha Kshirsagar
6.1 Introduction 119
6.2 Some Preliminaries about the Anatomy of a Face 120
  6.2.1 Skin 120
  6.2.2 Muscles 120
  6.2.3 Bone 121
6.3 Control Parameterization 122
  6.3.1 Interpolation 122
  6.3.2 FACS (Facial Action Coding System) 122
  6.3.3 FAP (Facial Animation Parameters) 123

6.4   Facial Deformation Models   123
       6.4.1   Shape Interpolation   123
       6.4.2   Parametric Model   123
       6.4.3   Muscle-Based Models   124
       6.4.4   Finite Element Method   128
       6.4.5   Other Models   129
       6.4.6   MPEG-4-Based Facial Animation   129
6.5   Tongue, Wrinkles and Other Features   136
6.6   Summary   137
6.7   Conclusion   137

7   Body Deformations   **140**
Amaury Aubel
7.1   Surface Models   140
       7.1.1   Rigid Deformations   140
       7.1.2   Local Surface Operators   141
       7.1.3   Skinning   141
       7.1.4   Contour Deformation   142
       7.1.5   Deformations by Example   144
7.2   Volumetric Models   145
       7.2.1   Implicit Surfaces   146
       7.2.2   Collision Models   147
7.3   Multi-Layered Models   148
       7.3.1   Skeleton Layer   148
       7.3.2   Muscle Layer   148
       7.3.3   Fat Layer   155
       7.3.4   Skin Layer   155
7.4   Conclusion   158
       7.4.1   Comparative Analysis   159
       7.4.2   Depth of Simulation   159
       7.4.3   Future Research Directions   160

8   Hair Simulation   **161**
Sunil Hadap
8.1   Introduction   161
8.2   Hair Shape Modeling   162
8.3   Hair Dynamics   164
8.4   Hair Rendering   165
8.5   Summary   168
8.6   Static Hair Shape Modeling Based on Fluid Flow   169
       8.6.1   Hair Shape Model   170
       8.6.2   Interactive Hair-Styler   173
       8.6.3   Enhancing Realism   176
8.7   Modeling Hair Dynamics Based on Continuum Mechanics   178
       8.7.1   Hair as Continuum   179
       8.7.2   Single Hair Dynamics   182

8.7.3	*Fluid Hair Model*	185
8.7.4	*Results*	189
8.8	Conclusion	190

9 Cloth Simulation   **192**
Pascal Volino, Frédéric Cordier

9.1	Introduction	192
9.2	Technology Summary	193
	9.2.1 *Historical Review*	193
	9.2.2 *Cloth Mechanics*	193
9.3	Mechanical Simulation of Cloth	198
	9.3.1 *Mechanical Modeling Schemes*	199
	9.3.2 *A Precise Particle-Based Surface Representation*	204
	9.3.3 *Numerical Integration*	207
9.4	Collision Techniques	211
	9.4.1 *Principles of Collision Detection*	212
	9.4.2 *Collision Detection for Cloth Simulation*	213
	9.4.3 *Collisions on Polygonal Meshes*	215
	9.4.4 *Collision Response Schemes*	216
9.5	Enhancing Garments	220
	9.5.1 *Mesh Smoothing*	220
	9.5.2 *Geometrical Wrinkles*	222
	9.5.3 *Advanced Fabric Lighting*	223
	9.5.4 *Toward Real-Time Garment Animation*	224
9.6	Designing Garments	226
	9.6.1 *Garment Design Tools*	227
	9.6.2 *Applications*	228
9.7	Conclusion	229

10 Expressive Speech Animation and Facial Communication   **230**
Sumedha Kshirsagar, Arjan Egges, Stéphane Garchery

10.1	Introduction	230
10.2	Background and Review	231
10.3	Facial Animation Design	231
10.4	Parameterization	233
10.5	High Level Control of Animation	234
10.6	Speech Animation	238
	10.6.1 *Using Text-to-Speech*	238
	10.6.2 *Phoneme Extraction from Natural Speech*	239
	10.6.3 *Co-articulation*	242
	10.6.4 *Expression Blending*	243
	10.6.5 *Enhancing Realism*	244
10.7	Facial Motion Capture and Analysis	245
	10.7.1 *Data Analysis*	245
	10.7.2 *Principal Component Analysis*	246
	10.7.3 *Contribution of Principal Components*	247

	10.7.4	*Nature of Analysis Data and the PCs*	250
	10.7.5	*Expression Blending Using PCs*	250
10.8	Facial Communication		252
	10.8.1	*Dialogue Generation*	253
	10.8.2	*Natural Language Processing and Generation*	255
	10.8.3	*Emotions*	255
	10.8.4	*Personality and Mood*	256
10.9	Putting It All Together		258
10.10	Conclusion		259

11 Behavioral Animation   **260**

Jean-Sébastien Monzani, Anthony Guye-Vuilleme, Etienne de Sevin

11.1	What Is Behavioral Animation?		260
	11.1.1	*Behavior*	261
	11.1.2	*Autonomy*	262
11.2	State-of-the-Art		262
	11.2.1	*Perception and Memory*	262
	11.2.2	*Defining Behaviors*	264
	11.2.3	*Interactions*	267
	11.2.4	*Animation*	268
	11.2.5	*Applications*	268
11.3	An Architecture for Behavioral Animation		269
	11.3.1	*Separate the Body and the Brain*	269
	11.3.2	*System Design*	270
	11.3.3	*Animation: A Layered Approach*	273
	11.3.4	*Intelligent Virtual Agent: Simulating Autonomous Behavior*	276
11.4	Behavioral Animation and Social Agents		277
11.5	Case Study		279
	11.5.1	*Storytelling*	279
	11.5.2	*A Mechanism of Motivated Action Selection*	281
11.6	Conclusion		285

12 Body Gesture Recognition and Action Response   **287**

Luc Emering, Bruno Herbelin

12.1	Introduction: Reality vs Virtuality		287
12.2	State-of-the-Art		289
12.3	Involved Technology		289
12.4	Action Recognition		289
	12.4.1	*Recognition Methods*	289
	12.4.2	*Model vs Data-Oriented*	291
	12.4.3	*Recognizable Actions*	293
	12.4.4	*Action-Analysis Levels*	294
	12.4.5	*Action Specification*	295
	12.4.6	*Action Recognition Algorithm*	297

12.5   Case Studies   298
        12.5.1   Interactive Fighting   300
12.6   Discussion   300
        12.6.1   Sense of Touching   300
        12.6.2   Reactivity   301
        12.6.3   Objective and Subjective Views   301
        12.6.4   Embodiment   301
        12.6.5   System Performance   301
        12.6.6   Delegate Sub-Tasks   301
        12.6.7   Semantic Modulation   302
        12.6.8   Event/Action Associations   302
        12.6.9   Realistic Behavior   302
        12.6.10   Verbal Response   302

13   Interaction with 3-D Objects   **303**
Marcello Kallmann
13.1   Introduction   303
13.2   Related Work   304
        13.2.1   Object Functionality   305
        13.2.2   Actor Animation   305
13.3   Smart Objects   307
        13.3.1   Interaction Features   307
        13.3.2   Interpreting Interaction Features   309
13.4   SOMOD   310
        13.4.1   Object Properties   310
        13.4.2   Interaction Information   310
        13.4.3   Behaviors   312
13.5   Interacting with Smart Objects   314
        13.5.1   Interpretation of Plans   314
        13.5.2   Manipulation Actions   315
13.6   Case Studies   317
        13.6.1   Opening a Drawer   318
        13.6.2   Interaction of Multiple Actors   319
        13.6.3   Complex Behaviors   320
13.7   Remaining Problems   321

14   Groups and Crowd Simulation   **323**
Soraia Raupp Musse, Branislav Ulicny, Amaury Aubel
14.1   Introduction   323
        14.1.1   Structure of this Chapter   324
14.2   Related Work   324
        14.2.1   Crowd Evacuation Simulators   325
        14.2.2   Crowd Management Training Systems   327
        14.2.3   Sociological Models   328
        14.2.4   Computer Graphics   329
        14.2.5   Classification of Crowd Methods   330

14.3   A Hierarchical Approach to Model Crowds   333
    14.3.1   Hierarchic Model   333
    14.3.2   Emergent Crowds   335
14.4   Crowd Visualization   338
    14.4.1   Virtual Human Model   338
    14.4.2   Crowd Creation   338
    14.4.3   Level of Detail   339
    14.4.4   Animated Impostors   339
    14.4.5   Impostor Rendering and Texture Generation   340
    14.4.6   Texture Refreshment Approach   342
    14.4.7   Visibility Issue   343
    14.4.8   Factored Impostor   344
    14.4.9   Z-Buffer Corrected Impostor   345
    14.4.10   Results   346
14.5   Case Studies   346
    14.5.1   Programmed Crowds   346
    14.5.2   Guided Crowds   348
    14.5.3   Autonomous Crowds   349
    14.5.4   Interactive Crowd in Panic Situation   350
14.6   Conclusion   351

15   Rendering of Skin and Clothes   **353**
Neeharika Adabala
15.1   Introduction   353
15.2   Rendering of Skin   354
    15.2.1   Texturing   354
    15.2.2   Illumination Models   356
    15.2.3   Interaction with the Environment   358
    15.2.4   Temporal Features   358
    15.2.5   Summary of Skin Rendering Techniques   360
15.3   Rendering of Clothes   361
    15.3.1   Modeling Color Variation from Images   362
    15.3.2   Illumination Models   362
    15.3.3   Representation of Milli-Geometry   364
    15.3.4   Rendering with Micro/Milli Geometric Detail and BRDF for
            Woven Clothes   365
    15.3.5   Macro-geometry and Interaction with the Environment   370
15.4   Conclusion   372

16   Standards for Virtual Humans   **373**
Stéphane Garchery, Ronan Boulic, Tolga Capin, Prem Kalra
16.1   Introduction   373
16.2   The H-Anim Specification Scheme   373
    16.2.1   The Need for a Standard Human Skeleton   373
    16.2.2   H-Anim Skeleton Convention   374

Contents

	16.2.3	*Benefits and Limitations of the Standard Skeleton*	375
	16.2.4	*Enforcing Motion Re-use*	376
16.3	The MPEG-4 FBA Standard	379
	16.3.1	*MPEG-4 Body Animation Standard*	380
	16.3.2	*MPEG-4 Face Animation Standard*	383
16.4	What's Next?	391

Appendix A: Damped Least Square Pseudo-Inverse $J^{+\lambda}$ 392

Appendix B: H-Anim Joint and Segment Topology 393

Appendix C: Facial Animation Parameter Set 396

References 400

Index 437

Preface

Scenes involving Virtual Humans imply many complex problems that researchers have been trying to solve for more than 20 years. Today, everyone would like to simulate or interact with believable Virtual Humans in various situations as in games, films, interactive television, cultural heritage or web-based situations. The field of applications is enormous and there is still a long way to go to achieve the goal of having realistic Virtual Humans who adapt their behavior to any real human interaction and real-life situation.

This book contains fundamental research in Virtual Human technology. It provides a state-of-the-art in face and body modeling and cloning, facial and body animation, hair simulation, clothing, image-based rendering, crowd simulation, autonomous behavioral animation etc. More than a dozen of the PhDs from both MIRALab, University of Geneva, and VRlab, EPFL, Switzerland, have contributed to this book. They have described their recent work taking into account the state-of-the-art in their field.

We would like to thank a few people who have helped the production of this book by editing the manuscript: Professor Prem Kalra from the Indian Institute of Technology and Dr. Chris Joslin from MIRALab. We would like to thank Mrs. Zerrin Celebi from VRlab for her editorial assistance. We are also very grateful to the John Wiley editors, particularly Ms. Laura Kempster, who have been very helpful in the production of this book.

As an extra resource we have set up a companion website for our title containing short movies and demos illustrating all Chapters. Please use the following URL to access the site:http://vrlab.epfl.ch/HandbookVHumans

Nadia Magnenat-Thalmann
Daniel Thalmann

List of Contributors

Nadia Magnenat-Thalmann and Daniel Thalmann

Wonsook Lee, Taro Goto, Sumedha Kshirsagar, Tom Molet

Pascal Fua, Ralf Plaenkers, WonSook Lee, Tom Molet

Hyewon Seo

Ronan Boulic, Paolo Baerlocher

Prem Kalra, Stephane Garchery, Sumedha Kshirsagar

Amaury Aubel

Sunil Hadap

Pascal Volino, Frédéric Cordier

Sumedha Kshirsagar, Arjan Egges, Stéphane Garchery

Jean-Sébastien Monzani, Anthony Guye-Vuilleme, Etienne de Sevin

Luc Emering, Bruno Herbelin

Marcello Kallmann

Soraia Raupp Musse, Branislav Ulicny, Amaury Aubel

Neeharika Adabala

Stéphane Garchery, Ronan Boulic, Tolga Capin, Prem Kalra

List of Figures

1.1   Representation of the head and face by Fred Parke, University of Utah, 1974.   4

1.2   Adam the Juggler created by Triple I, 1982.   5

1.3   Virtual Marilyn in 'Rendez-vous in Montreal' by Nadia Magnenat-Thalmann and Daniel Thalmann, 1987.   6

1.4   Real-time Virtual Marilyn as referee in a Virtual Tennis match.   7

1.5   JUST immersive VR situation training of health emergency personnel.   10

1.6   Virtual Terracotta soldiers in Xian.   11

1.7   Capturing the motion for the Namaz prayer.   12

1.8   Revival of life in Pompeii.   12

1.9   Virtual classroom for assessment and treatment of childhood disorders.   13

1.10   Virtual Clothing in Salon Lanvin.   14

1.11   Virtual Clothing in Musée Picasso.   15

1.12   Training in industrial applications.   16

1.13   Lara Croft.   19

2.1   (a) Three images of an uncalibrated video-sequence. (b) The reconstructed 3-D model.   30

2.2   Control points and the generic model.   31

2.3   Overflow of face and body photo-cloning.   32

2.4   Automatic 3-D facial feature detection flow.   35

2.5   Distribution graph of features.   35

2.6   Distribution graph of each feature's distance.   36

2.7   (a) Detected features. (b) Modification of a generic head with feature points.   40

2.8   (a) A geometrical deformation for the side views to connect to the front view. (b) before and after multi-resolution techniques.   40

2.9   Snapshots of a reconstructed head in several views and animation on the face.   41

2.10   (a) Input range data. (b) Delaunay triangles created with feature points and points collected for fine modification using Delaunay triangles. (c) The result of giving functional structure on a range data.   42

2.11   (a) Snapshots taken from the same angles.   43

2.12   Two surfaces in different colours in the same space.   43

2.13   2-D case to show the calculation of the distance for each point on the reconstructed curve to the original input curve by calculating the normal vector.   44

2.14   2-D case to get error percentage between 2-D curves.   44

2.15   Error distribution for the face cloning from orthogonal photograph where the bounding box of the head has the size $167.2 \times 236.651 \times 171.379$.   45

2.16   Points with error bigger than (a) 15 (b) 10 and (c) 5.   45

2.17   Use of OPTOTRAK™ for head and facial motion data.   47

2.18   Feature points optical tracking.   47

2.19   MPEG-4 feature points.   48

2.20   Successive feature point displacements from a speech sequence (without global motion compensation).   49

2.21   Facial captured expressions applied on various face models.   50

3.1   Layered body model: (a) Skeleton. (b) Volumetric primitives used to simulate muscles and fat tissue. (c) Polygonal surface representation of the skin. (d) Shaded rendering. (e) A cow and a horse modeled using the same technique.   54

3.2   (a) Cyberware Whole Body Color 3-D Scanner. (b) Polhemus mobile laser scanner. (c) Resulting 3-D model.   56

3.3   Scan of a human subject. (a) Its associated axial structure and (b) a similar scan of a different subject and the animated skeleton obtained by fitting our model to the data.   57

3.4   Five input photographs of a woman, Reconstructed 3-D body.   59

3.5   Comparison of measurement on the actual body and reconstructed body.   59

3.6   How do horses trot?   61

3.7   Eadweard Muybridge's photographic analysis of human and animal motion.   62

3.8   Magnetic (a) and optical (b) motion capture systems.   63

3.9   The importance of silhouette information for shape modeling. (a) One image from a stereo pair. (b) Corresponding disparity map. (c) Fitting the model to stereo data alone results in a recovered body model that is too far away from the cloud. (d) Using these outlines to constrain the reconstruction results in a more accurate model. (e) Only the dashed line is a valid silhouette that satisfies both criteria of section 2-D Silhouette Observations.   69

3.10   Results using a trinocular sequence in which the subject performs complex 3-D motions with his arms, so that they occlude each other.   72

3.11   Results using another trinocular sequence in which the subject moves his upper body in addition to abruptly waving his arms.   73

4.1   Leonardo da Vinci, a Renaissance artist, created the drawing of the Vitruvian Man based on the 'ideal proportions'.   76

4.2   Anthropometric landmarks (feature points) in H-Anim 1.1 specification.   78

4.3   Automatic measurement extractions from the scan data (Cyberware).   81

4.4   Anthropometric models for 'Jack'.   82

4.5   Automatically generated 'Anthroface' models.   83

4.6   Geometrical deformation methods for differently sized body models.   84

4.7   Overview of the system.   88

4.8   A scanned model example.   89

4.9   The template model.   90

4.10   Feature points used in our system.   91

4.11   Skeleton fitting procedure.   93

4.12   Skeleton fitting.   93

4.13   Fine fitting.   95

4.14	Result models.	97
4.15	Cross-validation result.	98
5.1	The realism assessment seen from the point of view of the application field.	100
5.2	Levels of abstraction of the musculo-skeletal system.	101
5.3	Influence of the posture on the action of a muscle through its line of action.	102
5.4	Two priority levels IK achieved with the cascaded control.	106
5.5	The two chain tips have to reach conflicting positions in space, the solution provided by the weight strategy is a compromise while the solution provided by the priority strategy favors the right chain tip.	108
5.6	Overview of the animation production pipeline.	112
5.7	Simplest redundant case.	113
5.8	The variation space with the minimal norm solution (a) and (b) the final solution including a lower priority task projected on the kernel of J (noted N(J)).	114
5.9	The simplest redundant case with two conflicting tasks.	115
5.10	The low level task is first compensated prior to the mapping.	115
5.11	Interactive optimization with four priority levels.	117
6.1	Frontal view of facial muscles.	121
6.2	Muscle types.	125
6.3	Three-layered structure.	126
6.4	Rational free form deformation.	127
6.5	Computing weights for animation.	131
6.6	Facial deformation based on FAPs.	134
6.7	Automatic process for designing FAT with an MPEG-4 face model.	135
6.8	Process for designing FAT construction by experienced animator's work.	135
6.9	Artistic MPEG-4 FAP high-level expressions.	136
7.1	Marilyn's skin is deformed by JLDs.	141
7.2	Characteristic defects of the skinning algorithm.	143
7.3	Arm deformation with cross-sections.	143
7.4	Comparison on shoulder deformation between the skinning algorithm (top row) and the Pose Space Deformation algorithm (Wyvill et al. 1998). (bottom row) using two extreme key-shapes.	144
7.5	Shape blending of various laser scans of a real person using a template subdivision surface.	144
7.6	Hand modeled with convolution surfaces.	146
7.7	Leg deformation including contact surface using FEM.	147
7.8	The material depth (encoded in psuedo-color) is used for computing the contact surface when the knee is bent.	148
7.9	Hand deformation based on Dirichlet FFDs.	149
7.10	Leg muscles mimicked by deforming metaballs.	149
7.11	Anatomically-based modeling of the human musculature using ellipsoids.	150
7.12	Isotonic contraction of the arm muscles followed by an isometric contraction when the hand is clenched into a fist.	151
7.13	A deformed-cylinder muscle model.	152
7.14	Leg muscles – reconstructed from anatomical data – are deformed by action lines and muscle interaction.	152

7.15 Each muscle is parameterized and deformed by a set of centroid curves (action lines). 153

7.16 Finite element model of the leg. 154

7.17 Layers in LEMAN. 155

7.18 Skin extraction by voxelizing the inner layers in a rest pose. 156

7.19 The layered model by Shen and Thalmann (1996). Ellipsoidal primitives (b) form an implicit surface, which is sampled by a ray-casting process. The sampling points (c) are used as control points of B-spline patches. The B-spline surface is ultimately polygonized at the desired resolution (d and e). 157

7.20 Three frames of the monkey shoulder animation by Wilhelms and Van Gelder. 158

7.21 Elastic skin that slides over the underlying surfaces. 158

7.22 The skin buckles and creases in the work of Hirota et al.. 158

8.1 Hairstyling by defining a few curves in 3-D. 162

8.2 Cluster hair model, by Yang et al.. 163

8.3 Hair model based on fluid flow paradigm. 164

8.4 Hair animation using the explicit model, by Kurihara. 165

8.5 Volumetric texture rendering by Kajiya and Kay (1989). 166

8.6 Rendering the pipeline of the method- 'pixel blending and shadow buffer'. 167

8.7 Fur using explicit hair model. 168

8.8 Modeling hair as streamlines of a fluid flow. 169

8.9 Ideal flow elements. 170

8.10 Linear combination of ideal flow elements. 171

8.11 Source panel method. 172

8.12 Subdivision scheme for ideal flow. 173

8.13 Polygon reduced geometry to define panels. 174

8.14 Hair growth map and normal velocity map. 174

8.15 Placing panel sources. 174

8.16 Simple hairstyles using few fluid elements. 175

8.17 Hair as a complex fluid flow. 176

8.18 Adding perturbations to a few individual hairs. 176

8.19 Adding overall volumetric perturbations. 177

8.20 Hair clumpiness. 177

8.21 Possibilities for enhancing realism. 178

8.22 Hair as a continuum. 180

8.23 Equation of State. 181

8.24 Hair strand as an oriented particle system. 182

8.25 Hair strand as rigid multibody serial chain. 184

8.26 Fluid dynamics: Eulerian and Lagrangian viewpoints. 186

8.27 Hair animation. 190

9.1 Early models of dressed virtual characters. 194

9.2 Different woven fabric patterns: plain, twirl, basket, satin. 195

9.3 A mechanical simulation carried out with particle systems and continuum mechanics. 200

9.4 Using lengths or angles to measure deformations in a square particle system grid. 204

9.5 Computing deformations in a fabric triangle. 206

9.6	Computing vertex forces for elongation, shear, bending.	206
9.7	Automatic hierarchization of a 50000 triangle object.	214
9.8	Using direction or bounding volumes to detect collisions within and between nodes, and propagation of the direction volumes up the hierarchy tree.	215
9.9	Hierarchical collision detection at work, showing the hierarchy domains tested.	216
9.10	Intersections and proximities in polygonal meshes.	216
9.11	Repartition of collision response on the vertices of a mesh element.	218
9.12	Combined corrections of position, speed and acceleration.	219
9.13	A rough sphere model with no smoothing, Gouraud, and Phong shading.	221
9.14	Polygon smoothing: Interpolation, vertex contribution and blending.	221
9.15	Smoothing the rough mesh of a coat, with texture mapping.	222
9.16	Dynamic amplitude variation of geometrical wrinkles, with respect to elongation and orientation.	223
9.17	An animated dress, mechanically computed as a rough mesh, and dynamically wrinkled according to the mesh deformation.	223
9.18	Enclosing cloth particles into spheres of dynamic radius resulting from the modeling of a catenary curve.	225
9.19	Building a real-time garment.	226
9.20	A typical framework for garment design, simulation and animation system.	227
9.21	Designing garments: pattern placement and seaming.	228
9.22	Simulating garments: draping and animation.	228
9.23	Fashion design: simulating animated fashion models.	229
9.24	Complex virtual garments.	229
10.1	Facial communication: a broad look.	232
10.2	Hierarchy of facial animation design.	233
10.3	Levels of parameterization.	233
10.4	Various envelopes for key-frame animation.	235
10.5	FAML syntax.	236
10.6	Example of expression track.	237
10.7	Interactive design of facial animation.	237
10.8	Typical speech animation system.	238
10.9	Two approaches to speech-driven facial animation.	240
10.10	Real-time phoneme extraction for speech animation.	241
10.11	Dominance functions for co-articulation.	243
10.12	FAP composition problem and solution.	243
10.13	Placement of cameras and facial markers.	245
10.14	Influence of first six principal components.	249
10.15	Generation of 'happy' speech in PC space.	251
10.16	Generation of 'sad' speech in PC space.	251
10.17	Speech animation using expression and viseme space.	251
10.18	Emotions-moods-personality layers.	257
10.19	Autonomous emotional dialogue system.	259
11.1	Results of Tyrrell's test.	266
11.2	Low and high level components in the system.	270
11.3	Snapshot of the Agents' Common Environment.	271

11.4   Verbal communication between two IVAs has to go through the low level.   273
11.5   Example callback for a walking task.   274
11.6   Reactivated tasks – Task stack for the walking tasks.   275
11.7   The Tasks Handler.   276
11.8   Inter-agent communication: the Secretary is talking to the Editor.   280
11.9   Simplified motivational model of action selection for Virtual Humans.   282
11.10   'Subjective' evaluation of the motivations (solid curve) from the value
         of the internal variables (dashed line) with a threshold system.   282
11.11   A part of the hierarchical decision graph for the *eat* motivation.   283
11.12   Results of the simulation in terms of achieved behaviors.   284
11.13   Virtual life simulation: by default.   285
12.1   MAI Box: Manipulation, Activity and Impact.   288
12.2   Overview of the VR immersive devices.   290
12.3   Model-oriented simulation system.   292
12.4   Data-oriented simulation system.   292
12.5   Decoding human walking with minimal body references.   294
12.6   Global, floor and body-coordinate systems.   295
12.7   A database of pre-defined postures.   296
12.8   Compromise between recognition data quantity and data analysis costs.   298
12.9   Interactive walk-through environment driven by action recognition events.   299
12.10   The virtual shop.   299
12.11   Interactive fight training with a virtual teacher.   300
13.1   The choice of which interaction features to take into account is directly
         related to many implementation issues in the simulation system.   309
13.2   Defining the specific parameters of a drawer.   310
13.3   Positions can be defined for different purposes.   311
13.4   The left image shows a hand shape being interactively defined. The
         right image shows all used hand shapes being interactively located with
         manipulators.   311
13.5   Defining interaction plans.   313
13.6   For each actor performing an interaction with an object, a thread is used to
         interpret the selected interaction plan.   314
13.7   Considered phases for a manipulation instruction.   315
13.8   Specific constraints are used to keep the actor's spine as straight as possible.   316
13.9   When the position to reach with the hand is too low, additional constraints
         are used in order to obtain knee flexion.   317
13.10   The reaching phase of a button press manipulation.   318
13.11   A state machine for a two-stage lift functionality.   321
13.12   A state machine considering intermediate states.   321
14.1   Helbing's crowd dynamics simulation.   325
14.2   EXODUS evacuation simulator (Exodus).   326
14.3   Simulex, crowd evacuation system.   327
14.4   Legion system, analysis of Sydney stadium.   328
14.5   Small Unit Leader Non-Lethal Training System.   329
14.6   Reynolds's flock of boids.   330
14.7   Bouvier's particle systems crowd.   331

14.8   Hodgins's simulation of a group of bicyclists.   331
14.9   Hierarchical structure of the model.   334
14.10   Autonomous crowd entry at the train station.   335
14.11   A person enters the interaction space, the virtual people react.   336
14.12   Emergent crowds.   337
14.13   Body meshes of decreasing complexity using B-spline surfaces.   340
14.14   A football player and its impostor.   341
14.15   Impostor rendering and texture generation.   342
14.16   Posture variation.   343
14.17   Virtual Human decomposed into several planes.   344
14.18   Actual geometry (a), single quadrilateral (b), multi-plane impostor (c),
         and factored impostor (d).   344
14.19   Actors performing a 'wave' motion.   346
14.20   Image of football stadium showing regions specified to place the crowd
         at the beginning of the simulation as well as the surfaces to be respected
         when agents pass through the doors.   347
14.21   Image of the simulation 'The Crowd goes to the Football Stadium'.   348
14.22   Image of simulation 'Populating the Virtual City with Crowds'.   348
14.23   Image of an autonomous crowd in a train station.   349
14.24   Crowd reacting as a function of actors' performance.   349
14.25   Images show the grouping of individuals at the political demonstration.   350
14.26   Agents at the train station.   350
14.27   Crowd in the virtual park: (a) before emergency, (b) after gas leak.   351
15.1   Process of facial simulation and wrinkle generation.   359
15.2   Wrinkle generation with real-time system.   360
15.3   Demonstration of visualization of aging with realistic rendering of
         wrinkles.   360
15.4   Artifact due to illumination.   362
15.5   Rendering of cloth with color texture and bump mapping (b) gives a
         zoomed in view of (a).   363
15.6   Outline of algorithm.   366
15.7   Example color scheme of a weave pattern.   366
15.8   Output of procedural texture (a) Very loosely twisted thread without shading.
         (b) More tightly twisted thread, noise is added to simulate the presence
         of fibers about the thread. (c) Thicker fibers twisted into thread. (d) Tightly
         twisted thread.   367
15.9   Example of color texture generated for the color scheme component in the
         tiled texture of cloth from photograph.   368
15.10   Versatility of the approach for generation of various weaves.   369
15.11   Directional dependence of the appearance of cloth when contrasting colored
         threads are woven together.   370
15.12   Illustration of ability to zoom in on detail.   371
16.1   Topologic relationships between the JOINT, SEGMENT and SITE node
         types.   374
16.2   Two H-Anim compliant characters.   377
16.3   Types of rotation distribution (for tilt, roll and torsion) over the three spine
         regions.   378

16.4   Three orthogonal projections (front, side and back) of various instants of a
       walking cycle (note the orientation of the pelvis and the vertebrae 'slices').   378
16.5   Facial Animation Parameter Units (FΛPU) and their definition.   385
16.6   Feature definition point set.   386
16.7   Six primary facial expressions.   389
16.8   Piecewise linear approximation of vertex trajectory.   389
A.1   Default posture and HUMANOID frame.   393

List of Tables

2.1 Possible ways to get a virtually cloned face. 29
2.2 Typical ways to get range data. 30
2.3 Comparison between photographs and laser scanner. 31
4.1 Important landmark terms and definitions. 79
4.2 Measurement definitions. 86
5.1 End effector tasks with their rank. 117
6.1 Facial deformation models: a comparative analysis. 138
8.1 Comparison of the various hair models. 168
9.1 Typical values of elastic mechanical properties of polyester fabric. 197
9.2 Some values for common fabrics. 198
10.1 Eigenvalues and percentage contribution. 248
10.2 Basic emotions. 256
10.3 Five personality dimensions. 257
12.1 Gesture specification. 296
13.1 Comparison of motion control methods. 307
13.2 The eight types of interaction features used in the smart object description. 308
13.3 Code for interactions of opening and closing a drawer. 318
13.4 How state variables are used to synchronize multiple actors. 319
14.1 Various behavioral approaches. 332
14.2 Characteristics of different types of crowd control. 333
15.1 Comparison of skin rendering techniques. 361
16.1 Animation classification with respect to spatial constraints and re-use potential. 376
16.2 Expressions of the coefficients C_i for a spine region containing n joints, indexed by i, varying from 1 (pelvis side) to n (skull side). 377
16.3 BodyDefTable content. 381
16.4 BAP groups. 383
16.5 Facial Animation Parameter Units (FAPU) and their definition. 385
16.6 FAP groups. 387
16.7 Textual description of the six basic facial expressions. 388
C.1 Facial Animation Parameter set. 396

1

An Overview of Virtual Humans

Nadia Magnenat Thalmann and Daniel Thalmann

Virtual Humans simulations are becoming more and more popular. Nowadays many systems are available to animate Virtual Humans. Such systems encompass several different domains: autonomous agents in Virtual Environments, human factors analysis, training, education, virtual prototyping, simulation-based design, and entertainment. Virtual Humans are commonly used nowadays in the entertainment industry, and most specifically in movies and video games. If the quality of pictures has been dramatically improved during the last years, the animation is still a major bottleneck in production. In this chapter, we first emphasize the role of Virtual Humans, then we present a history and the numerous applications of Virtual Humans. We conclude with a presentation of the main challenges of Virtual Humans that are discussed in this book.

1.1 Why Virtual Humans?

Today's cutting-edge technology in Virtual Environments offers a number of tools, where, rather than trying to describe an inaccessible building or structure using words, sketches, or pictures, the entire scene can be reconstructed in three dimensions and viewed from various angles and view points. Virtual Reality techniques have introduced a wide range of new methods and metaphors of interaction with these Virtual Environments.

Virtual Environments are generally composed of static and dynamic virtual entities and may include 3-D graphics objects, 3-D sounds, images, and videos. However, most of these Virtual Environments display static 3-D architectural models that can be navigated in real time in a passive manner and offer little for actual exploration, interaction and participation. Active engagement and participation require human interaction and communication between the user and the people of the era of the site. This demands virtual embodiments of the participant and the people. Inside these Virtual Environments, Virtual Humans are the key technology that can provide virtual presenters, virtual guides, virtual actors, and be used to show how humans should act in various situations. Scenes involving Virtual Humans involve many complex problems that researchers have been solving for several years. With the new developments of digital and interactive television and multimedia products, there is

Handbook of Virtual Humans Edited by N. Magnenat-Thalmann and D. Thalmann
© 2004 John Wiley & Sons, Ltd   ISBN: 0-470-02316-3

also a need for systems that provide designers with the ability to embed real-time simulated humans in games, multimedia titles and film animations.

The ultimate research objective is the simulation of Virtual Worlds inhabited by a Virtual Human Society, where Virtual Humans will co-operate, negotiate, make friends, communicate, group and break up, depending on their likes, moods, emotions, goals, fears, etc. But such interaction and corresponding groups should not be programmed. Behavior should emerge as a result of a multi-agent system sharing a common environment, in our case, sharing a Virtual Environment. For example, in a panic situation, we do not model group behavior, because each human reacts differently depending, for example, on his/her level of fear. If we model the individual entity, there will be groups of different behaviors (not programmed explicitly) as a result of the interaction of common individual behaviors. Simulations consist of groups of autonomous Virtual Human agents existing in dynamic 3-D Virtual Environments. Virtual Humans have some natural needs like hunger, tiredness, etc. which guide the choice of their behavior. In order to behave in a believable way, these agents also have to act in accordance with their surrounding environment, be able to react to its changes, to the other agents and also to the actions of real humans interacting with the virtual world. Behavior models should be developed that are simple enough to allow for real-time execution of a group of agents, yet still sufficiently complex to provide interesting behaviors. Virtual Humans have their own motivations and needs, are able to sense and explore their environment, and their action selection mechanism determines suitable actions to take at any time. For this purpose, architecture allowing merging of individuals' artificial life simulation with the current multi-agent model is being developed.

One important point in the simulation is the believability of the individual Virtual Humans; they should behave like real humans, including abilities such as: perception, language understanding and generation, emotions, goal-driven behavior, reactivity to the environment including with other Virtual Humans, memory, inference, appearance of thought and personalities, interpersonal interactions, social skills and possibly others.

Virtual Humans in a society require four main elements:

1. High-level behavior, which concerns decision-making and intelligence, motivation, and social behavior.
2. Perception: virtual sensors (for Virtual Worlds) and real sensors (for Real Worlds).
3. Animation: flexible motion control.
4. Graphics: realistic aspect including skin, hair, and clothes.

We can identify many areas where autonomous Virtual Humans are essential. Before discussing several types of applications in Section 1.3, where Virtual Humans are involved, we can cite the three main 'applications'.

- *Virtual people for inhabited Virtual Environments.* Their role is very important in Virtual Environments with many people, such as virtual airports or even virtual cities. In the next few years, we will see a lot of Virtual Humans in many applications. These Virtual Humans will be more and more autonomous. They will also tend to become intelligent.
- *Virtual substitutes.* A virtual substitute is an intelligent computer-generated agent able to act instead of the real person and on behalf of this person on the network. The virtual substitute has the voice of the real person and his or her appearance. S/he will appear on the screen of the workstation/TV, communicate with people, and have pre-defined behaviors planned by the owner to answer the requests of other people.

- *Virtual medical assistance*. Nowadays, it is difficult to imagine an effective solution for chronic care without including the remote care of patients at home by a kind of Virtual Medical Doctor. The modeling of a virtual patient with correspondence to medical images is also a key issue and a basis for telesurgery.

Mainly, telepresence is the future of multimedia systems and will allow participants to share professional and private experiences, meetings, games, and parties. Virtual Humans have a key role to play in these shared Virtual Environments and true interaction with them is a great challenge. Although a lot of research has been going on in the field of Networked Virtual Environments, most of the existing systems still use simple embodiments (avatars) for the representation of participants in the environments. More complex Virtual Human embodiment increases the natural interaction within the environment. The users' more natural perception of each other (and of autonomous actors) increases their sense of being together, and thus the overall sense of shared presence in the environment.

1.2 History of Virtual Humans

1.2.1 Early Models

Ergonomic analysis provided some of the earliest applications in computer graphics for modeling a human figure and its motion. One of the earliest figures used for ergonomic analysis was William Fetter's Landing Signal Officer (LSO), developed for Boeing in 1959 (Fetter 1982). The seven jointed 'First Man', used for studying the instrument panel of a Boeing 747, enabled many pilot actions to be displayed by articulating the figure's pelvis, neck, shoulders, and elbows. Possibly the first use of computer graphics in commercial advertising took place in 1970 when this figure was used for a Norelco television commercial. The addition of twelve extra joints to 'First Man' produced 'Second Man'. This figure was used to generate a set of animation film sequences based on a series of photographs produced by Muybridge (1955). 'Third Man and Woman' was a hierarchical figure series with each figure differing by an order of magnitude in complexity. These figures were used for general ergonomic studies. The most complex figure had 1000 points and was displayed with lines to represent the contours of the body. In 1977, Fetter produced 'Fourth Man and Woman' figures based on data from biostereometric tapes. These figures could be displayed as a series of colored polygons on raster devices.

Cyberman (Cybernetic man-model) was developed by Chrysler Corporation for modeling human activity in and around a car (Blakeley 1980). Although he was created to study the position and motion of car drivers, there was no check to determine whether his motions were realistic and the user was responsible for determining the comfort and feasibility of the position after each operation. It is based on 15 joints; the position of the observer is pre-defined.

Combiman (Computerized biomechanical man-model) was specifically designed to test how easily a human can reach objects in a cockpit (Evans 1976). Motions have to be realistic and the human can be chosen at any percentile from among three-dimensional human models. The vision system is very limited. Combiman is defined using a 35 internal-link skeletal system. Although the system indicated success or failure with each reach operation, the operator was required to determine the amount of clearance (or distance remaining to the goal).

Boeman was designed in 1969 by the Boeing Corporation ((Dooley 1982). It is based on a 50th-percentile three-dimensional human model. He can reach for objects like baskets but a mathematical description of the object and the tasks is assumed. Collisions are detected during Boeman's tasks and visual interferences are identified. Boeman is built as a 23-joint figure with variable link lengths.

Sammie (*S*ystem for *A*iding *M*an *M*achine *I*nteraction *E*valuation) was designed in 1972 at the University of Nottingham for general ergonometric design and analysis (Bonney et al. 1972). This was, so far, the best parameterized human model and it presents a choice of physical types: slim, fat, muscled, etc. The vision system was very developed and complex objects can be manipulated by Sammie, based on 21 rigid links with 17 joints. The user defined the environment by either building objects from simple primitives, or by defining the vertices and edges of irregular shaped objects. The human model was based on a measurement survey of a general population group.

Buford was developed at Rockwell International in Downey, California, to find reach and clearance areas around a model positioned by the operator (Dooley 1982). The figure represented a 50th-percentile human model and was covered by CAD-generated polygons. The user could interactively design the environment and change the body position and limb sizes. However, repositioning the model was done by individually moving the body and limb segments. He has some difficulty in moving and has no vision system. Buford is composed of 15 independent links that must be redefined at each modification.

In 1971 Parke produced a representation of the head and face in the University of Utah, and three years later achieved advances in good enough parametric models to produce a much more realistic face (Parke 1974). Figure 1.1 shows an example.

Another popular approach was based on volume primitives. Several kinds of elementary volumes have been used to create such models, e.g. cylinders by Poter and Willmert (1975) or ellipsoids by Herbison-Evans (1986). Designed by N. Badler et al. of the University of Pennsylvania (1979), Bubbleman is a three-dimensional human figure consisting of a number of spheres or bubbles. The model is based on overlap of spheres, and the appearance (intensity and size) of the spheres varies depending on the distance from the observer. The spheres correspond to a second level in a hierarchy; the first level is the skeleton.

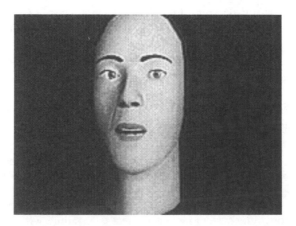

Figure 1.1 Representation of the head and face by Fred Parke, University of Utah, 1974 (Reproduced with permission of Fred Parke)

In the early 1980s, Tom Calvert, a professor of kinesiology and computer science at Simon Fraser University, Canada, attached potentiometers to a body and used the output to drive computer-animated figures for choreographic studies and clinical assessment of movement abnormalities. To track knee flexion, for instance, they strapped a sort of exoskeleton to each leg, positioning a potentiometer alongside each knee so as to bend in concert with the knee. The analog output was then converted to a digital form and fed to the computer animation system. Their animation system used the motion capture apparatus together with Labanotation and kinematic specifications to fully specify character motion (Calvert and Patla 1982).

1.2.2 Short Films and Demos

In the beginning of the 1980s, several companies and research groups produced short films and demos involving Virtual Humans.

Information International Inc, commonly called Triple-I or III, had a core business based on high resolution CRTs which could be used for digital film scanning and digital film output capabilities which were very advanced for the time. Around 1975, Gary Demos, John Whitney Jr, and Jim Blinn persuaded Triple I management to put together a 'movie group' and try to get some 'Hollywood dollars'. They created various demos that showed the potential for computer graphics to do amazing things, among them a 3-D scan of Peter Fonda's head, and the ultimate demo, Adam Powers, or 'the Juggler' (see Figure 1.2).

In 1982, in collaboration with Philippe Bergeron, Nadia Magnenat-Thalmann and Daniel Thalmann produced *Dream Flight*, a film depicting a person (in the form of an articulated stick figure) transported over the Atlantic Ocean from Paris to New York. The film was completely programmed using the MIRA graphical language, an extension of the Pascal

Figure 1.2 Adam the Juggler created by Triple I, 1982

language based on graphical abstract data types. The film won several awards and was shown at the SIGGRAPH '83 Film Show.

A very important milestone was in 1985, when the Film *Tony de Peltrie* used for the first time facial animation techniques to tell a story. The same year, the Hard Woman video for Mick Jagger's song was developed by Digital Productions and showed a nice animation of a woman. 'Sexy Robot' was created in 1985 by Robert Abel & Associates as a TV commercial and imposed new standards for the movement of the human body (it introduced motion control).

In 1987, the Engineering Society of Canada celebrated its 100th anniversary. A major event, sponsored by Bell Canada and Northern Telecom, was planned for the Place des Arts in Montreal. For this event, Nadia Magnenat-Thalmann and Daniel Thalmann simulated Marilyn Monroe and Humphrey Bogart meeting in a café in the old town section of Montreal. The development of the software and the design of the 3-D characters (now capable of speaking, showing emotion, and shaking hands) became a full year's project for a team of six. Finally, in March 1987, the actress and actor were given new life as Virtual Humans. Figure 1.3 shows the Virtual Actress.

In 1988 *Tin Toy* was a winner of the first Oscar (as Best Animated Short Film) for a piece created entirely within a computer. The same year, deGraf/Wahrman developed 'Mike the Talking Head' for Silicon Graphics to show off the real-time capabilities of their new 4-D machines. Mike was driven by a specially built controller that allowed a single puppeteer to control many parameters of the character's face, including mouth, eyes, expression, and head position. The Silicon Graphics hardware provided real-time interpolation between facial expressions and head geometry as controlled by the performer. Mike was performed live in that year's SIGGRAPH film and video show. The live performance clearly demonstrated that the technology was ripe for exploitation in production environments.

In 1989, Kleiser-Walczak produced Dozo, a (non-real-time) computer animation of a woman dancing in front of a microphone while singing a song for a music video. They captured the motion using an optically-based solution from Motion Analysis with multiple

Figure 1.3 Virtual Marilyn in 'Rendez-vous in Montreal' by Nadia Magnenat-Thalmann and Daniel Thalmann, 1987

cameras to triangulate the images of small pieces of reflective tape placed on the body. The resulting output is the 3-D trajectory of each reflector in the space.

In 1989, in the film *The Abyss*, there is a sequence where the watery pseudopod acquires a human face. This represents an important step for future synthetic characters. In 1989, Lotta Desire, star of *The Little Death* and *Virtually Yours* established new accomplishments. Then, the *Terminator II* movie in 1991 marked a milestone in the animation of synthetic actors mixed with live action. In the 1990s, several short movies were produced, the best-known being *Geri's Game* from Pixar which was awarded the Academy Award for Animated Short.

1.2.3 The Evolution towards Real-Time

Also at this time the Jack software package was developed at the Center for Human Modeling and Simulation at the University of Pennsylvania, and was made commercially available by Transom Technologies Inc. Jack provided a 3-D interactive environment for controlling articulated figures. It featured a detailed human model and included realistic behavioral controls, anthropometric scaling, task animation and evaluation systems, view analysis, automatic reach and grasp, collision detection and avoidance, and many other useful tools for a wide range of applications.

In the 1990s, the emphasis shifted to real-time animation and interaction in virtual worlds. Virtual Humans began to inhabit virtual worlds and so have we. To prepare our own place in the virtual world, we first develop techniques for the automatic representation of a human face capable of being animated in real time using both video and audio input. The objective is for one's representative to look, talk, and behave like us in the virtual world. Furthermore, the virtual inhabitants of this world should be able to see our avatars and to react to what we say and to the emotions we convey.

The virtual Marilyn and Bogart are now 17 years old. The Virtual Marilyn has acquired a degree of independent intelligence; in 1997 she even played the autonomous role of a referee announcing the score of a real-time simulated tennis match on a virtual court, contested by the 3-D clones of two real players situated as far apart as Los Angeles and Switzerland (Molet et al. 1999). Figure 1.4 shows the tennis match and Marilyn as a referee.

During the 1980s, the academic establishment paid only scant attention to research on the animation of Virtual Humans. Today, however, almost every graphics journal, popular magazine, or newspaper devotes some space to virtual characters and their applications.

Figure 1.4 Real-time Virtual Marilyn as referee in a Virtual Tennis match

Hundreds of researchers work in the area, and every single situation is being simulated. In the years when we were working in the background, we persevered because of the widespread public appeal of our topic and the satisfaction of following our own vision. The future is wide open now with VR and Augmented Reality (AR). We will be able to simulate every new situation and enjoy the past as if it still existed.

1.3   The Applications of Virtual Humans

1.3.1   Numerous Applications

The number of applications of Virtual Humans is unlimited as human activities are unlimited. In this section, we will first provide a list of the main applications. Then, in the next sections, we will present a few case studies showing some of these applications:

- Virtual people for simulation-based learning and training (transportation, civil engineering, etc.), skill development, team coordination, and decision-making.
- Virtual users for the ergonomic analysis in work environments and vehicles.
- Virtual patients for surgery and plastic surgery.
- Virtual presenters for TV and the Web.
- Virtual individuals and crowds for the simulation and training in case of emergency situations.
- Virtual mannequins for the clothing industry.
- Virtual actors for movies.
- Virtual patients for orthopaedics and prostheses and rehabilitation.
- Virtual teachers for distance learning, interactive assistance, and personalized instruction.
- Virtual people for the treatment of social phobia and virtual psychotherapies.
- Virtual inhabitants for virtual cities and architectural simulation with buildings, landscapes and lights, etc.
- Virtual characters for computer games and Lunaparks/casinos.
- Virtual athletes for sport simulation and teaching.
- Virtual soldiers for military applications such as battlefield simulation, team training, and peace-keeping operations.
- Virtual characters for interactive drama titles in which the user can interact with the characters and hence be involved in a scenario rather than simply watching it.
- Virtual workers for the simulation in industrial environments.
- Virtual ancient people for inhabited cultural heritage sites.
- Virtual representations of participants in virtual conferences in order to reduce the transmission bandwidth requirements.
- Virtual employees for design and maintenance of equipment: design for access, ease of repair, safety, tool clearance, visibility, etc.
- Virtual people for human factor analysis: human size, capabilities, behavior, and performance affect interactions with designed environments.

1.3.2   Virtual Presenters for TV and the Web

With the emergence of 3-D graphics, we are now able to create very believable 3-D characters that can move and talk. Multi-modal interaction with such characters is possible as the required technologies are getting mature (speech recognition, natural language dialogues, speech synthesis, animation, and so on).

For example, Matrox Graphics Inc. released the Matrox Virtual Presenter for Microsoft® PowerPoint®. A plug-in for this widely used presentation software, the Matrox Virtual Presenter uses photo-realistic talking heads made possible by LIPSinc and Digimask™ technologies, to provide an innovative and cost-effective way to deliver presentations electronically.

Ananova [http: Ananova] is an attractive 3-D, animated woman who can claim the distinction of being the world's first virtual news anchor. Created in NewTek's LightWave by London-based Ananova Ltd. and various technical partners, Ananova delivers short news stories to you around the clock. Ananova is not based on any one person. Designers spent many hours choosing a combination of facial features that would give her a distinctive, yet appealing, look. The technical challenge for Ananova's developers initially was how to engineer a fully-animated 3-D character capable of creating dynamically-generated news bulletins in a style and tone appropriate to specific pieces of content. To create Ananova's voice, text-to-speech synthesis software from Lernout & Hauspie (L&H) was integrated with Ananova's real-time information systems. Feedback from the L&H Realspeak generates the automatic lip-synching on her face. This ensures that her words are almost indistinguishable from human speech.

Interactive characters also provide a great improvement in the presentation of the content and enhance the enjoyment of the Web experience. Today, the core technology for such talking characters is maturing, and website implementation and integration phase is catching up. More and more websites are ready to integrate the technology of talking interactive characters for a variety of applications.

For example, 'Andy' the avatar talks with his hands. He is a 3-D animation, displaying a distinct personality and natural facial expressions that help him interpret words and phrases for hearing-disabled viewers on their computer screens. Andy is a 'signing avatar', one of a pool of Internet-enabled virtual people that translate English into sign language and help deaf and hard-of-hearing children develop language and reading skills. The SigningAvatar™ software, developed by Sims and Carol Wideman with assistance from the National Science Foundation (NSF), represents a step forward in providing universal access to technology. The software has been praised by teachers of the deaf and experts in computer technology for putting virtual 3-D technology, widely used in video games, to use for educational purposes. SigningAvatar™ is used in several Florida school districts and at schools serving deaf students around America.

1.3.3 Virtual Assistants for Training in Case of Emergency

The growing availability of powerful graphics hardware, able to support high-end immersive VR simulations, brings fresh interest, to a broadening spectrum of organizations, in the new potential offered by modern VR-based training and therapy applications. Originally, VR training systems focused on skills training involving the operation of strictly technological entities (airplanes, nuclear power stations, complex hardware devices, etc). Concerning VR therapy, applications were even more limited, if not marginal. Only recently have advanced virtual character simulation technologies reached a level of believability that extends the spectrum of VR applications to other domains such as medicine, emergency situations or psychotherapy, i.e. domains that require interaction with Virtual Environments featuring believable Virtual Humans. With powerful hardware and software technologies at hand, we face a problem: how to allow trainers and therapists to author and control the exposure required by these new application domains? An even bigger challenge is the shift from the well-known interactive scenes to the interactive narrations which trainees and patients should be exposed to.

In order to implement the social channel interaction, the introduction of a Virtual Assistant (VA) seems to be required. The VA is perceived by a trainee/patient as an inherent element of the evolving scenario. At the same time the VA's main role is to mediate the interactions between the system and the subject. In the course of the simulation, a trainee/patient (the decision-maker) is accompanied by VAs. The user navigates, assesses the situation and makes decisions by issuing natural voice commands. VAs (decision executors) wait for commands and execute actions showing expected skills. A VA may refuse to execute commands that would push the scenario development in an undesired direction. In such situations, he may prompt the user for retrial or may suggest an alternative possibility. This way, each step of the scenario offers the possibility of negotiation. In extreme cases, when the participant is unable or refuses to decide, the VA can automatically make the decisions of the default decision group.

Let us consider an immersive VR tool for situation training of health emergency personnel, as developed in the European project JUST (Ponder et al. 2003) [http: JUST]. During the interactive scenario, the trainee faces a huge rear-projection screen displaying stereo images of the simulation. He is immersed in surround sound. In course of the simulation he is able to navigate freely around the Virtual Environment in order to locate the sites of interest. The navigation paradigm is based on a single magnetic tracker attached to the trainee's head. The trainee is interacting with his Virtual Assistant using natural voice commands and hearing the respective replies and prompts from the Virtual Assistant. The role of the trainee is to assess the situation, make decisions and give respective commands to the Virtual Assistant who is executing them, showing proper physical skills. Figure 1.5 shows several images of such a immersive VR simulation training.

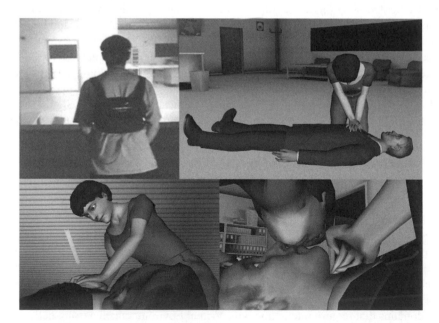

Figure 1.5 JUST immersive VR situation training of health emergency personnel: immersed trainee and execution of ordered basic life support procedures

1.3.4 Virtual Ancient People in Inhabited Virtual Cultural Heritage

Inhabited Virtual Cultural Heritage is a novel means of conservation, preservation and interpretation of cultural history. By simulating an ancient community within the virtual reconstructions of a habitat, the public can better grasp and understand the culture of that community.

One of the first example of the use of Virtual Humans in Virtual Heritage was the simulation of the Terracotta soldiers [http: TerraCotta] by MIRALab, University of Geneva. Excavation of the grave complex of the Ch'in emperor Shi Huang Ti in Xian in the 1970s revealed a vast field of lifesize terracotta statues depicting soldiers, servants, and horses, estimated to total 6,000 pieces. A sense of great realism was conveyed in the figures with remarkable simplicity. The figures were modeled on the emperor's real army, and each face was different. They were supposed to guard the grave and protect their ruler on his journey in the afterlife. The figures were carefully fashioned to resemble one of his real infantries, with well-outfitted officers, charioteers, and archers, as well as youthful foot soldiers. Now faded with the passage of time, the army was originally painted in a wide variety of bright colors. The Xian project was intended to recreate and give life again to this army using Virtual Humans. Figure 1.6 shows the Virtual Terracotta soldiers.

In the European Project CAHRISMA [http: CAHRISMA], the objective was the realistic VR simulation of cultural heritage involving architecture, acoustics, clothes and overall reproduction of ceremonial liturgies, in particular the architectural and acoustic simulation of sacred edifices: Sinan's mosques and Byzantine churches in Istanbul, Turkey. To reconstruct a Namaz crowd scenario we needed to create animation clips of particular motion sequences. Animation was captured with the VICON system (optical motion capture). The complete Namaz prayer was performed by a Muslim specialist. Figure 1.7 shows the motion capture process.

The European Project LIFEPLUS (Papagiannakis et al. 2004) [http: LifePlus] concerns cultural heritage reconstruction and preservation of ancient Pompeii, Italy. Therefore, it

Figure 1.6 Virtual Terracotta soldiers in Xian, (MIRALab, University of Geneva)

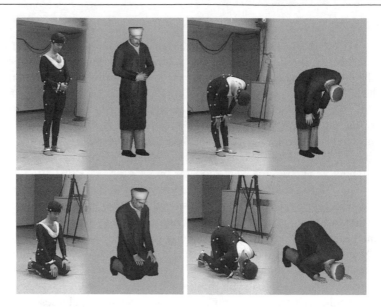

Figure 1.7   Capturing the motion for the Namaz prayer

proposes a new development for the innovative revival of life in ancient fresco-paintings in ancient Pompeii and the creation of narrative spaces. The revival is based on real scenes captured on live video sequences augmented with virtual Romans and plants, as shown in Figure 1.8. The metaphor, which inspires the project approach, is oriented to make the 'transportation in fictional and historical spaces', as depicted by fresco-paintings, as realistic, immersive and interactive as possible.

1.3.5   Virtual Audience for Treatment of Social Phobia

There is also an interesting development in Virtual Reality systems for the treatment of the fear of public speaking (Herbelin et al. 2002). Public speaking simulators have been developed for such a treatment. The imagery of the Virtual Environment consists generally

Figure 1.8   Revival of life in Pompeii

of a seminar room and virtual audiences. The main interesting point of this experience is that the therapist can control motions, facial expressions and voices of each virtual audience (chatting, yawning, agreement, disagreement, clapping).

Social phobia can be limited to only one type of situation – such as a fear of speaking in formal or informal situations, or eating or drinking in front of others – or, in its most severe form, may be so broad that a person experiences symptoms almost any time they are around other people. Social phobia can be very debilitating – it may even keep people from going to work or school on some days. Many people with this illness have a hard time making and keeping friends. Figure 1.9 shows a typical environment for the treatment of social phobia.

1.3.6 Virtual Mannequins for Clothing

The Internet has emerged as a compelling channel for the sale of apparel. However, online shoppers are reluctant to purchase apparel online because they could not try on the items. Furthermore, of particular note is the consumer's overwhelming concern with fit and correct sizing, concerns with having to return garments and the inability to fully evaluate a garment (quality, details, etc.). Consumers who purchase apparel online today base their purchase and size-selection decisions mostly on 2-D photos of garments and sizing charts. Recognizing the insufficiency of this customer experience, e-tailers have begun to implement improved functionalities on their sites. Recently introduced capabilities allow the customer to view items together, such as a blouse and a skirt, enabling the mix and match of color/texture combinations, and zoom technology, to give the customer a feel for garment details. LandsEnd.com uses My Virtual Model (http: MyVirtualModel), which provides a virtual mannequin, adjusted to the shopper's proportions. In the same manner, Nordstrom (http: NORDSTROM) is using 3-D technology from California-based 3-Dshopping.com, which offers 360-degree viewing, enabling complete rotation of the apparel item. Even with these improvements in product presentation, a number of things can go wrong when the consumer pulls the apparel item out of the box. Although there are a number of solutions available, the problem of a realistic 'Virtual mirror' still remains one of the main impediments. The most common problems include poor fit, bad drape, or unpleasant feel while

Figure 1.9   Virtual classroom for assessment and treatment of childhood disorders (ADHD and social phobia), (Skip Rizzo/Digital Media Works/The Psychological Corporation) (Reproduced with permission of Albert Rizzo)

wearing the item, or surprise as to the color of the garment. Customer dissatisfaction in any of these areas causes returns, a costly occurrence for e-tailors, and creates lost customer loyalty, an even more costly proposition. Macy's Passport 99 Fashion Show is one of the best quality Virtual Try On (VTO) show rooms that has been created so far. The primary benefit of Macy's VTO was to introduce dressed bodies animated in real time on the Web. Although the user interactivity has been of primary focus, the actual content lacks realism. The content is highly optimized and although it is optimal for web application, real cloth behavior is not visible.

Besides realism, modern applications require cloth simulation to accommodate modern design and visualization processes for which interactivity and real-time rendering are the key features. The University of Geneva MIRALab team has proposed an adaptation of Macy's approach to web visualization that provides a decent cross-platform and real-time rendering solution. However, this defines major constraints for the underlying simulation methods that should provide high-quality results in extreme time-constrained situations, and therefore with the minimal required computation. The approach additionally proposes a scheme that brings to the cloth an exact fit with the virtual body and physical behavior to fully evaluate the garment. This work uses a practical implementation of a simple and fast cloth simulation system based on implicit integration (Volino and Magnenat-Thalmann 2000). Figures 1.10 and 1.11 show examples.

1.3.7 Virtual Workers in Industrial Applications

There are a number of industrial applications where Virtual Humans in Virtual Reality and preferably in Augmented Reality could make a useful contribution. We will focus on training

Figure 1.10 Virtual Clothing in Salon Lanvin, (MIRALab, University of Geneva)

Figure 1.11   Virtual Clothing in Musée Picasso (MIRALab, University of Geneva)

and services such as planning maintenance and revamp. For these applications, we feel that
AR can help improve work efficiency, and reduce the risk of errors. This is useful both
economically (less cost) and humanely (less stress):

- *Training applications*: One of the most effective ways to train people to perform complex
  tasks is to show them films of experts in action. However, producing a realistic movie
  of an expert performing a complex task is not always easy. To be useful, the movie
  should show the exact setting of the factory where the work needs to be done, so
  that staff just have to reproduce the procedures demonstrated in the video. There are a
  number of problems with this. Experts are often too valuable to let them leave their jobs
  and go to distant sites to shoot training movies. If the expert comes to a site, his/her
  time is valuable and the video must be filmed quickly. In some cases, it may also be
  impractical to film certain actions, if they are dangerous, if they should only be performed
  in emergency situations or would damage expensive equipment. In addition, a movie
  often stops short of being effective because the trainee cannot share the viewpoint of
  the instructor. By contrast, using Augmented Reality applications with Virtual Humans,
  dangerous procedures can be simulated while real images and videos are used as a realistic
  background. Another advantage is that procedures described using Augmented Reality
  techniques can be visualized from different viewpoints. This helps the viewer gain a
  better understanding of the procedure.
- *Documentation applications*: Factory procedures are documented in reference manuals.
  However, to be useful, these manuals must be regularly updated. This is costly and time-
  consuming. To reduce these costs (by as much as 50%), some factories currently use
  on-line documentation of procedures, based on Virtual Reality techniques.

- *Planning applications*: Simulations can also be used to plan new procedures and minimize delays due to bad planning. Such simulations are more realistic when Augmented Reality techniques are used. Also in this case we gain benefit when the 3-D models of the planning environment and components are available. In huge companies it is usual to have 3-D models of new plants. This may not be the case for all small and medium-sized enterprises.
- *Maintenance applications*: Most maintenance work takes place during regularly scheduled inspections. They are designed to prevent catastrophic breakdowns, but also to enforce compliance with safety procedures. For instance, pipeline leakage in a chemical or power plant should be avoided at all costs. Careful planning, documentation of maintenance procedures and crew training are therefore necessary to maintain high security standards.

As an example, the STAR project (Vachetti et al. 2003) (http: STAR) targets Augmented Reality training of hardware maintenance professionals. It allows a trainee using a see-through HMD to walk around some real hardware devices and see a Virtual Human showing how to perform certain maintenance operations. Fig. 1.12 illustrates this approach: a virtual worker demonstrates the use of a machine in a complex industrial environment. The user of the Augmented Reality system can change the point of view at any time, and since the camera position is correctly registered to the real scene, the virtual worker is always correctly blended into the streaming video.

1.3.8 Virtual Actors in Computer-Generated Movies

Traditionally, roles for living beings in movies have been filled by human stars and stunt people, trained animals, animatronics, and other models or mechanical devices or by drawings assembled into cel animations. Today, computer graphics (CG) is being used instead. CG creatures and critters are replacing animatronics and live animals. Digital stunt people are being hired for roles too dangerous or impossible for humans to fill. Crowds of digital extras fill stadiums and street scenes. But most significantly, directors are casting 3-D characters in starring roles.

Figure 1.12   Training in industrial applications

While producing the film *Star Wars*, director George Lucas and the technical wizards at the Industrial Light & Magic (ILM) studios experimented with various modeling and simulation techniques for computer-generated imaging. Creatures sculpted in clay or plaster were translated by one of the ILM computer modelers into three-dimensional wireframe models, on to which skin textures were applied. ILM had to write its own software for this purpose – the goal was to make the computer simulate the real-world physics of skin, cloth, fur, feathers and hair.

In the film *The Catherine Wheel*, technicians at the New York Institute of Technology Computer Graphics Lab used a half-silvered mirror to superimpose videotape images of real dancers on to the computer screen to pose a computer-generated dancer. The computer used these poses as 'keys' for generating smooth animation.

By the early 1980s techniques motion capture and animatronics such as had been developed by universities and research labs. These techniques were adapted from traditional methods such as those used for analysing human movement to improve performance in Olympic sports. Production studios showed more interest in these techniques and began applying these in mainstream films. Some well-known examples of such films are *Ghostbusters* (1984), *Who Framed Roger Rabbit?* (1988), and *Terminator 2* (1992).

With the advent of powerful processors, rendering improved, textures were richer, movements smoother, and lighting effects more realistic. Taking advantage of the new technology, producers and directors in Hollywood started thinking about the realism factor. Was it possible to create a subject that was deceased or long extinct and put it on film? With *Jurassic Park*, Spielberg proved that it was possible to create on film something that didn't exist. With the right technology and sufficient computing power it was possible to digitally resurrect dead actors or extinct animals in films. Virtual film sets could be created on computer screens, eliminating the need to shoot at outdoor locations or to construct expensive backdrops or film sets.

Taking the concept of virtual characters further, the digital wizards at ILM studios showed Tom Hanks meeting President John F. Kennedy (handshake and all) in the 1994 film *Forrest Gump*. In another example, a recent advertisement shows actor Steve McQueen (who died in 1980) getting into a new car and driving away. In these films computer graphics technology was harnessed to blend old footage with new films.

But computer-generated characters need not only be modelled on actors or animals that once lived. Actors can also be fictitious and created digitally. For example, in *Terminator 2*, Robert Patrick's T-1000 character could not exist without computer effects such as morphing and warping.

In the movie *Titanic* (http: titanic), extensive use was made of virtual people, whose movements were generated from a library of precaptured motions.

The film *Final Fantasy* (http: finalfantasy) is the first feature film involving only Virtual Actors. The cast has physical and emotional characteristics that are virtually indistinguishable from live human beings. The Virtual Actors have realistic flowing hair and follicles, and physics-based clothes. Portraying the fluidity of human movement was also an integral part of the creation process. At times, *Final Fantasy* looked stunningly realistic with characters moving with human-like fluidity and remarkable attention to detail when modeling various surfaces.

For the trilogy *Lord of the Rings* (http: LordoftheRings), Weta developed innovative and efficient techniques. The Virtual Creature Gollum's performance is based on that of actor

Andy Serkis, with animators at Weta again using a mixture of motion capture, roto-motion (matching animation to a live-action plate), and key-frame animation.

1.3.9 Virtual Characters in Video Games

Video games involving Virtual Humans has become the Killer Application. The types of games we are talking about use the computer to create virtual worlds and characters for people to dynamically interact with – games such as Doom, Quake, Tomb Raider, Starcraft, Myth, Madden Football, Diablo, Everquest, or Asheron's Call. but what are the techniques used to animate these 3-D characters ? According to de Gelas (2000), most big gaming houses animate their 3-D characters using Motion Capture. As explained in Chapter 3, this means that each movement of a real human is captured on the computer, and those animations will be used to make the movements of the characters of the game more realistic. This technique is used for example in most of the Electronic Arts sports simulations. In any case, all the movements of a character must be stored on the gaming CD. The more lifelike the 3-D animation has to be, the more of the in-between steps of each move must be recorded and stored. For example, a karate kick should show the movement of the hip turning and then the movement of the thigh, then the knee, then the lower leg, and finally the ankle and the foot. Each little movement should take several frames to avoid choppy animation.

As a game has to run with decent frame rates on a low end computer, only the most important stages of a movement are used in the animation, with very few frames. A computer game that shows a karate kick probably shows only the turning of the hip and the kicking with the foot in very few frames. That is why computer characters climb and fight with wooden movements, because lifelike animation demands many frames in tenths of seconds.

Only the key-frames are stored, a frame where a certain movement starts and where it ends. The faster the PC, the more frames the game engine can algorithmically between key-frames. To create key-frames, the game engine simply interpolates between two key-frames. And that is why De Gelas (2000) believes that hardware key-frame interpolation will change the gaming world. As a result, game developers may use more polygons for the objects, as they do not have to worry that a certain movement, which makes a lot of polygons move, will appear too slow.

Current graphical engines can only deal with static geometry. To tackle this problem, game developers use skeletal animation. This kind of animation works with objects who have a 'skeleton' with 'bones' to which a polygonal mesh (a skin) is attached.

The heroine of Eidos Interactive's video game Tomb Raider (http: tombraider), Lara Croft (see Figure 1.13) is an animated archeologist adventurer in the vein of Indiana Jones. Buxom and brainy, Croft uses wits and weapons to beat the bad guys and rescue treasures, all while dressed in absurdly tight outfits. Lara continued her adventures in the video games Tomb Raider 2 and Tomb Raider Gold. Lara Croft is probably the best-known Virtual Woman in games. Creating all those animation sequences, where for example Lara Croft climbs, shoots and kicks, is a pretty labor-intensive and complex process.

Advances in technology and artificial intelligence are making game characters act increasingly lifelike. The more time you spend with games that simulate real people or critters, the more you may begin to wonder if they're alive. For example, in the 'Creatures' series from

Figure 1.13   Lara Croft (Reproduced with permission of Eidos)

Creature Labs. Norns are artificial life forms that you can raise, teach, and breed. Basically, Norns are digital pets that will interact with you and whose growth is dependent on how you treat them. If Norns are mistreated, they become sickly, injured, and depressed. Norms are not Virtual Humans but there are other creatures which are also based on Artificial Life but with human shapes: 'The Sims'. 'The Sims' is a strategy/simulation computer game, created by game designer Will Wright and published by Maxis. First released in 2000, it is the most successful PC game in history. Like other Maxis games, such as the earlier SimCity (also designed by Wright), 'The Sims' is sometimes described as a 'god game': a game that lets you create and control the lives of virtual people. The game focuses entirely on virtual people called 'Sims', placing the player in control of a 'virtual dollhouse', controlling their daily activities such as sleeping, eating, cooking and bathing, to name a few. The presentation of the game's artificial intelligence is very advanced, and the Sims will respond to outside conditions by themselves, although often the player/controller's intervention is necessary to keep them on the right track. 'Basically I want the games I program to surprise me,' said Will Wright, creator of 'The Sims'. 'And 'The Sims' does that on a daily basis. I see these hilarious things happen that were not explicitly programmed, but they were just a function of these simple rules interacting. And that to me is like the real core of artificial life. The really interesting part about it is the emergent behavior.'

Artificial Intelligence and Artificial Life can have an impact on games by creating enemies, partners, and support characters that act just like humans. The AI characters can be part of the continual evolution in the game industry to more realistic gaming environments. Increasing realism in the graphical presentation of the virtual worlds has fueled this evolution. Human-level AI can expand the types of experiences people have playing computer games by introducing synthetic intelligent characters with their own goals, knowledge, and capabilities. Ultimately it will be up to the gaming community at large to realize that the market for interactive entertainment has grown tremendously in the last several years, to the point where there are more gamers than non-gamers out there. Hopefully with some creative applications of artificial intelligence and attention to what other kinds of interactive experiences are possible to achieve in this medium, we will move more towards what mainstream audiences want to play with.

1.4   The Challenges in Virtual Humans

The simulation of Virtual Humans is an immense challenge as it requires to solve many problems in various areas. In the next sections, we try to survey the most important aspects. To reach the point that a Virtual Human looks like, behaves autonomously like a real person and interacts naturally, a lot of research effort is still needed. The twenty-first century may not be sufficient for a true imitation of the real complex human and her/his behavior.

1.4.1   A Good Representation of Faces and Bodies

Human modeling is the first step in creating Virtual Humans. For the head, although it is possible to create them using an interactive sculpting tool, the best way is to reconstruct them from reality. As explained in Chapter 2, several methods may be used for this:

1. Reconstruction from 2-D photos.
2. Reconstruction from a video sequence.
3. Construction based on laser technology.

The same methods could be used for body modeling, as shown in Chapters 3 and 4, but the main problem is still the body deformations which has been addressed by many researchers, but is still not 100% solved. Chapter 7 explains the main methods used to try to solve the problem. Concerning facial expressions in Networked VEs, four methods are possible: video-texturing of the face, model-based coding of facial expressions, lip movement synthesis from speech and pre-defined expressions or animations. But, believable facial emotions are still very hard to obtain, as shown in Chapter 6.

1.4.2   A Flexible Motion Control

The main goal of computer animation is to synthesize the desired motion effect which is a mixture of natural phenomena, perception and imagination. The animator designs the object's dynamic behavior with its mental representation of causality. S/he imagines how it moves, gets out of shape or reacts when it is pushed, pressed, pulled, or twisted. So, the animation system has to provide the user with motion control tools able to translate his/her wishes from his/her own language.

In the context of Virtual Humans, a Motion Control Method (MCM) specifies how the Virtual Human is animated and may be characterized according to the type of information it privileged in animating this Virtual Human. For example, in a key-frame system for an articulated body, the privileged information to be manipulated is the angle. In a forward dynamics-based system, the privileged information is a set of forces and torques; of course, in solving the dynamic equations, joint angles are also obtained in this system, but we consider these as derived information. In fact, any MCM will eventually have to deal with geometric information (typically joint angles), but only geometric MCMs explicitly privilege this information at the level of animation control.

But, how to do it? A database of motion capture sequences although well used in games is not the solution, key-frame is not the solution, inverse kinematics is not the solution. However, they are part of the solution. Once an acceptable motion segment has been created, either by key-framing, motion capture or physical simulations, re-use of it is important. By separating motion or skeleton generation into a time-consuming preprocess and a fast process based on efficient data representation, it fits well to real-time synthesis for applications such as game and virtual reality while taking advantage of a rich set of examples. Much of the recent research in computer animation has been directed towards editing and re-use of existing motion data. Stylistic variations are learned from a training set of very long unsegmented motion-capture sequences. Chapter 5 presents the main methods for controlling motion of the human models while standards for the skeleton are presented in Chapter 16.

1.4.3 A High-Level Behavior

Autonomous Virtual Humans should be able to have a behavior, which means they must have a manner of conducting themselves. Typically, the Virtual Human should perceive the objects and the other Virtual Humans in the environment through virtual sensors (Thalmann 1995): visual, tactile and auditory sensors. Based on the perceived information, the actor's behavioral mechanism will determine the actions s/he will perform. An actor may simply evolve in his/her environment or may interact with this environment or even communicate with other actors. In this latter case, we will consider the actor as a interactive perceptive actor.

A virtual actor inhabits a world which is dynamic and unpredictable. To be autonomous, it must be able to perceive its environment and decide what to do to reach the goal defined by its behavior. The relevant actions must then be transformed into motor control actions. Therefore, the design of a behavioral animation system raises questions about creating autonomous actors, endowing them with perception, selecting their actions, their motor control and making their behavior believable. They should appear spontaneous and unpredictable. They should give an illusion of life, making the audience believe that an actor is really alive and has its own will. As stated by Bates (1994), believability of an actor is made possible by the emergence of emotions clearly expressed at the right moment. The apparent emotions of an actor and the way it reacts are what gives it the appearance of a living being with needs and desires. Without it, an actor would just look like an automaton. Moreover, the use of emotions makes actors placed in the same context react differently. By defining different emergence conditions on different actors for their emotions, the generated emotions are ensured to be different and consequently derived behaviors are different. Behavioral animation is mainly presented in Chapter 11 while facial aspects are discussed in Chapter 10.

Another challenge is to simulate the behavior of a collection of groups of autonomous Virtual Humans in a crowd (Musse and Thalmann 2001). Each group has its general behavior specified by the user, but the individual behaviors are created by a random process through the group behavior. This means that there is a trend shared by all individuals in the same group because they have a pre-specified general behavior. Problems of crowd modeling are addressed in Chapter 14.

1.4.4   Emotional Behavior

Emotion may be defined as the affective aspect of consciousness; this is a state of feeling, a psychic and physical reaction (as anger or fear) subjectively experienced as strong feeling and physiologically involving changes that prepare the body for immediate vigorous action. Virtual Humans should be capable of responding emotionally to their situation as well as acting physically within it. Apart from making the Virtual Humans more realistic, visible emotions on the part of the Virtual Humans could provide designers with a direct way of affecting the user's own emotional state. Virtual Humans will therefore be equipped with a simple computational model of emotional behavior, to which emotionally related behavior such as facial expressions and posture can be coupled, and which can be used to influence their actions.

An emotion is an emotive reaction of a person to a perception. This reaction induces him or her to assume a body response, a facial expression, a gesture or select a specific behavior. An emotion takes place between a perception and a subsequent reaction. Two different persons can thus have different reactions to the same perception according to the way they are affected by this perception.

Ortony et al. (1988) describe an emotional model. The generated emotions belong to three classes which are the same as the perception classes. The emotions are generated in reaction to objects, actions of agents and events. The class of emotions caused by events is partitioned into three groups of emotion types. The first group concerns the emotions caused by potential events. The second group concerns events affecting the fortune of others and the last concerns events affecting the well-being of the actor. Each class is characterized by emergence conditions for each of its emotions and variables affecting its intensity. The emotions felt by an actor are caused by its perception. Although some perceived objects, actors or actions are necessary for the emergence of an emotion, they may not possess some required qualities with sufficient intensity to produce an emotion effectively felt by the actor. Chapter 10 discusses the modeling of emotions in the context of facial animation.

1.4.5   A Realistic Appearance

Even when Virtual Humans have nice bodies and faces and behave realistically, they still need a realistic appearance in terms of hair, skin, and clothes.

Along with the evolution of cloth simulation techniques, focus was primarily aimed to address realism through the accurate reproduction of the mechanical features of fabric materials. The early models, developed a decade ago, had to accommodate very limited computational power and display device, and therefore were geometrical models that were only meant to reproduce the geometrical features of deforming cloth (Weil 1986). Then, real mechanical simulation took over, with accurate cloth models simulating the main mechanical properties of fabric. While some models, mostly intended for computer graphics, aimed to simulate complex garments used for dressing virtual characters, (Carignan et al. 1992; Volino et al. 1995), other studies focused on the accurate reproduction of mechanical behavior, using particle systems (Breen et al. 1994) or finite elements (Eischen et al. 1996). Despite all these developments, all these techniques remain dependent on high computational requirements, limiting their application in the new trends toward highly interactive and real-time applications brought by the multimedia technologies. While highly accurate methods such as finite elements are not suitable for such applications, developments are now focusing on approximate models, that can render, using minimal computation, approximate, but realistic results in a very robust way. The simulation of dressed Virtual Humans is presented in Chapter 9.

On a scalp, human hair are typically 100,000 to 150,000 in number. Geometrically they are long thin curved cylinders having varying thickness. The strands of hair can have any degree of waviness from straight to curly. The hair color can change from white to grey, red to brown, due to the pigmentation, and have shininess. Thus, there arise difficulties of simulating hair stem from the huge number and geometric intricacies of individual hairs, the complex interaction of light and shadow among the hairs, the small scale of thickness of one hair compared to the rendered image and intriguing hair-to-hair interaction while in motion. One can conceive three main aspects in hair simulation – hair shape modeling, hair dynamics or animation, and hair rendering. Often these aspects are interconnected while processing hairs. Hair shape modeling deals with exact or fake creation of thousands of individual hair – their geometry, density, distribution, and orientation. Dynamics of hair addresses hair movement, their collision with other objects particularly relevant for long hair, and self-collision of hair. The rendering of hair involves dealing with hair color, shadow, specular highlights, varying degree of transparency and anti-aliasing. Each of the aspects is a topic of research and is explained in Chapter 8.

For the cloth appearance, but also for the skin appearance, rendering is important, as it is rendering that finally brings all the previously described models into a form that is perceived by the end user. Chapter 15 explains the problems and methods for rendering of cloth and skin.

1.4.6 Interacting with the Virtual World

Virtual Humans should interact in a natural way with the Virtual World. This means they should manipulate Virtual Objects as well as have social exchanges with other Virtual Humans.

The necessity to model interactions between an object and a Virtual Human agent (hereafter referred to as an agent), appears in most applications of computer animation and simulation. Such applications encompass several domains, as, for example, virtual autonomous agents living and working in Virtual Environments, human factors analysis, training, education, virtual prototyping, and simulation-based design. An example of an application using agent–object interactions is presented by Johnson and Rickel (1997), whose purpose is to train equipment usage in a populated Virtual Environment. Commonly, simulation systems perform agent–object interactions for specific tasks. Such an approach is simple and direct, but most of the time, the core of the system needs to be updated whenever one needs to consider another class of objects. To overcome such difficulties, a natural way is to include, within the object description, more useful information than only intrinsic object properties. An interesting way is to model general agent–object interactions based on objects containing interaction information of various kinds: intrinsic object properties, information on how-to-interact with it, object behaviors, and also expected agent behaviors. The smart object approach, introduced by Kallmann and Thalmann (1998) extends the idea of having a database of interaction information. For each object modeled, we include the functionality of its moving parts and detailed commands describing each desired interaction, by means of a dedicated script language. A feature modeling approach (Shah and Mäntylä 1995) is used to include all the desired information in objects. A graphical interface program permits the user to interactively specify different features in the object, and save them as a script file. Chapter 13 is dedicated to this interaction with complex Virtual Objects.

Behaviors may be also dependent on the emotional state of the actor. A non-verbal communication is concerned with postures and their indications of what people are feeling. Postures are the means to communicate and are defined by a specific position of the arms and legs and angles of the body. This non-verbal communication is essential to drive the interaction between people without contact or with contact. What gives its real substance to face-to-face interaction in real life, beyond speech, is the bodily activity of the interlocutors, the way they express their feelings or thoughts through the use of their body, facial expressions, tone of voice, etc. Some psychological researches have concluded that more than 65% of the information exchanged during a face-to-face interaction is expressed through non-verbal means (Argyle 1988). A VR system that aims to approach the fullness of real-world social interactions and to give to its participants the possibility of achieving quality and realistic interpersonal communication has to address this point; and only realistic embodiment makes non-verbal communication possible. Facial intercommunication is mainly discussed in Chapter 10.

1.4.7 Interacting with the Real World

The real people are of course aware of the actions of the Virtual Humans through VR tools such as head-mounted displays, but one major problem is to make the Virtual Humans conscious of the behavior of the real people. Virtual actors should sense the participants through their virtual sensors. For the interaction between Virtual Humans and real ones, face and gesture recognition is a key issue. Several ways exist to capture the human body posture in real-time. One uses video cameras which deliver either conventional or infrared pictures. This technique has been successfully used in the ALIVE system (Maes et al. 1995) to capture the user's image. The image is used for both the projection of the participant into the synthetic environment and the extraction of Cartesian information of various body parts. If this system benefits from being wireless, it suffers from visibility constraints relative to the camera and a strong performance dependence on the vision module for information extraction. A second technique is based on sensors which are attached to the user. Most common are sensors measuring the intensity of a magnetic field generated at a reference point. The measurements are transformed into position and orientation coordinates and sent to the computer. This raw data is matched to the rotation joints of a virtual skeleton by means of an anatomical converter (Emering et al. 1999). Chapter 12 is dedicated to body action recognition while Chapter 2 discusses Face Motion Capture and Chapter 3 presents Body Motion Capture.

1.5 Conclusion

Real-time realistic 3-D Virtual Humans will be essential in the future, but we will need more intelligent and emotional Virtual Humans to populate the Virtual Worlds. The ultimate objective in creating realistic and believable Characters is to build intelligent autonomous Virtual Humans with adaptation, perception and memory. These Virtual Humans should be able to act freely and emotionally. Ideally, they should be conscious and unpredictable. But, how far away are we from such a ideal situation? Current Virtual Humans are more and more realistic in terms of appearance and animation, they are able to perceive the virtual world, the people living in this world and in the real world. They may act based on their perception in an autonomous manner. Their intelligence is constrained and limited to the results obtained in the development of new methods of Artificial Intelligence. However, representation in the form of Virtual Humans is a way of visually evaluating the progress. In the near future, we may expect to meet intelligent Virtual Humans able to learn or understand a few situations.

2

Face Cloning and Face Motion Capture

Wonsook Lee, Taro Goto, Sumedha Kshirsagar, Tom Molet

In recent years, the Virtual Human face has attracted more and more attention from both the research and industrial communities. It is no longer a fantasy to imagine that one can see oneself in a Virtual Environment talking and interacting with other virtual figures or even with real humans. By advances in algorithms and new developments in the supporting hardware, this fantasy has become a reality. We describe research done in the last decades and how problems have been solved. A Virtual Human is composed of a face and body and we treat them separately depending on their character and this chapter is devoted to the face. We present a methodology of how to create Virtual Humans and how to capture the real-life movement for a virtual face. The methodology, algorithms and results are also illustrated and shown in figures and images in public demonstrations and many computer-generated films.

2.1 Introduction

There are more and more Virtual Humans in Virtual Environments, such as in computer games, computer-generated films, Internet-based entertainment services, etc. At the beginning of the Virtual Human modeling, a great amount of manual effort was needed and as time goes on, in the last decades many innovative ideas have been presented and it is no longer a fantasy to imagine that one can see oneself in a Virtual Environment moving, talking and interacting with other virtual figures or even with real humans. However, there are still limitations in terms of ease, variety, and usability. By advances in algorithms and new developments in the supporting hardware, this fantasy has become a reality. There has been a great deal of literature related to these topics and there are numerous industries interested in realizing these ideas.

In this chapter we would like to present a solution to how to produce a delicate Virtual Human in shape and motion with simple input data in an easy way. The input data format

Handbook of Virtual Humans Edited by N. Magnenat-Thalmann and D. Thalmann
© 2004 John Wiley & Sons, Ltd   ISBN: 0-470-02316-3

for the creation of Virtual Humans is mainly photographs, thanks to the easy accessibility for anybody in daily life. Motion capture is a mature technique in computer animation. Advanced contributions in face motion capture are based on and experimented on main hardware technologies currently available and achieve real-time performances. We will here especially focus our attention on the path leading from measured or raw data to the models in an animation parameter space.

2.2 Feature-Based Facial Modeling

2.2.1 Facial Modeling Review and Analysis

3-D modeling of the human face, especially face cloning, has wide applications from the video conference to facial surgery simulation. Face cloning means to make a virtual counterpart in 3-D, which resembles the shape of a given person's face. The diversity of facial forms in terms of sex, age, and race is enormous. In addition, face modeling is the basis for facial animation in a virtual world, in such a way that the three terms such as shape, texture, and animation structure are exactly matched to produce a convincing visualization. Cloning a real person's face has practical limitations in the sense of how long it takes to get a result, how simple the equipment is, and how realistic it looks.

We address the problem of how to acquire an animatable human face with a realistic appearance. It is our goal to develop a technique that enables the easy acquisition of the avatar model having the ability to be animated well and produced at a low cost. The issues involved in modeling a Virtual Human face are as follows:

- acquisition of human face shape data;
- realistic high-resolution texture;
- functional information for animation of the human face.

We first give a wide review of several methodologies and compare them to find the best way to get an animatable Virtual Human with accurate shape.

Equipment such as 3-D scanners (e.g. a laser scanner) able to capture the 3-D shape of a human seem to be an appealing way to model humans. Although the method seems as simple as taking a photo, the approach is not as straightforward and the resulting human shape cannot directly be used inside a Virtual Environment. The manipulation of such a device has various levels of difficulties to get acceptable results. For example, defining the appropriate settings of the device is generally not straightforward. The main drawback lies in the post-processing required to get a usable virtual actor. First, in order to get a proper 3-D shape, the result requires a geometric modeling post-process, particularly in terms of the amount of geometric data and surface correction, such as smoothing surfaces or filling holes. In order to animate the 3-D shape inside a Virtual Environment, it has to be combined with the animation structure. This requires additional information that the scanning process cannot provide. We can illustrate the problem with one example: animating the face requires having eyes independent from the rest of the head. When the face is built using a 3-D scanner, first, only the visible parts of the eyes are modelled, second, they make one single surface with the rest of the face, which makes the animation of full eyeballs impossible without post-processing.

We give the existing methods to generate a clone from a given input, such as simple equipment like cameras, more sophisticated equipment or a rather complicated algorithm.

- *Plaster models*: Magnenat-Thalmann and Thalmann (1987) used plaster models built in the real world. Pixar's animation character 'Geri' (Pixar 1998) is also sculpted, which was then digitized and used as a basis to create the 3-D model.

- *Arbitrary photographs*: With one or several photographs, the approach consists in using the sculpting method in a similar way as we do in the real world. Software Sculptor (LeBlanc et al. 1991), dedicated to the modeling of 3-D objects, is based on local and global geometric deformations. Blanz and Vetter (1999) proposed an extremely impressive appearance-based approach that uses a PCA-based statistical head model. This model has been taken from a large database of human heads, i.e. the 200 generic models from a laser scanner, and its parameters can be adjusted so that it can synthesize images that closely resemble the input image or images. While the result is outstanding, even when only one image is used, the recovered shape cannot be guaranteed to be correct unless more than one is used. Because the model is Euclidean, initial camera parameters must be supplied when dealing with uncalibrated imagery.

- *Features on photographs (organized) and a generic model*: There are faster approaches to reconstruct a face shape from a few photographs of a face, which use two or three photographs (Kurihara and Arai 1991; Akimoto et al. 1993; Ip and Yin 1996; Lee and Magnenat-Thalmann 1998). This utilizes a 3-D existing face model and very little information (only feature points) from photographs. The input photographs are taken or selected carefully to satisfy a certain requirement.

- *Range data*: The approach based on 3-D digitization to get a range data often requires special purpose high-cost hardware. However, it aims to produce a highly matched face. These data usually provide a large number of points for the static shape without having any functional structure for animation. There are several existing methods using either a laser scanner (Lee et al. 1996; Blanz and Vetter 1999), active light striper (Proesmans and Van Gool 1997), sequences of contours from cameras (Nagel et al. 1998; Zheng 1994), stereoscopic cameras (Fua 1998; Lee and Magnenat-Thalmann 2000), video with markers (Guenter et al. 1998) or without markers (Fua 2000; DeCarlo 1996). Even though many methods claim to be fully automatic, there is still a lot of user interaction in preparation (e.g. sticking markers on a face properly for video with markers) and trial-error procedures for individual dependent parameters. We consider practical points of view when we describe several methods one by one in detail here. Before starting, we define the terms such as 'active' and 'passive'. When we say input is 'active', it means that we actively create it with defined equipment in a defined environment. 'Passive' input data means that we take present input data. For the animation, we make a similar definition. 'Active' animation means we create the animation as we wish while the 'passive' animation implies that we just play existing animation without creating a new expression. Overall comparison is given in Table 2.1 and Table 2.2. The animation functional structure can be constructed when we get shapes or can be added post-processing.

- *Stripe generator*: As an example of structured light camera range digitizer, a light striper with a camera and stripe pattern generator (Proesmans and Van Gool 1997) can be used for face reconstruction with relatively cheap equipment compared to laser scanners.

- *Stereoscopy*: This method uses the geometric relation over stereo images to recover the surface depth (Fua 1998), which often results in very noisy data. Similarly, there are many other methods that concern precision and accuracy (Addleman 1997; Daanen et al. 1997; Gu et al. 1998; Fua 1999). The second type of technique concentrates on the shape and visual realism of the reconstructed models, such as those used in Virtual Reality applications.

Table 2.1 Possible ways to get a virtually cloned face. Passive animation means we receive animation from input. Active animation means we generate any animation

Input	Equipment	Acquisition method	Result	Time	Animation
plaster model	mono camera	manual marks on the model and take several views of photographs	detailed matching	days/weeks	Yes
photos (arbitrary)	mono camera	manual parameter input and automatic pixel matching process of the image with large database of generic heads	detailed matching	hours	no/active[1]
	mono camera	manual using user-friendly designing software		days/weeks	active[2]
photos (organized)	mono camera	(semi-)automatic feature[3] detection and a generic head modification	rough matching	minutes	active

Notes:
1 This depends on the database of the generic models. If all the generic models have animation structure, the resulted cloned head inherits the function for the animation. If the generic models have only static shape, we have to apply post-process to give animation of the cloned head.
2 It has 'no' animation unless we add the animation structure on the shape. However, we put it as 'active' since we usually add the animation structure together when we do shaping.
3 Feature part (point) means the easily recognizable parts such as nose, eyes, and lips.

- *Video sequences*: This uses a video stream, which needs a cheap and entirely passive sensor, such as an ordinary video camera. The more frames there are, the better the results. Fua and Miccio (1999) proposed an approach to fitting complex head animation models, including ears and hair, to registered stereo pairs and triplets. This approach was later extended (Fua 2000) so that it could use image sequences taken with a single camera, without requiring calibration data. It is based on bundle-adjustment and takes advantage of rough knowledge of the face's shape, in the form of a generic face model (Kalra et al. 1992), to introduce regularization constraints. As shown in Figure 2.1, this allows the robust estimation of head motion. The resulting image registration is accurate enough to use a simple correlation-based stereo algorithm (Fua 1993) to derive 3-D information from the data and use the earlier method (Fua and Miccio 1999) to refine the model. In this work, the generic face model was treated as a triangulated mesh whose degrees of freedom were the 3-D coordinates of the individual vertices. Shan et al. (2001) proposed a similar approach based on a purpose-built model controlled by a small number of degrees of freedom, thus allowing much faster convergence. Therefore, the technique proposed in Fua (2000) could be used to initialize the Blanz and Vetter (1999) system in an automated fashion.

Some of the above methods concentrate on recovering a good shape, but the biggest drawback is that they provide only the shape without structured information. Starting with a structured

Table 2.2   Typical ways to get range data

Equipment	Acquisition method	Result	Time	Animation
laser scanner	automatic methods	detailed matching (noisy possible)	minutes	no
a camera and pattern generator	automatic line reader	detailed matching		passive
stereoscopic camera	automatic pixel matching between two views	detailed matching (noisy possible)	minutes/ hours	no
cameras with special background	automatic silhouette extraction and sub-triangulation	detailed matching	minutes	no
video camera	marks on a person's face and get positions of marks automatically	detailed matching		passive
	no marks and manual fitting (small number of features/automatic matching for all areas)	detailed matching (noisy possible)		no

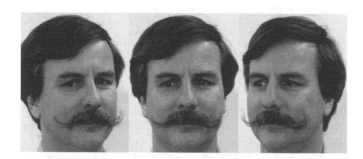

Figure 2.1   Top row: 3 images of an uncalibrated video-sequence. Bottom row: The reconstructed 3-D model

Table 2.3   Comparison between photographs and laser scanner.

	CG from photographs	Laser scanner
price	cheaper	expensive
accessibility	general	special
texture resolution	high	low
characteristic points	easy to catch	often very noisy
non-characteristic points to 3-D	difficult	good
hairy part	visible	problems

facial mesh, Lee et al. (1996) developed algorithms that automatically construct functional models of the heads of human subjects from laser-scanned range and reflection data.

The approach based on 3-D digitization to get a range data often requires special purpose (high-cost) hardware. A more common way of creating 3-D objects is reconstruction from 2-D-photo information, which is accessible at the lowest price.

Since laser scanners and computer-generated modeling using photographs are the most used input methods in practice, we first compare the two typical methods in Table 2.3 in terms of cost, resolution and results. Beside the price or accessibility by wide range of people, the laser scanner gives a better shape for large and smooth regions (e.g. forehead, cheeks) than computer-generated modeling using photographs. However, computer-generated modeling using photographs gives a better resolution for characteristic regions (e.g. eyes, node holes). So we present a methodology to take features from computer-generated modeling using photographs and to take non-features from scanned data, which means the scanned data can be animatable.

2.2.2   Generic Human Face Structure

The model used for the generic face can be constructed in any convenient way, and triangular polygonal mesh is one of the most favorable forms for simple manipulation purposes (see Figure 2.2). We generate a generic face in triangular mesh keeping two points in mind.

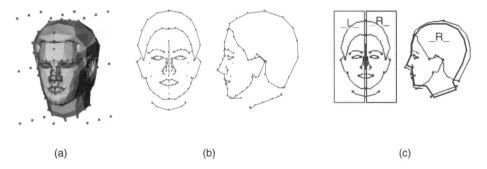

(a)   (b)   (c)

Figure 2.2   (a) Control points and the generic model. The control points on the surface correspond to feature points on photographs and the other control points are set as extras (b) Features of the frontal view and on the right side of the side view of the person (c) Feature points names are organized in a special way to indicate if the feature belongs to_R_,_L_ or centerline to make the algorithm to create 3-D points

First, the triangles must be well distributed, so that it shows finer triangles over the highly curved and/or highly articulated regions of the face and larger triangles elsewhere. It also includes eyeballs and teeth. Second, an animation structure (functional information) must be embedded inside. How to add functional information belongs to facial animation parts, which will be described in Chapter 6.

2.2.3 Photo-Cloning

As shown in Table 2.3, photographs are one of the easiest and cheapest equipment to get feature points. The features on photographs are very visible most of time even under various circumstances. The face-cloning component uses feature point detection on the frontal and side images and then uses Dirichlet Free-Form Deformations (DFFDs) for shape modification. Next a fully automatic seamless texture mapping is generated for 360° colouring on a 3-D polygonal model.

Two images are used as the input photographs for the face cloning using the methodology as 'photo-cloning' in Figure 2.3.

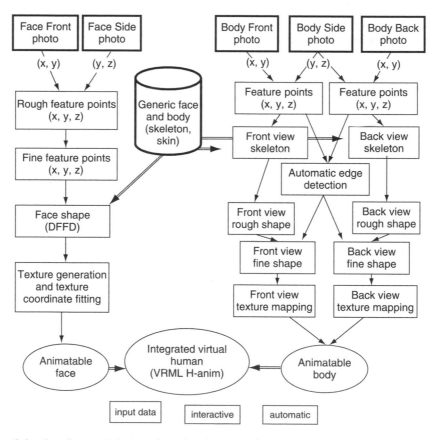

Figure 2.3 Overflow of face and body photo-cloning. In this chapter we focus on face cloning only

In this section, we present a way to reconstruct a photo-realistic head for animation from orthogonal pictures. First, we prepare a generic head with an animation structure and two orthogonal pictures of the front and side views. The pre-process is done to make the following:

1. A generic shape of the face.
2. Generic animation structure.
3. Definition of feature point and feature lines that show the connection of feature points.
4. Definition of control points on the generic model.
5. Coordinate relation calculation for Dirichlet Free-Form Deformations (DFFD) which is used for shape modification.
6. An expression database.

Whenever there is input for a new face data, the pre-defined feature points and lines need to be positioned properly. We process normalization and a semi-automatic feature positioning starting from a few key features to guide automatic feature detection.

The main idea to get an individualized head, is to detect feature points (eyes, nose, lips, and so on) on the two images and then obtain the 3-D position of the feature points to modify a generic head using a geometrical deformation.

2.2.4 *Feature Location and Shape Extraction*

Feature detection from 2-D image data is the one of the main steps. When we refer to feature detection, it means to catch the 2-D or 3-D positioning data of most visible points on a face such as eyebrow, eye outlines, nose, lips, the boundaries between hair and face, chin lines, etc. Some parts such as the forehead and cheeks are not always easy to locate exactly on 2-D photographs and they are called non-feature points.

Cootes and Taylor (1996) use statistical parameters of the shape variety to locate face features. This technique is more for tracking the movement of the pre-studied facial expression. (Brunelli and Poggio 1992) uses a feature-based face recognition technique. They first use a template matching method by means of a normalized cross-correlation coefficient. Then after the matching, gradient information of both the horizontal and vertical is used to recognize the edges. The face outline is extracted using the gradient intensity map of an elliptical shape. This method is quite useful since all human beings have the same facial structure, but can be weak at noise component, such as moustaches or cuts/scratches. On the other hand, Intrator et al. (1996) use a neural network model. This method has robustness against irregular individual features and noise. They use a generalized symmetry transform method, as the pre-processing and then warp the face to a standard location using these points. After this process, a back-propagation-type network is used to classify the features. The extraction of the feature positions (eyes and mouth) is robust enough, but the detailed shape is not considered in this method. Another neural network based approach is done by Reinders et al. (1995). They use a neural network model to locate facial micro features. Each feature, such as an eye, can be considered a structural assembly of micro features, which are small parts of the feature that are being sought. They construct the detailed shape from the micro features. They also try to adapt the 3-D face model to an image (Reinders et al. 1996) using a knowledge-based feature selection mechanism. Akimoto et al. (1993) try to detect feature points automatically from a knowledge-based model. They use simple filtering techniques, using the Sobel operator and constant threshold, and try to extract feature points. Ip and Yin (1996) propose a method for an automatic side feature detection using concave and convex curve information. This method works well for limited human ethnics of Asian features, but not for other ethnics. There is also another knowledge-based approach where the configuration of the features can help localize features and find the face position, since we have the knowledge that the features cannot appear in arbitrary arrangements. For example, given the positions of the two eyes, we know that the nose and the mouth can only lie within specific areas of the image. Leung et al. (1995) use such a knowledge-based approach to develop a method called random labelled graph matching that permits detection of facial feature positions. Garcia et al. (2000) recognize the global position of features using wavelet analysis and knowledge of the human face. However, they did not work on feature shape extraction.

A photograph does not convey motion information, but provides edge information, and also sometimes colour information. Thus, we have to recognize feature positions from the static image information. In general, a vision system constructs a face from this kind of image by the combination of the segment division of the features on the face and the detail region recognition after the segmentation. The segmentation of the face is based on knowledge of the human face. The facts such as 'there are two eyes around the centre of the face', or 'the mouth is below the nose' help the segment construction, the called a knowledge-based methodology. Detail recognition is based on the combined information of edge appearance and colour difference, called a vision-based methodology.

To mimic these two methodologies, we divide our feature detection into two steps: (1) global matching to find location of features; (2) detail matching to find each feature shape by a specific method designed for each feature.

In the global matching process, a generic 3-D facial model is used. Feature positions such as an eye position or nose position are different for each individual. As we explained, we use photographs from two views. An operator has to locate the generic face model on the face image by drawing a square for each photograph. This process to put the generic model on an image is done manually (see Figure 2.4(a)), because the search of the face position from the background image is not the main goal in this aspect. However, the global matching after indicating the facial region is fully automatic.

As a pre-process, the generic model is separated into several feature regions such as eyes, nose, eyebrows, mouth, and jaw regions as shown in Figure 2.4(b). By the global positioning of generic model on the photographs, the positions of the features, like eyes, are approximated even though they are not accurate. The feature positions are different due to the age, race, gender, etc. For example, young children do not have strong jawbones and this makes their eye positions lower than those of adults. Our strategy to find the feature positions is to use statistical data for image processing. Image analysis has limited accuracy, but knowledge of a face helps the processing. Therefore, we analyze 200 people to know the distribution of the facial features. Figure 2.5 and Figure 2.6 show the distribution graph of feature positions. The x-axis is a position of feature shown by ratio. The position of a 100% indicates the tip of jaw, 0% indicates the top of the head. The y-axis is the number of people. We randomly picked people from our database to compile the graph. This graph shows that the distribution can be considered a standard distribution. Therefore, they can be estimated by Gaussian curves of small dispersion, except at the position of the forehead. Thus, we can set a constant distribution value, which is calculated from the curve, to the equation to estimate positions. Since most humans have almost symmetrical faces, only the vertical

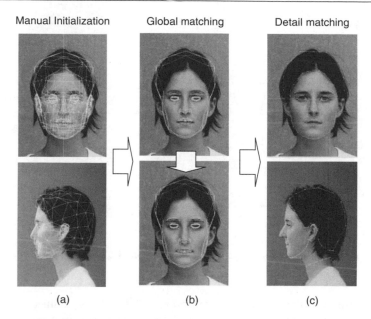

Figure 2.4 Automatic 3-D facial feature detection flow

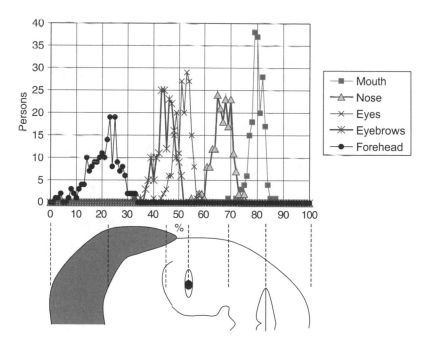

Figure 2.5 Distribution graph of features

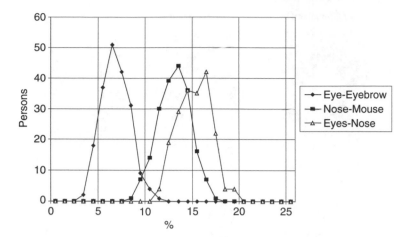

Figure 2.6 Distribution graph of each feature's distance. 5% of distance is the 1/20 length of the face

distribution is used to calculate the feature positions. Let α be a parameter for each region and σ^2 be a distribution value, and y_0 as a pre-defined average position of each feature. The Gaussian weight value of the position $W(y)$ is defined by the following equation:

$$W(y) = \alpha \exp\left(-\frac{(y-y_0)^2}{2\sigma^2}\right) \tag{2.1}$$

Equation (2.1) is used as a weight value for the feature position estimation. We multiply this value to a self-correlation value of the extracted edge image of the face. Therefore, the face image is processed to make feature edges clear. We first use Canny edge detector to extract the edges of the features, and use only the horizontal edges. This is because most features on the face, like eyes and mouth, are based on horizontal lines. Therefore, it is efficient to remove wrinkles on the cheeks because they do not have strong horizontal edges.

2.2.4.1 Individual feature location matching

First, all the regions are moved at the same time, and the best fitting positions are calculated considering the image matching and the distribution weight. Here we can define pixel value on the image as $P(x, y)$, and pixel value in the eye region as $P_e(x, y)$, also the weight function of the eye region as $W_e(y)$. The probability of the eye's position $E_e(Y)$ is calculated as follows.

$$E_e(Y) = W_e(Y) \sum_x \sum_y P_e(x, y)P(x, Y+y) \tag{2.2}$$

where Y is the fitting position. Now, considering the total balance of the regions, we use the probability of the eyes $E_e(Y)$, the mouth $E_m(Y)$, the eyebrows $E_b(Y)$ and the nose $E_n(Y)$ that are calculated in the same way. The result of the possibility $E(Y)$ is calculated by the following equation:

$$E(Y) = E_e(Y) + E_m(Y) + E_b(Y) + E_n(Y) \tag{2.3}$$

An approximated position is defined where the largest value of $E(Y)$ appears. Then these regions are separated into two parts for more detailed position extraction. Eye regions and eyebrow regions constitute one part while nose and mouth regions do the other. From database analysis, it is found that the distance between eye and eyebrow is not very different from one person to another. The distance from the nose to the mouth is also in a narrow range as shown in Figure 2.6. The dispersion ranges of the eye-eyebrow and the nose–mouth are narrower than the eye–nose. Thus, again the region fitting is done in the narrower region for each part. In this process, equations that are used for the calculation are the same as shown before, but the differences appear only at the distribution value σ^2. Finally, the parts are completely separated from each other, and the same position fitting calculation is applied.

Since the edge of a bottom line of the nose is not always strong, another dependency method is used for the calculations in this region. The positions of eyes and mouth are fixed before the nose position extraction. Then the distribution is calculated between eye and mouth in place of face size. Figure 2.6 shows the distribution of nose position. Using this distribution parameter, the bottom line of the nose is estimated with the similar approach. This process, while considering the face balance, gives a robust fitting result. Figure 2.4(b) shows that these regions fit to the proper position by this matching algorithm.

Using the method described above, 200 faces in our face database which was built during several public demonstrations are tested to check the accuracy of the global matching. The database contains a large range of human races, ages of both genders. Also there are people with facial hair. However, the database does not include people with glasses or other similar things. The extraction rate in finding the proper position of all features was 201 in 203 cases. The two missed detections occurred when either the photographs were very noisy, or the face was very far from the average.

The position of each feature is also applied to the side face. The difficulty in transferring the feature information from the front view to the side view comes from the non-orthogonal views and different illumination between two photographs. We normally take one photograph of a target person from the front view. Then the target turns about 90 degrees, and we take one more photograph for the side view. This means the pair of photographs is not taken at the same time and the direction of the light can be changed. In addition, the head angle is not always kept the same as a human can move. If the photographs are taken at the same time from his/her front and side, the data is more accurate. Thus, we have to consider the error from the front and the side. The global position detected from the front view is used on the side view, but these are not considered as accurate positions. The global matching has a 99.0% rate of success. The main reason for the high rate is that feature positions of most people are in a Gaussian distribution. Thus the image recognition with the feature position analysis makes the success rate high. Failure occurs when strong noise such as a moustache is present and the distribution of facial features is far from the average. The more accurate position of each feature is calculated in the detailed extraction phase of the side view.

2.2.4.2   Detail detection

In the global matching, the position of facial features is obtained. In this section, we describe the method of recognizing the feature shape of each region. This detail matching contains basically the recognition of the size, shape and exact location of features. The automatic shape extraction of the ears is not always easy since hairs sometimes hide ears. At present, ear position processing is not supported in our method. The shape extraction of each region is treated differently but the image processing methods we use are similar and the result is given as curves for each region as shown in Figure 2.4(c).

The analysis of detail shape is done with a kind of multi-orientation edge detection method. The detailed shape extraction part is separated into forehead, jaw, eyes, nose, mouth and side view. The jaw shape extraction is successful when the symmetry is kept. If the front photo is not taken exactly from the front view, the accuracy of the curve fitting drops. However, the success rate is more than 90% with photographs that are taken from the exact angle. The forehead extraction is also in the same situation, but is influenced more by the front hair. The nose shape extraction is sometimes influenced by a strong edge of a nose hole. Some nose holes can be seen from the front view, but not everything can be, which makes the appearance not clear. Our nose shape extraction algorithm is meant to extract very weak edge curves, and sometimes fits the nose holes. The success rate is about 70%. The eye and mouth shape extraction are about 80% successful. The side view silhouette extraction depends on the background image. The success rate of every shape extraction is calculated by the multiple of every region extraction. Thus, we cannot say this is a full automatic shape extraction. However, the method helps to fit features on the face. An operator has to edit misrecognized shapes after the extraction. In addition, feature extraction of silhouettes is currently not supported since the movement of the curve is influenced by the background intensity and long hair is difficult to deal with. An operator must also move these curves, but there are a few control points to make these curves. Thus, an auto fitting of these curves does not help to shorten the operation time. However, as we describe how to create 3-D features from two sets of 2-D features in next section, the accurate feature detection on the side view is not as important as the front view. Most information used for 3-D face creation comes from the front view and only missing information for depth comes from the side view.

With the image-processing technique, the time needed to place feature markers on the face becomes just a few seconds with a regular PC. This automatic feature detection method allows any unskilled operator to produce her/his 3-D animatable virtual clone. The total process time including automatic feature detection, 3-D surface deformation and texture generation and mapping is about one minute.

2.2.5   Shape Modification

We detected 2-D feature points on two photographs automatically in previous sections. The question is how to modify a generic model, which has more than a thousand points to make an individualized smooth surface. First, we have to choose if we do modification in 2-D and then combine two sets of 2-D to make 3-D or we do modification in 3-D directly. This is a critical issue for the data handling for error tolerance. We have to find a method to decrease the dependency of perfectly orthogonal photograph input. Several kinds of distance-related functions in 2-D have been employed by many researchers to calculate the displacement of surface points related to the feature points detected. However, these methods cannot recover the proper shape when the detected features are not perfectly orthogonal.

As we described earlier, the front and side view photographs are taken in an environment where the two views are not perfectly orthogonal and the illuminations are different. We apply an algorithm on detected 2-D features to make 3-D features aiming to decrease the dependency of orthogonality of photographs and then make modifications in 3-D. Since we know the feature point structure from photographs, it is possible to handle them in a proper way by filtering, using the knowledge of feature points.

2.2.5.1   Asymmetric 3-D features from two sets of 2-D features

Our input is two views of a person. One frontal view and one side view are the only input. Since only one side view is used, one may misunderstand that the final virtual clone has a symmetric face. However, the frontal view has almost all the information required for asymmetric information and the way to produce 3-D points from two 2-D points saves asymmetric information of the face. Two sets of feature points on frames have structure, which means every feature point has its own name. In our case, we use about 160 feature points. Some points have position values, which means they are visible on images, on both the frontal and the side views, while others have values only on the frontal view or on the side, for example, the back part of a head is not visible in the frontal view. The problem is how to make (x, y, z) from a given set of 2-D points. Since the perfect orthogonal pair photographs are not easily realized, an unexpected 3-D shape may occur if we take the average of y_s and y_f for the y coordinate where subscripts s and f mean side and frontal view. These are our criteria to combine two sets of 2-D features, say (x, y_f) and (z, y_s), to make 3-D features.

2.2.5.2   Making an individualized 3-D face

Then, two 2-D position coordinates in the front and side views, which are the XY and the ZY planes, are combined to be a 3-D point. After using a global transformation to move the 3-D feature points to the space for a generic head, Dirichlet Free Form Deformations (DFFD) (Moccozet and Magnenat-Thalmann 1997) are used to find new geometrical coordinates of a generic head adapting to the detected feature points. The control points for the DFFD are feature points detected from the images. Then, the shapes of the eyes and teeth are recovered from the original shape with translation and scaling adapted to a new head. Figure 2.7 shows the steps for head modification from photos.

2.2.6   Texture Mapping

Texture mapping is useful not only to cover the rough matched shape, as here the shape is obtained only by feature point matching, but also to get a more realistic colorful face.

The main idea of texture mapping is to get an image by combining two orthogonal pictures in a proper way to get the highest resolution for the most detailed parts. The detected feature points data is used for automatic texture generation by combining two views (actually three views by creating the left view by flipping the right view). We first connect two pictures with a pre-defined index for feature lines using a geometrical deformation as shown in Figure 2.8(a) and a multi-resolution technique to remove boundaries between different image sources as shown in Figure 2.8(b). The eyes and teeth images are added automatically on top of an image, and these are necessary for the animation of the eyes and mouth region.

To give a proper coordinate on a combined image for every point on a head, we first project an individualized 3-D head onto three planes such as the front (XY), right (ZY) and

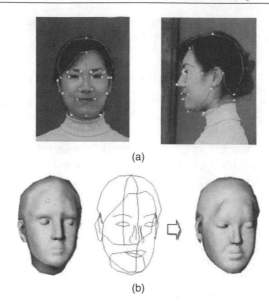

(a)

(b)

Figure 2.7 (a) Detected features. (b) Modification of a generic head with feature points

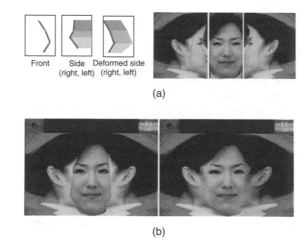

Front Side Deformed side
(right, left) (right, left)

(a)

(b)

Figure 2.8 (a) A geometrical deformation for the side views to connect to the front view. (b) before and after multi-resolution techniques

left (ZY) directions. With the information of the pre-defined index for feature lines, which are used for image merging above, we decide on which plane a point on a 3-D head is projected. Then projected points on one of the three planes are transferred to either the front feature points space or the side feature points space in 2-D. Finally, one more transform on the image space is processed to obtain the texture coordinates.

Figure 2.9 shows several views of the final reconstructed head from the two pictures in Figure 2.7 (a). When we connect this head with a body, we remove the neck since the neck is part of the body due to the body skeleton animation for face rotation. Face animation

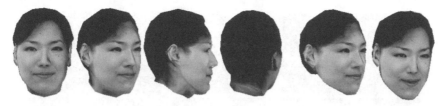

Figure 2.9 Snapshots of a reconstructed head in several views and animation on the face

is immediately possible as being inherited from the generic head. Look at the last face in Figure 2.9 to see an expression on a face.

2.2.7 Face Cloning from Range Data

The result of photo cloning is successful in approximating the shape of the laser-scanned body. The photo-cloned body has reasonably small error so that if we adapt the cloned body to remove the error, the final body has the same shape from the range data while it has the functional skin structure and skeleton for animation.

For many range data examples from scanners, the results are not always satisfactory, especially for feature regions on a face. When there is shadowy or complex area around hair, ear, eyes or nose, it creates error for the region for many scanners. Photo-cloned body has a better resolution for the feature parts, for example, the eye and lips regions, where range data often have large errors. The photo-cloned human shape inherited the functional structure from a generic human, where the points and triangles are designed to be good for the animation. So it is desirable to partition the surface depending on feature-superior area and surface-superior area. So we use a methodology to partition the surface into two regions with the criteria of whether they are acceptable or not. We use two methods depending on the range input data. We use fine adaptation removing error, if the vertex belongs to the region and if not, we use the photo-cloned vertexes. There the surfaces have a different structure, which means the resulted head has inside structure such as eyes and teeth differently from the laser-scanned head. So we have to make error measurements after taking out the inside structures. Of course we perform this measurement after aligning the output surface in the same space of the input surface using scaling and translation.

If the range input data has errors or only a front face is captured as shown in Figure 2.10a, we use Delaunay triangles created with feature points by checking errors between range input data and photo-cloned data. Since the features can be positioned properly from the photographs, we collect feature points only when their positions on a modified head are inside certain limitations of corresponding points on the original range data. Then we calculate Delaunay triangles of chosen feature points and collect non-feature points inside Delaunay triangles. We check it using barycentric coordinates. The Delaunay triangles and collected points on a surface are shown in Figure 2.10b. The points collected are suitable to be adapted by the range data while other points are kept as the photo-cloned position.

2.2.8 Validation of the Face Cloning Results

As we mentioned in the introduction, there are two main categories for obtaining 3-D human models, according to the different requirements for the output. The typical example of the

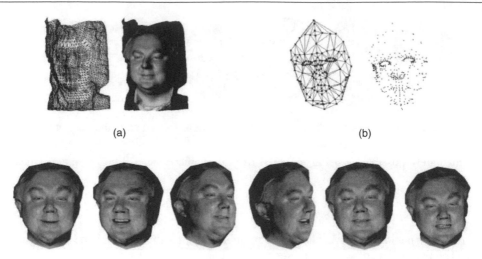

(a)   (b)

Figure 2.10 (a) Input range data. (b) Delaunay triangles created with feature points and points collected for fine modification using Delaunay triangles. (c) The result of giving functional structure on a range data. This reconstructed head is able to animate within given expression parameters

first category is either CAD or medical applications where the precise and exact location of the each pixel is important while the visual realism is not. The second category belongs mainly to the Virtual Reality application, where the real-time calculation and realistic and believable-looking effects are more important than precision. Since our aim is more focused on real-time Virtual Reality applications, the accuracy of the shape is less important than the visual resemblance for human cloning. Nevertheless, we present both validations to prove the efficiency of the feature-based approach.

To validate the result, we use the output from a laser scanner as our input. In this case, we do not need to worry about how to measure the real surface of the human subject nor the possible error produced by the laser scanner. We took a model in VRML 2.0 format from a freeware web site (http: tammy), which was produced by Cyberware Digitizer. This *tammy.wrl* contains both the face and body parts. We use only the face part in this section and the body part is discussed separately in the next chapter.

2.2.8.1   Visual validation

We take two orthogonal photos of the face part after loading the laser-scanned model. We use the generic model in Figure 2.2a. The first and fourth snapshots in Figure 2.11(a) are used as the input photographs (301×309) for the face cloning. The visual comparison of the original data and reconstructed data in Figure 2.11 shows that the result is very acceptable and the feature-based approach is efficient. The number of points on a head is 1257, where 192 of them are for teeth and 282 of them are used for the two eyes. This leaves only 783 points for the individualization of the face surface aside from eyes and teeth. As well as the small number of points, the output surface has animation information inside.

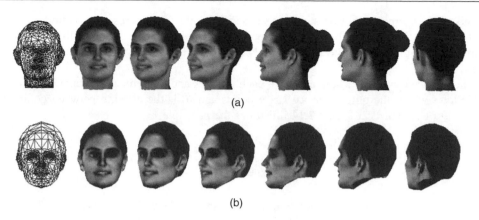

(a)

(b)

Figure 2.11   (a) Snapshots of the laser-scanned model 'Tammy' (b) Snapshots of the reconstructed model using feature-based face cloning program. Compare snapshots in (a) and (b) taken from the same angles

2.2.8.2   Error measurement

The input surface (from the laser scanner) is a set of 3-D points and so is the output surface (from the cloning program). However, the surfaces have a different structure, which means the resulting head has such an inside structure that the eyes and teeth are different from the laser-scanned head. So we have to make error measurements after taking out the inside structures. Of course, we perform this measurement after aligning the output surface in the same space of the input surface using scaling and translation. Figure 2.12 shows two heads in the same space after translation and scaling. The two surfaces show some mismatch, which is the error, for example, the back part of the hair shows only the input surface where the various hairstyles are not included in this face cloning system. So the points on the left side of the vertical line on the last image in Figure 2.12 are used for error measurement.

In order to compute the error between the two surfaces, we use 3-D distance measurement between two surfaces. For each point P_i on the output surface, we calculate the normal vector n_i by taking the average of normal vectors of connected triangle faces on the surface. Then we make the projection of n_i to the input surface and get the intersection Q_i. To calculate the projection of $n_{i,}$, we first calculate the intersection point between the normal vector and each extended plane of a triangle face on the input surface. Then we can decide if the intersection is inside the triangle face or not. Usually there are one or two intersection

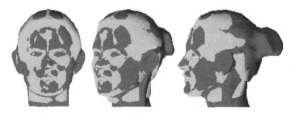

Figure 2.12   Two surfaces in different colours in the same space. The points on the left side of the vertical line on the last image are used for error measurement

points of the normal vector on the input surface. We select the nearest intersection point, Q_i, and calculate the distance between each point P_i on the output surface and the intersection point Q_i. The distance between the point P_i and Q_i is the error E_i of P_i. Figure 2.13 shows the 2-D case.

The surface error E is a summation of each error E_i and the error percentage is calculated as follows where the output surface has n points and R_i is the distance between Q_i and the centre O of the surface. Figure 2.14 illustrates the principle.

$$Error\% = 100.0 \frac{\sum\limits_{i=1}^{n} \frac{E_i}{R_i}}{n} \tag{2.4}$$

When the bounding Box of points on the output surface which are calculated for errors has the size *167.2 × 236.651 × 171.379* where *x(-84.1756, 83.0243)*, *y(-112.715, 123.936)* and *z(-99.808, 71.5709)*, the average error is 3.55236. Here, 756 points are used for error measurement, where the eyes, teeth and some of the back hair parts (indicated in Figure 2.10) are exempt.

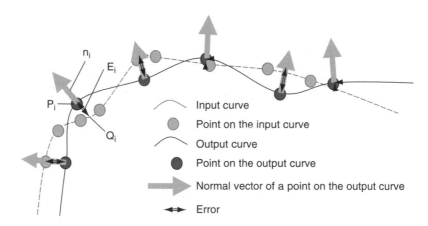

Figure 2.13 2-D case to show the calculation of the distance for each point on the reconstructed curve to the original input curve by calculating the normal vector

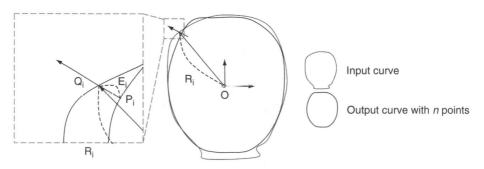

Figure 2.14 2-D case to get error percentage between 2-D curves

The errors are distributed as shown in Figure 2.15 with a minimum error = 0.00139932 and a maximum error = 29.6801. Figure 2.16 shows where the errors come from. The biggest error between two surfaces comes from the ear region, as shown in Figure 2.16(a). The structure of ears is so complicated and it is not possible to adapt it accurately with feature-based method and even with range data equipment. The hairlines between the hair and face regions create the next error source as shown in Figure 2.16(b) and 2.16(c). This error comes from the special hairstyle of the generic model. The final error is 2.84306% of the surface.

In this section, we introduce face modeling and animation techniques. A model-based approach to photo-realistic animatable Virtual Human cloning from several pictures uses as input two photos of the face of the subject. The efficient and robust face cloning method shows the processes of modifying a generic head for shape acquisition and producing texture images by combining orthogonal image pairs smoothly. Unlike other existing systems, which require a special environment to obtain input data, we seek the solution through a friendly user interface for an accurate localization of feature points.

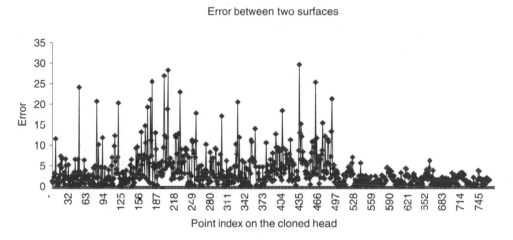

Figure 2.15 Error distribution for the face cloning from orthogonal photograph where the bounding box of the head has the size $167.2 \times 236.651 \times 171.379$

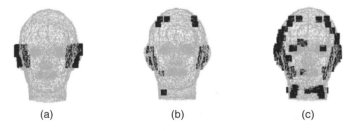

Figure 2.16 Points with error bigger than (a) 15 (b) 10 and (c) 5

2.3   Facial Motion Capture

Motion Capture can be referred to as the process of recording objects' motions in a computer-relevant format. While the techniques or systems used to perform motion acquisition vary greatly from optical, magnetic through acoustic, prosthetic, etc., they usually share a common issue whenever the target object to be animated is a complex structure (such as a Virtual Human body or face) rather than a simple solid object. This issue is the transformation of the raw captured data into the model's own parameter space (e.g. joints' rotations space of the body hierarchy). In this section, we will focus on this operation: transforming measured data into animation parameters.

2.3.1   Motion Capture for Facial Animation

We can broadly divide the facial motion capture techniques into video-based and non-video-based techniques. The video-based techniques are reviewed and studied in detail in the next chapter. In this section we concentrate on the non-video-based techniques. These comprise of using mechanical, opto-electronic, and optical trackers. The basic goal of such systems has been to extract animation parameters from a real-life performance, as against designing the character animation by hand. The manual design needs lots of effort on the part of experienced animators and requires a great deal of time to achieve desired accuracy and precision. On the other hand, use of motion capture techniques allows easier and quicker design of animation that is very realistic, as directly derived from a real-life performer in action. Furthermore, an animator is free to edit the capture data to modify the animation effects as desired.

Around 1992, the SimGraphics company (web: simg) developed one of the first facial motion capture systems called a 'face waldo'™. Using mechanical sensors attached to the chin, lips, cheeks, and eyebrows, and electro-magnetic sensors on the supporting helmet structure, it was possible to track the most important motions of the face and map them in real-time onto computer puppets.

Optotrack™ is a motion capture system that uses small infra-red markers attached to the skin of the performer. The system uses opto-electronic techniques to extract the 3-D position of these markers with an accuracy of 0.1 mm. Kuratate et al. (1998) have reported using such a system for facial capture, as demonstrated in Figure 2.17.

Recently, motion capture using retro-reflective markers tracked with cameras sensitive to light in the red region has become quite popular. Many such systems are commercially available and have been successfully used for computer graphics animation and analysis. Most systems, though originally designed for tracking body movements, can be easily adopted for facial motion capture.

Use of motion capture for facial animation is not limited to generate performance-driven facial animation. There are three different ways of using facial motion capture in Virtual Human animation:

- Direct application of motion capture data for face animation.
- Generation of static expressions and visemes for realistic animation.
- Analysis of facial movements to improve facial animation.

We discuss all these ways in details here.

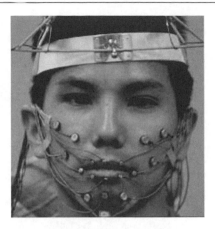

Figure 2.17 Use of OPTOTRAK™ for head and facial motion data. (Reproduced with permission of D. Burham, J. Robert-Ribes and E. Vatikiotis-Bateson.)

2.3.2 MPEG-4-Based Face Capture

Using an optical system, such as Vicon (http: metrics) we can track facial expressions and retarget the tracked features on to the facial animation engine. The results of the deformation algorithm can then be viewed. We use a subset of MPEG-4 (web: mpeg4) feature points corresponding to the Face Animation Parameter (FAP) values to track the face and extract the FAPs frame by the frame. For the capture, we use 8 cameras and 27 markers corresponding to the MPEG-4 feature point locations. Three additional markers are used for tracking the global orientation of the head. The image on the left of Figure 2.18 shows the feature points we use for tracking. The central image shows the tracking point representation as obtained from the software interface. Figure 2.19 schematically shows the feature points chosen by use for facial capture, according to the MPEG-4 standard. For a more detailed description of MPEG-4 facial animation, please refer to Chapters 6 and Chapter 16. The feature points along the inner lip contour cannot be used, as they touch each other in neutral position and many facial movements during speech, causing an error in the reconstruction of the marker trajectories.

We now explain the algorithm used to extract the global head movement from the 3-D capture data and subsequently achieve FAPs for animation. The discussion is based on the improved translation invariant method.

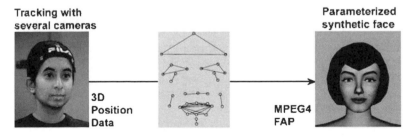

Figure 2.18 Feature points optical tracking

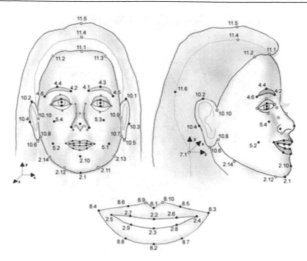

Figure 2.19 MPEG-4 feature points

We use three markers attached to the head to capture the rigid head movements (the global rotation and translation of the head). We use the improved translation invariant method. Let $(p_i, \; p'_i)$ be the positions of the points on the surface of the rigid body, observed at two different time instants. For a rigid body motion, the pair of points $(p_i, \; p'_i)$ obeys the following general displacement relationship:

$$p'_i = Rp_i + t \qquad i = 1, 2, \cdots, N \tag{2.5}$$

R is a 3×3 matrix specifying the rotation angle of the rigid body about an axis arbitrarily oriented in the three-dimensional space, whereas t represents a translation vector specifying arbitrary shift after rotation. Three non-collinear point correspondences are necessary and sufficient to determine R and t uniquely. With three point correspondences, we get nine non-linear equations while there are six unknown motion parameters. Because the 3-D points obtained from the motion capture system are accurate, linear algorithm is sufficient for this application, instead of iterative algorithms based on least square procedure. If two points on the rigid body, p_i and p_{i+1}, undergoing the same transformation, move to p'_i and p'_{i+1} respectively, then

$$p'_i = Rp_i + t \tag{2.6}$$

$$p'_{i+1} = Rp_{i+1} + t \tag{2.7}$$

Subtraction eliminates translation t; using the rigidity constraints yields:

$$\frac{P'_{i+1} - p'_i}{|P'_{i+1} - p'_i|} = R\frac{p_{i+1} - p_i}{|p_{i+1} - p_i|} \tag{2.8}$$

The above equation is defined as:

$$\hat{m}_i = R\hat{m}_i \tag{2.9}$$

If the rigid body undergoes a pure translation, these parameters do not change, which means the translation is invariant. After rearranging these three equations, we can solve a 3×3 linear system to get R and afterwards obtain t by substitution in equation (2.5). In order to find a unique solution, the 3×3 matrix of unit $\hat{m}$ vectors must be of full rank, meaning that the three $\hat{m}$ vectors must be non-coplanar. As a result, four point correspondences are needed. To overcome this problem of supplying the linear method with an extra point correspondence, a 'pseudo-correspondence' can be constructed due to the property of rigidity. We find a third $\hat{m}$ vector orthogonal to the two obtained from three points attached to the head. Thus, the system has a lower dimension, requiring only three non-collinear rigid points. Once we extract the global head movements, the motion trajectories of all the feature point markers are compensated for by the global movements and the absolute local displacements and subsequently the MPEG-4 FAPs are calculated. As FAPs are defined as normalized displacements for the feature points from the neutral position, it is simple to compute FAPs given the neutral position (typically captured as first frame of animation) and the displacement from this position (see Figure 2.20).

2.3.3 Generation of Static Expressions or Key-Frames

Using facial motion capture to directly drive facial animation results in a higher degree of realism. However, it is not always practical to apply such motion capture data for a 'performance-driven facial animation', because it is often restricted by the availability of the performer and the complexity of the equipment involved, which often needs tedious calibration and set-up. Considering these limitations, the output of such motion capture session can be used to design the 'building blocks' of the facial animation. This ensures an adequate degree of realism at the basic unit level. Designing static expressions is probably the most important task and it reflects the final quality of the animation to a great extent. Traditionally, it is possible to design these static expressions in two ways:

1. Use a parameterized facial model and user interface where the animator can interactively 'design' the expressions.
2. Use 3-D mesh modeling software to work directly on the mesh level with various out of box tools for global and local mesh deformation

Both these techniques require a lot of input from innovative designers, and the output depends on the skills and effort put into the design process. It would be much easier and faster to capture the actual expressions of an actor enunciating various emotions and making viseme shapes. The accuracy with which you can capture these expressions typically depends on

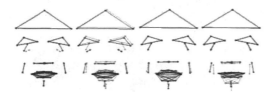

Figure 2.20 Successive feature point displacements from a speech sequence (without global motion compensation). Left image shows the initial neutral posture in dark gray

the technique used for capture and for re-targeting. A combination of this technique with traditional methods leads to a satisfactory facial animation design. Thus, we first capture an actor's facial movements using the motion capture system, to design the static expressions and visemes. These are transformed into the facial model using the parameters and the animator can further work on them to edit, change, enhance or modify. Figure 2.21 demonstrates how six basic facial expressions have been captured from a performer's actions and re-targeted to various synthetic faces by extraction of MPEG-4 FAPs. For more discussion on how these captured parameters are used to design animation sequences, please refer to Chapter 10.

2.3.4 Analysis of Facial Capture Data to Improve Facial Animation

The motion capture combined with statistical analysis techniques such as Principal Component Analysis (PCA) can be used for effective and efficient facial animation. Kuratate et al. (1998) used PCA and a linear estimator algorithm to drive the facial animation from opto-electronically captured facial movement data. Arsal and Talkin (1998) described an algorithm to extract the face point trajectories starting from a phonetically labelled speech signal. They tracked the subject's face using a multi-camera triangulation system. The principal components extracted from the tracked data were used as a compressed representation of this captured data along with the Line Spectral Frequencies (LSF) of the speech signal in a codebook. For each speech frame, a codebook search was performed to find the matching speech parameter values, and the corresponding Principal Components (PCs) for the matched codebook entry were then subsequently used to get the face point trajectories.

In the previous two paragraphs we have already seen the use of the facial motion capture in two different ways to create facial animations. We would like to combine the benefits of both the methods, namely enhanced realism and freedom for design. Designing key-frames of animation (static expressions and visemes) using the facial capture data alone is not enough to strike this balance. An animator applies various time envelopes and blending functions in the process of obtaining facial animation sequences from the static expressions. It is in this process that we need to be very careful in order to avoid artefacts and strange effects arising

Figure 2.21 Facial captured expressions applied on various face models

from combining various facial animation parameters. After all, a life-like facial animation is not merely a series of static expression glued together with simple functions. In order to bring realism to the dynamic movements of the face obtained by a combination of a series of static expressions, we need to do a statistical analysis of the actual speech data. This would help in improving the realism and robustness of the speech animation techniques. We consider the Principal Component Analysis (PCA) to be a powerful tool in achieving this goal. Unlike the two approaches for facial animation using motion capture data and PCA mentioned at the beginning of this section, our motivation behind using PCA is to study the dynamics of the facial feature points during fluent speech, in addition to reducing the dimensionality of the data. Furthermore, we also propose a method to blend various expressions during speech. We captured optical tracking data of a real person speaking a number of sentences from a database of phoneme rich sentences. Since the PCA can be carried out on any form of capture data irrespective of the tracking method, we defer the discussion of this topic till Chapter 10. Here we emphasize that accuracy of the optical tracking and the fact that we get the motion trajectories of the feature points directly in 3-D space (as against some video-based techniques) makes the analysis of data easy and more effective.

3

Body Cloning and Body Motion Capture

Pascal Fua, Ralf Plaenkers, WonSook Lee, Tom Molet

In recent years, there has been increasing interest in automatically extracting human shape and motion parameters from sensor data. This due partly to the fact that useful sensors are getting ever more prevalent and cheaper, and partly to the fact that computers have become powerful enough to take advantage of them in real time. This ability to model humans has many applications, such as smart interfaces, surveillance, electronic publishing, entertainment, sports medicine and athletic training among others. Such modeling, however, is an inherently difficult task, both because the body is very complex and because the sensor data is often incomplete, noisy and ambiguous.

In this chapter, we first review typical approaches to representing Virtual Human bodies and discuss their suitability to automated capture. We then review the existing techniques for deriving shape models and discuss the very active area of motion estimation using both active and passive sensors

3.1   Introduction

One of the oldest goals in computer animation has been the lifelike simulation of human beings. Human figure models have been studied in computer graphics almost since the introduction of the medium. In the last decade, the structure, flexibility, and fidelity of human models have increased dramatically. The human model has evolved from wire-frame stick figures, through simple polyhedral models, to curved surfaces, and volumetric representations.

With the increase in complexity of the models has also come the need to automate their generation from image data so as to reduce the amount of work required before a near-realistic performance can be achieved. At present, it takes an experienced graphics designer a very long time to build a complete and realistic model that closely resembles a specific person. Furthermore, a static shape is not enough for animation purposes. One also has to create an articulated

Handbook of Virtual Humans Edited by N. Magnenat-Thalmann and D. Thalmann
© 2004 John Wiley & Sons, Ltd   ISBN: 0-470-02316-3

skeleton, establish its relationship with a potentially deformable skin surface and derive realistic motion models. This, also, can be done manually but is extremely time-consuming and requires highly skilled animators. As a result, many automated approaches to addressing this problem have been developed and allow an increase in realism while reducing the cost.

Furthermore, cameras are becoming increasingly prevalent in our environment. At the same time, modeling human motion and understanding human gestures are essential in areas such as medicine, surveillance and smart interfaces. As a result, these sophisticated models and automated techniques can be used not only for animation purposes, but also to disambiguate potentially noisy image data and to analyze it more effectively.

In this chapter, we first review typical approaches to representing Virtual Human bodies and discuss their suitability to automated capture. We then review the existing techniques for deriving shape models and discuss the very active area of motion estimation using both active and passive sensors. Finally, we present our own work in that area.

3.2 Body Models for Fitting Purposes

The human body is a very complex structure. Furthermore, as humans, we are especially sensitive to the human form and computer-generated animations must be extremely convincing to satisfy our demands for realism. Modeling and animating the body are therefore one of the most difficult and challenging problems in computer graphics. Recovering human body-shape and motion from sensor-data is an equally demanding task because this data is often noisy, incomplete and ambiguous.

In both cases, a good model is crucial to success. In this section, we briefly review a few basic methodologies for representing humans and refer the interested reader to Chapter 7 for additional details. We take special interest in their potential use for automated modeling and fitting to data.

3.2.1 Stick Figure

Nearly all body models are based on some stick figure representation. A tree-like hierarchy of joints represents the intersections of links, which are an abstract representation of body parts. One such model is depicted in Figure 3.1(a). We call this hierarchy the *articulated structure*. It is referred to as an articulated skeleton as well, although it does not contain any geometry that one would associate with a skeleton made up of bones.

Most systems for tracking people make use of some variant of this stick figure definition. One of the rare exceptions is the model by Kakadiaris and Metaxas (1995) which is constructed as a physics-based spring system. Limbs are modeled by volumetric primitives that are attached by springs to each other. Relatively loose connections between the body parts replace an underlying rigid structure. This allows for more flexibility in the model. In some way, estimation errors introduced by a badly corresponding model can be taken into consideration. However, with such a model it becomes very difficult to constrain joint angles in order to enforce anatomically correct postures.

3.2.2 Simple Volumetric Primitives

The goal of motion capture or gait analysis Computer Vision algorithm is more to extract the motion parameters from video sequences than to produce visually pleasing models. Visual

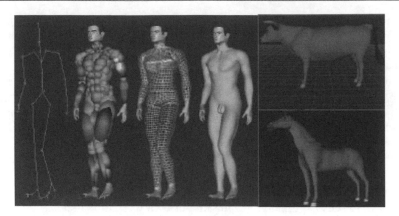

Figure 3.1 Layered body model: (a) Skeleton. (b) Volumetric primitives used to simulate muscles and fat tissue. (c) Polygonal surface representation of the skin. (d) Shaded rendering. (e) A cow and a horse modeled using the same technique

accuracy of the model is not required. Therefore, simple primitives such as ellipsoids and cylinders are a popular way to flesh out the models for tracking purposes. Even though humans cannot be modeled photo-realistically using such discrete primitives, they are popular because they are very simple and have some well-understood mathematical properties, which makes optimization and fitting to image-data easier.

For example, cones (Wachter and Nagel 1999), ellipsoids (Sminchisescu and Triggs 2001), and tapered super-quadrics (Kakadiaris and Metaxas 1995; Gavrila and Davis 1996) were successfully used to track human motions.

3.2.3 Multi-Layered Models

Such models retain the articulated skeleton structure but replace the simple primitives by multiple layers that represent the gross shape of bones, muscle and fat tissue. They have been extensively used for animation purposes and we refer the interested reader to Chapter 7 of this book for additional details.

At the root of our own approach to video-based shape and motion capture that is introduced in next section, is such a multi-layered human body-model. It is depicted in Figure 3.3(a–d). It was originally developed solely for animation purposes (Thalmann et al. 1996) and incorporates a highly effective multi-layered approach for constructing and animating realistic human bodies. The first layer is a skeleton that is a connected set of segments, corresponding to limbs and joints. A joint is the intersection of two segments, which means it is a skeleton point around which the limb linked to that point may move. Smooth implicit surfaces, also known as metaballs or soft objects, form the second layer (Blinn 1982). They are used to simulate the gross behavior of bone, muscle, and fat tissue. The metaballs are attached to the skeleton and arranged in an anatomically-based approximation. In the following section on shape and motion estimation we will argue that this representation is extremely effective for 2-D and 3-D data fitting purposes (Plänkers and Fua 2001; Plänkers and Fua 2003). Furthermore, this method is equally applicable to other vertebrates, such as the horse and cow in Figure 3.1e.

3.2.4 Anatomically Correct Models

A logical next step would be use anatomically correct models that include as much medical knowledge as possible. However, existing systems, such as those presented in Chapter 7, are so complex that no existing system integrates the various models for different layers into a complete human body model. The partial models are limited to certain applications such as medical dynamic simulation, deformation or realistic rendering. In order to fit these highly realistic models to image data, more research will have to be undertaken because these models contain too many parameters.

3.3 Static Shape Reconstruction

Recording the shape of objects has been done for quite a while. The very first painting can be considered a visual 2-D recording of the shape of the depicted object. Clay modeling would be the natural extension to 3-D. This kind of modeling is purely visual. In order to obtain a parametric description one has to measure the model in a certain way. This creates the problem of finding a good way to describe the model so that it could be rebuilt from the numbers alone without reference to the original subject or model.

Applications for parametric models are numerous, from reverse engineering to medical analysis or simulations. In the following sections we will present several approaches to obtaining shape models of objects. More specifically, we will discuss methods for obtaining more or less parameterized body models.

3.3.1 3-D Scanners

The Cyberware Whole Body Color 3-D Scanner captures the shape and color of the entire human body. The scanner acquires a full body model in 17 seconds. To capture the intricacies of the human body in one pass, the Cyberware scanner uses four scanning instruments mounted on two vertical towers. Each tower has a linear ball-bearing rail and servo-motor assembly that moves the scanning instrument vertically. A platform structure supports the subject, while a separate frame provides alignment for the towers. With a person standing on the scanner's platform, the scanning instruments start at the person's head and move down to scan the entire body.

The primary goal of Cyberware's scanner is to acquire an accurate computer model in one pass. The use of multiple instruments improves accuracy on the sides of the body and in difficult-to-reach areas, such as under a person's arms. While the simple anthropometric pose gives the best results, the scanner is designed to handle many different poses for a wide range of applications. The full system is depicted in Figure 3.2(a).

A much cheaper approach to laser scanning is the use of a single mobile scanning head. Cost drops substantially while acquisition time augments critically. It is difficult to have a live subject remain totally immobile during the full scan. For static objects, like the bust in Figure 3.2(b), this approach may be sufficient and a correct 3-D reconstruction can be obtained as shown in Figure 3.2(c).

Recently, advances in photogrammetry have allowed the slow and expensive laser scanners to be replaced by a set of standard cameras. Stereo correlation or space carving techniques are used to obtain the surface of the objects in the scene. Often, structured light is projected onto the subject to make the matching more robust. The system presented by Saito and Kanade (1999) goes one step further by extracting the surface at frame-rate, which allows the creation of 3-D movies that can be looked at from any angle.

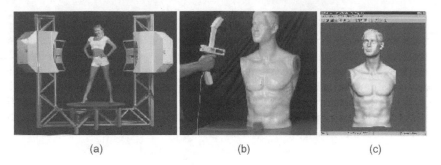

(a)   (b)   (c)

Figure 3.2   (a) Cyberware Whole Body Color 3-D Scanner. (b) Polhemus mobile laser scanner. (c) Resulting 3-D model. (Reproduced by permission of Polhemus and Cyberware.)

3.3.2   Finding Structure in Scattered 3-D Data

The data obtained by laser scanners or similar devices represents a static high resolution surface and deforming it realistically for animation purposes is difficult. This requires partitioning it into body parts and attaching those parts to an articulated skeleton.

Introducing a structure into 3-D scattered data without a-priori knowledge about the data is a very difficult and yet unsolved problem. Most research in this area focuses on fitting implicit surfaces or generalized cylinders (Bittar et al. 1995). Verroust and Lazarus (1999) introduced a method for extracting skeletal curves from an unorganized collection of scattered data points lying on a surface. These curves may have a tree-like structure to capture branching shapes. The main steps for the construction of the axes are, first, the computation of neighborhood relationships and geodesic distance graphs and, second, the computation of geodesic level sets, their centroids and the location of branching nodes. A surface or volume model, e.g. generalized cylinders, could then be constructed around this skeleton to describe the data in a more compact and structured manner.

They applied this approach to reconstructing blood vessels as well as the shape of a human and a horse. The results show that the algorithm recovers a well-positioned skeleton that runs through the 'middle' of the data. However, in the human case only the topology of the axial structure resembles the anatomic skeleton whereas its position inside the body is very different. Figure 3.3(a) shows a rendering of data obtained using a Cyberware laser scanner and the recovered axial structure. Deforming a surface fitted to the data by animating its axial structure like a skeleton would yield deformations that are not human-like, it would look highly unrealistic. Higher level knowledge about body structure needs to be integrated in order to obtain results usable for character animation.

Another problem is the non-uniqueness of automatically extracted skeletons because the axial structure is not unique for a given object (Verroust and Lazarus 1999). It depends on user-defined thresholds and the – more or less arbitrary – choice of a starting point for the algorithm, called the seed point. They also observe that the issue of finding a suitable axis in order to design a generalized cylinder is rarely discussed in the literature, even though, in practice, this task can be tedious.

Another important work about constructing algebraic surfaces from 2-D and 3-D data has been published in Sullivan et al. (1994). The authors fit implicit surfaces similar to those that we use in our own work (Plänkers and Fua 2001; Plänkers and Fua 2003) presented in

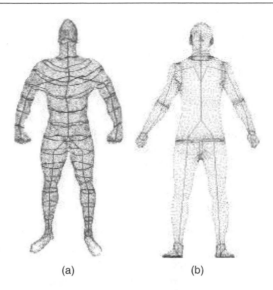

(a)   (b)

Figure 3.3 Scan of a human subject. (a) Its associated axial structure and (b) a similar scan of a different subject and the animated skeleton obtained by fitting our model to the data

this chapter on 3-D point data as well as 2-D silhouette data. Parameters defining shape and pose of a 3-D model are estimated in a constraint least-squares framework.

3.3.3 Conforming Animatable Models to 3-D Scanned Data

Recent work (Ju and Siebert 2001; Douros et al. 1999; Sun et al. 1999) explores ways to turn highest definition 3-D scans into animatable models. (Douros et al. 1999) concentrated on the task of generating a smooth and well-structured surface that fits the dense set of data points delivered by the scanner. Basic segmentation and feature point correspondences add first notions of semantics to the data as well as compressing the amount of information needed to define the model.

Promising work on animating directly the dense scanner data is presented in Sun et al. (1999). A relatively simple and H-Anim compatible body model is deformed globally and positioned in a way to match the data in a coarse way. A mapping between the coarse model and all scanner data points is established. The relative proximity of the coarse model mesh and the scanner points allows for a fairly realistic animation of the complex scanner data using a normal volume representation.

Taking ideas from both previously mentioned approaches, it was then proposed to first segment the 3-D scanner-data points and organize them into slices (Ju et al. 2000). This idea was then extended to deforming a complex but generic body model to correspond as closely as possible to the scanner data (Ju and Siebert 2001). A manual global deformation is followed by an automated local deformation of the model mesh to fit the data closely. This method preserves the structure of the model while, at the same time, it tightly fits the data. Using deformation capacities of standard modeling applications allows for animating the photo-realistic model.

Most current work on modeling human bodies from high definition input devices concentrates on the shape. The animatable model surface corresponds to the scanner data very closely. Little effort, however, is put into positioning the articulated structure inside the model surface and how the surface should be deformed in order to achieve realistic animations for a large variety of motions.

The result of applying our own fitting techniques to scanned data is presented in Figure 3.3(b). Simple vertex-to-skeleton association, called *skinning*, would already allow animation at acceptable quality. However, note the position of the elbows. The upper arm is too long compared to the forearm. Without using anthropometric constraints it is impossible to tell the location of the elbow on a stretched arm.

3.3.4 Photo-Based Shape Reconstruction

Much work has been devoted to reconstructing object geometry from images. In particular, early vision research was motivated by the desire to explain images, that is, to recover the shape, appearance and nature of the scene objects. The problem is difficult and no universal object reconstruction system exists. People argue that such a general system is impossible to build. Success has been claimed for systems that work in very constrained environments, usually putting strong assumptions on object types, object as well as background appearance and camera setup.

In Hilton et al. (1999), the authors propose a method for capturing realistic whole-body animated models of clothed people using model-based reconstruction from color images taken from orthogonal viewpoints in an environment with a specially prepared background and properly controlled lighting. Body outlines are extracted from the images and used to morph a 3-D generic humanoid model into the shape and appearance of a specific person. It is a low-cost approach to whole-body capture of clothed people from digital color images.

This technique is simple and efficient, and has been further refined to model the whole person, including a high-resolution animatable face (Lee and Magnenat-Thalmann 2000). This approach combines a generic face template and an H-Anim 1.1 compliant body model. To adjust the model's shape and texture using feature and edge information, it requires two orthogonal photos of the subject's face and three photos of his body. Figure 3.4 depicts the five input images for a particular subject and the resulting body model. The complete approach extends the face cloning technique of Chapter 2 to the whole body. It incorporates a user friendly interface for accurate localization of feature points. They are used for automatic skeleton modification, automatic edge extraction and personalization of the generic skin. A simple but effective heuristics-based boundary extraction algorithm is proposed to automatically extract the body silhouette from the images. To avoid potential overlaps of skin parts, a two-step modification is introduced: first, matching is performed using only feature-point information and, then, refined using edge information. The body texture map is computed from two images. In the end, connecting the individualized heads and bodies yields a complete animatable human model that can exist in Virtual Environments. Figure 3.5 shows the comparison between a tailor's measure and the reconstructed body's measure. The errors are only a few centimeters even on the very deformable parts such as waist and less than 1 cm on a fairly rigid part such as hip.

The accuracies shown in Figure 3.5 are entirely acceptable for virtual reality applications and do not detract from the quality of the animations that can be generated using these models. However, methods based exclusively on a few orthogonal views cannot produce

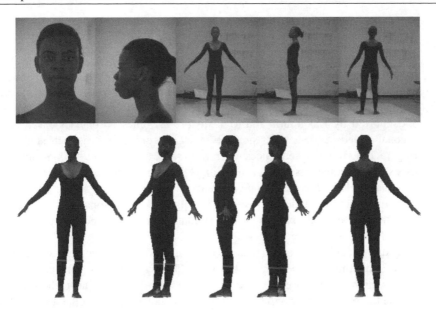

Figure 3.4 Top row: Five input photographs of a woman, Bottom row: Reconstructed 3-D body

		Tailor's (m)	model's (m)	Diff. (cm)
	Height	1.74	1.75029	1.029
	Waist	0.68	0.727171	4.7171
	Hip	0.894	0.88432	−0.968
	Chest	0.835	0.819402	−1.5598

Figure 3.5 Comparison of measurement on the actual body and reconstructed body

highly precise body shape for a specific individual. Realism is achieved through efficient texture mapping that is used to hide the innacuracies of the reconstructed shape. Recent research (Starck and Hilton 2002) has extended the single camera silhouette approach to multiple simultaneous views of a person. Shape-constrained deformable models are used to simultaneously estimate shape and appearance across multiple views, giving improved accuracy and overcoming some of the limitations in combining multiple separate views.

Other promising approaches to realistic shape modeling have been developed for face-modeling purposes, for example, as discussed in Chapter 2, a database covering many different heads, their 3-D shape as well as their texture or appearance, Principal Component Analysis allows for the definition of powerful bases that are able to yield nearly any given face when combined in the right way (Blanz and Vetter 1999). Unfortunately, adapting these approaches for full body modeling is not straightforward. The face can be considered a single rigid surface with many easily extractable feature points. The body, in contrast, is highly deformable and can be abstracted at best as an articulated set of piecewise rigid parts. No systems using a pure learning approach to body modeling have been found yet.

3.3.5   Video-Based Shape Reconstruction

In contrast to image-based systems that rely on several views of a subject taken at a single instant, video-based systems have to deal with a dynamic scene. The subject moves between instants, which makes analyzing its shape a challenge. Little work has been published on this subject and we believe that addressing the human shape and motion recovery problem simultaneously is one of the features of originality of the work presented in this section.

The work reported by Kakadiaris and Metaxas (1995) relies on physics-based modeling from orthogonal video sequences. It presents a framework that constructs a deformable model during tracking in video sequences taken from three mutually orthogonal cameras. The model consists of superquadrics representing limbs that are connected by a spring system. It does not use an articulated hierarchy. The extracted silhouettes of the subject were used as a physical force to attract the model and deform the quadrics both globally as well as locally. A spring system kept the body parts together, emulating an articulated structure. A Kalman filter was used for the estimation process.

Converting this model – a set of relatively loosely connected quadric surfaces – into an animatable body model is not straightforward. The system does not guarantee a specific topology, which would ease the conversion process. Also, similar to the image-based approaches mentioned in the previous section, the model projects well into the observed camera views; the model's shape in-between is approximated through simple interpolation techniques. The system does not make use of the possibility to refine the model by using previously unobserved viewpoints during a motion sequence.

The Virtualized Reality project (Saito and Kanade 1999) has access to a multi-camera video dome that is able to capture at frame rate a scene from many viewpoints all around. However, exploiting these huge amounts of data is very difficult. Current research was mainly centered around re-rendering captured scenes from new viewpoints using disparity maps and multiple textures to interpolate between observed viewpoints. Similarly, the approach reported by Davis et al. (1999) is also limited by the fact that it relies on a voxelized representation of the scene at each instant, without producing a parametric description.

In the work of Ju and Siebert (2001), the authors propose taking a single 3-D reconstruction of such a scene and apply the techniques for obtaining animatable models from laser scanners, such as those previously discussed. This, unfortunately, eliminates the main advantage of having access to motion sequences: obtaining information about the underlying articulated structure as well as the dynamic deformation of the surface, that is, the positions of the articulations inside the skin surface.

The system, proposed in Plänkers and Fua (2001; 2003), takes a two-step process. First, similar to most tracking applications, a rough model is obtained through quick user interaction and the system takes care of tracking it throughout a sequence. In a second phase, the system optimizes the shape of the model globally in all frames, taking advantage of all information from any viewpoint and every posture available.

3.4   Dynamic Motion Capture

Understanding and recording human and other vertebrae motion have a long tradition. Paintings from early cultures thousands of years old tried to describe the actions involved in certain tasks, e.g. hunting. Their only tool for observation were their own eyes and the only means of presentation were paintings of distinct parts of the motion.

More powerful tools for analysis and presentation became available through the invention of photographic procedures, later enhanced to moving images, films. In the following section we will present early studies on the subject of motion analysis from image sequences. Then, jumping to more recent times, we will discuss popular techniques for capturing motion with the help of magnetic or optical devices, followed by a more elaborate discussion on recent advances in the field of video-based motion capture.

3.4.1 Early Motion Analysis

3.4.1.1 Eadweard Muybridge

Eadweard Muybridge was one of the most significant contributors to the early study of human and animal locomotion. In 1872 Muybridge was enlisted by Leland Stanford to settle a wager regarding the position of a trotting horse's legs. Using the fastest shutter available, Muybridge was able to provide only the faintest image. He was more successful five years later when, employing a battery of cameras with mechanically tripped shutters, he showed clearly the stages of the horse's movement: at top speed, a trotting horse had all four hooves off the ground simultaneously, and in a different configuration from that of a galloping horse.

(International Center of Photography 1984)

Some of the original plates are shown in Figure 3.6.

Muybridge's technique falls into the category of visual motion capture. A motion is filmed or photographed at multiple instants and often from several viewpoints. The assembling of the individual frames to a single large-format print constitutes the final result and was meant mainly for artistic purposes. Muybridge considered the scientific study of motion only as a secondary aspect. Recent research at the Smithsonian National Museum of American History (Delaney 2000) suggests that the scientific value of his work is actually questionable because the sequences were 'post-processed' for aesthetic reasons. Yet his photography continues to influence artists, photographers, filmmakers, and researchers.

His work is still invaluable to designers for animating characters for games or general computer-generated entertainment. His plates of very detailed motion, taken often from several points of view simultaneously as the example in Figure 3.7, serve as a model for

(a)   (b)

Figure 3.6 How do horses trot? (a) Degas painting 'Le Faux Départ' (1870) demonstrating the common misperception that a horse had all four hooves off the ground when the legs were stretched out. (b) Muybridge's photographic analysis (1878) disproves this. A horse's legs are off the ground when they are close together

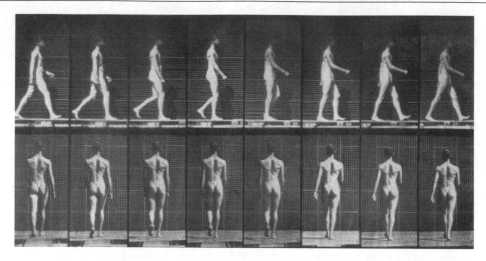

Figure 3.7 One example of Eadweard Muybridge's photographic analysis of human and animal motion. He often used several viewpoints, two in this example, to capture the 3-D aspect of the complex motions involved in even simple everyday tasks, e.g. walking or climbing stairs

key-framing today's heroes in computer games. However, 'captured' motions in Muybridge's plates cannot be used directly for animating new characters. Only the visual analysis of the motion is available, no quantitative assessment can be made from the plates. Animators need to manually adjust the parameters for their character so that its projection coincides with the subject on the plates.

3.4.1.2 Etienne-Jules Marey

In 1860 Etienne-Jules Marey started his work on studying the movements of humans and animals. His most influential publication *Le mouvement* (Marey 1994) was first published in 1894, in the same era as Muybridge's popular artwork. Sequences were generated by painting white stripes on tight black clothes and redoing the motion.

He can be considered to be the first person to analyze human and animal locomotion on video. In contrast to Muybridge's battery of photographic cameras, he used a single 'video camera' to capture a movement. His ambitions were more scientific as well, working on motion capture, motion analysis as well as motion measurements rather than concentrating on the artistic aspect of the plates.

3.4.2 *Electro-Magnetic and Optical Motion Capture Systems*

Electro-magnetic Motion Capture systems such as the Polhemus STAR∗TRAK™ or the Ascension MotionStar™ use magnetic field sensing technology to track motion from multiple sensors. A few wired magnetic sensors are attached to the body of the performer. Usually, one sensor per body part is sufficient because the sensors capture position as well as orientation. Tracking the sensor is done by the system and each sensor's unique identification and its full 'visibility' by design – occlusions cannot occur – make this step robust and fast. Sensor positions and orientations are processed in hardware and at rates of at least 100Hz in most recent systems.

As shown in Figure 3.8(a), joint angles can be inferred from such data and used to let a Virtual Human mimic the actions of the performer in real time. The approach depicted here (Molet et al. 1999) is orientation-driven and the position measurements are only used to recover the performer's global position. This method allows fast human gesture tracking for interactive applications as well as high rate recordings that are over 100Hz. This approach is well suited for magnetic-based systems that are more reliable and precise for orientation sensing, whereas position measurements necessitate difficult system calibration. This is in contrast to the majority of motion capture techniques that tend to rely on position, instead, because optical motion capture systems track orientation better than position and because known animation techniques, such as inverse kinematics or geometric algorithms, typically require position targets.

However, tests (Livingston and State 1997; Trefftz and Burdea 2000) have shown the sensors' accuracy to be low and highly influenced by the surrounding environment, especially in the presence of metal. This could be partially improved by look-up table techniques (Livingston and State 1997) provided that another measuring system, that does not disturb the magnetic field, is available to estimate the errors and build the lookup-table. In any event, the sensors have to be wired which is cumbersome and it limits the performer's actions. Newer systems lessen this drawback by introducing a 'wireless' solution where all cables only need to be connected to a kind of backpack that is worn by the performer. This is a tremendous improvement but it is still cumbersome to put on the markers and to fix the cables to the body. The weight of the backpack can have an unwanted influence on the motion of the performer.

By contrast, optical motion capture systems do not need cabling, they rely on optical markers that can be tracked visually, such as those shown in Figure 3.8(b). Several cameras are arranged around the capture space with the number of cameras directly influencing the robustness of the system and the size of the capture volume. A compromise between the amount of overlap or redundancy and the size of the capture volume has to be found, which means balancing robustness against volume.

Oxford Metric's Vicon system can use between six and 24 cameras to capture complex multi-body motions in great volumes. The capture rate or time frequency of optical systems can be very high, up to 250 Hz to capture even the slightest subtleties of the performer's

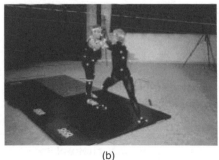

(a)   (b)

Figure 3.8 Magnetic (a) and optical (b) motion capture systems

motions. Latest systems even support real-time processing at frame rate. But a major problem of optical systems remains the robust tracking of the many retro-reflective markers. Each body part needs to have several markers attached to it in order to estimate its position and orientation. Performers may not behave naturally because they do not feel at ease with so many physical markers attached to their body.

But even these highly sophisticated systems can lose track of markers or interchange the trajectories of two markers, mainly because of frequent occlusions mostly caused by limb self-occlusion. As a result, manual post-processing of the trajectories is common practice, although it is tedious and time-consuming. In fact, some of the techniques that we present in following sections – notably, automated estimation of the performer's skeleton proportions and marker motion prediction based on the skeleton model – can help solve these problems (Herda et al. 2001).

3.4.3   Video-Based Motion Capture

In recent years there has been much interest in capturing complex motions solely by analyzing video sequences, as this would provide a much cheaper and more flexible alternative. This can be achieved by tracking the human body using 3-D models with kinematic and dynamic constraints. Some of the earliest efforts (O'Rourke and Badler 1980; Hogg 1983) used edge information to drive a kinematic model of the human body. These systems require precise hand initialization and cannot handle the full range of common body motions.

Single camera solutions such as (Bregler and Malik 1998; Wachter and Nagel 1999; Sminchisescu and Triggs 2001) would be ideal to process standard image sequences, including the incredible amount of movies and other films that have been produced until now. However, they are not always robust, in part because image data is very noisy and in part because it is inherently ambiguous (Morris and Rehg 1998). By contrast, using multiple cameras (Kakadiaris and Metaxas 1995; Kakadiaris and Metaxas 1996; Delamarre and Faugeras 2001) leads to a considerable reduction in the size of the search space, and a considerable improvement in robustness, at the cost of having to deal with large amount of data, most of which is redundant.

Below, we briefly review some of the classical work in this area and present some newer developments. For a more in-depth description, we refer the interested reader to recent surveys in the area of visual motion capture (Aggarwal and Cai 1999; Gavrila 1999; Moeslund and Granum 2001).

3.4.3.1   Unimodal parametric approaches

Digital Muybridge (Bregler and Malik 1998) is a successor to Muybridge's work discussed above. It recovers motion from mono or multi-ocular video sequences using a differential approach. An optical flow formulation was embedded in a new model-based framework that simplified the non-linear nature of 3-D articulated tracking to a linear 2-D problem. This was done by linearizing the angular rotations in the articulated chain using the concept of the product of exponential maps and projecting a simplified model based on ellipsoids with scaled orthographic projection. They were able to recover the 3-D articulated motion from Muybridge's original photo plates of human locomotion. Due to the differential nature of the algorithm, drifting may become a problem in longer sequences. This is one of the few works that introduces a sophisticated model for the dynamics of an articulated structure.

An extension to this work has recently been proposed by Drummond and Cipolla (2001). Statistics of probability distributions were used to linearize the problem of articulated tracking, again representing rotations by exponential maps and using coarse volumetric primitives. The proposed system is able to track a human body in real time in a multi-ocular environment. The authors note that most errors in the tracking are due to the model not being accurate enough. Our own work in this area, presented in this chapter, provides a method for recovering a more accurate model of the filmed person after minimal interaction.

A related approach has been proposed by Wachter and Nagel (1999). Here, edge as well as region information is used in a Kalman filter-based estimation framework. The 3-D articulated motion of a simple volumetric model is recovered from monocular video sequences. Although the combination of using edge as well as region information allows for some robustness, the model may drift in long sequences.

Again using a Kalman filter-based framework (Kakadiaris and Metaxas 1995) estimated shape as well as motion of articulated objects using physics based models. Given a scene with subtracted background in three mutually orthogonal cameras, they modeled the object by quadrics enhanced with local deformation. They were the first to use accurate shape models in a human tracking system. The orthogonal views allowed for some robustness with respect to self-occlusions.

Similar models were used by Gavrila and Davis (1996) in a multi camera search-based framework. They first obtain a realistic model that closely matches the person using a still image silhouette-based approach of the elbow on a stretched arm.

Then, the projection of the model is matched with the segmented body parts in all camera views. The person has to wear tight colored clothes to make the segmentation robust. They introduced the chamfer distance transform to perform the search efficiently.

More recently, Delamarre and Faugeras (2001) have proposed a related approach that can be seen as a mixture of earlier physics-based work (Kakadiaris and Metaxas 1996) and an articulated model-based framework. A simple volumetric model, roughly initialized to the size of the filmed person, is fitted to 3-D data obtained from a calibrated stereo rig or to extracted silhouettes from a few distant viewpoints. The data is interpreted as forces that attract the limbs of the model and motion prediction is provided by a Kalman filter.

3.4.3.2   Unimodal statistics-based approaches

One characteristic of the methods presented until now has been their independence from motion models. This means that these methods can be used to track arbitrary motions, a very important aspect of motion capture applications. Motions that are already known no longer need to be captured. The trade-off is to paid in terms of robustness. The simple prediction generated by the Kalman filter typically fails for abrupt motions. In the following paragraphs we present several techniques that take more elaborate motion models into account, mostly by learning 'probable' motions from training sequences.

The MIT Medialab group explored several methodologies in their quest for human motion recognition from video sequences. Most work is done towards real-time motion recognition for new human–machine interfaces. They explored both geometric model-based and model-free approaches. More emphasis is put on motion models that are exploited in both cases.

The model free approach relies on fixed viewpoints as well as robust silhouette extraction, which was realized in a highly controlled environment through background subtraction using a variant of blue screening or chroma keying. Short-term motion history was efficiently coded as motion gradient images, which could be compared to those of temporal templates via simple pattern matching techniques. The system proposed by Davis and Bobick (1997) allowed real-time interaction through a limited set of motions.

A more generic system used articulated blob models in a Kalman filter-based environment. This was initially limited to 2-D tracking (Wren et al. 1995), and was then extended to real-time 3-D tracking using scaled orthographical projection and a recursive filter approach in conjunction with learned motion models (Wren and Pentland 1999). This approach makes extensive use of the articulated model with special emphasis on guiding the lowest level image processing operations. The system relies on a fixed background as well as putting constraints on the color of clothes, notably uniformly colored clothes that must be distinct from the skin color, and both must be distinct from the background.

An extension of this system, presented by Davis et al. (1999), was able to capture the location of head, hands, and feet in real time in a multi-camera set-up. The recovered locations of the extremities were used to animate virtual characters, mimicking the performers' actions. However, due to the underlying overly simplistic model, the recovered motion is far from realistic.

3.4.3.3   Multi-modal or multiple hypothesis testing

Recently, particle filters have become a popular means of tracking objects in complex environments and with complex motions. The CONDENSATION algorithm and its variants (Isard and Blake 1998; Deutscher et al. 2000; Sidenbladh et al. 2002) are often used in this context. However, due to the enormous search space for highly articulated structures much thought has to be put into reducing the complexity of the algorithm. Later work, such as by Davison et al. (2001), suggests that the full multi-modal multiple-hypothesis approach in the form of particle filtering has to be replaced by less complex and more efficient techniques. In the work of Choo and Fleet (2001) a modified particle filter, called the 'Hybrid Monte Carlo Filter,' is introduced that reduces the computational complexity by several orders of magnitude. Its viability and robustness for long practical sequences have still to be proved but first results are promising.

A different approach is advocated by Cham and Rehg (1999). The authors argue that tracking articulated objects in 3-D is too difficult a problem to be solved directly. Instead, they break it down to a combined 2-D tracking and 3-D estimation approach. A 2-D model consisting of articulated scaled primitives is used for tracking in a single camera view. In a second step they fit a 3-D model to the results delivered by the previous tracking step. A unimodal tracker together with multiple hypothesis testing makes the system fairly robust.

3.4.3.4   Remarks

By taking into account the advantages and disadvantages of previous work, one may come to the conclusion that a mixture of local optimization together with testing several – possibly randomly distributed – hypotheses could be the optimal way for robust and precise tracking of articulated objects, especially human beings. Various methods for solving parameter estimation and tracking problems are discussed by Bar-Shalom and Li (1993). Incorporating constraints from anatomical modeling and a better understanding of its mathematical underpinnings should further improve system performance and robustness.

3.5 Articulated Soft Objects for Shape and Motion Estimation

The human layered body-model seen in the previous section in Figure 3.1 (a–d) is at the root of our approach. Our goal is to use video-sequences to estimate the model's shape and derive its position in each frame, and to this end, we have reformulated it as an *articulated soft object*. We outline our approach below and refer the interested reader to earlier publications for additional details (Plänkers and Fua 2001; 2003).

3.5.1 State Vector

Our goal is to use video-sequences to estimate our model's shape and derive its position in each frame. Let us therefore assume that we are given N consecutive video frames and introduce position parameters for each frame. Let B be the number of body parts in our model. We assign to each body part a variable length and width coefficient. These dimensions change from person to person but we take them to be constant within a particular sequence. This constraint could be relaxed, for example, to model muscular contraction.

The model's *shape* and *position* are then described by the combined state vector:

$$\Theta = \{\Theta^w, \Theta^l, \Theta^r, \Theta^g\} \tag{3.1}$$

where we have broken Θ into four sub-vectors, which control the following model components:

- Shape

$$\Theta^w = \{\theta_b^w | b = 1..B\}, \text{ the width of body parts.}$$
$$\Theta^l = \{\theta_b^l | b = 1..B\}, \text{ the length of body parts.}$$

- Motion

$$\Theta^r = \{\theta_{j,f}^r | j = 1..J, f = 1..N\}, \text{ the rotational degree of freedom of joint } j \text{ of the articulated skeleton for all frames } f.$$
$$\Theta^g = \{\theta_f^g | f = 1..N\}, \text{ the six parameters of global position and orientation of the model in the world frame for all frames } f.$$

The size and position of the metaballs are relative to the segment they are attached to. A length parameter not only specifies the length of a skeleton segment but also the shape of the attached metaballs in the direction of the segment. Width parameters only influence the metaballs' shape in the other directions. Motion parameters Θ^r are represented in terms of Euler angles. We can constrain joint motions to anatomically valid ranges by defining an allowable interval for each degree of freedom. Other methods for describing rotations, such as quaternions or exponential maps, could be used as well.

3.5.2 Metaballs and Quadratic Distance Function

Metaballs (Blinn 1982) are generalized algebraic surfaces that are defined by summation of n 3-dimensional Gaussian density distributions, which we refer to as *primitives*. The final surface S is found where the density function F equals a threshold T, taken to be 0.5 in this work:

$$S = \{[x, y, z]^\tau \in \mathbf{R}^3 | F(x, y, z) = T\} \tag{3.2}$$

$$F(x, y, z) = \sum_{i=1}^{n} f_i(d_i(x, y, z)) \tag{3.3}$$

$$f_i(x, y, z) = exp(-2d_i(x, y, z)) \tag{3.4}$$

where d_i represents the algebraic ellipsoidal distance described below. For simplicity's sake, in the remainder of the chapter, we will omit the i index for specific metaball sources wherever the context is unambiguous.

We use ellipsoidal primitives because they are simple and, at the same time, allow accurate modeling of human limbs with relatively few primitives, thus keeping the number of parameters low. To express simply the transformations of these implicit surfaces that are caused by their attachment to an articulated skeleton, we write the ellipsoidal distance function d of Eq. (3.4) in matrix notation as follows. Given a state vector Θ, the algebraic distance of point $x = [x, y, z, 1]$ to an ellipsoid attached to a particular joint can be written as

$$d(x, \Theta) = x^T \cdot S_\Theta^T \cdot Q_\Theta^T \cdot Q_\Theta \cdot S_\Theta \cdot x \tag{3.5}$$

where Q_Θ is a 4×4 matrix that defines the shape and center of the ellipsoid and S_Θ represents the skeleton-induced rotation-translation matrix from the world frame to the frame to which the metaball is attached. This formulation will prove key to effectively computing the Jacobians required to implement the optimization scheme presented in the next section.

We can now compute the global field function F of Eq. (3.3) by plugging Eq. (3.5) into the individual field functions of Eq. (3.4) and adding up these fields for all primitives. In other words, the field function from which the model surface is derived can be expressed in terms of the Q_Θ and S_Θ matrices, and so can its derivatives. These matrices will therefore constitute the basic building blocks of our optimization scheme's implementation.

3.5.3 Optimization Framework

Our goal is to instantiate the degrees of freedom of our model so that it conforms as faithfully as possible to the image data derived from motion sequences. The expected output of our system is the instantiated state vector Θ of Eq. (3.1) that describes the model's shape and motion. This is a highly non-linear problem: the model consists of an articulated set of implicit surfaces. As a result it contains rotations in Euclidean space as well as quadratic and exponential distance functions. Simplifying the volumetric models, replacing the perspective transform by an orthographic one, and using a different representation for rotational joints can be used to linearize parts of the problem (Bregler and Malik 1998). Such approaches, however, tend to lose in generality. Therefore, we chose to use a non-linear least squares estimator (LSE) to minimize the distance between the observations and the model. We implemented a variant of the standard Levenberg-Marquart least-squares solver (Press et al. 1986) that can handle large number of unknowns by using sparse matrices.

In practice, we use the image data to *nobs* write observation equations of the form:

$$F(\text{x}, \Theta) = T - \epsilon_i, 1 \leq i \leq nobs \tag{3.6}$$

where F is the global field function of Eq. (3.3), is the threshold of Eq. (3.2), x is a data point, and ϵ_i is an error term. We then minimize

$$v^T P_v \tag{3.7}$$

where $v = [\epsilon_1, \ldots, \epsilon_{nobs}]$ is the vector of residuals and P is a diagonal weight matrix associated to the observations. Because F is both well defined and differentiable, these observations and their derivatives can be estimated both simply and without search using the matrix formalism of the section on metaballs. This is valuable because our least-squares solver takes advantage of differential information for faster and more robust optimization, as do most powerful optimizers.

In our work, we concentrate on combining stereo and silhouette data. Figure 3.9 illustrates their complementarity: In this example, we used a single stereo pair. In Figure 3.9(c) only

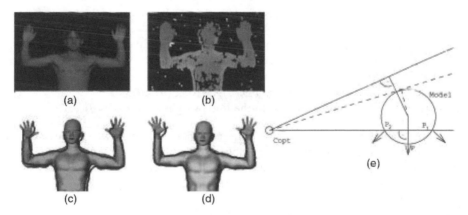

Figure 3.9 The importance of silhouette information for shape modeling. (a) One image from a stereo pair. (b) Corresponding disparity map. (c) Fitting the model to stereo data alone results in a recovered body model that is too far away from the cloud. The system compensates by incorrectly enlarging the primitives as shown by the fact the true body outlines, shown in black, are inside the model. (d) Using these outlines to constrain the reconstruction results in a more accurate model. (e) Only the dashed line is a valid silhouette that satisfies both criteria of section 2-D Silhouette Observations. The upper line is perpendicular to the normal of the surface at the closest point and points on the lower line are on the surface but the rays are not perpendicular to the surface normal

stereo-data, in the form of a cloud of 3-D points derived from the disparity map, was used to fit the model. The stereo data is too noisy and shallow to sufficiently constrain the model. As a result, the fitting algorithm tends to move it too far away from the 3-D data and to compensate by inflating the arms to keep contact with the point cloud. Using the silhouettes in addition to the stereo data, however, sufficiently constrains the fitting problem to obtain the much improved result of Figure 3.9(d). We now turn to the detailed implementation of these 3-D point and 2-D silhouette observations which are the main cues we obtain from the image sequences.

3.5.3.1   3-D point observations

Disparity maps such as those of Figure 3.9(b) are used to compute clouds of noisy 3-D points. Each one is used to produce one observation of the kind described by Eq. (3.6). Minimizing the corresponding residuals tends to force the fitted surface to be as close as possible to these points.

The properties of the chosen distance function allow the system to naturally deal with outliers and to converge even from rough initializations or estimates. The smooth shape of the inverted exponential that is used in our field function is responsible for both effects. It approaches zero asymptotically and, thus, provides an upper limit on the error resulting from distance between model and observation.

3.5.3.2   2-D silhouette observations

A silhouette point in the image defines a line of sight to which the surface must be tangential. Let $\theta \in \Theta$ be an element of the state vector. For each value θ, we define the implicit surface

$$S(\theta) = \left\{ [x, y, z]^T \in R^3, F(x, y, z, \theta) = T \right\} \qquad (3.8)$$

Let $[x(\theta),\ y(\theta),\ z(\theta)]$ be the point on the line of sight where it is tangential to $S(\theta)$. By definition, $[x(\theta),\ y(\theta),\ z(\theta)]$ satisfies two constraints:

1. The point is on the surface, therefore $F(x(\theta),\ y(\theta),\ z(\theta),\ \theta) = T$.
2. The normal to $S(\theta)$ is perpendicular to the line of sight at $[x(\theta),\ y(\theta),\ z(\theta)]$.

We integrate silhouette observations into our framework by performing an initial search along the line of sight to find the point x that is closest to the model in its current configuration. This point is used to add one of the observations described by Eq. (3.6). By construction, the point on the ray with the lowest field value satisfies the second constraint as depicted by Figure 3.9(e).

In order to keep the second constraint satisfied during the optimization process, the Jacobian has to be constructed accordingly. A change in model position or size induces a motion of x along the ray in order to remain the closest point on the ray with respect to the model. This involves computing first and second order derivatives for the Jacobian entries.

3.5.4   Implementation and Results

We use the framework presented above to both track the human figure and recover shape parameters. Our system is intended to run in batch mode, which means that we expect the two or more video sequences we use to have been acquired before running our system. It goes through the following steps:

1. *Initialization*: We initialize the model interactively in one frame of the sequence. The user has to enter the approximate position of some key joints, such as shoulders, elbows, hands, hips, knees and feet. Here, it was done by clicking on these features in two images and triangulating the corresponding points. This initialization gives us a rough shape, this is a scaling of the skeleton, and an approximate model pose.

2. *Data acquisition*: Clouds of 3-D points are derived from the input stereo-pairs or triplets using a simple correlation-based algorithm (Fua 1993). These points form a noisy and irregular sampling of the underlying body surface. To reduce the size of the cloud and begin eliminating outliers, we robustly fit local surface patches to the raw 3-D points (Fua 1997) and use the center of those patches to generate observations.

3. *Frame-to-frame tracking*: At a given time step the *tracking* process adjusts the model's joint angles by minimizing the objective function of Equation (3.7) with respect to the joint angle values that relate to that frame. This modified posture is saved for the current frame and serves as initialization for the next one. Optionally the system may use the model's projection into the images to derive initial silhouette estimates, optimize these using image gradients and derive from the results silhouette observations such as those introduced in the previous section.

4. *Global fitting*: The results from the *tracking* step serve as initialization for global *fitting*. Its goal is to refine the postures in all frames and to adjust the skeleton and/or metaball parameters to make the model correspond more closely to the person. To this end, it optimizes over all frames simultaneously, again by minimizing the objective function of Equation (3.7) but, this time, with respect to the full state vector including the parameters that control the length and width of body parts.

The final fitting step is required to correctly model the proportions of the skeleton and derive the exact position of the articulations inside the skin surface. This must be done over many frames and allows us find a configuration that conforms to every posture. To stabilize the optimization, we add to our objective function additional observations that favor constant angular speeds. Their weight is taken to be small so that they do not degrade the quality of the fit but, nevertheless, help avoid local minima in isolated frames and yield smoother and more realistic motions.

The result is a set of skeleton and primitive parameters $\Theta^{l,w}$ and a sequence of motion parameters $\Theta^{r,g}$ that make the recovered model mimic the subject's action as shown in Figures 3.10 and 3.11. They feature video sequences in which the subject performs complex and abrupt upper body motions that involve frequent self-occlusions. They were acquired by two progressive-scan cameras arranged in an inverted 'L' configuration and capturing non-interlaced images at 30 frames/sec with an effective resolution of 640×400. In the left column, we show one of the three original images; in the center one, we show a shaded image of the reconstructed model and, in the right one, superpose the original image with this shaded image. This allows a good visual estimation of the quality of fit.

3.6   Conclusion

Modeling people and their movements is an increasingly important topic in many areas such as entertainment, medicine, and surveillance. Furthermore, the ability to follow and interpret human motion can be expected to be a key component of tomorrow's interfaces. However,

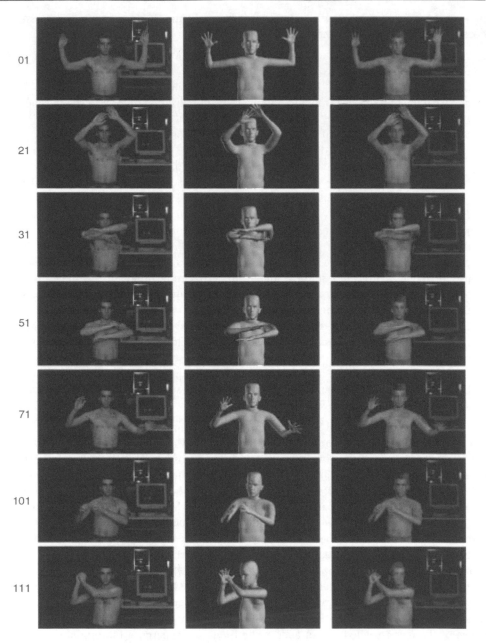

Figure 3.10 Results using a trinocular sequence in which the subject performs complex 3-D motions with his arms, so that they occlude each other

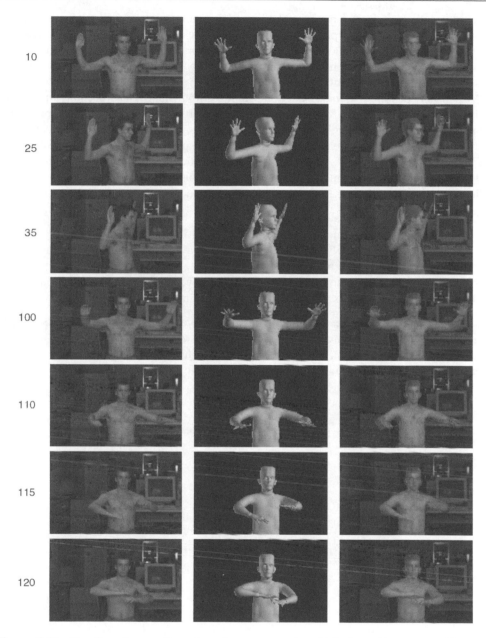

Figure 3.11 Results using another trinocular sequence in which the subject moves his upper body in addition to abruptly waving his arms

generating and animating sophisticated body models require a tremendous amount of manual labor. While this may be acceptable for big-budget movies, the television and game industries are much more cost-driven and would benefit greatly from using the techniques we discussed in this chapter. This is even truer if image-based motion capture is to succeed in the areas of sports medicine and athletic training.

As a result, capturing human shape and motion from images has become an increasingly popular research topic. Many investigators have proposed and implemented promising approaches, but automated solutions are still to achieve the kind of robustness that would be required in a truly practical system. This is due in part to the immense complexity of the human body and in part to the fact that humans often act in an unforeseeable manner that may defeat our existing mathematical prediction tools. To overcome these obstacles, we believe that the following research issues ought to be addressed:

- Designing more sophisticated body models that take biomedical constraints into account while remaining simple enough to be fitted to actual image data.
- Developing motion models that account for the way people actually perform various actions and using them to track more effectively.
- Allowing the system to simultaneously consider several possible interpretations of the data it sees, so that it does not get involved in unwanted local minima.

Successful completion of these tasks should result in practical systems that will be able to reliably model people from images and video sequences. As cameras become more and more prevalent in our environment, this can be expected to have an important impact wherever modeling, monitoring and understanding human activities are required.

4

Anthropometric Body Modeling

Hyewon Seo

Anthropometric human models are used in a wide number of applications in computer graphics. For instance, engineering human factor applications have long recognized the need for a variety of accurately scaled body dimensions to facilitate reach and fit analysis. Others use anthropometric data in order to include most likely human models in their 3-D-generated images. The aim of this chapter is to discuss some of the main issues and approaches when modeling anthropometric bodies. The chapter is divided into four sections. The first deals with introductive discussions; the second provides a historical background as well as a summary of different methodologies developed for anthropometry and anthropometric human models. The third outlines our approach to anthropometric body modeling that has been specially targeted on garment manufacturing and retail. Finally, we conclude this chapter in the final section. Examples of various models and validation of results are provided.

4.1 Introduction

Anthropometry means, literally, the measurement of people (Norgan 1994). It has come, however, to be used in a more restrictive sense to mean the comparative study of sizes and proportions of the human body. Whereas the kind of measurements selected in a broader scope can include physical performance such as joint limits, mass, strength and body composition such as fat percentage, our focus will be more on using sizes and proportions in modeling human bodies. Indeed, sizing survey continues to be a primary focus of many manufacturing areas such as design and sizing of clothing, military protective equipment, workstations and cars.

The description of the human form by proportions goes back to the ancient Greeks, as well as to the sculptors and painters of the Renaissance, who measured the human body to estimate body proportions in order to reproduce life-like images of varying sizes (see Figure 4.1).

Handbook of Virtual Humans Edited by N. Magnenat-Thalmann and D. Thalmann
© 2004 John Wiley & Sons, Ltd   ISBN: 0-470-02316-3

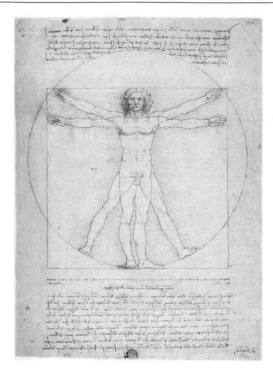

Figure 4.1 Leonardo da Vinci, a Renaissance artist, created the drawing of the Vitruvian Man based on the 'ideal proportions'

Since the first appearance of Virtual Humans in the early 1980s (Magnenat-Thalmann and Thalmann 1987), researchers in computer graphics have been interested in the application of anthropometric data in order to include the most likely human models in the 3-D-generated images and films. However, as the vast majority of modern anthropometry has been conducted to study effects of some environmental factors, the notion of the anthropometric human modeling has been extended to the systematic creation of a precise human model based on statistically processed population data or alternatively, a given person's dimensions can be directly used in the creation of a Virtual Human model. Nowadays, the computer graphics community and anthropometry experts have begun to exchange their expertise to come up with solutions that can satisfy the various needs of both. While anthropometry offers precise details of body proportion, the computer graphics provides the framework to test the environmental factor.

This chapter introduces problems and solutions to computer-aided anthropometric human modeling. Section 4.2 provides a historical background as well as a summary of different methodologies developed for anthropometry and anthropometric human models. Section 4.3 outlines our approach to anthropometric body modeling that has been specially targeted on garment manufacturing and retail. Finally, we conclude this chapter in Section 4.4. Examples of various models and validation of results are also provided.

4.2   Background

4.2.1   Anthropometry

4.2.1.1   Definition

Anthropometry, the biological science of human body measurement, systematically studies human variability in faces and bodies. The procedures for measurement in anthropometry are precisely specified, allowing data between individuals to be successfully compared, and permitting useful statistics of population groups to be derived.

Anthropometric evaluation begins with the identification of particular locations on a subject, called landmark points. Anatomical landmarks are features (usually points or curves) on the surface of a human body that indicate the location of a body organ or component. These features do not necessarily have consistent definitions in terms of differential geometry. However, their definitions are more intuitive and, since they are anatomically meaningful, they can easily be located by a human expert. Such landmarks are typically used not only in the clothing industry, but also in anatomy and anthropology. Typical examples include: nape of neck (7th cervical vertebra), top of the head, iliac crests, underbust and mid-clavicle point.

A series of measurements between these landmarks is then taken using carefully specified procedures and measuring instruments such as calipers and measuring tape. Typically the measurements are taken in scientific surveys, and involve careful positioning of people before measurements are taken. This is to enable the precise definition of what was measured. Figure 4.2 illustrates the anthropometric landmarks used in the CAESAR project (Burnsides et al. 2001), which then were adapted to become 'feature points' in H-Anim (http: hanimFeature) standard. Important landmarks and points defined by Carrere et al. (2000) are summarized in Table 4.1.

4.2.1.2   Computer graphics for modern anthropometry

Much of the anthropometric data currently in general use is derived from data acquired by manual measurement of a sample of the population nearly 50 years ago. Improvements in diet and healthcare in recent years have resulted in an increase in the average size of the population, thus making the 50-year-old data obsolete. Recent surveys conducted by the British and US Army and others have endeavored to remedy this situation by utilizing 3-D scanners to acquire dense, accurate three-dimensional human body data quickly and effectively. Manual techniques, which involve the use of callipers and measuring tapes, are extremely slow and costly, produce sparse data and are almost impossible to automate. Since the advent of 3-D image capture technology, there has been a great deal of interest in the application of this technology to the measurement of the human body and the goal is now to develop a 3-D image capture system capable of routinely providing dense, accurate anthropometric data (Daanen and van de Water 1998).

Accordingly, recent algorithms include automatic processing of scan data to extract features or measurements. Nurre (1997) presents an incremental approach that progressively refines the identification of data points. The first phase of identification is to orient and segment the human body data points. Algorithms for these tasks are presented, including the 'discrete point cusp detector', with a description of their use. In order to show the robustness of the software, it has been tested on twenty different body scan data sets. Works by Dekker (2000) on the identification indicates that there are robust ways to find about 100 anatomical

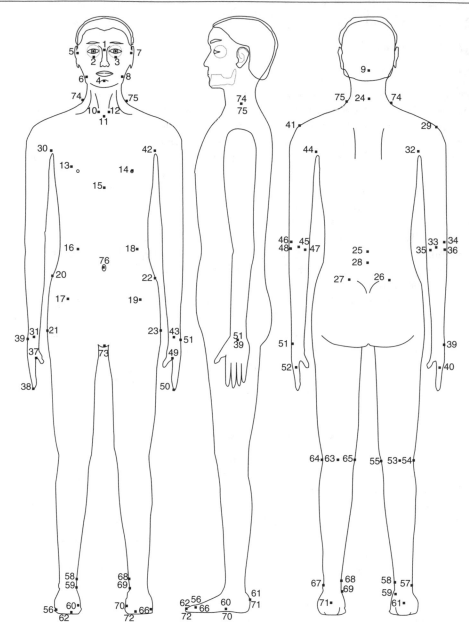

Figure 4.2 Anthropometric landmarks (feature points) in H-Anim 1.1 specification

landmarks on a human body, at least for specific categories. A partially automatic landmark detection method was used in CAESAR (Civilian American and European Surface
Anthropometry Resource) project (Burnsides et al. 2001).

Gu et al. (1998) concentrate on human body modeling for the purpose of measurement of
human body for the clothes industry. They use a hexagonal supporting framework to form

Table 4.1 Important landmark terms and definitions

Landmark	Definition
Abdominal Extension (Front High-Hip)	Viewed from the side, it is the measure of the greatest protrusion from one imaginary side seam to the other imaginary side seam usually taken at the high hip level; taken approximately 3 inches below the waist, parallel to the floor.
Acromion (Shoulder Point)	The most prominent point on the upper edge of the acromial process of the shoulder blade (scapula) as determined by palpitation (feeling).
Ankle (Malleolus)	The joint between the foot and lower leg; the projection of the end of the major bones of the lower leg, fibula and tibia, that is prominent, taken at the minimum circumference.
Armpit (Axilla)	Points at the lower (inferior) edge determined by placing a straight edge horizontally and as high as possible into the armpit without compressing the skin and marking the front and rear points or the hollow part under the arm at the shoulder. * See Scye.
Bicep Point	Point of maximum protrusion of the bicep muscle, the brachii, as viewed when elbow is flexed 90 degrees, fist clenched and bicep strongly contracted.
Bust Point	Most prominent protrusion of the bra cup.
Cervicale(Vertebra Prominous)	At the base of the neck portion of the spine and located at the tip of the spinous process of the 7th cervical vertebra determined by palpitation, often found by bending the neck or head forward.
Elbow(Olecranon)	When arm is bent, the farthermost (lateral) point of the olecranon which is the projection of the end of the inner most bone in the lower arm (ulna); the joint between the upper and lower arm.
Gluteal Furrow Point	The crease formed at the juncture of the thigh and buttock.
Hip Bone (Greater Trochanter)	Outer bony prominence of the upper end of the thigh bone(femur).
Iliocristale	Highest palpable point of the iliac crest of the pelvis, half the distance between the front (anterior) and back (posterior) upper (superior) iliac spine.
Kneecap	Upper and lower borders of the kneecap (patella) located by palpitation; joint between the upper and lower leg.
Neck	Front (anterior) and side (lateral) points at the base of the neck; points on each cervical and upper borders of neck ends of right and left clavicles.
Infrathyroid (Adam's apple)	The bottom (inferior), most prominent point in the middle of the thyroid cartilage found in the center front of the neck.
Shoulder Blade (Scapula)	Large, triangular, flat bones situated in the back part of the chest (thorax) between the 2nd and 7th ribs.
Scye	Points at the folds of the juncture of the upper arm and torso associated with a set-in sleeve of a garment. * See Armpit.

Table 4.1   Continued

Landmark	Definition
Top of the Breastbone (Suprasternal)	Bottom most (inferior) point of the jugular notch of the breastbone (sternum).
Tenth Rib	Lower edge point of the lowest rib at the bottom of the rib cage.
7th Thoracic Vertebra	The 7th vertebra of 12 of the thoracic type which covers from neck to lower back.
Waist (Natural indentation)	Taken at the lower edge of the 10th rib by palpitation; point of greatest indentation on the profile of the torso or half the distance between the 10th rib and iliocristale landmarks; location between the lowest rib and hip identified by bending the body to the side.
Waist (Omphalion)	Center of navel (umbilicus).
Wrist (Carpus)	Joint between the lower arm and hand; Distal ends (toward the fingers) of the ulna (the innermost bone) and radius (the outermost bone) of the lower arm.

a closed space for imaging with 12 cameras for upper and lower body parts in six views. Additionally a slide projector with a grid pattern is used to catch the chest area using the stereo pair of the intersections of horizontal and vertical lines.

Meunier and Yin (2000) propose two-dimensional, image-based anthropometric measurement systems that offer an interesting alternative to traditional and three-dimensional methods in applications such as clothing sizing. Their attractiveness lies in their low cost and the speed with which they can measure size and determine the best-fitting garment.

In the market, there are also now available some systems that are optimized either to extract accurate measurements from parts of the body, or for realistic visualization for use in games, Virtual Environments and, lately, e-commerce applications. Cyberware Inc.'s DigiSize was 'partially developed in a joint government project to improve and automate fitting and issuing of military clothing'. They claim they offer complete and state-of-the-art solutions to age-old tape measurements and trial-and-error fitting problems. Figure 4.3 shows an example.

Several approaches are under active development to endow semantic structure to the scan data. Dekker et al. (1999) have used a series of meaningful anatomical assumptions in order to optimize, clean and segment data from a Hamamatsu whole-body range scanner in order to generate quadmesh representations of human bodies and build applications for the clothing industry. Ju and others (Ju et al. 2000; Ju and Siebert 2001) introduced methods to automatically segment the scan model to make it conform to an animatable model.

4.2.1.3   Statistical issues

Systematic collection of anthropometric measurements has made possible a variety of statistical investigations of groups of subjects. Subjects are often grouped on the basis of gender, race, age, 'attractiveness' or the presence of a physical syndrome. Means and variances for

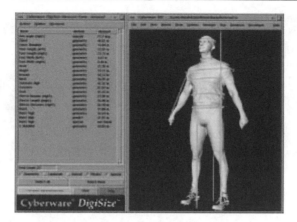

Figure 4.3 Automatic measurement extractions from the scan data (Reproduced with permission of Cyberware)

the measurements within a group effectively provide a set of measurements, which capture virtually all of the variation that can occur in the group.

One of the main aims of statistical analysis is to be able to identify factors for the purpose of prediction. For instance, multiple regression analysis can be used to examine how much variation can be explained using a large number of continuous and discrete variables.

Most of the anthropometric data available nowadays are in percentiles, even though more desirable statistical methods such as regression analysis or multivariate analysis were addressed by some of the recent studies (http: Cardlab).

4.2.1.4 Applications

Anthropometric data is used in many areas of manufacture to provide information for the design of products such as clothing, footwear, safety equipment, furniture, vehicles and any other objects with which people interact. In the armed services this data is of particular importance as the survival of the serviceman may depend upon it. For example, in the accurate shape of cloth-fitting protection equipment such as body armor or combat helmets, or in the optimum ergonomic design of combat vehicles.

4.2.2 Anthropometric Human Models in CG

4.2.2.1 Rigid scaling

Since anthropometry was first introduced in computer graphics by Dooley (1982), a number of researchers, including Azuola et al. (1994) and Grosso et al. (1989) have investigated the application of anthropometric data in the creation of Virtual Humans (see Figure 4.4). The Spreadsheet Anthropometry Scaling System (SASS) presented by Azuola et al. enables the user to create properly scaled human models that can be manipulated in their animation system 'Jack' (Badler 1997). The system creates a standardized human model based on a given statistically processed population data or, alternatively, a given person's dimensions can be directly used in the creation of a Virtual Human model. In the former case, this generates dimensions of each segment of a human figure based upon population data supplied as input.

Figure 4.4 Anthropometric models for 'Jack'. (Reproduced with permission of Norman P. Badler.)

Their initial Virtual Human was composed of 31 segments, of which 24 had a geometrical representation. For each segment or body structure with geometrical representation, three measurements were considered, namely the segment length, width, and depth or thickness. Measurements were compiled from the NASA Man-Systems Integration Manual (NASA-STD 3000) and the Anthropometry Source Book (NASA Reference Publication 1024).

Apart from these size measurements, they also explored kinematical properties of the human body such as center of mass, joint limits, and strength. They allow the user to select the desired anthropometric group to browse or modify. Despite their innovative efforts, however, the system was limited in some crucial points. First, they are based on percentile. The percentile is a very simple statistic and has undesirable properties in many cases. Second, although it may be grounded on accurate size information, the geometric representation did not correspond to it and was implemented by a rigid scale of each component and physical characteristics, even though they later on showed the extension of the system equipped with partially deformable models (Azuola et al. 1994).

4.2.2.2 Variational modeling

DeCarlo et al. (1998) use a limited set of measurements and proportions between a set of facial landmarks. Given base measurements, they produced a plausible set of constraints on the geometry using anthropometric statistics. The idea is to generate a shape that shares the important properties of a typical face as far as possible and yet still respect a given set of anthropometric measurements. They cast the problem as a constrained optimization one: anthropometric measurements are treated as constraints, and the remainder of the face is determined by optimizing a surface objective function. A variety of faces (see Figure 4.5) are then generated for a population through the random generation of face measurements according to anthropometric statistics.

This is an interesting approach that, unfortunately, cannot be easily extended to produce realistic shapes on the resulting models owing to the nature of variation modeling. The shape remains as passive element as the initial shape is changed to satisfy the measurement constraints while 'fairness', i.e. smoothness of the shape is being maximized. Later in this document, we adopt active shaping instead, wherein shape information is determined in relation to the given size and fed into the system to deform the mesh.

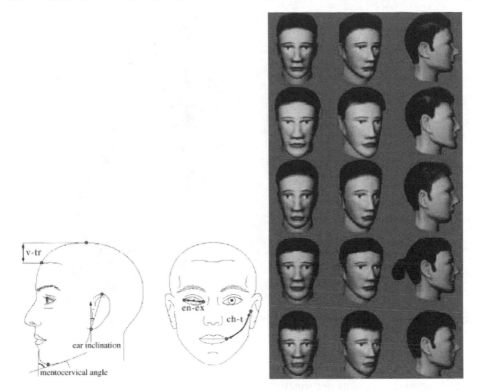

Figure 4.5 Automatically generated 'Anthroface' models from DeCarlo et al. (2000). (Reproduced with permission of Doug Decarlo.)

4.2.2.3 Geometric methods

The problem of correctly sized body models can be implemented by geometric deformation methods (see Figure 4.6). These methods often come with user interfaces with which the user can interactively manipulate the pre-defined parts of the given template models until s/he obtains the desired size. The modeling therefore consists of a series of 'modify and re-measure' processes and it is up to the user to appropriately manipulate the given mesh to obtain a good shape (Seo et al. 2000). Such an approach can often be found in commercial softwares such as 'C-Me' from Browzwear (http: Browzwear).

4.2.2.4 Example-based approaches

A variety of parameterized control techniques that exploit existing models have been introduced. Here, we will restrict our discussion to methods for modeling geometry. In works that are developed in facial modeling (Blanz and Vetter 1999) have presented a 'morphable face model' to manipulate an existing model according to changes in certain facial attributes. New faces are modeled by forming linear combinations of the prototypes that have been collected from 200 scanned face models. Manual assignment of attributes is used to define shape and texture vectors that, when added to or subtracted from a face, will manipulate a specific attribute.

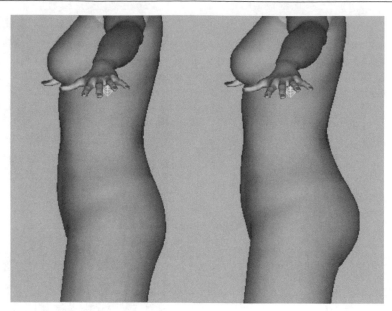

Figure 4.6 Geometrical deformation methods for differently sized body models. (Seo et al. 2000.)

Pose space deformation (Lewis et al. 2000) approaches the problem of overcoming geometric skeleton-driven skin deformation by using the pre-existing arm models at varying postures and blending them during animation. Recently, Kry et al. (2002) have proposed an extension of that technique by using Principal Component Analysis (PCA), allowing for optimal reduction of the data and thus faster deformation.

Until now, a number of approaches have been developed to model and animate realistic body models using example-based techniques. Previous authors, however, have taken only a subset of the whole body. Sloan et al. (2001) have applied a radial basis function to blend examples of facial models and of the arm. There are several key differences from our work. First, we take a broader scope by dealing with the whole body model. Second, we solve several linear systems that are defined per shape descriptor. Third, we focus on static shape while their focus is on dynamic shape.

Allen et al. (2002) present yet another example-based method to create a realistic skeleton-driven deformation. Our approach resembles theirs since it makes use of a template model and disorganized scanned data, although it adopts a unique and compact shape description of the body geometry, and, unlike other systems, it handles the whole body. Also, we focus on generating diversity of appearance, although they briefly show static deformation by altering the control points of the template model.

4.2.3 Motivating Applications

4.2.3.1 Virtual try-on

The Internet, along with the rapidly growing power of computing, has emerged as a compelling channel for sale of garments. A number of initiatives have arisen recently across the world (http: MyVirtualWorld) (http: NORDSTROM), revolving around the concepts of made-to-measure manufacturing and shopping via the Internet. These initiatives are fueled by the current Web technologies available, providing an exciting and aesthetically pleasing interface to the general public.

One of the most challenging research areas in this context is in developing a robust methodology to automatically build realistic 3-D body models that satisfy given size or measurement constraints in real-time performance. A significant step in this process is the application of 3-D graphics technology to help create and simulate the virtual store and here we discuss various relevant research problems; the creation of the body/garment, simulation of body/garment movement and online sizing. Although some authors claim that using Web 3-D technologies is unlikely to be of any advantage to e-commerce by distracting customers while causing increased maintenance costs (Wagner 2000), efforts to bring virtual reality to online garment sales have been constantly pursued not only to obtain visually pleasing results but also to provide a high level of interactivity.

4.2.3.2   Populating Virtual Environments

The range of variation in their body size and shape contributes greatly to the diversity and individuality of the people we encounter in daily life. Simulating Virtual Environments populated with virtual but realistic crowds requires hundreds of different face and body geometries, maybe even a distinct one for each person, as in real life. It is a monumental challenge to achieve such a spectrum with existing modeling techniques.

4.2.3.3   Anthropometric modeling and ergonomics

For product designers to test their designs, models that are driven by anthropometry play an important role. Timely detection of ergonomic deficiencies results in higher quality and prevents additional costs invoked by later corrections.

4.2.4   Challenging Problems

4.2.4.1   Size vs. shape

Arguably, anthropometric measurements allow the most complete control over the shape of the body but it would be almost impossible to provide all the measurements required to detail the model. Therefore it is not uncommon to use a subset of measurements. (Later in this chapter, we use 8 primary measurements to make 3-D mannequins for the clothing application.) In such cases, the problem of estimating other measurements and determining an appropriate shape for the full geometry needs to be solved. To take an example, there exists an infinite number of ways to determine the shape of a closed contour, given its length constraint. Until now, the shape has been dealt with as a passive constituent – the final body shape is a result of a series of deformations so that it satisfies the given measurement. At times, they have tried to keep as much as possible to the shape of the template model. In Section 4.3, we show how we exploit existing models to automatically derive realistic body shapes on the fly

4.2.4.2   Fast generation

In various applications of anthropometric body modeling technique, one cannot assume the potential users are 3-D artists who are familiar with graphics packages. If 3-D body creation techniques are to be meaningful in this context, they must be able to produce correctly sized body models and be efficient enough to be used in an interactive runtime setting with minimum user intervention. Thus, one key challenge is how to hide the complexities of the human body and to efficiently transform the information required for the manipulation of body geometry.

4.2.4.3   Making animatable models

A static body has limited sense. Many engineering applications require appropriately sized bodies to be at different postures or even animated. In order to obtain such animatable body models, the skin surface and the underlying skeleton structure often form an integrated part of the body modeling. This means the skeleton structure should remain at the correct locations inside the skin at all times during the size-driven deformation.

4.3   Our Approaches to Anthropometric Models

This section describes our example-based approach to generating realistic, controllable human whole-body models. This system consists of three major parts. First, each example from the 3-D range scanner is pre-processed so that the topology of all the examples is identical. Second, the system that we call the *modeling interpolator* learns from these examples the correlation between the *size parameters* and the *body geometry*. After this learning process, the synthesizer is devoted to the run-time generation of appropriate shape and proportion of the body geometry through interpolation.

The application uses 8 primary measurements (listed in Table 4.2) as size parameters, which have been defined in sizing surveys for apparel design. We assume that the users are aware of their own measurements or the measurements have been retrieved from 3-D scanners or tapes.

Table 4.2   Measurement definitions

Body measurement	Definition	Explanation
Stature	Vertical distance between the crown of the head and the ground	Only for subjects other than babies who are not yet able to stand upright
Crotch length	The vertical distance between the crotch level at center of body and the ground	Measured in a straight line with the body mass equally distributed on both legs
Arm length	The distance from the armscye shoulder line intersection (acromion) over the elbow to the far end of the prominent wrist bone (ulna) in line with small finger	Measured with the subject's right fist clenched and placed on the hip, and with the arm bent at 90°

Table 4.2 Continued

Body measurement	Definition	Explanation
Neck girth	The girth of the neckbase	The circumference is measured over the base of the 7th cervical vertebra, the neck shoulder points and the center front neck point – at the transition of the neck to the trunk
Chest/Bust girth	Maximum circumference of the trunk measured at bust/chest height	Horizontal girth measured under the armpits (without arms) and across the most prominent points of the breasts (nipples)
Underbust girth (optional; only for women)	Horizontal girth of the body immediately below the breasts	The measurement position is determined by the breast that is lower down the body
Waist girth	Horizontal girth at waist height	From the side view: The waist level is determined by the deepest part of the spinal curve or rather the point of tangential change
Hip girth	Horizontal girth of the trunk measured at hip height	From the side view: The position of the measurement is determined by the fullest part of the buttocks

4.3.1 Overview

The overall system is shown in Figure 4.7. The system relies on external modeling systems or geometry capture technology to create initial sample shapes. Given the sample models, the initial model preparation module ensures the correspondence between them by making use of a reference model. Furthermore, the dimensions of the model on each part of the body are measured and annotated. Based on the prepared samples and the corresponding measurements, the interpolator's construction module determines the coefficients of the function. According to the interpolator function calculated from this stage, the runtime evaluation module deforms the reference model in order to get the desired model on the fly through multi-way blending of examples.

4.3.2 Data Acquisition

4.3.2.1 3-D scanned data

At present, a variety of 3-D reconstruction methodologies are available that can capture shapes that exist in the real world. Our initial models or examples will rely on existing models or 3-D shape capture technology. Example data were acquired from Tecmath 3-D range scanner. Faces were intentionally removed owing to the privacy policy (scanned subjects were mostly customers of a clothing company). Starting from the initial polygonal models, additional pre-processing was done using commercial graphics packages (3ds max); holes were filled, the number of triangles was reduced (up to 50,000), and all triangles were

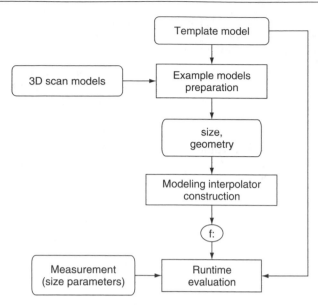

Figure 4.7 Overview of the system

connected to form one single mesh. As a result, each scan data is composed of one single mesh with no holes and no open edges. Throughout this chapter, we assume that the example 3-D geometry is a polygonal mesh with moderate complexity, and without texture data.

All subjects are in an erect posture with arms and legs slightly apart, and are lightly clothed (see Figure 4.8), which allowed us to carry out 'touchless' measurements. Each of the 3-D-scanned data was measured at various parts – mainly around the torso – and was annotated with its sizing parameters. The sizing parameters used in this chapter are tabulated in Table 4.2.

4.3.2.2   The template model

The template model is composed of a standard human skeleton structure (http: Hanim) and a skin surface that is composed of quadrilateral patches, as shown in Figure 4.9. Once the skeleton is appropriately located under the mesh, we define the skin attachment.

- *The skeleton*: The skeleton hierarchy we have chosen to use is an H-anim one, with the Level of Articulation (LoA) 2. It is composed of 33 joints, excluding the hands and feet.
- *The template mesh*: The template mesh has a grid structure – a set of vertical and horizontal lines that form a set of quadpatches. Measuring a model is done by simply computing the lengths of some of the horizontal or vertical contours.
- *The animation data*: Once the mesh model and the skeleton are ready, the skin-to-bone attachment is established. The attachment is considered as assigning for each vertex of the mesh its affecting bones and corresponding weights. To say that a vertex is 'weighted' with respect to a bone means that the vertex will move as the bone is transformed in order to stay aligned with it. This skin deformation technique, often called skeleton-driven deformation (Weber 2000), is perhaps the most widely used technique in 3-D character

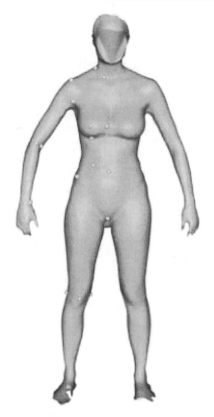

Figure 4.8 A scanned model example

skin deformation. A prerequisite of a successful skeletal-driven deformation is an appropriate attachment of the skin to the underlying skeleton. In our current implementation,
this is done using an external application (BonesPro). Later in the chapter, the skeletal
deformation is used not only for the skin deformation during animation but also to modify
the size and posture of the template model.

4.3.3 Pre-Processing

Given the template model and a set of scanned data, we need to obtain the conformation
of the template model onto each scanned model. Having a predetermined topology has both
theoretical and practical merits: first, it allows an easy way to describe the shape of the
objects (vector representation) we are dealing with at a desired level of detail. Second, we
can re-use the initial skin attachment information so that all resulting models are made
to be immediately animatable. Finally, different postures of examples are easily resolved
by applying appropriate transformations to the template skeleton that derives the linear
deformation of the template mesh. Section 4.3.2.2 presents a fast optimization algorithm
tailored to find these transformations.

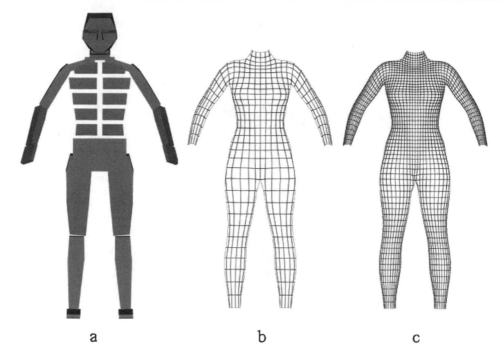

a   b   c

Figure 4.9   The template model

Our method consists of three successive phases:

- *Phase 1. Feature point identification*: A number of manually labeled feature points vary from application to application, but usually range from 30 to 50.
- *Phase 2. Initial skeleton fitting*: From the feature point specified, the goal of this phase is to determine the appropriate posture and proportions of the reference model. We define this problem as a multidimensional minimization problem. The variables in the optimization are the degree of freedom of each joint in the skeleton hierarchy. Optimizing joint variables are determined that minimize the distance of corresponding feature points location.
- *Phase 3. Fine skin fitting*: Starting with a roughly fitted template model that has been found from the skeleton fitting phase, this phase iteratively improves the fitting accuracy by minimizing the shape difference between the template and the scan model.

4.3.3.1   Feature point

Feature points need to be identified on both the template mesh and the scanned mesh, in order to guide the skeleton fitting phase. Despite an enormous amount of work in various fields of computer graphics, the problem of automatic feature detection is not yet completely solved (Lee and Lee 2002). In our approach, the user interactively provides the feature points location through the interface provided. The feature points used in this application are illustrated in Figure 4.10.

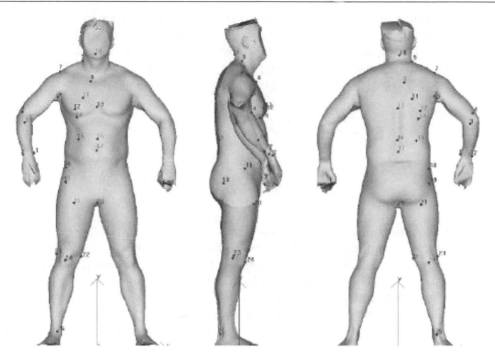

Figure 4.10   Feature points used in our system

4.3.3.2   Skeleton fitting

The first phase of the algorithm finds the relative position, proportion and the posture of scanned model by appropriately fitting the reference model to it. We refer to the transformations applied to each joint of the reference skeleton as *joint parameters*. When applying different joint parameters during fitting, we use skeleton-driven deformation to calculate the new positions of the skin surface according to the transformation of the underlying skeleton. The most likely joint parameters are the ones that drive the template skin so that it best matches the feature location by minimizing the error given by

$$E_F(X) = \sum_{i=1}^{m} ||P_i - P'_i(X)||$$ (4.1)

where X is the joint parameters, m is the number of feature points that are influenced by X, P_i and $P'_i(X)$ denote the location of feature point i in the scanned mesh and the calculated location of the corresponding feature point in the template model that is driven by the skeletal deformation, respectively.

Note that a bone affects only a few feature points and therefore the error distance is summed on the influenced feature points only. Using the skin attachment information, we can easily identify the feature points that are influenced by a bone. When there are no feature points that are attached to the current bone, feature points from its child or descendants from the highest depth are used. Using only a subset of the feature points provides sufficient accuracy for our purposes. At times, feature points that are weakly attached to a bone may result in distortion of the bone, finding an extreme scale transformation along one or two directions. Weighting the distance with the vertex-to-bone weight can prevent this, but it will result in loose fitting for some points. To overcome this problem, we add an internal energy term to the objective function that penalizes the joint configuration that violates the scale ratio uniformity. Thus, the energy given in Equation (4.1) is modified to:

$$E(X) = \alpha \cdot E_F + \beta \cdot E_D \qquad (4.2)$$

with

$$E_D(X) = \frac{S_x}{S_y} + \frac{S_y}{S_z} + \frac{S_z}{S_x} \qquad (4.3)$$

Optimization methods based on analytic function derivation as in (Allen et al. 2002) could be employed to find a solution. However, due to the complexity of the objects we are dealing with, it would be too time-consuming. In our work, we employ a direction set method (Press et al. 1988). End bones (the head, hand and feet) are excluded, as there are no closing markers to derive a meaningful search.

We find the joint parameters one bone at a time. For each new bone that is encountered in the depth first search (DFS), we form a search space that is defined by its DoF. The root joint has full DoF (translation, scale and rotation) while other joints excluding spinal joints have only scale (s_x, s_y, s_z) and rotation (r_x, r_y, r_z). Spinal joints have limited rotation, to avoid undesirable torsion and/or abduction of the spine joints due to the limited specification of feature points. We restrict the range of the rotation search space to $(-\pi/2 \sim \pi/2)$ and the scale to larger than 0.0.

An obvious problem with this approach is that the search may terminate with different parameters depending on the order of the degree of freedom in the search space. We have experimented with translation, rotation, and scaling (TRS) and scale, rotation and translation (SRT) and concluded changing the order of transformation does not affect the resulting skeleton configuration significantly. In our work, TRS was used and the X_j becomes:

$$X_j = (t_{x_j}, t_{y_j}, t_{z_j}, \theta_{x_j}, \theta_{y_j}, \theta_{z_j}, S_{x_j}, S_{y_j}, S_{z_j}) \qquad (4.4)$$

where t_{x_j} and s_{x_j} are the translation and scale along the x-axis respectively, and θ_{x_j} represents the rotation around the x-axis of the joint j.

Due to the hierarchy, each bone inherits the transformations from its parent bone. We found the inherited transformation serves as a good initial value. For the 'HumanoidRoot' bone, the default value from the template model was used as the initial transformation. In some instances, the shared influence of the bones on a feature point (for instance, markers around the elbow are influenced both by the 'upper arm' and the 'forearm' bones) can lead to a subsequent search with a child bone, that results in an increase of the distance of the feature point whose minimal solution is found earlier by its parent bone. Nevertheless, we found sequentially visiting bones in a depth first search manner (DFS) and finding locally optimizing transformations results in a good approximation of the subjects. A pseudocode for the skeleton fitting procedure is shown in Figure 4.11.

```
proc skeleton_fitting ()
{
    ←feature points on the scanned data;
    for each bone    encountered in the DFS order
    {
        if (  in an end-bone) continue;
            ←DoF of  ;
            ←feature_points_under_influence ( );

            ← ;  ←1;
        While (  =∅)
        {
            for each  , a child in the level  in a tree with   as a root
                ←add ( , feature_points_under_influence ( ));
            ← +1;
        }
        direction_set_method (      ');
    }
}
```

Figure 4.11   Skeleton fitting procedure

While this generally produces acceptable linear approximation, the user has the option of selectively defining the transformation of each bone after the automatic fitting. Repeated application of the optimization procedure resulted in a fairly good skeletal configuration. Figure 4.12 shows the skeleton and the template skin control mesh that has been fitted accordingly through the skeleton-driven deformation.

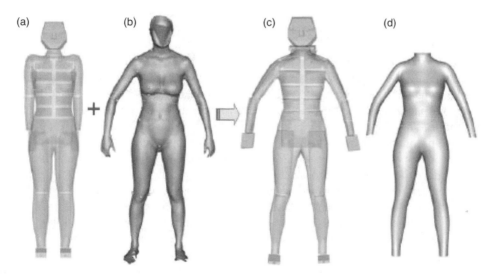

Figure 4.12   Skeleton fitting. The template model (a) is fitted to the scan data (b), resulting in the linear approximation of the scan model as shown (c) (with the skeleton) and (d) (mesh only)

4.3.3.3   Fine skin refinement

Starting with a roughly fitted template model that has been found from the skeleton fitting phase, this phase iteratively improves the fitting accuracy by minimizing the shape difference between the template and the scan model. The found shape difference is saved onto the displacement map. The fine refinement operates according to the following procedure:

1. *Initial mapping*: First, initial mapping of the template mesh onto the scan mesh is found. Each vertex on the template mesh is projected onto the closest vertex, edge or triangle on the scan mesh through collision detection. Barycentric coordinates are generated for each template vertex.
2. *Relaxation*: Then, the vertex positions of the template mesh are updated by minimizing the energy function that (1) minimizes the amount of mesh deformation and (2) constrains vertices that belong to the same feature contour to be co-planar. A displacement vector between the previous and the new position is calculated.
3. *Mapping*: New vertices are projected onto the surface of the scan mesh. Barycentric coordinates that are initially calculated from step (1) are updated with optimized collision detection using the displacement vectors.
4. If the new shape is satisfactory, the algorithm terminates, otherwise step (2)–step (3) is repeated.
5. *Skeleton refitting*: Now that we have found the displacement map, we can refine the skeleton fitting from Section 5.1 so that the thickness of the displacement map is minimized. The idea is to compute the transformation of each joint that minimizes the distance between the two segments – one the result of the skeletal deformation only and the other with the displacement map added. The cost function in this minimization computes the summation of the vertex distances between the source and the target. The direction set method is used to do that. Figure 4.13 shows the fine fitting.

4.3.4   Interpolator Construction

Once the system has been provided with example models prepared in Section 4.3.2, we build modeling interpolators for each component of the body geometry by a scattered data interpolation. These interpolators allow the runtime evaluation of the shape from the given input parameters. We separate the linear component and residual components for the deformation. The joint interpolator handles each DoF of the joints. Displacement interpolators find the appropriate displacements on the skin from the input parameters.

In both cases, we adopt PCA (Principal Component Analysis) (Press et al. 1988), one of the common techniques to reduce the data dimensionality. Upon finding the orthogonal basis called eigenvectors, the original data vector x of dimension n can be represented by the projection of itself onto the first $M(\ll n)$ eigenvectors that correspond to the M largest eigenvalues. In our case, 25 bases were used both for the joint and the displacement interpolators. Our template models are made of 33 joints, each having 6 DoF, and 841 vertices with 3 DoF.

At the time of the interpolator's construction, we define a parameter space where each measurement represents a separate axis. Eight primary measurements shown in Table 4.2 are used to construct the dimension space. Each example model after the fitting is measured

(a)   (b)   (c)

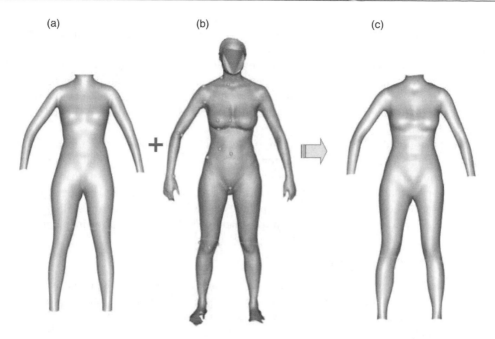

Figure 4.13 Fine fitting. (a) We start with a roughly fitted model from the previous phase. (b) The scanned model. (c) After the fine refinement

in various parts to find its corresponding location in the parameter space. A smooth varying interpolation of a particular component of the body geometry can then be obtained across the measurement space by using these examples as interpolation nodes. When solving for the coefficients of the associated linear system of size $N \times N$, with N the number of examples, we use LU decomposition.

We use a Gaussian function $\Phi(r) = e^{-ar^2}$ as the basis function for the multi-way blending. Gaussian Radial Basis Functions (GRBF) (Bishop 1995) are reputed to behave well in a very mild condition. Thus, the interpolators are in general of the following form:

$$s(x) = p_m(x) + \sum_i^N w_i \cdot \Phi\left(||x - x||\right), x \in R^d, w_i \in R, \tag{4.5}$$

where p_m is a low degree polynomial, $||\cdot||$ denotes the Euclidean norm and d and N are the dimension of the parameter space and the number of examples, respectively.

4.3.4.1 Joint interpolation

Although the transformations computed independently for each bone may be used, significant redundancy exists in the bone, e.g. neighboring bones often undergo similar transformations. For instance, when the bone 'sacroilliac', whose main influence covers the hips part, has a large scaling transformation, the neighboring bone 'l_hip' also tends to undergo a similar transformation, depicting a large thigh. This also results partially due to the fact that the size parameters themselves have correlations, when they are from a real individual. As mentioned earlier, PCA of bone transformations serves to find an optimal orthogonal basis. At first, the eigenskeletons for each DoF are computed. We truncate the eigenskeleton basis and still have a good basis for approximating the observed bone transformations.

Each interpolator is responsible for one element of the joint parameters. As mentioned earlier, there are $25N$ (N: DoF, 6 in our case) interpolators, which are responsible for the scale and translation transformation of the joints in x, y and z directions. Note that the joint interpolators do not contain rotation transformation, as they are considered to be independent of the body size.

It should be noted that the human body is a hierarchical structure and there are two ways of describing the transformation (scale, for instance) of a joint: relative or absolute. Relative transformation specifies the transformation of each segment relative to its parent whereas absolute transformation specifies the transformation of each segment independently relative to the origin. Since the interpolator is ignorant of the hierarchical nature of the joint, we chose an absolute description of the joint parameters, each independent of its parent nodes.

4.3.4.2 Displacement interpolation

As described earlier, we use point vectors to represent the residual component of the body geometry. As is the case of the joint parameters, there is a significant spatial coherence in the skin displacement. Thus, we start by finding eigen-displacements through PCA. In our application here, the first 25 principal components were sufficient to reconstruct the original body shape. Consequently, three sets of interpolators of size 25 were constructed for x, y, and z directional displacements.

Analogous to the joint interpolators, displacements interpolators exploit the size to shape correlations that exist in the example bodies, to regulate the estimation of realistic shapes given sizing parameters as input. Unlike the joint interpolators, however, they contain no linear term p_m in the approximation function (see Equation (4.5)). This is due to the fact that the fat, i.e. muscles, is highly nonlinear and can be better modeled by purely elastic deformation.

4.3.5 Results and Implementation

Using the system described in Section 4.3, a variety of different body models have been created. The models that are shown in Figure 4.14 have been generated from a database of 57 scanned female subjects. Eight sizing parameters were used. The preprocessing steps are implemented in the 3-D Studio Max™ environment while the runtime modeler application is based on our real-time human simulation platform (Magnenat-Thalmann et al. 2002).

The evaluation of interpolators (30 joint interpolators and 20 shape interpolators) upon the receipt of the user input parameters takes less than one second on a 1.0 GHz Pentium 3. This includes the time for the update of the vertex-to-bone weight in order to continue the motion sequence that is constantly applied to the resulting models. By virtue of the skeletal deformation, we can obtain the resulting models, including the original scan models in any desired posture, after the vertex-to-bone is appropriately calculated. In Figure 4.14, a captured, key-frame-based motion data sequence is used for the animation.

In the following we report the results of the synthesizers by the cross-validation using all examples in the database. From the example database, each example has been excluded in

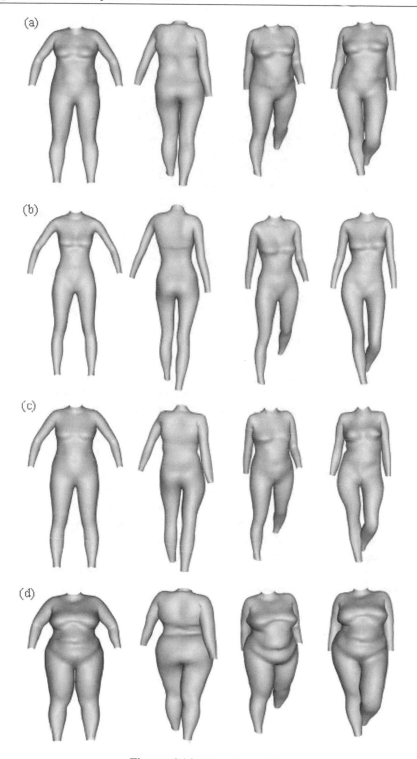

Figure 4.14 Result models

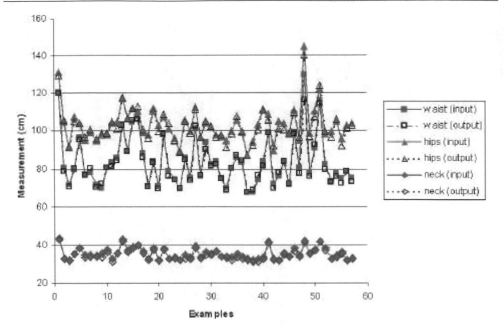

Figure 4.15 Cross-validation result

training the synthesizer and was used as a test input to the synthesizer. The output model was then measured to compare with the input measurements. Figure 4.15 shows that our modeler faithfully reproduces models that are consistent with the input parameters.

4.4 Conclusion

Some of the main issues and approaches have been discussed in anthropometric body modeling. Of the different approaches that have been presented, the example-based approach is justified for a variety of reasons. First, the captured body geometry of real people arguably provides the best available resource to model and estimate correlations between parameters and the shape. Second, a very fast model generation is made possible by efficiently blending the prepared examples through the interpolator function evaluation.

To illustrate, an example-based system, capable of automatically generating properly sized body geometries, has been presented.

5

Body Motion Control

Ronan Boulic, Paolo Baerlocher

Motion control of a 3-D character body is considered here in the animation production perspective. We examine especially how simulation techniques can improve motion realism. We open the discussion on productivity and efficiency issues by considering also metaphors of motion editing and re-use. Links are provided to closely related fields such as motion planning, behavioral animation, and deformation control at large (body deformation and cloth simulation are treated extensively in Chapters 7 and 9 respectively). The chapter is organized as follow: first, we clarify the purpose of animation prior to a discussion on the current state of the art. Then we focus on the issue of providing user-centered tools while coping with the intrinsic complexity of 3-D character posture control. In that respect, we choose to examine the potential of the Multiple Priority Levels Inverse Kinematics (MPL-IK).

5.1 Introduction

Motion control of a 3-D character body is considered here from the animation production perspective. As with other aspects of 3-D characters' control, motion control aims at conveying a sense of *realism* through the coordinated evolution of the character body. However, we feel it is important to clarify the term *realism* as it is often the ultimate justification for most of the proposed approaches in motion control. We identify the source of the confusion concerning this word from the fact that modern motion control techniques are at the crossroads of two independent fields: animation and simulation (Figure 5.1). In these two fields the same word 'realism' has different meanings.

In traditional animation, the motto is 'motion conveys emotion', thus realism is judged by the believability of the resulting motion. Subjective evaluation by a target human audience, animator or public at large, is the means of assessing the quality of the motion, hence the quality of the underlying motion control technique. Indeed, the human visual system has a remarkable ability to extract complex 3-D information even from sparse clues such as moving dots

Handbook of Virtual Humans Edited by N. Magnenat-Thalmann and D. Thalmann
© 2004 John Wiley & Sons, Ltd   ISBN: 0-470-02316-3

Figure 5.1   The realism assessment seen from the point of view of the application field

on a uniform background (Johanson 1973). Very low-level stimuli suffice to infer a motion types such as walking, running, dancing, bicycling, with attributes like carrying a load, and more general intention. Viewers are also able to report whether the motions are derived from real-world motions or are synthesized. This evaluation method, known as the Turing test, has been used extensively by Hodgins et al. (1995) to judge human motion simulation approaches. Another recent study has shown that the subjective evaluation runs at an unconscious level; in this work (Oesker et al. 2000) the statistical analysis of observers' answers to the viewing of animations with levels of details highlighted a correlation between answers and levels of details although, when asked about it, none of the observers reported changes in the animation style.

Simulation, by essence, targets a deeper understanding of motion generation through the finer modeling of the elements of the musculo-skeletal system and their physically-based interaction. The methodology is completed by the objective measurement of the motion quality through *experimental validation*. A simulation must be able to make predictions with reasonable precision within the working hypothesis framework. The difficulty in assessing such predictions comes from the complexity of the biological articulated body system. The validation set-up is further complicated by the uneasy if not impossible identification of the biologic tissue characteristics and the control parameters of the simulated living system. Generally, systems aiming at simulating full body motion have to make the drastic modeling simplification of the musculo-skeletal system as a hierarchy of rigid bodies linked by ideal mechanical joints (henceforth referred to as a Multi-Body System). As a consequence, their validity is reduced to the study of passive motions, as in crash tests, or to the comfort of postures and strictly defined gestures, as in ergonomics.

To conclude this discussion on the meaning of 'realism', current animation techniques providing full body motion can be said to be realistic in the *believability* sense but not in the *experimental validation* sense due to the difficulty of comparing prediction with real-world data. This second criterion is too strong to evaluate the present body animation techniques. For this reason we privilege the criterion of believability in the rest of this chapter. Additional criteria of *user-friendliness* of the control interface, *productivity* through re-use and *performance* are considered when relevant.

The next section covers the state of the art in motion control techniques. Then we focus on the issue of providing user-centered tools while coping with the intrinsic complexity of 3-D character posture control. In that respect, we choose to examine in more detail the potential of the Multiple Priority Levels Inverse Kinematics (or MPL-IK). The final section summarizes the major trends of motion control techniques and offers a conclusion.

5.2 State of the Art in 3-D Character Animation

The state of the art is divided into several parts. We first review the different levels of abstraction used for the musculo-skeletal system together with related motion control techniques. In particular, we examine how simulation know-how could contribute to improving animation techniques. Then we give an overview of motion control approaches for Multi-Body Systems prior to focusing more on Inverse Kinematics algorithms. The final section discusses a road map for motion re-use, highlighting methods suitable for on-line exploitation.

5.2.1 The Levels of Abstraction of the Musculo-Skeletal System

For the purposes of efficiency, animation systems traditionally split the motion control problem into two sub-problems (see Figure 5.2a): the animation of the internal motion (primary motion) and the animation of the external envelope and cloth (secondary motion). At this level of abstraction the body volume and mass distribution is modeled as a Multi-Body System (or MBS) while the external envelope is modeled as a surface associated with a model of attachment to the body. Presently, all the commercial systems, as well as the most recent research in motion control, rely on this paradigm. The next section reviews in detail the various motion control techniques based on this paradigm.

It is nevertheless important to present finer models used in various simulation systems. Such models will allow us in the future to progressively uncover precious data about the mechanical properties of real joints. Once these are well understood, normalized equations establishing their values can be integrated within the ideal mechanical model of joint. Presently such knowledge is very incomplete and difficult to find. This is in contrast with robots where the characteristics of the motors and mechanical parts are available from the start.

One a major element to take into account when improving the simulation of the musculo-skeletal structure is how to integrate the activity of all the muscles through their action lines (see Figure 5.2(b)). While still relying on the MBS paradigm, this approach reflects the fact that the muscles greatly depend on the posture. Figure 5.3 highlights the varying lever arm position appearing between the line of action of a muscle and the joint center of rotation.

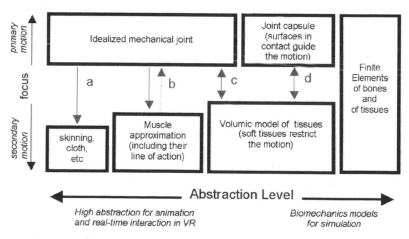

Figure 5.2 Levels of abstraction of the musculo-skeletal system

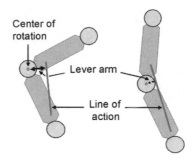

Figure 5.3   Influence of the posture on the action of a muscle through its line of action

Two applications are then possible:

- The muscles' activity and their lines of action allow them to derive the torques acting at the joints which in turn produce the motion of the body by applying Newton's laws. Pioneer work has been done by Delp et al. (1990) in orthopaedics to predict walking motions of the lower body after some surgery. More recently Komura et al. have exploited the same musculo-skeletal structure for two goals: first, quantitatively assess, along all the possible directions, the maximum torque of a joint (Komura et al. 1999) (called its strength), and, second, re-target a given motion so that it becomes biomechanically valid (Komura et al. 2000).
- Given a desired motion, various approaches have searched for the combination of muscles achieving the motion. This is an inverse problem as there may exist an infinite number of solutions (the musculo-skeletal system is said to be *redundant*). Optimal control techniques have been used by Pandy (1990) to obtain a jumping motion for a musculo-skeletal model of the lower body.

The next refinement step is to integrate the motion control problem with soft tissue deformation control (see Figure 5.2(c)). These two problems are coupled as the motion also can be subject to the influence of the deformation, especially as a restriction when soft tissues reach their elasticity limit or collide with tissues from another body segment. The recent work by Hirota et al. (2001) specifically highlights this later influence on the knee region (the knee being modeled as an ideal joint).

The following refinement is to get rid of the ideal mechanical joint model and solve the problem of bone surfaces contact (see Figure 5.2(d)). It is surprising that an ideal mechanical joint gives such a good approximation of a biologic joint. However, in reality the continuous modification of contact points (knee) or surface (hip, shoulder) over the joint range, leads to small variations of the joint rotation axis or center of rotation (expressed in a bone coordinate system). This phenomenon is well known for the knee (Blacharski and Somerset 1975). Another development is to evaluate precisely the joint range of motion as in the hip joint where the motion of the head of the femur is restricted by the pelvic bone.

The complete integration of motion and deformation models is obtained by modeling all the tissues, including bones, with finite elements. As the computing cost of such approach is very high, it cannot be generalized currently to the full musculo-skeletal structure.

Note: a presentation of the parameters characterizing soft tissues can be found in Chapter 7 on body deformation and Chapter 9 on cloth simulation.

5.2.2 Techniques for the Animation and the Control of the Multi-Body System

In this section, we first detail how the idealized mechanical joint model can integrate some key characteristics of biological joints. Then once a body is modelled, it can be manipulated, animated or used for simulation purposes. By *manipulation*, we mean that its posture is adjusted in an interactive manner, directly by the user. The design or adjustment of realistic postures is an important issue in computer animation, where the generation of motion often relies on a set of well-designed key postures.

The *animation* of a figure is the generation of a sequence of postures. In some applications, such as video games, this must be performed in real-time.

Simulating human articulated figures is important for prediction purposes in ergonomics. Within the restricted MBS framework and under the assumption of proper modeling of range and strength, it can answer questions related to the suitability of a posture with respect to accessibility and visibility constraints.

5.2.2.1 Idealized mechanical joints

We have seen that ideal and simplified joint models must be defined in order to be tractable on the whole body scale. A joint is the body component concerned with motion: its essential feature is to allow some degree of relative motion between the two segments it connects. Ideal kinematic joint models are defined in order to formalize this permitted relative motion, called range of motion, characterized by the number of parameters that describe the motion space and are constrained by joint limits. Korein (1985) uses spherical polygons as boundaries for the directional component of spherical joints such as the shoulder. Some biomechanical studies on the motion range of the human shoulder (Engin and Tuemer 1989; Wang and Verriest 1998) and the scapula (Maurel and Thalmann 2000) provide precious data and models to master the coupling of this complex region.

The second key aspect that should be integrated into the joint model is a model of its strength. The motion of an articulated figure, and the postures it assumes, are mainly due to the forces that the skeletal muscles apply on the bones. Hence, the muscular strength, which is highly variable from person to person, is an important component of a human model for prediction purposes, in manual lifting tasks, for example (Ayoub and Mital 1987). Typically, an ergonomist is interested in the maximum force that a person may exert at a given point, in a given direction. Another question is how to determine the safest (or most comfortable) posture for exerting a force. Hence, a model of strength available at the joint level may help to answer to questions on the force exertion in Cartesian space. Strength is complex information and is difficult to measure for each muscle separately. Usually indirect measures are performed at the joint level: the measured torque is due to the group of muscles acting on that joint, for a given direction of exertion (e.g. flexion or extension). A joint strength is also influenced by its own position and velocity, as well as those of adjacent joints. Moreover, strength decreases over time, according to the endurance of a person: this variability may be described by a *fatigue* model. Other global factors such as age and gender also affect the strength of a person. Many studies (Ayoub et al. 1981) have been performed to collect strength data with the aim of developing an *atlas of strength*. However, it is an arduous task to establish the whole human strength model: at the present time only partial results based on various simplifying assumptions are available. Because of the inherent difficulty in dealing with strength at the joint level, a number of researchers bypass the joint level and directly relate postures to the forces that can be exerted by an end-effector in the Cartesian space. A review of such studies has been made by Daams (1994) with the aim of developing an *atlas of force exertion* for product design.

Garg and Chaffin (1975) present a three-dimensional simulation of human strength, that predicts the maximum hand forces that an individual would be able to exert safely. A complete program, called 3-D-SSPP (Static Strength Prediction Program), has been developed from this early study (Chaffin et al. 1999).

Lee et al. (1993) describe a system that generates motions of lifting tasks (Badler et al. 1993) based on a static strength model of the arm (Pandya et al. 1992). The strength information is exploited to define a comfort criterion whose maximization allows the selection of realistic joint trajectories.

5.2.3 What Is Motion?

Motion is a change in the position of an object with respect to a reference, and mechanics is the science that studies the motion of objects. For practical purposes, its treatment is split into two fields:

- *kinematics* deals with the geometry of motion regardless of its physical realization (in other words, is concerned with the position, velocity and acceleration of bodies);
- *dynamics*, based on Newton's laws of motion, relates the causes of motion (i.e. the forces) to the acceleration of a body, taking into account its mass.

This distinction leads to two classes of techniques for the animation of articulated figures: kinematic methods and dynamic methods.

5.2.3.1 Kinematic manipulation techniques

Manipulating a virtual articulated figure is similar to the manipulation of a doll: the objective is to obtain a desired posture. A first option is to control the relative rotation of the segments by adjusting the joint angles: determining the posture corresponding to a given set of joint parameters is called the direct kinematics problem. This is a very handy tool for the designer, as shown by Watt and Watt (1992). However, when the position of a body part matters, it is difficult to adjust the joints to obtain the given position. The typical example is to adjust the joint angles of the shoulder, elbow and wrist joints so that the hand exactly reaches an object. This problem is known as the inverse kinematics problem, and can be seen as a constraint on the set of possible joint parameters. Solving this problem is hence very useful in the manipulation of articulated figures, and indeed has been extensively studied, first in robotics and later in computer graphics.

5.2.3.2 Kinematic animation techniques

The goal of any animation technique is to generate believable motion. Technically, the simplest solution is to rely on skilled animators, who manually define key postures of the articulated figure by directly setting the parameters of its joints. Then, the postures are smoothly interpolated over time to generate the full set of frames required for an animation, and the animator is free to adjust the resulting postures if they are not correct. This is known as the keyframing technique. Although tedious, it allows the fine tuning of complex motion when used with a coarse to fine motion refinement methodology (i.e. first the primary motion of the whole body and major segments, then the secondary motions of hands, feet, etc.).

The motion capture technique (Menache 2000) consists of the tracking and recording of a set of markers strategically positioned on the object of interest (typically a person). To obtain its posture, the Cartesian positions of the markers have to be converted into a set of joint angles (Molet et al. 1999; O'Brien 2000; Herda et al. 2001); this technique is fully developed in Chapter 3. This approach requires expensive hardware but also results in natural-looking motion, hence it is extensively used in the entertainment industry (special effects and video games). Due to the errors introduced by the measurement, the data should be corrected (manually or automatically) in order to obtain more accurate motions.

However, as with key-framing, captured motions only suit a particular figure with fixed dimensions. To overcome this limitation, a large number of motion retargeting techniques has been proposed, each focusing on a specific aspect of the problem: dynamics of the motion (Hodgins and Pollard 1997; Popović and Witkins 1999; Pollard 1999; Choi 2000), Cartesian constraints (Bindiganavale and Badler 1998), balance (Tak et al. 2000), differing skeleton topologies (Monzani et al. 2000; Shin et al. 2001), space-time approach (Gleicher 1998; Gleicher and Litwinowicz 1998), multi-resolution (Lee and Shin 1999), and comparison of techniques (Gleicher 2001).

Procedural techniques have been developed in order to generate specific motions such as walking or grasping. An example of a purely kinematic model based on biomechanical data is given by Boulic et al. (1990): the resulting gaits are controlled by a set of high-level parameters in order to personalize the style of the walk.

When the Cartesian position of particular end effectors is important, inverse kinematics techniques are needed. Goals for end effectors may be animated over time, and a sequence of postures satisfying them is generated (when possible). In computer animation, one of the first examples of articulated figure animation based on inverse kinematics is due to Girard and Maciejewski (1985): the feet of multi-legged figures are constrained on the floor, while a kinematic model of locomotion controls the coordination of the legs. Moreover, simple dynamics are used to provide an overall feel of inertia.

However, inverse kinematics (IK) is merely a constraint-satisfaction tool, and there is no guarantee that the resulting 'motion' is continuous or looks 'right': actually, a very small change of the goal in Cartesian space may result in a huge change in the configuration, because the inverse kinematic problem is intrinsically ill-conditioned near singular config-urations, as shown in (Maciejewski 1990). He proposed a damping factor cancelling the instability at the cost of a slightly slower convergence. Within that framework, IK can be used on the fly to locally adjust motions, as first shown with the coach-trainee metaphor (Boulic and Thalmann 1992). Despite its real-time ability this approach only focuses on enforcing half-space constraints without any timing requirement; this is too restrictive for animators. The fine control of the constraints' timing has been taken into account in Gleicher's work within a space–time optimization framework (Gleicher 1998; Gleicher and Litwinowicz 1998). Some other retargeting techniques rely to some degree on an IK solver (analytic such as Lee and Shin (1999) or numeric such as Pollard (1999)) integrated into a physically-based optimization framework (Popović and Witkin 1999). The more general problem of retargeting motion for skeleton models with different topologies and/or proportions has been described by Monzani et al. (2000) for off-line editing and Shin et al. (2001) for online character animation.

5.2.3.3 Balance control

Balance control is an essential problem in the realistic computer animation of articulated figures, and of humans in particular. While people take for granted the action of keeping their balance, it is still a challenge for neurophysiologists to understand the mechanisms of balance in humans and animals (Roberts 1995). Here, we focus on techniques for balance control in static equilibrium developed in the computer graphics community, and well suited to the postural control problem. It requires only the additional information of the body mass distribution. Clearly, more advanced methods are required in dynamic situations.

The center of mass is an important characteristic point of a figure. In the computer graphics community, Phillips offered the first control of the center of mass by constraining the angular values of the ankle, knee and hip joints of the leg that supports most of the weight (Phillips and Badler 1991). A more general approach for the control of the center of mass, called Inverse Kinetics, has been proposed by Boulic et al. (1994, 1996). The constraint on the position of the center of mass is solved at the differential level with a special-purpose Jacobian matrix that relates differential changes of the joint coordinates to differential changes of the Cartesian coordinates of the center of mass. In Figure 5.4(a) the control of the center of mass is constrained to remain on the vertical line passing through its base; the tip of the chain on the left stresses the reachable space under that implicit balance requirement. The same control set-up with two priority levels is applied in a 3-D context to obtain a 'remove a thorn from the foot' posture (an extended aproach handling multiple support is proposed in Boulic et al. (1997)). Recently, Baerlocher and Boulic (2000) has extended the control of mass properties to the moments of inertia of the articulated structure.

An alternate static balance control approach proposes acting on the total amount of torque perceived by the figure (Aydin and Nakajima 1999). The balance of the body may be ensured by constraining the total torque to be null. This method allows consideration of the external forces in addition to weight, and hence may be used to simulate static pushing or pulling of heavy objects. More general dynamic balance control methods are discussed in the next section.

5.2.3.4 Dynamics-based animation techniques

A great deal of work exists on the dynamics of articulated bodies (Huston 1990), and efficient direct dynamics algorithms have been developed in robotics for structures with

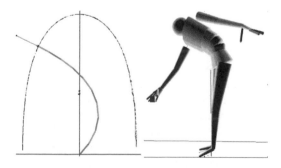

Figure 5.4 Two priority levels IK achieved with the cascaded control

many degrees of freedom (Featherstone 1986; SDFAST 1990). In computer animation, these algorithms have been applied to the dynamic simulation of the human body (Mac Kenna and Zeltzer 1996). Some Software Development Toolkits are now available to handle a wide range of simulations (KARMA 2003; Smith 2003). Basically, given a set of external forces (such as gravity or wind) and internal forces (due to muscles) or joint torques, direct dynamics algorithms compute the motion of a complex articulated body according to the laws of rigid body dynamics. Impressive animations of *passive* structures such as falling bodies on stairs can be generated in this way with little input from the animator. On the other hand, such an approach can turn adjustments into a tedious task as the animator has only indirect control over the animation. More generally, it is impractical for an animator to specify a temporally coordinate sequence of force/torque activation to generate a desired *active* behavior (Multon et al. 1999). This is the Inverse Dynamics problem, a complex one, that has been addressed for walking by Ko and Badler (1996). Impressive results have also been achieved by Hodgins et al. (1995) with the simulation of dynamic human activities such as running and jumping. Providing an intuitive framework for animators to control the outcome of a simulation with dynamic constraints is a difficult problem addressed by Liu and Popović (2002). Motion generation is often a control problem as it results from an active coordination of a multi-bodies system. Following the early work of Raibert and Hodgins (1991) on generalizing controller design for virtual characters, some controller architectures have also been proposed to generate a wide range of gaits (Lazlo et al. 1996) and to combine elementary behaviors (Faloutsos et al. 2001).

A first evaluation of simulation levels of details is described by Carlson and Hodgins (1997) as in some contexts, such as games, the computational cost restricts the number of entities that can be animated with dynamics. However, due to the nature of dynamic systems, it is impossible to modify the simulation level of detail without changing the long-term evolution of the system, thus, their exploitation leads to a viewpoint-bundled determinism that might be acceptable only for games.

The use of constraints to avoid the direct specification of torques has also been researched: for example, in the computer graphics community, the satisfaction of 'space-time constraints' has been proposed by Witkin and Kass (1988) with the minimization of an objective function such as the total energy expenditure. This family of techniques has been further improved to reduce their important computational cost with hierarchical wavelets (Lui et al. 1994). Nevertheless, as noted by Multon et al. (1999), an important drawback of this technique still remains: interaction with the environment must be planned from the start, thus unplanned collisions are not detected nor treated automatically.

5.2.4 Background to Inverse Kinematics

As we have seen, the Inverse Kinematics technique is useful both for the manipulation and animation of articulated figures. More specifically, it lies at the heart of constraint-based motion editing tools (Gleicher 2001). Thus it is important to be aware of the issues raised by its resolution. Basically, the problem is to determine a joints configuration for which a desired task, usually expressed in Cartesian space, is achieved. For example, the shoulder, elbow and wrist configurations must be determined so that the hand precisely reaches a position in space. The equations that arise from this problem are generally non-linear, and are difficult to solve in general. In addition, a resolution technique must also deal with the difficulties described hereafter.

5.2.4.1 Dealing with multiple constraints (or tasks), and resolving conflicts

In the remainder of this chapter, the words *constraints* and *tasks* are used interchangeably.

It is highly desirable for a resolution technique to manage multiple constraints simultaneously. As a consequence, it may happen that some of them cannot be satisfied at the same time, whereas they can be separately. This conflicting situation is resolved with one of the two following strategies (see Figure 5.5):

- Weights can be assigned to each constraint to define their relative importance and a compromise is found that, however, satisfies none of the constraints exactly.
- Or, constraints are optimized at different hierarchical levels. In this mode, every constraint is satisfied as much as possible but without affecting the satisfaction of more important ones.

The solution provided by the weight strategy is a compromise while the solution provided by the priority strategy favors the right chain tip.

For the positioning and animation of articulated figures, the weighting strategy is the most frequent: some typical examples are given by Badler et al. (1987) and Zhao et al. (1994) for posture manipulation and by Phillips et al. (1990) to achieve smooth solution blending. In the field of robotics however, researchers have developed *task-priority strategies* to precisely arbitrate conflicts by establishing a clear priority order among the constraints (Hanafusa et al. 1981; Maciejewski and Klein 1985; Nakamura and Hanafusa 1986; Siciliano and Slotine 1991).

5.2.4.2 Dealing with over-constrained and under-constrained problems

Two different situations can occur:

- *The problem has no exact solution*: This arises when a constraint cannot be satisfied (i.e. when a goal is unreachable), or when two or more tasks are in conflict and cannot be

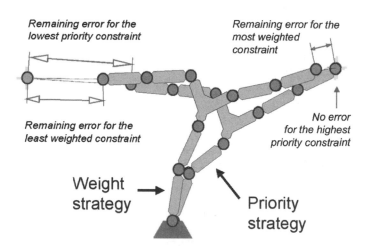

Figure 5.5 The two chain tips have to reach conflicting positions in space, the solution provided by the weight strategy is a compromise while the solution provided by the priority strategy favors the right chain tip

satisfied simultaneously. Numeric IK solvers are particularly sensitive to such *singular context* as shown in (Maciejewski 1990); the proposed approach is to control the norm of the solution through a damping coefficient (Appendix A).

- *The problem possesses one, two or more solutions, or even an infinity of solutions*: This case occurs when there are more degrees of freedom in the structure than constraints: the problem is said to be *under-constrained* or *redundant*. In robotics, criteria to exploit the redundancy are typically used for joint limits avoidance (Liégeois 1977) and singularities avoidance (Klein and Huang 1983). These criteria are not necessarily valid for computer graphics applications: in the natural standing posture, many joints (such as the knee) are at their limit, and also at a singular configuration with respect to an end-effector controlling a foot. Instead, the minimization of the distance with respect to a reference posture is a convenient choice (Boulic et al. 1994). More sophisticated criteria are based on mechanical or biomechanical considerations, e.g. minimization of joint torques due to the weight (Boulic et al. 1997). A degree of comfort can also be associated with each joint posture, and the total comfort is a criterion that can be maximized (Aydin and Nakajima 1999).

5.2.5 Review of Inverse Kinematics Resolution Methods

Analytic solutions do not exist for general articulated structures but, when considered in isolation, the limbs of 3-D characters can exploit robust and fast analytical solutions (Korein 1985; Tolani et al. 2000; Lee and Shin 1999). A non-exhaustive selection among the vast amount of other approaches can be found in Baerlocher (2001).

5.2.5.1 The resolved motion-rate method

In his pioneering work, Whitney (1969) introduces the resolved motion-rate control, which is the basis of more complex resolution schemes. Given an initial configuration, Whitney performs a linearization of the non-linear equations, characterized by a Jacobian matrix relating differential changes of the joint coordinates to differential changes of constraint coordinates. The linear system is solved in order to obtain a new configuration closer to the goal. By repeated resolution of this process, the system usually converges to a solution satisfying the constraint if the initial configuration was 'sufficiently close' to it. This method is inspired by the well-known iterative Newton–Raphson method for the resolution of non-linear equations.

The main research issue has been to extend this method to exploit the redundancy of the problem at the differential level. Whitney uses a generalized inverse to minimize the weighted norm of the variation of joint coordinates. Liégeois (1977) has proposed an extension for the optimization of a criterion expressed in joint space, by exploiting the null space of the Jacobian matrix. Klein and Huang (1983) provide more insight on this topic and on the meaning of the pseudo-inverse solution in terms of the Singular Value Decomposition (Press et al. 1986) representation of the Jacobian matrix. Hanafusa et al. (1981) further extend the redundancy exploitation with criteria expressed in Cartesian space: hence a secondary Cartesian constraint that can be satisfied without affecting the primary constraint. This simultaneous resolution of two constraints with different priorities is known as the task-priority strategy. Maciejewski and Klein (1985) improved the resolution scheme of Hanafusa et al. (1981) by exploiting pseudo-inverse properties. The scheme has then been generalized to an arbitrary number of priority levels by Siciliano and Slotine (1991). So-called algorithmic singularities appear in the task-priority strategy when two constraints are in conflict: the damped least square formulation also handles this case (Maciejewski 1990).

5.2.5.2   Optimization-based methods

The IK can be formulated as a constrained optimization problem and thus solved with non-linear programming methods. For real-time or interactive applications, local optimization methods are preferred to the much more expensive global optimization methods even if there is a risk of being stuck in a local optimum of the objective function. In computer graphics Zhao and Badler (1994) use an optimization method for the manipulation of an articulated figure: a non-linear function (describing the degree of satisfaction of all constraints) is minimized under a set of linear equality and inequality constraints describing joint limits. An application of this method in the manipulation of articulated figures is the Jack system (Badler et al. 1993).

5.2.5.3   Database-guided (or model-based) inverse kinematics algorithms

Methods or extensions specific to the human body have also been developed: human behavior is directly integrated into the process to obtain more realistic, natural-looking, solutions. Some of the approaches discussed here lie at the frontier of the motion planning field as they structure a priori data into information that guides the choice of the solution. For the purpose of posing a human arm with a given hand position, Wang and Verriest (1998) describe an efficient geometric inverse kinematic algorithm for the human arm that incorporates realistic shoulder limits. Koga et al. (1994) exploit a two-step algorithm: first, an approximate arm posture is found based on a sensorimotor transformation model developed by neurophysiologists, and based on measurements; second, the approximate posture is refined to precisely match the hand position constraint, with the help of a simple numerical method. In the domain of force-exerting postures, Aydin and Nakajima (1999) use a huge database of realistic, pre-defined body postures, also with a final refinement process.

Recently, a new generation of methods has been proposed that aims at exploiting databases of captured motions to provide a higher level control for the end-user. These methods exploit mainly interpolation, motion samples chaining or statistical modeling. For a set of walking cases Guo and Roberge (1996) and Golam and Kok (2000) guide the interpolation with motion-specific events; one important point to stress is that the normalized phase coordinate of each event generally changes from sample to sample, thus requiring a dedicated interpolation scheme to ensure the coherence of interpolated motions. Wiley and Hahn (1997) interpolate between a set of pre-recorded postures to generate real-time reach and walk sequences. A more general technique requiring less example motions is described in (Rose et al. 2001); an abstract motion space is constructed from example motions of the same family (a *verb*) parameterized along a few user-centered dimensions (*adverbs*). A scattered data interpolation scheme is set by combining radial basis functions and linear functions to build a cardinal basis out of the example motions while minimizing residual positioning errors.

An alternate strategy is to gather a large database of different motion samples and to chain the most correct ones depending on the context. This idea was first exposed by Lamouret and van de Panne (1996); it clearly stated one important problem: if we want a smooth transition between two successive motion samples, which motion from the database is the closest to the current one? This problem reduces to the question: which metrics is appropriate to compare posture or motion? They proposed a mass–distance metrics that relies on a discretization of the character into a set of mass points; the distance between two postures is then the sum of the squared Euclidian distances between the mass points in the two postures. A similar approach has been chosen by Kovar et al. (2002) to build their motion graph. The alternate metrics is to directly compute a distance in the state space of the articulated figure, basically between the position of the root and between the orientations of the joints. This approach is highly dependent on the choice of parameterization for the orientations. Lee et al. (2002) have chosen to work with quaternions to avoid singularities but distal joints (wrist, ankle, neck, etc.) are not included in the metrics which makes it less general then the previous strategy. For both choices of metrics, the addition of a term measuring a velocity's distance is generally considered for motion comparison.

Stemming from the computer vision field, statistical and probabilistic techniques have become more popular to produce animations. Principal Component Analysis (PCA) is generally the first step to reduce the dimensionality of a motion sequence data set. It can be exploited directly to produce new motions but it lacks vital information such as the temporal structure of the motion (Alexa and Mueller 2000). Some authors have explored the potential of Markov chains and Hidden Markov Models (HMM) to capture and generalize the temporal pattern information for a set of related motions (Molina-Tanco and Hilton 2000). Very convincing results based on theses techniques were obtained by Brand and Hertzmann (2000) with their *stylistic* HMM (SHMM).

The advantage of all these methods is that they are likely to produce more realistic solutions than those resulting from purely constraint-satisfaction-based methods. A second advantage is the relative ease in obtaining highly believable motion through motion capture. On the other hand, the expressive power of statistical methods is constrained by the underlying database; their ability to generalize the desirable features of the motions provided depends strongly on the number of sample motions and their distribution in the feature space. While the addition of new samples can enlarge the repertoire of controlled features, it can also blur the generalization of former features.

5.2.5.4 Comparison of resolution methods

As we have seen, there are a large number of methods to solve the inverse kinematics problem. Each has its own advantages and disadvantages. They can be compared on the following important criteria: efficiency (speed), robustness, generality, believability, and complexity of the method. For real-time applications, analytic methods are always preferable, if a closed-form solution exists. Otherwise the main advantage of numerical methods is their generality and flexibility: they can deal with arbitrary linkages, and new types of constraints can easily be integrated and combined. The price to pay for this generality is a higher computational cost and complexity of the resolution methods (due to their iterative nature), and low reliability since the convergence to a solution is not guaranteed. Moreover, for articulated figure positioning, realistic results can only be obtained if a sufficiently detailed model of the figure being manipulated is provided (with joint limits, joint coupling, comfort criteria, and so on). This modeling task may require a significant effort. For this reason, database-guided techniques are a simpler way to obtain more realistic results, but their scope is limited to a particular problem, in a particular situation.

5.2.6 Other Issues in the Production of 3-D Character Animation

The previous sections have tried to give an overall view of specialized animation techniques. The purpose of the present section is to see how to integrate them to provide a production pipeline capable of efficiently generating believable animations (Figure 5.6).

Among the current challenges faced by animation techniques is the growing demand of gamers for permanent on-line worlds. Within such environments an always more diversified population of 3-D characters should be able to endorse a wide range of skills (*variety*) and be able to select and activate anyone depending on the context, at will (*flexibility*).

We are faced here with four problems: (1) the fast production of families of motions reflecting precise skills; (2) their automatic adjustment to a wide population of more or less human-like characters; (3) the possibility of chaining and/or combining their activation on the fly and last but not least; (4) their adaptation resulting from interaction with the environment. Presently the productivity of the animation pipeline is low due to the intrinsic complexity of the 3-D human structure and our unconscious ability to perceive (un)natural animation artifacts (Oesker et al. 2000). The shift in research and development is to provide methods able to *re-use* the growing amount of captured and physically-based motions. All approaches aim at retaining most of the original natural dynamics while enforcing additional constraints either for editing purpose or for generalization of the motion to a different skeleton.

Among the difficulties faced by this operation is the lack of standardization of the human skeleton resulting in additional conversion between representations. The retargeting operation is more efficient, both off-line and on-line when the source and the destination skeletons adopt the same coordinate system conventions. Chapter 16 discusses in more detail the strengths and weaknesses of the H-anim proposal (H-Anim 2003).

More research is necessary to identify automatically structuring events within a given family of motions. This is the key to automating the constitution of pertinent encapsulated skills that end-users or autonomous characters can pilot through high level parameters (such as normalized velocity for walking).

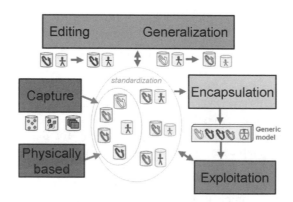

Figure 5.6 Overview of the animation production pipeline

In any case, all the stages of retargeting, encapsulation and exploitation involving inter-action with the environment, require an IK solver to bridge the action in Cartesian space to the joint space expressive power. In many cases simultaneous constraints will have to be accepted. While the weighting strategy is comparatively cheaper, we favor the ability to enforce strict priorities as it is superior in a number of cases (e.g. for balance control). Furthermore, we foresee applications necessitating a much larger number of priority levels than have been used until now in animation.

There is still one point to distinguish which retargeting methods can be exploitable in a real-time on-the-fly fashion, at least if we imagine the computing power is sufficient: they have to be one-pass and exploit only the knowledge of the past and present. They can exploit a priori information of the motion to give a smart prediction of the immediate future. Presently most of the methods rely on multiple passes to guarantee the believability of the resulting animation (Lee and Shin 1999; Gleicher 2001). Only (Choi and Ko 2000) and (Shin et al. 2001) propose on-line motion retargeting.

To conclude this state-of-the-art report, it is vital to stress the importance of the interface offered to animators or end-users. A user-centered approach such as (Rose et al. 2001) can be more efficient than another tool based on a more powerful algorithm but lacking an intuitive interface.

5.3 The Multiple Priority Levels IK (MPL-IK)

As suggested in the previous section, we need a robust IK solver able to handle an arbitrary high number of priority levels. The present section first recalls the most simple IK architecture, then moves to the two priority levels and finally generalizes to p priority levels. A complexity analysis of the associated algorithm can be found in (Baerlocher and Boulic 2003).

5.3.1 Background to Numeric IK

Figure 5.7 shows the simplest redundant case with a two degrees of freedom chain $\{\theta_1, \theta_2\}$ and a one-dimensional constraint along the x dimension for the chain tip, called the Effector. The relationship between the x coordinate of the chain tip and the degrees of freedom values $\{\theta_1, \theta_2\}$ is non-linear. Also, by construction the system is redundant, so its inversion leads to an infinite number of solutions. For this reason, the IK control scheme is based on a linearization of the equation linking the joint space to the Cartesian space for the current state of the system.

An *Effector* is a location on the articulated body
that the user wants to constrain in Cartesian
space (for example along dimension x)

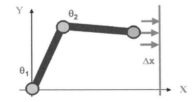

Figure 5.7 Simplest redundant case

The result of this stage is the Jacobian matrix J, gathering the partial derivatives of the constraint with respect to the two degrees of freedom. The Jacobian matrix J needs to be inverted to map the desired constraint variation Δx to a corresponding posture variation $\Delta\theta = \{\Delta\theta_1, \Delta\theta_2\}$. We use the pseudo-inverse, noted J^+, as it ensures desirable properties to build powerful projection operators. Among them, the norm of the solution mapped by J^+ is minimal, i.e. it is the smallest posture variation realizing the desired constraint variation. As the system is highly non-linear, the validity of this operation is limited to small variations, so the target constraint goal is approached incrementally by looping through the linearization process for each update of the chain state. Fortunately the building of the Jacobian is an easy step for the classical position or orientation constraints (Watt and Watt 1992).

Here is the general solution where all the end effector(s) constraints are controlled at the same priority level. In addition, a projection operator allows optimization of a *secondary constraint* $\Delta\alpha$, expressed in the joint variation space, at a lower priority level. The discrete form of the solution is:

$$\Delta\theta = J^+\Delta x + P_{N(J)}\Delta\alpha \qquad (5.1)$$

$$P_{N(J)} = (I_n - J^+J) \qquad (5.2)$$

where:

$\Delta\theta$ is the unknown vector in the joint variation space, of dimension **n**.

Δx describes the *main task* as a constraint variation toward a target. Its dimension, noted **m**,

J is the Jacobian

J^+ is the unique pseudo-inverse of J

$P_{N(J)}$ is a projection operator on the *Null space* of the linear transformation J (with I_n being the identity matrix of the joint variation space (n x n)). Any element belonging to this sub-space is mapped by J into the null vector in the constraint variation space.

$\Delta\alpha$ is an arbitrary n-dimensional vector, usually the gradient of a cost function to minimize $f(\theta)$. It is called the *secondary task* as it is partially realized by the projection on the *Null space* (Figure 5.8).

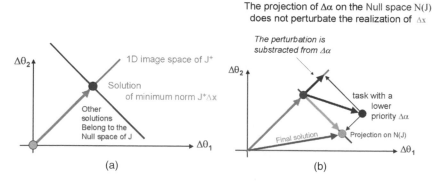

Figure 5.8   The variation space with the minimal norm solution (a) and (b) the final solution including a lower priority task projected on the kernel of J (noted N(J))

5.3.2 Handling Two Conflicting Constraints

Equation (5.3) has been proposed for enforcing two priorities levels of end effector control. Figure 5.9 illustrates this context; worth noting is the conflicting nature of the two constraints, both cannot be achieved simultaneously. Let Δx_1 be the highest priority constraint, Δx_2 the lowest priority constraint: we have to construct a $\Delta\alpha$ contribution belonging to the joint variation space and enforcing these two priority levels (Figure 5.10).

Two mechanisms are used: the first one removes the contribution of the main constraint Δx_1 from the secondary constraint Δx_2 with the term $-J_2(J_1^+\Delta x_1)$. Then the compensated term is projected, along $N(J_2)$, on $N(J1)$.

This architecture introduces an algorithmic singularity when the low-level constraint cannot be fully achieved (i.e. when $N(J_1)$ and $N(J_2)$ coincide). A regularization technique must be applied in this context (Appendix A summarizes the construction of the damped pseudo-inverse proposed in (Maciejewski 1990)). The final formula, after simplification, is:

$$\Delta\theta = J_1^+\Delta x_1 + \left[J_2 P_{N(J_1)}\right]^+ (\Delta x_2 - J_2(J_1^+\Delta x_1)) \tag{5.3}$$

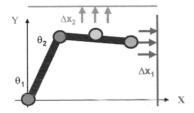

A two dofs chain has to constrain
the chain tip on a vertical line and
a second effector on an horizontal line.

Figure 5.9 The simplest redundant case with two conflicting tasks

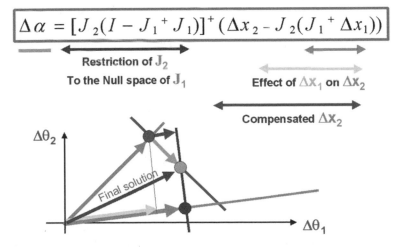

$$\Delta\alpha = [J_2(I - J_1^+ J_1)]^+ (\Delta x_2 - J_2(J_1^+ \Delta x_1))$$

Restriction of J_2
To the Null space of J_1

Effect of Δx_1 on Δx_2

Compensated Δx_2

Figure 5.10 The low level task is first compensated prior to the mapping

5.3.3 Generalizing to p Priority Levels

The human structure being highly redundant, there is a large solution space for the realization of much more than two constraints. A first general framework has been described by Siciliano and Slotine (1991). In this approach a new Jacobian matrix has to be defined:

The Augmented Jacobian, noted J_i^A piles all the individual constraint Jacobians J_i from level 1 to level i.

Then, if we denote p, the total number of priority levels, the solution is computed incrementally by accumulating the contributions of each priority level starting from the highest one, indexed by 1:

$$\Delta\theta_1 = J_1^{+\lambda_1}\Delta x_1 \tag{5.4}$$

and for i = 2 to p (the final solution is obtained in $\Delta\theta_p$)

$$\Delta\theta_1 = \Delta\theta_{i-1} + (J_i P_{N(J_{i-1}^A)})^{+\lambda_1}(\Delta x_i - J_i\Delta\theta_{i-1}) \tag{5.5}$$

where a pseudo-inverse superscripted with λ_i denotes a damped pseudo-inverse to handle singularities. The choice of the damping factor λ_i is made to ensure that the solution norm is bounded by a pre-defined value. In the approach described in (Siciliano and Slotine 1991), the computing cost of the projection operator $P_{N(J^A)}$ grows in $O(p^2)$ with the number of priority levels p. We have proposed a solution with a cost in $O(p)$. Our improvement lies in its recursive computation (Baerlocher 2001). Starting with $P_{N(J_0^A)} = I_n$ we have:

$$P_{N(J_i^A)} = P_{N(J_{i-1}^A)} - (J_i P_{N(J_{i-1}^A)})^{+}(J_i P_{N(J_{i-1}^A)}) \tag{5.6}$$

5.4   MPL-IK Results

The robustness of the Multiple Priority Levels IK has been thoroughly tested with an interaction optimization framework where any aspect of the optimization context can change while the convergence runs. The user is able to add and remove constraints, as well as change their relative priorities, at any time during the simulation (multiple constraints can share the same priority level). Similarly, the lowest-level cost function is activated and deactivated whenever necessary. The interaction also brings a deeper understanding of the human body configuration space.

A simplified human model is used to study various reach postures. Table 5.1 lists all the end effectors and the associated constraints activated permanently or temporarily during that session. In addition, an optimization function expressed in the joint space was optimized at the lowest level of priority. For the present case study we have used the following cost function: leg-flexion, leg-extension or leg-symmetry.

For this example, the articulated figure is rooted at the right toe which remains fixed in a world coordinate system (the choice of the root is also interactive, in case no choice is made the default location is the spine base). The initial posture is standing up. Figure 5.11 shows some solutions complying with the specification of Table 5.1. The trajectories highlight the reachability of the right hand starting from the squat posture.

Table 5.1 End effector tasks with their rank

End effector	Function of the task	rank
left toe	maintain contact with the floor (position)	1
eyes	orienting toward the sphere (lookat-orientation)	1
left hand center	holding the vertical bar (position and orientation)	1
center of mass	projecting on a point or a line in-between the feet	2
right hand center	reaching the blue sphere (position)	3
pelvis, elbow, knee	activated temporarily to readjust locally the posture (position)	4
cost function(θ)	activated temporarily to readjust globally the posture	5

Figure 5.11 Interactive optimization with four priority levels

5.5 Conclusion

Motion control is an extremely rich topic especially when dedicated to the animation of such complex entities as active human beings. A large and growing panel of approaches is available depending on the desired compromise between believability and predictability of the method. When focusing on pure animation, the production cost becomes the major concern; presently most of the efforts are oriented towards improving the reusability of realistic motions (generally captured). Re-using and generalizing motions to a wide range of characters often require constraint it of some body parts (in position and/or orientation), thus the emphasis of the present chapter on inverse kinematics techniques. Relying on a powerful and robust IK solver architecture is one of the key elements in the success of a motion retargeting technique. In that respect we have briefly discussed how to build an IK solution enforcing an arbitrary number of strict priority levels. The performances and the general robustness of the algorithm are compatible with interactive use. Associated with the control of the center of mass, this technique offers a much greater spectrum of posture optimization.

The remaining aspects to be improved are on the biomechanic and the neuroscience side of the problem. First, the knowledge of each joint's available strength is essential to distribute the internal torques preferably to stronger joints, thus resulting in an overall improvement of the posture comfort. Yet human strength data are sparse and difficult to generalize for virtual characters. Motion control as a whole is such a complex task that we certainly have a lot to learn from the mechanisms taking place within the human brain; recent results demonstrating the inherent predictive capacity of cognition and perception are extremely stimulating in that regard (Berthoz 2002).

6

Facial Deformation Models

Prem Kalra, Stephane Garchery, Sumedha Kshirsagar

This chapter presents various deformation models, which are used for facial animation. These models have been categorized into classes based on the manner in which the geometry of the face is manipulated. Broadly speaking, these may be purely geometric without accounting for any physical properties of facial tissues and muscles, and models, which are based on the physical properties and use mechanics of forces. The chapter also includes a brief description of the anatomy of a human face, which gives an insight into the development of some models. Many of these models use a parameterization scheme, which helps control the animation. A brief outline of some popular parameterization schemes is also provided. An example of MPEG-4-based facial deformation/animation is presented for real-time applications. Various deformation models are compared with respect to the realism, computational speed, and some other characteristic features.

6.1 Introduction

There is increasing interest in facial modeling and animation due to the appearance of virtual characters in film and videos, inexpensive desktop processing power, and the potential for a new 3-D communication paradigm for human-computer interaction. Generation of facial deformation is an issue, which is particularly important for animating faces. A face model without the ability to deform is a passive object and has little role in Virtual Humans. The deformation model needs to ensure that facial movements are naturalistic and realistic, in the sense of improving accuracy to enhance comprehension. This involves study and investigation of facial anatomy, and the motion and behavior of faces involving the generation of facial expressions, which are readily comprehensible.

This chapter is intended as an accessible reference to the range of reported facial deformation techniques. Often these models are seen as geometric manipulations using methods such as key-framing and geometric interpolations, parameterizations, finite element methods, physical based muscle modeling, pseudo-muscle models using procedures, spline models

Handbook of Virtual Humans Edited by N. Magnenat-Thalmann and D. Thalmann
© 2004 John Wiley & Sons, Ltd   ISBN: 0-470-02316-3

and free-form deformations. These models are closely linked to the controlling motion parameterization. Thus, we also present some popular schemes of control parameterization.

This chapter is organized as follows. First, we give a preliminary note on the anatomy of a face. In Section 6.3 we present the control parameterization schemes. Section 6.4 provides the various deformation models, followed by a comparative chart of these models in Section 6.5. Finally, we conclude in Section 6.6.

6.2 Some Preliminaries about the Anatomy of a Face

The study of anatomy and physiology helped artists in olden days to create lively pictures and drawings. Similarly, this can give better insight for modeling and animating faces. We give here a brief outline of the structure and movement of skin, muscles and their characteristics of movement, and the major bones of the skull.

6.2.1 Skin

Skin is significant in providing both the appearance and the movement of the face:

- *Structure*: Human skin comprises several layers (Danielson 1973). The outermost layer is epidermis, below which lies dermis. Beneath the dermis lies a layer of soft irregular connective tissues, which form fascia also known as hypodermis or the subcutaneous surface. This structure enables skin to move freely over the muscles and bones underneath.
- *Motion*: The motion characteristics are due to the mechanical properties of skin, interaction of layers and muscle activation. The major components that determine the mechanical properties of skin are collagen, elastin fibres and ground substance. Collagen fibres are the major constituent in skin. They are strong and stiff. The behavior of elastin depicts almost all linear stress strain response (Lanir 1987). The ground substance is responsible for skin's visco-elastic behavior. The main mechanical properties are: non-linearity, anisotropy, visco-elasticity, incompressibility and plasticity (Wu 1998). Ageing changes the properties of skin and causes the emergence of wrinkles.

6.2.2 Muscles

Muscles are the principal motivators of facial actions and thus determine facial movement:

- *Structure*: Muscle lies between the bone and skin. Attached at the bone end is the origin, which is fixed and the connection to the fascia is the insertion, which is free. Some of the muscles such as the obicularis oris, have both ends, the origin and insertion, attached to the skin.
- *Contraction and movement*: All facial actions occur as a consequence of muscular contraction. Muscles in general are of a large variety of sizes, shapes and complexity. However, they are essentially bundles of fibers that operate in unison. It is the arrangement of these fibers that determines both the relative strength and range of movement that a muscle can produce. There are two types of muscular contractions: isotonic which causes shortening, and isometric, which develops tension but does not shorten the muscle. All facial muscles contrast isotonically (Patel 1992).

- Facial muscles are, in general, thin, voluntary and subcutaneous. They also occur in pairs with one for each side of the face. Often muscles tend to be considered according to the region in which they occur. Figure 6.1 shows the frontal view of facial muscles (Parke and Waters 1996). There are three types of facial muscles in terms of their actions: linear/parallel muscles which pull in an angular direction, elliptical/circular sphincter muscles which squeeze, and sheet muscles which act as a series of linear muscles.

6.2.3 Bone

The bones of the head, collectively termed the skull, determine the proportion and shape of the face. The nature and shape of the skull vary with race, age, and gender. The skull consists of two parts: the cranium and mandible. The upper part of the cranium protects the brain and is called the calvaria, and the rest of the skull is the facial skeleton, of which the upper part is fixed and the lower part is the freely moving mandible. Relative sizes, shapes and distances between these bones are responsible for the unique characteristic of each face.

In addition to above, there are facial features with a distinct form and specific motion, e.g., eyes, tongue and teeth. Eyes are a particularly noticeable attribute and significant regarding the appearance and motion of the face.

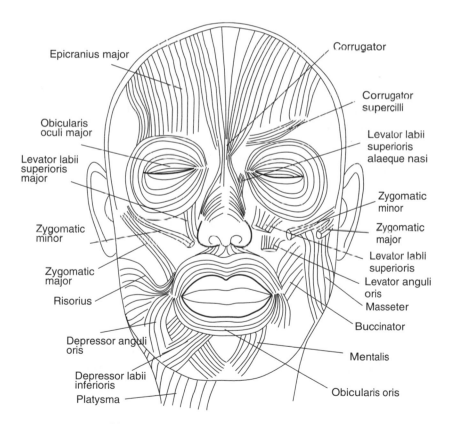

Figure 6.1 Frontal view of facial muscles

6.3   Control Parameterization

The development of facial animation may be considered as dealing with: defining control parameterization and development of techniques and models for facial animation based on these parameterizations (Parke and Waters 1996). From an animator's point of view, facial animation is manipulation of the parameters and therefore parameterization is an important aspect of the animation model. There are three main schemes of parameterization, which have been used in the context of facial animation models. These are interpolation, FACS (Facial Action Coding System) and FAP (Facial Animation Parameters). We now present these schemes.

6.3.1   Interpolation

Interpolation is a general technique of animation and was also applied to facial animation. Interpolation basically involves finding an intermediate value with given end values. The intermediate value can be related through the parameter that combines the extreme values. In a simple situation, one can consider the extreme values as the expressions or poses of the face and the intermediate value is obtained by interpolating the data points, i.e., the vertex positions of the two extreme positions. Here, the type of interpolating function (e.g., linear or non-linear) defines the type of control.

6.3.2   FACS (Facial Action Coding System)

Though several systems or languages have been developed to describe facial expressions, the most popular and widely used is the Facial Action Coding Systems (FACS) (Ekman and Frisen 1978). The FACS was developed by Ekman and his colleagues, and was not intended for use in animation. The primary goal of FACS was to develop a comprehensive system, which could reliably describe all possible visually distinguishable facial movements. It defines fundamental basic actions known as Action Units (AUs). Each AU describes the contraction of one facial muscle or a group of related muscles. Thus, FACS was derived by analysis of the anatomical basis for facial movements. There are 46 action units. This repertoire of action units can be regarded as a 'kit' for creating and compositing facial expressions. FACS is, however, limited to those muscles that can be controlled voluntarily. FACS seems complete for reliably distinguishing actions of the brows, forehead and eyelids but it does not include all the visible actions for the lower part of the face particularly related to oral speech. In addition, it does not include the head movements. However, the use of FACS in facial animation goes beyond what was intended.

There have also been variants of FACS. For example, a basic facial motion parameter can be defined in terms of minimum perceptible action (MPA) (Kalra et al. 1991). Each MPA has a corresponding set of visible facial features such as movement of the eyebrows, the jaw, the mouth or other motions that occur as a result of contracting muscles associated with the region. The MPAs also include non-facial muscle actions such as nods and turns of the head and movement of the eyes. The MPAs for the mouth region are designed so that rendering of speech can be done reliably.

Some efforts have also been made to further refine the action units of FACS and extend it to FACS+ (Essa and Pentland 1997).

6.3.3 FAP (Facial Animation Parameters)

SNHC (Synthetic Natural Hybrid Coding), a subgroup of MPEG-4, has devised an efficient coding method for graphics models and the compressed transmission of their animation parameters specific to the model type. For synthetic faces, the Facial Animation Parameters (FAP) are designed to encode animation of faces reproducing expressions, emotions and speech pronunciation. Chapter 16 on 'standards' provides the necessary details on these parameters. The 68 parameters are categorized into 10 different groups related to parts of the face. FAPs represent a complete set of basic facial actions, and therefore allow the representation of most natural facial expressions. The parameter set contains two high level parameters, the viseme and the expression.

Since the FAPs are required to animate faces of different sizes and proportions, the FAP values are defined in Face Animation Parameter Units (FAPU). The FAPU are computed from spatial distances between major facial features on the model in its neutral state. It must be noted that the standard does not specify any particular way of achieving facial mesh deformation for a given FAP. The implementation details such as resolution of the mesh, deformation algorithm, rendering etc. are left to the developer of the MPEG-4 facial animation system. The standard also specifies use of a Facial Animation Table (FAT) to determine which vertices are affected by a particular FAP and how. The Facial Animation Tables model is very useful, guaranteeing not only the precise shape of the face, but also the exact reproduction of animation.

6.4 Facial Deformation Models

Various models of deforming a face have been developed over the years (Noh and Neumann 1998). Many of these models are adaptations of general deformation models to facial deformation. Some of the models are based on merely creating believable visual effects without considering physical and structural laws, and others are derived using a physical basis comprising forces, muscular contractions and skin bio-mechanics. We can categorize these models based on the mechanism in which the geometry of the face model is manipulated. There have been number of deformation models developed in each category, as follows, we present some of these models.

6.4.1 Shape Interpolation

This was one of the earliest approaches employed for animating faces (Parke 1972, 1991; Enmett 1985). This is primarily based on running an interpolation function (linear or non-linear) on the vertex positions of the extreme poses or expressions of faces. Thus deformation at any instance is in terms of the displacement of the vertices determined by the interpolating parameter and the extreme positions. The method is rather simple. However, the approach has several limitations: the range of expressions obtained is restricted and the method is data-intensive as it needs explicit geometrical data for each pose/expression. The control is through the interpolation parameter defined through a linear or non-linear function.

6.4.2 Parametric Model

The parametric model overcomes the restrictions of the interpolation technique (Parke 1974, 1982, 1989). Here, a collection of polygons is manipulated by a set of parameters. This allows a wide range of faces by specifying a small set of appropriate parameters associated with different regions of a face. However, the design of the parameters set is based on hard-wiring the vertices to manipulate a part of the face, which makes the model dependent on the facial topology. This curtails the generality of the model. In addition, a complete set of such parameters is difficult to obtain which would define all possible expressions. The deformation control is through the time series of the parameter set.

6.4.3 Muscle-Based Models

The complete anatomical description of a face is rather complex. It is not practical to design a model, which entails the intricacies of the complete description of the face anatomy. However, efforts have been made to create models, which are based on simplified structures of bones, muscles, skin and connective tissues. These models provide the ability to manipulate facial geometry based on simulating the characteristics of the facial muscles. This approach offers generality as the same set of muscles is valid for all faces. We consider here two types of methods, one is based on the physics or mechanics involved in the process of deformation and in the other method, a visual simulation is produced by simplifying the underlying anatomy and the mechanics involved. Most of these muscle-based models use the parameterization scheme of FACS or its variant.

6.4.3.1   Physics-Based Muscle modeling

In this category, we consider the models which are based on the physics or mechanics of the underlying phenomena that model the muscle behavior. Three kinds of models are considered: mass spring systems, vector representations, and layered spring meshes. Mass-spring methods propagate muscle forces in an elastic spring mesh that models skin deformation. The vector approach deforms a facial mesh using motion fields in delineated regions of influence. A layered spring mesh extends a mass spring structure into three connected mesh layers to model anatomical facial behavior more faithfully:

- *Spring mesh muscle*: The work by Platt and Badler (1981) is one of the earliest attempts of the research focused on muscle modeling and the structure of the human face. In this model, the skin is considered as elastic plane of surface nodes. Forces applied to elastic mesh through muscle arcs generate realistic facial expressions. The muscles are collection of fibers modeled as arcs connecting the skin and the bone. The skin nodes behave like Hookean springs where the extension is proportional to the force divided by the spring constant. The model used by Platt and Badler consists of 38 regional muscle blocks interconnected by a spring network. When a muscle contracts, a force is applied to a muscle node in the direction of its bone attachment. Action units of FACS are used for specifying the animation.
- *Vector muscle*: Waters (1987) proposed a model based on a delineated deformation field that models the action of muscles upon skin. A muscle definition includes the vector field direction, an origin, and an insertion point. Real muscles in general consists of many individual fibers, here a single vector emulates the effect. Three kinds of muscles have been considered: linear, sphincter and sheet. In linear muscle, the affected or the surrounding skin is contracted toward the attachment on the bone. The field extent on the skin is defined by cosine functions and fall-off factors that produce a cone shape

when visualized as a height field. The sphincter muscle contracts around the center of the ellipsoid (or ellipse in a planar case) and is primarily responsible for the deformation of the mouth region. Sheet muscle, as opposed to the linear muscle, does not emanate from a point source, instead consider a broad flat area on which the parallel fibers spread. Figure 6.2 shows the three types of muscles. Waters animates human emotions such as anger, fear, surprise, disgust, joy, and happiness, using vector-based muscles implementing the FACS. The vector muscle model provides a compact representation of muscles that is independent of the facial topology. It has been successfully used in many animations, an example of vector muscles is seen in Billy, the baby in the movie *Tin Toy*, who has 47 Waters' muscles on his face. The positioning of vector muscles into anatomically correct positions, however, can be a tedious task. There has not been any automatic way reported for placing muscles beneath a surface mesh. The process in general involves manual trial and error with no guarantee of efficient or optimal placement. Incorrect placement results in unnatural or undesirable animation of the mesh.

- *Layered spring mesh muscles*: Terzopoulos and Waters (1990) proposed a facial model that models a more detailed anatomical structure and dynamics of the human face. A three-layered structure is considered, which corresponds to skin, fatty tissue, and muscle respectively (see Figure 6.3). These layers encompass different parameters for each tissue type. The topmost surface represents the epidermis and thus has parameters, which enable a stiff behavior. The layer beneath with pentahedral elements represent the dermis. The hexahedral elements in the second layer represent the fatty tissues, which are highly deformable and thus have the parameters, which enable this behavior. Nodes at the bottom of the second layer represent the fascia that connect to the muscle fibers. Elastic spring elements connect each mesh node and each layer. Muscle forces propagate through the mesh systems to create animation. This model achieves great realism, however, simulating volumetric deformations with three-dimensional lattices requires extensive computation.

A simplified mesh system reduces the computation time while still maintaining visual realism (Wu et al. 1994). Here, visco-elastic properties of skin are considered. Lee et al. (1995) presented models of physics-based synthetic skin and muscle layers based on earlier work (Terzopoulos and Waters 1990). Here, the face model consists of three components: a biological tissue layer with non-linear deformation properties, a muscle layer knit together under the skin, and an impenetrable skull structure beneath the muscle layer. The model accounts for volume preservation and skull penetration force. The synthetic tissue is modeled as triangular prism elements that are divided into the epidermal surface,

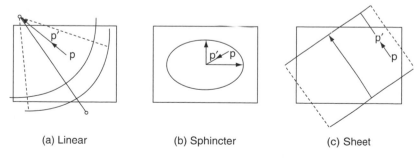

(a) Linear   (b) Sphincter   (c) Sheet

Figure 6.2   Muscle types

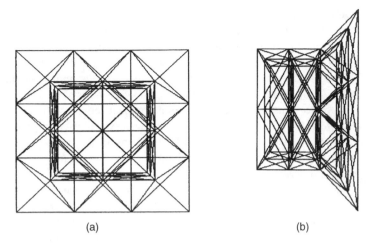

(a)   (b)

Figure 6.3 Three-layered structure

the fascia surface, and the skull surface. Spring elements connecting the epidermal and fascia layers simulate skin elasticity. Spring elements that effect muscle forces connect the fascia and skull layers. The model achieves a great degree of realism and fidelity, however, the model remains computationally expensive. In another model (Kahler et al. 2001), a three-layer structure is used and mass-spring system is employed for deformation. An editing tool is provided to design a course shape of muscles interactively, which is then used for automatic creation of a muscle fitting to the face geometry.

6.4.3.2 Pseudo-Muscle modeling

Physics-based muscle modeling is inspired by the physical phenomenon that is considered to model the muscle behavior. It may produce realistic results. However, it may be a daunting task to consider the exact modeling and the parameters needed to simulate a specific human's facial structure. Simulated muscles offer an alternative approach by deforming the facial mesh in muscle-like fashion, but ignoring the complicated underlying anatomy and the physics. Deformation usually occurs only at the thin-shell facial mesh surface. Muscle forces can be simulated in the form of operators arising through splines (Nahas et al. 1988, 1990; Waite 1989; Wang and Forsey 1994) or other geometric deformations (Kalra et al. 1992).

- *Abstract muscle actions*: Abstract Muscle Action (AMA) (Magnenat-Thalmann et al. 1988) refers to a procedure for driving a facial animation system. These AMA procedures are similar to the action units of FACS and work on specific regions of the face. Each AMA procedure represents the behavior of a single or a group of related muscles. Facial expressions are formed by group of AMA procedures. When applied to form facial expression, the ordering of the action unit is important due to the dependency among the AMA procedures.
- *Free form deformation*: Free form deformation (FFD) is a deformation technique for deforming solid geometric models by manipulating control points arranged in a three-dimensional lattice (Sederberg and Parry 1986). Conceptually, a flexible object is embedded in an imaginary, clear, and flexible control box containing a 3-D grid of control

points. As the control box is deformed i.e., squashed, bent, or twisted into arbitrary shapes, the embedded object follows the deformation accordingly (see Figure 6.4). The embedded object can be represented in any form such as polyhedral object, a high ordered parametric surface or an implicit surface. A mapping is established from one 3-D space to another 3-D space using a trivariate tensor product Bernstein polynomial. Rational free form deformation (RFFD) incorporates weight factors for each control point, adding another degree of freedom in specifying deformations (Kalra et al. 1992). Hence, deformations are possible by changing the weight factors instead of changing the control point positions. When all weights are equal to one, then RFFD becomes an FFD. The main advantage of using FFD (or RFFD) to abstract deformation control from that of the actual surface description is that the transition of form is no longer dependent on the specifics of the surface itself (Magnenat-Thalmann and Thalmann 1996).

Kalra et al. (1992) simulate the visual effects of the muscles using Rational Free Form Deformation (RFFD) using a region-based approach. To simulate the muscle action on the facial skin, surface regions corresponding to the anatomical description of the muscle actions are defined. A parallelepiped control volume is then defined on the region of interest. The skin deformations corresponding to stretching, squashing, expanding, and compressing inside the volume are simulated by interactively displacing the control points and by changing the weights associated with each control point. Linear interpolation is used to decide the deformation of the boundary points lying within the adjoining regions. Displacing a control point is analogous to actuating a physically modeled muscle. Compared to Waters' vector muscle model (Waters 1987), manipulating the positions or the weights of the control points is more intuitive and simpler than manipulating muscle vectors with delineated zone of influence. However, RFFD (or FFD) does not provide a precise simulation of the actual muscle and the skin behavior so that it fails to model

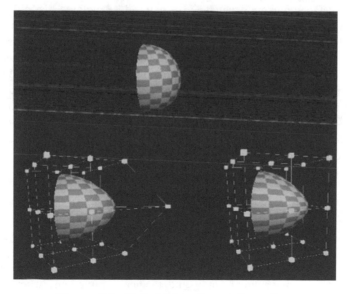

Figure 6.4   Rational free form deformation

furrows, bulges, and wrinkles in the skin. Furthermore, since RFFD is based upon surface deformation, volumetric changes occurring in the physical muscle is not accounted for.

- *Spline muscles*: Polygonal representation of a surface mesh is widely used to approximate the irregular and curved shape of a face primarily due to the simplicity and its hardware rendering support. This, however, often fails to adequately approximate the smoothness or flexibility of the form of a human face. The polygonal models require a large number of polygons to produce a smooth-looking surface for a human face. For an ideal facial model it is desirable to have a surface representation that supports smooth and flexible deformations. Parametric surfaces or spline-based surfaces offer a solution. These provide higher order continuity usually up to C2. Furthermore, the affine transformations can be applied to a small set of control points instead of all the vertices of the mesh, hence reducing the computational complexity. These transformations or the displacements of the control points simulate the muscle actions.

There have been some models based on parametric surfaces used to define the facial model (Nahas et al. 1988, 1990; Waite 1989; Wang and Forsey 1994). Many animation films have used these models. For example, bicubic Catmull-Rom spline patches are used for modeling Billy, the baby in animation *Tin Toy* by Pixar, and recently, they used a variant of Catmull and Clark's (1978) subdivision surfaces to model Geri, a human character in the short film *Geri's Game*. This technique is mainly adapted to model sharp creases on a surface or discontinuities between surfaces (Catmull 1974). Eisert and Girod (1998) used triangular B-splines to overcome the drawback that conventional B-splines do not refine curved areas locally since they are defined on a rectangular topology.

Wang and Forsey (1994) showed a system that integrated hierarchical spline models with simulated muscles based on local surface deformations. A simple B-spline surface enables smooth modeling of the surface. However, to produce finer resolution of the surface, the entire surface is affected. Thus, more control points are added even where the details are not required. In contrast, hierarchical splines provide the local refinements of B-spline surfaces and new patches are only added within a specified region. As a consequence, changes to a single control point affects the surface up to two control points. Gradient-based approach is used to obtain the deformation caused by muscles. Hierarchical B-splines are an economical and compact way to represent a spline surface and achieve high rendering speed. Muscles coupled with hierarchical spline surfaces are capable of creating bulging skin surfaces and a variety of facial expressions.

Dubreuil and Bechmann (1996) used DOGMA (Deformation of Geometrical Model Animated), a subset of generalized n-dimensional space deformation model called DOGME (Bechmann and Dubreuil 1993). For a 4D model, the deformation is defined in terms of displacement constraints and the fourth dimension is time. A limited set of muscles is modeled using splines.

6.4.4 Finite Element Method

The finite element method (FEM) has been used widely in structural analysis of materials in CAD/CAM. The FEM is basically a method to approximate the solution of a continuous function with a series of shape functions. In the context of facial deformation these have been employed for biomechanical study and medical simulations, where accuracy is of importance.

Larrabee (1986) proposed the first skin deformation model using FEM. The skin is simplified as elastic membrane with nodes spaced at regular intervals. The linear stress–strain relationship is employed for the skin membrane. This approach attempted modeling the effect of skin flap design for preoperative surgical simulation. A more rigorous model is proposed by Deng (1988) comprising three-layered facial tissue. The model is constructed as a thick shell including a skin layer, a sliding layer and a muscle layer. The model was used for simulating the closure of skin excision. Pieper et al. (1992) further extend Deng's model employed on facial data obtained from CT (Computer Tomography) for surgical simulations. Koch et al. (1996) developed a model using data from a patient using CT and MRI (Magnetic Resonance Imaging) data. The approach uses a combination of techniques to build a prototype system for surgical planning and prediction of facial shape after craniofacial and maxillofacil surgery. One may notice that these models have not been used for facial animation, however, they do have the potential for it.

Guenter (1992) proposed a simpler scheme of attaching muscles and wrinkle lines to any part of the face and used a global stiffness matrix to compute the deformation. The skin is modeled as a linear elastic rectangular mesh. Contraction of muscles is computed in 2-D and then mapped onto 3-D. FACS is used for control parameterization where muscles can be specified as one or more action units. Thus, this model combines muscle-based modeling with a simpler model of FEM.

6.4.5 Other Models

There are other deformation models, which do not strictly fall into any of the above classes. Many of these models are based on local deformation of facial geometry.

In some of the performance-driven animations (Williams 1990; Patterson et al. 1991; Guenter et al. 1998), the deformation for the neighboring zone of the dot is computed through a distance function. For example, a cosine window function can be used for this purpose, the size of the window is interactively specified (Patterson et al. 1991). A normalization or composition scheme is often desirable to overcome the unwanted effects when two regions overlap.

In another approach, a transformation method is used for modeling an individualized face from a canonical model (Kurihara and Arai 1991). The same method is also extended for animating a face. A set of control points is selected and the transformation gives the displacement of these control points. The displacements of other points are computed using a linear combination of the displacements of the control points. The actual computation is done in 2-D using a cylindrical projection. FACS is used for control parameterization.

6.4.6 MPEG-4-Based Facial Animation

As explained earlier in Section 6.3.3 and in more detail in Chapter 16, MPEG-4 defines a parameter set for facial animation. The precise method of deformation is not, however, standardized. In this section we demonstrate two ways to implement an MPEG-4-compliant facial animation. In the first method, we use a local deformation technique based on feature definition point (FDP) for the facial mesh. The second technique uses the Facial Animation Table defined by MEPG-4 and is essentially an interpolation method. Both techniques produce real-time animation.

6.4.6.1   Geometric Deformation

Many local deformation models have been developed complying with the MPEG-4 facial animation standard (Kshirsagar et al. 2000; Lavagetto and Pockaj 1999; Lande and Francini 1998). Here, one such deformation method is explained in details. We present a robust, fast, and simple geometric mesh deformation algorithm. The algorithm is feature points based i.e. it can be applied to enable the animation of various mesh objects defined by the placement of their feature points. We then explain how this algorithm can be effectively used for MPEG-4 facial mesh deformation and animation in real-time.

Generalized mesh deformation.   We assume that the object to be deformed is defined by the locations of the pre-defined feature points on the surface of the mesh. Further, the deformation of the mesh can be completely defined by the movements of these feature points (alternatively referred as control points) from their neutral positions either in absolute or in normalized units. This method of definition and animation provides a concise and efficient way of representing an object. Since the control points lie on the geometric surface, their locations are predictable, unlike in FFD techniques. In order to get realistic-looking deformation and animation, it is necessary that the mesh has a good definition of the feature points, i.e. the control point locations should be defined considering the animation properties and real-life topology of the object under consideration. Additionally, movement constraints should be defined for the feature points. A constraint in a direction indicates the behavior of the control point in that direction. For example, if a control point is constrained along the x axis, but not along the y and z axes, it means that it still acts as an ordinary vertex of the mesh along the y and z axes. Its movement along these axes will be controlled by the other control points in the vicinity.

Given a geometric mesh with control point locations and constraints, the next step is to compute the regions influenced by each of the control points. Each vertex of the mesh should be controlled by not only the nearest feature point, but other feature points in the vicinity, in order to avoid patchy animation. The number of feature points influencing a vertex and the factor by which each feature point influences the movement of this vertex is decided by the following:

- the distances between the feature points, i.e. if the feature points are spread densely or sparsely on the mesh;
- the distances between the ordinary (non-feature point) vertices of the mesh and the nearest feature point;
- the relative spread of the feature points around a given vertex.

The algorithm is divided into two steps. In the *initialization* step, the above mentioned information is extracted and the coefficients or *weights* for each of the vertices corresponding to the nearest feature points are calculated. The distance between two points is computed as the sum of the edge lengths encountered while traversing from one point to the other. We call this the *surface distance*. The surface distance measure is useful to handle holes and discontinuities in the mesh, e.g. mouth and eye openings in the facial mesh models. The *deformation* step actually takes place during the real-time animation for each frame.

Initialization.   The initialization can further be divided into two sub-steps: computing feature point distribution and computing the weights.

For computing feature point distribution, the information about all the neighboring feature points for each feature point is extracted. The mesh is traversed starting from each feature point, advancing only one step in all the possible directions at a time, thus growing a mesh region for each feature point, called the *feature point region*. Neighboring feature points are those feature points that have a common feature point region boundary. As a result, for each feature point defined on the mesh surface, we get a list of the neighboring feature points with *surface distances* between them. This information is further used for computing the weights.

Next, extract possible overlapping influence regions for each feature point and compute the corresponding weight for deformation for all the vertices in this influence region. Consider a general surface mesh as shown in Figure 6.5. During the process of mesh traversal starting from the feature points, assume that the vertex P is approached from a feature point FP_1. FP_1 is added to the list of the influencing feature points of P.

From the information extracted in the previous step of mesh traversal, FP_2, and FP_3 are the neighboring feature points of FP_1. FP_2 and FP_3 are chosen so that the angles θ_2 and θ_3 are the smallest of all the angles θ_i for neighboring feature points FP_i of FP_1. Also:

$$\theta_2 < \frac{\pi}{2}, \theta_3 < \frac{\pi}{2} \tag{6.1}$$

The surface distances of the vertex from these feature points are respectively d_{1P}, d_{12} and d_{13} as shown in Figure 6.5. While computing the weight of FP_1 at P, we consider the effect of the presence of the other neighboring feature points, namely FP_2 and FP_3 at P. For this, we compute the following weighted sum d:

$$d = \frac{d_{12} \cos \theta_2 + d_{13} \cos \theta_3}{\cos \theta_2 + \cos \theta_3} \tag{6.2}$$

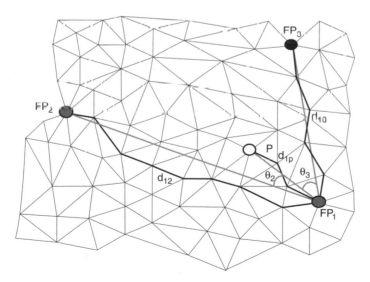

Figure 6.5 Computing weights for animation

Thus, d is the weighted sum of the distances d_{12} and d_{13}. The feature point in a smaller angular distance from the FP_1 is assigned a higher value of weight. If there is only one neighbouring feature point of FP_1 such that $\theta_2 < \pi/2$, then d is simply computed as $d_{12}/\cos\theta_2$.

We compute the weight assigned to the point P for the deformation due to movement of FP_1 as:

$$W_{1,P} = \sin\left(\frac{\pi}{2}\left(1 - \frac{d_{1p}}{d}\right)\right) \tag{6.3}$$

or more generally:

$$W_{i,P} = \sin\left(\frac{\pi}{2}\left(1 - \frac{d_{ip}}{d}\right)\right) \tag{6.4}$$

Thus, point P has a weight for displacement that is inversely proportional to its distance from the nearest feature point FP_1. This determines the local influence of the feature point on the vertices of the mesh. At the same time, nearer the other feature points (FP_2 and FP_3 in this case) to FP_1, this weight is less according to equations (6.2) and (6.3). This determines the global influence of a feature point on the surrounding region, in the presence of other feature points in the vicinity.

It is possible that a vertex is approached by more than one feature point, during the process of mesh traversal. We compute the weight for this feature point following the same procedure, as long as the angular distance criterion (1) is satisfied, and the *surface distance* $d_{iP} < d$, d as defined in equation (6.2). This second criterion ensures that the feature points FP_j whose nearest neighbors are nearer to the vertex P than FP_j are not considered while computing the deformation for vertex P. Thus, for the example taken here, weights will be computed for vertex P for the feature points FP_1 as well as FP_2 and FP_3, provided d_{2P} and d_{3P} are less than d. As a result, we have for each vertex of the mesh, a list of control points influencing it and an associated weight.

We tested the algorithm on simple meshes with different values of limits in equation (6.1), and different weighting functions in equations (6.2) and (6.3). The ones giving the most satisfactory results were chosen. In equation (6.3), we chose *sine* function, as it is continuous at the minimum and maximum limits.

Deformation. Once the weights for the vertices have been computed, the mesh is ready for real-time animation. Note that *initialization* step is computationally intensive, but carried out only once. The computed weights take into consideration the distance of a vertex from the feature point and relative spread of the feature points around the vertex. Now, from the displacements of the feature points for animation, we calculate the actual displacement of all the vertices of the mesh. Here, we have to consider the effects caused when two or more feature points move at the same time, influencing the same vertex. We calculate the weighted sum of all the displacements caused at the point P due to all the neighboring feature points. Let $FP_i, i = 1, 2, \ldots, N$ be the control points influencing vertex P of the mesh. Then with:

D_i = the displacement specified for the control point FP_i
$W_{i,P}$ = the weight as calculated in the *Initialization* for vertex P associated with the control points
$d_{i,P}$ = the corresponding distance between P and FP_i.

Equation (6.5) gives the resultant displacement D_P caused at the vertex P:

$$D_P = \frac{\displaystyle\sum_{i=0}^{N} \frac{W_{i,P}D_i}{d_{i,p}^2}}{\displaystyle\sum_{i=0}^{N} \frac{W_{i,p}}{d_{i,p}^2}} \tag{6.5}$$

This operation is performed for every frame during the computation of the animation of the mesh.

FDP-based deformation.   The deformation model as described in the previous section is a generic model. Here, we show how the generic model is applied to an MPEG-4 compliant facial model. Given a facial mesh, we can define the locations of the MPEG-4 feature points as per the specification, as shown in Figure 16.5 in Chapter 16. In addition, for each feature point, we add the constraints as required by the deformation model. This facial mesh is now ready to be animated using any FAP. Figure 6.6 shows some results of facial animation produced using the deformation model.

The deformation model is well suited for real-time facial animation. The most important advantage of this method is that it calculates the mesh regions of influence automatically, given the distribution of feature points. Thus, it becomes very easy and fast to animate a variety of faces. The method works best on medium to high-resolution meshes. If the facial mesh is designed with care to support different resolution in different areas (less number polygons on the forehead, but more in the lip region), the results of the animation are much more realistic.

6.4.6.2   FAT-based deformation

The Face Animation Tables (FATs) define how a model is spatially deformed as a function of the amplitude of the FAPs. Each facial model is represented by a set of vertices, and associated information about the triangles joining them is often called as *IndexedFaceSet* in a geometric representation. We consider two different cases: if a FAP causes a transformation such as rotation, translation or scale, a transform node can describe this animation, and if a FAP, such as *open jaw*, causes flexible deformation of the facial mesh, the FAT defines the displacements of the *IndexedFaceSet* vertices. These displacements are based on piece-wise linear motion trajectories (see Chapter 16).

We have developed two different methods for the FATs construction (Garchery and Magnenat-Thalmann 2001). The first method is automatic and is based on the FDP-based deformation model for an MPEG-4 compliant facial model. The process starts with a facial model with corresponding FDP data. Then, for each FAP, the procedure consists of applying various intensities of FAPs to the facial mesh, and then taking the difference of the position of each vertex with its neutral position (see Figure 6.7). Thus the tables of deformations are built for each FAP and for each vertex. If one needs more precision for a certain FAP, it is possible to use different intensities and different intervals (using a 'true piece-wise linear function') to generate FAT. However, with various interval borders and intensities, the size of the animation data increases, but so does the computation overhead.

Figure 6.6 Facial deformation based on FAPs

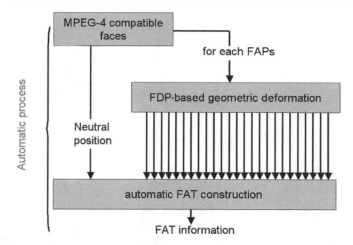

Figure 6.7   Automatic process for designing FAT with an MPEG-4 face model

In the second method, we provide tools to generate the 'artistic FAT' in order to have the freedom of using any model (not necessarily a human face), as well as to have a variety in deformation used for animation. When an animator develops a model that will be animated by set of FAPs, the definition of the neutral position is important, as it is used for animation later. A definition of the neutral state is given in Chapter 16.

Often construction of only one linear interval by each FAP is enough, however, the animator can use multiple intervals if required to obtain a more precise and realistic animation.

Once the whole set of the FATs has been designed, we compile the set of the deformations into the FAT information. The program developed for this parses all the files and compiles the information then to be used by the FAT-based animation (see Figure 6.8). We currently use the VRML files format but it is very easy to integrate another file format supporting *IndexedFaceSet* or a similar structure.

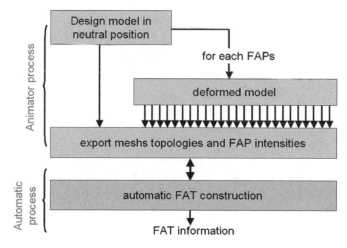

Figure 6.8   Process for designing FAT construction by experienced animator's work

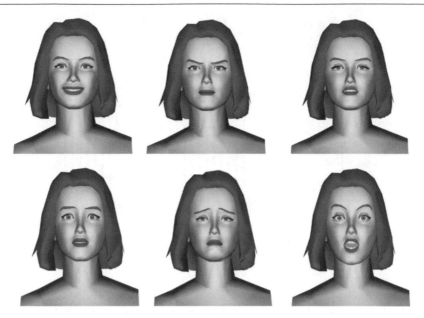

Figure 6.9 Artistic MPEG-4 FAP high-level expressions

The advantage of this method is that it enables exact control of facial deformation in terms of the FAP intensity. We have extended this control to the high level FAP, where visemes and expressions can be used. This allows us to construct animation with high level specifications (see Figure 6.9), this may however, constrain the flexibility from the designer's perspective. Furthermore, this may not be suitable when animation requires mixing of visemes and expressions.

This method of artistic FAT construction takes longer than the automatic one but the deformations can be controlled better, especially for the high level FAPs. We can also combine the two methods.

6.5   Tongue, Wrinkles and Other Features

In most facial animation, the tongue and its movement are omitted or oversimplified. When modeled, it is often represented as a simple geometric primitive like an ellipsoid or a parallelepiped. Although only a small portion of the tongue is visible during normal speech, the tongue shape is important for realistic synthesized mouth animation. Stone (1991) proposes a 3-D model of the tongue defined as five segments in the coronal plane and five segments in the sagittal plane. This model may deform into twisted, asymmetric, and groove shapes. This relatively accurate tongue model is simplified by Pelachaud et al. (1994) for speech animation. They model the tongue as a blobby object (Wyvill et al. 1986). This approach assumes a pseudo-skeleton comprised of geometric primitives (9 triangles) that serve as a charge distribution mechanism, creating a spatial potential field. Modifying the skeleton modifies the equi-potential surface that represents the tongue shape. The palate is modeled as a semi-sphere and the upper teeth are simulated by a planar strip. Collision detection is also proposed using implicit functions. The shape of the tongue changes to maintain volume preservation. Equi-potential surfaces are expensive to render directly, but an automatic method adaptively computes a triangular mesh during animation. Tongue animation was performed along with lip animation based on FACS taking co-articulation into account. Some simpler geometric models based on NURBS have also been used for modeling the tongue (King and Parent 2002).

Most of the deformation models discussed so far may not be appropriate for features like wrinkles, folds and bulges. These features require special attention. Some models, being physically based, are able to produce wider folds and contour lines as a consequence of the deformation process, however, there is no explicit control on their formation. There are two kinds of wrinkles: temporary wrinkles that appear during a facial expression and permanent wrinkles due to ageing. A hybrid model using spline has been proposed to model wrinkles (Viaud and Yahia 1992). Wu et al. (1999) have proposed a more detailed model. A three-layer structure (skin, connective tissues, and muscle) is employed in skin deformation process. Skin is represented as triangular mesh, whereas muscles are generally designed as B-spline patches. Muscle contraction causes the skin surface to deform following a biomechanical model. Patterns of skin surface and potential wrinkles are synthesized in a texture image. The dynamics of a 3-D model is transferred as strain measures to modify the texture image. Some rendering issues for skin incorporating details like wrinkles are described in Chapter 15 on rendering models.

6.6 Summary

The various deformation models have been relatively compared with respect to the different features and properties as shown in Table 6.1. Qualitative measures such as low, medium, high, easy, hard are used for the relative characterization/placement. In the first column, computational effort is considered, the ones marked 'low' were intended for rapid generation of deformation as opposed to the ones marked 'high' which may require computation in the order of minutes per frame. Model complexity shows in some sense the mathematical complexity of the model. For example, a model using the finite element method requires a complex mathematical model. Geometry dependency of the face conveys how the model is sensitive to the changes in the geometry for example transformations like scaling. A model, which provides unpredictable results when a transformation is applied to the geometry means it has 'high' dependency. Physical realism pertains to the physical functional relevance and analogy considered for the model design. Visual realism refers to a subjective grading of the visual results as reported in the literature. The user-control relates to the degree of ease for achieving what is conceived.

6.7 Conclusion

This chapter has included most of the major techniques and approaches for the basic facial deformation models proposed over the years in facial animation. Basically they address the questions of what portion or region of a face is to be moved and how. The various methods developed simulate movement in different ways. Broadly, they can be categorized as geometric methods and physical methods. Some approaches using either geometric or

Table 6.1 Facial deformation models: a comparative analysis

1.1.1. Model	1.1.2.	Model complexity	Geometry dependency	Physical realism	Visual realism	User control	Control parameterization
Interpolation	Low	Low	High	Low	Medium to High	Easy	Interpolation
Parametric	Low	Low	High	Low	Medium	Easy	Interpolation
Muscle (Physical Based)							
a) Spring	Medium	Medium	Low to Medium	Medium	Low to Medium	Medium	FACS
b) Vector	Medium	Medium	Low to Medium	Medium	Medium to High	Medium	FACS
c) Layered Pseudo-Muscle	High	High	Low to Medium	High	Medium to High	Hard	FACS
a) Procedures	Low	Low	High	Medium	Medium	Easy	–
b) Spline	Low to Medium	Low	Low	Medium	Medium	Easy	FACS
c) Free form deformation	Low to Medium	Low	Low	Medium	Medium	Easy	MPA
FEM	High	High	Medium	High	Medium to High	Hard	FACS
Others							
a) Spatial mapping	Medium	Low	Low to Medium	Low	Medium	Easy	–
b) Transformation method	Low	Low	Low to Medium	Low	Medium	Medium	FACS
c) Feature point based	Low	Low	Low	Low	Medium	Easy	FAPs

physical methods models dynamics of the face based on the underlying muscles, which are instigators of facial movement. A detailed classification is done on the basis of the mechanism used for deforming the facial geometry. A relative comparison of the various models is also done on the basis of different properties – speed of computation, realism, ease of control, etc.

7

Body Deformations

Amaury Aubel

The modeling of the human being is one of the most arduous tasks in computer graphics. Because of the complexity of the human body, no current biomechanical or computer graphics model comes close to its true nature. Additionally, we are subconsciously attuned to the details of humans because of our extreme familiarity with human shapes. Hence, when we see a Virtual Human on screen, we know immediately if something is wrong, if one detail is missing, etc. In this survey, we review the various approaches to body (or skin) deformation of virtual characters. We begin with surface deformation models that consist of only two layers. Then we describe volumetric models that add the notion of inside/outside and are thus particularly well suited to collision detection and processing. Finally, we focus on multi-layered deformation models, in which the main anatomical layers of the body are explicitly represented and deformed.

7.1 Surface Models

Surface models rely on just two layers:

- An *articulated structure* or *skeleton*, which forms the backbone of the character animation system. This structure is arranged as a hierarchy and is covered by skin.
- An external geometric envelope or *skin*, whose deformations are driven by the underlying articulated structure.

7.1.1 Rigid Deformations

The simplest skin model consists of a collection of independent polygonal meshes placed on top of the skeleton, with generally one mesh by body part. By rigidly anchoring each mesh to a specific joint, one obtains a skin that roughly follows the motion of the underlying articulated structure. However, body parts interpenetrate in the vicinity of joints or appear unconnected during movement. Furthermore, muscle bulging is not rendered using this approach.

Handbook of Virtual Humans Edited by N. Magnenat-Thalmann and D. Thalmann
© 2004 John Wiley & Sons, Ltd   ISBN: 0-470-02316-3

7.1.2 Local Surface Operators

Some of the above problems can be solved by a continuous deformation function with respect to the joint values. Komatsu (1988) applied such a function to deform the control points of biquartic Bézier and Gregory patches. A distinction between bending and twisting motions is made and local deformations rules are applied to the control points accordingly. The outcome is a smooth shape (thanks to the Bézier patches) that bends and rounds near joints upon flexion, with some crude approximation of muscle swelling.

At roughly the same time, Magnenat-Thalmann and Thalmann (1987) introduced the concept of *Joint-dependent Local Deformation* (JLD). Similar to Komatsu's approach, JLDs deform the skin algorithmically. In a first pass, the skin vertices are mapped to skeleton segments, thus restricting the influence of a joint to the two segments it connects. Afterwards, the vertices are deformed (using their parameterization in terms of segments) by a function of the joint angles. The numerous function parameters serve to adjust the amount and the extent of rounding near the joints as well as muscle inflation. The approach is demonstrated effectively on the body and the hand (Magnenat-Thalmann 1988) (see Figure 7.1). For the latter, an exponential function is applied on inner finger vertices to mimic muscle inflation.

Komatsu and Magnenat-Thalmann and Thalmann showed that fairly realistic skin deformations could be derived from the application of specialized algorithms. However, their approach suffers from three problems. First, each joint type needs to be handled by a specific function. Second, the mathematical functions are perhaps too limited to depict the complexity and individual variability of real anatomy. Last but not least, the graphics designer cannot easily control the deformations since they are determined algorithmically. This last limitation is somewhat alleviated in the work of Forsey (1991), in which the skin is approximated by hierarchical B-spline patches, whose control points move as a function of joint angles.

7.1.3 Skinning

Skinning is another type of surface deformer that works locally. It differs from earlier local surface operators in that the algorithm is generic enough to be applied to all kinds of joints and in that full control of the deformations is handed over to the graphics artist. Skinning

Figure 7.1 Marilyn's skin is deformed by JLDs. (Magnenat-Thalmann et al. 1988.)

is basically an interpolation algorithm. A multitude of different names have been coined for it (even though they all refer to the same technique): skinning (Lander 1998), skeleton-subspace deformation (Lewis et al. 2000), smooth binding (Maya 2001), transform blending (Sloan et al. 2001), matrix blending, etc. The basic idea can be summarized as follows. Every skin vertex P is expressed as a linear combination of offset points P_i, each of which is rigidly transformed by an associated skeletal coordinate frame, as shown in Equation (7.1).

$$P = \sum_{i=1}^{n} w_i M_i P_i \qquad \sum_{i=1}^{n} w_i = 1 \tag{7.1}$$

More precisely, the 3-D world coordinates P of the vertex are transformed into the coordinate systems M_i of n relevant joints in an initial skeletal posture. The weights, which add up to 1, are assigned to the various joints that influence the vertex. When the skeleton is moved, the new position of the skin vertex is found by the same equation.

As demonstrated by video games, skinning is a very simple technique that works rather well. Its initially low computational cost is further reduced by hardware support of matrix blending on recent graphics cards. Skinning is also fairly versatile. Dynamics can be faked by moving the joints dynamically, which in turn leads to a dynamic motion of the bound vertices. To do so, new imaginary joints are usually introduced in the articulated structure. More generally, new joints can be inserted into the articulated structure in order to simulate secondary deformation such as breathing or muscle action (Maya 2001).

Recent work focuses on increasing the speed of the skinning procedure. Sun et al. (1999) restrict the number of computations by mapping a high-resolution mesh onto a lower-resolution control mesh using the concept of normal-volume. Singh and Kokkevis (2000) introduced surface-based FFDs to deform skins. These surface-oriented control structures bear a strong resemblance to the geometry they deform and can be constructed from the deformable geometry automatically. As in (Sun et al. 1999), the advantage of the approach is that one can skin the low-resolution surface control structure and use it to deform the high-resolution object. Houle and Poulin (2001) produce skinned meshes with continuous level of detail. When simplifying the mesh, the global displacement of a skin vertex after an edge collapse is simply injected back into Equation (7.1).

The skinning technique has, however, severe limitations. First of all, assigning weights is at best semi-automatic. A good deal of manual work is ordinarily required to attain acceptable deformations. Indeed, the graphics artist often spends hours to manually adjust the weights, vertex by vertex. Moreover, in areas with considerable mobility like the shoulder, *some* combination of weights may produce good results in certain skeleton postures and yield unacceptable ones in others, leading to considerable frustration by designers. As identified by Lewis et al. (2000), the problem basically is that the desired deformation may not necessarily lie in the subspace defined by the skeletal frames. Consequently, one may very well tweak the skinning weights endlessly, since the 'right' combination does not always exist. Two visual defects, depicted in Figure 7.2, can be recognized as typical products of deformations actually lying outside the skeletal subspace. Nevertheless, due to the simplicity of the method, skinning remains the most widespread technique for skin deformation.

7.1.4 Contour Deformation

The human trunk and limbs exhibit a roughly cylindrical shape. This property can readily be exploited by considering the different body parts as generalized cylinders and manipulating

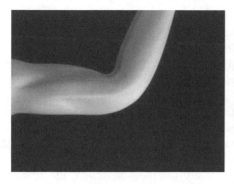
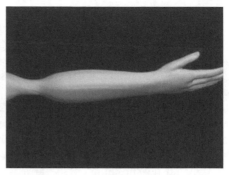

Figure 7.2 Characteristic defects of the skinning algorithm (reproduced from (Lewis et al. 2000)). Left: The elbow collapses upon flexion. Right: The elbow also collapses when the forearm is twisted. (Reproduced with permission of John Lewis and Nickson Fong.)

the cross-sections to approximate skin deformations. Thus Thalmann et al. (1996) group the skin vertices in contours. By setting the orientation and position of each contour, they obtain a smooth deformation of human limbs and trunk. As deformations are not computed on an individual vertex basis but for grouping contours, real-time results are easily achieved (Kalra et al. 1988).

The algorithm for setting the position and orientation of a cross-section is surprisingly simple. If we consider the deformation of the arm, as illustrated in Figure 7.3, we have three joints and two segments whose directions are l_1 and l_2. Let N_u, N_0 and N_1 be the normal vectors of the cross-section planes at the ends of the segments. Typically, the end normals are set to the directions of the segments while the middle normal is assigned the normal of the bisecting plane (Equation 7.2):

$$N_o = \frac{N_u + N_l}{2} \tag{7.2}$$

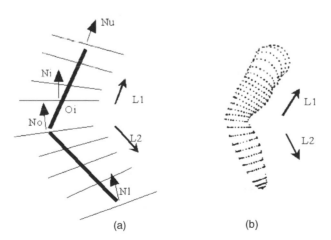

(a)   (b)

Figure 7.3 Arm deformation with cross-sections

Then, simple linear interpolation of the two closest end normals gives the normal for the i-th intermediate cross-section. A similar operation is performed for tangent vectors so that a local frame is eventually constructed for each cross-section. The origin of the frame can be conveniently placed on the skeleton segment. Equipped with these local frames, it becomes straightforward to compute local coordinates for every vertex of the i-th contour and use these for subsequent deformations.

This technique produces very smooth deformations at a low computational cost because deformations are not computed one skin vertex at a time but for an entire contour. Besides, as vertices are transformed into local coordinate systems, one of the characteristic defects of the skinning algorithm disappears: when the arm is twisted, the cross-sections rotate accordingly, so no shrinking of the arm is produced. On the other hand, the elbow still collapses upon flexion (see Figure 7.3(b)), yet the effect can easily be reduced by adequately scaling the local coordinates within a cross-section. This scheme can also be used for coarsely simulating muscle inflation. On the downside, a contour is solely influenced by the two closest joints, which may lead to poor results in some regions like the shoulder. Furthermore, a specific organization of the mesh is required, which may create additional stitching problems between the limbs and the trunk.

7.1.5 Deformations by Example

Recently, there has been a growing interest in producing skin deformation by blending pre-defined examples or *key-shapes* (Lewis et al. 2000; Sloan et al. 2001; Allen et al. 2002). These key-shapes are simply triangle meshes in various skeletal poses. They are acquired by digitizing devices such as laser scanners or sculpted by hand in traditional modeling software. The basic idea for deformation is that the key-shapes form an abstract space, from which new shapes can be created by interpolation or extrapolation. Unlike 3-D morphing algorithms, which essentially try to solve a correspondence problem, the deformation-by-examples approach is confined to the problem of smooth interpolation and possibly of coherent extrapolation. A unique topology (i.e., the same number of vertices and the same connectivity) shared by all key-shapes is, therefore, a prerequisite.

As key-shapes are arbitrarily and, thus, irregularly placed in the skeletal parameter space (i.e., the joint angles), shape deformation can be thought of as a scattered data interpolation problem. Radial basis functions (RBFs) are typically used for scattered data interpolation, since these are controllable, smooth, and have a large literature of techniques and extensions. Lewis et al. (2000) settle on a Gaussian RBF while Sloan et al. (2001) select a RBF with a cross-section of a cubic B-spline. The notable exception is the work of Allen et al. (2002), in which a k-closest neighbor interpolation is used instead.

These shape blending techniques are quite powerful (see Figure 7.5) and elegantly solve the typical problems associated with skinning algorithms (see Figure 7.4). They also perform fast by comparison with multi-layered deformation models and can even achieve real-time results on modest PCs by taking advantage of matrix blending hardware acceleration (Sloan et al. 2001). The greatest strength of the method is that the deformation process can be accurately controlled by adding as many key-shapes and as many details as desired. So, unlike skinning, muscle inflation is faithfully reproduced from the pre-defined examples and can even be exaggerated by extrapolation in the abstract space. But this strength is also the weakness of the method since the number of reference shapes needed grows exponentially

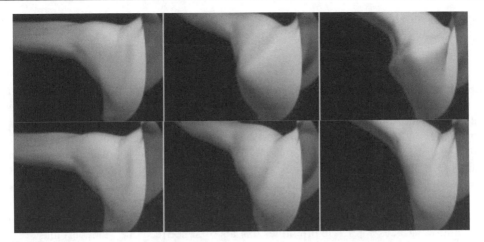

Figure 7.4 Comparison on shoulder deformation between the skinning algorithm (top row) and the Pose Space Deformation algorithm (Wyvill et al. 1998). (bottom row) using two extreme key-shapes. (Reproduced with permission of John Lewis.)

Figure 7.5 Shape blending of various laser scans of a real person using a template subdivision surface. (Reproduced from (Allen et al. 2002.)) (c) 2002 Association for Computing Machinery, Inc.

with the number of parameters (e.g. degrees of freedom in the articulated structure). This imposes a high workload on the graphics artist when key-shapes are created by hand as in (Lewis et al. 2000; Sloan et al. 2001).

This problem is partly solved by the recent work by Allen et al. (2002): they use a cyberware scanner to acquire the data in a large number of sampled poses. Evidently, replacing the hand-designed poses by laser scans introduces new technical problems since the 3-D rangefinder produces meshes that can have any topology. Their solution consists in converting the range data to a single consistent parameterization using a template subdivision surface and a displacement-map model. Thus, in the same way skeletal motion is now traditionally captured by optical or magnetic devices, body deformations are captured and played back for any skeletal pose by interpolation.

7.2 Volumetric Models

The first volumetric models relied on elementary geometric primitives such as ellipsoids and spheres to approximate the shape of the body. They were developed in the early age of computer graphics when systems still had very limited capabilities. Implicit surfaces present an interesting generalization of these early models. It must be noted that volumetric models share some similarities with multi-layered models (see Section 7.4). Unlike multi-layered models, however, they allow gracefully handling of collisions between body parts.

7.2.1 Implicit Surfaces

Implicit surfaces are frequently used to represent organic forms because of their natural smoothness. Early on, Blinn (1982) created a 'blobby man' from an implicit surface generated by point sources with an exponentially decreasing field function. A decade later, Yoshimito (1992) showed that a complete realistic-looking Virtual Human could be created with metaballs at a reduced storage cost. He demonstrated the approach with a ballerina made up of 500 ellipsoidal metaballs and a few ellipsoids on a low-end PC. The author reckons that about 100,000 polygons would have to be used to obtain a comparable visual quality. More complicated implicit formulations have been used as well. Bloomenthal simulates a human arm (Bloomenthal and Shoemake 1991) and hand (Bloomenthal 1993) with convolution surfaces applied to primitives that approximate the bones, tendons, muscles, and veins (see Figure 7.6).

Implicit surfaces possess many properties that make them suitable for body modeling. Their main distinctive quality is that they smoothly blend into one another because the field functions have C1 or higher continuity, thus yielding very aesthetic shapes. An exception is found in (Thalmann et al. 1996) where there is only geometric continuity so as to increase speed. Another advantage is that implicit surfaces defined by point or polygon skeletons are simple to edit. Finally, they offer a very compact formulation, which requires little memory and storage capacity. On the other hand, many issues arise when the model is animated. First of all, unwanted blending typically occurs as the character's skeleton moves. In Figure 7.6 for instance, the fingers are likely to blend. Thalmann et al. (1996) prevent this by dividing

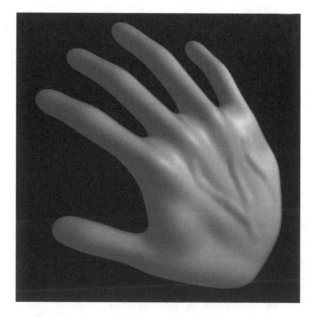

Figure 7.6 Hand modeled with convolution surfaces. (Reproduced with permission of Jules Bloomenthal)

the body into coherent parts (right upper leg, left upper leg, etc.) and labeling skeleton points with specific body parts, thus strictly restricting the influence of a metaball to a localized region. More generally, unwanted blending is avoided through the use of *blending graphs*, which specify how the contributions from different skeletal primitives are to be summed (Cani-Gascuel and Desbrun 1997; Wyvill et al. 1998). Polygonizing the implicit surface is another issue that is further complicated by the animation. Since the polygonization of the implicit surface is required for the application of texture maps among other things, a fixed topology of the polygonization is desirable during the animation. Hybrid techniques mixing surface deformation models and implicit surfaces are generally brought in to resolve this problem. In (Thalmann et al. 1996), B-spline patches are fitted to the iso-surface using contour deformation and a ray-casting procedure, while in (Leclercq et al. 2001) a skinning algorithm is applied to a polygonal mesh followed by a normal-directed projection of the skin vertices onto the implicit surface.

7.2.2 Collision Models

Some volumetric models allow gracefully handling of collisions between different models (or different parts of a same model) and accordingly generate deformed surfaces in contact. Gascuel (1993) integrates elastic properties directly into the formulation of distance-based implicit surfaces and thus establishes a correspondence between the radial deformation and the reaction force. In this way, a stable, precise, C1 contact surface is elegantly defined between colliding models and the resulting reaction forces can be integrated in a physically-based simulation at the next animation step. Various extensions, which preserve the C1 continuity of the surface, allow the spread of the deformation in the region surrounding the contact surface (Gascuel 1993), to locally control the volume variation (Gascuel et al. 1991), and to introduce anisotropy in the deformation (Cani-Gascuel 1998).

Recently, Hirota et al. (2001) proposed a non-linear finite element model of a human leg derived from the Visible Human Database (National Library of Medicine 1995). The demonstration of their system highlights the contact area between the calf and the posterior side of the thigh when the knee is flexed and achieves a high level of realism in the deformation (see Figure 7.7). In order to estimate the amount of penetration at every skin

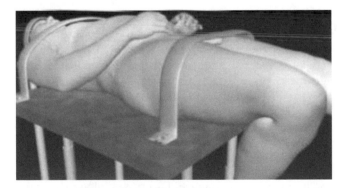

Figure 7.7 Leg deformation including contact surface using FEM. (Reproduced with permission of Department of Computer Science, University of North Carolina, Chapel Hill.)

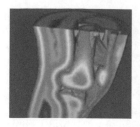
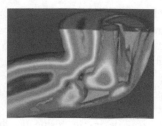
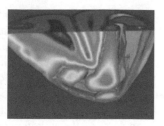

Figure 7.8 The material depth (encoded in psuedo-color) is used for computing the contact surface when the knee is bent (Reproduced with permission of Department of Computer Science, University of North Carolina, Chapel Hill.)

vertex, the authors introduce the notion of *material depth* (see Figure 7.8), which is a continuous approximation of the distance fields in a deformed configuration.

Frisken et al. (2000) propose using adaptively sampled distance fields (ADF) representations for handling soft body collisions (Frisken and Perry 2001). Analogous to implicit surfaces, inside/outside and proximity tests can be performed rapidly using ADFs because the notion of interior and exterior is inherent to the formulation. Furthermore, potential contact regions can be quickly localized by exploiting the spatial hierarchy of the data. Moreover, the region of overlap can be accurately represented by simply subtracting the ADFs of different objects (Frisken et al. 2000). Finally, as for (Hirota et al. 2001), a continuous penalty force can be defined over the whole volume overlap.

7.3 Multi-Layered Models

Chadwick et al. (1989) first coated their character with an additional muscle layer. Since then, most researchers have used a layered approach to character modeling, with more or less attention to the anatomical accuracy. Earlier models rely on a combination of ordinary computer graphics techniques like skinning and implicit surfaces, and tend to collapse several anatomical layers into one. Recent works are more inspired by the actual biology of the human body and attempt to represent and deform every major anatomical layer, and to model their dynamic interplay.

7.3.1 Skeleton Layer

The skeleton is defined by an articulated structure, which consists of a hierarchy of segments or, in a few instances, of parallelepipeds (Gascuel et al. 1991). The articulated structure is sometimes covered by material bones, which are approximated by simple geometric primitives or triangle meshes (see Hirota et al. 2001; Porcher-Nedel 1998; Scheeppers et al. 1997; Wilhelms 1997; Wilhelms and Van Gelder 1997) among others.

7.3.2 Muscle Layer

Geometric models: in the Critter system devised by Chadwick et al. (1989), the foundations for the muscles and fat deformations are based on Free Form Deformations (FFD). In practice, a muscle is encased in a pair of adjoining FFDs oriented along the skeleton link. In total, seven planes of control points slice the muscle. The two control planes at either end function to ensure C1 continuity with other connected muscles. The deformation of the central cubical volume via the three remaining control planes produces muscular deformation. Kinematic deformations are controlled by establishing a relationship between the control points of the mid-planes and the joint angles in the skeleton while dynamic deformations result from the elastic deformation of an embedded mass-spring network built from the FFD control points. Similarly, Moccozet (1996) models the behavior of the hand muscles using Dirichlet Free Form Deformation (DFFD) (DFFD is an interesting generalization of FFD that removes the severe limitation imposed on the shape of the control box and provides a more local control of the deformation). The resulting geometric deformations look convincing despite the complicated branching structure of the hand (see Figure 7.9).

Implicit surfaces have been recognized as highly suitable for modeling organic forms. Hence, they have been extensively used to model the muscle layer too. Turner and Thalmann (1993) approximate muscles by implicit primitives like spheres and super quadrics. Thalmann et al. (1996) use grouped ellipsoidal metaballs with a simplified quadratic field function to mimic the gross behavior of bones, muscles, and fat. The contraction and release behavior of muscles is simulated by binding the nine degrees of freedom of an ellipsoid (i.e., rotation, translation, and scaling) to the degrees of freedom of the skeleton. For example, the bulging and the flattening of the leg muscles can be engendered by ellipsoidal metaballs whose scaling parameters are tied to the knee flexion (see Figure 7.10). The technique reaches its

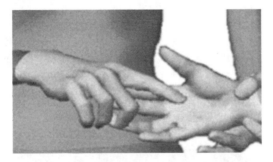

Figure 7.9   Hand deformation based on Dirichlet FFDs. (Moccozet 1996.)

Figure 7.10   Leg muscles mimicked by deforming metaballs

limits in regions of high mobility (the shoulder, typically), in which each ellipsoidal primitive is simultaneously influenced by several joints. In that case, the (linear) interpolation of the contributions of the various joints as in (Thalmann et al. 1996) may lead to unsatisfactory deformations. More recently, Leclercq et al. (2001) also modeled muscles with ellipsoidal metaballs. They do not say, however, whether muscle inflation is faked.

The first attempts at building anatomically accurate replicas of the musculature of humans (Scheeppers et al. 1997) or animals (Wilhelms 1997) made use of the ellipsoid as the basic building block. It is a natural choice because an ellipsoid approximates fairly well the appearance of a fusiform muscle. Besides, an ellipsoid has an analytic formulation that lends itself well to inside/outside tests. When the primitive is scaled along one of its axes, the volume of the primitive can moreover be preserved by adequately adjusting the lengths of the two remaining axes. The ratio of the height to width can be kept constant in the same manner. This is why two independent research teams (Scheeppers et al. 1997; Wilhelms 1997) use a volume-preserving ellipsoid to represent a fusiform muscle. Scheeppers et al. (1997), for instance, detail every superficial muscle of the upper body and explicitly introduce tendons that connect the muscle bellies to the bones (see Figure 7.11). For multi-belly muscles such as the pectorals in the chest, they position a set of ellipsoids along two spline curves.

A distinctive feature of the system by Scheeppers et al. (1997) is that, besides isotonic contractions, isometric contractions of the muscles can also occur. A tension parameter, which controls the ratio of a muscle's height to its width, is bound to articulation variables and thus allows alteration of the form of a muscle that does not undergo any change in length. This effect is noticeable in the biceps as the hand is clenched into a fist (see Figure 7.12).

Both research teams nevertheless admit that the ellipsoid, albeit a good approximation in simple cases, fails to capture the shape of more complicated muscles. Hence, Scheeppers et al. (1997) also provide a general model that consists in tubular-shaped bicubic patches

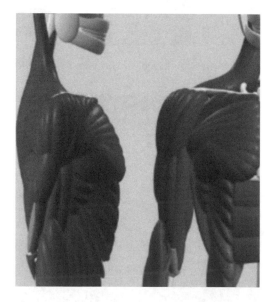

Figure 7.11 Anatomically-based modeling of the human musculature using ellipsoids. (Scheeppers et al. 1997) (Reproduced with permission of Richard Parent.)

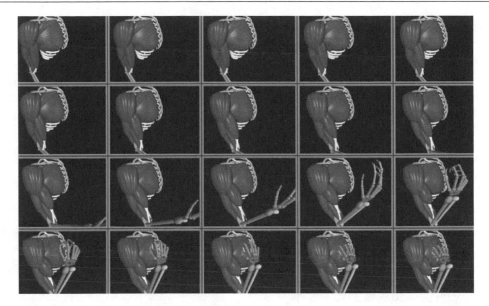

Figure 7.12 Isotonic contraction of the arm muscles followed by an isometric contraction when the hand is clenched into a fist. (Reproduced with permission of Richard Parent.)

capped with elliptic hemispheres at either end and use it for modeling muscles that bend such as the *brachialis* in the arm. Exact volume preservation remains possible because the general muscle model still has an analytic description. Likewise, Wilhelms and Van Gelder (1997) resort to generalized cylinder versions of the muscles in their latest work on animal modeling. A muscle is made up of seven elliptic cross-sections that consist in turn of a certain number of points that can be edited to adjust the overall shape. Initially, the axis of the cylinder runs in a straight line from the origin on the proximal bone to the insertion on the distal bone. Two pivot points can, however, be inserted to bend the axis (see Figure 7.13) and reduce the penetration of other anatomical structures. During animation, whenever a joint lying between muscle origins and insertions moves, a new deformed cylinder shape is computed. Based on the change in length of the cylinder's axis, the width and thickness of every cross-section are scaled to maintain approximately constant volume.

It must be noted that the generalized cylinder muscle model had already been proposed previously by Dow and Semwal (1993). In their work, cross-sections are represented by B-spline curves, whose control points move radially according to the tension of the muscle. Inter-muscle collisions are detected based on polygonal versions derived from the cross-sectional splines, and control points are accordingly pushed towards the cylinder axis.

The work of Dong et al. (2002) goes one step further than previously cited works towards the anatomical accuracy of the muscle layer (see Figure 7.14). Geometric muscle models are (semi-)automatically obtained from segmented anatomical slices derived from the Visible Human (National Library of Medicine 1995). From key contours detected in the slices, profile curves along the muscle's main axis are constructed and ultimately converted to meshes. Upon skeletal motion, the muscle profile curves are deformed in response to the movement of the muscle action lines (an action line is an imaginary line or curve along which the force produced by the muscle is exerted onto the bone, see references in biomechanics such as

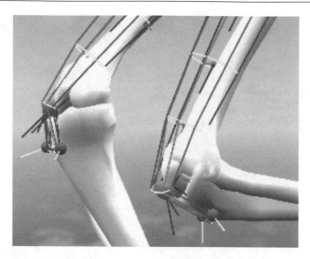

Figure 7.13 A deformed-cylinder muscle model. Pivot points ensure a smooth bending of the muscle around joints ellipsoids. (Reproduced from (Wilhelms and Van Gelder 1997).) (Reproduced with permission of J.Wilhelms)

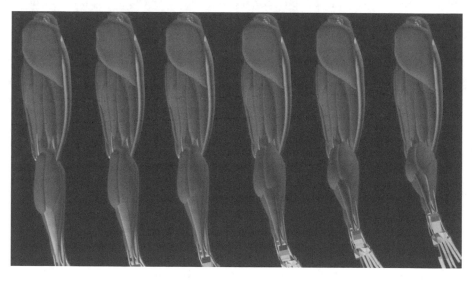

Figure 7.14 Leg muscles – reconstructed from anatomical data – are deformed by action lines and muscle interaction. (Reproduced with permission of G. Clapworthy.)

(Delp, Loan 2000) for more details). A generic and specific deformation model is created so as to fit the wide variety of muscle shapes. Similarly to (Wilhelms and Van Gelder 1997), cross-sections are scaled to maintain approximately constant volume. Unlike most other works, however, muscle interaction is also taken into account. Collisions between adjacent muscles are first detected for each animation frame. Penetrating vertices are then moved repeatedly along their normals until the collision is completely resolved. Non-penetrating vertices are also moved to support volume conservation.

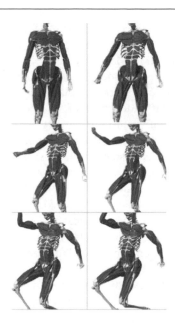

Figure 7.15 Each muscle is parameterized and deformed by a set of centroid curves (action lines). Each action line moves under the influence of the skeleton joints and deflective ellipsoidal surfaces

Finally, Aubel (2002) recently proposed a generic two-layered muscle model that can capture all muscle shapes and produces visually convincing and anatomically accurate deformations (see Figure 7.15) at interactive rates. A skeleton, defined by a set of (cubic) centroid curves (action lines), parameterizes the (vertex-based) outer shape of the muscle and thus governs its deformation. Action lines deform as a function of the underlying skeletal state, while ensuring that tendons maintain a constant length upon motion. Deflective ellipsoidal surfaces eventually refine the path taken by the action lines.

Regarding physically-based models, Gourret et al. (1989) first generated tissue deformation by applying the engineering Finite Element Modeling (FEM) technique. A human hand grasping an elastic ball is shown as an example. A linear constitutive law for the flesh tissue is used in the context of small stresses and quasi-static analysis produces for each frame a large linear system, which relates the displacement of the nodes to the forces via the stiffness matrix (see Equation (7.3) in matrix form):

$$Ku = f \tag{7.3}$$

Where K is the stiffness matrix and u the displacement vector.

Boundary conditions can be imposed by assigning fixed values to some components of u. Theoretically, this equation is valid provided that the displacement field and the displacement gradient are small. Obviously, neither condition is met when soft tissues deform. This two-fold hypothesis is, however, often assumed in computer graphics so as to avoid the non-linearities produced by finite (i.e., large) deformations. Similarly, biological material is in reality non-linear but a linear stress-strain relationship is frequently chosen for simplicity's sake.

Zhu et al. (1998) deform the *anconeus* muscle using FEM and volume graphics. They use eight-node 3-D brick elements to represent a muscle as a collection of voxel elements. Chen and Zeltzer (1992) also rely on the FEM technique to obtain muscle deformation. They use twenty-node 3-D bricks and a muscle model that is based on the work of Zajac (1989) in biomechanics. In both cases, muscles work in isolation and are not covered by a skin.

More recently, Hirota et al. (2001) deal with the geometric non-linearity induced by large deformations and model more realistic non-linear soft tissues. Their non-linear FEM solver makes use of tetrahedral elements. For each integration step, the equation of motion is linearized by taking Newton-Raphson steps. In their system, they not only deform the leg muscle layer but also the other anatomical structures with a finite element mesh made up of 40,000 tetrahedrals and 10,000 nodes that comprise the major bones of the leg, some muscles, tendons, and ligaments, and a monolithic skin-fat layer (see Figure 7.16).

Gascuel el al. (1991) rely on the simpler mass-spring model to deform the muscles and flesh of the character. They associate deformable components to each skeleton link. Cones of flesh are arranged in a star-shaped way around the center of mass of the link and radially deformed by damped springs. The deformations are propagated from one flesh cone to the others by a second module so as to meet dynamic or geometric criteria (e.g. constant volume). The deformable components are well suited for detecting collisions and responding to them.

Nedel and Thalmann (1998) abstract a muscle by an action line (a polyline in practice) and a surface mesh deformed by an equivalent mass-spring network. An elastic relaxation of the surface mesh is performed for each animation frame, thus yielding a collection of static postures. The authors acknowledge that their model can work only on fusiform muscles. Furthermore, they do not state how they constrain the surface mesh to follow the action line when it consists of more than one segment.

Ng-Thow-Hing (2000) uses B-spline volumes for modeling muscles. He points out that the B-spline solid can capture the multiple muscle shapes (fusiform, triangular, bipennate, etc.) and can also render various sizes of attachments including the aponeurosis, which is a wide sheet of tendon. Muscle reconstruction involves fitting the control points of the B-spline solid to raw data acquired by different modalities (the data are typically represented by a 3-D cloud of points). A 3-D mass-spring-damper network implanted in the B-spline solid forms the basis for muscular deformation. The network does not correspond to the B-spline control points because these may be immaterial, but to spatial points of maximum influence. Unfortunately, an inevitable consequence of the duality between the B-spline control points

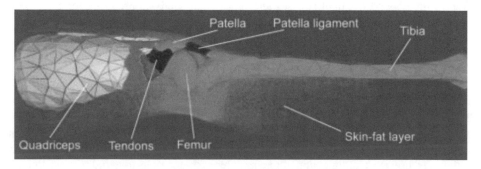

Figure 7.16 Finite element model of the leg. (Reproduced with permission of Department of Computer Science, University of North Carolina, Chapel Hill.)

and the spatial material points is an increase in the computational complexity. Varying force magnitude in the network results in non-uniform physical effects. While most physics-based models simulate a sequence of static equilibrium problems (i.e., quasi-static), the approach of Ng-Thow-Hing permits viscosity or inertia effects such as creep or oscillations. The author also incorporates muscle/(muscle, bone) collision forces as reaction constraints (Platt and Barr 1988) but no explicit solution is given as to how multiple collisions between muscles can be resolved within the same integration step.

7.3.3 Fat Layer

Few models explicitly represent fatty tissues and model their behavior. In fact, the fat layer is frequently blended into the muscle layer ((Delp and Loan 2000) or (Thalmann et al. 1996) for example). In the LEMAN system (Turner and Thalmann 1993), the fat layer is modeled as a thickness below the skin. The thickness is adjusted globally, or locally, skin vertex by skin vertex. When the model is animated, the behavior of the fatty tissues is approximated by hookian springs connecting skin vertices to the nearest perpendicular points of the muscle layer (see Figure 7.17). In practice, the fat springs are not created but equivalently replaced by reaction constraints (Platt and Barr 1988) applied to the skin vertices that penetrate the muscle layer surface displaced by the fat layer thickness. Similarly, Wilhelms and Van Gelder (1997) as well as Ng-Thow-Hing (2000) model the elastic behavior of the fatty tissues by springs anchoring the skin vertices to the muscle layer beneath. In (Wilhelms and Van Gelder 1997), the anchor points on the muscle layer are computed using a parametric trilinear transformation over two adjacent slices of deformed-cylinder muscles.

When implicit surface techniques are used to extract the skin from the muscle and skeletal layers, an offset can easily be applied to account for the thickness of the adipose tissues. Scheeppers et al. (1997) adjust the radius of influence of the density functions derived from the implicit versions of the muscle primitives. Wilhelms and Van Gelder (1997) voxelize the region around the character in a rest pose and extract an iso-surface at some distance from the bones and muscles by choosing an appropriate threshold (see Figure 7.18).

7.3.4 Skin Layer

Skin has been modeled by every type of surface: polygonal (Chadwick et al. 1998; Hirota et al. 2001; Wilhelms and Van Gelder 1997), parametric (Gascuel et al. 1991;

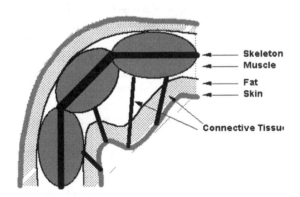

Figure 7.17   Layers in LEMAN. (Turner and Thalmann 1993.)

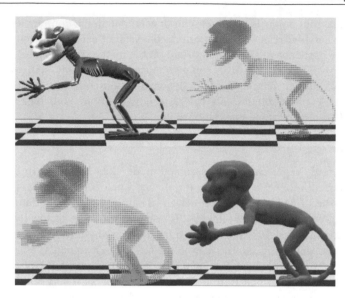

Figure 7.18 Skin extraction by voxelizing the inner layers in a rest pose (Wilhelms and Van Gelder 1997). The initial density function (upper right) is blurred and moved away from the underlying components (lower left) by a filter and an appropriate threshold (Reproduced with permission of J.Wilhelms)

Wilhelms 1997; Thalmann et al. 1996), subdivision (DeRose et al. 1998; Scheeppers et al. 1997) and implicit (Bloomenthal and Shoemake 1991; Cani-Gascuel 1998). Polygonal surfaces can directly be processed by the graphics unit. So, when speed or interactivity are called for, polygonal meshes are most eligible. However, various schemes may be needed to smooth out the surface discontinuities. Wilhelms and Van Gelder (1997) filter the voxelization of the muscle and skeleton layers by a Gaussian kernel (see Figure 7.18). The side-effect of the filter is that it also removes – somewhat indiscriminately – the possible fine details in the muscle layer.

Parametric surfaces, such as bicubic patches, are appealing candidates for modeling the skin because they naturally yield smooth shapes. Note that in the end, however, B-spline or Bézier patches must be polygonized for rendering purpose. Thalmann et al. (1996) relax the continuity constraints usually placed on soft object field functions and derive a lower degree polynomial field function for the inner layers because they compensate the loss of C1 continuity of the inner layers by the use of cubic B-spline blending for the skin (see Figure 7.19).

As noted before, implicit surfaces are quite appropriate for representing organic forms. They nevertheless suffer from a number of problems, which become conspicuous when the model is animated. The chief obstacle to their use is that the application of texture maps is difficult or even impossible. This is why they are rarely used for directly extracting a skin and used more often for deeper invisible anatomical layers.

There basically exist three ways to deform the skin in multi-layered models:

- Surface deformation models are first applied to the skin. In a second stage, the skin is projected back onto the inner anatomical layers. Alternatively, both stages may happen concurrently, as in (Thalmann et al. 1996).

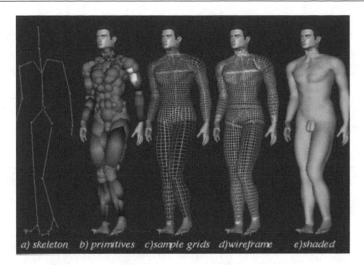

Figure 7.19   The layered model by Shen and Thalmann (1996). Ellipsoidal primitives (b) form an implicit surface, which is sampled by a ray-casting process. The sampling points (c) are used as control points of B-spline patches. The B-spline surface is ultimately polygonized at the desired resolution (d and e)

- The skin is deformed by a mechanical model of elastic membrane and constrained to stay a certain distance away from the material beneath.
- The skin is defined as the surface of a volume finite element/mass-spring model of the body.

The former deformation model is used by Leclerq et al. (2001) who subdivide a coarse skin mesh using an N-adic decomposition of the triangles and project the created vertices along their normals onto an implicit surface generated from ellipsoidal metaballs. In (Thalmann et al. 1996), regular skin cross-sections are sampled by casting rays from the skeleton segments in a star-shaped manner. The orientation of the cross-sections is determined by contour deformation. The outermost points where rays intersect the implicit surface, which is also defined by ellipsoidal primitives, are subsequently used as skin B-spline control points (see Figure 7.19).

The second case is mainly illustrated by (Turner and Thalmann 1993) and (Wilhelms and Van Gelder 1997). Wilhelms and Van Gelder (1997) simulate the motion of the skin by elastic relaxations of an equivalent mass-spring system (see Figure 7.20). Each skin vertex is anchored to the closest underlying component and each edge of the skin mesh becomes a spring whose stiffness is set to the area of the two adjacent triangles divided by the edge's length squared (Van Gelder 1998). This formula provides a more accurate model of uniformly elastic skin that would uniform stiffness. In the LEMAN system designed by Turner and Thalmann (1993), the skin is deformed by a mechanical model based on (Terzopoulos et al. 1987) that leaves it free to slide over the underlying surfaces (see Figure 7.21). The skin resistance to bending is ignored in the mechanical simulation since real skin bends much more easily than it stretches. Unlike (Wilhelms and Van Gelder 1997), the emphasis in LEMAN is laid on producing a dynamic skin motion with typical squash and stretch effects.

Figure 7.20 Three frames of the monkey shoulder animation by Wilhelms and Van Gelder (reproduced from (Wilhelms and Van Gelder 1997)). The skin mesh is deformed by a mass-spring network with varying stiffness and elastically anchored to the underlying muscles (Reproduced with permission of J.Wilhelms)

Figure 7.21 Elastic skin that slides over the underlying surfaces. (Turner and Thalmann 1993.)

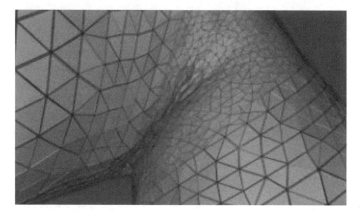

Figure 7.22 The skin buckles and creases in the work of Hirota et al. (Reproduced with permission of Department of Computer Science, Univeristy of North Carolina, Chapel Hill.)

The main limitation of the system is that the skin mesh is topologically restricted to a rectangular grid.

Finally, the third and last deformation model is exemplified by the excellent work of Hirota et al. (2001). In their system, the skin triangle mesh is chosen to be a subset of the sides of the tetrahedral finite elements that mesh the interior of the body. Unlike other works, they manage to obtain fold and crease patterns in the skin (see Figure 7.22). In contrast, their simulation is far from real-time, reaching a whopping computation time of 376 minutes on a 300MHz R12000 processor for a fifty-frame animation of leg flexion.

7.4 Conclusion

In this section, we first draw a comparison between the various approaches that have been proposed. We then discuss the issue of simulation depth. Finally, we list the remaining unsolved problems in the area.

7.4.1   Comparative Analysis

Predictably, surface deformation models have a rather low computation time. Most of them execute in real-time for moderately detailed skin meshes on low-end hardware. The major flaw of specialized surface operators is that the deformation is algorithmically determined. As a result, graphics designers cannot interactively improve the deformation. Additionally, mapping a deformation algorithm designed for a specific model to another model is bound to be problematic. Skinning and contour deformation techniques approximately produce the same visual quality at roughly the same (low) computational cost. They both allow a fine control through the manipulation of weights. In contrast, both require lots of manual intervention from the designer who may have to get down to the vertex level to improve the deformation. Though physically more realistic, 2-D mass-spring systems and other elastic surface models have seldom produced visually appealing results. Key-shape interpolation in an abstract space stands out as the best compromise among surface models. Nevertheless, as noted before, the visual quality entirely rests with the graphics artist. Moreover, the number of key-shapes grows exponentially with the number of parameters. These parameters include the joint axes around which rotations may occur and possibly less obvious ones such as the degree of muscle activation. Eventually, this may lead to an explosion in the number of required key-shapes. Also, the impact of the interpolation function on the deformation is not well known.

Among multi-layered models, those based on FEM generally produce good-looking deformations. They are, however, extremely slow and unwieldy. Because of the high computational cost associated with the FEM technique, most models simulate the deformation of only a few muscles, usually working in isolation. Most of them would probably become intractable if one tried to simulate the numerous muscles of the human body at the same time. In fact, only recently has a relatively complete model been demonstrated (Wilhelms and Van Gelder 1997). It is important to note, however, that there exists a huge body of literature on FEM and that various acceleration techniques have been proposed, especially in the context of virtual surgery. Another considerable drawback of FEM models is their poor reusability. Transforming a skinny character into a muscular character for instance requires remeshing the model and re-assigning elastic and mass properties to the finite elements. Muscle models based on mass-spring networks run faster than FEM models but have not produced any convincing deformations thus far. On the contrary, geometric deformation models have shown promising results both in terms of aesthetics (Scheepers et al. 1997; Dong et al. 2002; Aubel 2002), in particular, and accuracy (Dong et al. 2002; Aubel 2002).

7.4.2   Depth of Simulation

We have seen that many different research teams have tackled the difficult problem of body deformation in the past two decades. Two clearly distinct approaches recently emerged from the wealth of research work and literature in the area.

First, a data-based approach: recent shallow approaches like the Pose Space Deformation (Lewis et al. 2000) paved the way for fast synthesis of realistic-looking deformation by turning the deformation problem into a modeling problem.

Second, an anatomically-based approach: at the other extreme, researchers have proposed anatomically correct musculo-skeletal models that produce great-looking results. These deep models promise universally accurate simulation. However, producing anatomically plausible models is a daunting task, as shown by the huge body of literature in biomechanics.

Very much similar to character animation where optical and magnetic motion capture, a data-based approach, is complemented by motion synthesis techniques (forward/inverse kinematics/dynamics), the future of body deformation probably lies in a combination of 'shallow' and 'deep' approaches. One can very well conceive an anatomically-based system whose output is used for generating the various key-shapes required by recent example-based deformation techniques, thus combining the precision of deep simulation models with the speed of shallow deformation models. Inversely, muscle modeling for biomechanics or orthopedics purposes could benefit from laser scanning technology.

7.4.3 Future Research Directions

Research in body deformations has still a large potential of development. In particular, the following aspects need a specific effort on research:

- *Anatomically-based models*: In particular, it is important to take into account the different deformations resulting from the different fiber arrangements in the two muscles.
- *Scalability and re-use of internal components*: A few parameters should suffice to change a skinny character into a muscular character, or a tall character into a short character.
- *Surface self-intersection prevention*: Contact surfaces between different body parts may form in the vicinity of joints.
- *Simulation of fatty tissues*: Most of the work to date on inner anatomical layers has been concerned with the musculature. Obviously, the importance of fatty tissues on the surface form has been under-estimated.
- *Bi-directional propagation of the deformation between layers*: If the skin is displaced because of the application of external forces (e.g. virtual clothes pressing on the body), the deformation should be spread to the fatty tissues and muscles.

8

Hair Simulation

Sunil Hadap

In this chapter, we summarize the technological advances in hair simulation for computer graphics. There are mainly three tasks in hair simulation – hair shape modeling, hair dynamics and hair rendering. Various models developed for these tasks fall into the categories of particle systems, explicit hair models, cluster hair models and models based on volumetric textures. We discuss advantages and disadvantages of each of these approaches. We further elaborate on our hair modeling research with a new hair shape model and hair dynamics model. Both use the paradigm of fluid flow but in a different context.

8.1   Introduction

One of the many challenges in simulating believable Virtual Humans has been to produce realistic-looking hair. The Virtual Humans, two decades ago, were given polygonal hair structure. Today, this is not acceptable. Realistic visual depiction of Virtual Humans has improved over the years. Attention has been given to all the details necessary to produce visually convincing Virtual Humans and many improvements have been done to this effect. On a scalp, human hair strands are typically 100,000 to 150,000 in number. Geometrically they are long, thin curved cylinders having varying thickness. The strands of hair can have any degree of waviness from straight to curly. The hair color can change from white to gray, red to brown, due to the pigmentation. Further, it has shininess of varying degrees. Thus, difficulties of simulating hair stem from the huge number and geometric intricacies of individual hair, the complex interaction of light and shadow among the hairs, the small scale of thickness of one hair compared to the rendered image and intriguing hair-to-hair interaction while in motion. One can conceive of three main aspects in hair simulation – hair shape modeling, hair dynamics or animation, and hair rendering. Often these aspects are interconnected while processing hairs. Hair shape modeling deals with exact or fake creation of thousands of individual hair – their geometry, density, distribution, and orientation. Dynamics of hair addresses hair movement, their collision with other objects particularly

Handbook of Virtual Humans Edited by N. Magnenat-Thalmann and D. Thalmann
© 2004 John Wiley & Sons, Ltd   ISBN: 0-470-02316-3

relevant for long hair, and self-collision of hair. The rendering of hair involves dealing with hair color, shadow, specular highlights, varying degree of transparency and anti-aliasing. Each of the aspects is a topic of research in itself. Much work has been done in hair simulation research, some dealing only with one of the aspects of simulation – shape modeling, dynamics or rendering. Several research efforts were inspired by the general problem of simulation of natural phenomena such as grass and trees. These addressed a more limited problem of simulating fur or short hair. We divide hair simulation models into four categories depending upon the underlying technique involved: *particle systems, volumetric textures, explicit hair models* and *cluster hair model*. We discuss models presented by researchers in each of these model categories and state their contribution to the three aspects of hair simulation, i.e. hair shape modeling, hair dynamics and hair rendering. We then introduce our approach for hair shape-modeling and hair dynamics simulation for animation.

8.2   Hair Shape Modeling

An intricate hairstyle is indeed a consequence of the physical properties of an individual's hair and complex hair–hair and hair–body interactions. As we will see in the subsequent sections, modeling complex hair dynamics, also at interactive speeds, is currently impractical. For these reasons, it would be worthwhile to treat *hair shape modeling* as a separate problem and use some heuristic approach. Early attempts of styling long hair were based on *explicit hair models*. In the explicit hair model, each hair strand is considered for the shape and the dynamics. Daldegan et al. (1993) proposed that the user could interactively define a few characteristic hair strands in 3-D and then populate the hairstyle based on them. The user is provided with a flexible graphical user interface to sketch a curve in 3-D around the scalp. A few parameters such as density, spread, jitter and orientation control the process that duplicates the characteristic hairs to form a hairstyle. Figure 8.1 illustrates the method of

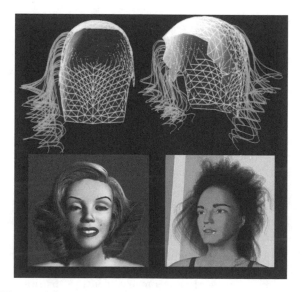

Figure 8.1   Hairstyling by defining a few curves in 3-D

defining a few characteristic curves and the resulting hairstyles from the method. Similarly, even for fur modeling, (Daldegan and Magnenat-Thalmann 1993), (Van Gelder and Wilhelms 1993) and (Bruderlin 1999) followed a similar explicit hair modeling approach.

The explicit hair models are very intuitive and close to reality. Unfortunately, they are tedious for hairstyling. Typically, it takes days to model a complex hairstyle, as in Figure 8.1, using the method in (Daldegan et al. 1993). They are also numerically expensive for hair dynamics. These difficulties are partially overcome by considering a bunch of hair instead of individual hair in the case of the wisp/cluster models. This assumption is quite valid. In reality, due to the effects of adhesive/cohesive forces, hairs tend to form clumps. Watanabe introduced the wisp models in (Watanabe and Suenaga 1989, 1992). More recently, Yan et al. (1999) modeled the wisps as *generalized cylinders* (see Figure 8.2). One of the contributions of the work was also in rendering of hair using the blend of ray-tracing generalized cylinders and the *volumetric textures*. The wisp model is also evident in (Chen et al. 1999). Surprisingly, till now, the wisp models have been limited to only static hair shape modeling and we feel that this offers an interesting research possibility, i.e. how to model hair dynamics, efficiently. It would be interesting to model how hair leaves one wisp and joins another under dynamics.

Nature exhibits some interesting fuzzy objects such as clouds, fire, eroded rocks and fur for which it is hard to have an explicit geometric definition. Using the volumetric texture approach, fur can be modeled as a volumetric density function. Perlin and Hoffret (1989) introduced *hypertextures*, which can model fur. Here, fur is modeled as intricate density variations in a 3-D space, which gives an illusion of the fur like medium without defining the geometry of each and every fiber. The model is essentially an extension to procedural solid texture synthesis evaluated throughout the region, instead of only on the surface. They demonstrated that combinations of simple analytical functions could define a furry ball or a furry donut. They further used 3-D vector valued noise and turbulence to perturb the 3-D texture space. This gave a natural look to the otherwise even fur defined by the hypertexture. A good discussion on the procedural approach to modeling volumetric texture and fur in particular is found in (Ebert et al. 1998). Hypertexture method by Perlin and Hoffret is only limited to geometries that can be analytically defined.

Figure 8.2 Cluster hair model, by Yang et al. (Reproduced with permission of Dirc Dong Yang.)

Copyright @ MIRALab, University of Geneva, 2000

Figure 8.3   Hair model based on fluid flow paradigm

As evident from the previous discussion, one of the strengths of the explicit hair models is their intuitiveness and ability to control the global shape of the hair. On the contrary, volumetric textures give a nice way of interpreting complexity in nature and they are rich in details. We notice that the fluid flow has both these characteristics, which we would like to exploit for hair shape modeling. We model hair shape as streamlines of a fluid flow (Hadap and Magnenat-Thalmann 2000). Figure 8.3 shows a hairstyle obtained as a result of our model. The modeling of hair as streamlines of fluid flow is discussed in detail.

8.3   Hair Dynamics

Anjyo et al. (1992), Rosenblum et al. (1991) and Kurihara et al. (1993) developed dynamic models that are essentially based on individual hair. An individual hair is modeled as connected particles by tensile springs having bending stiffness at each joint. Then the dynamics of individual hair is solved for the movement due to the inertial forces and the collision with the body. Though the cantilever dynamics and collision avoidance with the body of each hair is within the scope of current computing power, modeling complex hair-to-hair interaction is still a challenge. Figure 8.4 illustrates the effectiveness of the dynamic model even though no hair–hair interaction is considered. Recently, Hadap and Magnenat-Thalmann (2001) have developed an elaborate stiffness dynamics model for individual hair strand. This is also probably the first detailed attempt to model complex hair–hair interactions.

In the case of animating fur, which is mostly modeled as volumetric texture, one cannot take the approach as in explicit models. In this case, a time-varying volume density function can facilitate animation of fur. One can simulate effects of turbulent air on the fur using stochastic space perturbation such as turbulence, noise, Brownian motion etc. Apart from (Lewis 1989) and (Perlin and Hoffert 1989; Perlin 1985), work by Dischler (1999) gave a generalized method for these animated shape perturbations.

Figure 8.4   Hair animation using the explicit model, by Kurihara

8.4   Hair Rendering

In the field of Virtual Humans, hair presents one of the most challenging rendering problems. The difficulties arise from various reasons: large number of hairs, detailed geometry of individual hair and complex interaction of light and shadow among the hairs and their small thickness. The rendering of hair often suffers from the aliasing problem because many individual hairs reflect light and cast shadows on each other contributing to the shading of each pixel. Further, concerning display of hairs, we do not see only individual hairs but also a continuous image consisting of regions of hair color, shadow, specular highlights, varying degree of transparency and haloing under backlight conditions. The image, in spite of the structural complexity, shows a definite pattern and texture in its aggregate form. In the past decade, the hair-rendering problem has been addressed by a number of researchers, in some cases with considerable success. However, most cases work well in particular conditions and offer limited (or no) capabilities in terms of dynamics or animation of hair. Much of the work refers to a more limited problem of rendering fur, which also has a lot in common with rendering natural phenomena such as grass and trees. We discuss the related work in hair rendering, focusing on their salient features and limitations.

Particle systems introduced by (Reeves 1983) were primarily meant to model class of fuzzy objects such as fire. Despite the particles' small size – smaller than even a pixel – the particle manifests itself by the way it reflects light, casts shadows, and occludes objects. Thus, the subpixel structure of the particle needs to be represented only by a model that can represent these properties. A particle system is rendered by painting each particle in succession onto the frame buffer, computing its contribution to the pixel and compositing it to get the final color at the pixel. The technique has been successfully used to render these fuzzy objects and integrated in many commercial animation systems. However, the technique has some limitations for shadowing and self-shadowing. Much of it is due to the inherent modeling using particle systems: simple stochastic models are not adequate to represent the type of order and orientation of hair. Also, it requires an appropriate lighting model to capture and control the hair length and orientation. The specular highlights in particular owing to the geometry of the individual strands are highly anisotropic. Impressive results have been obtained for the more limited problem of rendering fur, which can be considered as very short hair.

As we have already discussed in the case of hair shape modeling, (Perlin and Hoffert 1989) introduced hypertextures that can model fur-like objects. Hypertexture approach remains limited to geometries that can be defined analytically. Kajiya and Kay (1989) extended this approach to use it on complex geometries. They used a single solid texture tile, namely texel. The idea of texels was inspired by the notion of volume density used in (Perlin and Hoffert 1989). A texel is a 3-D texture map where both the surface frame and lighting model parameters are embedded over a volume. Texels are a type of model intermediate between a texture and a geometry. A texel is, however, not tied to the geometry of any particular surface and thus makes the rendering time independent of the geometric complexity of the surface that it extracts. The results are demonstrated by rendering a teddy bear (Figure 8.5). Texels are rendered using ray casting, in a manner similar to that for volume densities using a suitable illumination model. Kajiya and Kay reveal more about the particular fur illumination model and a general rendering method for rendering volume densities. The rendering of volume densities are also covered in great detail in (Ebert et al. 1998).

In another approach by Goldman (1997), emphasis is given on rendering visual characteristics of fur in cases where the hair geometry is not visible at the final image resolution – the object being far away from the camera. A probabilistic rendering algorithm, also referred to as fake-fur algorithm, is proposed. In this model, the reflected light from individual hairs and from the skin below is blended using the expectations of a ray striking a hair in that area as the opacity factor. Though the volumetric textures are quite suitable for rendering furry objects or hair patches, rendering of long hair using this approach does not seem obvious. A brute force method to render hair is to model each individual hair as a curved cylinder and render each cylinder primitive. The sheer number of primitives modeling hair poses serious problems with this approach. However, the explicit modeling of hair has been used for different reasons when employing different types of primitives. An early effort by Csuri et al. (1979) generated fur-like volumes using polygons. Each hair was modeled as a single triangle laid out on a surface and rendered using a Z-buffer algorithm for hidden surface

Figure 8.5 Volumetric texture rendering by Kajiya and Kay (1989). (Reproduced with permission of Jim Kajiya.)

removal. Miller (1988) produced better results by modeling hair as pyramids consisting of triangles. Oversampling was employed for anti-aliasing. These techniques, however, impose serious problems considering reasonable number and size of hairs.

In another approach, a hardware Z-buffer renderer was used with Gouraud shading for rendering hair modeled as connected segments of triangular prisms on a full human head. However, the illumination model used was quite simplistic and no effort was made to deal with the problem of aliasing. LeBlanc et al. (1991) proposed an approach of rendering hair using pixel blending and shadow buffers. This technique has been one of the most effective in the practical hair rendering approach. Though it could be applied for the variety of hairy and furry objects, one of the primary intentions of the approach was to be able to render realistic different styles of human hairs. Hair rendering is done by a mix of ray tracing and drawing polyline primitives, with an added module for the shadow buffer (Reeves et al. 1987). The rendering pipeline has the following steps: first, the shadow of the scene is calculated for each light source. Then, the hair shadow buffer is computed for each light source for the given hair style model; this is done by drawing each hair segment into a Z-buffer and extracting the depth map. The depth maps for the shadow buffers for the scene and hair are composed giving a single composite shadow buffer for each light source. The scene image with its Z-buffer is generated using a scene model and composite shadow buffers. The hair segments are then drawn as illuminated polylines (Zckler et al. 1996) into the scene using a Z-buffer of the scene to determine the visibility and the composite shadow buffers to find the shadows. Figure 8.6 shows the process and Figure 8.7 gives a final rendered image of a hairstyle of a synthetic actor with a fur coat.

Special effects such as rendering wet hair require a change in the shading model. Bruderlin (1999) presented some simple ways to account for the wetness of hair such as changing the specularity. That is, hairs on the side of a clump facing the light are brighter than hairs on a clump away from the light. Kong and Nakajima (1999) presented the approach of using a visible volume buffer to reduce the rendering time. The volume buffer is a 3-D cubical space defined by the user depending upon the available memory and the resolution required. They consider the hair model as a combination of coarse background hair and detailed surface hair determined by the distance from the viewpoint or the opacity value. The technique considerably reduces the rendering time, however, the quality of results is not as impressive.

Yan et al. (1999) combine volumetric texture inside the explicit geometry of hair cluster defined as a generalized cylinder. Ray tracing is employed to find the boundaries of the

Figure 8.6 Rendering the pipeline of the method- 'pixel blending and shadow buffer'

Figure 8.7   Fur using explicit hair model

generalized cylinder and then the standard volume rendering is applied along the ray to capture the characteristics of the density function defined. This may be considered a hybrid approach for hair rendering.

8.5   Summary

So far, we have presented the state of the art in hair simulation, one of the most challenging problems of Virtual Humans. We have considered three aspects in hair simulation: hair shape modeling, hair rendering and hair dynamics. Different approaches have been proposed in the literature dealing with one or more aspects of hair simulation. We divide them into four categories based on the underlying technique: particle systems, volumetric textures, explicit hair models and cluster hair model. Some of these techniques are appropriate and effective only for one of the aspects in hair simulation. Before we discuss in detail our approach to hair simulation, we summarize the effectiveness and limitations of various aspects of the hair simulation, in Table 8.1. The rest of the chapter is devoted to the recent models proposed by us for static hair shape modeling and dynamic hair simulation.

Table 8.1   Comparison of the various hair models

	Hair modeling	Hair animation	Hair rendering

Explicit models	effective
	– tedious to model
	– not suitable for
	  knots and braids
		adequate
		– expensive due to size
		– inappropriate for
		  hair-hair interaction
			fast
			– inadequate for
			  self-shadowing

Particle systems	inappropriate	adhoc – lacks physical basis – no hair-hair interaction	effective – lacks shadowing and self-shadowing

Table 8.1 Continued

	Hair modeling	Hair animation	Hair rendering
Volumetric textures	effective – not suitable for long hair	limited – via animated shape perturbation	effective – expensive
Cluster model	effective – not suitable for simple smooth hair	not done – via animated shape perturbation	effective
Hair as a fluid	effective – not suitable for knots and braids	not done	not done

8.6 Static Hair Shape Modeling Based on Fluid Flow

Hair styling is one of the oldest human passions. Recently, even the Virtual Humans are involved in this form of art. It needs special attention because of the shape complexity. We try to simplify the problem and notice that hair has many properties that are similar to a fluid flow. The comparison is only limited to static hair shape with a snapshot of a fluid flow rather than its dynamics. Figure 8.8 illustrates how we can think of hair as selective streamlines of a well set-up fluid flow. Probably the first thing to notice is that long hair has an overall tendency to go down under gravitational influence. The hair-to-hair collision avoidance is too prominent an issue to be ignored. Consequently, though hair is thin in geometry, collectively it has a volume. The hair-to-hair collision avoidance is similar to the *continuum property* of fluid, i.e. no two streamlines of a fluid flow intersect, however close they may get, with an exception of flow singularities. This observation is significant in hair-to-hair interaction. Further, hair to body collision avoidance is the same as a flow around an obstacle. Flow component normal to an obstacle boundary is zero, as the flow does not penetrate the obstacle. As depicted in Figure 8.8 (near the neck and the shoulder), the hair follows a similar pattern. It is tangential to the body except from where it originates (on the scalp).

Hair strand tends to stand out on the scalp as it originates. This situation is different from the hair to body collision avoidance. In the flow context, we can visualize it as a secondary

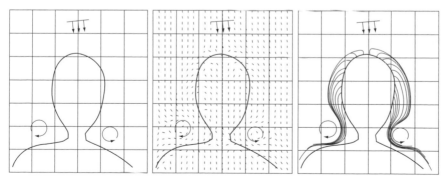

Figure 8.8 Modeling hair as streamlines of a fluid flow

flow forcefully oozing out from within an obstacle boundary that has fine holes. So the velocity component normal to the boundary is non-zero and constant. The greater the normal velocity component, the more the streamlines will stand out.

Apart from this, hair shape has some other similarities with fluid flow such as hair curls being analogous to vorticity and hair waviness being analogous to the turbulence in the flow. Even the hair parting line appears as the *flow stagnation point* in a flow around an obstacle. Observe in Figure 8.8 how the streamlines follow opposite directions at the stagnation point, that is the top of the scalp. In spite of the similarities discussed above, hair is not precisely like a fluid flow. For example, hair tends to form clumps, which is not true in the case of flow streamlines. In fact, some hair care products try to bring more streamline like order to one's hair, by reducing the clumsiness. Furthermore, though overall hair shape follows a fluid flow-like structure, individual hair has perturbations and may break away from the flow at several places. We discuss these issues later in this section. We first develop hair shape model based on the observations made so far.

8.6.1 Hair Shape Model

The choice of the fluid model for the purpose of modeling hair can be debatable. As we try to equate only a snapshot of fluid flow to hair, the natural choice would be to consider a stable flow. Stable flow is a flow, which does not change over time. A good example of this kind of flow is the flow around a thin body in a very stable wind tunnel. We further choose the flow to be an *ideal flow* (Wejchert and Haumann 1991), which is inviscid, hence, stable, irrotational and incompressible. We find that the model is simple, fast and adequate. The governing equation for the flow is the Laplace equation:

$$\nabla^2 \phi = 0$$
$$\vec{V} = \vec{\nabla} \phi \qquad (8.1)$$

where $\vec{V}$ is velocity, a gradient of a scalar potential ϕ.

As Equation (8.1) is a linear partial differential equation, the sum of the particular solutions is also a solution of the equation. There are a few interesting particular solutions we would like to combine. Figure 8.9 illustrates the *ideal flow elements*. We have an analytic form for the velocity field induced by the elements. For a detailed discussion on the ideal flow elements refer to (Wejchert and Haumann 1991; Anderson 1991). Generation of a typical complex flow by a linear combination of these elements is illustrated in Figure 8.10. Let the

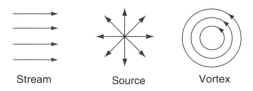

Stream   Source   Vortex

Figure 8.9   Ideal flow elements

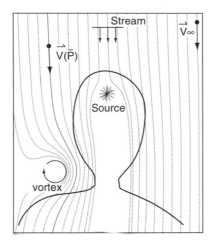

Figure 8.10   Linear combination of ideal flow elements

velocity induced at a point $\bar{p}$ by a user-defined ideal flow element be $\vec{V}_{users}(p)$. Thus, the linear combination of flow elements is:

$$\vec{V}(p) = \sum \vec{V}_{user}(p) \qquad (8.2)$$

We propose to model hair as streamlines of such a complex flow set-up. Though there are numerous possibilities for the user to combine these elements, in order to get close to a hair shape we would design a flow set-up considering the observations stated in the beginning of this section. First, we put a *stream* to give the flow an overall downward direction. Then we may place a few other elements such as a *source* and a *vortex*, as shown in Figure 8.10. Note that the hair-to-hair collision avoidance is intrinsic to the fluid flow equation, hence it is always ensured. Consider an obstacle, the body, placed in the flow field as shown in Figure 8.10. Notice that the flow streamlines would penetrate the geometry. In order to model the flow obstacle collision avoidance, we use the *panel method* (Anderson 1991; Ling et al. 1996). Let us approximate the boundary by dividing it into a number of planar segments, namely panels. There are many variations of the panel method based on the choice of flow elements, we choose the simple *source panel method*. We place one source per panel, slightly away from the center of the panel along the inward normal. Note that the source has a singularity at its center. The user can vary the *panel source offset* to achieve desired numerical accuracy. As depicted in Figure 8.10, a source in a flow has the property of generating an obstacle to the flow. Thus, as shown in Figure 8.11, setting up small sources along the boundary will ensure that flow does not penetrate the geometry. We find this set-up adequate to ensure obstacle avoidance.

For N such panels, let the source strengths be λ_1, λ_2, ... λ_N. We incorporate the panel sources into Equation (8.2).

$$\vec{V}(\bar{p}) = \sum \vec{V}_{user}(\bar{p}) + \sum_{i=1}^{N} \lambda_j \vec{S}_j(\bar{p}) \qquad (8.3)$$

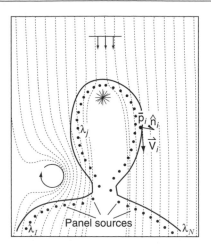

Figure 8.11   Source panel method

where $\vec{S}_j(\bar{p})$ is velocity induced by a unit source positioned near the panel j. In order to solve for these unknown strengths, let us sample the flow at N panel centers and set up a boundary condition. The velocity at the i th panel center $\bar{p}_i$ is

$$\vec{V}(\bar{p}_i) = \sum \vec{V}_{user}(\bar{p}_i) + \sum_{j=1}^{N} \lambda_j \vec{S}_j(\bar{p}_i) \tag{8.4}$$

For an inviscid flow, the velocity at the boundary can be non-zero. However, as the flow cannot penetrate the boundary surface, the velocity vector must be tangential to the surface. This ensures that the streamline will be parallel to the boundary surface. This is the typical situation of long hair rolling over the neck and shoulders. However, we would also like to accommodate the cases where the streamline oozes out, just like hair originating from the scalp. Both cases are addressed by stating the wall boundary condition in terms of the velocity component normal to the boundary. If $\hat{n}_i$ is unit normal to the boundary surface at panel center i, the wall boundary condition is:

$$\vec{V}(\bar{p}_i) \cdot \hat{n}_i = b_i \tag{8.5}$$

$$\left(\sum \vec{V}_{user}(\bar{p}_i) + \sum_{j=1}^{N} \lambda_j \vec{S}_j(\bar{p}_i) \right) \cdot \hat{n}_i = b_i$$

$$\sum_{j=1}^{N} \left((\vec{S}_j(\bar{p}_i) \cdot \hat{n}_i) \lambda_j \right) = b_i - \left(\sum \vec{V}_{user}(\bar{p}_i) \right) \cdot \hat{n}_i$$

$$\sum_{j=1}^{N} S(i, j) \lambda_j = b_i - \left(\sum \vec{V}_{user}(\bar{p}_i) \right) \cdot \hat{n}_i \tag{8.6}$$

where b_i is the user-specified magnitude of the normal velocity. In Equation (8.5), the quantity $\vec{S}_j(\bar{p}_i) \cdot \hat{n}_i$ represents the velocity induced by a unit panel source near j th panel on the center of the i th panel. This is constant for a given geometry and a particular set-up of the panel sources for that geometry. We call it the *flow boundary form* and denote it by $S(i, j)$. To solve the system of linear Equation (8.6) in N unknowns (λ_j), we use LU decomposition followed by a back substitution. Thus, for a given constant flow boundary form matrix and its LU decomposition, one can quickly get a set of λ_j for the boundary condition b_i and variation of the complex user flow set-up. This is particularly important for fast user interaction. Figure 8.12 shows how the streamlines avoid the obstacle after setting appropriate panel source strengths. There are new streamlines standing out from the scalp as a result of the non-zero normal velocity specified on the scalp region. Elsewhere the streamlines are parallel to the body. By selecting the appropriate streamlines (the ones which ooze out from the scalp), we thus have a hairstyle.

We carry out hair rendering by drawing individual hair. This requires that we compute a large number of streamlines. We approximate a streamline by a polyline and we compute it by space marching the velocity field using small constant steps. Observing Equation (8.3), computation of velocity at each point, as we compute the streamline, involves the contribution of a large number of panel sources. This is numerically expensive considering a few hundred thousand hair strands to be drawn. To address this problem, we use a subdivision scheme for fluid flow introduced recently (Weimer and Warren 1999). The user defines a basic flow resolution as shown in Figure 8.12. We compute the flow field at each point of the coarse grid and, in order to compute the flow at any point in the field, we use the subdivision flow. Thus, we have reduced the computation of flow at any point to computation of contributions by only a few neighboring points on the coarse grid. For a detailed discussion on the subdivision flow, refer to (Weimer and Warren 1999).

8.6.2 *Interactive Hair-Styler*

As described in the previous section, flow computation with an obstacle is done by the source panel method, which involves solving a large, fully dense system of linear equations. To keep the computation within acceptable limits, the user starts modeling hair on a coarse mesh model as shown in Figure 8.13. It should be noted that the choice of a structured mesh is not a requirement for the method.

The user then defines the total number of hair and paints the *hair growth map* (see Figure 8.14) directly on the model. The hair growth values can be varied smoothly by using

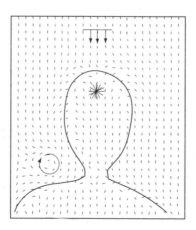

Figure 8.12 Subdivision scheme for ideal flow

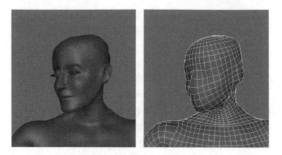

Figure 8.13 Polygon reduced geometry to define panels

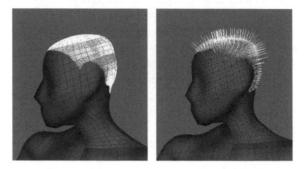

Figure 8.14 Hair growth map and normal velocity map

pressure on the pressure-sensitive stylus. From the probability density function in the form of the hair growth map, the placement of individual hair is pre-computed.

In order to place sources corresponding to each panel, the user defines the panel source offset along the inward normal of the panel. Figure 8.15 shows the typical 3-D configuration of panel sources. The user can finalize the source panel set-up after visual examination. Upon acceptance, the flow boundary form is computed along with its LU decomposition as explained in Section 8.6.1. This typically takes a minute for one thousand panels (on a Pentium II 400MHz, 512MB RAM). As the geometry of the face remains constant throughout the hair styling, this needs to be computed only once as long as the source panel set-up does not change.

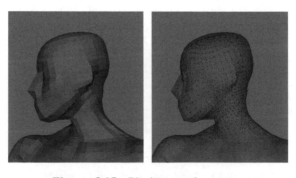

Figure 8.15 Placing panel sources

To define the boundary condition of the flow described in Section 8.6.1, the user paints the *normal velocity map*. During this, the hair growth map is also presented for visual feedback along with the normal velocity map. The user will define zero normal velocity everywhere except for the regions where the hair originates. He/She can control how the hair will stand out from the scalp by varying the magnitude of the normal velocity. Figure 8.14 shows the painted normal velocity map.

The user is provided with 3-D versions of ideal flow elements: streams, sources and vortices and can interactively place them around the model to define the hairstyle. After the user places a stream (the first fluid element in the hairstyle) in a downward direction to define the overall direction of the hair, a few hair strands are displayed for the interaction as shown in Figure 8.16(a). The user defines the overall length of the hair. One can use a source from the toolbox and place it in front of the face to turn the hair away from the face as shown in Figure 8.16(b). The other alternative is to trim hair on the face by using a trimming tool as shown in Figure 8.16(c).

For deciding the detail *hair length map*, which defines the length of each streamline, the user is provided with a trim tool. Though the definition of the hair length map is similar to that of the hair growth map, it is not intuitive to paint the length map on the scalp as in the case of the hair growth map. Instead, the user takes any polygonal geometry, and after adjusting it appropriately, cutting across the displayed hair, she can trim the hair. The hair length map is recalculated by tracing back the streamlines from the point of intersection with the trim tool.

The user can then place a few other fluid elements, mostly vortices, to add further details to the hairstyle. For every change in the flow set-up and the boundary condition, source panel strengths are evaluated using the LU decomposed flow form factor. The effects of placing or moving the flow elements are computed in about a second. The computation speed does not permit the user to interact with the flow in real time. This interactivity and only a few flow elements are sufficient to model a complex hairstyle. Figure 8.16(d) illustrates a hairstyle, which is designed using only 5 fluid elements, 1 stream (not in the frame), 2 sources and 2 vortices. The hairstyle in Figure 8.17 is the result of setting up a complex ideal flow. Typically, the complete design of a complex hairstyle takes about an hour.

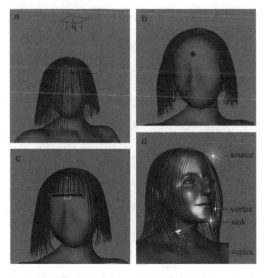

Figure 8.16 Simple hairstyles using few fluid elements

Figure 8.17   Hair as a complex fluid flow

8.6.3 Enhancing Realism

As depicted by the hairstyle in Figure 8.17, modeling hair as fluid flow followed by appropriate rendering scheme, gives results close to reality. Nevertheless, we try to break away from the theme and introduce variations inspired from the volumetric textures (Perlin and Hoffert 1989; Lewis 1989; Neyret 1998). This will further add realism to hair.

It is desirable to avoid the synthetic look of the hair, which is the result of the strict order of the individual streamlines. For this, we add an empirical model. The user defines a vector-valued volumetric function such as noise and turbulence to define a volumetric perturbation. There are two possibilities in using the perturbations. The user can define a breakaway behavior of the individual hair as a probability function on the lengthwise parameter. Typically, the probability of the individual hair breaking away from the flow (and then follow the vector field defined by the volumetric perturbation) increases with the length from the scalp. Figure 8.18 illustrates added

Figure 8.18   Adding perturbations to a few individual hairs

Figure 8.19 Adding overall volumetric perturbations

realism due to few hairs breaking away from the flow. Alternatively, the user can add overall perturbation to the flow field to define a new character to the hairstyle (see Figure 8.19). Notice that the contribution of the noise increases linearly with the length of the hair. In the illustrations we use three independent Perlin's noises (Perlin and Hoffert 1989) to form a vector-valued noise. A wide range of 'out of box' volumetric textures such as fractals, waves, turbulence and noise are available to the user for the volumetric perturbations.

Fluid-like hair may be everybody's dream. Though in reality, under cohesive/adhesive forces, hair tends to form clumps, i.e. a set of hair gets close to follow a common path. The clumpy behavior is added to the model as follows. We observe that the clumps follow a typical pattern. Individual hairs of the clump originate from the scalp, follow the overall flow for some length, then join a clump near to it and again after some length i.e. towards the tip may leave the clump. The user defines (a) clumsiness; (b) number of hair per clump; (c) minimum clump length; and (d) maximum clump length. The factor clumsiness defines the maximum change in the radius of a clump on a relative scale. Figure 8.20

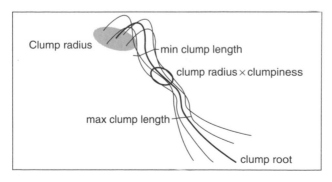

Figure 8.20 Hair clumpiness

Figure 8.21 Possibilities for enhancing realism

illustrates some of these parameters. From the number of hairs per clump and the overall density of the hair (defined by the total number of hairs), we compute the number of clumps and the clump influence region. We then place clumps randomly on the scalp. The central hair of the clump influence region, namely the clump root, defines the shape of the clump. An individual hair originating from the scalp follows the fluid flow till minimum clump length. Then it follows the clump root till maximum clump length and follows the flow again. As the volumetric perturbations are available at both the levels, one can apply perturbations to the clump and/or to the individual hair. Use of clumsiness is evident in Figure 8.19 along with the noise. Further, we use a color map to give individual hair a color.

Figure 8.21 shows three hairstyles. The left-most image shows the result of the uniform fluid flow that gives a synthetic look. The central hairstyle shows the presence of noise and perturbations giving a more natural look. Finally, the right-most image shows a hairstyle as a result of adding waviness and clumsiness.

8.7 Modeling Hair Dynamics Based on Continuum Mechanics

In this section we address the difficult problem of hair dynamics, particularly hair–hair and hair–air interactions. To model these interactions, we propose to consider hair volume as a continuum. Subsequently, we treat the interaction dynamics to be fluid dynamics. This proves to be a strong as well as a viable approach to an otherwise very complex phenomenon. However, we retain the individual character of hair, which is vital to visually realistic rendering of hair animation. For that, we develop an elaborate model for stiffness and inertial dynamics of individual hair strands. Being a reduced coordinate formulation, the stiffness dynamics is numerically stable and fast. We then unify the continuum interaction dynamics and the individual hair's stiffness dynamics.

Shape modeling and the dynamics of long hair are a difficult task. The difficulties stem from the sheer number of hair strands, their geometric intricacies and associated complex physical interactions. We have reviewed previous attempts at modeling hair dynamics in Section 8.3. Appreciably, none of the previous attempts considered hair–hair and hair–air interactions. Even individual hair dynamics was grossly approximated to suit available computational power. However, in recent years computing power has grown many times. The supercomputing power of the past is becoming increasingly available to an animator's workstation. Hence we feel a need to develop new hair dynamics models in light of current and future computing advances. We contribute to hair dynamics modeling in two important ways:

1. We address the problem of hair–hair, hair–body and hair–air interactions. We make a paradigm shift and model these interactions, in a unified way, as fluid dynamics. We use smoothed particle hydrodynamics (SPH) (Gascuel et al. 1996; Monaghan 1992) as a numerical model.
2. We give an elaborate model for the stiffness dynamics of individual hair. We treat a hair strand as a serial rigid multi-body system. This reduced coordinate formulation eliminates stiff numerical equations as well as enables a parametric definition of bending and torsional dynamics.

8.7.1 Hair as Continuum

Hair–hair interaction is probably the most difficult problem in achieving visually pleasing hair dynamics. Though there have been many advances in collision detection and response (Lin and Gottschalk 1998), they are simply unsuitable for the problem at hand, because of sheer number complexity of hair. We take a radical approach by considering hair as a continuum. The continuum assumption states that the physical properties of a medium such as pressure, density and temperature are defined at each and every point in the specified region. Fluid dynamics regards liquids and gases as a continuum and even elastic theory regards solids as such, ignoring the fact that they are still composed of individual molecules. Indeed, the assumption is quite realistic at a certain length scale of the observation but at smaller length scales the assumption may not be reasonable. One might argue, hair–hair spacing is not at all comparable to inter-molecular distances to consider hair as a continuum. However, individual hair–hair interaction is of no interest to us apart from its end effect. Hence, we treat the size of individual hair and hair–hair distance as much smaller than the overall volume of hair, justifying the continuum assumption. As we develop the model further, it will be apparent that the above assumption is not just about approximating the complex hair–hair interaction. An individual hair is surrounded by air, as it moves, it generates a boundary layer of air. This influences many other hair strands in motion. This aerodynamic form of friction is comparable to hair–hair contact friction. In addition, there are electrostatic forces to take part in the dynamics. It is not feasible to model these complex multiple forms of interactions. This inspires us to consider the dynamics of a single hair interacting with other surrounding hairs in a global manner through the continuum assumption. Thus, we hope to have a sound model for an otherwise very complex phenomenon.

As we start considering hair as a continuum, we look at the properties of such a medium, namely the hair medium. There are two possibilities: the hair medium could be considered as a solid or a liquid, depending on how it behaves under shearing forces. Under shearing stresses, solids deform till they generate counter-stresses. If the shearing stresses are removed, the solids exhibit the ability to retain their original shape. The liquids are not able to withstand any shearing stresses. Under the influence of the shearing stresses they continue to deform indefinitely and they do not have any shape memory. In the case of hair, if we apply a lateral shearing motion, it acts like a liquid. At the same time, lengthwise, it acts as a solid. Thus, there is a duality in the behavior of hair as a continuum.

However, from an animation point of view, we cannot treat hair solely as a continuum, unless the viewpoint is far enough and individual hair movement is not perceived. Thus, we have to retain the individual character of hair as well, while considering hair as a continuum. We split hair dynamics into two parts:

- Hair–hair, hair–body and hair–air interactions, which are modeled using continuum dynamics, and more precisely fluid dynamics.
- Individual hair geometry and stiffness, which is modeled using the dynamics of an elastic fiber.

Interestingly, this approach even addresses the solid–liquid duality effectively. The model can be visualized as a bunch of hair strands immersed in a fluid. The hair strands are cinematically linked to fluid particles in their vicinity. The individual hair has its own stiffness dynamics and it interacts with the environment through the kinematical link with the fluid. Density, pressure and temperature are the basic constituents of fluid dynamics. The density of the hair medium is not precisely the density of individual hair. It is rather associated with the number density of hair in an elemental volume. In Figure 8.22, we can observe that the density of hair medium is less when the number density of hair is less. The density of the hair medium is thus defined as the mass of the hair per unit occupied volume and is denoted as ρ. The notion of density of hair medium enables us to express the conservation of mass (it is rather conservation of the number of hair strands) in terms of the continuity equation (Panton 1995):

$$\frac{1}{\rho}\frac{\partial \rho}{\partial t} = -\nabla \vec{\nu} \tag{8.7}$$

where, $\vec{\nu}$ is the local velocity of the medium. The continuity equation states that the relative rate of change of density $(\frac{1}{\rho}\frac{\partial \rho}{\partial t})$, at any point in the medium, is equal to the negative gradient of the velocity field at that point $(-\nabla \vec{\nu})$. This is the total outflow of the medium at that point. The physical interpretation of the continuity equation in our case means that, as the hair strands start moving apart, their number density, and hence the density of the hair medium drop and vice

Figure 8.22   Hair as a continuum

versa. The pressure and the viscosity in the hair medium represent all the forces due to various forms of interactions of hair strands described previously. If we try to compress a bunch of hair, it develops a pressure such that hair strands will tend to move apart. The viscosity would account for various forms of interactions such as hair–hair, hair–body and hair–air. These are captured in the form of the momentum equation (Panton 1995) of a fluid:

$$\rho\frac{d\vec{v}}{dt} = \nu\nabla \cdot (\nabla\vec{v}) - \nabla p + F_{BD} \tag{8.8}$$

The acceleration of fluid particles $\frac{d\vec{v}}{dt}$ with spatial pressure variation ∇p would be such that it will tend to even out the pressure differences and as the fluid particles move, there will be always resistance $\nu\nabla \cdot (\nabla\vec{v})$ in the form of the friction. The body forces F_{BD}, i.e. the inertial forces and gravitational influence are also accounted for in the equation.

Temperature considerably affects the properties of hair. However, we do not have to consider it in dynamics. We treat the hair dynamics as an isothermal process unless we are trying to simulate a scenario of hair being dried with a hair dryer. Second, the temperature is associated with the internal energy of the fluid, which is due to the continuous random motion of fluid molecules. At the length scale of our model, i.e. treating hair as a continuum, there is no such internal energy associated with the hair medium. Subsequently, we drop the energy equation of fluid, which is associated with the temperature and the internal energy.

The equation of state (EOS) (Panton 1995) binds together all the fluid equations. It gives a relation between density, pressure and temperature. In our case of hair–hair interaction, EOS plays a central role along with the viscous fluid forces. The medium we are modeling is not a real medium such as gas or liquid. Hence, we are free to 'design' EOS to suit our needs:

$$p = \begin{cases} 0 & \text{if } \rho < \rho_0 \\ K_c\left(\dfrac{\rho - \rho_0}{\rho_c - \rho_0}\right)^n & \text{if } \rho_0 \leq \rho < \rho_c \\ K_r & \text{if } \rho_c < \rho \end{cases} \tag{8.9}$$

We define hair rest density ρ_0 as a density below which statistically there is no hair–hair collision. In addition, we define hair close packing density as ρ_c that represents the state of the hair medium in which hair strands are packed to the maximum extent. This density is slightly lower than the physical density of hair, ρ_h. Figure 8.23 illustrates the relation between the density and the pressure of the hair medium. In the proposed pressure/density relationship, notice that there is no pressure built up below the hair rest density ρ_0. As one starts squeezing the hair volume, pressure starts building up. As a consequence, the hair

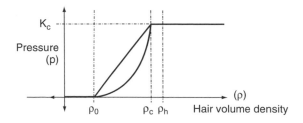

Figure 8.23 Equation of State

strands are forced apart. At the hair compaction density ρ_c, the pressure is maximum. K_c is the compressibility of the hair volume. The power n refers to the ability of hair volume to get compressed. If the hair is well aligned, the power is high. As we compress the hair volume, suddenly hair strands start to form close packing and build the pressure quickly. On the contrary, if hair is wavy and not very well aligned, the pressure build-up is not abrupt.

Instead of modeling collisions of individual hair strand with the body, we model them, in a unified way, as boundary condition of the fluid flow. There are two forms of fluid boundary conditions:

- *Flow tangency condition*: The fluid flow normal to the obstacle boundary is zero.
- *Flow slip condition*: The boundary exerts a viscous pressure proportional to the tangential flow velocity.

Formulation of the flow boundary condition is deferred to the later section.

8.7.2 Single Hair Dynamics

In the previous section we discussed how we could think of hair–hair interaction as fluid forces by considering hair volume as a continuum. However, for the reasons explained there, we still need to retain the individual character of a hair strand. The stiffness dynamics of an individual hair is discussed in this section.

In a very straightforward manner, one may model hair as a set of particles connected by tensile, bending and torsional springs (Daldegan et al. 1993; Rosenblum 1991), as shown in Figure 8.24. If the hair strand is approximated by a set of n particles, then the system has $6n$ degrees of freedoms (DOFs) attributed to three translations, two bendings and one twist per particle. Treating each particle as a point mass, we can set up a series of governing differential equations of motion and try integrating them.

Unfortunately this is not a viable solution. Hair is one of the many interesting materials in nature. It has remarkably high elastic modulus of 2–6GPa. Moreover, being very small in diameter, it has very large tensile strength when compared to its bending and torsional rigidity. This proves to be more problematic in terms of the numeric aspect. We are forced to choose very small time steps due to the stiff equations corresponding to the tensile mode of motion, in which we are barely interested. In fact, the hair fiber hardly stretches by its own weight and body forces. It just bends and twists.

Hence, it is better to choose one of the following two possibilities. Constrain the differential motion of the particles that amounts to the stretching using *constrained dynamics* (Baraff 1996). Alternatively, reformulate the problem altogether to remove the DOFs associated with the stretching, namely a *reduced coordinate formulation* (Featherstone 1987). Both methods are equally efficient, being linear time. Parameterizing the system DOFs by an exact number of generalized coordinates may be extremely hard or even impossible for the systems having complex topology. In this case, a constrained method is preferred for its generality and

Figure 8.24 Hair strand as an oriented particle system

modularity in modeling complex dynamical systems. However, for the problem at hand, the reduced coordinate formulation is a better method for the following reasons:

- Reduced coordinates are preferred when in our case the $3n$ DOFs remaining in the system are comparable to the $3n$ DOFs removed by the elastic constraints.
- The system has fixed and simple topology where each object is connected to maximum of two neighbors. We can take advantage of the simplicity and symbolically reduce the most of the computations.
- Reduced coordinate formulation directly facilitates the parametric definition of bending and torsional stiffness dynamics.

Subsequently we model an individual hair strand as a *serial rigid multibody chain*.

8.7.2.1 Hair as serial rigid multibody chain

The first step is to clearly define the serial rigid multibody system that approximates the motion of individual hair strand. We divide the strand into n segments of equal length. The advantages of defining segments of equal length will be made clear, subsequently. The segment length l may vary from strand to strand. The n segments are labeled as $link_1$ to $link_n$. Each link is connected to two adjacent links by a three DOF spherical joint forming a single unbranched open-loop kinematics chain. The joint between $link_{i-1}$ and $link_i$ is labeled $joint_i$. The position where the hair is rooted to scalp is synonymous to $link_0$ and the joint between head and hair strand is $joint_1$.

Further, we introduce n coordinate frames F_i, each attached to the corresponding $link_i$. The coordinate frame F_i moves with the $link_i$. The choice of coordinate system is largely irrelevant to the mathematical formulations, but they do have an important bearing on efficiency of computations, discussed later. Having introduced the link coordinates, we need to be able to transform representations of the entities into and out of the link coordinates. $_iX_{i-1}$ is an adjacent-link coordinate *spatial transformation* which operates on a *spatial vector* represented in coordinate frame F_{i-1} and produces a representation of the same spatial vector in coordinate frame F_i. $_iX_{i-1}$ is composed of a pure translation, which is constant, and a pure orientation which is variable. We use a unit quaternion q_i to describe the orientation. Then, we augment components of n quaternions, one per joint, to form $q \in \Re^{4n}$, the system state vector. Note that, additional n unit quaternion constraints, $i.e. |q_i| = 1$, make system have $3n$ coordinates. Thus system is optimally represented to have $3n$ DOFs. Moreover, the angular velocity across the spherical joint is described by conventional 3×1 angular velocity vector w_i. These form $w \in \Re^{3n}$, the derivative state vector of the system.

The spatial motion of the rigid body, $link_i$ in our case, is fully characterized by its 6×1 *spatial velocity* v_i, 6×1 *spatial acceleration* a_i and 6×6 *spatial inertia tensor* I_i. Figure 8.25 illustrates the definition of a hair strand as a serial multibody rigid chain.

8.7.2.2 Kinematic equations

A 6×3 motion sub-space $\hat{S}$ relates the angular velocity w_i to spatial velocity across the joint, which is the only allowed motion by the spherical joint. Since the position of the link in its own coordinate frame remains fixed, we can express the spatial inertia $\hat{I}_i$ and the motion sub-space S as a constant. Further, by proper choice of coordinate system, $\hat{I}_i$ assumes a

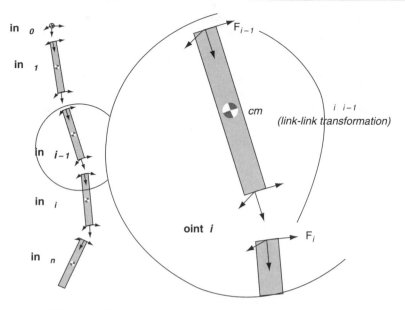

Figure 8.25 Hair strand as rigid multibody serial chain

rather simple form. Subsequently, the velocity and acceleration across the spherical joint are given by the following equations:

$$\hat{v}_i = {_i}\hat{X}_{i-1}\hat{v}_{i-1} + \hat{S}w_i \tag{8.10}$$

$$\hat{a}_i = {_i}\hat{X}_{i-1}\hat{a}_{i-1} + \hat{v}_i\hat{X}\hat{S}w_i + {_i}\hat{S}\dot{w}_i \tag{8.11}$$

$$\hat{S} = \begin{bmatrix} 1 & 0 & 0 \\ 0 & 1 & 0 \\ 0 & 0 & 1 \\ 0 & 0 & 0 \\ 0 & 0 & 0 \\ 0 & 0 & 0 \end{bmatrix}$$

Equations (8.10) and (8.11) enable us to recursively compute the link velocities $\hat{v}_i$ and the link accelerations $\hat{a}_i$, starting from $\hat{v}_0$ and $\hat{a}_0$, given joint angular velocities w_i and joint angular accelerations $\dot{w}_i$. In our case $\hat{v}_0$ and $\hat{a}_0$ are the spatial velocity and the spatial acceleration of hair root, $i.e$ the scalp. We need to successively integrate the derivative vectors of the system $i.e.$ $\dot{w}_i$ and w_i to w_i and q_i respectively. The following equation relates the joint variable rates $\dot{q}_i$ expressed as quaternions to the angular velocities w_i:

$$\begin{bmatrix} \dot{q}_0 \\ \dot{q}_1 \\ \dot{q}_2 \\ \dot{q}_3 \end{bmatrix} = 1/2 \begin{bmatrix} -q_1 & -q_2 & -q_3 \\ q_0 & -q_3 & q_2 \\ q_3 & q_0 & -q_1 \\ -q_2 & q_1 & q_0 \end{bmatrix} \begin{bmatrix} w_1 \\ w_2 \\ w_3 \end{bmatrix} \tag{8.12}$$

$$q_0^2 + q_1^2 + q_2^2 + q_3^2 = 1 \tag{8.13}$$

The next step is to identify various external forces acting on the links, which induce the joint angular accelerations and make hair strand bend and move.

8.7.2.3   Forward dynamics of hair strands

A number of forces act on each link apart from the gravitational influence $\hat{g}$. The explicit definition of the point of action of the spatial force on link is irrelevant as it is embedded in the definition of the spatial force.

- The gravitational influence is accommodated by giving the base a fictitious additional negative gravitational acceleration, *i.e.* by subtracting $\hat{g}$ from $\hat{a}_0$.
- Force $\hat{f}_{ci}$ is the interaction spatial force (aggregate of line force and torque) on $link_i$ coming from the kinematics link with the hair medium as discussed in Section 8.7.1. The actual form of $\hat{f}_{ci}$ is given in Sections 8.7.3 and 8.7.4. This force accounts for all the interaction effects such as hair–hair collision, hair–body collision and hair–air drag.
- In order to account for the bending and torsional rigidity of the hair strand, the $joint_i$ exerts an actuator force $Q_i^a \in \Re^3$ on both $link_{i-1}$ and $link_i$ in opposite directions. The actuator force is not a spatial force but rather a force expressed in joint motion space. The joint actuator force is a function of joint variables q_i incorporating the bending and torsional stiffness constants.

Given the set of forces acting on the system, we now need to calculate the induced joint angular accelerations $\dot{w}_i$. This is a forward dynamics problem involving a rigid multibody system. We use the Articulated Body Method to solve the hair strand forward dynamics. This method has a computational complexity of $O(n)$. The detailed discussion of this algorithm is beyond the scope of this chapter. It is comprehensively covered in (Featherstone 1987; Mirtich 1996).

8.7.3   Fluid Hair Model

Establishing the kinematical link between the individual hair dynamics and the dynamics of interactions is a crucial part of the algorithm, which is done in this section.

The conventional fluid dynamics formulation uses a Eulerian viewpoint. One way to think of the Eulerian method is to think of an observer watching the fluid properties such as density, temperature and pressure change at a certain fixed point in space, as fluid passes through this point. In the numerical simulations, the space is discretized using a rectangular grid or a triangular mesh to define these few observation points for computations. Hence using the Eulerian viewpoint, we will ultimately get fluid forces acting or this fixed set of points. We would like to transfer the fluid force at each of these points onto the individual hair, which is in the vicinity of the point. There is no simple correlation between the grid points and the hair strands, unless they coincide. Also the hair strand will be in the vicinity of new set of grid points every time it moves. This makes it difficult to formulate the kinematical link between the two. There are methods such as the particle-in-cell method, which try to do the same. However, we opted for the other, less popular but effective, Lagrangian formulation of fluid dynamics.

In the Lagrange formulation, the physical properties are expressed as if the observer is moving with the fluid particle. *Smoothed Particle Hydrodynamics* (SPH) (Monaghan 1992) is one of the Lagrangian numerical methods, that utilizes space discretization via a number of discrete points that move with the fluid flow. One of the first applications of SPH in computer animation was done by (Gascuel et al. 1996). For a good overview of SPH, refer to (Morris 1995).

Figure 8.26 illustrates the concept of smoothed particles. The physical properties are expressed at the centre of each of these smoothed particles. Then the physical property at any point in the medium is defined as a weighted sum of the properties of all the particles.

$$A_s(r) = \sum_b A_b \frac{m_b}{\rho_b} W(r - r_b, h) \tag{8.14}$$

The summation interpolant $A_s(r)$ can be thought of as the smoothed version of the original property function $A(r)$. The field quantities at particle b are denoted by a subscript b. The mass associated with particle b is m_b and density at the center of the particle b is ρ_b, and the property itself is A_b. We see that the quantity $\frac{m_b}{\rho_b}$ is the inverse of the number density (*i.e.* the specific volume) and is, in some sense, a volume element.

To exemplify, the smoothed version of density at any point of medium is

$$\rho(r) = \sum_b m_b W(r - r_b, h) \tag{8.15}$$

Similarly, it is possible to obtain an estimate of the gradient of the field; provided W is differentiable, simply by differentiating the summation interpolant:

$$\nabla A_s(r) = \sum_b A_b \frac{m_b}{\rho_b} \nabla W(r - r_b, h) \tag{8.16}$$

The interpolating kernel $W(r - r', h)$ has the following properties:

$$\int W(r - r', h) dr' = 1 \tag{8.17}$$

$$\lim W(r - r', h) = \delta(r - r') \tag{8.18}$$

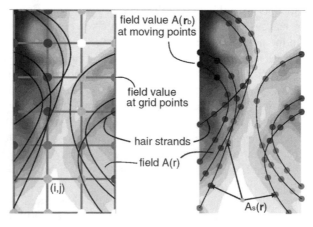

Figure 8.26 Fluid dynamics: Eulerian and Lagrangian viewpoints

The choice of the kernel is not important in theory as long as it satisfies the above kernel properties. For practical purposes we need to choose a kernel, which is simple to evaluate and has compact support. The *smoothing length h* defines the extent of the kernel. We use the cubic spline interpolating kernel.

$$W(r, h) = \frac{\sigma}{h^\nu} \begin{cases} \left(1 - \frac{3}{2}s^2 + \frac{3}{4}s^3\right) & if..0 \leq s \leq 1 \\ \frac{1}{4}(2 - s)^3 & if..1 \leq s \leq 2 \\ 0 & otherwise \end{cases} \tag{8.19}$$

Where $s = |\mathbf{r}|/h$, ν is the number of dimensions and σ is the normalization constant with values $\frac{2}{3}$, $\frac{10}{7\pi}$, or $\frac{1}{\pi}$ in one, two, or three dimensions, respectively. We can see that the kernel has a compact support, i.e. its interactions are exactly zero at distances $|\mathbf{r}| > 2h$. We keep the h constant throughout the simulation to facilitate a speedy search of neighborhood of the particles. The nearest neighbor problem is well known in computer graphics.

There is no underlying grid structure in the SPH method, which makes the scheme suitable for our purpose. We are free to choose the initial positions of the smoothed particles as long as their distribution reflects the local density depicted by Equation (8.15). Eventually the particles will move with the fluid flow. In order to establish the kinematical link between the individual hair dynamics and the dynamics of interactions, we place the smoothed particles directly onto the hair strands as illustrated in Figure 8.26. We keep the number of smoothed particles per hair segment constant, just as we have kept the hair segment length constant, for reasons of computational simplicity. As the smoothed particles are glued to the hair strand, they can no longer move freely with the fluid flow. They just exert forces arising from the fluid dynamics onto the corresponding hair segment and move with the hair segment (in Figure 8.26, the hair strand is not discretized to show the segments). Using this method, we have incorporated both, the elastic dynamics of individual hair and the interaction dynamics into hair dynamics.

Apart from providing the kinematical link, the SPH method has other numerical merits when compared to a grid-based scheme:

- As there is no need for a grid structure, we are not defining a region of interest to which the dynamics must confine to. This is very useful considering the fact that, in animation the character will move a lot and the hair should follow it.
- No memory is wasted in defining field in the region where there is no hair activity, which is not true in the case of grid-based fluid dynamics.
- As the smoothed particles move with the flow carrying the field information, they optimally represent the fluctuations of the field. In the case of grid-based scheme, it is necessary to opt for tedious adaptive grid to achieve similar computational resolution.

In the rest of the section, we discuss the SPH versions of the fluid dynamics equations. Each smoothed particle has a constant mass m_b. The mass is equal to the mass of the respective hair segment divided by the number of smoothed particles on that segment. Each particle carries a variable density ρ_b, variable pressure p_b and has velocity v_b. The velocity v_b is actually the velocity of the point on the hair segment where the particle is located, expressed in the global coordinates r_b is the global position of the particle, i.e. the particle location on the hair segment in the global coordinates. Once initially we place the particles on the hair strands, we compute the particle densities using Equation (8.15). Indeed, the number density of hair at a location reflects the local density, which is consistent with the definition of the density of the hair medium given in Section 8.7.1.

For brevity, introducing notation $W_{ab} = W(r_a - r_b, h)$ and let $\nabla_a W_{ab}$ denote the gradient of W_{ab} with respect to r_a (the coordinates of particle a). Also quantities such as $v_a - v_b$ shall be written as v_{ab}.

The density of each particle can be always found from Equation (8.15), but this equation requires an extra loop over all the particles (which means the heavy processing of nearest neighbor finding) before it can be used in the calculations. A better formula is obtained from the smoothed version of the continuity equation (Equation 8.7):

$$\frac{d\rho_i}{dt} = \sum_{j=1}^{N} m_j v_{ij} W_{ij} \tag{8.20}$$

We now can update the particle density without going through the particles just by integrating the above equation. However, we should correct the densities using Equation (8.15) to avoid the density being drifted.

The smoothed version of the momentum equation, Equation (8.8), without the body forces, is as follows:

$$\frac{dv_i}{dt} = -\sum_{j=1}^{N} m_j \left(\frac{P_j}{\rho_j^2} + \frac{P_i}{\rho_i^2} \prod_{ij} \right) \nabla_i W_{ij} \tag{8.21}$$

The reason for dropping the body force F_{bd} is that, the comprehensive inertial and gravitational effects are already incorporated in the stiffness dynamics of the individual strand. Otherwise, we would be duplicating them.

As the particles are glued to the respective hair segment, they cannot freely achieve the acceleration $\frac{dv_i}{dt}$ given by the momentum equation. Instead we convert the acceleration into force by multiplying it with the mass of the particle m_i. The force gets exerted ultimately onto the hair segment. In the previous section, we referred the total of all the fluid forces due to each particle on the segment as the interaction force $\hat{f}_{ci}$. Although we need to convert the Cartesian form of forces into the spatial forces, this is straightforward.

In Equation (8.21), $\prod_{ij}$ is the viscous pressure, which accounts for the frictional interaction between the hair strands. We are free to design it to suit our purpose, as it is completely artificial viscosity, i.e. it has no relation to the viscous term $\nu \nabla \cdot (\nabla \vec{v})$ in the momentum equation (Equation 8.8). Taking inputs from the artificial viscosity form for SPH proposed by (Morris 1995), we set it to

$$\prod_{ij} = \begin{cases} \dfrac{-c\mu_{ij}}{\bar{\rho}_{ij}} & if \mu_{ij} < 0 \\ 0 & if \mu_{ij} \geq 0 \end{cases}$$

$$\mu_{ij} = h \frac{v_{ij} \cdot r_{ij}}{|r_{ij}|^2 + h^2/100}$$

$$\bar{\rho}_{ij} = (\rho_i + \rho_j)/2 \tag{8.22}$$

The constant c is the speed of sound in the medium. However, in our case, it is just an animation parameter. We are free to set this to an appropriate value that obtains satisfactory visual results. The term incorporates both bulk and shear viscosity.

It is quite straightforward to model solid boundaries, either stationary or in motion, with special boundary particles. The boundary particles do not contribute to the density of the fluid and they are inert to the forces coming from the fluid particles. However, they exert a boundary force onto the neighboring fluid particles. A typical form of boundary force is as given in (Morris 1995). Each boundary particle has an outward pointing unit normal n and exerts a force

$$f_n = f_1(n \cdot \Delta r) P((t) \cdot \Delta r) n$$
$$f_t = K_f(t \cdot \Delta v) t \tag{8.23}$$

Where, n is outward normal at the boundary particle, t is the tangent. Function f_1 is any suitable function, which will repel the flow particle away. P is the Hamming window, which spreads out the effect of the boundary particle to neighboring points in the boundary. That way, we have a continuous boundary defined by discrete set of boundary particles. The coefficient of friction K_f defines the tangential flow slip force f_t.

At each step of the integration, first we obtain the density at each particle ρ_i using Equation (8.20). To correct numerical errors from time to time, we use Equation (8.15). The only unknown quantity so far is the pressure at each particle p_i. Once we know the particle densities ρ_i, the equation of the state (Equation 8.7.1), directly gives the unknown pressures. This is the central theme of the algorithm. Subsequently, we compute the fluid forces acting on each particle using the momentum equation (Equation 8.21). We know now the interaction forces $\hat{f}_{ci}$ for each hair segment and we are ready to integrate the equation of the motion for individual hair strand.

8.7.4 Results

The hair animation system is implemented to incorporate single hair dynamics as well as the continuum hair medium. Efficient implementation of the algorithm enables to simulate about 10,000 hair strands having 30 segments each in less than 2 minutes. We report three animations using the described methodology. They are in increasing order of scene complexity (see Figure 8.27). However, they utilize the same underlying models discussed so far. The simplest of the animations highlight a multitude of the dynamics in minute detail and the more complex ones illustrate the effectiveness of the methodology in animating real-life hair animations.

- In the first animation, from the initial spread, individual hair strands collapse under gravity. Hair strands have their shape memory working against gravity. Otherwise they would have straightened up at frame 24. Also, as the hair strands get close, the pressure builds up due to an increase in the number density in the 'hair fluid', which further retains the volume, throughout the animation, by keeping individual hair apart. The inertial forces and the influence of air are evident in the oscillatory motion of hair. The air drag is most effective towards the tip of hair strands. Observe the differential motion between the tips. Hair strands on the periphery experience more air drag than the interior ones. This is only possible due to the fluid hair mixture model; the movement of hair does set air in motion like a porous obstacle.

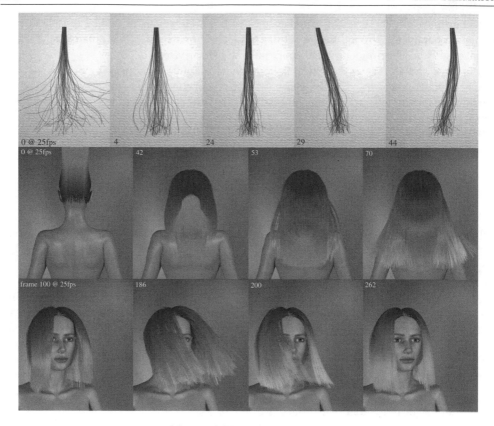

Figure 8.27   Hair animation

- The second animation scenario is to illustrate the 'fluid' motion of hair without losing the character of individual hair. The hair volume starts falling freely under gravity. Quickly, the individual hair's length constraint and stiffness restrict the free falling motion to give it a bounce, towards end of the free fall (frame 53). At the same time, 'hair fluid' collides with the body and bursts away sidewise (frame 70). The air interaction gives an overall damping. Observe that the hair quickly settles down, even after the sudden jerk in the motion, due to air drag and hair friction with the body.
- The third animation exclusively illustrates the effectiveness of the model in animating hair blown by wind. Needless to say that there is an influence of airfield on individual hair. More importantly, body and hair volume acts as a full and partial obstacle to air altering its flow.

8.8   Conclusion

Despite the inherent difficulty, no doubt, the hair simulation research has been encouraging and shown remarkable improvements over the years. People in general are not ready to accept a bald digital actor or an animal without fur. Such realism to computer graphics characters is also becoming more widely available to the animators. Many of the commercial software applications provide suitable solutions and plug-ins for creating hairy and furry characters.

However, the quest for realism increases after noticing what one can already achieve. This demands continued research for better solutions. Hair dynamics, for instance, remains an area, where existing computing resources impose constraints. It is still very hard to imagine real-time hair blowing with full rendering and collisions. Hair dressing and styling also require flexible and convenient modeling paradigms. Fast and effective rendering methods for all types of hair styles, short or long, in all conditions, dry or wet, and modeling the optical properties of hair are still to be explored. So there is still long way to go.

9

Cloth Simulation

Pascal Volino, Frédéric Cordier

Garments are the most visible features that people wear, and take advantage of to express their style. Their motion is a complex combination of the body's motion and subtle animation features resulting from the complex mechanical behavior of the cloth, and needs to be reproduced accurately to achieve high realism levels. Their simulation involves the combination of many technologies which are not only related to mechanical simulation of deformable surfaces to relate accurately the mechanical properties of fabrics, but also to collision detection and response, rendering, and design tools which fashion designers need to express their creativity.

9.1   Introduction

Essential for perceiving the identity – and the beauty – of a human being and its virtual counterpart, garments not only protect the body from the cold and rain, but also construct the social appearance of the being.

They are the most 'customizable' attributes that the human can exhibit in his/her social life. Unlike skin color, eye color and hairstyle, choice can be made from very large variations of garment shape, color and style. This choice is not perfectly random, but is also directed by social conventions and fashion.

Toward the goal of reproducing Virtual Humans in their beauty and also in their social life, the accurate modeling of garments is quite essential. Garments furthermore contribute to the realism of virtual worlds by adding many visual clues related to physically-based animation, which will dim out the inherent imperfections of the modeling of the virtual world.

Garment simulation and animation are at the crossroads of many technologies, which essentially involve physically-based mechanical simulation to adequately reproduce the shape and the motion of the garment on the virtual body, collision detection for modeling the interactions between the garments and the body, and also modeling techniques to enable a designer to construct any complex garment in a simple and intuitive way.

Handbook of Virtual Humans Edited by N. Magnenat-Thalmann and D. Thalmann
© 2004 John Wiley & Sons, Ltd   ISBN: 0-470-02316-3

9.2　Technology Summary

Among the various problematics to be addressed for garment simulation the following points are particularly important.

- *Mechanical modeling of cloth properties*: This aims to turn the mechanical behavior of cloth (how cloth deforms according to constraints and solicitations) into mathematical equations that can be managed by a simulation system.
- *Mechanical simulation of virtual cloth*: This deals with the algorithmic and numerical techniques that are used to turn the mechanical model into an actual simulation and animation of the virtual cloth object.
- *Collision detection and response*: This specifically handles the management of the contact between cloth surfaces and other objects, such as the garments and the body.
- *Garment design tools*: This deals with the techniques used to design complex garments, and their applications in the fields of computer graphics and garment industry.

9.2.1　Historical Review

Garment simulation, which started in the late 1980s with very simple models, has gained tremendous benefits from the progress in computer hardware and tools as well as the development of specific simulation technologies which have nowadays led to impressive applications not only in the field of simulation of virtual worlds, but also as design tools for the garment and fashion industry.

In the field of computer graphics, the first applications for cloth simulation appeared in 1987 (Terzopoulos et al. 1987) in the form of a simulation system relying on the Lagrange equations of motion and elastic surface energy. Solutions were obtained through finite difference schemes on regular grids. This allowed, for example, the accurate simulation of a flag or the draping of a rectangular cloth and could distinguish it from any stiff material such as a metal, or plastic. However, the first applications which really simulated garments started in 1990 with the considerations of many other technologies complementing cloth simulation, such as body modeling and animation, and collision detection and response (Lafleur et al. 1991; Carignan et al. 1992; Yang and Magnenat-Thalmann 1993) (see Figure 9.1).

Since then, many new advances have improved achievements, notably by the use of particle systems which are more adapted to the large deformation of cloth (Breen et al. 1994; Eberhardt et al. 1996), and advanced numerical integration methods (Baraff and Witkin 1998). Collision technologies have also benefited from advances, in terms of collision detection (Volino and Magnenat-Thalmann 1994(a) and (b)) as well as response (Volino and Magnenat-Thalmann 2000). These developments are complemented by rendering techniques for enhancing cloth realism, as well as new garment design interfaces providing fashion designers to release efficient tools with their creativity.

9.2.2　Cloth Mechanics

The mechanical properties of fabric material account for how it reacts to given stimuli, such as imposed deformations, constraints or force patterns. While any number of parameters may be defined for modeling behaviors that may occur in some application or other, a standard

Figure 9.1   Early models of dressed virtual characters. (Carignan et al. 1992.)

set of parameters is usually used to reproduce the most important mechanical characteristics of fabric materials.

9.2.2.1   Fabric materials

The mechanical behavior of fabric is inherent in the nature and molecular structure of the fiber material constituting the cloth, as well as the way these fibers are arranged in the fabric structure. Fabric fibers can be organized in several ways in the cloth surface. The main structures are:

- *woven fabrics*: Threads are orthogonally aligned and interlaced alternately using different patterns (such as plain or twirl).
- *knitted fabrics*: Threads are curled along a given pattern, and the curls are interlaced on successive rows.
- *non-woven fabrics*: There are no threads, and the fibers are arranged in an unstructured way, such as paper fibers.

Woven fabrics are the most commonly used in garments. They are relatively stiff though thin, easy to produce, and may be used in a variety of ways in many kind of design. In contrast, knitted fabrics are loose and very elastic. They are usually employed in woolens or in underwear. This structure greatly influences the mechanical behavior of the fabric material, which is mainly determined by:

- *the nature of the fiber*: wool, cotton, synthetic;
- *the thread structure*: diameter, internal fiber and yarn structure;
- *the thread arrangement*: woven or knitted, and particular pattern variation;
- *the pattern properties*: tight or loose.

These properties are critical to the stiffness of the material, its ability to bend, and its visual appearance (see Figure 9.2).

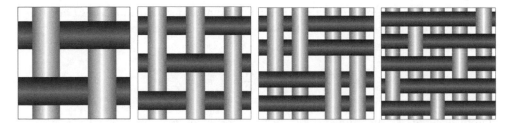

Figure 9.2   Different woven fabric patterns: plain, twirl, basket, satin

9.2.2.2   Mechanical properties of cloth

The mechanical properties of deformable surfaces can be grouped into four main families:

- *Elasticity*, which characterizes the internal forces resulting from a given geometrical deformation.
- *Viscosity*, which includes the internal forces resulting from a given deformation speed.
- *Plasticity*, which describes how the properties evolve according to the deformation history.
- *Resilience*, which defines the limits at which the structure will break.

Most important are the elastic properties that are the main contributor of mechanical effects in the usual contexts where cloth objects are used. Deformations are often small and slow enough to make the effect of viscosity, plasticity and resilience insignificant. One major hypothesis is that *quasi-static models* in the domain of elastic deformations will suffice for models intended to simulate the rest position of the garment on an immobile mannequin (draping). However, when a realistic animation is needed, the parameters relating energy dissipation through the evolution of the deformation are also needed, and complete *dynamic models* including viscosity and plasticity should be used.

Depending on the amplitude of the mechanical phenomena under study, the curves expressing mechanical properties exhibit shapes of varying complexity. If the amplitude is small enough, these shapes may be approximated by straight lines. This *linearity* hypothesis is a common way to simplify the characterization and modeling of mechanical phenomena.

It is common in elasticity theory to consider that the orientation of the material has no effect on its mechanical properties (*isotropy*). This, however, is inappropriate for cloth, as its properties depend considerably on their orientation relative to the fabric thread.

Elastic effects can be divided into several contributions:

- *Metric elasticity*, deformations along the surface plane.
- *Bending elasticity*, deformations orthogonally to the surface plane.

Metric elasticity is the most important and best studied aspect of fabric elasticity. It is usually described in terms of strain-stress relations. For linear elasticity, the main laws relating the strain e to the stress s involve three parameters, which are:

- *the Young modulus E*, summarizing the material's reaction along the deformation direction.
- *the Poisson coefficient ν*, characterizing the material's reaction orthogonal to the deformation direction.
- *the Rigidity modulus G*, pertaining to oblique reactions.

Along the two orthogonal directions i and j, these relations, named *Hook's Law, Poisson Law* and *Simple Shear Law* relating the stress ε to the strain σ are respectively expressed as follows:

$$\varepsilon_{ii} = \frac{1}{E_i}\sigma_{ii} \quad \varepsilon_{jj} = \frac{\nu_{ij}}{E_i}\sigma_{ii} \quad \varepsilon_{ij} = \frac{1}{G_{ij}}\sigma_{ij} \tag{9.1}$$

Cloth materials are two-dimensional surfaces for which two-dimensional variants of the elasticity laws are suitable. They are not isotropic, but the two orthogonal directions defined by the thread orientations can be considered as the main orientations for any deformation properties. In these *orthorombic* cloth surfaces, the two directions are called *warp* and *weft*, and they have specific Young modulus and Poisson coefficients, E_u, ν_u and E_v, ν_v respectively. The elasticity law can be rewritten in terms of these directions as follows:

$$\begin{bmatrix} \sigma_{uu} \\ \sigma_{vv} \\ \sigma_{uv} \end{bmatrix} = \frac{1}{1-\nu_u\nu_v} \begin{bmatrix} E_u & \nu_v E_u & 0 \\ \nu_u E_v & E_v & 0 \\ 0 & 0 & G(1-\nu_u\nu_v) \end{bmatrix} \begin{bmatrix} \varepsilon_{uu} \\ \varepsilon_{vv} \\ \varepsilon_{uv} \end{bmatrix} \tag{9.2}$$

Energetic considerations imply the above matrix to be symmetric, and therefore the products $E_u\nu_v$ and $E_v\nu_u$ are equal. Considering isotropic materials, we also have the following relations:

$$E_u = E_v\nu_u = \nu_v G = \frac{E}{2(1-\nu)} \tag{9.3}$$

A similar formulation can be obtained for bending elasticity. However, the equivalent of the Poisson coefficient for bending is usually taken as null. The relation between the curvature strain τ and stress γ is expressed using the flexion modulus B and the flexion rigidity K (often taken as null) as follows:

$$\begin{bmatrix} \tau_{uu} \\ \tau_{vv} \\ \tau_{uv} \end{bmatrix} = \begin{bmatrix} B_u & 0 & 0 \\ 0 & B_v & 0 \\ 0 & 0 & K \end{bmatrix} \begin{bmatrix} \gamma_{uu} \\ \gamma_{vv} \\ \gamma_{uv} \end{bmatrix} \tag{9.4}$$

While elasticity expresses the relation between the force and the deformation, viscosity expresses the relation between the force and the deformation speed in a very similar manner. To any of the elasticity parameters can be defined a corresponding viscosity parameter obtained by substitution of the stresses ε and γ by their derivatives along time ε' and γ'.

While the described linear laws are valid for small deformations of the cloth, large deformations usually enter the non-linear behavior of cloth, where there is no more proportionality between strain and stress. This is practically observed by observing a 'limit' in the cloth deformation as the forces increases, often preceding rupture (resilience), or remnant deformations observed as the constraints are released (plasticity). A common way to deal with such non-linear models is to assume weft and warp deformation modes as still being independent, and replace each linear parameter E_u, E_v, G, B_v, B_v by non-linear strain-stress behavior curves.

9.2.2.3 Measuring mechanical properties of cloth

The garment industry needs the measurement of major fabric mechanical properties through normalized procedures that guarantee consistent information exchange between the garment industry and the cloth manufacturers. The *Kawabata Evaluation System for Fabric* (KES) is a reference methodology for the experimental observation of the elastic properties of the fabric material. Using five experiments, fifteen curves are obtained, which then allow the determination of twenty-one parameters for the fabric, among them all the linear elastic parameters described above, except for the Poisson coefficient.

Five standard tests are part of KES for determining the mechanical properties of cloth, using normalized measurement equipment. The *tensile test* measures the force/deformation curve of extension for a piece of fabric of normalized size along weft and warp directions and allows the measurement of E_u and E_v along with other parameters assessing non-linearity and hysteresis. The *shearing test* is the same experiment using shear deformations, which allows the measurement of G. The *bending test* measures the curves for bending deformation in a similar way, and allows the measurement of B_u and B_v. Finally, the *compression test* and the *friction test* allow the measurement of parameters related to the compressibility and the friction coefficients.

While the KES measurements allow determination of parameters assessing the non-linearity of the behavior curves and some evaluation of the plasticity, other methodologies, such as the FAST method, use simpler procedures to determine the linear parameters only.

As an example, for a plain wool-polyester fabric of $125 \, g/m^2$ density, experimental tests yield the following approximate values, shown in Table 9.1.

While high variations may be observed between different fabric materials, and particularly for knitted fabrics, these values constitute 'average' values for common fabric types. However, for most common fabric materials, the following ranges are observed as shown in Table 9.2.

While the Kawabata measurements and similar systems summarize the basic mechanical behaviors of fabric material, the visual deformations of cloth, such as buckling and wrinkling, are a complex combination of these parameters with other subtle behaviors that cannot be characterized and measured directly.

Table 9.1 Typical values of elastic mechanical properties of polyester fabric

Young modulus, warp	3600 N/m
Young modulus, weft	3200 N/m
Young modulus, diagonal	1200 N/m
Rigidity modulus	35 N/m
Poisson coefficient, warp	0.16
Poisson coefficient, weft	0.18
Flexion modulus, warp	5.1 μNm
Flexion modulus, weft	4.4 μNm
Flexion modulus, diagonal	3.7 μNm
Flexion rigidity	1.5 μNm

Table 9.2 Some values for common fabrics

Young modulus, warp (E_u)	2000–10000 N/m
Young modulus, weft (E_v)	1000–5000 N/m
Rigidity modulus (**G**)	20–60 N/m
Flexion modulus, warp (B_u)	5–20 μNm
Flexion modulus, weft (B_v)	4–10 μNm

In order to take these effects into account, other tests focus on more complex deformations. Among them, the draping test considers a cloth disk of given diameter draped onto a smaller horizontal disc surface. The edge of the cloth will fall around the support, and produce wrinkling. The wrinkle pattern can be measured (number and depth of the wrinkles) and used as a validation test for simulation models.

Tests have also been devised to measure other complex deformation of fabric material, mostly related to bending, creasing and wrinkling.

9.3 Mechanical Simulation of Cloth

Mechanical simulation intends to reproduce virtual cloth surfaces with given parameters, which are often expressed as strain-stress curves for weft and warp elongation elasticity, shear elasticity, weft and warp bending elasticity. While simple linear models approximate these curves to the linear parameters E_u, E_v, G, B_u, B_v and possibly v, more accurate models would model the curves with non-linear analytic functions such as polynomials on interval-defined functions. Advanced models might also consider plasticity through the modeling of hysteresis in the curves, and viscosity by adding the deformation speeds in the expression of the internal forces of the fabric. Additionally to be considered is the density of the fabric (mass per surface unit).

The cloth also has to react to its environment. These interactions are obviously collisions with the environment objects which account for reaction and friction (most importantly for virtual garments, the body that wears the garment) as well as self-collision between various garment parts. Also comes gravity, which exerts a force proportional to the mass of the object, and thus a constant acceleration that pulls objects toward the floor. Advanced models might also consider aerodynamic forces, which in simple implementations are only viscosity forces related to the speed difference between the cloth and the surrounding air (wind speed), and in complex models result from an advanced computation of the motion of the surrounding air masses that interact with the cloth and other objects.

Whatever modeling is chosen for representing the behavior of the cloth material, additional equations are required to illustrate to fundamental laws of mechanics. Among them, *Newton's Second Law*, which relates the acceleration of objects to the force applied on it divided by its mass, is the most fundamental. Additionally, various *conservation laws* express the conservation of motion momentum within mechanical systems. These laws may be combined in an integral of variational forms in many different ways to obtain formulations that are suitable to the chosen mechanical simulation scheme.

Several different contexts have to be considered for garment simulation. Among them are *draping problems*, where the draping rest shape of a garment has to be computed on an immobile body, and *animation problems*, where the accurate garment animation has to be computed on a moving body. While a draping problem only needs the numerical solver to find the equilibrium of the equations as efficiently as possible using only elasticity laws, an animation problem requires the solver to compute accurately the evolution of the mechanical state along time, and necessitates the simulation of dissipative mechanical behaviors such as viscosity and plasticity. While a *quasi-static* solver which does not consider speed can be sufficient to deal with a draping problem, a *dynamic* solver simulating speed and inertia is necessary for an animation problem.

9.3.1 Mechanical Modeling Schemes

Combining the equations of material behavior with mechanical laws yields complex systems of mathematical equations, usually partial differential equations or other types of differential systems. Mathematics provides analytical solutions only for a limited class of simple equations, which would only solve very elementary situations involving simple models, and which have no interest for usual cloth simulation contexts. For complex cloth simulations, such solutions are not available, and the only practical solution is to implement numerical methods.

The numerical solution of a system of differential equations requires discretization, explicit computation of the physical values at precise points in space and time. *Space discretization* can either be accomplished through numerical solution techniques, such as in models derived from continuum mechanics, or be part of the mechanical model itself, as in particle system models. Usual discretizations consider polygonal meshes which allow convenient representation of the discrete mechanical representation. Mostly used are triangular meshes, regular or irregular, or regular square meshes. It is also possible to use meshes of curved patches (spline, Bézier, subdivision) allowing reduction of the number of elements, or even implicit surfaces although they cannot be explicitly used to represent mechanical entities. *Time discretization* results from the numerical computation of a sequence of states during the time period. Interpolation of the successive states provides an approximation to the entire trajectory. There are several schemes for performing mechanical simulation, differing mainly on where the discretization takes place in the process. The two major families are:

- *Continuum mechanics*, which studies the state of material surfaces and volumes through quantities varying continuously in space and time. Each physical parameter of the material is represented by a scalar or vector value continuously varying with position and time. Mechanical and behavior laws can then be represented as a set of partial differential equations which hold throughout the volume of the material. While the mechanical representation of the object only depends on the model itself, numerical resolution often requires the discretization of the equations in the volume space.
- *Particle systems*, which discretize the material itself as a set of point masses ('particles') that interact with a set of 'forces' which approximately model the behavior of the material.

The difference between these two schemes is that a particle system is a discrete model built on a related discrete surface representation, whereas continuum mechanics defines a continuous model which is then discretized (see Figure 9.3).

Aside from these mechanical simulation techniques, we can also define geometrical simulation techniques which, instead of computing the system position and evolution using mechanical laws, only attempt to reproduce it in a realistic way by imitating the expected phenomena geometrically. While such models are unable to deal with 'unexpected situations'

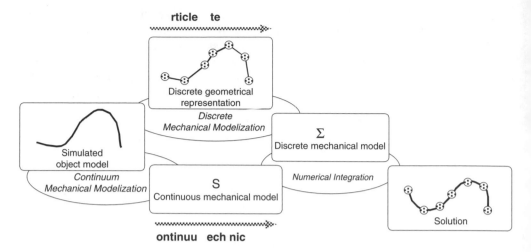

Figure 9.3   A mechanical simulation carried out with particle systems and continuum mechanics

for which the result has not been explicitly foreseen, they can be efficient for limited contexts for which object deformations are deterministic within a well-defined range, using very little computation.

9.3.1.1   Continuum mechanics models

A continuum mechanic model describes the mechanical state of an object using continuous expressions defined on the geometry. For deformable surfaces, such expressions are usually the surface deformation energy related to the local surface deformation (elongation, shearing, curvature), formulated as differential expressions. Mechanical laws are directly derived on them, providing the trains exerted on infinitesimal surface elements.

The main advantage of continuum mechanical techniques is that they provide accurate models of the material derived directly from mechanical laws and models of material properties. They are inherently capable of reproducing the non-linearities of most visco-elastic models, as their formulation as continuous expressions is straightforward. Furthermore, object representation is constant and discretization need only be performed for numerical solution, and can be adapted dynamically. Besides the heavy computing requirements of continuum mechanics techniques, however, they also suffer from several drawbacks which can render them inappropriate for certain applications. For instance, the formal and analytical description they require for the mechanical behavior of the material cannot easily be altered to represent transitory and non-linear events. Hence, phenomena such as frequent collisions or other highly variable geometrical constraints cannot be conveniently taken into account.

While highly adapted to the accurate computation of the dynamics of objects having well-defined mechanical constraints and relatively stable mechanical contexts, continuum mechanical approaches are less promising for the rapid simulation of highly deformable materials involved in numerous collisions, such as cloth simulation

The Lagrange equations are the basis of the most common continuum mechanic models. They were initially used by Terzopoulos et al. (1987) in the field of simulation of deformable surfaces, and are the starting point of many current models. Such models consider the equation of motion of an infinitesimal surface element of the surface, expressed by the variation of internal energy produced by the particle motion. The equation of motion is derived from variational calculus and described in the Lagrange form, while the mechanical behavior of the material is described as the local deformation energy related to the actual material deformation, and expressed locally for any surface point. The first step is to compute the local deformation properties of the surface. Most of the time, the model would allow a separate consideration of elongation and curvature deformations. In that case, the elastic surface energy is represented by two components derived from the elongation and curvature elasticity deformation, namely the metric tensor of the first fundamental form and the curvature tensor of the second fundamental form.

The internal energy is then derived from these expressions. The mechanical behavior of the material is integrated at this point in its mechanical deformation energy expression. In the general case, the curves relating the deformation energy with respect to any kind of elementary deformation have to be expressed.

The resulting expression is then integrated into the Lagrange equation, which is turned into a differential system which has to be solved to obtain the evolution of the deformable surface. Such a system cannot be solved analytically, and has to be processed numerically using surface discretization along the material coordinates. The differential expression of this energy for each grid point finally yields a sparse linear system, that can be solved using a numerical method, such as the Gauss-Seidel method.

Terzopoulos and Fleischer (1988) has extended his model to various applications where deformable objects are simulated using physically based animation. These include cloth simulation, other applications showing simple surfaces with geometrical or collision constraints as well as flag animations and cloth tearing. This model has been used and further developed for garment simulation on virtual actors, using adapted elastic models and collision response, as described in (Lafleur et al. 1991) and (Carignan et al. 1992). This work has shown a real integration of the cloth simulation system into a framework for building and animating garments on virtual actors, including developments on octree-based collision detection (Yang and Magnenat-Thalmann 1993) and pattern-based design techniques (Werner et al. 1993). Different variations include specialized variations for wrinkle propagation in quasi-static models (Aono et al. 1990), inclusion of aerodynamic models (Ling et al. 1996), implementation with constraint-based collision response (Liu et al. 1996).

The formulation of continuum models does not include any hypothesis on the surface description. It is possible to increase performance using advanced surface representations, such as recursive quadtree meshes for which the resolution is dynamically adapted to the expected deformations. Moreover, a continuous scheme is highly suited for surface representations that include surface curvature in an analytical way, such as spline or Bézier patches. The computation of the deformation energy of such patches is highly simplified, as the shape can be expressed analytically by the geometrical parameters of the patch without any form of discretization.

9.3.1.2 Finite element models

Finite elements are a powerful way of integrating continuum mechanics models. Different from the previously described model which discretizes the mechanical equations on a grid representing the surface using finite differences, finite elements compute mechanical energies within a pre-defined discretization.

A discrete element of the surface is basically defined as an interpolation function over a patch (usually a triangle or a quadrangle). This interpolation function has a given order (bilinear, trilinear, quadrilinear), and an associated set of parameters (degrees of freedom) that give the actual shape to the interpolation surface over the element. The higher the order, the more accurately the element would fit the actual surface shape, but also the more degrees of freedom there is to deal with. Beside polynomial functions, other shape functions can also be used.

From the mechanical properties of the material is computed the energy, related to the deformation of the surface for given values of the interpolation parameters. Depending on the kind of mechanical simulation to be performed, these values have to be processed globally on the whole system (for example, energy minimization to compute an equilibrium position).

Surface continuity between the interpolation surface of adjacent elements imposes a constraint relationship on the degrees of freedom of these elements. All these relationships are summarized in a huge and sparse linear system defined on all the degrees of freedom, and completed by additional constraints (boundary conditions) which can, for example, constrain the motion of some edges of the surface. The huge linear system is built by assembling successively the contributions of all the elements of the surface. This operation is eased by using elements defined as regular meshes, for which some mechanical parameters as well as the neighboring relationships are uniform.

To perform the simulation, the huge and sparse linear system has to be solved. This is done using optimized iterative techniques, such as the conjugate gradient method. Several factors influence the performance, such as the matrix conditioning which can be improved by an adequate numbering of the elements that reduces the diagonal band width of the sparse matrix.

Finite elements have only had a marginal role in cloth simulation (Collier et al. 1991; Gan et al. 1991, 1995). The work presented in (Eischen et al. 1996) is restricted to rectangular cloth surfaces of a few hundred elements, for which an accurate non-linear elastic model is built from experimental curves of fabric characteristics obtained from KES experiments. The study focuses on model accuracy by precisely simulating fabric behavior and comparing bending and buckling properties with those inferred from real fabric experiments for a range of values of the mechanical properties. While the accuracy of finite element models, which are techniques of choice for mechanical engineering, is clearly demonstrated by this study, the limitations of this methodology clearly show up for garment simulation applications. The computation time is 'excessive for use in complex 'real-world' garments'(Eischen et al. 1996). Furthermore, accurate modeling of highly variable constraints is difficult to integrate into the formalism of finite elements, and this sharply reduces the ability of the model to cope with the very complicated geometrical contexts which can arise in real-world garment simulation on virtual characters.

9.3.1.3   Particle system models

Rather than consider the mechanical properties of the material volume as a whole, another approach is to discretize the material itself as a set of point masses ('particles') that interact with a set of 'forces' which model approximately the behavior of the material.

Particle systems are used to simulate a wide range of phenomena, ranging from models of crowds, where each particle is an autonomous entity reacting to its environment, to gas or fluid flow, and finally, to deformation of solids, where the particles constitute a discretization of material volume. The latter application is characterized by interaction involving only neighboring particles which are linked together in a relatively fixed topology, while the others do not maintain constant neighbor particle relations (free particles).

Implementing a particle system is the most common way to animate cloth represented by polygonal meshes. The geometrical discretization corresponds to the discretization of the mechanical model. Each vertex of the mesh is a particle, representing a small surface region of the object. The particle interacts mechanically with the neighboring particles in various ways, depending on the kind of mesh and on the elasticity representation chosen.

The usual way to numerically simulate a mechanically based particle system is to directly integrate Newton's Second Law for a mass particle over all the particles, P being the particle position, F the sum of the forces applied to the particle, and M its mass:

$$F(t) = M \frac{d^2 P}{dt^2} \tag{9.5}$$

The forces exerted on each particle depends on the current state of the system, which is represented by the positions and speeds of all the particles. These forces usually represent all mechanical effects on the system, which include internal elasticity and viscosity forces, gravity and aerodynamic effects, and different kinds of other external constraints. However, some particular kinds of geometrical constraints may also be integrated geometrically, by altering directly the position or speed of particles.

Formulating the equation of motion of all the particles of the system leads to a large second-order ordinary differential equation system that has to be integrated using a standard integration method.

Mass-spring systems are the simplest way to design a volume model using a particle system. In this approach, each particle represents a point mass, part of the material discretization, which is linked to its neighbors by a 'spring' representing the elastic behavior of the material. The springs tend to keep the particles at their initial resting positions. Various types of springs are available for representing the usual mechanical parameters. Using regular grids, metric, shearing and bending elasticities can be modeled using elongation springs, as well as flexion springs (see Figure 9.4). While metric elasticity is usually defined by elongation springs along the lattice edges, shearing elasticity can be modeled either by lattice angle springs, or by diagonal elongation springs. In the same way, curvature elasticity may be defined either by flexion springs between opposing edges, or by elongation springs between opposed vertices.

Using elongation springs clearly simplifies the model, as this simple kind of spring element can be easily modeled. This will not, however, be accurate for high deformations. These change edge orientations significantly, and also interfere with 'normal' metric elasticity, a combination that makes precise modeling of strain-stress behavior difficult. Flexion springs can model shearing, and particularly curvature elasticity more accurately. However, this requires more intensive computation, and makes use of surface orientation information that cannot always be precisely computed.

More complex formulations exist, that consider not only mesh edges, but also interactions between all the particles of a full polygon, or even a more extended group of polygons. Such representations are necessary to accurately reflect all the elasticity behaviors of surfaces. Accurate curvature representation usually needs several polygons for an accurate evaluation.

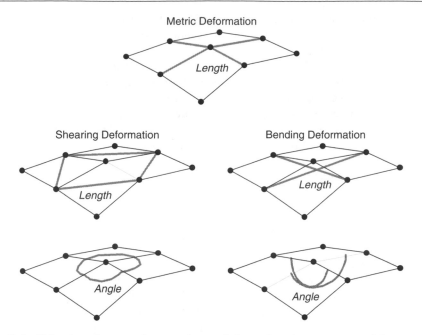

Figure 9.4 Using lengths or angles to measure deformations in a square particle system grid

In the case of irregular meshes, such models are often required, as there are no geometrical symmetries to be exploited. These models are, however, essential if all the mechanical parameters of anisotropic cloth materials have to be simulated accurately.

Among the main contributions on particle system models, early works considered simple visco-elastic models on regular grids, such as (Sakagushi et al. 1991) with applications for draping problems with simple numerical integration schemes. Accurate models started with (Breen et al. 1994) on modeling the microstructure of cloth using parameters derived from KES behavior curves and integration based on energy minimization. Such accurate models, however, required much computation on problems that were restricted to draping. On the other hand, more recent models trade accuracy for speed, such as the grid model detailed in (Provot 1995) which additionally includes geometric constraints for limiting large deformation of cloth. Additional contributions are detailed in (Eberhardt et al. 1996) with the simulation of KES parameters and comparison of the efficiency of several integration methods. Advanced surface representations were used in (DeRose et al. 1998), where the simulation model and collision detection take advantage of the hierarchical structure of subdivision surfaces. Modeling animated garments on virtual characters is the specific aim of the work described in (Volino et al., Volino and Magnenat-Thalmann 1997), which investigate improved mass-spring representations for better accuracy of surface elasticity modeling on irregular meshes. Most recent work, however, focuses on improvements of the numerical integration methods in order to improve efficiency of the simulation.

9.3.2 A Precise Particle-Based Surface Representation

As an example of a precise full surface model, we propose the implementation of a particle system model that offers the same accuracy properties as a first-order finite element model.

We consider the weft and warp orientations as the main referential for the computation of strains and stresses in each triangle of a mesh. For this, we build a local 'fabric' two-dimensional surface coordinate system that is normalized to the equilibrium deformation of the surface: The two unit vectors U and V describing this coordinate system are aligned to the weft and warp directions, which initially are orthogonal, and their length on the fabric at rest deformation is unity. Using the values (Pua, Pva), (Pub, Pvb), (Puc, Pvc) being the (u, v) coordinates of the triangle vertices A, B, C respectively, we compute as pre-processing some values to be used in subsequent computations. First, the determinant D is computed:

$$D = Pua(Pvb - Pvc) - Pub(Pva - Pvc) + Puc(Pva - Pvb) \qquad (9.6)$$

The following co-determinants are also defined, these values actually being the algebraic lengths of the triangle edges opposite to the vertex A, B, C projected along the direction U, V, normalized by D:

$$Rua = D^{-1}(Pvb - Pvc) \qquad\qquad Rva = -D^{-1}(Pub - Puc)$$

$$Rub = -D^{-1}(Pva - Pvc) \qquad\qquad Rvb = D^{-1}(Pua - Puc)$$

$$Ruc = D^{-1}(Pva - Pvb) \qquad\qquad Rvc = -D^{-1}(Pua - pub) \qquad (9.7)$$

At any moment, the deformation state of the triangle is computed for a given geometrical position of the triangle vertices using simple geometry. The starting point for that is the current value of the U and V referential vectors in the deformed triangle, computed from the current position of the triangle vertices A, B, C as follows:

$$U = RuaA + RubB + RucC \qquad V = RvaA + RvbB + RvcC \qquad (9.8)$$

Using the hypothesis that the U and V vectors are orthonormal in the triangle in its undeformed state, in-plane deformation stresses are computed as follows (Figure 9.5):

- Elongation stress along the U (weft) direction: $\varepsilon_{uu} = |U| - 1$.
- Elongation stress along the V (warp) direction: $\varepsilon_{vv} = |V| - 1$.
- Shearing stress between the U and V directions: $\varepsilon_{uv} = (U.V)/(|U|.|V|)$.

In a similar manner, stress deformation speeds to be used in viscosity force evaluations can be computed from the speed of the triangle vertices A', B', C', using the referential vector evolution speeds U' and V' as follows:

$$U' = Rua\ A' + Rub\ B' + Ruc\ C' \qquad V' = Rva\ A' + Rvb\ B' + Rvc\ C' \qquad (9.9)$$

- Along the U (weft) direction: $\varepsilon_{uu}' = (U.U')/|U|$.
- Along the V (warp) direction: $\varepsilon_{vv}' = (V.V')/|V|$.
- Between the U and V directions: $\varepsilon_{uv}' = (U.V' + U'.V)/(|U|.|V|)$.

The mechanical model of the fabric material computes the strains $\gamma_{uu}, \gamma_{vv}, \gamma_{uv}$ from the corresponding stresses (elasticity) and stress evolution speeds (viscosity), using mechanical parameters or behavior curves. Each of these strains contribute to equivalent forces applied

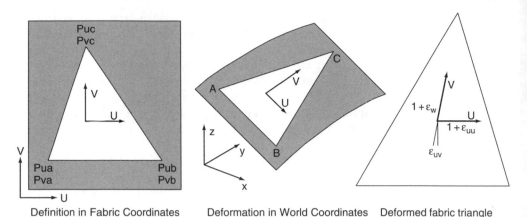

Definition in Fabric Coordinates   Deformation in World Coordinates   Deformed fabric triangle

Figure 9.5 Computing deformations in a fabric triangle

on the triangle vertices, each vertex force being equal to the strain integral applied on the corresponding opposite edge. Calling U^* and V^* the normalized vectors U and V, they are expressed as follows (here written for vertex A):

$$Fa = -0.5D(U^*(\gamma_{uu}Rua + \gamma_{uv}Rva) + V^*(\gamma_{uv}Rua + \gamma_{vv}Rva)) \qquad (9.10)$$

This can also be established by expressing the deformation energy of the triangle and differentiating against displacement of the vertices along weft and warp directions.

Curvature is not directly modeled by this formulation. However, a rotation momentum of value M_u and M_v around the U and V axis can be applied on an element by computing W^* the normalized normal vector $U^\wedge V$ and computing the following vertex forces (here written for vertex A):

$$Fa = (MvRua - MuRva)W^* \qquad (9.11)$$

Curvature effects are then generated by imposing adequate opposite momentums on couples of triangles of the mesh, depending on the curvature measured between them, measured from the angle between their normals and the distance separating them (see Figure 9.6).

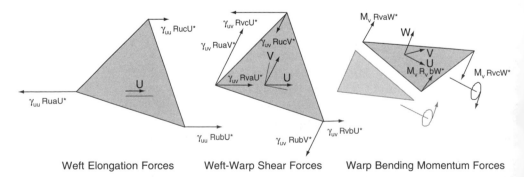

Weft Elongation Forces   Weft-Warp Shear Forces   Warp Bending Momentum Forces

Figure 9.6 Computing vertex forces for elongation, shear, bending

This model is accurate enough to simulate precisely all mechanical parameters measured by standard procedures, such as KES and FAST. It also models the Poisson effect, as well as all viscosity parameters for which no standard measurement procedures are available, and which are, however, essential to accurately reproduce the energy dissipation necessary for the accurate simulation of cloth in motion. Plasticity effects can be integrated ad well, using non-linear behavior laws based on deformation history. Iterating this accurate model has shown to be only around five times slower than iterating the simplest and very inaccurate mass-spring system. An efficient system would allow switching between both models, giving speed for cloth manipulation (garment design and assembly) and accuracy for simulation (draping and animation on the virtual character). Both models also suit efficient implicit integration methods, as detailed in (Volino and Magnenat-Thalmann 2000(b)), as discussed in the next section. It can also be noted that both models can quite simply be extended for modeling 3-D volumes without much additional complications, using tetrahedrons as primitive elements.

9.3.3 Numerical Integration

The mechanical model equations cannot be solved analytically, and the simulation has to be carried out using a numerical process. Implementation of efficient numerical techniques is a key issue in an efficient simulation system.

In some models derived from continuum mechanics, and particularly for optimized techniques, the numerical resolution is embedded in the model, as, for example, with finite element methods. Other methods apply a discretization scheme to convert the analytical system into a set of equations that have to be solved numerically, for example, using finite differences. For particle system models, the system state and evolution are described by the position and evolution of the particles. The discretization of the mechanical laws on the particles usually produces a system of ordinary differential equations that has to be solved numerically along time evolution.

Except for the very simple 'school' problems considering elementary mechanical systems with one or two degrees of freedom and linear mechanical models, it is quite impossible to analytically resolve the differential equation systems describing the evolution of mechanical systems. Numerical resolution approximates the solution by a form of extrapolation from time step to time step, using the derivatives as evolution information. One of the main drawbacks of numerical simulation is the simulation error which accumulates from step to step. Optimized numerical methods can perform the numerical resolution by efficiently minimizing this error and the resulting simulation inaccuracy. This section will focus on the particular techniques that can be directly used with the particle system described in the previous section.

9.3.3.1 Numerical integration of particle systems

For mechanical simulation using particle systems, the problem can usually be reduced to the resolution of second-order ordinary differential equation system where the variables are the particle positions along the evolving time. Let $P(t)$ be the position vector of the entire system at time t, whose size is three times the total number of vertices (we are working with three-dimensional coordinates in the Euclidian space). $P'(t)$ and $P''(t)$, the first and second derivatives with respect to t, are the speed and acceleration vectors, respectively. As detailed earlier, the mechanical model computes $P''(t)$ from $P(t)$ and $P'(t)$ at a given time t. The role of the numerical integration is to compute the state of the system after a given time step dt. The most intuitive method is to perform two successive integrations: Compute $P(t + dt)$ from $P(t)$ and $P'(t)$ and compute $P'(t + dt)$ from $P'(t)$ and $P''(t)$. There are, however, several drawbacks with this. The main problem is the accumulation of error during successive integrations, leading to potential instability artifacts after several time steps.

A better solution is to consider the state of the system as being represented by the position $P(t)$ and the speed $P'(t)$. A vector $Q(t)$ is defined as the concatenation of $P(t)$ and $P'(t)$. The size of this vector is six times the number of vertices. Then $Q'(t)$ is the concatenation of $P'(t)$ and $P''(t)$. The task is now to compute $Q(t + dt)$ from $Q(t)$ and $Q'(t)$. Solving the first-order ordinary differential equation obtained this way is a common problem of numerical analysis, well covered in the literature (Press et al. 1992). Numerous integration techniques exist, of different complexities and having optimal accuracy and efficiency in different contexts.

Explicit numerical integration methods. Explicit integration methods are the simplest methods available to solve first-order ordinary differential systems. They consider the prediction of the future system state directly from the value of the derivatives. The best-known techniques are the Runge-Kutta methods. Among them, the *first-order Euler method*, used in many early implementations, considers the future state as a direct extrapolation from the current state and the derivative. Higher order and more accurate methods also exist, such as the *second-order Midpoint method*, used for instance in (Volino et al. 1995), and the *fourth-order Runge-Kutta method*, used for instance in (Eberhardt et al. 1996).

In typical cloth simulation situations, the fourth-order Runge-Kutta method has proven to be far superior to the second-order Midpoint method, which itself is significantly more efficient than the first-order Euler method. Although computationally more expensive than the Midpoint and Euler methods for each iteration, the larger time step which can be used makes it worthwhile, especially considering the benefits in stability and accuracy. Increasing order, however, does not translate indefinitely into increasing precision. The situation is analogous to polynomial interpolation, where fewer points are needed to interpolate a function with a polynomial of higher order, but only with smooth functions that can be effectively approximated by these polynomials. This is not the case with highly irregular and discontinuous functions, for which such an approximation is not valid. Furthermore, trying to represent a discontinuous function using high-order regular functions may actually lead to catastrophic artifacts near the discontinuities. Simulating these functions using low order, or even linear functions using small time steps greatly increases the robustness and reduces the errors in such situations.

As the time step increases, the inaccuracy for large time steps is degraded by the same order than the one of the method. This imposes a particularly tight control of the suitable time step for high order methods. To take advantage of their performance, an efficient adaptive control algorithm is therefore required to tune the time step in order to remain within optimal values. The evaluation of the computation error is a good way to control the adequacy of the time step which is used for the computation. It is possible to embed within the computation of the solution of the next step the computation of the possible error interval, which provides a way of judging the appropriateness of the time step size.

Derived from the fourth-order method described above, a convenient way of doing this is to use a derivation of the fifth-order Runge-Kutta algorithm detailed in (Press et al. 1992(b)), modified to compute the error for comparison with an embedded fourth-order evaluation. Using six derivation stages instead of four, we gain an order of accuracy as well as the error evaluation. The time step control is then carried out by increasing or decreasing the time step according to the amplitude of the error. The iteration might even be recomputed with a smaller time step if the error exceeds a certain threshold. This algorithm was used in the implementations described in (Volino and Magnenat-Thalmann 1997).

Other families of techniques have different strategies for further reducing the integration error, sometimes at the expense of numerical robustness. Among them, the *Burlish-Stoer method* and its variations based on the Richardson extrapolation, which tries to guess the 'limit value' of the result while the time step decreases to 0, by comparing and extrapolating the evolution of the computed solution as the size of the computation time step changes. While these methods are very efficient for functions that are more or less derived from analytic expressions, they are not very robust for handling discontinuities, such as those encountered with collision models.

Numerical stability and implicit integration methods. Numerical integration, like any other numerical process, is by nature inaccurate. A small and controlled numerical inaccuracy is of no harm to the result, particularly in our case where only the visual aspects are important. However, numerical inaccuracy may produce a more serious side effect: the simulation may become unstable. In such a model, numerical errors accumulate with successive iterations and may diverge, eventually to near-infinite values without any resemblance to physical reality. The model seems to 'explode' and there is no hope of recovery.

We stated above that accuracy could always be obtained at the expense of computation time. The opposite is unfortunately not always true. While many very simple mechanical models have enough realism for them to be integrated in real-time computation systems, the major limiting factor is not further realism degradation, but the numerical instability that is likely to arise.

It is this instability, rather than the numerical inaccuracy itself, which quite often must be controlled in a simulation. The main reason for paying attention to simulation accuracy is not for visual realism, but to prevent the simulation from 'exploding'. While small unrealistic artifacts would often go unnoticed in real-time simulation systems, a numeric explosion due to instability systematically leads to unrecoverable effects.

Given a surface of density D, Young modulus E, bending modulus B and discretized into elements of size l, instability for elongation and bending limit the time step to values roughly proportional to $l(D/E)^{1/2}$ or $l^2(D/B)^{1/2}$ respectively. Given the fact that the total number of elements to process (and therefore the computation time per iteration) is also inversely proportional to l^2, we can see that discretization is indeed a drastic limiting factor of efficiency. In order to circumvent the problem of instability, implicit numerical methods are used. For cloth simulation, this was first outlined in (Baraff and Witkin 1998).

The most basic implementation of the implicit method is the Euler step, which considers finding the future state for which the 'backward' Euler computation would return the initial state. It performs the computation not using the derivative at the current time step, but using the predicted derivative for the next time step. Besides the inverse Euler method, other, more accurate higher-order implicit methods exist, such as the inverse Midpoint method, which remains quite simple but exhibits some instability problems. A simple solution is to interpolate between the equations of the Euler and Midpoint methods, as proposed in (Volino and Magnenat-Thalmann 2000(b)). Higher-order methods, such as the Rosenbrook method, however, do not exhibit convincing efficiencies in the field of cloth simulation. Multistep methods, which perform a single-step iteration using a linear combination of several previous states, are other good candidates for a good accuracy-stability compromise. Among them, the second-order BDF method has shown some interesting performances, as detailed in (Eberhardt et al. 2000; Hauth and Etzmuss 2001) and (Choi and Ko 2002).

Whatever variation is chosen, the major difficulty in using implicit integration methods is that they involve the resolution of a large and sparse linear equation system for each iteration. This being the 'frightening' aspect of implicit integration, various approaches have been proposed to resolve this issue.

One of the problems encountered is that the system matrix varies along time, mostly because of the orientation change of the forces between the particles, and also possibly because of the non-linearities of the mechanical model. In order to optimize the resolution process, one approach is to linearize the problem in order to obtain a matrix which remains constant throughout the simulation, and is constructed once during initialization (Kang and Cho 2000). This allows most of the existing numerical resolution libraries to be used. A constant matrix would also allow its inverse to be computed and each iteration then carried out by a simple matrix-vector multiplication, as proposed in (Desbrun et al. 1999). The major problem is that the inverse of a sparse matrix is usually not sparse, and unless drastic approximations are carried out, the storage difficulty and vector multiplication time severely reduce the interest of this method when the system becomes large.

When system resolution at each iteration is the chosen method, the most suitable resolution scheme seems to be the Conjugate Gradient method, as suggested in (Baraff and Witkin 1998). While most contributions linearize the problem to obtain a constant matrix, in (Volino and Magnenat-Thalmann 2000(b)) is detailed a method that embeds the matrix evaluation in the Conjugate Gradient algorithm itself 'on the fly' for each iteration. As well as removing the need for matrix storage, this furthermore removes the difficulties related to the variation of the matrix as the mechanical system evolves. Using the real matrix rather than a constant approximation significantly enhances the dynamic behavior of the system, as less numerical damping preserves dynamic motion in a better way. This is particularly important in applications intending to reproduce the dynamic motion of cloth accurately. Some 'partial' linearization might, however, bring more stability in highly anisotropic systems which might exhibit significant orientation changes and non-linear effects between each iteration.

Most models using implicit integration schemes restrict themselves to mass-spring systems, as their simple formulation eases the process of defining the linear system to be resolved. However, implicit integration methods can also be used to integrate accurate surface-based particle systems as the one described above, from derivation of the particle force expressions relatively to the particle positions and speeds. This is quite simply integrated into the implicit formulations described in (Volino and Magnenat-Thalmann 2000(b)), and extended toward other advanced methods such as (Hauth and Etzmuss 2001). These formulations actually blur the line between particle systems and finite element methods, as the described particle system is indeed a first-order finite element method where the implicit resolution scheme corresponds to the energy minimization scheme of finite elements and the build of the linear system matrix to the assembly process of elements into the global system to be resolved.

Choosing a suitable integration method.   Obviously, implicit methods have their advantage in most applications for computer graphics, where numerical stability is the main issue. Most particle systems used for cloth simulation are stiff systems, where the important behavior to be reproduced is the global cloth motion, discarding the unwanted high-frequency phenomena related to particle vibration, which are only the result of the discrete structure. While explicit methods need to have time steps adapted to the frequencies of these vibrations to prevent numerical instability, implicit methods can afford to deal with time steps only adapted to the macroscopic behaviors of the cloth. Unfortunately, the computation time required for one implicit step is quite higher than for most explicit methods.

Implicit methods are, however, not a universal panacea that resolves efficiently any kind of simulation. Despite their stability, the solution they propose is not necessarily an accurate solution, particularly when using large time steps. Actually, they only ensure stability by 'guessing' the equilibrium state of the system (through additional computation requiring the knowledge of the state derivatives and system resolution) and converging to this guess when the time step becomes large. Many dynamic effects may disappear in these approximations, leading to disturbing artifacts such as excessive damping as well as 'burned-in' wrinkles that fail to evolve during the simulation. They also may anyway exhibit instability in cases where the equilibrium guess obtained by the first-order derivatives is fooled by the non-linearity of the model (particularly through significant orientation changes between each step).

You get what you pay for, whatever technique you use to perform the simulation. In the case of explicit methods, you have to pay for accurate computation of the motion of every particle. This may take a lot of computational resources, but the result will be very accurate through the use of high-order methods describing the whole evolution completely. This guarantees that a cloth animation will actually behave in the right way in any simulation context. With implicit methods, you find a way to 'cheat' in order to allow higher computation inaccuracy without compromising numerical stability that may arise from the local dynamic properties of your mesh, and pay less for a more approximate result (but possibly less realistic, as you care only for the macroscopic motion and not for all individual particles). While this is suitable for most draping applications where the aim is to converge to equilibrium as quickly as possible, the resulting approximations are likely to prevent the reproduction of complex global dynamic motions of very refined meshes.

In (Volino and Magnenat-Thalmann 2001) is performed a formal comparison of implicit and explicit models in terms of simulation accuracy and computational performance.

9.4   Collision Techniques

Virtual objects are determined only by a formal description in the computer's memory. They do not occupy any 'real' volume in space. Nothing prevents several such objects from occupying the same volume in virtual space. However, if these objects were to represent solid objects simultaneously existing in a common scene, they would be unrealistically interpenetrating. Collision management aims to produce, in the virtual world, what is 'built in' to the real world: objects should interact to prevent geometrical interference. The obvious mechanical interactions that occur during contact of real objects have to be completely remodeled in the computer world.

Collision effects are the consequences of the fact that two objects cannot share the same volume at the same time. When objects touch, interaction forces maintain this volume exclusion. The most important are reaction forces, which oppose geometrical intersection, and then friction forces which prevent objects from sliding against each other. From the point of mechanical simulation, dealing with collisions involves two types of problem:

- *Collision detection*: To find the geometrical contacts between the objects.
- *Collision response*: To integrate the resulting reaction and friction effects in the mechanical simulation.

These two problems are different in nature: The former is essentially geometrical whereas the latter is more relevant to mechanical modeling. The following sections describe how to manage collision detection efficiently, how to translate this information to collision geometry relevant for response on a polygonal mesh, and the approaches used for collision response.

9.4.1 Principles of Collision Detection

Detecting object contacts and proximities is, by itself, not very difficult. Depending on the kind of geometrical objects considered, it is always possible to subdivide them into simple primitives. Appropriate mathematical tools are available to determine the geometrical properties of the collisions.

The major difficulty of collision detection is actually related to the number of geometrical primitives that might be implied in collisions. Collision detection would imply testing if every possible couple of potentially colliding primitives do actually collide. Most of the time, a brute-force exploration of all potential couples would lead to a computation time proportional to the square of the number of elements. Thus the real problem is one of complexity. Given a large number of objects of various configurations, the problem concerns how we can efficiently determine the collisions between them.

Complexity reduction aims to reduce this quadratic behavior to a smaller function, such as logarithmic or linear. This is done in two ways:

- *The use of tests between pertinent primitive groupings* that might eliminate the need to perform tests between individual elements of these groups. This is usually done by taking advantage of some structural and geometrical consistency between the primitives to be tested.
- *The assumption of structural continuity* of some structural or geometrical properties between successive frames in an animation, allowing incremental computation from frame to frame.

The extraction of relevant geometrical structures from the primitive arrangements to be tested and the consideration of their evolution are the basis of all the optimized algorithms for collision detection. Each of them is adapted to different geometrical contexts, most of them relying on geometrical attributes specific to the context in which they are implemented. Nevertheless, they can be classified into groups depending on the general idea which leads to the complexity reduction. The main groups are:

- *Bounding volumes*, where complex objects or object groups are enclosed within simpler volumes that can be easily tested for collisions. No collision with the volume means no collision with the contained objects to be tested. Most known are bounding boxes, which are defined by the min and max coordinates of the contained objects either in world or in local coordinates (Gottschalk et al. 1996), or bounding spheres (Palmer and Erimsdale 1995; Hubbard 1996), defined by their center and their radius. More advanced are Discrete Orientation Polytopes, bounding polyhedrons defined along arbitrary directions (Klosowski et al. 1997). Choice of adequate volume is based on how tightly they enclose the objects, how easily they can be geometrically transformed and combined, and how efficiently collision detection is performed between them.

- *Projection methods*, which evaluate possible collisions by considering projections of the scene along several axes or surfaces separately (Cohen et al. 1995). No collision between two projected objects implies no collision between those objects to be tested.

- *Subdivision methods*, based either on the scene space or on the objects, which decompose the problem into smaller components. They can be space defined, such as voxel methods obtained by subdividing the space with a grid. Objects that do not share a common voxel do not collide. They can also be object regions, usually evaluated through bounding volume techniques. Hierarchical subdivision schemes add efficiency (Held et al. 1995). Space can be defined as octree hierarchies (Fujimura et al. 1983; Yamaguchi et al. 1984), whereas objects can be represented as primitive hierarchies, mostly in the form of bounding volume hierarchies (Webb and Eigante 1992; Volino and Magnenat-Thalmann 1994). Collision detection is propagated down the hierarchy only if the current level presents a collision possibility. Most issues involve efficiently updating the structure as the objects evolve.

- *Proximity methods*, which arrange the scene objects according to their geometrical neighborhood, and detect collisions between these objects based on the neighborhood structure. Such a structure can be based on 3-D Voronoi domains of the space (Mirtich 1998) or use Minkowski representations (Gilbert and Foo 1990). Sorting algorithms can also order objects in conjunction with projection methods. Collision detection is only performed between neighboring objects. Issues are related on how to update efficiently the structure as the objects evolve.

These techniques can be combined in different ways, depending on the various optimizations made possible by the context of the scene. Among possible optimizations, it is possible to take advantage of the consistency of the objects (their size and repartition), and for animations the fact that the scene does not change very much from one frame to another (simple incremental updates made possible by small displacements and constant topologies).

9.4.2 Collision Detection for Cloth Simulation

Most objects used for cloth and garment simulation are complex and deformable geometries described as polygonal meshes. Collision detection aims to detect geometrical contacts between mesh elements (vertices, edges polygons). Most of the time also, the meshes are animated (even the relaxation process taking place for computing static draping problems is a form of animation). The collision detection algorithms has to take advantage of the small incremental displacements of the meshes which mostly keep constant topology (constant neighborhood relations and local geometry between mesh elements) during the process.

While implementations using octree subdivisions have been used for this purpose (Yang and Magnenat-Thalmann 1993), bounding volume hierarchies, however, seem more adapted, as the structure of the hierarchies which should reflect to some extent the neighborhood relations between the mesh elements, can remain constant, and build during pre-processing. Between each frame, only the update of the bounding volumes is required.

Each node of the hierarchy represents a mesh region of the surface, which is in most cases deformable. There is no interest in using transformation-insensitive bounding spheres or object-oriented bounding boxes, but rather axis-oriented volumes that can be recomputed and combined in a very efficient way. While bounding boxes (Volino and Magnenat-Thalmann 1994) represent a good choice, the elongated nature of cloth regions would, however, benefit from volumes that can be elongated into many directions, such as Discrete Orientation Polytopes (Klosowski et al. 1997). Among good compromises between direction orientations and computation requirements is to use directions defined by the faces and vertices of a cube, or defined by the faces of a dodecahedron.

A suitable hierarchy can be built using a recursive process, starting from each mesh polygon as a leaf node of the tree (see Figure 9.7). A grouping process then merges two adjacent nodes into parent nodes using a 'shape quality' criteria to select the best candidates. Typically, this shape quality can be the maximization of the {region area}/{square region perimeter} ratio for obtaining surface regions as rounded as possible. A well-balanced hierarchy tree should have $O(1)$ children per node and $O(\log(n))$ depth.

Collision detection between two surface regions is carried out by testing the collision between the bounding volumes of the nodes representing the regions, and propagating the test to their children, if it is positive. Collision between leaf nodes indicates possible collision between the corresponding mesh polygons. Self-collision detection is carried out by detecting self-collisions within all children nodes, as well as between all possible children couples, with no self-collision within a leaf node. Between each frame of the animation, only the bounding volume geometries have to be updated in the tree to reflect the displacements of the mesh vertices.

The particular case of self-collision detection raises a performance issue, any surface region might potentially be self-colliding because of the adjacent (but not colliding) mesh elements it contains. More practically, as there are no bounding-volume criteria to limit the algorithm from recursing down to all the tree leaves, even if the surface is flat enough not obviously to contain any self-collision at all. This causes a major performance hit for most collision detection algorithms if self-collisions within a cloth object have to be detected (for instance, to prevent self-penetration of garment folds), however marginal they are.

This issue can be resolved by considering that self-collisions only occur within surface regions that are curved enough to exhibit 'loops' between the colliding parts, as presented

Figure 9.7 Automatic hierarchization of a 50000 triangle object. Shown levels: 5 to 10

in (Volino and Magnenat-Thalmann 1994). Such a curvature test would then be added in the self-collision detection algorithm, by only detecting self-collisions within nodes that are curved enough according to this criteria, and also by replacing the bounding-volume test between two adjacent nodes by a curvature test on the whole surface they represent.

The curvature test can be practically implemented by finding the existence of a direction which always 'sees' the same side of the whole surface region, and therefore the dot product to the normal directions of all mesh polygons has a constant sign. This is done by building a 'direction volume' stored in each hierarchy node containing the sign of these normal dot products for a set of sample directions for the leaf nodes. They are then propagated up the hierarchy by a simple merge process that discards each sample direction that has contradictory signs in the nodes to be merged. No directions left means possible self-collisions. This update has to be carried out between each frame of an animation, along with bounding volume recomputation.

Another tricky part of the algorithm is to be able to efficiently identify whether two arbitrary nodes of the hierarchy are adjacent (if there is at least a common vertex in the mesh region they represent). This can be done by storing a particular set of boundary vertices for each node (only those separating two different surface regions among those of the highest hierarchy level that also do not include the region being considered) and finding a searching for a common vertex between the sets of the two nodes to be tested (see Figure 9.8). This set is $O(1)$ size whatever the hierarchy level of the node, and ensures an adjacency detection process of $O(\log(n))$.

This algorithm allows the hierarchical bounding-volume algorithm to recover most of its efficiency, even to detect self-collisions, which is typically the number of collisions multiplied by the logarithm of the total number of polygons. For sparsely self-colliding objects such as garments, the computation overhead to detect self collisions between garment parts remains low compared to the detection of the collisions between the body and the garment (see Figure 9.9).

9.4.3 Collisions on Polygonal Meshes

Once the colliding polygons of the mesh have been extracted, they need to be expressed as geometric information that carries some meaning on how the surfaces are colliding. Usually,

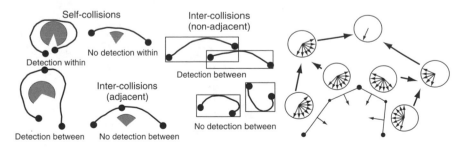

Figure 9.8 Using direction or bounding volumes to detect collisions within and between nodes, and propagation of the direction volumes up the hierarchy tree

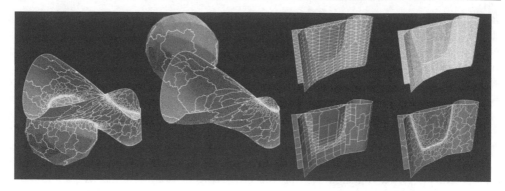

Figure 9.9 Hierarchical collision detection at work, showing the hierarchy domains tested

collisions can be divided into *intersections*, where two surface elements interpenetrate each other, and *proximities*, where two surface elements are separated by a distance below a given threshold, usually representing the 'thickness' of the surface. In the case of collisions between polygonal meshes, we can identify the cases shown in Figure 9.10.

Collision response has to enforce the fact that real surfaces cannot cross each other. It may either handle intersections usually by backtracking the motion leading to the surface crossing and integrating the collision effect, and, in the case of proximities, by maintaining a minimum separation distance between the surfaces. In either case, the collision effect is usually applied on the mesh vertices of the colliding elements, which carries the geometrical information of the mesh.

9.4.4 Collision Response Schemes

Collision response has to reproduce reaction and friction effects through adequate action in the ongoing mechanical simulation. Its integration in the mechanical simulation system

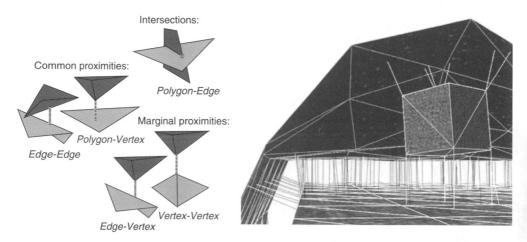

Figure 9.10 Intersections and proximities in polygonal meshes: different examples

changes the mechanical quantities from the value they would have without the collision effects. There are two main ways to handle collision response:

- *mechanical response*, where the collision reaction is simulated by forces or by force adjustments which reproduce the contact effect;
- *geometrical response*, where the collision reaction is simulated by direct corrections on the positions and velocities of the objects.

The mechanical approach is the most formal way of dealing with the problem. The forces or energetic contributions generated by the response can be directly integrated into the mechanical model and simulated. As all the effects are taken into account in the same computation step, the resulting simulation produces an animation where collision response and other mechanical forces add their effects in a compatible way. Reaction is typically modeled by designing a collision penalty force which will make the colliding objects repel each other and prevent them from intersecting. The repulsion force function is usually designed as a continuous function of the collision distance, and as a piecewise function using simple linear or polynomial intervals. Such an approach is, for example, used in (Lafleur et al. 1991). Designing the optimal shape is difficult, because of these compromises which depend on the actual mechanical context of the simulation. The biggest issue is to model in a robust way geometrical contact (a very small collision distance), in which collision response forces only act in a very small range when considered on the macroscopic scale. This implies the use of very strong and rapidly evolving reaction forces, which are difficult to simulate numerically, since a suitable numerical process should discretize the collision contact duration into time steps that are numerous enough for an accurate reproduction of the collision effects and which cause problems with the usual simulation time steps which are normally too large.

The geometrical approach aims to directly reproduce the effects of collision response on the geometrical state of the objects without making use of mechanical forces, and thus uses a process separated from the mechanical simulation. It has been extensively used by Volino et al. (1995) Volino and Magnenat-Thalmann (1997). The advantages are obvious: geometrical constraints are directly enforced by a geometrical algorithm, and the simulation process is freed from high intensity and highly discontinuous forces or other mechanical parameters, making it faster and more efficient. One drawback, however, results from this separation: as collision response changes the geometrical state of the objects separately from the mechanical process, nothing ensures the compatibility of this deformation to a correct variation of the mechanical state that would normally result from it. Furthermore, there is no compatible 'additivity' of geometrical variations such as there is for forces and energy contributions. The resulting collision effects may be incompatible with mechanics, but also between several interacting collisions. All these issues have to be addressed when providing a collision response model that provides acceptable and steady responses between all the frames of an animation.

Collision effects are decomposed into *reaction effects* (normal components), which are the obvious forces preventing the objects penetrating each other, and *friction effects* (tangential components), which model additional forces that oppose the sliding of objects. The most common friction model is the solid Coulombian friction, where friction forces opposing the motion do not exceed reaction forces times a friction coefficient.

9.4.4.1   Collision response for particle systems

Before any collision response can be applied, a precise quantification of the geometrical property of the collision has to be computed from the geometrical data carried out by the mesh vertices, as well as the actual involvement of these vertices with respect to the basic laws of mechanical momentum conservation.

A good collision response scheme has to exhibit continuity properties: a slight change in the state of the colliding elements should only produce a slight change in the collision response. This property is essential when producing high quality animations where the objects do not 'jump' as they slide on each other.

In (Volino and Magnenat-Thalmann 2000(a)) a geometric collision response scheme is described which fulfills these constraints by a precise computation of the collision 'contact points' on the polygonal meshes. These points are expressed as a linear combination of mesh vertex positions, velocities and acceleration. An alteration scheme on these mesh vertex properties is then defined to correct the corresponding properties of the contact points while preserving the mechanical momentum conservation according to the masses of the mesh vertices. Position, velocity and force can thus be corrected independently to satisfy the collision constraints (see Figure 9.11).

It is quite simple to include constrained particles in this scheme, by considering that such particles do not react to external forces by having infinite mass. This scheme can even be generalized to particles constrained to move along particular directions by considering inertia matrices for each constrained mesh vertex, that has null eigenvalues along the constrained directions.

A particular problem arises as some particles of the mesh are involved into several collisions. Any correction performed on one of these vertices by a collision might perturb the geometry of another. This can be addressed partially by handling the correction of each collision successively, each collision being corrected from the state already corrected by the previous collisions. Accuracy can be improved by performing this correction after sorting the collision process order from the largest correction to the smallest, and iterating the correction process several times if necessary. Another approach, detailed by Volino and Magnenat-Thalmann (2000(a)) is to compute the nominal correction to be applied on each collision that would add up in a way to produce the wanted correction for each collision in a global way. This is done by constructing a linear system that is resolved using a

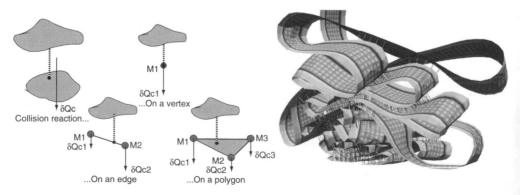

Figure 9.11   Repartition of collision response on the vertices of a mesh element

particular implementation of the Conjugate Gradient algorithm where the system matrix is expressed dynamically 'on the fly' depending on the current collision state. Unknowns might be collision corrections δQc, providing robustness and good efficiency for sparse collisions, or cumulated particle corrections δQi, providing better efficiency for dense collisions and better integration in the mechanical model.

Collision correction models. The collision response model detailed by Volino and Magnenat-Thalmann (2000(a)) enforces collision constraints to be respected through correction of the position, speed and acceleration of the particles:

- The *position correction* alters the position P of the colliding vertices so that the collision distance is maintained at the current frame. Given the wanted collision position $Pc_0(t)$ at the current frame, the correction should be:

$$\delta Pc(t) = Pc_0(t) - Pc(t) \tag{9.12}$$

- The *speed correction* alters the speed P' of the colliding vertices so that the collision distance is obtained at the next frame. Given the desired position $Pc_0(t+dt)$ at next frame, the speed correction should be:

$$\delta Pc'(t) = \frac{Pc_0(t+dt) - Pc(t)}{dt} - Pc'(t) \tag{9.13}$$

- The *acceleration correction* alters the acceleration P'' of the colliding vertices so that the collision distance is obtained two frames thereafter with null distance evolution. Given the wanted position $Pc_0(t+2dt)$ and (usually null) speed $Pc_0'(t+2dt)$ at second next frame, the acceleration correction should be:

$$\delta Pc''(t) = \frac{Pc_0(t+2dt) - Pc(t)}{dt^2} - \frac{0.5 Pc_0'(t+2dt) + 1.5 Pc'(t)}{dt} - Pc''(t) \tag{9.14}$$

Depending on the simulation context, the use of these three successive schemes appears to be the most robust solution, using specific collision distances for each one (see Figure 9.12).

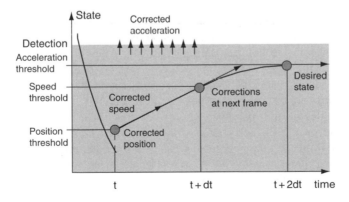

Figure 9.12 Combined corrections of position, speed and acceleration

Practically, position correction is first applied in order to replace the particles in 'reasonable' configurations, speed correction then orients the particle evolution toward a better configuration, and acceleration correction finally ensures a smooth evolution toward the desired configuration. Collision response should in practice rely mostly on the latter, whereas the two others act depending on the collision severity, typically during initial shock.

Collision reaction is simulated by performing these corrections on the normal component of the collision according to the collision orientation. Friction is carried out on the tangential component.

Position and speed corrections do not participate directly in the mechanical behavior, and are processed as a corrective process between each iteration of the mechanical model. Acceleration corrections are, however, somehow part of the mechanical model, as accelerations are only the result of the forces that produces them. It is thus possible to use this equivalence between force and acceleration to give a 'mechanical appearance' to a collision response scheme actually based on geometrical corrections. The major interest of this is to integrate the collision response in the mechanical simulation itself, for better interaction between the mechanical effects and the collision reaction and friction. Volino and Magnenat-Thalmann (2000(b)) detailed a method that takes advantage of this force expression in order to compute force/state derivatives, and by this to take advantage of the benefit of implicit integration to deal with collision effects as well.

Extensive research is still being carried out to enhance the robustness of collision response toward complex situations, by involving coherence checking, collision history and geometrical consistency. Some information can be found in (Bridson et al. 2002).

9.5   Enhancing Garments

The computation requirements of mechanical simulation impose some practical limitations on the size of the cloth meshes that can be simulated in a realistic amount of time. A basic rendering of such rough meshes would not produce visually satisfactory results, mainly because the size of the mesh elements are unable to reproduce smooth curvature and all the tiny wrinkles that appear on moving cloth. The visual results can be improved using post-processing techniques that either improve the geometry through refinement techniques, or even enhance realism through specific rendering techniques.

9.5.1   Mesh Smoothing

One of the most important problems to address is that the polygons, supposed to represent smooth surfaces, become visible if the mesh is too rough. The simplest way to deal with this is to use smooth shading techniques during rendering. Among them, the simple *Gouraud shading* interpolates the light color computed on the vertices over the mesh polygons, while the *Phong shading* interpolates the shading normal direction. More advanced models, such as the *Blinn shading*, are also used in sophisticated rendering systems (see Figure 9.13).

Shading techniques do not, however, change the real shape of the surface, and this is particularly visible on the surface contours, as well as the lack of self-shadowing effects between the folds. Replacing the polygonal mesh by a smoother representation is one way to address this. Among others, one method is to replace the mesh polygons by smooth patches, derived from Bézier or Spline surfaces (Bajaj and Ihm 1992). Another is to build subdivision surfaces using a recursive division scheme of the polygons (Sabin 1986; Halstead et al. 1993; Zorin et al. 1996; DeRose et al. 1998).

Figure 9.13 A rough sphere model with no smoothing, Gouraud, and Phong shading

An efficient approach, detailed in (Volino and Magnenat-Thalmann 1998), proposes a polygon interpolation method that computes a near-smooth surface from any polygonal mesh described by its vertex positions P_i and surface normals N_i. Given any point P on the polygon described by its barycentric coordinates r_i, the method computes a new point Q, that describes a smooth surface all over the polygon. The computation is carried out first by interpolation of the polygon positions and normals:

$$P = \left(\sum_i r_i P_i\right) \qquad N = \left(\sum_i r_i N_i\right)_{Normalized} \qquad (9.15)$$

Each polygon vertex then produces a 'smooth' contribution Q_i to be computed as follows, using an intermediate point K_i:

$$K_i = P + ((P_i - P) \cdot N)N \qquad Q_i = K_i + \frac{(P_i - K_i) \cdot N_i}{2 + ((N \cdot N_i) - 1)}N \qquad (9.16)$$

The contributions are then blended together using the barycentric coordinates and a shape function $f(r)$ that can be chosen as $f(r) = r^2$:

$$Q = \frac{\sum_i f(r_i) Q_i}{\sum_i f(r_i)} \qquad (9.17)$$

The resulting patches are smooth and orthogonal to the vertex normals at each corner of the polygon (see Figure 9.14). If evenly distributed, curvature on an even very rough mesh can model perfectly spherical or cylindrical surface patches. While their curvature is slightly

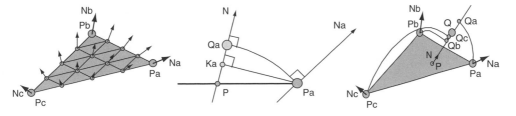

Figure 9.14 Polygon smoothing: interpolation, vertex contribution and blending

discontinuous along the edges, this is mostly not visible for most surfaces to be smoothed. However, Volino and Magnenat-Thalmann (1998) describe a more complicated perfectly continuous version.

An even simpler scheme, described by Vlachos et al. (2001), gives away the perfect sphericity of the patches in a method that does not require any normalizations. This method is particularly suitable for hardware implementations.

9.5.2 Geometrical Wrinkles

Rough meshes are unable to represent curved features that are smaller than the size of the mesh polygons, and therefore unless a garment is represented by several millions of polygons, many wrinkle features would not appear, which can be a severe limitation on the realism of a simulation.

Wrinkles can, however, be rendered on the surface by bump mapping techniques, where the normal used for shading is altered by a pre-defined height map constructed on the surface in a way similar to texture mapping. Another technique is to use surface subdivision to actually deform the surface in accordance to this height map (see Figure 9.15).

Wrinkles do, however, behave dynamically during an animation. They move in accordance to the motion of the fabric, they appear when the fabric becomes loose and disappear when the fabric is stretched. A simple way to produce dynamical wrinkles in to modulate the amplitude of the wrinkle rendering dynamically according to the current stretch of the fabric, computed from the mechanical model on the original mesh (see Figure 9.16). Volino and Magnenat-Thalmann (1999) described a simple and fast method to perform this computation using comparison of the current length of the mesh edges and their initial length. The dynamic nature of wrinkles is furthermore improved by blending several wrinkle patterns, each reacting differently to the current deformation depending on the local orientation of its folds. In (Hadap et al. 1999) is detailed a more accurate wrinkle amplitude computation based on cloth area conservation.

Figure 9.15   Smoothing the rough mesh of a coat, with texture mapping

Figure 9.16 Dynamic amplitude variation of geometrical wrinkles, with respect to elongation and orientation

Dynamic wrinkles can be combined either with geometrical subdivision or with bump mapping, or possibly both of them, the first for large-scale folds and the second for small-scale wrinkles (see Figures 9.16, 9.17).

9.5.3 Advanced Fabric Lighting

For high-quality realistic rendering of cloth, the specific nature of the textile and its particular thread and fiber structure produce particular lighting effects that have to be considered. Different techniques are available, depending on the visualization scale to be considered and the visibility of the corresponding fiber structure.

The structure of fabric materials is not isotropic. For woven textiles, the fibers are usually oriented along orthogonal directions, while for knitted fabrics, they follow a complex but repetitive curved pattern. The global reflectance of all the fibers therefore depends on the light direction and on the position of the observer. Some specific models are detailed in (Poulin and Fournier 1990) and (Ward 1992). For complex models, additional parameters may be taken into account, such as the wavelength of the light and polarization. These parameters are particularly important for physically-based lighting models (Cook and Torrance 1982).

Several approaches have been developed for computing and rendering accurately the lighting of fabrics. In one approach, the whole surface is described as a tiling of the texture cell. Lighting can then be computed using advanced texture and bump map techniques, such as described in (Cabral et al. 1987). Accurate lighting on such structures would take into

Figure 9.17 An animated dress, mechanically computed as a rough mesh, and dynamically wrinkled according to the mesh deformation

account the masking effects between the bump features occurring if the view incidence angle is small, and self-shadowing of the bump features when the light incidence angle is small (Becker and Max 1993). Most of the time it is not necessary to consider the rendering of fiber arrangements, which appear too small to be visible. However, some rendering issues for close-ups are addressed in Chapter 15 on rendering models. Macroscopic lighting models can either be determined experimentally by measuring the reflectance of cloth with various light and camera orientations, or by carrying out the accurate rendering of a sample model of the fiber arrangement. Volume rendering techniques in which fibers are modeled as density functions may also be used when the 'softness' of the fabric material has to be visualized in small-scale views.

9.5.4 Toward Real-Time Garment Animation

While simple computation models are able to simulate in real-time the animation of small fabric samples, simulation of virtual garments on animated virtual characters is a very time-consuming process. The biggest performance issues result from the complex and refined meshes necessary to describe the garment geometry in an accurate way. Mechanical simulation of such meshes requires a lot of computational resources dedicated to the mechanical evaluations of each mesh element, along with the numerical integration of the resulting equations. Collision detection furthermore remains an important performance issue despite the use of sophisticated optimization algorithms, the virtual character itself being represented as a very complex geometrical object.

The still huge performance leap necessary to obtain the real-time simulation of complete garments cannot be obtained by further optimization of classic simulation techniques, despite the recent developments on simple models using particle systems, implicit integration and optimized collision detection. They require more drastic simplifications of the simulation process to be carried out, possibly at the expense of mechanical and geometrical accuracy. Among the possibilities are:

- *Geometrical simplification* of the mechanical description of the garment object, using rendering techniques (texturing, bump mapping, smoothing) to reproduce small details (design features, smooth shapes, folds and wrinkles).
- *Approximations in the collision interactions* between the cloth and the body, for instance, using approximate bounding volumes of force fields.
- *Low-cost simplified geometric models* to animate the cloth object, which approximate the mechanical behavior and motion of the cloth into pre-defined geometric deformations. Problems involve the design of adequate pre-defined motions that would represent the properties of the cloth in the many different mechanical contexts garments could be involved. These motions are usually defined using analytic functions adapted to a particular context, or by automatic processes such as neural networks 'learning' the cloth behavior from actual simulations (Grzezczuk et al. 1998).
- *Hybrid context-sensitive simulation frameworks* which simplify the computation according to the current interaction context of garment regions, possibly mixing together rough mechanical simulation with small-scale specific simulation of features such as wrinkles (Kang and Cho 2002).
- *Integrated body-and-garment simulations* where the cloth is defined directly as a processing of the skin, either as texture and bump mapping (suitable for stretch cloth) or using local deformations reacting to the body motion using simplified mechanics.

All these techniques can be combined for designing a real-time system for garment animation, provided that the body animation system and the rendering pipeline is efficient enough to support these features with adequate frame rate.

9.5.4.1 An example of real-time dressed virtual characters

Cordier and Magnenat-Thalmann (2002(a) and (b)) described a complete system that can display real-time animations of dressed characters. It is based on a hybrid approach where the cloth is segmented into various sections where different algorithms are applied.

- Tight and stretched garment parts are modeled directly with textures and bump maps on the skin surface itself. An offset on the skin mesh possibly models cloth thickness. These garment parts directly follow the motion of the body without any extra impact on the processing time.
- Loose cloth which remains within a certain distance around the body (sleeves, pants) are simulated by mapping the cloth mesh into a simple simplified particle system where the particles are constrained to move freely within a sphere of varying attached to the original skin position. The particles remain independent and only subject to constant gravity forces, which allows the simple computation of a very simple and fast explicit parabolic motion curve for them. This is, however, enough to reproduce some realistic dynamical motion as the body moves. They are constrained to remain inside their respective spheres using a simple geometrical projection on their position and speed. The radius of the sphere is dynamically computed according to the desired cloth looseness and the current angle of the corresponding skin surface relative to gravity minus skin surface acceleration direction, so as to roughly model a catenary curve (see Figure 9.18).
- Loose cloth which is not specifically related to a body part (skirts) are computed using a very simple mass-spring system following the triangle mesh structure integrated with the implicit Euler method, using the techniques described in (Volino and Magnenat-Thalmann 2000(b)). This layer, which requires the implementation of a numerical integration scheme,

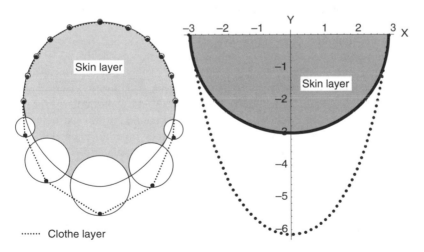

Figure 9.18 Enclosing cloth particles into spheres of dynamic radius resulting from the modeling of a catenary curve

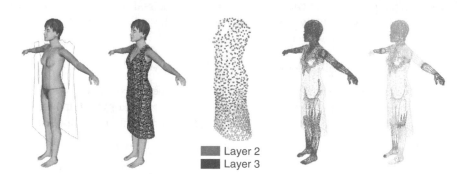

Figure 9.19   Building a real-time garment: designing and assembling a garment with traditional methods, isolating garment regions for simulation contexts, removing invisible skin regions, attaching cloth to the body animation

is the heaviest in terms of computation. Collisions with the body are processed by enclosing body parts into bounding cylinders animated by the body skeleton and applying simple projections of particle position and speed on the cylinder surface in case of contact. This scheme, which cannot model accurately contacts, is, however, robust enough to prevent flying cloth entering the body. Pre-processing determines the potential colliding particles for each cylinder, limiting computation.

Garment appearance is further improved by additional tesselation of the cloth surface using a smooth interpolation technique as described in the previous section.

The specific cloth regions are established during a pre-processing phase, where the garment mesh (typically resulting from a non-real-time garment design software) is mapped onto the body using a specific posture. In the cases where cloth surfaces cover the skin, their vertices are automatically related to the corresponding skin surface animation parameters (usually computed from skeleton animation), and the covered skin regions are discarded from the data structures.

Linked to a real-time body animation system able to compute the skin surface directly from the skeleton animation, this hybrid scheme adds garments to the body with very low performance impact (see Figure 9.19). Of course, such method does not have the versatility available in the standard approach (multilayer garments, reaction to environment, putting garment on and off . . .), and remains quite limited in accuracy, particularly for reproducing real mechanical properties of cloth, and in the allowed complexity of garment features. On the other hand, the animation is very robust (cloth does not jam even with inconsistent body motion), and is visually realistic enough to suit most applications requiring real-time animation of virtual characters.

9.6   Designing Garments

Whatever the simulation technology behind a garment software, no model would be realistic if adequate tools did not allow a fashion designer to build complex garments easily and accurately. Garment simulation is indeed a powerful tool to enable the garment design to be carried out interactively, with rapid feedback on any design choices and actions.

9.6.1 Garment Design Tools

The most intuitive and natural approach for making garments takes its inspiration from the traditional garment industry, where garments are created from two-dimensional patterns and then sewn together. Working with 2-D patterns remains the simplest way of keeping an accurate, precise and measurable description and representation for a cloth surface. In the traditional garment and fashion design approach, garments are usually described as a collection of cloth surfaces, tailored in fabric material, along with the description of how these patterns should be sewn together to obtain the final garment. Many computer tools are already available in the garment industry for this purpose. A powerful virtual garment design system reproduces this approach by providing a framework for designing the patterns accurately with the information necessary for their correct seaming and assembly (see Figure 9.20). Subsequently, these are placed on the 3-D virtual bodies and animated along with the virtual actor's motion.

Examples of virtual garment design tools are described in (Carignan et al. 1992; Werner et al. 1993). With these tools, garments are defined as polygonal pattern shapes carrying information on fabric material and seaming designed with a 2-D interface. Using a 3-D interface, these patterns are given an initial position around the body. The garment assembly is then carried out using adapted forces that pull the seaming lines together using a relaxation process, involving mechanical simulation with collision detection on the body. The resulting draped garment may then be the initial position of an animation which is computed using mechanical simulation, the garment reacting and moving with the animated body (see Figure 9.21 and Figure 9.22).

The designer benefits largely from dedicated design tools adapted to particular pattern design features (particular cuts and seams, creases) which might be edited on the 2-D patterns as well as on the 3-D garment, as well as automated placement and update of the edited patterns around the body. Enhancements of such systems are mostly oriented toward enhanced interactivity (pattern edition tasks are quickly propagated on the garment shape) and automatism (simplified simulation set-up and automated garment size adjustments).

Other approaches for generating garments are based on direct design of the 3-D garment surface, possibly resulting from a matching of the body skin surface. Such surfaces may then be 'unfolded' into garment pattern shapes. Such approach is mostly useful for designing tight garments, such as underwear. An example of such techniques are described in (Aono et al. 1990).

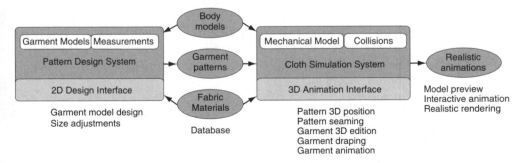

Figure 9.20 A typical framework for garment design, simulation and animation system

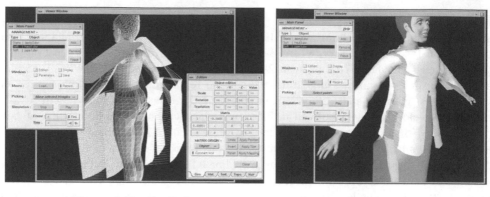

Figure 9.21   Designing garments: pattern placement and seaming

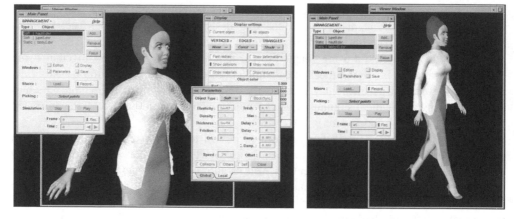

Figure 9.22   Simulating garments: draping and animation

9.6.2 *Applications*

Many applications benefit from virtual garments. The most obvious application is the dress-ing of virtual characters for computer graphics applications. This might for instance be simple garment models animated in real-time for interactive applications such as computer games. The physically-based motion of mechanically animated garments do make a huge contribution to making a virtual scene appear realistic, and this also improves the perception of motion. More complex models may be used to dress virtual characters taking part in the scenario of movie productions. Such garments are quite necessary when dressing an animated virtual actor that should look real.

The other field of interest is the garment industry. The major application is garment prototyping, to enable a fashion designer to visualize a creation without spending time and resources building a test prototype. The visual appearance of the garment can be previewed on an animated mannequin, as well as fitting and comfortability measurements obtained by mechanical evaluation of cloth deformations and body contacts (see Figure 9.23). Such preview features may also be extended to e-commerce applications, by letting a consumer

Figure 9.23 Fashion design: simulating animated fashion models

Figure 9.24 Complex virtual garments

view how he/she will appear wearing a particular garment model, and let him/her customize the model according to his/her measurements and fashion interests.

9.7   Conclusion

While numerous advances have been made to improve the accuracy and efficiency of the simulation techniques used to reproduce the shape and motion of virtual garments, the integration of these techniques into actual applications is just beginning. There are still some needs to be addressed for the simulation techniques themselves, mostly being able to simulate dynamic wrinkling of cloth in a mechanically sound manner and deal with the dynamic mechanical complexity of cloth assemblies used in complex fashion designs (see Figure 9.24). However, another important part of the research is the integration of these technologies into applications that industry would benefit from, as well as letting everybody take advantage of the unlimited creative possibilities available in virtual worlds.

10

Expressive Speech Animation and Facial Communication

Sumedha Kshirsagar, Arjan Egges, Stéphane Garchery

In Chapters 2 and 6, we discussed various techniques for face modeling and facial deformation and schemes used for parameterized facial animation. Designing realistic facial animations remains a challenging task. Several models and tools have been developed to automate the design of facial animations synchronized with speech, emotions and gestures. In this chapter, we take a brief overview of the existing parameterized facial animation systems and how they can be used to design facial animations effectively. We further elaborate on speech animation techniques including lip synchronization, co-articulation and expression blending. The final goal is for realistic facial animation to be used in a facial communication system. Such systems use Virtual Human representations to enhance user interaction. We elaborate on such facial communication systems and discuss the requirements and some proposed solutions.

10.1 Introduction

Virtual Humans have been the focus of computer graphics research for several years now. Believable animation of virtual faces and bodies has interested computer users and challenged animators and researchers alike. Recently, very believable virtual characters have been seen in 3-D animation movies. However, such production demands many days or even months of manual design work from highly skilled animators. On the other hand, computer users increasingly demand to be able to interact with such characters on the Internet and in games. Such real-time interactive character animation cannot be pre-defined with the accuracy and the artistic precision evident in the computer-generated movies. Thus, the interest in the Virtual Human research is very broad, ranging from pre-defined scenarios to interaction in real-time. Correspondingly, the range of applications of animated Virtual Humans varies from movies to Internet to interactive games.

Handbook of Virtual Humans Edited by N. Magnenat-Thalmann and D. Thalmann
© 2004 John Wiley & Sons, Ltd   ISBN: 0-470-02316-3

The scope of this chapter is the facial communication of autonomous Virtual Humans in real-time interactive applications. By facial communication, we refer to the interaction by means of speech, facial expressions, head movement and eye gaze in real-time. We need to strike the balance between precision, speed of design and speed of animation. We review the vast field of facial communication and previous work done on specific topics. We explain in detail the speech animation techniques, elaborating on lip synchronization, co-articulation and expression blending. We focus on various effects in facial animation in order to enhance realism. Further, we discuss different schemes devised for easy design of facial animation. Finally, we discuss new challenges in facial communication using autonomous dialogue systems.

10.2   Background and Review

Facial communication encapsulates a plethora of techniques of facial and speech animation, analysis and synthesis of expressions, emotions and non-verbal signals, dialogue and interaction. The face is the most observed and well-known landmark in the human figure, and thus it is probably the most challenging aspect to simulate in graphics, without any loss of realism. At the same time, it forms the most basic and necessary part of any Virtual Human animation system. No wonder the field of computer facial animation is vast and well explored. There are many dimensions, directions and levels in this field. As a result of years of research, various techniques have been developed and accepted as standard practice and a certain terminology has been established. We take a look now at the background, expectations, and the avenues of research.

The field of facial communication has evolved over the years, starting with facial modeling and animation pioneered as early as 1972 by Parke. Subsequently, facial communication has grown and diversified, absorbing inputs from the areas as diverse as computer vision, speech processing, linguistics, natural language processing and psychology. Figure 10.1 takes a broad look at different stages of developments and techniques that constitute the area of facial communication. The figure also depicts how diverse and multidisciplinary is the field of facial communication. The left column shows various disciplines of computer science providing inputs to different tasks in facial communication. The right column shows the most prominent published work in that field. We have enumerated only the work that is pioneering and significant in the corresponding area. A more detailed consideration of the published literature is given subsequently.

As we concentrate on various aspects of simulating Virtual Humans in a facial communication application, this study is naturally divided into facial parameterization and deformation (detailed in Chapter 6), expression and animation design, speech animation, facial expressions and non-verbal signals, response generation and emotion and personality modeling. Where necessary, each section is divided into two parts, the first explains the background and related concepts in brief, whereas the second lists the previous work done in that area.

10.3   Facial Animation Design

The basic part of any facial communication system, of course, is the facial animation front-end. Here we begin by presenting the fundamental ideas of facial animation design. A complete facial animation design system typically incorporates the following steps

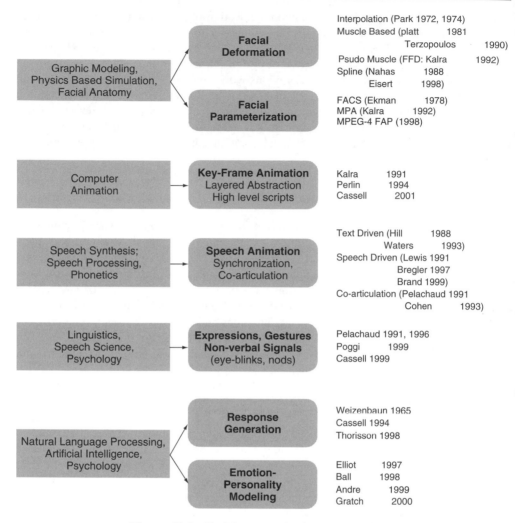

Figure 10.1 Facial communication: a broad look

demonstrated in Figure 10.2. These steps are very similar to the layered abstraction in facial animation described by Kalra et al. (1991).

1. Define a desired face model geometry: male/female, realistic/cartoon, etc.
2. Define an animation structure on the facial model by parameterization.
3. Define 'building blocks' or basic units of the animation in terms of these parameters, e.g. static expressions and visemes (visual counterparts of phonemes).
4. Use these building blocks as key-frames and define various interpolation and blending functions on the parameters to generate words and sentences from visemes and emotions from expressions.
5. Generate the mesh animation from the interpolated or blended key-frames.

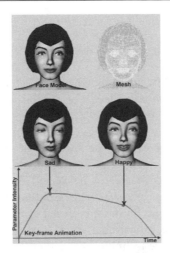

Figure 10.2   Hierarchy of facial animation design

Of these, step 1 corresponds to facial modeling and has been covered in Chapter 2. Step 2 has been explained in Chapter 6. We begin with a closer look at parameterization, in step 2 and subsequently cover the other steps in this chapter.

10.4   Parameterization

A detailed analysis and comparison of various facial animation systems and parameterization schemes have been already given in Chapter 6. Here, we briefly review the parameterization schemes in the perspective of high level design of facial animation, rather than as an interface for facial deformation. Of course, the facial deformation techniques depend on the underlying parameterization scheme to a great extent. Not all the deformation techniques can be used with all parameterization schemes and vice versa.

We consider two levels of parameterizations for a facial animation design system, as depicted in Figure 10.3. At a low level, parameterization should take into account the finest control over the facial mesh and realistic deformations. This parameter set is usually dependent on the face model as well as the technique used for mesh deformation. On a

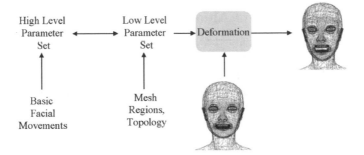

Figure 10.3   Levels of parameterization

higher level, the parameter set should provide an easy-to-use powerful control over facial movements. These parameters should account for possible global and local facial movements, their interdependence, and fast and versatile design considering visemes and expressions as basic units of animation. Further, it should provide a wide range of natural and intuitive expression control, having subtlety and orthogonality as additional requirements. There can be a possible overlap between these two levels of parameter sets and definitely they should be interconvertible. For example, on a higher level 'open mouth' parameter should affect all the low-level parameters affecting various movements of lips (upper lips, lower lips, corner lips, etc.), jaw and cheek. Though each of the low-level movements is a combined effect of several muscle actions and hence control parameters, a single high-level parameter ('open mouth' in this case) is highly desirable for quick and intuitive definition. A conversion between such high- and low-level parameters can be defined by empirical mapping based on the observation of facial movements during speech and expressions. Alternatively, it can also be derived from a systematic statistical analysis of low- and high-level facial movements extracted by using motion capture techniques. In either case, it is important to extract the redundancy in highly correlated facial movements and optimally represent the movements in order to design, reproduce and edit facial expressions and visemes. The structure of facial muscles is naturally a starting point for devising a parameterization scheme. Understanding muscle actions not only provides a natural basis to design facial deformation algorithms, but is also useful for evaluating the facial animation systems for realism. Various facial parameterization schemes such as FACS, MPA, and MPEG-4 FAPs have already been described in Chapter 6. More details of the MPEG-4 FAPs can be found in Chapter 16. Any of the parameterization schemes can be used for designing visemes, facial expressions and for building animation, with the help of interactive tools. The choice has often been driven by availability. For the animators, the parameter set should fulfill all the requirements of a high-level parameter set, as explained in the previous paragraph. Given such a parameter set, it is up to the creativity of an animator to define various visemes and facial expressions. Six expressions (joy, sadness, anger, fear, disgust, surprise) have been recognized as universal by emotion researchers (Ekman 1982). A very good study of facial expressions from the researchers' and artists' point of view is given by Faigin (1990). This chapter presents a detailed explanation of facial bone and muscle structure and an in-depth analysis of various expressions and their relations to the facial muscles, with historical references to the study on emotion and expression by the research community.

10.5   High Level Control of Animation

In this section we focus on steps 4 and 5 of the animation design sequence enumerated at the beginning of the previous section. They involve time positioning of the key-frames and transition from one key-frame to the next in a manner that creates a realistic animation. For a rich quality facial animation, a variety of blending and interpolation functions have been considered. These are important especially for speech animation and expression blending, taking into account the effects of co-articulation and realistic transitions from one expression to the other. These blending functions have varied from simple triangular functions for phonemes and attack-sustain-decay-release type of envelopes for expressions to user-defined non-linear interpolation functions. However, these functions have always been designed by

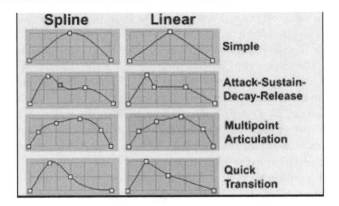

Figure 10.4 Various envelopes for key-frame animation

the rules based on observation and intuition. Figure 10.4 demonstrates various typical time envelopes used for facial animation design.

The key-frame-based animation has been often used for non-real-time animation applications. For more interactive and real-time applications, techniques need to be developed for high-level facial animation control. Such techniques often employ scripting languages defining facial (and body) animation. The scripts can be generated on-the-fly by an animator (IMPROV, Perlin and Goldberg 1996), from text (BEAT, Cassell et al. 2001) or by an intelligent agent controlling the Virtual Human (such as Avatar Markup Language, Kshirsagar et al. 2002), (Virtual Human Markup Language (http://www.vhml.org) or Affective Presentation Markup Language, Carolis et al. 2002). By use of a high-level scripting language, a user can define a complete animation scenario not by key-frames, but by text, expressions and actions as the basic building blocks. Such a high-level description of the animation enables the re-use of smaller animation units leading to variety and richness in the animation. It also facilitates interfacing animation systems with intelligent agents. Here we explain

The animation language called the Facial Animation Markup Language. FAML is a part of AML, based on XML syntax, and uses pre-defined expressions to build up the animation. It has the potential to create a rich variety of animations because of the options it offers to combine pre-defined animations.

We use MPEG-4 FAP as low-level parameters for animation. However, any animation parameters can be used, as the FAML is independent of the underlying animation method used. A FAP database contains a variety of pre-defined facial expressions. The <Settings> tag contains the information such as the frame-rate, length of animation, and the local path of the FAP database as well as pre-defined speech animations, if any. A number of tracks can be defined in the FAML. Each track can be given a name, e.g. emotions, head movements, eye movements, etc. This separation enables distinct control over various parts of the face. There may be as many <ExpressionsTrack> elements as required. Further, there may be as many <Expression> elements as required in each <ExpressionsTrack>. The expressions may or may not be overlapping. Each <Expression> has a start time, a name, and a time envelope defined. The name, in fact, refers to the static expression file from the FAP database. Each time envelope is defined by as many <Point> elements as required. The shape defines the interpolation from the previous point to the current one, and can take the value of logarithmic, exponential or linear. The first default point is with zero intensity at the start time. The intensity is normalized and the duration is specified in seconds. The <SpeechTrack> is reserved for the viseme or FAP files corresponding to a pre-defined speech animation. The viseme file contains timing information for each of the viseme and the FAP file contains frame-by-frame information of the low-level facial animation parameters for the speech animation. The speech track also specifies the audio file for the pre-recorded speech by the <AudioFile> tag. It should be noted that the inclusion of the speech track enables the use of pre-defined or pre-recorded speech animations. Unlike the expression track, the speech track cannot be overlapping. The syntax of FAML is shown in Figure 10.5. Figure 10.6 shows a typical expression track.

Thus, the FAML easily defines an animation and software can be developed that generates low-level animations from the high-level definition. Figure 10.7 shows a snapshot of the GUI developed where an animator can define various tracks, key-frames and speech animations to generate and test facial animations quickly.

The complexity of the key-frame-based facial animation system increases when we incorporate effects such as co-articulation for speech animation and blending between a variety of facial expressions during speech. The next section addresses the issues related specifically to speech animation.

```
<FAML>
<Settings>
        <Fps>FramesPerSecond</Fps>
        <Duration>mm:ss:mmm</Duration>
        <FAPDBPath>"path of folder containing high level expression
(.ex) files"</FAPDBPath>
        <SpeechPath>"path of folder containing speech animation (.vis)
files"</SpeechPath>
</Settings>
<ExpressionsFiles>
        <File>"name of expression file (.ex) from the path defined
above"</File>
</ExpressionsFiles>
<ExpressionsTrack name = "Name of track">
<Expression>
        <StartTime>mm:ss:mmm</StartTime>
        <ExpressionName>"name"</ExpressionName>
        <Envelope>
                <Point>
                    <Shape>{log or exp or linear} </Shape>
                    <Duration>InSeconds</Duration>
```

Figure 10.5 FAML syntax

```
<ExpressionsTrack name = "Emotions">
<Expression>
        <StartTime>00:00:800</StartTime>
        <ExpressionName>smile.ex</ExpressionName>
        <Envelope>
                <Point>
                <Shape>log</Shape><Duration>0.5<Duration><Intensity>1
        <Intensity>
                </Point>
                <Point>
                <Shape>log</Shape><Duration>0.5<Duration><Intensity>0
        .7<Intensity>
                </Point>
                <Point>
                <Shape>exp</Shape><Duration>0.8<Duration><Intensity>0
        <Intensity>
                </Point>
        </Envelope>
</Expression>
</ExpressionsTrack>
```

Figure 10.6 Example of expression track

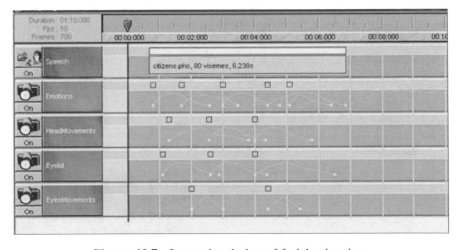

Figure 10.7 Interactive design of facial animation

10.6   Speech Animation

Speech animation is the process of animating a synthetic face, synchronized with a natural–language sentence generated either by computer (synthetic speech) or recorded from a real person speaking using a microphone. The advances in speech synthesis technologies are resulting in better quality computer-generated voices. Nevertheless, using natural voice for the animation of synthetic faces remains an interesting as well as challenging area of research in computer animation. For example, if we have to represent a person by his avatar in a Virtual Environment, it becomes necessary to drive the speech animation by the real voice of the person, rather than the synthetic voice. Whether using computer-generated speech or real speech, some of the issues addressed by the facial animation systems are the same. Figure 10.8 shows the typical steps involved in any speech animation system. Given speech or text as input, phonemes are extracted with timing information. A pre-defined database of facial animation parameters is used to map these phonemes to visemes (visual counter-parts of phonemes) and subsequently to the appropriate mouth shapes. A process of co-articulation is necessary to obtain smooth and realistic animation. The resulting animation parameters with appropriate timing information are rendered on the 3-D face model in synchronization with the audio.

10.6.1   Using Text-to-Speech

The first speech synthesizer was developed as long as ago 1939. Since then, the advances made in this field have resulted into various text-to-speech (TTS) systems being

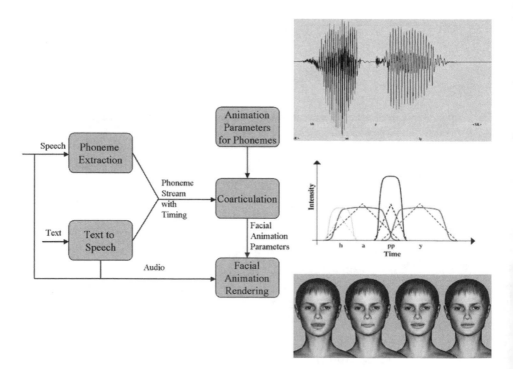

Figure 10.8   Typical speech animation system

available commercially (Microsoft, IBM, Dragon, Elan Informatique, AT&T etc.) or through research initiatives (e.g. Festival at University of Edinburgh http://www.cstr.ed.ac.uk/ projects/festival/)). In order to integrate a TTS system in a talking head, it is necessary to extract audio corresponding to text and corresponding phonemes with associated timing information. The phonemes are the smallest units of speech, broadly classified as the vowels and consonants. There are 46 such phonemes in English. A viseme is defined as the visual counter-part of phoneme and can be understood as the smallest unit of speech animation. Several phonemes can correspond to the same viseme. For example, phonemes /b/ and /p/ (classified as plosives) correspond to the same mouth movements and hence are classified under the same viseme. Refer to (Rabiner and Schafer 1978) for a detailed explanation of the phoneme classification. The phonemes obtained from the TTS system are mapped on to the corresponding visemes or mouth shapes and animation is rendered on the synthetic face in synchronization with the audio.

One of the early text-driven visual speech synthesis systems was reported by Hill et al. (1988). This provided automatic generation of speech animation from typed text. Several talking heads have been developed since then, each integrating different TTS systems and different face animation models (Beskow 1995; DECface, Waters and Levergood 1995; Grandstrom 1999). Talking heads have been developed in several languages including French (Goff and Benoit 1996), Italian (Pelachaud et al. 2001), Finnish (Olives et al. 1999), Turkish, Chinese (Perng et al. 1998). Korean, and to name a few. The quality of the voice and the face model and animation determine the quality of the resulting talking head system. But one more important aspect is the realism, which is governed by effects such as co-articulation and expression blending. We study these effects later in this section.

10.6.2 Phoneme Extraction from Natural Speech

The use of a TTS software to drive animated talking heads allows the use of the phoneme timing information generated by the TTS. On the contrary, additional processing is required to extract phoneme timing information from natural voice for a speech-driven talking head. Indeed, generation of timing information from natural speech is a challenging task. The extraction of visually relevant parameters from auditory information is the main research issue. It is necessary to extract parameters from the speech signal, which are directly or indirectly related to the mouth/lip movements. The parameters extracted from speech signal are pitch, energy, Fourier Transform (FT) coefficients, Linear Predictive Coding (LPC) coefficients, Mel-frequency Cepstral (MFC) coefficients, etc. For a detailed explanation of standard speech processing techniques, we recommend the classical book by Rabiner and Schafer (1978). The parameters required for facial animation are usually FACS, MPEG-4 FAPs, or simply positions of certain feature points or system-specific parameters such as face states. The goal of the speech-driven talking head system is to develop the techniques to map audio-derived parameters to the facial animation parameters. Such techniques should ideally work in real-time, independent of language and speaker. The majority of such techniques reported use a video camera or optical tracking sensors to record the face of the speaker while speech data is collected. The Neural Network (NN) and/or Hidden Markov Models (HMM) are trained using both the processed audio and processed visual data. The processed auditory data may or may not be mapped to intermediate parameters such as phonemes, words or sentences Yamamoto et al. (1998) used mel-cepstral coefficients as audio-derived parameters. They modeled HMMs for phonemes and mapped the HMM states directly onto the lip parameters (height, width, protrusion) from the training data. Tamura et al. (1998) took a similar approach but used dynamic parameters and concatenated syllable HMMs to construct sentence HMMs. The video rewrite technique proposed by Bregler et al. (1997) utilized the HMM to automatically label tri-phones in the recorded audio visual database. Mouth images for new audio are obtained by matching the pre-labeled tri-phones from the trained database. Brand (1999) developed a Voice Puppetry system for generating facial animation from expressive information in an audio track. An entropy minimization algorithm was used to train the HMM. The complete system integrates various sophisticated techniques in image processing, computer vision and speech analysis. McAllister et al. (1997) used mouth shape descriptors called moments computed from the FT coefficients of the speech signal. Predictor surfaces were computed from the moments and the mouth shape parameters such as lip protrusion, lip width and lip opening height recorded on training sequences of vowels. These predictor surfaces are then used to extract the mouth shape parameters from speech. The last two approaches mentioned above did not use explicit representation of data into phonemes or visemes.

It is possible to develop phoneme extraction techniques based on acoustic data analysis alone (see Figure 10.9). Use of neural networks have also been tried by many researchers in order to recognize the phonemes from speech. Massaro et al. (1999) used cepstral parameters

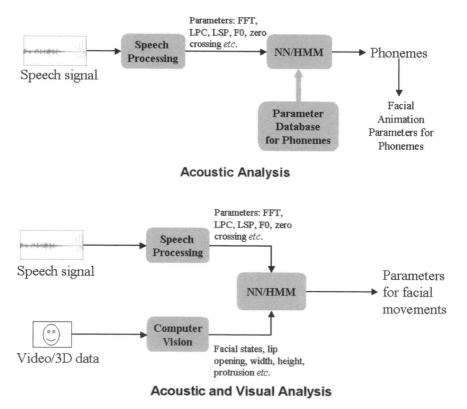

Figure 10.9 Two approaches to speech-driven facial animation

for speech to train a multilayer perceptron (a neural network) using a database of monosyllabic words. The training dataset was phoneme-labeled and the facial animation parameters for a proprietary model were directly mapped from the phonemes, thus avoiding use of any visual data. Curinga et al. (1996) used a similar approach, but also used video data to extract lip shape parameters (e.g. distance between lip corners, distance between chin and nose). Thus, the speech parameters were not intermediately converted into phonemes. Morishima (1998) described a real-time voice-driven talking head and its application to entertainment. He used LPC-derived cepstral coefficients to extract mouth shape parameters using neural networks.

The systems using mouth shape parameters need extra processing of the data in order to animate any generic head model, whereas the techniques using phoneme representation in the extraction process are easier to adopt to any facial animation system. Further, results from such systems also influence the facial animation resulting in an animation resembling the style of the speaker whose data was used for training, as reported by Brand (1999). HMMs may result into more accurate recognition of phonemes or facial features subject to the amount and nature of training data. However, they are normally slow in training as well as real-time process. Also, such approaches are data-intensive, require a lot of effort to implement a complete system and are usually less adaptable to any animation system. The reproducibility and repeatability of such techniques are also not proven. On the other hand, NN-based techniques are faster for real-time implementation. Though they are also data-intensive and the training phase may take longer, the results are reproducible. Also, NN-based techniques are often easy to implement and plug into any big animation system. We believe, for a system to work independent of speaker, it is advisable to focus on reorganizing groups of phonemes, rather than accuracy.

Figure 10.10 shows the real-time phoneme extraction system developed by Kshirsagar and Magnenat-Thalmann (2000). Input speech is sampled at 10 kHz with a frame size of 20 ms. Pre-processing includes pre-emphasis and Hamming windowing of the signal. Currently, no filtering is done for noise reduction. Twelve reflection coefficients are calculated as a result

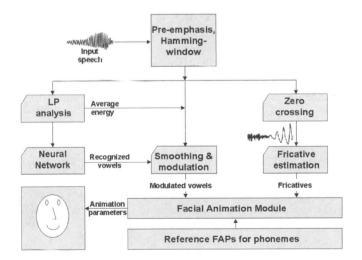

Figure 10.10 Real time phoneme extraction for speech animation

of LP analysis. These are the parameters that are directly related to the mouth shape during utterance of a vowel. Each parameter represents the cross-sectional area of the mouth cavity from throat to lips, at 12 equally spaced points along the length of the mouth cavity. The coefficients are obtained from sustained vowel data recorded from 12 male and 5 female speakers. This data is used to train the neural network. As a result of the training, the neural network can predict the presence of one of the five vowels (/a/, /e/, /i/, /o/, /u/) given a speech frame as input. These five vowels are chosen since we notice that the vowels in many languages can be roughly classified into these basic sounds or their combinations/variations. We use median filtering to smooth the resulting recognized vowels. The average energy of the signal is calculated as the zeroth auto-correlation coefficient over the frame and is used to decide the intensity of the detected vowel. The average energy is approximately related to the opening of the mouth. Zero crossings are calculated to decide the presence of the unvoiced fricatives and affricates (/sh/, /ch/, /zh/ etc.). Finally, the Facial Animation Module generates the FAPs depending upon the phoneme input. Any 3-D parameterized facial model can be used here. The speech animation is then easy using the pre-defined parameters for these extracted phonemes.

10.6.3   Co-articulation

In order to obtain realism in speech animation, it is important to have continuity from one viseme to the other in rendering. If the facial animation parameters corresponding to the visemes in the speech are applied to the synthetic face simply one after the other, a jittery animation would result. It is thus necessary to obtain a smooth transition between the animation parameters. Use of triangular envelopes as shown in Figure 10.4 can be one simple solution. However, this alone is not sufficient for realism. It is necessary to incorporate the effects of co-articulation.

Co-articulation is a phenomenon observed during fluent speech, in which facial movements corresponding to one phonetic or visemic segments are influenced by those corresponding to the neighboring segments. In the process of articulating a word or a sentence our brain and mouth do some on the fly 'pre-processing' in order to generate a fluent and continuous speech. Among these complex processings is the combination of lip/jaw movements to compose basic sounds or phonemes of the sentence. For instance, when we pronounce the word 'hello', even before saying the 'h', the mouth is taking the shape of the 'e' that is coming afterwards. During the pronunciation of the 'll' the mouth is also making the transition between the 'e' and the 'o'. Thus, the rendering timings for the visemes can be different than those obtained directly from phoneme extraction or Text-to-Speech. It is possible that two or more visemes are required to be rendered at the same time, with varying intensities.

In order to compute such co-articulation effects, two main approaches were taken by Pelachaud (1991) and Cohen et al. (1993). Both these approaches are based on the classification of phoneme groups and their observed interaction during speech pronunciation. Pelachaud arranged the phoneme groups according to the deformability and context dependence in order to decide the influence of the visemes on each other. Muscle contraction and relaxation times were also considered and the Facial Action Units were controlled accordingly. Cohen et al. defined non-linear dominance functions based on the work of Lofqvist (1990) (Figure 10.11). These dominance functions have to be defined for the facial

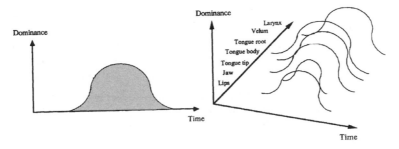

Figure 10.11 Dominance functions for co-articulation. (Reproduced from (Lofqvist 1990.) with permission of A.Lofqvist)

control parameters for each viseme. Subsequently, a weighted sum is obtained for the control parameter trajectories of co-articulated speech animation. The details of the co-articulation algorithm in this case also depend on the parameterization used by the particular facial animation system.

10.6.4 Expression Blending

Another factor affecting realism in speech animation is the addition of facial expressions during speech. This blending between expressions and visemes becomes serious when several such expressions affect a single facial animation parameter. We use MPEG-4 Facial Animation Parameter (FAP) here, but the discussion applies to other animation parameters as well. As shown in Figure 10.12, discontinuity can happen at the activation or at the termination of each expression or viseme when combined with another one. If we take the two FAP frame sequence of Figure 10.12(a) and compute the average of each frame, one can see that at the beginning of action two and at the end of action one we have a large discontinuity, as shown in Figure 10.12(b). The simple solution is to add to each expression

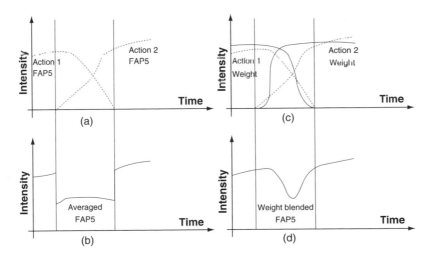

Figure 10.12 FAP composition problem and solution

or viseme a weighting curve (Fig. 10.12(c)), which minimizes the contribution of each high-level action at its activation and at its termination (Fig. 10.12(d)). The weighting curve values are generally set between 0 and 1. Another problem comes when it is necessary to control excessive deformation caused by a particular parameter. For example, consider blending between smile and phoneme /i/ (as in 'sleep'). Addition of the FAPs corresponding to smile and /i/ may result into excessive stretching of lips and thus unrealistic facial animation.

A simple way to handle this is to define the limits to each of the FAPs. Later in this chapter we describe a method to handle all these issues using the expression and viseme space. This space has been obtained by the statistical analysis of facial movements captured from a real person speaking and thus is effective in taking into account the physical restrictions posed by facial movements.

10.6.5 Enhancing Realism

Enhancing the realism of speech animation requires obtaining appropriate facial expressions associated with the meaning of the response, as well as mood or emotion. Humans do not have their eyes and head stationary while talking. We emphasize words with nods, eyebrow movements, and blink from time to time. The non-verbal signals such as eye gaze, head nods and blinks add to the believability and have to be coordinated with the content of the speech. Cassell and Thorisson (1999) reported that users prefer interacting with an agent showing non-verbal behaviors than a stationary agent. Pelachaud (1991) has made a detailed analysis of these additional facial movements and has emphasized that these factors affect realism in a talking head to a great extent. She demonstrated this by building several rules governing facial movements linked to speech. It is necessary to link these facial movements to the semantics (the meaning), of the speech. The facial movements are synchronized with information content, emotion and emphasis of the speech. Blinking is controlled at the phoneme level whereas the nodding and eyebrow movement are controlled at word level, mostly derived from intonation patterns. Recently, Poggi et al. (2000) have presented a methodology to synchronize verbal and non-verbal signals, considering different types of information conveyed during the conversation and the role played mainly by eye gaze during presenting such information.

As characterized by Ekman (1982), the following groups of facial expressions are effective during speech animation:

1. *Emblems*: These correspond to the movements whose meaning is well known but culturally dependent. They tend to replace verbal expressions, e.g. head nod to express 'yes'.
2. *Emotion emblems*: These convey signals about emotion, not necessarily felt by the speaker at the same time. For example, when we talk about a cheerful person, we smile as we talk.
3. *Conversational signals*: They are used to punctuate or emphasize the speech. For example, an accented vowel is accompanied by raising one's eyebrows.
4. *Punctuators*: Movement occurring at pauses, blinks are good examples of these.
5. *Regulators*: Movements that help the interaction between the speaker and listener, for example, slight raising of eyebrows when expecting an answer or comment.
6. *Manipulators*: These correspond to the biological needs of the face, like wetting lips and blinking from time to time to keep eyes wet.
7. *Affect display*: Finally, these are the expressions actually used to display the emotions felt.

Any complete facial animation system should take into account these facial movements in order to enhance realism. However, it is necessary to integrate certain language analysis techniques in order to extract the necessary information leading to the appropriate inclusion of the corresponding facial movements.

10.7 Facial Motion Capture and Analysis

The use of facial motion capture to animate the face was explained in Chapter 2. Contrary to the previously described key-frame approach, in such methods the movements of the facial feature points are captured for every frame. The animation parameters derived from this captured data are retargeted to various facial models to obtain animation for every frame. It is, however, not always practical to apply such motion capture data for a performance-driven facial animation, because it is often restricted by the availability of the performer and complexity of the equipment involved, which often needs tedious calibration and set-up. However, it is also very interesting to use such motion capture data for facial movements analysis leading to increasing realism in animated faces. We can study and analyze the facial movements as captured by a real performer and apply the result of the analysis to real-time animation. We believe that the statistical analysis of the actual speech data helps to improve the realism and robustness of the speech animation techniques already discussed. We consider the Principal Component Analysis (PCA) to be a powerful tool for achieving this goal. The results have been previously published by Kshirsagar et al. (2001) and are elaborated in this section.

10.7.1 Data Analysis

We use the same set-up to acquire speech animation data, as explained in Chapter 2. We use a commercially available optical tracking system (VICON 8) to capture the facial movements. For the capture, we used 6 cameras and 27 markers corresponding to the MPEG-4 feature point locations, as shown in Figure 10.13. We obtain the 3-D trajectories for each of the marker points as the output of the tracking system. As we focus on speech animation, 9 out of the 27 markers shown in the figure, only 8 markers along the outer lip border, 2 markers

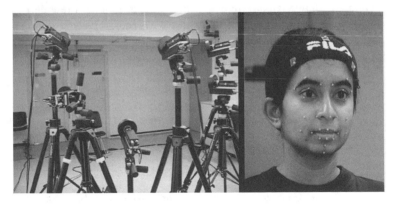

Figure 10.13 Placement of cameras and facial markers

on the chin, and 4 markers on the cheeks are used for the statistical analysis. The speaker is made to speak 100 randomly selected sentences from the TIMIT database (http: TIMIT) of phoneme-rich sentences fluently.

For each of the recordings, movements of all the 14 markers were extracted after removing the global head movements. Thus, for each of the 14 selected markers, 3-D positions are obtained for each frame. As a result, we have a vector of 42 components for every frame (3 coordinates for each of the 14 selected markers for a frame). Thus, each vector in 3-D space is represented as:

$$d = (x_1, y_1, z_1, x_2, y_2, z_2, \ldots x_n, y_n, z_n)^T \in \Re^{3n}, n = 14 \qquad (10.1)$$

It can easily be observed that the data is highly interdependent, because of the very nature of the facial movements. For example, the displacements of the points around the lip area are highly correlated to each other, and to the jaw movements, as they cannot be physically moved independent of each other. The lower lip movements are directly linked to the global jaw movements. In addition, there can be local movement of the lips independent of the jaw movement. Similarly, movement of the corner lips as in lip puckering and lip sucking directly affects the movement of the cheeks. However, just observing the captured data in the form of 3-D position trajectories does not throw much light on how these movements are inter-related. This inter-relation is the key factor for realistic animation and we employ PCA to extract this relation that occurs due to natural constraints.

10.7.2 Principal Component Analysis

PCA is a well-known multivariate statistical analysis technique aimed at reducing the dimensionality of a data set, which consists of a large number of inter-related variables, while retaining as much as possible of the variation present in the data set. This is achieved by transforming the existing data set into a new set of variables called the principal components (PC). These are uncorrelated and are ordered so that the first few PCs retain most of the variation present in all of the original data set. We explain the basic concepts behind the PCA here for completeness. This description is based on (Jollife 1986).

Let x be a vector of p random variables under consideration. In order to study the correlations between the p random variables, it is not simple to observe the data as it is, unless p is very small. Hence, an alternative approach is to look at a few derived variables, which preserve most of the information about these variations. The first step is to look for a linear function $\alpha_1' x$ of the elements of x which has maximum variance, where α_1 is a vector of p constants; $\alpha_{11}, \alpha_{12}, \ldots, \alpha_{1p}$, and $'$ denotes transpose, so that

$$\alpha_1' x = \alpha_{11} x_1 + \alpha_{12} x_2 + \ldots \alpha_{1p} x_p = \sum_{j=1}^{p} \alpha_{1j} x_j \qquad (10.2)$$

Next, look for a linear function $\alpha_2' x$, uncorrelated with $\alpha_1' x$, which has maximum variance, and so on. Thus at the kth stage, a linear function $\alpha_k' x$ is found which has maximum variance subject to being uncorrelated with $\alpha_1' x, \alpha_2' x, \ldots, \alpha_k' x$. The kth derived variable, $\alpha_k' x$ is the kth principal component (PC). Like this, up to p PCs can be found, but it is hoped that the number of PCs found is much less than p.

To find the PCs, let us consider that the random variables x has a known covariance matrix, C. This is the matrix whose (i, j)th element is the covariance between the ith and

jth elements of x when $i \neq j$, and the variance of the jth element of x when $i = j$. It turns out that, for $k = 1, 2, \ldots, p$, the kth PC is given by $z_k = \alpha_k' x$ where α_k is an eigenvector of C corresponding to its kth largest eigenvalue λ_k. Furthermore, if α_k is chosen to have unit length ($\alpha_k \alpha_k' = 1$), then $var(z_k) = \lambda_k$, where $var(z_k)$ denotes the variance of z_k. Thus, from the point of view of the implementation, finding the PCs is finding the eigenvectors of the covariance matrix C. For the derivation of this result, the reader is referred to (Jollife 1986).

We use the entire set of motion trajectory data of the 3-D positions of the selected markers as an input to the PCA analysis. Thus, each input vector is 42 dimensional. As a result of the PCA on all the frames of the captured data, the matrix T, whose columns are the eigenvectors corresponding to the non-zero eigenvalues of the above mentioned covariance matrix C, forms the transformation matrix between the 3-D vector space and the transformed *expression and viseme space*. Thus, each 42-dimensional vector d can be mapped onto a unique vector e in this space.

$$e = Td \tag{10.3}$$

The inverse transformation is appropriately given by:

$$d = T^T_e \tag{10.4}$$

where T^T denotes the transpose of the matrix T. Each distinct viseme and expression is represented as a point in this transformed multidimensional space. The very nature of the dynamic speech input data ensures that the transitions between these points in the newly formulated *expression and viseme space* correspond to the real-life like transitions of the markers in 3-D position space. We exploit this for smooth and realistic speech animation. The next subsection explains what these 'abstract' principal components represent in real life.

10.7.3 Contribution of Principal Components

Once we obtain the principal components, we can easily establish their role in generating facial animation. Nearly 99% of the variation has been accommodated in only the first 8 principal components. This is computed as follows. Each eigenvector of the covariance matrix represents variation in one principal direction of the newly formed space. Thus, the total variation is represented by all the eigenvectors put together. Given this, a percentage variation attributed to each eigenvector λ_i (or each principal component in turn) is calculated as

$$\frac{\lambda_i}{\sum_{j=0}^{N} \lambda_j} \times 100 \tag{10.5}$$

where N is the number of eigenvalues. Table 10.1 lists the eigenvalues and their percentage variation. Note that the absolute value of the eigenvalue is not of much significance here.

The lower order components do not contribute much to the deliberate facial movements. Thus, we represent each viseme and expressions by an 8-dimensional vector, each component indicating a weight for the corresponding PC. In general, the principal components may or may not represent any real-life parameters. We notice, however, that, for the facial capture

Table 10.1 Eigenvalues and percentage contribution

Eigenvalue	Percentage variation
210.02	72.34
50.50	17.40
13.11	4.52
5.86	2.02
3.00	1.03
1.87	0.64
1.49	0.51
1.03	0.36

data, they are closely related to facial movements. For this, we allow only one principal component to vary at a time keeping others at the default neutral position. Then we apply an inverse transformation to obtain the 3-D position of the markers. From these 3-D positions, the MPEG-4 FAPs are extracted. Figure 10.14 shows the influence of the first 6 principal components. The first column shows the profile view, the central column show the effect of the PC in one direction (decreasing from neutral) and the third column shows the effect of the same PC in the opposite direction (increasing from neutral).

The PC actions are described below:

1. PC1 Open Mouth: This component results into the global movement of the opening of the jaw, slight rotation of the jaw forcing the lips to part. This is by far the most common facial movement necessary for many phonemes pronunciations.
2. PC2 Pucker Lips: This movement causes the lips to form a rounded shape, necessary for the pronunciation of vowels such as /o/ and /u/. This also causes the protrusion of the lips.
3. PC3 Part Lips: Causes separation between the lips, without opening the jaw. In the other direction, this causes pressing of lips against each other. Notice the peculiar shape of lips caused by pressing, without penetrating. This movement is more local to the lips and does not affect the cheek region much.
4. PC4 Raise Cornerlips: This movement causes the vertical movement of the corner of the lips, causing a smiling action causing the lips to part slightly. In the other direction, it causes depressing of the corner lips, as in a sad expression.
5. PC5 Raise Upperlip: This movement is typically observed in a disgust expression. Notice the change in the nose shape because of change in the upper lip (exaggerated here) that is also observed in real life. PC5 combined with open mouth (PC1) and part lips (PC3) can give rise to a variety of mouth shapes.
6. PC6 Protrude Lowerlip: This is a peculiar movement, sometimes observed in an expression 'who knows!'. This causes curling of the lower lip and slight raising of chin.

PC7 appears to be a combination of PC5 and PC6, without any movement of chin. This, though it could be useful for facial expression design, in our opinion, cannot be controlled independently. The subsequent components appear to be a slight combination of the first components, and in fact cause less and less visible movement for a given percentage deviation from neutral position. We observe that there is no single component causing the movement

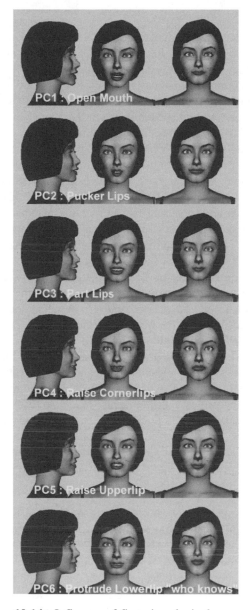

Figure 10.14   Influence of first six principal components

of lower lip alone. However, such a movement can easily be obtained by combining PC3 (to part the lips without jaw movement), PC5 (to lower the upper lip) and finally PC6 (slightly curling and lowering the lower lip). Thus, the principal components can be used to define a new parameter space for facial animation and a more intuitive interface for the designers of the facial animation. These parameters will be directly linked to the correlated facial movements.

10.7.4   Nature of Analysis Data and the PCs

The expression and viseme space formed by the PCA reflects the data it is operated on. This can be clearly visualized by taking an example of the data that contains only the opening of the jaw movement. If PCA is applied on this data, the only significant principal component obtained would be the opening of the jaw. On the other hand, any movements not present in the original data cannot be represented by a combination of the PCs obtained by the analysis on that data. Normal conversational speech does not include asymmetric movements, hence the space formed by such data cannot reproduce asymmetric movements. This is true in our case, as we have used only symmetric visemes and expressions. Any asymmetry required for naturalness of especially the facial expressions has to be added using lower level MPEG-4 parameters. Thus, wherever necessary, we use an expression to be a combination of the principal components and low level MPEG-4 parameters. This is also true in the case of the eye region of the face, that does not have any PCs in our analysis.

In order to study the subjectivity of the principal components, we collected two more data sets on a different subject. In one case, we used fluent speech, whereas in the other case, we used a set of syllable units. A syllable is a basic unit of speech that can be spoken independently and is the next bigger unit than a phoneme. Thus, each syllable contains at least one vowel and one or more consonants. For example, in the case of word 'phoneme', there are six phonemes (/f/, /o/, /n/, /i/, /m/ and /a/). Whereas the syllable content is only three, /f-o/, /n-i/ and /m-a/. We used the most complete possible set of syllables based on the phonetic studies (Roach 1983). Theoretically, thus, since this set includes all possible syllable units, the corresponding visual data should approximately include the majority of the viseme combinations and facial movements possible during speech in English. We performed the data capture and analysis in a similar manner as before. We obtained very similar results in terms of contribution of the principal components. The main difference was the ordering of the principal components. Mainly, PC1 and PC2 are exchanged in one case and PC3 and PC4 are exchanged in the other. This change can be attributed to the style of the speaker and is not significant as far as using the PCs for further animation design is concerned.

10.7.5   Expression Blending Using PCs

We addressed the problem of expression blending in Section 10.6.4. In this section, we describe how the results of the principal component analysis can be used for expression blending.

From the analysis of the expressive speech capture data, we observe that suppressing or enhancing certain components results into a good effect of mixing facial expressions with speech. When a particular expression needs to be blended with speech animation, the suppression or enhancement corresponds to adding an expression vector with the viseme vector resulting into an expressive viseme in the expression and viseme space. The result is transformed back to the 3-D position space to calculate the FAPs. The addition in the expression and viseme space appropriately scales all the parameters in the 3-D position space in a more natural way than the scaling of individual facial animation parameters.

Thus, we create the effect of the 'expressive viseme'. It is easier to add expressions to speech using the principal components, as we need to find out only the principal components affecting a particular expression, and enhance that component in the expression and viseme space, as against adjusting many FAPs in the 3-D space. Figure 10.15 and Figure 10.16

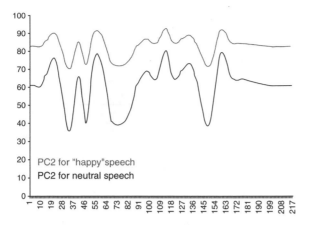

Figure 10.15 Generation of 'happy' speech in PC space

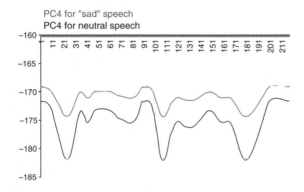

Figure 10.16 Generation of 'sad' speech in PC space

show the variation for the principal components after adding expressions to the neutral case. For a happy expression, PC2, that corresponds to the puckering of lips, is more significant and affects the resulting animation the most. Similarly, for the sad expression, PC4 is more significant and relates to the vertical movement of the corner of the lips.

We look at an application where synthetic or real speech is used along with phoneme segmentation to generate speech animation. For all the phonemes used for speech animation, we capture a speaker's static facial postures. This is equivalent to using designer-defined static expressions as explained in Section 10.3. We transform the 3-D position vectors into the newly generated expression and viseme space, thus the key-frames are represented now in the expression and viseme space, one key-frame corresponding to each phoneme in the speech. It is possible to apply co-articulation rules further to extract the modified timing information and to know which phonemes are required to be activated at the same time. The appropriate blending and interpolation functions are then applied in the expression and viseme space. After interpolation, the principal components are transformed back to the 3-D position space and the FAPs are calculated. This 'marching' through the viseme space results

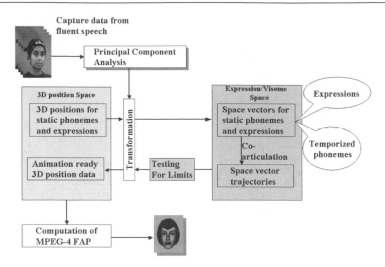

Figure 10.17   Speech animation using expression and viseme space

in realistic speech animation. There are two reasons for the effectiveness of working in the expression and viseme space. As the principal components are orthogonal components, fewer data is required for computation. Precisely, only 8 principal components are enough as against 30 FAPs for lips, mouth, and cheeks. Second, it is easier and more intuitive to devise the rules of co-articulation and expression blending as the principal components correspond to major facial movements. Figure 10.17 shows the processing for speech animation using the expression and viseme space.

In conclusion, we would like to state that the techniques derived from the statistical analysis of the facial motion capture have given us deeper insight into the dynamics of the facial movements. This not only resulted in a new parameter space useful for quick design of facial expressions, but also has brought new ways of generating convincing and realistic speech animation combined with expressions.

10.8   Facial Communication

Having discussed expressive talking faces and realism in facial animation, it is time to look at some of the applications. Popular as they have become, the talking heads find promising applications in Human Computer Interaction (HCI). The focus has shifted from mere text or speech-driven talking heads to autonomous Virtual Humans that can communicate with us in real-time. In this section, we discuss the issues involved in the autonomy of such Virtual Humans and the considerations involved in the communication with them using facial animation. In particular, we focus on the emotional aspect of the autonomous Virtual Humans. We concentrate on the evolution of the emotional state of the virtual actor through dialogue. The personality of an emotional autonomous virtual actor is defined and modeled to help the evolution of emotional state in a dialogue. Researchers have shown that employing a face as the representation of an agent is engaging and makes a user pay more attention (Koda and Maes 1996). The use of animated agents in an interface improves the appeal of the system. This leads users to perceive the agent as being more intelligent due to this high level of interaction. In order to achieve a more useful HCI, in addition to talking faces, we would like to have a conversation with a Virtual Human. It has been the dream of many computer scientists and researchers to be able to generate software they can converse with. Enabling autonomy in the Virtual Humans is an interesting research area. In an attempt to make a Virtual Human more 'life-like', we must consider how humans communicate with each other. Human communication is governed by certain social rules that occur through gestures, emotions and speech. Above all, this communication generally takes place via cooperative dialogue. When developing autonomous communicative agents, we must consider these aspects.

We can divide the problem of believable facial communication into several elements:

- Generation of temporized phonemes and audio from the input text and the application of co-articulation for realistic speech animation.
- Extraction of features, such as pauses and emphasis from the text. These features have been successfully used to generate facial movements such as blinking, nodding etc.
- Extraction of 'meaning' from the text in order to obtain appropriate facial expressions associated with mood or emotion.
- Linking all above points together to obtain a synchronized facial animation system.

The first two points have been discussed at length in the previous sections. The goal of this section is to focus on the third point leading to a believable facial communication. In order to realize a truly autonomous Virtual Human, amalgamation of expertise from the field of speech processing, computer graphics, natural language processing and artificial intelligence is required. To start with, we briefly consider the issues involved in the generation of dialogue for such an application. Further, we would like to consider an important aspect of autonomous Virtual Humans, namely, personality. This can be very important when communication between the real and virtual world is under consideration. We consider personality as an important aspect when modeling autonomous behavior. Though there have been numerous attempts at modeling facial animations, expressions, gestures and body animation, modeling personality and behaviors is relatively recent and less explored area. André et al. (1999) have given a detailed description of the work done for three projects focused on personality and emotion modeling for computer-generated lifelike characters. They emphasize the use of such characters for applications such as a virtual receptionist (or user guide), an inhabited marketplace and a virtual puppet theatre. They use the 'Cognitive Structure of Emotions' model (Ortony et al. 1988) and the Five Factor Model (FFM) of personality (McCrae and John 1992). Ball and Breese (1998) used Bayesian Belief network to model emotion and personality. They discuss two dimensions of the personality: dominance and friendliness. El-Nasr et al. (1999) use a fuzzy logic model to simulate emotions in agents. Various other systems have been developed to simulate emotions for different applications. A good overview can be found in (Picard 1998).

10.8.1 Dialogue Generation

One of the basic requirements of a Virtual Human able to communicate in a natural way is a good dialogue system and associated natural language understanding module. The main question arising in this area is 'How does a Virtual Human maintain its knowledge about the

world, the user and the history, and how does it use this knowledge to respond to the user?'
This forms the cognitive representation of the Virtual Human. Further, we need to link the
knowledge of the autonomous Virtual Human with his expressions and gestures, the visual
representation, which is discussed in the subsequent subsections.

One of the first attempts to create a system that can interact with a human through natural
language dialogue was ELIZA (Weizenbaum 1966). It used pattern-matching techniques to
extract information from a sentence. ELIZA had no sophisticated dialogue model; it just had
a simple trigger-reaction mechanism. Although the approach is very limited and dialogue
systems have evolved, it is still popular, see for example AIML (http::AIML). We begin
by presenting a brief survey of the state of the art in dialogue systems. We discuss various
types of dialogue management as well as a general theory of dialogue: the information state
theory.

10.8.1.1   Dialogue management systems

This subsection presents the different methods that exist for modeling dialogue. A more complete survey is given in (Churcher et al. 1997). In general, there are three main approaches to
dialogue modeling: dialogue grammars, plan-based dialogue management and collaborative
dialogue.

To describe the structure of a dialogue, one of the first methods was to use dialogue
grammars. Dialogue grammars define sequences of sentences in a dialogue. Often, such a
grammar described the whole dialogue from beginning to end, but recent approaches used
these grammars to describe frequently occurring sequences in a dialogue, such as question-
answer pairs. Constructing such a grammar can be done by using Chomsky-like rules or
a finite-state machine. The latter is especially suited when the dialogue structure is the
same as the task structure, that is, in every state the user has certain choices and these
choices correspond to state transitions. Because the system always takes the initiative in this
approach, it can anticipate the user's response, since there are only a few choices presented
to the user.

Plan-based approaches can model more complex dialogues than dialogue grammars. The
idea of a plan-based approach for the listener is to discover the underlying plan of the
speaker and respond properly to this. If such a plan is correctly identified, this approach
can handle indirect speech acts well. However, a plan-based approach does not explain *why*
dialogue takes place; the dialogue manager has no explicit goal.

A collaborative approach views a dialogue as collaboration between partners in order to
achieve a mutual understanding of the dialogue. This commitment of both participants is
the reason that dialogues contain clarifications, confirmations, and so on. Every partner has
certain beliefs about the other partner and uses these beliefs to respond to him/her. Also, two
partners can share mutual beliefs: statements that both participants regard to be true. This
concept of mutual belief is present in the model of conversational agency in (Traum 1996)
as an extension to the BDI model (Bratman 1987; Rao and Georgeff 1991). BDI stands for
belief, desire, intention, which are the three possible kinds of statements that can occur in an
agent's state. A lot of BDI systems use some kind of extension of logic to express beliefs,
desires and intentions. This is called a BDI logic (for an example of this, see Wooldridge
2000). Applications that use the BDI model to develop a conversational agent are described
in (Sadek et al. 1997; Egges et al. 2001; Ardissono et al. 1998).

10.8.1.2   Information state theory

Altogether, several approaches to developing dialogue systems can be compared through the information state theory, which was defined in the TRINDI project (Larsson and Traum 2000). In fact, the information state theory is an attempt to develop a model for best practice in the development of the dialogue management component of a spoken dialogue system. Key to this approach is to identify the relevant aspects of information in dialogue, how they are updated and how updating processes are controlled. This framework can then allow comparison to determine empirically which is the best practice.

10.8.2   Natural Language Processing and Generation

To process natural language, one needs a parser that analyses the sentence and that extracts information from this sentence. Normally, a distinction exists between shallow parsing and deep parsing. An example of shallow parsing is the pattern recognition approach of AIML. Deep parsing uses a formal grammar to analyze an utterance syntactically and then a semantic analysis delivers a meaning representation of the utterance. A recommended textbook about natural language understanding is (Allen 1995), which thoroughly discusses syntactic and semantic analysis of natural language. Both methods – shallow and deep parsing – have their advantages and disadvantages. Deep parsing can deliver more detailed information about the contents of an utterance than shallow parsing, but it is very bad at ignoring grammar errors in the sentence. Shallow parsing is more error-tolerant. Interpreting human speech differs substantially from interpreting a written text, because human speech is constructed of smaller sentences and has disfluencies (Cole et al. 1997). Shallow parsing could do a good job, but for a better semantic analysis, deep parsing is preferred. A combination of these two approaches delivers very promising results, it was for instance implemented in the Verbmobil project (Wahlster 2000).

Another important aspect is the generation of natural language, which transforms a semantic representation into a natural language utterance. Natural language generation (NLG) consists of three important elements:

- *Text planning*: determine what has to be communicated and how this is rhetorically structured
- *Sentence planning*: decide how information will be divided over different sentences (and perhaps paragraphs)
- *Syntactic realization*: generate every sentence according to a given language grammar.

Given these elements, two areas of research then arise: research in multi-sentence text generation (story-telling systems) and single-sentence text generation (applied in interactive scenarios). For communicative Virtual Humans, the latter category is particularly of interest since dialogue systems will very often create a single-sentence response. To generate a single-sentence response, the most important part is the syntactic realization, because the text planning has already been done by a dialogue system. Also sentence planning is not necessary, since there is only one sentence. For an overview of the state of the art in NLG, see (Dale et al. 1992) or (Reiter and Dale 1997).

10.8.3   Emotions

Emotions are closely related to facial expressions. By emotion, we understand a particular state of mind that is reflected visually by way of facial expressions. Hence, though we use emotion and expression as two different words, conceptually, we refer to the same thing by either of them. We use the emotion model proposed by Ortony et al. (1988), commonly known as the OCC model. The model categorizes various emotion types based on the positive or negative reactions to *events, actions,* and *objects*. The OCC model defines 22 such emotions. Table 10.2 shows these emotions with high-level categorization (positive and negative). The OCC model also describes how the intensities of the emotions are governed by internal as well as external factors.

Many researchers in facial expression analysis have recognized the six basic facial expressions defined by Ekman as universal. These basic expressions are joy, sadness, anger, surprise, fear, and disgust. They are very useful for facial animation, and can be combined to obtain other expressions. There is a partial overlap between the expressions proposed by Ekman and the ones stated by the OCC model. Only four expressions out of these six (joy, sadness, fear and anger) are defined in the OCC model. Surprise and disgust do not find a place in the OCC model, mainly because they do not involve much cognitive processing and do not correspond to valenced reactions. The major difference in these two classifications come from the fact that the OCC model tries to look deep into the state of mind of a human being, whereas the six expression model simply looks at how these states of mind are rendered on the face. As it appears, combinations of the six basic expressions can display different states of mind. The emotions described by the OCC model are numerous to be directly used in the computation of the emotional states in a real time interactive system. However, they are important and necessary to make the dialogue rich with expressions.

10.8.4 Personality and Mood

In psychology research, the Five Factor Model (FFM) (McCrae and John 1992; Digman 1990) of personality is one of the most recent models proposed so far. The model was proposed not only for a general understanding of human behavior but also for psychologists to treat personality disorders. The five factors are considered to be the basis or dimensions of the personality space. They are detailed in Table 10.3.

Table 10.2 Basic emotions

Positive emotions	Negative emotions
Happy-for	Resentment
Gloating	Pity
Joy	Distress
Pride	Shame
Admiration	Reproach
Love	Hate
Hope	Fear
Satisfaction	Fear-confirmed
Relief	Disappointment
Gratification	Remorse
Gratitude	Anger

Table 10.3 Five personality dimensions

Factor	Description	Adjectives used to describe this
Extraversion	Preference for and behavior in social situations	Talkative, energetic, social
Agreeableness	Interactions with others	Trusting, friendly, cooperative
Conscientiousness	Organized, persistent in achieving goals	Methodical, well organized, dutiful
Neuroticism	Tendency to experience negative thoughts and feelings	Insecure, emotionally distressed
Openness	Open mindedness, interest in culture	Imaginative, creative, explorative

All these dimensions of personality are closely related to the expressional, logical and emotional personification to varying degrees. For example, extraversion affects the logical behavior (choice of linguistic expressions) whereas neuroticism affects the emotional behavior more closely. Nevertheless, we prefer using all the dimensions in the model, even though the focus is on emotional personality. Since the model states that these five factors form the basis of the personality space, one should be able to represent any personality as a combination of these factors.

The FFM describes the personality, but it is still a high level description. We need to link the personality with displayed emotions that are visible on the virtual face. This is difficult to do unless we introduce a layer between the personality and the expressions. This layer, we observe, is nothing but mood. We clearly distinguish between mood and personality. Personality causes deliberative reactions, which in turn cause the mood to change. Mood is defined as a conscious state of mind that directly controls the emotions and hence facial expressions; it is also affected by momentary emotions as a cumulative effect. Thus, mood is affected from the level above it (personality) as well as the level below it (emotional state). The expressions can exist for a few seconds or even shorter, whereas mood persists for a larger time frame. The personality, on the highest level, exists and influences expressions as well as moods, on much broader time scale. This relation is shown graphically in Figure 10.18.

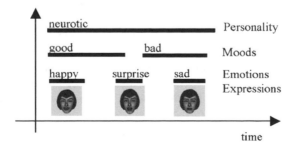

Figure 10.18 Emotions-moods-personality layers

To summarize, the following relations are made between the layers:

1. Personality practically does not change over time. It causes deliberative reaction and affects how moods change in a dialogue over time.
2. Mood, from a higher level, is affected by the personality, and it is also affected from the lower level by the emotional state.
3. On the lowest level, the instantaneous emotional state, which is directly linked with the displayed expressions, is influenced by mood as well as the current dialogue state.

Considering the FFM, we observe that Agreeableness, Neuroticism, and Extraversion are the most important dimensions of the personality, as far as emotions are concerned. A neurotic person will change moods often, and tend to go into a negative mood easily. On the other hand, an Extravert person will tend to shift to a positive mood quickly in a conversation. An Agreeable person will tend to go to positive mood more often, but frequent mood changes may not be shown.

A simple model based on probability matrix definition for personality was proposed by Magnenat-Thalmann and Kshirsagar (2000). Basic emotional states were defined, and probabilities can be assigned for transition from one state to the other. For example, a happy personality has a higher probability of changing to a happy state than to a sad state. Further, each change in emotional state is characterized by particular changes in facial expressions and periodic actions such as blinking, nodding and eye movements. For example, a fearful state is not only associated with an expression of fear, but also by increased blinking rate. This emotion and personality model is linked with the conversation using the tags embedded in the text responses of the dialogue database. When more sophisticated dialogue systems are available, the semantic analysis would result in generation of such tags in accordance with the state of conversation, rather than 'embedding' such tags.

10.9   Putting It All Together

So far we have reviewed various techniques in facial animation, speech animation, dialogue analysis and generation and emotion and personality modeling. All these technology bricks need to be combined in order to realize the interactive, autonomous, and expressive communicative Virtual Human. In conclusion, we will take a brief look at a possible scheme of integration. Figure 10.19 shows the system that partly combines some of the aspects discussed so far.

A text processing and response generation module processes the input text. This system can employ any of the dialogue techniques discussed above. The main requirement is that the output of the response generation, i.e. the response should have emotional tags embedded in it. These emotional tags would be calculated considering the dialogue state. Further, the emotional tags have probability values associated with them. The details of the system using ALICE as the dialogue system and prototype implementation has been explained by Kshirsagar and Magnetat-Thalmann (2002). In this system, multiple emotional tags were coded into the AIML. The emotional tags are passed on to the personality model. It is possible to implement the personality model using simple probability transition matrices as explained in previously. The personality model, depending upon the current mood and the input emotional tags, updates the mood. As mood is relatively stable over time, this mood switching is not a frequent task. Depending upon the output of the personality model, mood

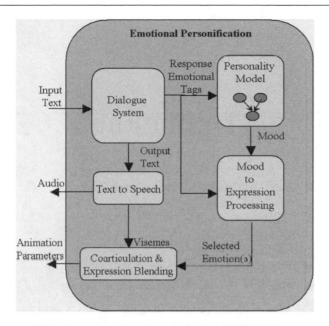

Figure 10.19 Autonomous emotional dialogue system

processing is done to determine the next emotional state. This processing determines the probabilities of the possible emotional states. The synchronization module analyzes previous facial expression displayed and output probabilities of the mood processing. It determines the expression to be rendered with the appropriate time envelopes. It also generates lip movements from the visemes generated by the Text to Speech engine. It finally applies blending functions to output the facial animation parameters depicting 'expressive speech'. It is this module that involves implementing various techniques discussed in Sections 10.6 and 10.7. A separate facial animation module renders the FAPs (described in Chapter 6) in synchrony with the speech sound.

10.10   Conclusion

The field of facial animation has matured after several years of research, experimentation and commercial exploitation. There is no doubt in the research community that facial communication with speech and expressions is a necessary component of the modern Human Computer Interaction systems. The problems related to visual representation of a face model, animation and rendering have been tackled and solved to certain extent already. What still remains in the less-explored area is the part of real-time conversation. For this, a greater interaction between computer graphics, artificial intelligence, cognitive science and psychology research communities is desired. It is often more difficult to integrate several components into a unified and convincing system than to develop the individual components. It is the truly interdisciplinary nature of the problem at hand that poses new challenges in the integration of various technology bricks. However, we have no doubt that with current advances in these fields, soon we will be able to talk with Virtual Humans in a truly interactive manner.

11

Behavioral Animation

Jean-Sébastien Monzani, Anthony Guye-Vuilleme, Etienne de Sevin

Creatures controlled by behavioral animation are immersed in a Virtual Environment and are able to perceive it, take decisions and finally interact with it. A lot of research has been dedicated to autonomous animals such as birds or fish. We will focus here on specific problems for animating Virtual Humans.

11.1 What Is Behavioral Animation?

Virtual Humans are commonly used nowadays in the entertainment industry, and most specifically in movies and video games. If the quality of pictures has been dramatically improved during the last years, the animation is still a major bottleneck in production. For movies, one can afford to spend months in order to produce a realistic animation for each character, but for real-time applications (and this is particularly true in video games) it is still very difficult to handle the behavior of virtual agents, especially when we try to make them autonomous. In behavioral animation, Virtual Humans acquire the ability to perceive their environment and are able to react and take decisions, depending on this input (it is important to note that agents need to be *situated* in a common environment: otherwise, no interaction could be possible).

Reynolds (1987) introduced this notion during the Siggraph 1987 conference, by stating that 'typical computer animation models only the shape and physical properties of the characters, whereas behavioral or character-based animation seeks to model the behavior of the character'. Reynold's first application was to model the flocking behaviors of birds and fish, but the idea of behavioral animation has been applied since then to various domains. What intrigues us in this book is of course its application to Virtual Humans, who are certainly more difficult to animate than animals.

Applications of behavioral animation have already created research, especially in the entertainment industry. The game 'Creatures' was the first to add neural networks to games, and let you teach your fantasy creature how it should behave. The game was a great success,

Handbook of Virtual Humans Edited by N. Magnenat-Thalmann and D. Thalmann
© 2004 John Wiley & Sons, Ltd ISBN: 0-470-02316-3

and generated follow-ups. More recently, 'The Sims' focused on the simulation of Virtual Humans in their everyday life, with successful and fun results. Even if behaviors are still limited, these games have proved that people are attracted to play with autonomous agents and the new success of the recent game 'Black and White' proves this once again. Please refer to the excellent site *Gamasutra* (http: gamasutra) for technical discussions on these games.

Of course, autonomous agents are not restricted to entertainment. They help train people in difficult situations, such as the pedagogical system STEVE (Rickel and Johnson 1997), in which a special immersive application for peace-keeping in Bosnia has been demonstrated with special attention paid to producing strong emotional content. Also, even if some applications do not especially require autonomous characters (for instance, chatting in large virtual worlds), it can be convenient to add some more creatures without having to bother about each individual behavior.

Before going further, we need to explain what behavior and autonomy mean for an autonomous agent. We continue by presenting some major contributions in this field, then summarize our most recent research in this domain and finally study some concrete applications.

11.1.1 Behavior

It is not easy to define the notion of behavior: quoting the Merriam-Webster Dictionary, it can be seen as:

- the manner of conducting oneself;
- anything that an organism does involving action and response to stimulation;
- the response of an individual, group, or species to its environment.

Starting with a system capable of displaying and animating virtual creatures (and especially humans), one can see as a 'behavior' some very simple actions like 'turning head to the left' to very general goals such as 'go to the closest bank in the city and withdraw enough money to buy something to eat'. Throughout this chapter, we will generally use terms such as 'actions' or 'gesture' to refer to the most simple behaviors that an agent is able to perform and employ 'behavior' for more abstract capabilities, such as executing a sequence of actions.

This chapter will not describe in detail all the available methods for performing actions: please refer to Chapter 5. To summarize, motions are usually either synthesized with proper models (e.g. walking, Inverse Kinematics) or recorded and played back (e.g. motion capture), with optional real-time adjustments (e.g. motion retargeting). Consequently, all other animation issues such as facial expressions, lip synchronization, and so forth will not be discussed, since the goal of behavioral animation is not to add new animation capabilities to an agent, but to select the 'best' action in a certain situation, giving a set of all possible actions.

We will, however, address the representation and mixing of actions, since this animation issue is traditionally linked to behavioral animation. Combining actions altogether is indeed a behavior, even if it also involves some geometric knowledge: for instance, it is possible to walk while holding a book in our hands, while it is impossible to sit and walk at the same time, simply because these two actions are controlling the same body elements. This will be discussed in detail in the corresponding section.

11.1.2 Autonomy

We generally consider autonomy as the quality or state of being self-governing. As we said, it relies on different factors: *perception* of the elements in the environment is essential, as gives the agent this awareness of what is changing around it. It is indeed the most important element that one should simulate before going further. Most common perceptions include (but are not limited to) simulated visual and auditive feedback. *Adaptation* and *intelligence* then define how the agent is capable of reasoning about what it perceives, especially when unpredictable events happen. On the other hand, when predictable elements show up again, it is necessary to have a *memory* capability, so that similar behavior can be selected again. Finally, *emotion* instantaneously adds realism by defining affective relationships between agents.

11.2   State-of-the-Art

Behavioral animation requires various capabilities, that we categorize into four elements: the awareness of the agent starts with a simulated *perception* of its environment (and the capability to memorize it). Based on this input, the agent will adapt its *behavior*, take the proper decisions and then *interact*, either with elements of the environment or with other Virtual Humans (when conversing, for example). Of course, it is not that easy to generate proper and convincing results without solving some *animation* problems, which are closer to computer graphics than AI.

11.2.1 Perception and Memory

It is tempting to simulate perception by directly retrieving the location of each perceived object straight from the environment. This is of course the fastest solution (and was extensively used in video games until the mid-1990s) but no one can ever pretend that it is realistic at all (although it can be useful, as we will see later on). Consequently, various ways of simulating visual perception have been proposed, depending on whether geometric or semantic information (or both) are considered. We are now going to compare synthetic vision, geometric vision and database access.

11.2.1.1 Synthetic vision through off-line rendering

Synthetic vision, introduced by Renault et al. (1990), is achieved by rendering off-screen the scene as viewed by the agent. During the process, each individual object in the scene is assigned a different color, so that once the 2-D image has been computed, objects can still be identified: it is then easy to know which object is in sight by maintaining a table of correspondences between the colors and objects' IDs. Furthermore, highly detailed depth information is retrieved from the view z-buffer, giving a precise location for each object.

Synthetic vision has been then successfully applied to animals ((virtual fishes (Tu and Terzopoulos 1994), and the SILAS dog (Blumberg et al. 1996)). Noser et al. (1995), showed how one can simulate a memory for agents: the 2-D rendering and the corresponding z-buffer data are combined in order to determine whether the corresponding voxel of the scene is occupied by an object or not. By navigating through the environment, the agent will progressively construct a voxel-based representation of it. Of course, a rough implementation of this method would suffer from dramatic memory cost, because of the high volume required to store all voxels. Noser et al. proposed to use octrees instead which successfully reduces the amount of data. Once enough information has been gathered through exploration, the agent is then able to locate things and find its way. Another application of synthetic vision is real-time collision avoidance for multiple agents: in this case, each agent is perceiving the others, and dynamically creates local goals so that it avoids others while trying to reach its original global goal.

Synthetic vision is the most elegant method, because it is the more realistic simulation of vision and correctly addresses vision issues such as occlusion for instance. However, rendering the whole scene for each agent is very costly and for real-time applications, one tend to favor *geometric vision*.

11.2.1.2   Geometric vision

Bordeux et al. (1999) have proposed a perception pipeline architecture into which filters can be combined to extract the required information. The perception filter represents the basic entity of the perception mechanism. Such a filter receives a perceptible entity from the scene as input, extracts specific information about it, and finally decides to let it pass through or not. The criteria used in the decision process depends on the perception requirements. For virtual objects, they usually involve considerations about the distance and the relative direction of the object, but can also be based on shape, size, color, or generic semantic aspects, and more generally on whatever the agent might need to distinguish objects. Filters are built with an object-oriented approach: the very basic filter for virtual objects only considers the distance to the object, and its descendants refine further the selection.

Actually, the structure transmitted to a filter contains, along with the object to perceive, a reference to the agent itself and previously computed data about the object. The filter can extend the structure with the results of its own computation, for example, the relative position and speed of the object, a probable time to impact or the angular extension of the object from the agent's point of view. Since a perception filter does not store data concerning the objects that passed through it, it is fully re-entrant and can be used by several agents at the same time. This allows the creation of a common pool of filters at the application, each agent then referencing the filters it needs, thus avoiding useless duplication.

As an example of filters, Bordeux has implemented a basic range filter which selects objects in a given range around the agent. The field of view filter simulates an agent's field of view with a given angular aperture. The collision filter detects potential impacts with other objects in the agent neighborhood and estimates, if needed, the time to impact, the object's relative speed and a local area to escape from. This has been used again in a safe-navigation behavior which dynamically computes a collision-free path through the world. It is even possible to specify how long an object will stay in the list after it was perceived, in order to simulate short-term memory.

However, the major problem with geometric vision is finding the proper formulas when intersecting volumes (for instance, intersecting the view frustum of the agent with a volume in the scene). One can use bounding boxes to reduce the computation time, but it will always be less accurate than synthetic vision. Nevertheless, it can be sufficient for many applications and, as opposed to synthetic vision, the computation time can be adjusted precisely by refining the bounding volumes of objects.

11.2.1.3 Database access

Data access makes maximum use of the scene data available in the application, which can be distributed in several modules. For instance, the object's position, dimensions and shape are maintained by the rendering engine whereas semantic data about objects can be maintained by a completely separate part of the application. Due to scalability constraints as well as plausibility considerations, the agents generally restrain their perception to a local area around them instead of the whole scene. This method is generally chosen when the number of agents is high, as in Reynolds' flocks of birds (Reynolds 1987), and schools of fish. In Musse and Thalmann's (2001) crowd simulation, agents directly know the position of their neighbours and compute coherent collision avoidance trajectory. Please refer to Chapter 14 for further details. As said before, the main problem with the method is the lack of realism, which can only be avoided by using one of the other methods.

11.2.2 Defining Behaviors

As seen in the introduction, the agents' behavior can range from very simple reactions to high level abstract definitions and is a tedious notion to define: consequently, a broad range of architectures have been proposed. We describe here the conventional AI planning methods, connectionism, motivated action selection and other hybrid approaches.

11.2.2.1 Planning

An agent determines its behavior by reasoning about what it knows to be true at a specific time. In the classical *planning systems* (Rao and Georgeff, 1991), *plans* provide step-by-step instructions on how to satisfy some goals; they basically require some *preconditions* to be fulfilled in order to activate their *effects*. Giving a *goal* to the agent will trigger some plans and generally activate some sub-goals. For instance, if a plan states that whenever the agent is thirsty (*the precondition*), it has to drink, the effect of the plan is to set up a *goal*: 'need drinking'. This goal in turn triggers some *subgoals*: the agent should pick up a glass and fill it with water.

Generic plans are often specified by adding *variables* to the preconditions. For example, imagine that our agent is aware that if an elevator is broken, it should use the stairs instead: we could specify the following plan:

```
preconditions:
   need go to ?x
   ?x is broken
conclusion:
   REMOVE need go to ?x
   ADD need go to Stairs
```

By using the variable ?x in this example, the preceding plan can be applied to every elevator in our world. In order to use it, a *pattern-matching* should be computed, to check if the required preconditions can be matched. That is, if the agent plans to take the first elevator, it should have stored somewhere in its knowledge base 'need go to Elevator1'. Of course, if 'Elevator1 is broken1' is also true, it will then use the stairs instead.

11.2.2.2 Connectionism

Artificial Neural Network (ANN) is often used for the specific case of learning. An in-depth description of the *connectionism* approach goes far beyond the goals of this book, and we will just give an overview of it, for readers who are unfamiliar with this methodology. Inspiration for ANN comes from the desire to reproduce artificially a system into which computations are more or less similar to the human brain. An Artificial Neural Network is a network of many simple processors (*units*), each possibly having a small amount of local memory. The units are connected by communication channels (*connections*) and there is often a *training* phase in order to help the ANN reasoning in a specific case. For instance, ANN can be used to model a creature with basic behaviors, as in the game 'Creatures': in this software, virtual 'pets' called Norn grow under the player's attention. The user tries to educate them so that, for example, they can remember how to use the objects in their environment.

Connectionism is an interesting approach, but suffers from being tightly linked to training: once the creature has been trained to learn something, it will tend to be able to solve this particular problem, but it will still have problems dealing with new situations. It is suited to specific tasks, but lacks generalization. Consequently, dealing with multiple tasks involves the creation of multiple neural networks, which is very complicated. On-going research tries to avoid these limitations; check Ziemke's article (1998) for a good review of algorithmic vs connectionist approaches.

11.2.2.3 Motivated action selection mechanism

Rather than using a top-down approach as in Artificial Intelligence, researchers have tried bottom-up solutions by using Artificial Life techniques. As pointed out by Christopher Langton, Artificial Life is literally 'life made by Man rather by Nature'. It mainly relies on the notions of *evolution* and *emergence*. The idea is to first model simple entities and then, by simulating virtually natural-life evolution and complexifying both the entity and its environment, when time passes, new behaviors will emerge. Since the entity always repeats a sequence of three behaviors (perception of the environment, action selection, and reaction), it continuously modifies its environment, which, in turn, influencies the entity.

The motivated action selection mechanism approach is to consider both the motivations of the agent and Artificial Life techniques. Motivations include for instance, *drink*, *eat*, and so forth, as described by ethology. It implies the action selection problem: the creature should constantly choose the best action so that it can survive into its environment. Ethology describes different models to do so, such as Tinbergen's (1951), or Baerends's (1976), hierarchical decision structure (HDS), Rosenblatt and Payton's free flow hierarchy (Rosenblatt and Payton 1989), modified by Tyrrell or associated Maes's network (Maes 1991) (see Figure 11.1).

Tyrrell has tested these models in complex simulated environments with many motivations and close to a wild animal environment. Results show that the free flow hierarchy, improved by Tyrrell (1992), is the most suitable mechanism of action selection in the context of Artificial Life.

From his test, Tyrrell defines six criteria to respect in a mechanism of action selection:

1. Take into account motivations.
2. Take into account environment information.

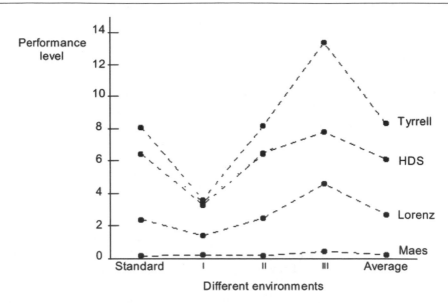

Figure 11.1 Results of Tyrrell's test. For the robust results, different models of action selection model have been tested with many motivations in different environments (standard, I, II, III, and then averaged)

3. Prefer to choose physiological actions over locomotion actions.
4. Continue the current sequence of actions until the end.
5. Stop the current sequence of actions if another motivation is urgent to satisfy.
6. Prefer compromise behaviors, i.e., which respective actions satisfy more motivations.

A new approch for inserting virtual life in Virtual Environments is to apply a motivated action selection mechanism to Virtual Humans. Agents become more adaptative and autonomous with motivations and emotions and, maybe one day, Virtual Humans could 'live' in their virtual world as we do in the real world and communicate with us.

11.2.2.4 Hybrid approaches

Apart from these classical approaches, Maes (1989) proposed merging traditional planners and reactive systems by organizing the agent's knowledge into interlinked *competence modules*. Action selection then becomes an emergent property of the system, when activating or inhibiting the corresponding modules. Each module encapsulates a list of preconditions, some effects (either adding or deleting beliefs) and a level of activation. Competence modules are linked in a network, with three different relationships: successors links indicate that the effects of a module are the preconditions of another one; the predecessor is just the reverse relationship; finally, a conflicter link is added whenever the effects of a module conflict with the preconditions of another one. These relationships between modules and a kind of energy circulating within the network will determine which modules can be activated, with the intuitive notion that activated modules 'pass on' energy to their successors. When the energy exceeds the level of activation of the module, it is activated. This architecture can help favor the selection of a particular kind of actions, but it is not easy to set up.

Cognitive modeling is another proposal for defining behaviors introduced by Funge et al. (1999). It is divided into two related sub-tasks: domain knowledge specification and character instruction: the first defines what can be found in the environment and how it changes, whereas the latter stores how to behave in order to modify the world. It relies on a strong mathematical notation called *situation calculus* which we will not describe in detail here. Functions (*fluent* in situation calculus) can define properties of elements of the world in a specific situation. Axioms then specify which preconditions are required before an action can be performed, but also how an action applied to an object with certain properties results in new effects, e.g. *'the effect of dropping a fragile object x is that the object ends up being broken'*. Based on this, optimizations can be applied to reduce the complexity of searches in the *situation trees* that list the future situations for each possible action. These concepts have been implemented in the Cognitive Modeling Language (CML) with a very nice demonstration of complex chasing behaviors (a shark is pursuing a mermaid who is avoiding it by hiding behind rocks).

11.2.3 Interactions

Communication between agents begins with non-verbal interaction. This kind of communication involves each agent managing some emotions and feelings about itself or others. Postures, gestures or particular motion (like *walking sadly* for instance) then visually reflect the agent's feelings, making them perceptible to the users but also to the other agents. It is interesting to notice that, usually, people do not consciously use non-verbal communication, but they instinctively understand it to a considerable extent and respond to it without any explicit reasoning. Bécheiraz and Thalmann (1996) presented a demonstration using these concepts, into which Virtual Humans are walking around in a garden and depending on there feelings, they can follow others (attraction), avoid them (repulsion) or try to engage or break contact. Interesting emerging behaviors can be observed, for instance, when a male character is jealous that the woman he loves is presently talking to someone else, he can come closer and break their communication with specific gestures. Even with very simple behavioral rules, a kind of story very quickly emerges, and since there is a lot of interactions, people feel that the method is more complex than it actually is.

Cassell et al. (1994) proposed a very complete model for verbal communication, although it is not a really an attempt to create intelligent autonomous agents, since all text as well as the intonation of the utterances is pre-computed by a dialogue planner. The system is then able to infer from these parameters the corresponding facial expressions, lip motions, eye gaze, head motion, and gestures. Special efforts have been made to create meaningful gestures: for instance, if the sentence is *'Are you sure that you can stay here?'*, then the agent can point a finger to the ground while pronouncing the latest word, to notify that it actually refers to the current room. As we can see from this example, there is a need to synchronize gestures, facial movements and speech, since the presence or absence of confirmatory feedback by one conversational participant, via gaze or head movement, for example, affects the behavior of the other. Synchronization is indeed a very difficult issue, because it is very context-dependent, for instance, in the case of hesitation, gesture occurs usually before speech, in order to take more time to think. Or, if two gestures have to be performed within one sentence, the first one might be interrupted in favor of the second one, because speech is faster than gesturing. The PaT-Net paradigm proposed by

Badler et al. (1998), was used here in order to deal with theses constraints (see the next section on animation for details).

Apart from the inter-agents' interactions, Kallmann and Thalmann (1999) proposed a model for human–object interactions. In Chapter 13, a general scheme is discussed on how to model objects with behaviors that can provide information about their functionality, changes in appearance from parameterized deformations, and a complete plan for each possible interaction with a Virtual Human. Such behaviors are described with simple primitive commands and special attention is given to correctly interpret object behaviors in parallel (e.g. when many human agents interact at the same time with the same object).

11.2.4 Animation

Animation in the specific case of Virtual Humans raises the problems of handling tasks in parallel: for instance, we are able to perform concurrent actions such as holding a cup of coffee in one hand while answering the phone with the other. In behavioral animation, we would like to automate this as much as possible. We will present in a special section our own approach to solving this problem, but let's have a look first at the Parameterized Action Representation (PAR) proposed by Balder et al. (1998).

PARs help to precisely define how an action is accomplished, not only by providing the usual data structures for temporal and spatial information (involved objects for instance), but also by specifying a manner like *slowly* or *carefully*. The PAR structures can also be created by analyzing natural language definitions, which is indeed a very convenient way for the animator to interact with the Virtual Humans. Furthermore, since complex actions might be performed at the same time or sequentially, PAT offer ways to synchronize actions with the help of parallel transition networks or PaT-Nets. This is a network architecture where nodes represent processes and arcs contain predicates, conditions, rules, or other functions that cause transitions to other process nodes. The main benefit is a non-linear animation model, since actions can be activated, suspended, changed, or stopped by transition to other nodes.

11.2.5 Applications

As said in the introduction, video games are the best-known application of Behavioral Animation: from 'Creatures' to 'Unreal' bots, from 'The Sims' to 'Black and White', new games appear in the shops every month, and they are incorporating more and more research results. Before continuing with a presentation of our latest research topics, we are going to briefly point out some other applications.

11.2.5.1 Storytelling

In the last few years, a lot of applications involving autonomous creatures have been merged under the notion of Virtual Storytelling, leading to the first special conference dedicated to this topic (International Conference ICVS). As example of interactive storytelling, we mention the contribution of Cavazza et al. (2001). Interactive storytelling is split into two approaches: either the plot is explicitly specified in the system, and actors' behaviors derive from it (*explicit approach*), or each individual actor pursues its own goals and by distributing roles between the actors, a story will emerge (*implicit approach*). Cavazza adopted the second approach, where characters' behaviors are generated from plan-based representations using an implicit approach, but *narrative concepts* are embedded into plans instead of just generic beliefs and desires. It is interesting to note that, even if in theory interesting behaviors can be derived from generic high-level beliefs, there is no guarantee that the selected actions will be narratively relevant. Consequently, in the 'sitcom' scenario presented by Cavazza, goals are chosen to add interest to the plot, typically 'gaining affection', 'betraying', and so on. Plans are formalized into Hierarchical Task Networks representing a hierarchy of sub-goals and actions. It is essential that each character keeps track of its long-term goals (in order to conserve the storyline) while replanning in real-time when the situation changes. The presented application demonstrates these concepts in a basic scenario: the main character (Ross) wants to invite the female character (Rachel) out on a date. In order to gather some information about Rachel's feelings, Ross first tries to read Rachel's diary, but he fails, because she just took it. Replanning occurs, and Ross decides to go and talk to Rachel's best friend. Unfortunately, Rachel notices this, and becomes jealous. Even if the interactions with other agents or with the environment are somewhat crude (there is no speech, for instance), the application succeeds in exhibiting an interesting storyline.

Back in the mid-1990s, the Oz project (Bates 1994), from Carnegie Mellon University was one of the earliest attempts to create believable creatures that use emotions and have rich personalities. However, this project did not focus on simulating Virtual Humans in a 3-D virtual Environment. Simple creatures called Woggles are inhabiting a 2-D world, and the project itself focuses on their interactions. Woogles' behaviors rely on the well-known Ortony, Clore and Collins emotion theory OCC (Ortony et al. 1988) (see Chapter 10): there is no planning, but just some simple goals that determine their emotional reactions to events. For instance, a Woogle becomes angry if another creature prevents it from achieving its goal. Special attention has been paid within the Oz Project to using natural language interactions, especially to generate text according to emotional states. Adding pauses, restarts and other variations helps to create convincing personalities, even if the graphical representation of creatures is simplified.

11.2.5.2 Specific animation platforms

Either for prototyping video games or to demonstrate research results, a lot of animation platforms have been proposed, ranging from the well-known (and early) Improv system by Perlin and Goldberg (1996), to commercial applications, such as Motion Factory's Motivate (Moltenbrey 1999), or Virtools' NeMo (Teven 1999). Most of these approaches are, however, very goal-oriented, and propose paradigms to define behaviors (with Finite State Machines, scripts or networks of animation elements interconnected like LEGO bricks). They are somewhat more focused on helping the animator in the creation of basic behaviors, rather than simulating a bunch of autonomous creatures.

11.3   An Architecture for Behavioral Animation

11.3.1   Separate the Body and the Brain

Automatically animating a Virtual Human is such a complex task, that one has to divide it into simpler elements. In this chapter, we will use the terms low and high levels. Saying that a task belongs to the low level does not means that it is something easier or faster to achieve! We will rather regroup in the low level the *physical elements* (for the Virtual Human, this includes the body, and basic animations like locomotion or objects interaction), and the *behavior* will be handled by the high level, simulating the Virtual Human's brain.

The low-level structures are responsible for physical elements that include: the 3-D graphical representation of Virtual Humans or objects, their animation and the simulation of sound. Virtual Humans are able to interact with objects, or with other humans (for instance, giving a paper to someone else). They also communicate verbally, and naturally exchange greetings and information with artificial speech. On the other hand, high-level modules give to the agent some *beliefs* (about itself, others or the environment) and depending on personal needs, the agent tries to fulfill its *goals* with the help of provided *plans*. Of course, both low level and high level are interconnected so that the agent's behavior can be reflected physically (walking, for instance) and similarly, if something changes in the environment (like someone speaking), the low level will warn the high level of the event, just as our brain and body are working altogether.

Such a low/high level separation is helpful. Imagine that you have to go to the train station. Would you really take care in each of your subtle motions, watch your steps, or even notice that you are avoiding other people? In your mind, you just have the *goal* of going to the station: this is your high-level decision. The low-level walking motion with obstacle avoidance is a very complex task, but you do not notice it. This simple example clearly demonstrates how useful it is to separate the behavior from the motion.

As we will see later on, this separation greatly helps to focus on behaviors without having to deal with low-level considerations. Furthermore, it is then easier to test, maintain and extend the code: either when implementing a new kind of facial expression or when creating new behavioral plans, one might concentrate on the animation factors or simply ignore the physical aspects and test the plans without a graphical feedback.

11.3.2   System Design

The previous considerations in low- and high-level separation have led to the construction of the system depicted in Figure 11.2. We are now going to present the low-level components

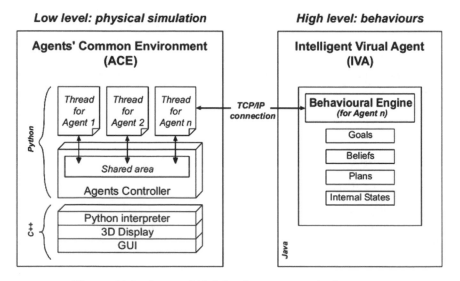

Figure 11.2   Low and high level components in the system

(*Agents' Common Environment*, hence referenced as ACE) and the high-level decisions making (the *Intelligent Virtual Agent* or IVA).

11.3.2.1 Agents' Common Environment (ACE)

To simulate the physical word, Kallmann et al. (2000) have developed a system called ACE for *Agents' Common Environment*. It comprises a set of different commands for controlling the simulation, such as the creation and animation of 3-D objects, Virtual Humans, and smart objects (Kallmann and Thalmann 1999) (see Chapter 13). Virtual Humans encapsulate various motion motors and may have facial expressions. They are able to replay a recorded animation (key-frames animation), can walk, or use Inverse Kinematics (Baerlocher and Boulic 1998), for better interactions with objects. Finally, they can visually perceive their environment with a geometric method (Bordeux et al. 1999).

ACE is mainly coded in C++ to ensure high performances. For convenient user-interaction, it also provides a Python layer which interprets commands on the fly and animates the Virtual Humans, as represented in Figure 11.3. Python is an all-purpose scripting

Figure 11.3 Snapshot of the Agents' Common Environment. One can note the left window defining obstacles (used when computing collision-free trajectories). A sample object manipulation window is used to move the agent name secretary on the right. The bottom window shows simple Python code that is interpreted on the fly

language that has been extended to fit the needs. More precisely, when the application is launched, a simple environment is created and displayed in a window, and a command shell is prompted, ready for entering Python scripts. This way, ACE provides the basic commands for loading, moving, animating humans and objects, giving a powerful set of functionalities straight from the scripting language. It is very convenient indeed to re-use a language and extend it to match our purposes, rather than developing a new syntax from scratch: this saves time and gives the opportunity to re-use third-party modules, which have been already implemented and tested by others.

In ACE, each agent is running in a separated process or *thread*, so that they can independently interact with the 3-D environment. When we want to create an agent, we code the corresponding Python script and load it into the *Agents Controller*: this layer, added on top of ACE, provides a shared area which helps the inter-agents' communication and synchronization with the environment. Otherwise, each agent would be left on its own, with no way of knowing what the others are doing, or when they are speaking, for instance. This shared area is especially useful for verbal inter-agents communication.

11.3.2.2   Intelligent Virtual Agent (IVA)

The *Intelligent Virtual Agent* relies on a Beliefs, Desires and Intentions architecture, as described by Rao and Georgeff (1991), so that each agent manages its own beliefs and makes decisions by itself. While agents in the low level have to share a common area and are handled by the *Agents Controller*, there is no such need for the IVA. Therefore, even if each IVA runs into a separated Java thread over the same application, there is no inter-threads communication (Figure 11.2 only shows one IVA for *Agent n*). This is in accordance with real human interaction: we do not have direct connections between our brains, but we need to use our body for communicating.

The knowledge of the agent is decomposed into its *beliefs* and *internal states* (anxiety, for instance), the *goals* to achieve, and the *plans*, which specify a sequence of actions required to achieve a specific goal. Based on these, the agent is then able to select the correct actions to perform in order to achieve its goals. Beliefs and goals may evolve over time, and the agent is able to take into account new elements, such as elements changing in the environment and dynamically react. More details on the *Intelligent Virtual Agent* will be given later.

11.3.2.3   Interconnecting low and high levels

By using sockets and TCP/IP connection, the system can run in a distributed way, reducing the CPU cost on the machine which is responsible for the 3-D environment display. A connection is established between each ACE agent thread and the corresponding IVA. It is then pretty easy for the IVA to send orders to the low level (making the agent move, or speak). Similarly, incoming input (verbal messages, perception) will be carried and sent by the low level to the high level behavioral module (see Figure 11.4). This is demonstrated in Figure 11.2: when Agent 1 speaks to Agent 2, the message goes first to the low level, then the thread for the first agent puts the message in the shared area. Agent 2 is then able to retrieve the message and hear it.

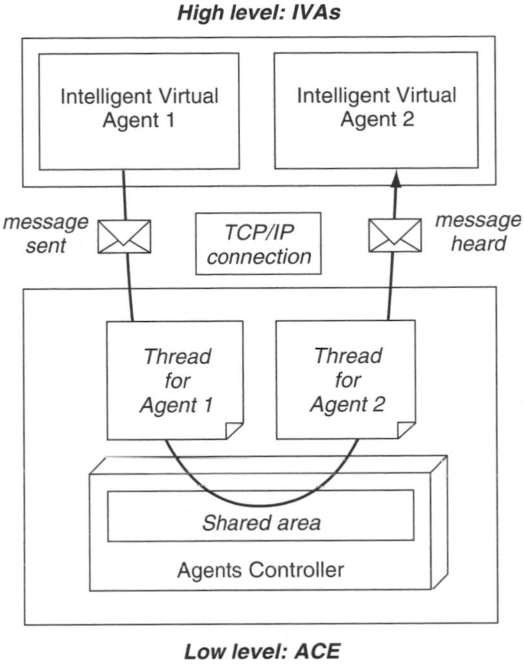

Figure 11.4   Verbal communication between two IVAs has to go through the low level

11.3.3   Animation: A Layered Approach

11.3.3.1   Concurrent tasks: mixing actions

We propose a layered architecture to help animation of Virtual Humans: Actions provide basic behaviors such as *walk*, *look* and coherently mix them. Tasks and Tasks Stacks ease the automatic activation and inhibition of actions, all under the responsibility of the Tasks Handler.

11.3.3.2   Actions

Actions are the simplest way to control the posture of the Virtual Human. They can be either activated or not, and smooth transitions between these states are computed by adjusting the individual actions weights. The library included in ACE (Boulic et al. 1997), can animate and coherently combine walking, looking, object interaction, facial expression and replay of recorded key-frame sequences.

   This approach is elegant and produces smooth animations, but is unfortunately not sufficient to specify high-level behaviors, as every action has to be triggered individually: for instance, sequencing actions like *'do action 1 then do action 2'* requires to check when *action 1* is finished, then remove it and activate *action 2*. Therefore, for something as simple as following a path (which we decompose into *go to location 1*, then *go to location 2*, . . .), one has to check each location individually. We found that this becomes quickly complicated and we introduced *Tasks* to deal with this problem.

11.3.3.3   Combining actions into tasks

Tasks are a convenient way to execute actions and monitor their evolution over time. They are implemented as Python classes, and all inherit from the same generic task which contains the task callback: this is a reference to one or more actions that should be executed when the Task is activated. Similarly, the termination callback checks regularly if the Task is terminated and if so, the Task will be automatically removed from its Tasks stack, as we will see later on. Other attributes include the state of the Task (*Suspended* or *Activated*), some timing attributes and some reference to the Virtual Human that it is controlling (vh_id). Two important attributes are remaining: the activation which takes one of the values {*Reactivated, Repeated, Once*}, and the list of next tasks to trigger once the task is terminated. They will be presented in the next section.

As an example, Figure 11.5 shows some of the attributes of a Walk Task. This task first stores a reference to the Virtual Human which is under control (vh_id) and the destination point, which is the location that the Virtual Human should reach. The task callback uses the `vhwalk` function provided by ACE control Virtual Human and the termination callback regularly checks the position of the agent to see if it has arrived at the destination.

11.3.3.4   Managing priorities with Tasks Stacks

To avoid conflicts when tasks of the same type are about to simultaneously control the same elements of the body, we regroup them into stacks, with one stack for each type per agent. We use stacks for walking, looking, interacting with objects, playing a key-frame, and manipulating the agent's face. Into each stack, only one task can be *executed* at a specific time, and tasks at the top of the stack have higher priorities than those below. In each frame, Tasks Stacks are responsible for updating Tasks, activate them, delete terminated ones, etc. Since tasks have two states (*Suspended* or *Activated*), only *Activated* Tasks are taken into account, as one can expect. The activation attribute of the task controls when the callback is called: if set to *Once*, task is activated once (playing a key-frame, for example); *Repeated* is for continuous tasks which should be performed at each frame (visual tracking of a moving object) and *Reactivated* only executes the task callback when the task becomes active.

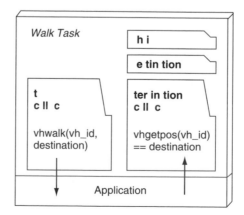

Figure 11.5   Example callback for a walking task

The Task inspection algorithm for each individual Tasks Stack starts from the top of the stacks and looks for the first *Activated* task (*Suspended* ones are ignored). This task is called the *top task*. Then, depending on the activation of the task: if set to *Once* and the task has never been executed, execute it; a *Repeated* will always be executed. And, if the activation is set to *Reactivated* and the top task is not the same as for the previous frame, execute the task. Once the top task has been found, we do not execute the pending tasks, but we still go through the stack in order to detect tasks which are terminated, by testing their termination callback. Terminated tasks are removed from the stack, and possibly activate other suspended tasks stored in their next tasks list.

As an example of *Reactivated* tasks, consider Figure 11.6: we have represented the stack of walking Tasks for one agent. At the beginning, there is only one activated task, which asks the agent to go to location A. But before the agent could actually arrive there, two new tasks are appended on the top of the stack: one order to go to location B (which is ignored, since it is *Suspended*) and an order to go to location C, which becomes the *top task* and consequently initiates the lower level action 'go to location C'. When location C has been reached, the task is removed, and the Tasks stack reactivates 'go to location A' again. Note that by default, if the agent reaches location A while going to location C, then task Walk to A is considered to be terminated and removed from the stack. To prevent this kind of behavior, one can suspend tasks and use the next tasks lists to activate each intermediate location when following a trajectory.

11.3.3.5 Multiple tasks altogether: the Tasks Handler

The Tasks Handler gathers all the Tasks stacks for one agent and repetitively activates each stack sequentially, in order to let them execute/purge their tasks. Tasks stacks are launched into threads so that the user only has to append tasks and does not need to check when they are terminated or not. Since all stacks are regrouped into one object, it is easier to link them, as shown in Figure 11.7: in this example, the next tasks lists sequentially activates two walking Tasks and a key-frame. As expected, the generated behavior drives the agent from location 1, then 2, then 3 and once the agent has arrived, make it applaud. In parallel, the visual attention of the agent is focused on a car.

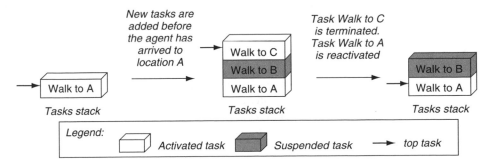

Figure 11.6 Reactivated tasks – Task stack for the walking tasks

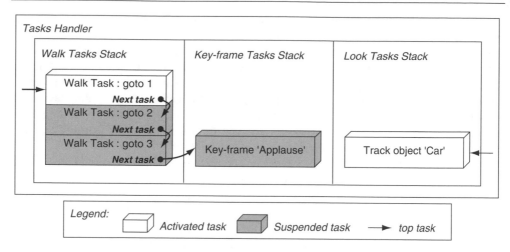

Figure 11.7 The Tasks Handler

11.3.3.6 Discussion

If we compare this approach with the PAR (Badler et al. 1998) architecture introduced previously, we might first think that PAR provides more information in its data structure, for instance, the manner of performing the action. We believe, however, that this specialization of action can be easily transported into the agent's planning system (see next section): depending on the agent's mood, it will for example pick up a walking style which reflects it. This is demonstrated in our scenario, as you will see in the Storytelling case study. The PAR preconditions and post-assertions can similarly be specified using plans, or, for a list of consecutive tasks, with the next tasks list. The interconnection of PAR using PaT-Nets is also similar to what we can achieve with the Tasks Stacks and Tasks Handler: PaT-Nets is a network organization while our approach is a two-layer method, but both can provide similar functionalities.

11.3.4 Intelligent Virtual Agent: Simulating Autonomous Behavior

The *Intelligent Virtual Agent* (IVA) (Caicedo and Thalmann 2000), represents the brain of the Virtual Humans, and is controlling its body (immersed in the 3-D environment). IVAs are based on the *Beliefs, Desires and Intentions* architecture, widely described by Rao and Georgeff (1991). Their approach is promising but needs some extensions to achieve our goal: we organize the IVA's knowledge into sets, distributed according to their functionality: *Beliefs, Goals, Competing Plans, Internal states, Beliefs About Others*. The *Behavioral Engine* then uses planning (as described previously) in order to achieve the goals.

To make plans more generic, we of course adopted the common approach of *pattern matching*: a parser is responsible for instantiating *variables* so that the same plan can be re-used for different cases. One should note that symbols beginning with a question mark will be instantiated by the pattern matcher. For instance `working-on Correcting-Text from Secretary` will match `working-on ?job from ?boss`. Furthermore, the user can add his/her own internal parameters in order to model continuous values which can be altered dynamically. For instance, the happiness of the agent might range from -1 (unhappy) to 1 (happy). This integration of internal states is very effective for difficult situations (which could not be solved with pattern matching only).

Apart from its name and the required *preconditions*, a plan is composed of *internal states* than can be tested after the preconditions. If both preconditions and internal states are fulfilled, the *effects* are executed. They are basically of four types: adding or deleting beliefs from the agent's beliefs, changing the internal states, and sending orders to the low level (animations, gestures, speech, etc.).

To help their management, plans can be categorized and regrouped. Apart from agent-specific plans (that is, plans that are only available for one agent, depending on its abilities), we introduce plans for job execution and delegation, plans for displacements into the environment and for inter-agents' communication. These plans make the Virtual Humans behave in a socially correct way: for instance, agents will exchange greetings before starting a conversation. Or, they can suspend the job that they are doing currently to favor a more important one. Of course, if one wants to simulate an agent which is not as polite as the others, it is easy to remove some of these plans and simulate a rude person.

11.4   Behavioral Animation and Social Agents

An important aspect of behavioral animation is the realistic simulation of how humans interact with each other in their everyday life. Which individuals meet frequently and which do not? What is the state of mind of the participants when they interact and how do they express it? How do they position their bodies relatively to each other in terms of distance and angle? Such questions are crucial for any behavioral animation engine dealing with multiple Virtual Humans, and must be addressed, explicitly or implicitly, in the design of the system's deliberative components. The development of such a socially intelligent behavioral animation system is useful in applications such as interactive games and production animations to realistically populate the scenes with lifelike synthetic actors, to enrich shared Virtual Environments, for the visual simulation of social phenomena, emergency situations, fire evacuations, etc.

The introduction of emotional states into the modeling of virtual beings is an important topic, which has received much attention in the behavioral animation field and has been successfully implemented in a number of systems. Nevertheless, as with simple goal-oriented behavior, adding purely emotional behavior may not be sufficient since it only corresponds to a small part of our daily activities. Every day, we engage in many interactions and social activities, adapting our behavior to the situation and people, dealing with complex motivations and different cultures, and also simply following routines which cannot be considered as the simple fulfillment of a precise goal or as a response to an emotion. Many social researchers like Berger and Luckmann (1966) have demonstrated that emotions are not sufficient to model human behavior; our group belonging, gender or cultural origin for example, are very important criteria to explain our behavior. Taking into account the sociological and social-psychological body of science is therefore an important challenge for the field of behavioral animation.

In order to implement these social features, agent-oriented technology is generally used. When the behavioral animation field's implicit definition of social behavior often refers to crowd and group activities (Bouvier and Guilloteau 1996), agent researchers usually link the concept to a communication task and define social ability as the ability to interact with other agents or humans (Wooldridge and Jennings 1995). It should be noted that the concept has an even broader meaning in sociology, where all human behaviors are considered social since they are always the product of a social-cultural context. While focused on different aspects, these views all tackle the same underlying issue, and agent technology and its associated standard are certainly an adequate approach for developing what could be referred to as social-behavioral animation. In fact, the BDI agent architecture which has proved to be a useful abstraction to model autonomous agents and offers a convenient and intuitive way to structure the agent's action selection, already makes a central use of mentalistic notions derived from psychology (Belief, Desire, Intention). Nevertheless, researchers such as Panzarasa et al. (1999), have pointed out that this architecture, in its current state, is not sufficient for the simulation of social behavior since it is solely based on the Bayesian decision theory, and must be enriched so that it takes into account the socially situated nature of human behavior and allows the inclusion of such important phenomena as social constraint, moral standards, routine behaviors, etc.

Designing believable social agents is a challenging task because the behaviors to reproduce are very complex and require a multi-disciplinary approach. Social behaviors make intensive use of many human abilities, such as vision, hearing, form recognition, memory, subtle body control, etc. Related work includes 3-D visualization, human animation with articulated and deformable bodies, and sound propagation modeling, which have recently shown impressive progress. Nevertheless, reasoning is still a major issue as strong theoretical oppositions exist within the AI field. In this context, the adequate conceptualization and formalization of artificial social reasoning is a crucial task, which is gaining importance in the AI and ALIFE fields.

Carley and Newell (1994), at Carnegie Mellon University, were among the first to construct a consistent definition of the social agent for Virtual Environments, based on two dimensions which are (1) the agent's information processing capabilities; and (2) the type of knowledge handled. In a complex environment, the social agent, using a specific cognitive apparatus, has to engage into information gathering tasks, e.g. by querying another agent. They can initiate and maintain social relationships for this purpose, and may be mutually supportive in the execution of joint actions. The social agent must also be able to handle complex and differentiated knowledge about the self, task domain and environment in a cultural and historical context.

More recently, Dautenhahn (1998), has been extremely prolific on the topic of socially intelligent agents and has provided a very good overview of the field. Like others, her work is focused on creating agents that are able to recognize each other, establish and maintain relationships as well as collaborate, but much attention is also given to other important aspects such as empathy, embodiment and historical grounding. Her ideas are implemented in the framework of the AURORA project.

In the context of social simulation, Conte et al. (1999), have produced interesting work on such topics as social norms' representation, cognitive emergence and agent rationality. The development of benevolent agents that can adopt other agents' goals spontaneously, i.e. without being asked by the recipient agents, is an example of a kind of social rationality which differs greatly from the usual economic rationality found in many agent models. Other researchers like Boman and Verhagen (1998), have also made interesting contributions to the study of how social norms acceptance and learning can be modeled. In a similar approach to Conte and Castlefranchi's, Sichman (1995), proposes a computational model of autonomy and inter-agent relationships based on dependence relations.

Other less specialized architectures are based on psycho-social attitudes and goal-based or emotional behaviors. As presented previously, the Oz Project (Bates 1994) integrates goal-directed and reactive behavior, as well as emotions and social behavior, in a global architecture. Rousseau and Hayes-Roth (1998) propose a social-psychological model based on moods and attitudes. Sengers (1997), among other interesting contributions, emphasizes the importance for social agents to clearly communicate their desires and intentions and has explored the ways to appropriately achieve action expression.

A connectionist approach has been used by Channon and Damper (1998), who argue that evolutionary emergence is the best technique to obtain socially intelligent agents. They describe a multi-agent system using neural networks and genetic algorithms that generates basic social behaviors such as cooperation and competition.

Finally, the work by Guye-Vuillème and Thalmann (2000), aims at enriching the previously described behavioral animation system with several high-level concepts derived from sociology and their associated mechanisms: social roles, norms, social values and perceptual types. Designers are able to model the Virtual Humans' behavior at a higher level, adding social identities, social motivations and social reasoning to the agents, on top of their specific competency. The role (e.g. woman, salesperson, football fan) is here used as a container for the agent's social identity, encapsulating a given world-view, specific rules of conduct, etc. An inheritance mechanism allows data to be re-used from one role to another, and several roles can be assigned to one agent. In this approach, the Virtual Human is composed of a set of roles and his/her 'freedom', defined as his/her behavior's unpredictability, emerges from the contradictions between these roles. This high-level architecture is implemented as a layer on top of the agent's standard BDI apparatus, driving its goals, beliefs and intentions in a socially realistic way. It is hybrid in nature: reactive mechanisms process the perceptual input to activate a subset of the agent's behavioral and cognitive data, then standard symbolic reasoning (rules matching) is performed on the lower-level information to complete the action-selection process.

The heuristic goal of automatically and realistically simulating social interaction using behavioral animation engines is very challenging and can be compared to the task of developing agents capable of passing a 3-D Turing test, involving both verbal and nonverbal communication. We think that the presented concepts and architectures, based on the social sciences corpus, will help realize this goal.

11.5 Case Study

11.5.1 Storytelling

This section describes an example of storytelling using the system proposed by Monzani et al. (2001). The scenario presents some employees working in an office and editing a journal. Characters endow some roles and this influences their ability to perform or delegate jobs (see Figure 11.8). At the top of the hierarchy is the Editor. He chooses stories or events to investigate, and asks the Secretary to give him an article on this topic. The Secretary then delegates the job to the Journalist who will finally send it to the Editor. This scenario has a lot of potential inter-agent cooperations and interactions: they have to speak, give and pick up some objects, and interact with elements such as computers on the desks. Depending on their roles, they can delegate jobs, since they are only able to handle one job at a time, they have to suspend an on-going job if a more important job comes along. Finally, it is possible

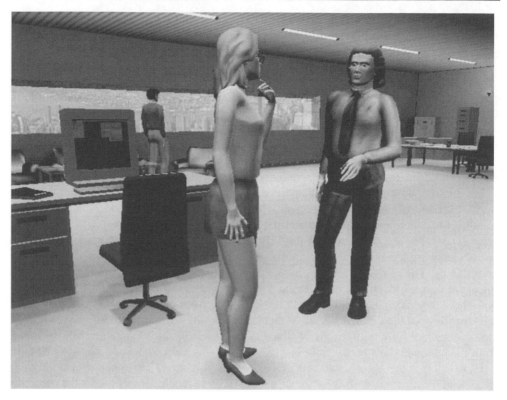

Figure 11.8   Inter-agent communication: the Secretary is talking to the Editor

to modify some elements during the simulation (like the time taken to complete a job) and
see how agents react. It is interesting to note that the agents' internal states can be inferred
from the way they perform an action. For example, we modified the scenario so that the
Journalist's computer crashes while he is typing his article: consequently, he feels ashamed,
walks sadly to the Editor's office and excuses himself for the delay.

Let's have a look now at a sample plan:

```
Plan:
name:
   execute-one-important-job
states:
hierarchy.get("?boss") >
current_job_priority.value
preconditions:
   asked execute-job ?job from ?boss
   is working
   working-on ?prevjob from ?prevboss
effects:
   Del (asked execute-job ?boss ?job)
Del (working-on ?prevjob from ?prevboss)
```

```
Add (working-on ?job from ?boss)
Add (need suspend-job ?prevjob from ?prevboss)
Eval (current_job_priority.value =
hierarchy.get("?boss");)
Add (need do-job ?job from ?boss)
Add (say ?boss (informed ?self working on ?job)
"I stop my job to do this immediately.")
```

Given the fact that our agent is working on a job assigned by somebody, if someone else comes with a new and more important job, then the previous job will be suspended to favor the new one.

From the agent's point of view, this can be summarized by *'If I'm working on the job named ?prevjob* (assigned by ?prevboss) and if ?boss asks me to do a new ?job, I will suspend my previous job ?prevjob and take the new one if this new job is more important than my current one.'

In order to model this, the agent needs to know the importance of everyone in the company. This is stored in a hash table hierarchy from which we retrieve a number representing the person's importance. Consequently, when the agent is working, this number is stored in the state current_job_priority to reflect the importance of the job. It is then easy to test this value when someone comes with a new job, as reflected in the states part of the plan.

To briefly describe the plan, the preconditions can first be translated to *'I'm working on a job and someone else is coming with a new job.'* As we have seen, the internal states are then evaluated to see if the incoming plan is more important than the current one. If so, the agent deletes and adds some beliefs so that it suspends the previous job and takes the new one. Consequently, two new goals are set: the need to suspend the previous job (?prevjob), and the need to perform the new one (?job). The current_job_priority is of course updated accordingly (Eval statement). Finally, one can notice that a verbal communication will be established between the agents, so that the ?boss is informed of the decision taken by the agent. An order to say something is sent to the low level (latest statement Add (say ...)).

It is interesting to notice that the verbal communication does not rely on natural language analysis: it would be a waste of time to compute a translation from the representation of beliefs to natural language, transmit the text in English and then compute the reverse transformation. To avoid this, we split the message into the *semantic* and the verbal realization of the *sentence*: the pattern for speech act is of the form (say agent semantic sentence). The semantic will be transmitted to agent and usually added to its beliefs, while the sentence is pronounced by the speech generation system. The semantic (informed ?self working on ?job) is using the special variable ?self which is always replaced by the name of the agent who is executing the plan. If the Graphic designer warns the Secretary that he is working on some illustrations, then the Secretary receives (informed Graphics-Designer working on Illustrations). There is one drawback to this approach, though: due to the separation of the semantic and the verbal realization of the message, the designer of the plans has to carefully maintain the coherence between them.

11.5.2 A Mechanism of Motivated Action Selection

De sevin et al. (2001) have implemented in Python a mechanism of action selection based on a free flow hierarchy (Tyrrell 1993), associated with a hierarchical classifier (Donnart and Meyer 1996). This approach respects Tyrrell's criteria and permits taking into account different types of motivations and also information coming from the environment perception. The key idea is that, during the propagation of the activity in the hierarchy, no choices are made before the lowest level in the hierarchy represented by the actions is reached.

The hierarchical classifier provides a good solution to model complex hierarchies by reducing the search domain of the problem using weighted rules. We can also easily make behavioral sequences (composed by a sequence of actions). So the Virtual Human can move to a specific place to perform a physiological action and satisfy the motivations no matter where it is. The hierarchy of our model contains four levels (depicted in Figure 11.9):

- *Level 1.* Internal variables evolving linearly during time, representing different states of the Virtual Human. The later levels represent the hierarchical classifier with rules to pass the activity to another level.
- *Level 2.* Motivations corresponding to a 'subjective evaluation' of the internal variables. A threshold system helps to reduce or enhance motivations values according to the internal variables. Whenever an internal variable is high, the agent will rapidly react in order to satisfy the related motivation. Figure 11.10 shows the result obtained at this level.

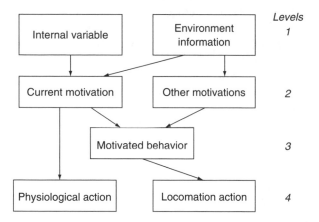

Figure 11.9 Simplified motivational model of action selection for Virtual Humans, i.e., —> propagation of activities

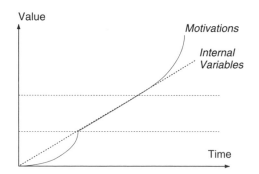

Figure 11.10 'Subjective' evaluation of the motivations (solid curve) from the value of the internal variables (dashed line) with a threshold system

The rules associated with the motivations to propagate the activity in the hierarchy are for example:

> IF hungry and no food around THEN go to food location.
> IF hungry and food around THEN eat.

- *Level 3*. Motivated behaviors generate actions so that the agent moves to a place where it can satisfy the correspondent motivation. The rules associated with the motivated behaviors to propagate the activity in the hierarchy are, for example:

> IF go to the food location and known food source THEN walk to this place.
> IF go to the food location and food source visible THEN walk to this place.

- *Level 4*. Actions are directly influencing the internal variables. Locomotion actions increase the internal variables, while the physiological actions decrease them. If the agent has the choice between these two kinds of actions, it will choose a physiological one, as it is more beneficial for it. Indeed, the rule weight for physiological actions equals twice the rule weight of a locomotion action in the model.

The activity is propagated similarly as a free flow hierarchy in the system according to the rules of the hierarchical classifier, and whatever the situation is, the system always chooses the most activated action (at each iteration). Take as an example the eat motivation depicted in Figure 11.11. The behaviors 'go to known location' or 'go to a visible food' control the agent displacement to a specific direction, using the low-level action of walking.

In other words, the main role of the action selection mechanism is to maintain the internal variables under the threshold by choosing the correct actions. Actions involving interactions with objects are preferably chosen because they are defined to be directly beneficial for the Virtual Human. Otherwise, the Virtual Human is instructed to walk and reach the place where the motivation can be satisfied.

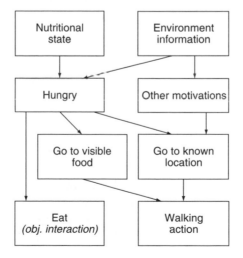

Figure 11.11   A part of the hierarchical decision graph for the *eat* motivation, which is evaluated on each iteration. Some compromises can be made with other motivations

The six criteria of Tyrrell have been respected in our model. First, the motivations and the environment information have been taken into account in the model. Second, the physiological actions are preferably chosen compared to locomotion actions due to the difference of their rule weights. Motivated behaviors satisfy motivations by generating behavioral sequences of actions. The agent can move to a specific place to perform a physiologic action. However, the system always chooses the most activated action, that is why if a motivation becomes urgent, exceeding the current motivation, the system switches to perform the one with the higher priority. At the end, motivated behaviors sum activities from different motivations (including behaviors), and their chances of being chosen increase when their values are higher.

The first graph of Figure 11.12 shows the linear evolution of the internal variables. The second graph shows the resulting actions. The system allows behavioral sequences where locomotion actions are followed by physiological actions, which decrease internal variables. The jump of activity between physiological actions and the locomotion ones is due to the weights of physiological rules, which equals twice the locomotion weights. The system will therefore preferentially choose the physiological actions because their values are higher than the locomotion actions. The chosen action always corresponds to the highest value in the second window. The action selection mechanism fulfills its function because each internal variable is maintained under the threshold over the time.

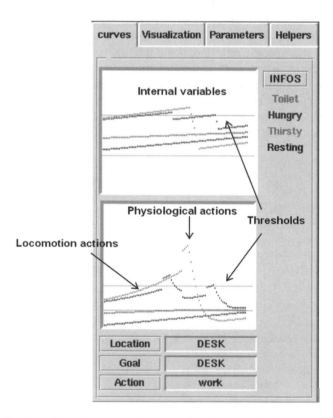

Figure 11.12 Results of the simulation in terms of achieved behaviors. It shows the upper and the lower level of the action selection hierarchy

Figure 11.13 Virtual life simulation: by default, the agent is working, waiting for a motivation (for instance, drinking) to be activated. The food is kept into the kitchen, as seen in the background

The simulation being presented in this chapter uses five main motivation types: eat, drink, rest, work (default action), and go to the toilet. Five smart objects (see Chapter 13) are directly related to each motivation: a hamburger, a cup of coffee, a sofa, a desktop computer, and a toilet. However, the action selection mechanism is not limited in the number of motivations and can thus be easily extended. During the simulation, the model is fed with parameters describing the current state of the agent concerning each of the motivations, and by flowing inside the hierarchical structure, will correctly trigger the concerned actions (see Figure 11.13).

After an action is selected as a response to satisfy one of the actor's motivations, the state parameter of the internal variable is adapted accordingly. For example, after the action of eating is completed, the 'Nutritional state' parameter will decrease. In this way, each action needs to be associated to an internal variable, closing the loop: motivation parameter evaluation, action selection, action animation, and internal variable parameter adjustment.

11.6   Conclusion

The scenario presented in the virtual storytelling application shows the possibilities and limitations of this approach. The resulting animation is fairly realistic, but autonomy is still limited because the user has to enter a lot of plans to create the agents' behavior. The simulation will more or less always look the same if no modifications are made. However, it clearly differs from a prerecorded static animation: if we move an agent around or a piece of furniture, the behaviors will quickly adapt to this new situation without any problem, as we separate the semantical information (the behaviors stored in the Intelligent Virtual Agents) from their realization (by the Agents' Threads in the ACE system).

Furthermore, new plans might be triggered as agents perceive their environment. If an agent hears a message, it can react to it even if it was not in the intended receivers' list of the message (that is something we experienced at the beginning: the Journalist heard the Editor calling the Secretary and he joined them). Similarly, visual perception helps to adapt behaviors: if an object is not there any more, the agent has to find it again in the environment before using it. Finally, the user has the possibility of modifying the agents' beliefs at run-time. For instance, we can crash the computer of the Journalist while he was typing his article: this forced him to plan again.

Motivated action selection mechanism enhances the autonomy of the agents: it simulates human motivations with different levels of priority without necessary requiring plans. However, for complex behaviors such as 'writing an article' (in the virtual storytelling example), elaboration of plans is necessary. Combining the two approaches could be a good solution to simulating complex behaviors while combining various levels of autonomy.

12

Body Gesture Recognition and Action Response

Luc Emering, Bruno Herbelin

With the overwhelming quantity of accessible knowledge, we clearly need new communication channels, which have to be easy to use, three-dimensional and tailored to a given task. In this chapter we explore one of these innovative communication channels: human gesture recognition and response by a computer. The idea is to project a real performer inside a virtual space where a computer analyzes the body gestures and generates meaningful action response. In particular, the examined virtual spaces consist of 3-D worlds where a real performer interacts with Virtual Humans.

12.1 Introduction: Reality vs Virtuality

Virtual Humans are widely found in entertainment and their visual quality has sufficiently increased to reasonably explore their liveliness in innovative communication channels between Reality and Virtuality. Bridging these two worlds by means of body-oriented action recognition is the aim of this chapter.

As we will present a whole range of interactive systems, it is convenient to present a classification that refers to all possible methods of projecting real entities into Virtuality and projecting virtual entities into Reality (Maes et al. 1995). In the 1990s a name for such projections was coined: *Projective Virtual Reality* (PVR) (Freund and Rossmann 1999). Rather than just considering one axis (Reality vs. Virtuality), we propose an extension with three different axes or spaces:

1. *Manipulation space*: the space owning the objects that are manipulated by the performer. Such objects are, for example, a graphical user interface (GUI), a 3-D model of a car, or a joystick. The associated manipulation spaces are respectively 2-D Virtuality, 3-D Virtuality and Reality.

Handbook of Virtual Humans Edited by N. Magnenat-Thalmann and D. Thalmann
© 2004 John Wiley & Sons, Ltd   ISBN: 0-470-02316-3

2. *Activity space*: the space where a performer believes himself to be. His beliefs are influenced by environmental properties and feedback such as vision, scene, sound, odor and touch.
3. *Impact space*: the target space of the performer's activity. For example, a performer manipulates a virtual robot model and indirectly controls a physically existing robot on Mars. The impact space is the robot's space, i.e. reality.

Each space is represented in a bounded interval (from 'real' to 'virtual'), on an axis that leads to a cube-shaped representation: the MAI-box (Figure 12.1). Some examples for each vertex of the MAI-box are:

- **(r,r,r)**, our everyday space, so-called *Reality*.
- **(v,r,r)**, for example a video stream incorporated inside a Virtual Environment, the manipulated video stream is recorded to tape or broadcast.
- **(r,v,r)**, easily done with head mounted see-through displays and typical tele-operation systems.
- **(v,v,r)**, similar to (r,v,r) but with an immersive head-mounted display (PVR).
- **(r,r,v)**, widely used computer input paradigms such as the mouse-cursor metaphor.
- **(v,r,v)**, similar to (v,r,r) but the manipulated video stream serves as texture map in virtual scene, call *TV-view* metaphor in (Freund and Rossmann 99).
- **(r,v,v)**, a typical interface configuration in Virtual Reality (VR) (Shih et al. 1996).
- **(v,v,v)**, so-called Virtuality, the user is entirely immersed into virtual space.

In the present chapter, we focus on human – humanoid interaction, which are the main opposite corners, 'Reality' and 'Virtuality', of the MAI-box. In particular, we emphasize an interface that is almost entirely based on a participant's a-priori knowledge and daily experiences, namely body gestures such as grasping, waving, sitting down or walking.

In the following sections we will first look at existing recognition and reaction systems. Then we present in more detail a system for body and hand recognition, which will be illustrated with some virtual reality test beds that were accessible to a larger public. Finally, we share our experiences collected during research.

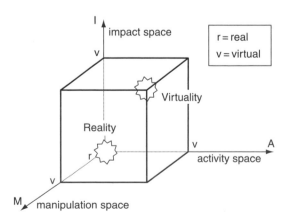

Figure 12.1 MAI Box: Manipulation, Activity and Impact

12.2 State-of-the-Art

In the following section we explore some of the most representative interactive environments that integrate body communication. Some of them aim to enhance our living space (so-called 'smart rooms'), some are storytelling (e.g. for artistic or museum-like purposes) and others are prototypes for entertainment and education.

The ALIVE (Artificial Life Interactive Video Environment) (Maes et al. 1995) is a representative interactive environment for smart rooms. It uses a high-tech mirror-effect. The live participant is performing in front of a big screen that displays an augmented video view of the participants' activity space. Augmented, because the video image is mixed with a virtual character, namely a reactive virtual dog. The video image is also used to extract the positions of the participant's head, hands and feet as well as the body location. The evident advantage of the system is the ease-of-use and minimal set-up time. However, activity recognition is limited to the possibilities offered by an optical tracking system.

A technically similar set-up is given by the virtual PAT (Davis and Bobick 1998) (the virtual personal aerobics trainer). The goal of this educational/entertainment system is to create personalized aerobics sessions where the instructor gives feedback according to the participant's performance.

The session automatically starts when the participant enters the activity area in front of the TV screen. The instructor feedback consists of announcing the type of exercise and giving positive or negative comments, such as 'Good job', 'Get moving' or 'Concentrate!'. The recognition is based on background-subtracted video in order to obtain the performer's silhouette motion-templates.

Conversational Characters aim to model face-to-face communication either between synthetic actors or between a live participant and a synthetic character. One of these educational systems is called 'Gandalf' (Thórisson 1997): 'Gandalf is a voice, a hand and a face, which appears on a small monitor in front of the user. To Gandalf's left is a large-screen display on which he can show a (crude) model of the solar system'.

Gandalf has speech recognition skills and answers to spoken questions. It also reacts to the participant's gestures and eye movements in order to navigate in the solar system model.

12.3 Involved Technology

Gesture recognition and action response involve a large range of software and hardware solutions. In particular, the projection of a participant into Virtuality asks for advanced sensor technology. The most common systems are shown in Figure 12.2. Details are found in Chapters 2 and 3 of the present book and in specialized literature.

12.4 Action Recognition

We use 'action' as a generic term for body-oriented gestures and postures. Before presenting our approach to real-time action recognition we briefly present possible recognition.

12.4.1 Recognition Methods

Concerning Static Posture-recognition, template-matching methods were one of the first to be developed. Unfortunately their efficiency is limited by the size of the database (Baudel et al. 1992). That is why computer-based learning approaches are now commonly

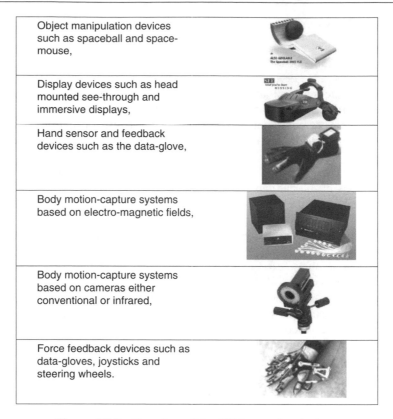

Object manipulation devices such as spaceball and space-mouse,	
Display devices such as head mounted see-through and immersive displays,	
Hand sensor and feedback devices such as the data-glove,	
Body motion-capture systems based on electro-magnetic fields,	
Body motion-capture systems based on cameras either conventional or infrared,	
Force feedback devices such as data-gloves, joysticks and steering wheels.	

Figure 12.2 Overview of the VR immersive devices

investigated. Basically, learning algorithms solve a classification problem: given a set of inputs, they propose a type or a class of recognized output:

- *Logical learning*: Symbolic learning algorithms (C4.5 based) gives a logical and well-structured working area for classification, but their learning algorithms can only consider one attribute at a time. Therefore, they can segment the solution-space only into 'orthogonal' parts. The class boundaries are poorly approximated and it would be too slow to enhance the approximations. Instance-Based Learning techniques are much more flexible as they work essentially by keeping typical attribute-examples for each class (algorithms IBL 1 to 3 are 'classical' AI techniques (Aha et al. 1990)). One gesture-based learning application has been fully evaluated by W.Kadous (1996), and in a precise comparison of those solutions, he gives IBL1 as the more appropriate.
- *Neural networks*: There are a number of ways for using a neural net as a classifier. One is to have an output neuron for each possible class, thus each output neuron will give a value closer to '1' when that particular class is indicated. The real power of a neural network comes from its internal structure and the way that connection weights are set. Using supervised learning, those weights are adjusted in order to fit the input and output conditions for a set of learning examples. What makes them difficult to use is the great number of variables to be tuned: input and output encoding, number of hidden

layers, number of neurons in each layer, interconnection of neurons, output function, bias node ... What is worse, however, is that there is no structured way of choosing the correct configuration for a particular task. As a simple but useful application, Vaananen and Bohm (1992) and Fels and Hinton (1998) suggest the ease of static hand posture recognition with neural networks.

In the same way that one statically connects one posture to a network input- layer, one can connect a succession of postures to a larger network input-layer. The neural net will still work 'statically' but on a set of N successive postures representing a gesture. The main job is to stack those N postures in time, in order to learn one or more movements, and then dynamically test the last N postures to see whether the network proposes a corresponding class. This works only very brief movements, otherwise the neural net cannot respond fast enough (Bohm et al. 1994). One other research field concerns recurrent neural nets and dynamic networks. The property of structures such as the Jordan networks (Jordan 1986) or Elman networks (Elman 1990) is to recursively plug the output layer to the inputs in order to add a dependency on the last state. This makes a neural net capable of learning a sequence of measures (Cracknell et al. 1994).

- *Hidden Markov Models*: HMM are commonly used for speech processing, but also for computer vision gesture recognition (Starner 1995; Marcel and Bernier 2000). Similar to neural nets, they suffer from a large number of parameters. As a particularly interesting example, Lee and Xu (1995) describe the possibility of interactive (opposed to supervise) training: if the system is in any way uncertain of its classification, it can query the user for confirmation, correct its decision, or add a new gesture class. Static posture recognition can be extended for dynamic gesture recognition, such as template matching on 3-D motion curves. Although fast and accurate, its efficiency highly decreases for large amounts of data (Sagawa et al. 1996).

  As with neural networks, one can change the topology in order to impose an order dependency, and thus represent a time constraint. Lee and Kim (1999) give one interesting usage of HMM for 2-D hand movements where involuntary hand motions can be separated from intentional gestures.

- *Grammar based*: In a Logical Learning approach; Hand et al. (1994) propose a system which recognizes hand gesture by matching them with a grammar of tokens and productions. This set of rules, derived from taxonomy of hand positions, is extended in order to include movement components. The basic idea is to take the result from a posture recognition system and to concatenate them into phrases.

12.4.2 Model vs. Data-Oriented

Recognition systems are easily classified into two categories: model-oriented and data-oriented. A data-oriented system is built directly on top of the raw data provided by the sensor system (Figure 12.3). In a model-oriented system, the raw sensor data is first mapped to a logical model before being processed by the recognition module (Figure 12.4).

The advantage of the model-oriented approach is that the recognition module does not depend on technology and can be used with various motion capture systems (such as optical or magnetic). The only pre-condition is the existence of an adequate sensor-data converter that maps the raw measurements to the logical model.

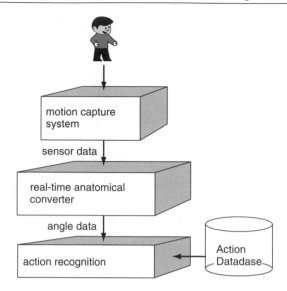

Figure 12.3   Model-oriented simulation system

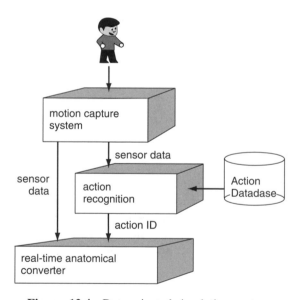

Figure 12.4   Data-oriented simulation system

In comparison with the data-oriented approach there is a loss of data precision. Indeed, the mapping of the raw sensor data onto a virtual model inevitably introduces some loss in data quality and most likely also alters their quantity.

We choose the model-oriented approach and use a magnetic motion capture system with a maximum of 16 sensors. The logical human model has 60 Degrees Of Freedom, and more if hands and feet are included. An in-house anatomical converter maps the raw sensor data onto a virtual skeleton model.

12.4.3   Recognizable Actions

The purpose of human activity is to achieve common or individual goals. In order to identify these goals by a software process, we divide human activity into smaller units called 'actions'. As human activity is driven by multiple motivations such as biological needs, rational decisions and social goals, we limit our model to action types having the following characteristics:

- *Goal-oriented*: The initiation of the action is motivated by a unique final goal. The action has a rational character, i.e. its goal is the result of a conscious decision. The goal is often underlined by a final permanent body posture or a characteristic set of constraints in Cartesian space. We do not consider actions of biological or physiological character such as fidgeting or balance gestures. We consider fidgeting as a noise whose amplitude is not big enough to have a significant impact on the action specifications. Finally, we do not consider actions of social character, although they are interesting for higher-level behavioral interactions. Social actions can be modeled as a composition of rational actions. For example, 'having a glass of wine with somebody' can be decomposed into (1) grasping the glass; (2) clink glasses; (3) drink; and (4) put the glass down. Actions of social character have many sub-goals, which is in contradiction with our previous requirement of unique goal-oriented actions.
- *Finite duration*: Time is a good criterion for delimiting the set of actions that we are interested in. We consider only actions of short duration, that is, actions of a few seconds. Actions of social nature have a longer lifetime, in the order of minutes and more. For periodic actions, such as walking, the definition of one motion cycle is sufficient. During the recognition phase, periodic actions will be recognized each time a cycle of the periodic motion is identified.
- *Postures and gestures*: Actions are expressed through the performer's body configuration, either in joints or Cartesian space. Postures are given by a permanent body configuration (absolute values at a given time) by opposition to gestures (variations over time).
- *Involved body parts*: Actions do not necessarily involve the complete body. A set of body parts can be sufficient to perform an action. A body part is one of the following: upper or lower arm or leg, a hand, a foot, the neck, the head, the pelvis, the abdomen or the thorax. Reducing an action definition to a set of body parts does not necessarily imply a loss of action relevant information.
- *Parallelism*: Sometimes, actions are performed in parallel rather than sequentially. Making a phone call with a mobile telephone while walking is considered as two different actions. The execution of actions can be sequential, overlapping or parallel, i.e. the 'phoning' action may start and end at any time before, during, or after the walking action. We also state that distinguishing parallel actions in an unambiguous way implies the use of non-intersecting sets of body parts for both actions.

On the basis of these observations, we define an action as follows, with a BNF-like (Backus-Naur-Form) notation:

$$\text{Action} := <\text{posture}> \mid <\text{gesture}> \mid <\text{constraint}> \mid <\text{gesture}> \times <\text{posture}> \mid$$
$$<\text{action}> + <\text{constraint}>$$

(where '×' means „followed by" and '+' means a parallel evaluation of both operands).

An action is defined by a gesture followed by a final posture. For example, 'sitting down' is decomposed into the 'sitting down' gesture and the permanent 'sitting' posture. Starting postures are not taken into account, as we are mainly interested in goal-oriented actions expressed with a well-defined final body state. Another reason is that for an action such as 'sitting down', a large number of starting postures can be considered. We are not interested in the performer's state at the beginning of an action.

Besides postures and gestures, we also consider actions that are defined by constraints. Constraints are actions such as 'holding an object'. Their evaluation results in a Boolean value: verified or not, true or false. They are evaluated in parallel to other actions.

Tracking and analyzing all DOF of a human body model for a large sampling rate is a time-consuming computation process. As we target real-time applications where only a small time slice of computation resources can be allocated for recognition algorithms, we have to balance data quantity with recognition precision. We propose a hierarchy of three data levels as explained in the next section.

12.4.4 Action-Analysis Levels

At the top level, we consider the Center of Mass (CoM). The CoM is a rough criterion that carries information regarding the global body configuration and motion direction. At the second level, we consider end effectors (EE): hands, feet, head and spine root. We include the spine root because it reveals the position of the upper body relative to the lower body. End effectors represent a remarkable compression of body information. Indeed, one can decode a human action solely by looking at the position evolution of these strategic body references (Figure 12.5).

A slightly larger set of body landmarks has been used by Hodgins et al. (1995) in order to compare real and simulated motions. At the lowest level, we analyze skeleton joint angles. They are the most detailed body information source available.

Cartesian data and joints angles heavily depend on the live performer's anatomical differences. We propose to normalize all Cartesian data with the body height of the performer. Indeed, statistical studies have measured high correlation between the body height and the major body segment lengths (Kroemer et al. 1990). We use three coordinate systems (Figure 12.6): a Global, a Body and a Floor Coordinate System (in short GCS, BCS, FCS). The BCS is attached to the spine base of the body and its up-axis is aligned with the main spine direction. The FCS is located at the vertical projection of the spine root onto the floor level and re-uses the GCS up-axis.

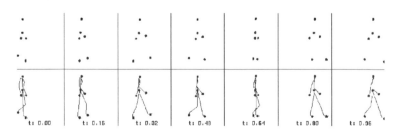

Figure 12.5 Decoding human walking with minimal body references

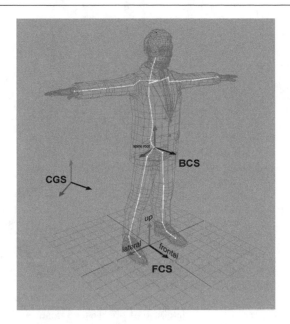

Figure 12.6 Global, floor and body-coordinate systems

An approximate CoM position is derived from the positions and the masses of the geometric volumes attached to the body skeleton. It is referenced in the FCS. The EEs, except the spine root, are referenced in the BCS. Indeed the spine root is referenced in the GCS, so that it indicates global body location and movements.

12.4.5 Action Specification

Knowing now that our hierarchical recognition model is based on three levels (CoM, EE, and JOINT), we introduce the concept of action primitives. An action primitive is an elementary unit required for action specification.

Postures are defined by a Boolean equation of posture primitives whose values are extracted from a body posture database (Figure 12.7). When inserting a posture into the database, some body parts can be tagged as relevant while others are not. Body parts are, for example, a forearm, a leg or the head. Reducing the posture specifications on a small set of body parts enhances the resolution and accuracy of the recognition system. Also, postures defined on non-intersecting sets of body parts can be recognized in parallel, for example, a posture defined on the left arm can be recognized in parallel to a posture defined on the right arm.

Gestures are defined by a Boolean equation of gesture primitives as shown in Table 12.1. Definitions can be more or less constrained, by adding more or less 'not_moving' primitives:

- *Posture primitive*

    Posture primitive $:= \sum (\text{body location, 3-D position}) + \sum (\text{JOINT, angle value})$

Where 'body location' is either the CoM or one EE. Explicitly specifying 3-D positions and angle values is tedious. Therefore, we use a specify-by-example approach: for each

Figure 12.7   A database of pre-defined postures

Table 12.1   Gesture specification

Gesture name	Gesture specification
Walking forward:=	((spine_root, forward) AND (left foot, forward)) OR ((spine_root, forward) AND (right foot, forward))
Side walking right:=	((CoM, nop) AND (spine root, right) AND (left foot, right)) OR ((CoM, not_moving) AND (spine root, right) AND (right foot, right))
Say yes:=	(head, up) OR (head, down)
Welcome:=	(right hand, up) AND (right hand, right) AND (left hand, up) AND (left hand, left)
Wave right hand:=	((right hand, left) AND (left hand, not_moving)) OR ((right hand, right) AND (left hand, not_moving))
Point right hand right:=	(right hand, right) AND (right hand, up) AND (left hand, not_moving)
Point right hand forward:=	(right hand, forward) AND (right hand, up) AND (left hand, not_moving)
Sit down:=	(CoM, backward) AND (spine, backward) AND (spine, downward)
Get up:=	(CoM, forward) AND (spine, forward) AND (spine, upward)

posture, we record a prototype and store it in a database. The system then extracts the posture primitives directly from these prototypes.
- *Gesture primitive*

$$\text{Gesture primitive} := \sum (\text{body location, velocity direction})$$

Where 'body location' denotes either the CoM or one EE. The 'velocity direction' is a sampled value describing the average motion direction: up, down, forward, backward, left, right. Its value is set whenever the velocity norm is above a normalized threshold along one of the FCS, BCS or GCS frame vectors. The threshold is empirically fixed. It delimits voluntary motions from noise, caused by fidgeting, for example. Additionally a not_moving value for the 'velocity direction' specifies a still CoM or EE. The head end effector is a special case as we consider rotation directions rather than translation directions. This is useful to express messages like 'yes' and 'no'. The rotation direction is determined by analyzing the average rotation of the look-at vector. For gesture primitives, we do not use JOINT level information because pattern recognition on joint angle evolution functions is incompatible with real-time constraints.
- *Constraint primitive*

$$\text{Constraint primitive} := \sum (\text{EE}i, \text{EE}j, f)$$

Where $i \neq j$ and f a distance-comparison function. A constraint primitive is either verified or not, true or false, depending on the result of f applied to both end effectors. In the simplest case, f is a function that compares the relative distance between the end effectors against a threshold value. An example is the 'holding an object' action: both hands are constrained to a constant distance, independently of the current posture or gesture. More sophisticated constraint functions are possible, such as checking the relative orientation between end effectors or checking whether an end effector is inside a bounding volume.

12.4.6   Action Recognition Algorithm

We now describe an action recognition algorithm that takes advantage of the hierarchical action-data structure. It starts by initializing a candidate database with all the defined actions: the Candidate Action Set (CAS). Then it proceeds sequentially with a candidate selection. Candidates that do not correspond to the performer's current action are eliminated from the CAS. If at any level the CAS becomes empty, the system returns an 'unknown action' message.

There is a constant balance between the number of action candidates and the amount of data per candidate (Figure 12.8).

- *Gestures (Levels 1 and 2).* Here we compute the current gesture primitives of the avatar. The primitives are substituted into each action's Boolean gesture equation. Those actions, whose equation result in a TRUE value, remain in the CAS. The others are discarded in order to avoid unnecessary computation at lower levels.
- *Postures (Levels 3, 4 and 5).* Here we compute the 3-D position of the CoM. For all the actions in the CAS, the squared distance between their CoM and the avatar's CoM is calculated. We call Min. and Max, the respectively smallest and largest squared distances.

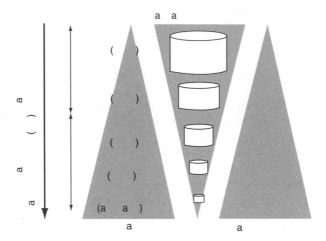

Figure 12.8 Compromise between recognition data quantity and data analysis costs

Actions remain in the CAS exclusively if their distance is smaller than a selectivity radius R. A selectivity parameter 'S' within [0, 1] controls how 'aggressively' candidates are removed at each level.

$$R = Min + (1 - S) \times (Max - Min)$$

- *The dimension of the Cartesian vector varies at the three levels*: 3-D for the CoM, 18D for the EEs (concatenation of six end effector's 3-D positions) and 68D for the joints (68 DOF). Note that this algorithm always selects at least one posture among the posture candidates. This is true even if the avatar's posture does not correspond to any of the postures defined in the database. This artefact may or may not be desirable, depending on the compromise of interaction misinterpretation and its ignorance. If misinterpretation happens too often, a simple remedy is to add some neutral postures into the database, for example, a 'stand still' posture.
- Constraints are evaluated in parallel to the gesture and posture levels. The method consists of evaluating the constraint functions with the performer's current body configuration.

Performance measurements with an action database of 35 actions showed an average recognition time of 1.2 ms (R4400 CPU, 200 MHz) with a standard deviation lower than 0.1 ms.

12.5 Case Studies

In this section, we describe some illustrations using action recognition and response. All set-ups are designed for a single performer and one or several Virtual Humanoids. We use a magnetic motion capture system and, optionally, a head-mounted display and data-gloves. Upon performer-activity recognition, the virtual participants react with specific behaviors. Their animation has been implemented with a generic motion integration framework (Emering 1999; Emering et al. 1999).

In the first example, we use action recognition as a means of controlling and guiding a Virtual Human in a Virtual Environment (Figure 12.9). The live performer is hooked up

Figure 12.9 Interactive walk-through environment driven by action recognition events: the performer approaches the green plant, grabs it and continues to walk

with ten magnetic sensors, which sample the body configuration at a maximum speed of 100Hz. The raw sensor measurements are transferred over the network to a computer where they are mapped to anatomical joint angles. These anatomical joint angles are the input for the action recognition system associated to a virtual participant. As the virtual camera is fixed on the head of this Virtual Human, the performer has a subjective scene view. Based on the recognition results and a finite-state behavior automaton, the Virtual Human can walk in all directions, grasp and drop the flower, switch on and off a virtual lamp. Some of the reactions are context-dependent: the same action triggers different responses depending on the agent's current state and location. For example, grasping the flower succeeds only within a short distance range centered on the flower's current location.

In the second example (Figure 12.10), the performer is immersed into a virtual shop environment where he meets a friend named Mary. The performer is supposed to buy a nice gift for Mary. The shopkeeper and Mary are autonomous virtual agents. They recognize the performer's actions and react in consequence: when the performer points to a desired object, the shopkeeper selects it and waits for confirmation. By nodding the head, the performer may either agree or refuse. On confirmation, the shopkeeper lifts the object and waits until the participant performs a grasping action. Then the participant is supposed to offer the object to Mary. If she is happy, she will accept the gift and go for a walk. In the opposite case, she adopts spiteful manners and leaves the scene. As the performer is supposed to move in Virtuality, a head-mounted display is necessary.

Figure 12.10 The virtual shop

12.5.1   Interactive Fighting

In the third example, an interactive fight-training scenario is exclusively based on recognition of posture-actions (Figure 12.11). The user is hooked up with nine motion capture sensors so that the computer creates an avatar in the virtual arena. Already present in the arena is a virtual autonomous trainer that waits for the performer's attack gestures. If the autonomous trainer recognizes the performer's fight gesture, it reacts with a complementary defense gesture. This scenario has been extensively tested in public exhibitions.

12.6   Discussion

Based on the previous interaction examples between a live performer and an inhabited virtual world, we gathered a lot of interesting and important hints to improve acceptance, presence and efficiency of action recognition as a communication channel between Reality and Virtuality.

12.6.1   Sense of Touching

This was obvious in the 'fight' set-up. By 'touching', we do not necessarily mean that haptic feedback is required, although this would greatly enhance the sense of presence in Virtuality. We mean that the performer should 'see' when he/she touched an object. For example the virtual fight opponent should notice when the performer tries to touch it and react, maybe by simply moving a step backwards. Similarly a flower pot could fall off a table when a collision has been detected with the performer's virtual hand.

Figure 12.11   Interactive fight training with a virtual teacher

12.6.2   Reactivity

As we usually recorded relatively small action databases (approximately 15 actions) and as it is difficult to ask the performer to accurately perform recognizable actions, the virtual participants did not sufficiently react. One solution is to have a larger database, so that the opponent becomes more reactive and tolerant to the performer's activity.

12.6.3   Objective and Subjective Views

It is easy to switch the virtual camera from an objective to a subjective scene view. For a subjective view, a head-mounted display greatly enhances the performer's projective experience of Virtuality. The subjective view is less attractive for external spectators because they have no virtual embodiment and therefore no impact at all on what they see on the screen. However, external spectators enjoy controlling an objective camera view with a mouse or a space-ball.

12.6.4   Embodiment

Many performers performed finger signs during the session, although we were not actually tracking fingers. They forgot about the absent data-gloves and expected to see the finger motions on their avatar. Adding a data-glove would certainly help here, but it means more cables and therefore, again a technological restriction to imagination.

12.6.5   System Performance

Some participants performed very fast motions, which could not be satisfyingly tracked by the system. We had average animation frame rates of 12 to 19 frames per second, which is insufficient for fast body motion capture. The frame frequency variation is mainly due to the graphical scene: depending on the virtual camera position, the scene switches to different levels of detail. Other participants were not sufficiently 'dynamic', thus not triggering the recognizable actions. For example, they did not sufficiently extend the arm or lift the leg as required by the action specifications in the recognition database. Finally, for a few rare exceptions, the system performs badly, mostly due to qualitatively poor motion capture results. We suspect that the concerned performers were too different from our virtual skeleton model and they would have required calibration fine-tuning. This happened in particular with small children.

12.6.6   Delegate Sub-Tasks

Imagine a performer moving a virtual object from one place to another. The final position of the object is the goal. Grabbing and releasing the object are sub-tasks. We should in no way let the participant waste time on grabbing the object with an extremely complex hand model and finger–object collision detection management. Although this is a very interesting and challenging topic, it does not contribute to the goal of the task. Sub-tasks can be left up to the computer's decision knowledge base and algorithmic know-how.

12.6.7 Semantic Modulation

Human gestures are often performed in parallel with speech. They can either modulate the emotional context of the dialogue or drastically change its semantics. If used as a stand-alone channel, gestures are self-contained, semantically meaningful units. A method for isolating the emotional motion components of gestures is described by Amaya et al. (1996). We did not develop any test environment for integrating action-recognition with a speech synthesizer, but this is important when focusing on dialogues between performers and virtual citizens, as noticed by Cassell et al. (1999).

12.6.8 Event/Action Associations

An action recognition system generates events that are associated with reactions. Those associations have to be chosen with great care as the convenience of the human–computer interface directly depends on them. Adjusting the displacement direction by raising the left or right arm is an example of a bad association. We experienced this in our interactive walk-through environment. A direction control connected directly to the relative orientation of the performer is much more intuitive and efficient. Yet, there are some examples of associations that cannot be performed in a natural way. 'Walking' is such an example. Technical limitations make it impossible for a performer to just 'walk' through an environment. Some researchers like (Pratt et al. 1997) experienced with 'treadmills', but treadmills do not allow an easy solution for the walking direction. We propose a splitting the event: when the performer performs a few steps forwards, then activate the displacement generator and keep it performing even though the performer stops walking. De-activate the displacement generator when the recognition system detects the performer walking backwards. This approach is a compromise between limited activity space and the need of long-range displacements in a virtual world. A practical hint: the walk forward and backward mechanism works fine as long as it approximately corresponds to an identity operation, i.e. globally the performer must not drift away form the activity space.

12.6.9 Realistic Behavior

If we create life-like environments and inhabitants, realistic behavior is a strong requirement. When a 'grasp' recognition event triggers the attachment of a nearby object to the performers' hands, then the object has to stay attached only as long as the performer keeps a grasp-like posture. When the performer changes his posture, the object must drop to the floor due to elementary gravity properties. Such examples are the main motivation for using constraint recognition, in parallel to actions.

12.6.10 Verbal Response

Independently of the form used, whether visual, audio or haptic, feedback is of major importance in interfaces. In our illustrations, feedback consists of behavioral responses from Virtual Humans. The communication is entirely non-verbal. In more elaborate environments, response must be extended by speech and facial expression. Verbal communication greatly enhances believability and the feeling of presence inside a virtual world.

13

Interaction with 3-D Objects

Marcello Kallmann

Among the several issues related to real-time animation of Virtual Human actors, the ability to interact with virtual objects requires special attention. Take as an example usual objects as: automatic doors, general furniture, or a lift. Interaction with such objects can easily become too complex for real-time applications. Some of the related problems involve: recognition of manipulation places, automatic arm and hand animation, and motion synchronization between actors and objects. The *smart object* approach is described here and can overcome many of these difficulties by storing all necessary interaction information within the object description. Interaction information is defined during the modeling phase, forming a complete 'user guide' to the object. In this way, virtual actors can simply access and follow such interaction descriptions in order to accomplish a given task. Solutions to related sub-problems such as programming an object's behaviors, interactions with multiple actors, or actor animation to manipulate objects are discussed here, and detailed case studies are analyzed.

13.1 Introduction

Computer graphics systems no longer represent just a static scene showing 3-D objects. In most applications nowadays, objects are animated, they have deformable shapes and realistic movements. Such objects 'exist' in Virtual Environments and are used to simulate a number of different situations. For instance, costs are saved whenever it is possible to simulate and predict the result of a product before manufacture.

Although many technical issues have not been fully solved, a lot of attention has been given to a next step: *lifelike behaviors*. The issue is to have virtual entities existing in Virtual Environments, deciding their actions on their own, manipulating virtual objects, etc. As a natural consequence, computer animation techniques today are strongly related to artificial intelligence and robotics techniques.

It is still a challenge to animate a virtual actor that can decide its motions, reacting and interacting with its Virtual Environment, in order to achieve a task given by the animator.

Handbook of Virtual Humans Edited by N. Magnenat-Thalmann and D. Thalmann
© 2004 John Wiley & Sons, Ltd ISBN: 0-470-02316-3

This virtual actor might have its own way to decide how to achieve the given task, and thus, many different sub-problems arise in many areas.

One of these sub-problems is how to give enough information to the virtual actor so that it is able to interact with each object in the scene. That means, how to give to an actor the ability to interact with general objects, in a real-time application. This includes different types of interactions that can be considered. Some examples are: the action of pushing a button, opening a book, pushing a desk drawer, turning a key to then open a door, and so on.

A human-like behavior would recognize a given object with vision and touch, and then, based on past experiences and knowledge, the correct sequence of motions would be deduced and executed. Such an approach is still too complex to be handled in a general case, and not suited for interactive systems where real-time execution is required.

To avoid complex and time-consuming algorithms that try to model the full virtual actor's 'intelligence', an alternate approach is to use a well-defined object description where all properties, functionality features and descriptions of the steps to perform each available interaction are added to the geometrical shape description of the object. In that way, part of the most difficult thing to model, the knowledge of the virtual actor, is avoided. Instead, the designer of the object will use his/her own knowledge assigning to the object all the information that the virtual actor needs to access in order to interact with the object. This more direct approach has been called the smart object approach (Kallmann and Thalmann 1999) to animate actor–object interactions.

13.2   Related Work

The need to model actor–object interactions appears in most applications of computer animation and simulation. Such applications encompass several domains, for example, autonomous agents in Virtual Environments, human factors analysis, training, education, virtual prototyping, and simulation-based design. A good overview of such areas is presented by Badler (1997), and one example of a training application is described by Johnson and Rickel (1997).

The term *object interaction* has been employed in the literature, mainly for the direct interaction between the user and the environment (Hand 1997), but less attention has been given to the actor–object interaction case.

Actor–object interaction techniques were first specifically addressed in a simulator based on natural language instructions using an *object specific reasoning* (OSR) module (Levinson 1996). The OSR holds a relational table informing geometric and functional classification of objects, in order to help interpretation of natural language instructions. The OSR module also holds some interaction information: for each graspable object site, the appropriate hand shape and grasp approach direction. This set of information is sufficient to decide and perform grasping tasks, but no considerations are made concerning interactions with more complex objects with some proper functionality.

In most cases, actors and objects have proper behaviors, and behavioral animation techniques (Millar et al. 1999; Ziemke 1998) can be employed. Behaviors can follow the *agent* approach, where actions are decided based on sensing the environment (Woolridge and Jennings 1995; Franklin and Graesser 1996). These domains provide techniques that can be employed to solve some issues of the general actor–object interaction problem. The term *object functionality* will sometimes be employed here instead of *object behavior*, reflecting the fact that the objects considered here have simpler behaviors than actors. The following two sections will present the method done: the definition of object's functionality, and the actor animation to perform interactions.

13.2.1 Object Functionality

In general, objects contain some proper functionality that needs to be defined. Some simple examples are: after pressing a button the lift door will open, or only after turning on the printer, can it print. Such rules need somehow to be programmed inside objects, and different techniques may be employed.

Okada et al. (1999) proposed composing object parts equipped with input and output connectors that can be linked to achieve different functionalities. State machines are also widely used. In particular, most game engines like Motivate (http: Motivate) or NeMo (http: NeMo) use hierarchical finite state machines, defined graphically through user interfaces.

One important point is the ability to interpret the defined functionality in parallel, in a synchronized way. As will be shown later, it may happen that several actors interact with a same object, e.g. to enter a lift.

Several techniques used for general behavior definition cover some of these aspects. One specific structure to define parallel behaviors is the *parallel transitions network* (PaTNets) (Granieri et al. 1995; Bindiganavale et al. 2000), presented in Section 11.2.4. Other works (Lamarche and Donikian 2001) cover the aspect of sharing resources with concurrent state machines.

It is natural to think that the description of the object functionality should be associated with the object geometric description as well. Current standards (such as VRML) for object description are normally based on scene graphs containing nodes to connect animation to external events, such as events from the user interface (mouse, keyboard, etc.). This provides a primitive way to describe basic object functionality, but as it is not generic enough, it is always necessary to use complete programming languages such as Java scripts. Thus, there is still a place for standards in the description of functionalities.

A similar scenario appears in the *feature modeling* area, mainly regarding the scope of CAD/CAM applications (Shah and M. Mäntylä 1995) where the main concern is to represent not only the shape of the object, but also all the other important features regarding its design choices and even manufacturing procedures. In fact, suppliers of CAD systems are starting to integrate some simulation parameters in their models (Berta 1999). The *knowledgeware* extension of the Catia system can describe characteristics such as costs, temperature, pressure, inertia, volume, wet area, surface finish, formulas, link to other parameters, etc. but still no specific considerations to define object functionality or interactivity.

The main point is that none of these techniques specifically cover the problem of describing object functionality for actor–object interaction purposes. As will be shown later, object functionality, expected actor behaviors, parallel interpretation of behaviors, and resources sharing need to be solved in a unified way.

13.2.2 Actor Animation

Once the object functionality is somehow defined and available, actors need to access this information and decide which motions to apply in order to complete a desired interaction.

The actor motion control problem is very complex, and mostly has been studied by the computer graphics community, mainly targeting movie and game industries. Boulic et al. (1997) and Chapter 5 of this book offer a good overview of the employed techniques. Recently the motion control problem has also received attention from the robotics and artificial intelligence domains.

For instance, from the robotics area, a classification of hand configurations for grasping has been proposed by Cutkosky (1989). Following the same idea, but targeting animation of virtual actors, Rijpkema and Girard (1991) introduce a knowledge-based grasping system based on pre-defined hand configurations with on-line adaptation and animation. This approach has been extended to two hand grasping by Mas and Thalmann (1994). Huang et al. (1995) also propose a system for automatic decision of hand configurations for grasping, based on a database of pre-defined grasping postures.

Also from the robotics domain, planning algorithms are able to define collision-free paths for articulated structures. Koga et al. (1994) have applied such algorithms in the animation of the arms of a virtual actor, obtaining interesting results. The main drawback of the method is conversely also its main advantage: because of its random nature, complicated motions can be planned, but with high and unpredictable computational cost, thus not currently applicable for interactive simulations. A huge literature about motion planning is available, mainly targeting the motion control of different types of robots (Latombe 1991; Laumond 1998), and companies such as Kineo (www.kineocam.com) have started to provide this technology.

Artificial intelligence techniques such as neural networks and genetic algorithms have been applied to the control of virtual bodies (Nolfi and Floriano 2000; Sims 1991; Panne and Fiume 1993). Currently, these algorithms are too costly and can be only applied in limited cases. However, artificial intelligence techniques will probably become more powerful and usable in a near future.

Inverse kinematics (Watt and Watt 1992) is still the most popular technique for articulated structure animation. Some works can handle the animation of complex structures, taking into account several constraints (Baerlocher 2001). Some works present specific implementations regarding only the movement of the actor's arm (Tolani and Badler 1996; Wang and Verriest 1998). Although interesting results can be obtained, it is still difficult to obtain realistic postures, specially concerning the automatic full body animation to reach objects with hands, for instance, to determine a coherent knee flexion when the actor needs to reach with its hand a very low position. For a complete overview of the possibilities of Inverse Kinematics techniques, as well as other related issues, please see Chapter 5.

In another direction, database-driven methods can easily cope with full body postures. The idea is to define pre-recorded (thus realistic) motions to reach each position in the space inside a discrete and fixed volumetric grid around the actor. Then, when a specific position is to be reached, the respective motion is obtained through interpolation of the pre-recorded motions relative to the neighboring cells. This is exactly the approach taken by Wiley and Hahn (1997) with good results achieved, but limited to the completeness of the database. Complementary works (Bindiganavale and Badler 1998) propose techniques to adapt pre-recorded motions to respect some given constraints. Database methods were also successfully used to determine grasping postures (Aydin and Nakajima 1999b). The main drawback of such methods is that they are not general enough: it is difficult to adapt motions to all given cases and also to handle collisions with the environment. However, some works have started to propose solutions to handle collisions (Nebel 1999).

Table 13.1 Comparison of motion control methods, regarding the realism of the generated movements, the real-time ability of computation, generality of being applied to different types of interactions, and the ability to handle and solve collisions with the environment and self-collisions

	Realism	Real-Time	Generality	Collisions
Motion database	+	+	−	−
Path planning	−	−	+	+
Inverse kinematics	−	+	+	−

As a final conclusion, Table 13.1 shows a comparison of these methods, from the point of view of animating actors for general interactions with objects.

13.3 Smart Objects

In order to simplify the simulation of actor object interactions, a complete representation of the functionality and interaction capabilities of a given object is proposed. The idea is that each interactive object contains a complete description of its available interactions, like forming a 'user guide' to be followed by actors during interactions. Once objects contain such information, they are considered here to become 'smart'.

13.3.1 Interaction Features

A feature modeling approach is used, and a new class of features for simulation purposes is proposed: *interaction features*. Interaction features can be seen as all parts, movements and descriptions of an object that have some important role when interacting with an actor. For example, not only buttons, drawers and doors are considered to be interaction features in an object, but also their movements, purposes, manipulation details, etc.

Interaction features can be grouped into four different classes:

- *Intrinsic object properties*: properties that are part of the object design, for example: the movement description of its moving parts, physical properties such as weight and center of mass, and also a text description to identify general objects' purpose and the design intent.
- *Interaction information*: useful to aid an actor to perform each possible interaction with the object. For example: the identification of interaction parts (like a knob or a button), specific manipulation information (hand shape, approach direction), suitable actor positioning, description of object movements that affect the actor's position (as for a lift), etc.
- *Object behavior*: to describe the reaction of the object to each performed interaction. An object can have various different behaviors, which may or may not be available, depending on its state. For example, a printer object will have the 'print' behavior available only if its internal state variable 'power on' is true. Describing object's behaviors is the same as defining the overall object functionality.
- *Expected actor behavior*: associated with each object behavior, it is useful to have a description of some expected actor behaviors in order to accomplish the interaction. For example, before opening a drawer, the actor is expected to be in a suitable position so that the drawer will not collide with the actor when opening. Such a suitable position is then proposed to the actor during the interaction.

This classification covers most common actor–object interactions. However, many design choices still appear when trying to specify in detail each needed interaction feature, in particular concerning features related to behavioral descriptions. Behavioral features are herein specified using pre-defined plans composed with primitive behavioral instructions. This has proved to be a straightforward approach because, in this way, to perform an interaction, actors will only need to 'know' how to interpret such interaction plans.

In the smart object description, a total of eight interaction features are identified, which are described in Table 13.2.

Table 13.2 The eight types of interaction features used in the smart object description

Feature	Class	Data contained
Descriptions	Object Property	Contains text explanations about the object: semantic properties, purposes, design intent, and any general information.
Parts	Object Property	Describes the geometry of each component part of the object, their hierarchy, positioning and physical properties.
Actions	Object Property	Actions define movements, and any other changes that the object may undertake, such as color changing, texture, etc.
Commands	Interaction Info.	Commands parameterize and associate with a specific part the defined actions. For example, commands *open* and *close* can use the same translation action.
Positions	Interaction Info.	Positions are used for different purposes, such as for defining regions for collision avoidance and to suggest suitable places for actors during interactions.
Gestures	Interaction Info.	Gestures are any movement to suggest to an actor. Mainly, hand shapes and locations for grasping and manipulation are defined here, but also specification of other actions or pre-recorded motions can be defined.
Variables	Object Behavior	Variables are generally used by the behavioral plans, mainly to define the state of the object.
Behaviors	Object and Actor Behavior	Behaviors are defined with plans composed of primitive instructions. Plans can check or change states, trigger commands and gestures, call up other plans, etc., specifying both object behaviors and expected actors' behaviors. These plans form the actor–object communication language during interactions.

13.3.2   Interpreting Interaction Features

Once a smart object has been modeled, a simulation system is able to load and animate it in a VE. For this, the simulator needs to implement a *smart object reasoning module*, able to correctly interpret the behavioral plans.

There is a trade-off when choosing which features to be considered in an application. As shown in Figure 13.1, when taking into account the full set of object features, less reasoning computation is needed, but less general results are obtained. As an example, minimum computation is needed to have an actor pass through a door following strictly a proposed path to walk. However, such a solution would not be general in the sense that all agents would pass the door using exactly the same path. To achieve better results, external parameters should also take effect, as, for example, the current actor's emotional state.

Note that the notion of a realistic result is context-dependent. For example, pre-defined paths and hand shapes can make an actor manipulate an object very realistically. However, in a context where many actors are manipulating such objects exactly in the same way, the overall result is not realistic.

A design choice appears while modeling objects with too many potential interactions. Especially in the case of composed objects, it is possible to model the object as many independent smart objects, each one containing only basic interactions. For example, to have an actor interacting with a car, the car can be modeled as a combination of different smart objects: car door, radio, and the car dashboard. In this way, the simulation application can explicitly control a sequence of actions such as: opening the car door, entering the car, turning on the radio, and starting the engine. On the other hand, if the simulation program is concerned only with traffic simulation, the way an agent enters the car may not be important. In this case, the general behavior of entering the car can be encapsulated in a single smart object car.

The smart object approach introduces the following main characteristics into a simulation system:

- *Decentralization of the animation control*: Object interaction information is stored in the objects, and can be loaded as plug-ins, so that most object-specific computation is released from the main animation control.
- *Reusability of designed smart objects*: Not only by using the same smart object in different applications, but also by designing new objects by merging any desired feature from previously designed smart objects.
- *A simulation-based design is naturally achieved*: Designers can take full control of the loop: design, test and re-design. Designed smart objects can be easily connected with a simulation program, to get feedback for improvements in the design.

Figure 13.1   The choice of which interaction features to take into account is directly related to many implementation issues in the simulation system

13.4   SOMOD

The Smart Object Modeler application (SOMOD) (Kallmann and Thalmann 2002) was developed specifically to model smart objects. It was developed using Open Inventor (Wernecke 1994) as graphics library, and FLTK for the user interface.

SOMOD permits geometric models of the component parts of an object to be imported, and then all the needed interaction features can be interactively specified. Features are organized by type, and a main window permits management of lists of features. According to the feature type, specific dialog boxes can edit the related parameters.

13.4.1   Object Properties

Text input windows are used to enter any text descriptions, with specific fields to describe a semantic name for the object, and its overall characteristics. These definitions can then be retrieved by simulators for any kind of processing.

An object is composed by assembling its different parts. The geometry of each part is imported from commercial modeling applications. Parts can then be positioned interactively using Open Inventor manipulators (see Figure 13.2). The same technique of using manipulators is adopted to define the movement actions that can be applied to each part. For example, to define a translation, the user displaces a part using a manipulator, and the transformation movement from the initial position to the user-selected position is then saved as an action. Note that actions are saved independently of parts, so that they can later be parameterized differently (defining commands) and applied to different parts.

13.4.2   Interaction Information

Commands are specified simply by associating actions to parts, and giving a parameterization of how the motion should be applied to that part. Commands fully specify how to apply an action to a part and are directly referenced from the behavioral plans whenever a part of the object is required to move.

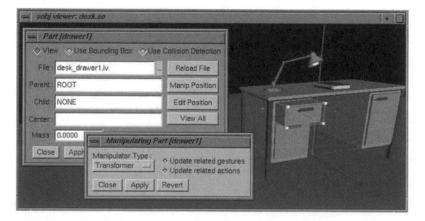

Figure 13.2   Defining the specific parameters of a drawer. The drawer is a part of the smart object desk, which contains many other parts. The image shows in particular the positioning of the drawer in relation to the whole object

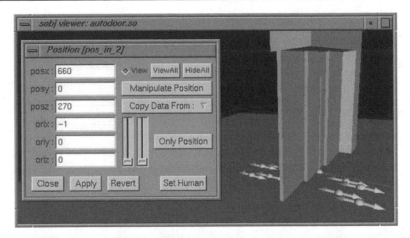

Figure 13.3 Positions can be defined for different purposes. Here many different positions (and orientations) are placed to propose possible places for actors to walk when arriving from any of the door sides

Positions and directions (see Figure 13.3) can be specified for different purposes. Each position (as each feature) is identified with a given name for later referencing from the interaction plans. Note that all features related to graphical parameters can be defined interactively, which is important in order to see their location in relation to the object. Positions are defined in relation to the object skeleton's root, so that they can be transformed to the same reference frame of the actor whenever this is needed, during the simulation. Note that smart objects can be loaded and positioned anywhere in the Virtual Environment and all associated information needs to be transformed accordingly.

Gestures are normally the most important interaction information. Gesture parameters are defined in SOMOD and proposed to actors during interactions. The term gesture is used to refer to any kind of motion that an actor is able to perform. A gesture can only reference a pre-recorded animation to be played, but the most used gesture is to move the hand towards reaching a location in space using inverse kinematics. Figure 13.4 illustrates the process of

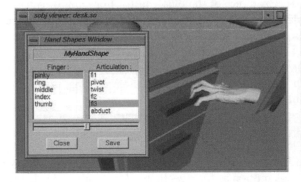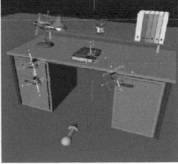

Figure 13.4 The left image shows a hand shape being interactively defined. The right image shows all used hand shapes being interactively located with manipulators

defining hand configurations and locations to be reached. Such information can then be used during simulations to animate the actor's arm to perform manipulations with the object. It is left to the simulator to decide which motion algorithm should be applied. As will be shown in Section 13.5, inverse kinematics was used for the examples shown here.

Some extra parameters can be set in order to define if after the reaching motion has been completed, the associated part should be taken, put, or just followed. Following is used to simulate interactions such as pressing buttons or opening drawers.

13.4.3   Behaviors

The behavioral animation solutions presented here are specific to the actor–object interaction problem. For a more general and complete overview on behavioral animation techniques, please refer to Chapter 11 of this book.

In smart objects, behaviors are defined using pre-defined plans formed by primitive instructions. It is difficult to define a closed and sufficient set of instructions to use, and a complex script language to describe behaviors is not the goal. The idea is to keep a simple format with a direct interpretation to serve as guidance for reasoning algorithms, and that non-programmers are able to create and test it.

A first feature to recognize in an interactive object is its possible states. States are directly related to the behaviors one wants to model for the object. For instance, a desk object will typically have a variable state for its drawers, which can be assigned two values: 'open' or 'close'. However, depending on the context, it may be needed to consider another midterm state value. Variables are used to keep the states of the object and can be freely defined by the user to approach many different situations. Variables are defined by assigning a name and an initial value, and can be also used for other purposes from the interaction plans, as for instance to retrieve the current position of the actor in order to decide from which side of a door the actor should enter.

Interaction plans are defined using a specific dialog box (see Figure 13.5), which guides the user through all possible primitive instructions to use. The following key concepts are used for the definition of interaction plans:

- An interaction plan describes both the behavior of the object and the expected behavior of actors. Instructions that start with the keyword 'user' are instructions that are proposed to the user of the object, i.e., the actor. Examples of some user instructions are: UserGoto to propose it to walk to some place, UserDoGest to tell it to manipulate some part using pre-defined gesture parameters (Figure 13.5), UserAttachTo to say that the actor should be attached to some object part, as when entering a lift, etc.
- In SOMOD, an interaction plan is also called a behavior. Many plans (or behaviors) can be defined and they can call each other, as subroutines. Like programming, this enables complex behaviors based on simpler behaviors to be built.
- There are three types of behaviors (or plans): private, object control, and user selectable. Private behaviors can only be called from other behaviors. An object control behavior is a plan that is interpreted all the time since the object is loaded in a Virtual Environment. They enable objects to act like agents, for example, sensing the environment to trigger some motion, or to have a continuous motion as for a ventilator. Object control behaviors cannot have user-related instructions. Finally, user selectable behaviors are those that are visible to be selected by actors, in order to perform a desired interaction.

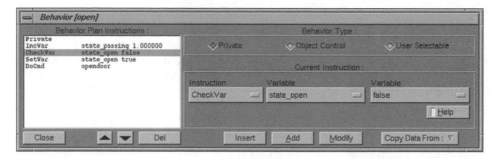

Figure 13.5 Defining interaction plans: menu-buttons are used to list all possible instructions to use, and for each instruction, the possible parameters are listed in additional menu-buttons. In this way complex behaviors can easily be created

- Selectable behaviors can be available or not, depending on the state of specified variables. For example, for a door, one can design two behaviors: to open and to close the door. However, only one is available at a time depending on the open state of the door. Behavior availability is controlled with an instruction CheckVar. Its use is exemplified in Figure 13.5, and will be explaining in Section 13.6.

Other important features to consider are:

- *Multi-Actor Interactions*: If the object is required to interact with many actors at the same time, synchronization issues need to be taken into account. There are two levels of synchronization. The first is to guarantee the interaction coherence. For this, interaction plans are responsible to correctly make use of variables, for example, to count the number of actors currently interacting with the object, correctly setting states and testing conditions to ensure correctness when multiple actors are accessing the same object, etc. Section 13.6.2 details a smart object door that is able to deal with several actors at the same time.

  Another level of synchronization is to correctly manage the interpretation of several interaction plans in parallel. This is independent of the object type and should be done by the simulator. A proposed procedure for this kind of synchronization is described in Section 13.5.1.

- *Graphical State Machines*: SOMOD plans are very simple to use when describing simple interactions and functionalities. They can cope with much more complex cases, but then plans start to get more complex to design. It is like trying to use a specific purpose language to solve any kind of problems.

  To simplify modeling the behaviors of more complex objects, SOMOD proposes a dialog box to graphically design finite state machines. The proposed solution is to start designing basic interaction plans, using the standard behavior editor (see Figure 13.5). Then, when all the components have had their functionality defined, the state machine window is used, to define the states of the whole object, and the connections between the components. At the end, designed state machines are automatically translated into interaction plans so that, from the simulator point of view, a single representation is kept, and all behaviors are treated as plans. Section 13.6.3 exemplifies how a state machine is used to simplify the creation of a smart lift.

- *Templates*: One important concept is to re-use previously defined objects and functionalities, and a specific template loader was designed for this goal. The template loader window can import any kind of features from other smart objects. Note that some features have dependencies on other features. These dependencies need to be tracked and coherently loaded. In addition, names are automatically updated whenever conflicts with previously created names appear.
- *Extensions*: SOMOD has been used for different purposes and different types of extensions have been integrated. Positions can be automatically generated to define regions for collision avoidance when actors are walking. Behavioral instructions can simply call a user-defined function in Python language (Lutz 1996), virtually enabling any complex behavior to be coded. A VRML exporter was also developed, however, with limited animation capabilities.

13.5   Interacting with Smart Objects

When a smart object is loaded into a Virtual Environment, actors are able to access the available interaction plans and interpret them. Two main issues should be considered when interpreting plans: how to synchronize the interpretation of plans in parallel, and how to animate the actor's skeleton whenever a manipulation action is required.

13.5.1   Interpretation of Plans

Each time an actor selects an interaction plan to perform, a specific thread is created to follow the instructions of the plan (Figure 13.6). The situation is that simultaneous access to the smart object is available when interpreting instructions, for example, that access variables or trigger motions.

A simple synchronization rule to activate and block the many processes interpreting plans in parallel is adopted. However, interaction plans still need to be well designed in order to cope with all the possible combinations of simultaneous access. For example, complex situations such as the *dining philosopher's* problem (Andrews 1991) are not automatically solved.

A simple built-in synchronization rule between threads is used. For this, plan instructions are grouped into two categories: *long* instructions, and *local* instructions. Long instructions

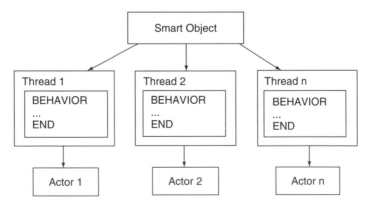

Figure 13.6   For each actor performing an interaction with an object, a thread is used to interpret the selected interaction plan. Each thread accesses and controls, in a synchronized way, its related actor and object, according to the plan's instructions

are those that cannot start and complete in a single time step of the simulation. For example, instructions that trigger movements will take several frames to be completed, depending on how many frames the movement needs to finish. All other instructions are said to be local.

Plans are interpreted instruction by instruction, and each instruction needs to be finished before the next one is executed. When a plan is being interpreted by some thread T, all other threads are suspended until a long instruction is found. In this way, T will fully execute sequences of local instructions, while all other threads remain locked. When a long instruction is reached, it is initialized, the other threads are activated, and T stays observing if the instruction has finished. This scheme results in the situation where all activated threads are in fact monitoring movements and other long instructions, and each time local instructions appear, they are all executed in a single time step, while other threads are locked.

This approach automatically solves most common situations. For example, suppose that a smart lift has an instruction: 'if state of calling button is *pressed* do nothing; otherwise set state of calling button to *pressed* and press it'. Suppose now that two actors, exactly at the same time, decide to call the lift. The synchronization rule says that while one thread is interpreting local instructions, all others are locked. In this way, it is guaranteed that only one actor will actually press the button. Without this synchronization, both actors would press the button together at the same time, resulting in serious inconsistent results.

13.5.2 Manipulation Actions

To animate the actor's skeleton for manipulation actions, inverse kinematics is used, with different constraints based on the type of manipulation and on the goal location to reach with the hand.

An unified approach was designed to target general manipulations with one arm. First of all, a manipulation movement is divided in three phases: reaching, middle, and final phases (Figure 13.7).

All manipulation movements start at the reaching phase. In this phase, inverse kinematics is used in order to animate the actor's skeleton to have its hand in the specified position. Then three cases can happen, depending on the parameters retrieved from the smart object: *follow, take,* or *put.* Parameters *follow* and *take* are used to specify the attachment of objects to the actor's hand. The *follow* parameter indicates that the actor's hand should then follow a specified

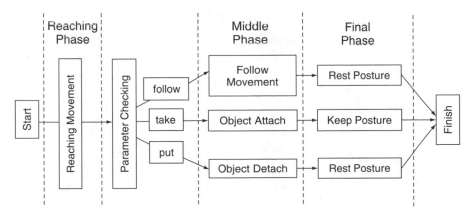

Figure 13.7 Considered phases for a manipulation instruction

movement. This is the case, for example, to press buttons and open drawers: the specified translation movement to animate the object part is followed by the actor's hand, while inverse kinematics is used in order to adjust the posture of the actor's skeleton. The final phase has the default behavior to either keep the actor's posture unchanged or to change it to a standard rest posture. This can be configurable and can chain other actions' instructions or allows the user to leave the actor in the rest posture. In this way long and complex manipulations can be subdivided into small pieces, each piece matching the schema of Figure 13.7.

In addition to the inverse kinematics motion to control the actor's arm towards the specified location, the current hand fingers configuration is interpolated towards the specified final configuration, and the actor's head is set to look to the place of manipulation.

To control the full actor body with different types of constraints, inverse kinematics (Baerlocher 2001) is used (see Chapter 5 for more details). The skeleton's root is a node between the pelvis and the spine, and which separates the hierarchies of the legs and feet from the hierarchies of the spine, head and arms.

At the beginning of a manipulation, the actor's skeleton's sizes and the task position to reach with the hand are analyzed and different constraints are set.

- First, the inverse kinematics module is set to only animate the joints of the arm, shoulder, clavicle, and the upper part of the spine. This set of joints makes the reach volume space larger, as the actor can reach further positions by flexing the spine. However, a side effect is that even for closer positions to reach, the spine can move, generating weird results. To overcome this, two new constraints are created. Positional and orientation constraints, with low priority, are used in order to keep the spine straight as long as possible (see Figure 13.8).
- Second, if the goal position to reach with the hand is lower than the lowest position achievable with the hand in a straight rest position, a special knee flexion configuration is set. The joints of the hip, knee, and ankle are added to the allowed joints to be animated by the inverse kinematics module, and two new constraints, with high priorities, are added to keep each foot in its original position and orientation. This configuration makes the actor flex the knees, keeping its feet attached to the ground, while the actor's skeleton root is gradually lowered (see Figure 13.9).

Figure 13.8 Specific constraints are used to keep the actor's spine as straight as possible

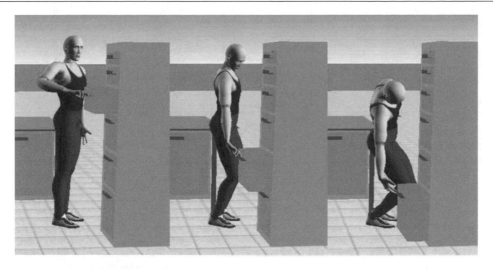

Figure 13.9 When the position to reach with the hand is too low, additional constraints are used in order to obtain knee flexion. The images show, from left to right, the postures achieved when reaching lower positions each time

After the initial phase of constraints and joints control distribution is done, the hand task is set with highest priority. In order to animate the arm from the initial configuration to the desired one, the initial hand position and orientation are extracted and interpolated towards the goal hand position and orientation, generating several interpolated sub-goals. Interpolations can be simply linear, but should consider biomechanical properties. Inverse kinematics is then used to generate the final actor posture for each interpolated sub-goal.

After the reaching phase is completed, a *follow* movement might be required (see Figure 13.7). In this case, the hand keeps its orientation, and only its position is updated to follow the movement of the object being manipulated. Figures 13.10 exemplifies both reaching and middle phases.

13.6 Case Studies

This section details how interaction plans can actually be coded. The focus is on explaining how different issues can be solved using simple scripted plans, and not to give a complete description of SOMOD instructions. The first case shows how simple interactions such as opening a drawer can be defined. The second example shows how concurrent object access can be handled when multiple actors want to interact with the same automatic door. A final example shows how the graphical state machine editor can be used to simplify the definition of more complex interactions.

The examples shown here were generated with the Agents Common Environment (ACE) system (Kallmann et al. 2000), which integrates smart objects with higher-level behavioral control modules. For more information about ACE, and for higher-level animation examples obtained with ACE, please refer to Chapter 11.

Figure 13.10 The reaching phase of a button press manipulation. Note that the actor's head is also controlled to look at the button, and the hand configuration is gradually interpolated towards the final button press shape

13.6.1 Opening a Drawer

Interaction plans are grouped as a set of behaviors, each one containing a list of instructions, similar to the procedures of a program. The code in Table 13.3 exemplifies interactions of opening and closing a drawer, as shown in Figure 13.9.

The instruction CheckVar determines if the behavior is available or not. For example, the behavior open_drawer is only available if the state variable var_open is false. In this way, at any time, actors can ask for a list of available interaction plans, i.e., available object behaviors according to the object's state.

Table 13.3 Code for interactions of opening and closing a drawer

```
BEHAVIOR open_drawer
    CheckVar v    ar_open false
    UserGoTo      pos_front
    UserDoGest    gest_drawer
    DoCmd         cmd_open
    SetVar        var_open true
END

BEHAVIOR close_drawer
    CheckVar      var_open true
    UserGoTo      pos_front
    UserDoGest    gest_drawer
    DoCmd         cmd_close
    SetVar        var_open false
END
```

In the example, when an actor receives the plan `open_drawer`, it will execute each primitive instruction in the plan starting with the `User` keyword. That is, it will walk to the proposed position and then it will apply inverse kinematics to animate the actor to perform the specified motion in the gesture `gest_drawer`. In this case, the motion includes a *follow* movement that is set to follow the movement of the drawer part. The drawer itself will be animated by the smart object, according to the specified `cmd_close` parameters. At the end, the object state is changed, allowing the `close_drawer` behavior to be available. Note that both instructions, which are interpreted by the object and by the actor, are combined in the same behavior.

This same kind of solution can be applied to all interactions consisting of reaching a place and then following an object's movement. This is the case of interactions such as pushing a button, opening the cover of a book, opening doors, etc.

13.6.2 Interaction of Multiple Actors

The code in Table 13.4 exemplifies how state variables are used to synchronize multiple actors passing through the same automatic door.

Each time an actor desires to pass through the door, it will interpret the behavior `enter`, that will give it the correct positions to pass through the door without colliding with other actors. The behavior `enter` is the only one visible to the actor, as all others are

Table 13.4 How state variables are used to synchronize multiple actors

```
BEHAVIOR open                          BEHAVIOR enter_l_r
    Private                                Private
    IncVar                                 UserGoTo        pos_l_in
  var_passing 1                            DoBh            open
    CheckVar                               UserGoTo        pos_r_out
  var_passing 1                            DoBh            close
    DoCmd        opendoor        END
END
                                       BEHAVIOR enter_r_l
                                           Private
                                           UserGoTo        pos_r_in
BEHAVIOR close                             DoBh            open
    Private                                UserGoTo        pos_l_out
    IncVar                                 DoBh            close
  var_passing -1
    CheckVar                   END
  var_passing 0
    DoCmd        cmd_close
END


BEHAVIOR enter
    UserGetClosest   pos pos_l_in, pos_r_in
    If               pos==pos_l_in
    DoBh             enter_l_r
    Else
    DoBh             enter_r_l
    EndIf
END
```

declared private. It starts by deciding from which side the actor will enter, using the `UserGetClosest` instruction that asks if the actor is closest to a position on the left side (`pos_l_in`), or on the right side (`pos_r_in`). Then, according to the result, the behavior to enter from the correct side is called.

Behaviors `enter_l_r` and `enter_r_l` simply send the actor to an initial position, open the door, send the actor to the final position on the other side, and close the door. But some more things are needed in order to cope with multiple actors. When modeling this smart object, several positions were created for each of four cases: going in from the left and right side, and going out from the left and right sides. Positions of a same case are given a same name, so that when the instruction `UserGoTo` is called, the object is able to keep track, among all the defined positions with the same name, those that currently have no actor using it. Figure 13.3 illustrates this automatic door and the used positions. The figure shows four positions for each case, which are associated to orientations and are represented as arrows. Note, however, that such a strategy relies entirely on the correct definition of the positions, for a more general solution, actors should be also equipped with sensors to avoid colliding with other entities which are not in the smart object control.

Behaviors `open` and `close` are called to actually close or open the door. These behaviors maintain a state variable that counts how many actors are currently passing through the door (`var_passing`) to correctly decide if the door needs really to be open or closed. Remember that actors interpret the same script concurrently, so that all actors will ask to close the door, but only the last one will actually close it.

13.6.3 Complex Behaviors

Consider the case of modeling a two-stage lift. Such a lift is composed of many parts: doors, calling buttons, a cabin, and the lift itself. These parts need to have synchronized movements, and many details need to be taken into account in order to correctly control actors interacting with the lift.

Similar to the examples already explained, the modeling of the lift functionality is done in two phases. First, all basic behaviors are programmed, e.g., opening and closing doors, pressing the calling button, and moving the lift from one stage to another. If the lift is to be used by multiple actors, then all corresponding details need to be taken into account. Then, a higher-level interaction of just entering the lift from the current floor to go to the other floor is coded using calls to the basic behaviors.

To simplify the modeling behaviors of such complex objects, a state machine can be used permitting definition of the states of the object as a whole, and the connections between the component behaviors.

Figure 13.11 shows a state machine example for the lift case. This state machine has two global states: `floor_1` and `floor_2`. When the lift is in `floor_1`, the only possible interaction is `enter_12`, that will call a private behavior which calls the full sequence of instructions: pressing the calling button, opening the door, entering, closing the door, move the cabin up, opening the other door, and going out.

In the lift behavior example of Figure 13.11, there is a single interaction of entering the lift, which can be too long, giving no options to the actor during the interaction. Figure 13.12 shows another solution, which models the functionality of the lift by taking into account possible intermediate states. In this case, the actor needs to select, step by step, a sequence of interactions in order to take the lift to the other floor.

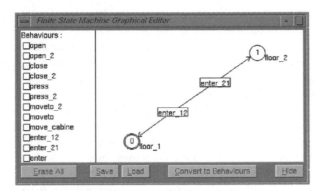

Figure 13.11 A state machine for a two-stage lift functionality. The double circle state is the current state, and the rectangular boxes show the interaction needed to change of state. For example, to change from floor_1 to floor_2 state, interaction enter_12 is required

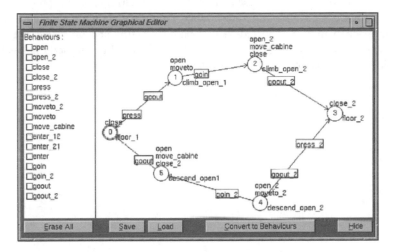

Figure 13.12 A state machine considering intermediate states. Also shown are behaviors associated with states, to be triggered whenever the object enters that state

13.7   Remaining Problems

The smart object approach proposes software architecture able to coherently control actor–object interactions for real-time applications. However, this architecture means that difficult sub-problems can be solved:

- *Simple yet powerful definition of concurrent behaviors*: The smart object approach proposes a simple script language organized as interaction plans to describe the object functionality. Even if such a solution can cope with complex cases, a more general, intuitive and simple way to define functionalities and behaviors is still the topic of intense research.
- *Planning and learning low-level manipulation procedures*: Rather than always using pre-defined geometric parameters for general manipulations, robust algorithms still need

to be developed in order to calculate feasible motions, taking into account collision detection with the manipulation space, and automatic decision and dynamic update of hand configurations and placements. For instance, the actor's hand configuration should change during opening a door, and the same for the whole skeleton configuration. Opening a door realistically would also involve a combination of walking and hand manipulation.

- *Realistic human motion*: Even when a feasible and correct motion has been calculated, how to make this motion display natural and realistic? This is a difficult issue, which involves psychological states, and comfort issues. The most reasonable direction to research is to fill the gap between motion-capture animation and simulation/procedural animation. Some ideas are to mix pre-recorded motion (database driven or not), corrected with simple interpolation or inverse kinematics methods. The goal is to re-use realistic recorded human movements, parameterized for a wide range of object manipulations, and optimized to reach comfort criteria.

- *Learning and adaptation*: Virtual actors should be able to learn the motions, and also the usefulness of objects, while interacting with them. This would an adaptation of the motions towards more realistic results. Learning and adaptation processes from the artificial intelligence field are still to be applied to enhance actor–object interactions. Smart objects have been used, connected to rule-based systems and or virtual life algorithms controlling the decisions of which interactions to perform, but still nothing has been done on learning and adaptation at the motion level.

14

Groups and Crowd Simulation

Soraia Raupp Musse, Branislav Ulicny, Amaury Aubel

A crowd is not only a group of many individuals: crowd modeling involves problems arising only when we focus on crowds. For instance, collision avoidance among a large number of individuals in the same area requires different resolving strategies in comparison with the methods used to avoid collisions between just two individuals. Also, motion planning for a group walking together requires more information than needed to implement individual motion planning. This chapter presents related works on the subject of groups and crowd simulation as well as discussing the requirements to model behaviors of groups and crowds of virtual actors; current applications, recently applied approaches and the challenges of crowd simulations are described.

14.1 Introduction

The aggregated motion is both beautiful and complex to contemplate: beautiful due to the synchronization, homogeneity and unity described in this type of motion, and complex because there are many parameters to be handled in order to provide these characteristics.

History reveals a great amount of interest in understanding and controlling the motion and behavior of crowds of people. As described by Sommer (1979):

> In a pioneer investigation into group size, James and his students recorded the groupings they observed in two Oregon cities. They observed 7,405 informal groupings of pedestrians, playground users, swimmers and shoppers, and 1,458 people in various situations. They found 71% of all groups, both informal and formal, contained only 2 individuals, 21% contained 3, 6% contained 4 and only 2% contained 5 or more.

Psychologists and sociologists have studied the behavior of groups of people for several years. They have been mainly interested in the effects when people with the same goal become only one entity, namely a crowd or a mass. In this case, persons can lose their individuality and adopt the behavior of the crowd entity, behaving in a different way than if they were alone (Benesch 1995).

The mass behaviors and movements of people have also been studied and modelled in computers with different purposes. To simulate a realistic motion of numerous virtual

Handbook of Virtual Humans Edited by N. Magnenat-Thalmann and D. Thalmann
© 2004 John Wiley & Sons, Ltd   ISBN: 0-470-02316-3

people, which can be directed as easily as one only agent. Recent films such as *Bug's Life* and *AntZ*, made by the entertainment industry, are a few examples. To simulate crowd motion showing the evacuation of people in complex environments (normally using fluid mechanics), for example, in a football stadium and in buildings. To populate collaborative and distributed Virtual Environments (CVE) in order to increase the credibility of people's presence. And finally, applications concerning the sociological and behavioral simulation of people in closed environments in order to analyze the relationship between different people, the hierarchy inside a crowd, the leadership and membership relations, among others.

14.1.1 Structure of this Chapter

The discussion on crowd behavior includes the description of different levels of behaviors and autonomy. While the crowd can represent a multi-layer architecture as it is composed by groups and agents, different levels of behaviors are also included, dealing with basic problems as well as complex ones. The focus of this chapter is on presenting different approaches as well as discussing the models we have developed in last few years.

This chapter is organized into five sections. The next section (Related Work) presents an overview of the works in the domain of crowds and related areas. In section 14.3 we present two different approaches we have been involved in: first, the hierarchical model called ViCrowd where the group is a more sophisticated structure in comparison with individuals, and, second, the emergent crowd with emphasis on complex individuals. Then, Section 14.4 is concerned with the issues of crowd visualization. Section 14.5 (Case Studies) deals with the several levels of autonomy and control of crowds describing results obtained with programmed, guided and autonomous crowds simulations. Section 14.6, finally, draws conclusions and discusses further topics on the subject.

14.2   Related Work

In this section we will present an overview of the selected works related to the simulation of groups and crowds. Although collective behavior was studied as long ago as the end of the nineteenth century (LeBon 1895), attempts to simulate it by computer models are quite recent, with most work done only in the mid and late 1990s. In the past years researchers from a broad range of fields such as architecture (Penn and Turner 2001; Tecchia and Chrysanthou 2000), computer graphics (Bouvier and Guilloteau 1996; Musse and Thalmann 2001; Ulicny and Thalmann 2001), physics (Helbing et al. 2000), robotics (Molnar and Starke 2001), safety science (Simulex), (Still 2000; Thompson and Marchant 1995), training systems (Bottaci 1995; Varner et al. 1998; Williams 1995) and sociology (Jager et al. 2001; McPhail et al. 1992) have created simulations involving collections of individuals. However, despite the apparent breadth of the crowd simulation research basis, it should be noted that interdisciplinary exchange of ideas is rare – researchers in one field are usually not very aware of work done in other fields.

Most approaches were application specific, focusing on different aspects of collective behavior, using different modeling techniques. Techniques employed range from those that do not distinguish individuals such as flow and network models in some of the evacuation simulations (Takahashi and Shiizuka 1992), to those that represent each individual as being controlled by more or less complex rules based on physical laws (Helbing et al. 2000; Hosoi et al. 1996), chaos equations (Saiwaki et al. 1999) or behavioral models in training systems (Williams 1995) or sociological simulations (Jager et al. 2001).

We can distinguish two broader areas of crowd simulations. First, one focusing on realism of behavioral aspects with usually simple 2-D visualizations such as evacuation simulators, sociological crowd models, or crowd dynamics models (see Figure 14.1)In this area simulated behavior is usually from a very narrow, controlled range (e.g. people just flying to exit or people forming a ring crowd structure) with efforts to quantitatively validate results correspondence to real-world observations of particular situations. Visualization is used to help to understand simulation results.

In the second area the main goal is high quality visualization (e.g. movie production, computer games), but usually realism of behavior model is not a priority. A convincing visual result is important, which is achieved partly by behavior models, partly by human intervention in the production process (see Figure 14.2). Here behavior models do not necessarily aim to match quantitatively the real world, their purpose is more to improve the human animator's work. However, recently both trend seem to be converging, where visualization-oriented systems are trying to incorporate better behavior models to ease the creation of convincing animations (*AntZ*) (CharacterStudio) and behavior-oriented models are trying to achieve better visualization, especially in the domain of evacuation simulators (STEPS) (Exodus).

Next we will present some representative works from most the typical domains in more detail.

14.2.1 *Crowd Evacuation Simulators*

One of the largest areas where crowd behaviors have been studied and modeled is the domain of safety science and architecture with the dominant application of crowd evacuation simulators. Such systems model the movement of a large number of people in usually closed, well-defined spaces such as inner areas of buildings (Thompson and Marchant 1995), subways (Hareesh et al. 2000), ships (Klüpfel et al. 2000) or airplanes (Owen et al. 1998).

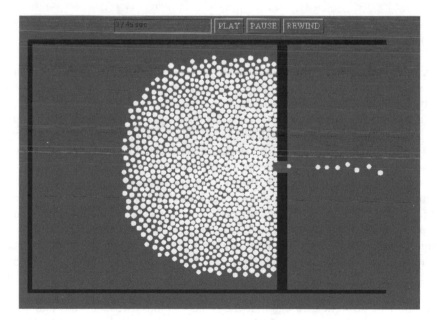

Figure 14.1 Helbing's crowd dynamics simulation. (Reproduced with permission of Dr. Helbing.)

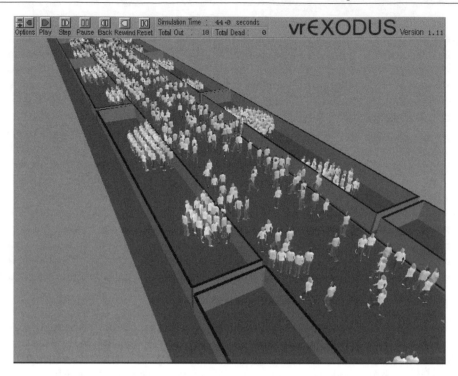

Figure 14.2 EXODUS evacuation simulator (Exodus). (Reproduced with permission of Professor Edwin Galea.)

Their goal is to help designers understand relations between organization of the space and human behavior (Okazaki and Matsushita 1993).

The most common use of evacuation simulators is a modeling of crowd behavior in case of a forced evacuation from a confined environment due to some threat like fire or smoke. In such a situation, a number of people have to evacuate the given area, usually through a relatively small number of fixed exits. Simulations are trying to help answering questions like: Can the area be evacuated within a prescribed time? Where do the hold-ups in the flow of people occur? Where are the likely areas for a crowd surge to produce unacceptable crushing pressure? (Robbins 1999) The most common modeling approach in this area is the use of cellular automata representation of individuals.

Simulex (Thompson and Marchant 1995) is computer model aimed at the simulation of the escape movement of occupants through large, geometrically complex building spaces defined by 2-D floor plans, and connecting staircases (see Figure 14.3). Each individual has attributes such as position, angle of orientation and walking speed. Various algorithms such as distance mapping, way finding, overtaking, route deviation and adjustment of individual speeds due to proximity of crowd members are used to facilitate the progress of the simulation.

An early prototype of Legion™ was developed by Still for simulation and analysis of crowd dynamics in pedestrian environments like stadia (Still 2000). Extensive, multi-disciplinary experimental and theoretical research at the Maia Institute (Monaco), has culminated in a state-of-the-art multi-agent system. In this third-generation algorithm (Kagarlis 2004), which is incorporated in the commercial product Legion™ v.1.7, every person in the crowd is treated

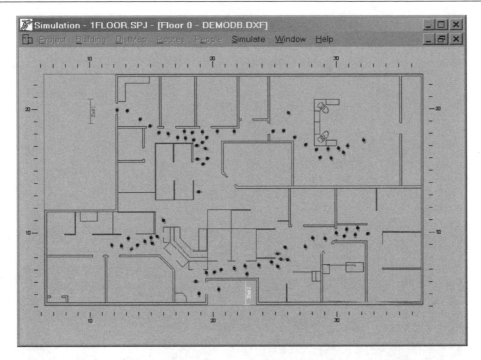

Figure 14.3 Simulex, crowd evacuation system. (Reproduced with permission of Dr. Peter and Thomson.)

as a virtual individual, with authentic pedestrian attributes drawn probabilistically from empirically established profiles. Their decisions, enabled by faculties akin to perception, cognition and memory, entail wayfinding facilitated by computer vision, and multi-objective microscopic searches in continuum space for every step. Each individual scans its local environment and chooses an action that aims to minimize the effort required to arrive at its destination. The decision is made according to the individual's preferences, location, objectives and recent experience; and is sensitive to local conditions, context, and intentions of neighbours. Legion v1.7 has been used by consulting engineers to model complex and challenging real-life environments such as Olympic parks and three-line railway intersections (see Figure 14.4, for an example of stadium).

14.2.2 Crowd Management Training Systems

Modeling of the crowds is essential in police and military simulator systems used to train how to deal with mass gatherings of people. CACTUS (Williams 1995) is a system developed to assist in planning and training for public order incidents such as large demonstrations and marches. The software designs are based on a world model in which crowd groups and police units are placed on digitized map and have probabilistic rules for their interactive behavior. The simulation model represents small groups of people as discrete objects. The behavioral descriptions are in the form of a directed graph where the nodes describe behavioral states (to which correspond actions and exhibited emotions) and transitions represent plausible changes between these states. The transitions depend on environmental conditions and probability

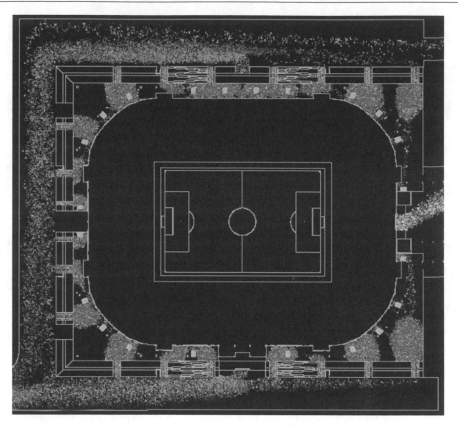

Figure 14.4 Legion system, analysis of Sydney stadium. (Still 2000.) (Reproduced with permission of Legion System)

weightings. The simulation runs as a decision-making exercise that can include pre-event logistic planning, incident management and de-briefing evaluation.

The Small Unit Leader Non-Lethal Training System (Varner et al. 1998) is a simulator for training US Marines Corps in decision-making with respect to the use of non-lethal munitions in peacekeeping and crowd control operations. Trainees learn rules of engagement, the procedures for dealing with crowds and mobs and the ability to make decisions about the appropriate level of force needed to control, contain, or disperse crowds and mobs. Crowds move within simulated urban environment along instructor-pre-defined pathways and respond both to actions of trainee and to actions of other simulated crowds. Each crowd is characterized by a crowd profile – a series of attributes like fanaticism, arousal state, prior experience with non-lethal munitions, or attitude toward Marines. During an exercise, crowd behavior computer model operates in real-time and responds to trainee actions (and inactions) with appropriate simulated behaviors such as loitering, celebrating, demonstrating, rioting and dispersing according to set of Boolean relationships defined by experts (see Figure 14.5).

14.2.3 Sociological Models

Despite being a field primarily interested in studying collective behavior, relatively small number of works on crowd simulations have been undertaken in sociology.

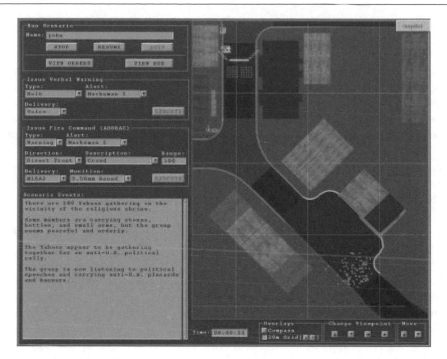

Figure 14.5 Small Unit Leader Non-Lethal Training System. (Reproduced with permission of Southwest Research Institute.)

McPhail et al. (1992) studied individual and collective actions in temporary gatherings. Their model of the crowd is based on perception control theory (Powers 1973) where each separate individual is trying to control his or her experience in order to maintain particular relationships to others; in this case it is spatial relationships with others in a group. A simulation program called GATHERING graphically shows movement, milling, and structural emergence in crowds. The same simulation system was later used by Schweingruber (1995) to study the effects of reference signals in common on coordination of collective behavior and by Tucker et al. (1999) to study formation of arcs and rings in temporary gatherings.

Jager et al. (2001) modeled clustering and fighting in two-party crowds. A crowd is modeled by multi-agent simulation using cellular automata with rules defining approach-avoidance conflict. Simulation consists of two groups of agents of three different kinds: hardcore, hangers-on and bystanders, the difference between them consisting in the frequency with which they scan their surroundings. The goal of the simulation was to study effects of group size, size symmetry and group composition on clustering, and 'fights'.

14.2.4 Computer Graphics

In the area of computer graphics, the goal of behavioral animation is to simplify designers' work by letting virtual characters perform autonomously or semi-autonomously complicated motions which otherwise would require large amount of human animators' work.

Reynolds (1987) described distributed behavioral model to simulate the aggregate motion of a flock of birds. The flock is simulated as a particle system, with the simulated birds (called boids) being the particles. Each boid is implemented as an independent actor that navigates according to its local perception of the dynamic environment, the laws of simulated physics, and a set of behaviors where the boids try to avoid collisions with one another and with other objects in their environment, match velocities with nearby flock mates and move towards center of the flock. The aggregate motion of the simulated flock is the result of the dense interaction of these relatively simple behaviors of the individual simulated birds (see Figure 14.6).

Bouvier and Guilloteau (1996) and Bouvier et al. (1997) used a combination of particle systems and transition networks to model human crowds in the visualization of urban spaces. Lower level behavior enabled people to avoid obstacles using attraction and repulsion forces analogous to physical electric forces. Higher level behavior is modeled by transition networks with transitions depending on timing, visiting of certain points, changes of local densities and global events (see Figure 14.7).

Hodgins and Brogan (1994), and Brogan and Hodgins (1997) simulated group behavior for systems with significant dynamics. They presented an algorithm to control the movements of creatures traveling as a group. The algorithm has two steps: first, a perception model determines the creatures and obstacles visible to each individual and then a placement algorithm determines the desired position for each individual, given the locations and velocities of perceived creatures and obstacles. Simulated systems included groups of legged robots, bicycle riders and point-mass systems (see Figure 14.8).

14.2.5 Classification of Crowd Methods

Previous research on behavioral modeling has mainly focused on various aspects of human control, such as particle systems, flocking systems and behavioral systems. Table 14.1 has been modified from the original version (Parent 2002) to include our approach (ViCrowd Model (Musse and Thalmann 2001)).

Figure 14.6 Reynolds's flock of boids. (Reproduced with permission of Craig W. Reynolds.)

Figure 14.7 Bouvier's particle systems crowd. (Bouvier and Guilloteau 1996.) (Reproduced with permission of Springer)

Figure 14.8 Hodgins's simulation of a group of bicyclists. (Hodgins and Brogan 1994; Brogan and Hodgins 1997.) (Reproduced with permission of Kluwer)

The methods presented in Table 14.1 can be chosen as a function of the nature of crowds required in the applications. Indeed, there are different types of constraints depending on the goal of the application. For instance, if the application is to model a crowd motion during an evacuation, the interactive control as well as the behavior simulation cannot be ignored. We have classified these applications into four types based on their different purposes.

The *entertainment* applications include film productions and games. In this case, the groups as well as individuals have to be easily controlled and directed. Some examples are

Table 14.1   Various behavioral approaches

Aspects	Particle systems	Flocking systems	ViCrowd model	Behavioral systems
Structure	non-hierarchical	levels: flock, agents	levels: crowd, groups, agents	can present hierarchy
Participants	many	some	many	few
Intelligence	none	some	some$^{(*)}$	high
Physics-based	yes	some	no	no
Collision	detect and respond	avoidance	avoidance	avoidance
Control	force fields, global tendency	local tendency	different degrees: pre-defined behavior, rules and guided control	rules

Note: * The intelligence of individuals in the ViCrowd model can vary from 'none' to 'some' depending on the behavioral rules specified. In the same way the intelligence of groups can vary from some to high.

the recent films (*AntZ*) and (*Bug's Life*). The challenges include the simulation of several people as well as the automatic generation of individuals that are important in the visual aspects. In addition, the easy control of groups represents a requirement of this kind of application.

The *crowd motion simulation* aims at evaluating the motion of several people in a constrained environment. It normally involves a simple visualization (embodiment of crowd) and a strong compromise with the numerical results in order to evaluate the environment. Some commercial software applications, e.g. (Simulex) and Legion (Still 2000) are examples of this kind of crowd application. The main challenges in this case include a realistic method of collision avoidance, a strong connection with the environment and a compromise with the numerical and statistical results.

In order to *populate collaborative Virtual Environments*, e.g. in a CVE system, the crowd requires real-time simulation, as well as many aspects of interactivity in order to guide and direct crowds during the simulation. The facility to program crowd behavior represents an important challenge in collaborative Virtual Environments, where participants can create and interact with crowds. Some experiments have been made in the context of the COVEN project (Tromp and Snowdon 1997).

The last type of crowd application is the *behavioral modeling of crowds*. In this case, the goal is to provide autonomous or semi-autonomous behaviors that can be applied by self-animating agents, who form the crowd. In order to deal with the constraints of having a large number of actors (hundreds or thousands), this kind of application presents the following challenges: description of sociological and social aspects which arise in crowds, dealing with directed and emergent behaviors and connection with the Virtual Environment. Also, necessary optimizations and simplifications are required in order to model and simulate crowd intelligence and decision ability.

14.3 A Hierarchical Approach to Model Crowds

14.3.1 Hierarchic Model

ViCrowd (Musse and Thalmann 2001) presents a model to automatically generate human crowds based on groups, instead of individuals. In our case, the groups are more 'intelligent' structures, while individuals follow the groups' specification. This decision is due to the real-time requirements of our work and aims to optimize the information needed to provide intelligent crowds.

ViCrowd is based on local rules applied to the groups, similar to flocking systems (Reynolds 1987), but where the groups are not a rigid structure possibly being changed during simulation. Also, a definition of behavioral rules using conditional events and reactions is included to provide more autonomous crowds. Thus, the user can decide to use conditional events to create more complex behaviors, as well as to randomly distribute action and motion to create static and simple behaviors.

The control in ViCrowd is presented in different degrees of autonomy ranging from totally interactive to totally autonomous control (without user intervention during the simulation). Table 14.2 presents some characteristics of crowd control types.

While guided crowds keep a better frame rate of simulations than autonomous crowds, they are not able to act as autonomously as the autonomous crowd, which can self-generate behaviors based on rules. On the other hand, the autonomous crowds can present more complex behavior but normally cannot provide a real-time simulation, consequently, the interaction with crowds during the simulation is difficult to obtain.

In ViCrowd, the autonomous crowds are reactive entities. Conditional events and reactions are included to model behavioral rules and to obtain different responses from the crowd. Previous works have discussed the importance of such a reactive nature to provide more realistic behavior (Arbib and Lee 1993; Arkin 1990; Drogou and Ferber 1994; Giroux 1996).

In comparison with other methods, ViCrowd presents the following advantages:

1. Multi-level hierarchy formed by crowd, groups and agents.
2. Various degrees of autonomy mixing very known methodologies: scripted and interactive control with rule-based behaviors (reactive behaviors).
3. Group-based behaviors, where agents are simple structures and the groups are more complex structures.

14.3.1.1 ViCrowd structure

We defined a crowd as a set of groups composed of virtual agents. Our model distributes the crowd information and behaviors to the groups generating information and behaviors to

Table 14.2 Characteristics of different types of crowd control

Behavior control	Guided crowds	Programmed crowds	Autonomous crowds
level of autonomy	low	medium	high
level of intelligence	low	medium	high
execution frame-rate	high	medium	low
complexity of behaviors	low	medium	high
level of interaction	high	medium	low

groups (GIB) and then, to the individuals. Also, GIB can be directly specified using script control, as can be seen in Figure 14.9.

Moreover, there are two ways of setting the parameters of our model: scripted and external control. Scripted control defines *scripted behaviors* of the crowd (using a script language) whereas external control (external module which communicates with ViCrowd) specifies *guided behaviors*.

As mentioned before, our crowd model is represented by a hierarchical architecture where the minor entity to be handled consists of groups. The crowd is an independent entity that contains information which can be distributed among groups. The groups are independent of each other and can be generated according to the crowd information or specified (using the script or external controller), without taking into account the crowd behaviors. The agents are less autonomous than the groups because they share the groups' information. Also, each group may contain a leader. This leader can be chosen randomly by ViCrowd, or can emerge using sociological rules.

Turning our attention now to the crowd control, ViCrowd aims at providing several degrees of autonomy, which can be applied depending on the complexity of the problem. At a lower level, the individuals have a repertoire of basic behaviors called *innate behaviors*. An innate behavior is defined as an 'inborn' way to behave. Goal-seeking behavior, the way trajectories are processed and collisions avoided, the ability to follow scripted or guided events/reactions are examples of innate behaviors of individuals.

While the innate behaviors are included in the model, the specification of scripted behaviors is done by means of a script language. *Group behaviors* like flocking (group ability to walk respecting a group structure) can be defined in the script language to program groups. We call these groups of virtual agents *<programmed groups>* who apply the scripted behaviors and do not need user intervention during simulation, nor are able to perform

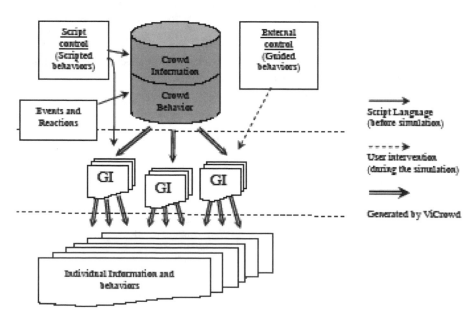

Figure 14.9   Hierarchical structure of the model

complex behaviors. Using the script language, the user can directly specify the crowd or group behaviors. In the first case, the system automatically distributes the crowd behaviors among the existing groups.

Complex behaviors can also be specified in order to improve the intelligence of virtual crowds. Events and reactions have been used to represent behavioral rules. This reactive character of the simulation can be programmed into the script language (scripted control) (see Figure 14.9). Also, other complex behaviors can be applied as sociological behaviors and decisions using memory and communication. We call these groups of virtual agents *<autonomous groups>*. Figure 14.10 shows an example of autonomous crowds.

Externally controlled groups, called *<guided groups>*, no longer obey their scripted behavior, but act according to the external specification. Indeed, in order to provide the interaction with virtual crowds (see Figure 14.11), several paradigms of interaction have been proposed aimed at modeling the information, which can be sent and received to/from the crowd.

14.3.2 Emergent Crowds

Our work aims at the simulation of larger number of Virtual Human agents for interactive Virtual Environments such as virtual reality training systems (Ulicny and Thalmann 2001; Ulicny and Thalmann 2002). Compared to the other crowd modeling approaches we focus on more complex behaviors of many agents in dynamic environments with possible user interaction.

In previous works crowds have been considered as already formed units with more or less uniform behavior placed in particular environments corresponding only to the limited purpose of the simulation: for example, pedestrians just fleeing from a burning building (Helbing et al. 2000; Still 2000), or a marching crowd during a demonstration (Varner et al. 1998; Williams 1995). However, in the real world there is no global controller of the crowd assigning

Figure 14.10 Autonomous crowd entry at the train station

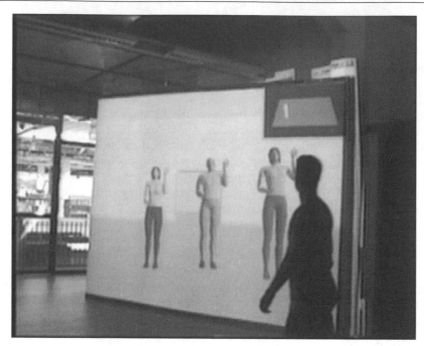

Figure 14.11   A person enters the interaction space, the virtual people react

people to particular groups and determining their behaviors. Collective behavior emerges from the interaction of individuals (Gilbert 1996), crowds are dynamically assembled and disassembled, and over the time they change their behavior. We take inspiration from the field of sociology: McPhail (1991) argues that members of a gathering do not act as a whole but rather that subsections of the number assembled react in a similar way, which, when observed externally appears as collective behavior. In our system, the crowd is modeled as a collection of individuals, which react to the environment, other agents and real human participants of the simulation and can have very different behaviors both for one agent in different situations and for many agents in the same situation. Figure 14.12 shows an example of the emergent crowd.

The simulation consists of a group of autonomous Virtual Human agents existing in a dynamic Virtual 3-D Environment. In order to behave in a believable way these agents have to act in accordance with their surrounding environment, be able to react to its changes, to the other agents and also to the actions of real humans interacting with the virtual world. Agents contain a set of internal attributes corresponding to various psychological or physiological states (e.g. level of curiosity, tiredness, etc.), a set of higher-level complex behaviors and a set of rules determining selection of these behaviors. Events provide agents with a way of interacting with the environment, other agents or human participants of the simulation. Each agent is able to receive events from the environment objects, other agents or the user interface. Combinations of different received events and different levels of agents' attributes can produce both changes in internal attributes and change in overt behavior.

Our behavior model is based on a combination of rules (Kalra and Barr 1992; Rosenbloom et al. 1993) and finite state machines (Cremer et al. 1995), to control the agent's behavior

Figure 14.12   Emergent crowds

using a layered approach. The first layer deals with the selection of higher-level complex behaviors appropriate to the agent's situation, the second layer implements these behaviors using low-level actions provided by the Virtual Human (Boulic et al. 1997). At the higher level, rules select complex behaviors (such as flee) according to the agent's state (constituted by attributes) and the state of the Virtual Environment (conveyed by the events). In the rules we specify for whom (e.g. particular agent, or agents in particular group) and when the rule is applicable (e.g. at a defined time, after receiving an event or when some attribute has reached specified value), and what the consequence is of rule firing (e.g. change of agent's high-level behavior or attribute). An example of such rule is:

```
FOR ALL
WHEN EVENT = in_danger_area AND ATTRIBUTE fear >50%
THEN BEHAVIOR FLEE
```

At the lower level, complex behaviors are implemented by hierarchical finite state machines. Each behavior is realized by one FSM which drives the selection of the low-level actions for the Virtual Human (such as move to location, play short animation sequence), manages connections with the environment (such as path queries, or event sending) and also can call other FSMs to delegate subtasks such as path following.

There are two types of complex behaviors. First, we can specify scripted behavior which is more precise, but less autonomous and with less environment coupling by using explicit sequences of low-level actions. Or, second, we can let agents perform autonomously complex behaviors with the feedback from the environment. Examples of such autonomous behaviors are: wandering, fleeing, neutralizing the threat, or requesting and providing help.

We can illustrate the semantics of the autonomous behaviors with the example of two agents performing coupled behaviors – requesting and providing help. When the first agent's health attribute is below a certain level, rule triggers help requesting behavior FSM. The agent stops at the place and starts to play the animation corresponding to asking for help (such as waving the hand) and sends as event conveying his request to the other agents. Reception of this event leads to the activation of the rule for the second agent, which then starts performing help-providing behavior FSM. He asks the environment (Farenc et al. 1999) for the path leading to the first agent, executes the path following FSM to perform the movement to the injured agent and after arriving he starts playing help-giving animation (such as giving first aid). Upon finishing animation the first agent is notified and the level of his health attribute is increased. In the end both involved agents quit these behaviors and return to their previous behaviors.

14.4   Crowd Visualization

Creating a visually compelling crowd can be a long and difficult task that requires much design experience. However, a few simple ideas may be applied so as to automate the process to a certain extent and model a sufficiently heterogeneous crowd in a reasonable time, as we shall see.

Rendering numerous Virtual Humans also poses a problem of speed. Even when the algorithm for crowd simulation is not real-time, it is still desirable to display the characters as quickly as possible for testing purposes. We propose here a few simple optimizations that help to sustain the highest possible frame rate of display. In the end, this enables the animator to render in real-time a few hundred characters on a modern PC.

14.4.1   Virtual Human Model

All human modeling/animation systems rely on (at least) two layers for modeling and deforming a Virtual Human: an invisible *skeleton* and an outer envelope (or *skin*). The underlying skeleton is essentially an articulated structure, whose nodes match real human joints. In the vast majority of cases, the skin is simply a mesh due to hardware requirements (graphics chips perform best when processing triangles). For more details, see Section 7.2.

14.4.2   Crowd Creation

The key feature of a realistic crowd is its diversity. As a basic principle, two individuals should never look the same. Yet, memory considerations and modeling time obviously impose some constraints.

We split the human body into several parts: the head, the hands, the feet, and the rest, which includes the limbs, trunk, and pelvis. This decomposition takes several factors into account. We, as human beings, identify people mainly from their face. The face is also the most expressive part of our body. Thus, it makes sense to keep heads as separate objects. Hands and feet are fairly complex because of the high mobility of the underlying skeleton in these regions. The hands alone have, for example, more joints than the rest of the body. Hence, their representations are also kept separately.

The design of a number of digital persons proceeds as follows. We start with a small set of body envelopes (that is without head, hands, and feet), e.g. two male bodies, one looking fit, the other one a bit plump, the same for female bodies. From this basic set, new bodies of distinct shape and proportions are generated automatically by applying free-form deformation (FFD) techniques (Coquillart 1990; Sederberg and Parry 1986) in a non-ambiguous skeleton posture. A good idea is to pose the body in an erect position with the arms raised (by roughly 90 degrees) rather than lying by the side of the body, and the feet reasonably apart.

The number of bodies should remain relatively small compared to the number of simulated characters, so that each body can be shared among several actors, thus lowering memory consumption. Memory usage can be further reduced by applying the FFD parameters for each animation frame instead of explicitly storing the mesh. However, this may notably impact the rendering speed.

To complete the modeling of the crowd, static meshes for the head, hands, and feet are attached onto the body. These meshes are chosen from a set of pre-defined objects so that they are also shared among several characters. Different materials can be applied so as to simulate various skin complexions. Finally, clothes are approximated with adequate shared textures.

14.4.3 Level of Detail

Even though graphics processors become faster by the day, the graphics unit becomes quickly burdened as the number of rendered Virtual Humans grows. Geometric level of detail (LOD) is a traditional computer graphics technique that has been used to remedy such situations. The idea behind LOD basically consists in reducing the number of rendered polygons by using several representations of decreasing complexity of a same object. The appropriate model or resolution is selected for each frame based on some criteria such as the distance to the viewer.

Many ways exist to produce multiple resolutions from a reference mesh: decimation techniques, subdivision surfaces, etc., all of which are being actively researched. However, the human body exhibits a specific geometric property: most body parts are roughly cylindrical. Consequently, one can easily think of the human body as a collection of slices or *cross-sections* (Shen et al. 1996). This leads to the natural choice of B-spline patches to represent the different body parts (Shen et al. 1996; Krishnamurthy and Levoy 1996).

B-spline surfaces offer many advantages. They exhibit C1 continuity, which results in a smoothly varying surface. It is also straightforward to generate meshes of increasing complexity, which addresses our multi-resolution problem (see Figure 14.13). Finally, they provide us with well-defined and stable texture coordinates.

For the head, hands and feet, we still rely on a traditional decimation technique. The body extremities are replaced with simple textured geometry for the lowest resolution.

14.4.4 Animated Impostors

Even when rendering a complex, moving, self-deforming figure such as a Virtual Human, changes from frame to frame in the animation remain small. Besides, since the human brain

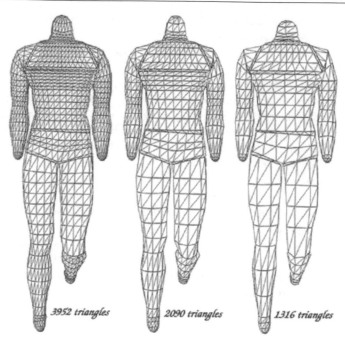

3952 triangles   2090 triangles   1316 triangles

Figure 14.13 Body meshes of decreasing complexity using B-spline surfaces. Body parts are stitched together using a simple contour connection algorithm

tends to reconstruct the missing data when shown only certain frames, a few key postures often suffice to understand the whole animation. This principle has been demonstrated successfully for decades in the cartoon industry.

We apply this idea to Virtual Humans: *animated impostors* extend the concept of dynamic impostors (Schaufler and Stürzlinger 1996) by taking into account changes in the character's appearance. Our system is currently implemented in software for want of a dedicated architecture such as Torbog's work (Torborg and Kajiya 1996). Hardware requirements include texture mapping and alpha channel support.

As defined by (Maciel and Shirley 1995), what we mean by impostor is a set of transparent polygons onto which we map meaningful opaque images. In our case we use a single textured plane. The quadrilateral is placed in such a way that it faces the camera continuously and its texture is updated regularly enough for it not to be visually distracting. The generation of the texture in an off-screen buffer is discussed in the next section.

The texture that is mapped onto this quadrilateral is merely a 'snapshot' of the Virtual Human. Under these conditions, if we take for granted that the picture of the Virtual Human can be re-used over several frames we have virtually decreased the complexity of a human character to two triangles (see Figure 14.14).

14.4.5 Impostor Rendering and Texture Generation

Two coordinate spaces are involved in the rendering of an impostor. We denote as *eye space* the viewing frustum defined by the scene camera. It is used for rendering the global

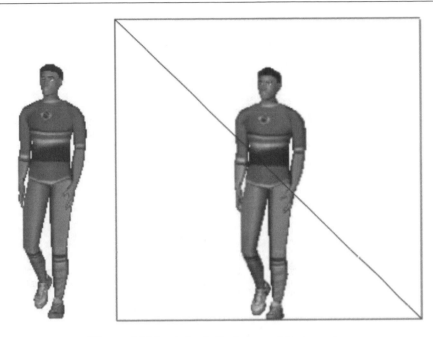

Figure 14.14   A football player and its impostor

scene with impostors. A perspective projection transforms impostors from *eye space* to two-dimensional *screen space*. Two coordinate systems are also involved in the generation of the texture that is mapped onto an impostor. We denote as *impostor space* the 3-D box associated with the orthographic camera used for taking snapshots of a Virtual Human. An orthographic projection transforms coordinates from *impostor space* to two-dimensional *texture space*. We direct the unfamiliar reader to (Watt and Watt 1992) for general information on viewing transformations.

Figure 14.15(a) represents a top view of a scene containing two articulated characters in eye space. The orientation of the camera is defined by a 3×3 rotation matrix: $R = (\vec{H}, \vec{V}, \vec{U})$ where $\vec{V}$ is the viewing vector along the line of sight, $\vec{U}$ is the 'up' vector, and $\vec{H}$ is the 'horizontal' vector that completes the right-handed coordinate system. Figure 14.15(b) shows a top view of the same scene rendered with impostors. The geometry of a character is replaced by a single textured quadrilateral, whose normal vector $\vec{N}$ points back to the eye. The quadrilateral is also rotated around its axis $\vec{N}$, so that it stands upright in screen space. Figure 14.15(c) shows how the textures mapped onto the impostors are generated. The orthographic camera that is used to take a snapshot is oriented according to the rotation matrix $R_0 = (\vec{H}_0, \vec{V}_0, \vec{U}_0)$. The viewing direction $\vec{V}_0$ is the unit vector derived from the location of the eye (i.e. position of the scene camera) and the center $\vec{T}_a$ of the bounding box of the Virtual Human. The 'horizontal' vector is given by the cross-product: $\vec{H}_0 = \vec{V}_0 \times \vec{U}$ where $\vec{U}$ is the normalized 'up' vector of the scene camera. Another cross-product yields the 'up' vector: $\vec{U}_0 = \vec{H}_0 \times \vec{V}_0$. In addition, the orthographic camera must be set up so that the Virtual Human should be entirely visible in both impostor and texture space. During the simulation, the orthographic camera is placed at distance D from $\vec{T}_a$ i.e. $\vec{T}_o = \vec{T}_a - D \cdot \vec{V}_o$. Due to the orthographic projection, D does not actually affect the size of the Virtual Human

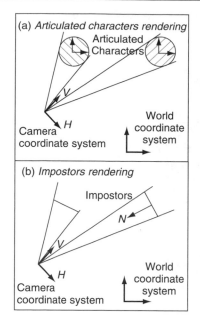

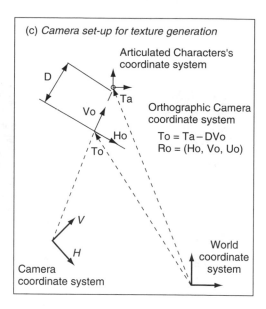

Figure 14.15 Impostor rendering and texture generation

in *texture space*. To ensure no parts of the character are cut off, we set the viewing box associated with the orthographic camera to the Virtual Human's bounding box, and we accordingly scale the textured quadrilateral in order to maintain a constant size in *screen space*. Note that the tighter the bounding box of the synthetic actor, the better the ratio of opaque texels to transparent ones in the texture. More details must be found in (Aubel et al. 2000)

14.4.6 Texture Refreshment Approach

The algorithm that decides whether the texture of a Virtual Human is stale has to be executed quickly because it must be performed for every Virtual Human. We rely on two factors to rapidly cull the actors that do not need to be refreshed: change in posture and relative orientation of the actor with respect to the camera.

(Squared) distances between particular joints are first computed. This is immediate since the skeleton is updated each frame. As soon as the variation between new distances and those computed when the texture was last generated exceeds a certain threshold, we mark the texture as stale. Four tests suffice to reflect any significant change in the posture (see Figure 14.16).

To test the orientation of the actor we use the fact that every character is always seen from a certain viewing angle which varies due to camera motion or actor's motion. In practice, we compute the matrix that corresponds to the transformation under which the viewer sees the Virtual Human. We then construct the transformation matrix from the old view matrix (i.e. when the texture was last generated) to the new one. We extract from the rotation matrix the rotation angle, which we check against a pre-defined threshold.

These first two tests result in a list of candidates for refreshment. In the next stage, the list is sorted according to several criteria. The first and most important criterion is the variation

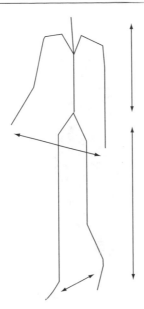

Figure 14.16 Posture variation

ratio, which reflects how poorly the current texture represents the new position/posture of the Virtual Human. It is calculated as follows:

Variation ratio = max (posture ratio × angle ratio, max (posture ratio, angle ratio))

Note that changes in both the posture and the orientation are cumulated if both ratios are greater than one. Second, the (normalized) distance from the virtual character to the viewer is taken into consideration so that distant characters and those on the periphery contribute less. Third, the rendering cost (based e.g. on the number of polygons) can also be brought into play. Eventually, the first k actors of the list are re-rendered.

14.4.7 Visibility Issue

Replacing a polygonal model of a Virtual Human with a single textured quadrilateral may introduce visibility problems: depth values of the texels are unlikely to match those of the actual geometry, which may lead to incorrect visibility (legs and right arm in Figure 14.4(b)).

The most natural solution to this problem is to augment impostors with depth information per texel (Schaufler 1997). However, this approach requires specific hardware and is usually expensive. Another way to overcome the visibility limitation consists in identifying geometry that forms the lowest level parts that are expected to have coherent motion and render them at different z-values. It is easy to divide a Virtual Human into coherent parts by using the natural segmentation of joints (see Figure 14.17). Moreover, since all the body parts are not necessarily involved in a motion, the refreshment of an actor may be less costly. However, even though it does solve the actor-on-chair visibility problem depicted in Figure 14.18, body parts are not smoothly connected, thus leading to unacceptable results (see hands and feet in Figure 14.18(c)). In addition, new visibility problems may occur between quadrilaterals overlapping in screen space and with close depth values. For example, the neck may incorrectly be occluded by long

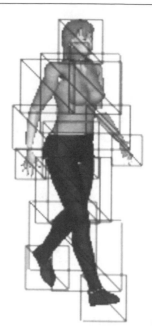

Figure 14.17 Virtual Human decomposed into several planes

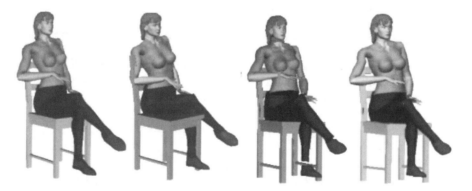

Figure 14.18 From left to right: actual geometry (a), single quadrilateral (b), multi-plane impostor (c), and factored impostor (d)

hair (see Figure 14.18(c)) in one frame, and visibility correctly resolved in the next one, thus adding an unpleasing popping effect to the list of visibility problems.

14.4.8 Factored Impostor

The solution advocated by Snyder and Lengyel (1998) is to detect mutual occluders and factor them in a single layer. This idea can be adapted to the context of Virtual Humans interacting with objects of their environment. First, the author identifies the few objects that might cause visibility problems (e.g. chair, table). At run-time, potential occlusions between a synthetic character and one of these objects are detected by checking if the bounding boxes of the character and object overlap. If so, a new impostor, consisting of both the actor and object, is created (see Figure 14.18(d)). If more than one object interferes with the Virtual Human, the additional objects are merged into the same impostor. For example, for an actor sitting at a table, the final texture will contain the Virtual Human, the chair, and the table. The construction of a factored impostor is done exactly as previously described, except that the bounding box now encompasses all factored objects.

However, the factoring scheme suffers from two problems:

1. The parallax effect cannot be reproduced (unless the refreshment rate is very high), which might prove disturbing when the aggregated objects have great differences in distance from the camera.
2. The relative velocities and/or dynamics of objects within the same impostor may considerably impact the texture refreshment rate, e.g. two moving characters within one impostor.

Virtual Humans rarely interact with very large objects, so the first problem can usually be ignored. On the other hand, the second item is more worrisome. Let us consider as an example two Virtual Humans sitting on a bench. It makes little sense to factor both actors and the bench into the same impostor, since the induced texture refreshment rate would become prohibitively expensive due to 2. Using two impostors, one for each actor, and factoring the bench into both impostors is not any better: the bench is drawn twice, thus causing new visibility problems let alone the 'superposition effect'. Breaking the bench into two pieces is impractical from a designer's viewpoint, and cracks could moreover appear in the final image of the reconstructed bench. Hence, when situation 2. occurs, we use another type of impostor.

14.4.9   Z-Buffer Corrected Impostor

The idea here is to render each Virtual Human with a separate impostor, and to use a special Z-buffer-corrected impostor for each interfering object (e.g. the chair in Figure 14.18). The Z-buffer-correction is done as follows: instead of clearing the Z-buffer plane of the off-screen buffer before taking a snapshot, we dump in it the Z-buffer content of the off-screen buffers associated with the (occluding) Virtual Humans. For the actor-on-chair problem, this has the effect of generating a texture, whose opaque texels correspond precisely to the elements of the chair that are not obscured by the actor. In order to avoid disocclusion errors, a Z-buffer-corrected impostor must be refreshed whenever one of the (occluding) actors is refreshed or the camera moves. This high refreshment rate is counter-balanced by the benefit of using, without constraints, impostors for the synthetic characters.

The Z-buffer re-use has a number of restrictions. If orthographic cameras are used for generating textures, depth values vary linearly in the distance from the camera, so that a simple scaling and translation of the depth values during the copy suffice (scaling and translation are native OpenGL operations for pixel transfers). If perspective cameras are used, depth values vary non-linearly, and the near and far planes of the various cameras must be set to the same values.[1] Another problem comes from the different orientations of the quadrilaterals. When the bounding boxes of two objects intersect, the two corresponding quadrilaterals are not exactly parallel, which introduces errors in the Z-buffer correction such

---

[1] Depth values only depend on the near and far planes for perspective projection.

Figure 14.19   Actors performing a 'wave' motion

as holes. We deal with this problem by setting the quadrilaterals to the same orientation, usually the bisecting plane of the quadrilaterals. In this way, we trade visually unacceptable errors such as holes for less disturbing ones, namely some distortion in the displayed image. In practice, the introduced distortion is barely perceptible, as objects whose bounding boxes intersect are necessarily close to one another, and thus close to being parallel.

14.4.10   Results

An example, we show in Figure 14.19 a simulated circular wave motion propagating through a gathered crowd of 120 Virtual Humans, each consisting of around 800 triangles. We set a fairly high angular threshold in order to avoid camera motion causing too frequent texture updates. By doing so, we managed to view and navigate through the crowd at an interactive frame rate. We achieve a steady rate of 24 frames a second by setting the posture variation threshold to 10%. In this configuration there was no visible degradation of the animation. Setting the posture variation threshold to 30% increases the frame rate to 36Hz with minimal loss of quality. In comparison, the frame rate drops to a low 3Hz when the actual geometry is rendered.

14.5   Case Studies

14.5.1   Programmed Crowds

Using programmed crowds we have produced two simulations. The scenario of the first simulation describes a crowd entering a football stadium during a match between Brazil and Switzerland. Three groups of virtual people are programmed: Brazilian supporters, Swiss supporters and journalists. The crowd intention is programmed in order to have Brazilians occupying one side of the football stadium and the Swiss people occupying the other. Journalists use the central door of the stadium. This simulation involved 100 agents. The goal of this simulation is to distribute the group behaviors among individuals as well as to deal with the basic behaviors as collision avoidance, trajectories computing, spatial distribution, etc., as already discussed in previous sections. The Virtual Environment is a football stadium where people can enter through the doors. At the beginning of the simulation, the information is IPs – Interest Points (the football stadium entries) and the regions where the crowd is placed. Also, some obstacles have been placed in the crowd's way in order to show the collision avoidance method. All this information was defined using a graphical interface to capture some locations and regions from the Virtual Environment. Figure 14.20 shows an image of the stadium.

The crowd in the football stadium is a programmed crowd. Intentions (which team to support), knowledge (obstacles, entries location and regions) and movement (list of IPs to be followed by the groups) are programmed and distributed to the groups. Afterwards, the programmed information is distributed among agents who follow the group tendency. An image of this simulation is presented in Figure 14.21.

The scenario of the second simulation is a crowd behaving in a virtual city according to urban knowledge stored in a database associated with the environment. In this case, the places to walk, to sit down, to wait or meet others are described in the database and dealt by ViCrowd. This simulation presented the integration of ViCrowd with an Informed Environment (Farenc et al. 1999). This film involved 80 agents. The goal of this simulation was to show the integration with a database and also to describe group control, which does not require individual controlling even in a more complex environment such as a virtual city. Also, group behavior such as adaptability was important in this simulation in order to describe a large number of agents who walk within a small surface (sidewalks), then creating an emergent behavior where people walk almost in line. The database associated with the virtual city generates the regions where the crowd can walk, the paths to be followed by the groups (list of IPs) and the location of obstacles to be avoided. This data is described as crowd knowledge in ViCrowd script to be dealt with by the virtual crowd. The behaviors of people are described in the script and concern different intentions: walk, take a bus, interact with smart objects (Kallmann and Thalmann 2002) (see Chapter 13). The APs where smart object interactions are to occur are programmed in the script language. The intentions are distributed among groups and individuals are able to walk according to the information

Figure 14.20 Image of football stadium showing regions specified to place the crowd at the beginning of the simulation as well as the surfaces to be respected when agents pass through the doors

Figure 14.21 Image of the simulation 'The Crowd goes to the Football Stadium'

stored in the database, interact with smart objects as defined in the APs, avoid objects informed in the database, etc. Figure 14.22 shows some images of this simulation.

14.5.2 Guided Crowds

This simulation occurs in the train station placed in a virtual city. Various behaviors and events to be triggered in a train station are programmed, e.g. wait for others, look at the

Figure 14.22   Image of simulation 'Populating the Virtual City with Crowds'

timetable, buy a ticket, etc. These actions are activated using an external module written in Lisp which requires the state of agents and evaluates the behavioral rules. As a result, orders are sent by the Lisp Client (RBBS) and are performed by the virtual crowd. The goal of this simulation is to show the integration with a system that uses Lisp through the City server. In this case, the guided agents are completely non-self-animated and do not perform autonomous behaviors during the simulation. The communication between the Lisp system and ViCrowd is made through the server, which translates and sends orders from one to the other clients. Figure 14.23 shows some images of this simulation.

14.5.3 Autonomous Crowds

To illustrate the autonomous crowds, we will describe three different simulations. In a first simulation, the Virtual Environment is a theater where virtual actors present their performance. The public is composed of 200 agents, which are able to react negatively and positively depending on the actors' actions. Indeed, each action performed by the actor triggers an event to which the crowd reacts. The structure of the crowd in this simulation includes groups with some different beliefs and intentions, causing them different reactions. When no events are triggered, the agents apply their programmed behaviors, that means heterogeneous behaviors of the audience: change position, touch the hair, look at other agents, etc. The goal of this simulation is to show some autonomous reactions applied by the crowd as a function of events generated by the actors in the theatre. Two images of this simulation are presented in Figure 14.24.

The second simulation includes 400 agents who apply different actions and reactions. Five groups of people can be recognized in this demo: participants in a demonstration, audience

Figure 14.23 Image of an autonomous crowd in a train station

Figure 14.24 Crowd reacting as a function of actors' performance

at the speech in the park, the speaker in the park, the people which are sited in the park and some agents which are just walking and do not react as a function of the demonstration. The groups have different intentions and beliefs and react differently. Behavioral rules defined in the script language have been created to group individuals, define their behaviors and their reactions. The goal of this simulation is to show the various possibilities for reactions that can be programmed in the script language and distributed to a large number of groups and agents. Figure 14.25 shows examples.

The last simulation shows a sequence of a crowd in a metro station in Lausanne (see Figure 14.26). The sequence uses regions to establish locations where actions have to be applied as well as regions where the people move. Also, an event is triggered to simulate the instant when the metro doors open, and agents react by entering using the nearest door.

14.5.4 Interactive Crowd in Panic Situation

Panic situations are specific instances of collective behavior where people flee from established patterns of social interaction in order to save their life, property or power after being confronted with a real or imaginary threat (Smelser 1962). Because such situations are quite

Figure 14.25 Images show the grouping of individuals at the political demonstration

Figure 14.26 Agents at the metro station

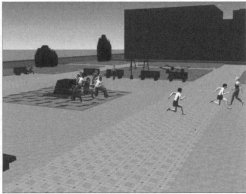

Figure 14.27 Crowd in the virtual park: (a) before emergency, (b) after gas leak

rare in natural conditions and it would be unethical to artificially expose real people to them, it is not easy to study them. By computer models of collective behavior involving Virtual Humans we can get a better understanding of the panic phenomenon without exposing anybody to real danger. Such experimental knowledge can be used to prevent the occurrence of panic both in advance by planning the spatial arrangement of the environment and also by learning which actions are in order to minimize panic effects by e.g. policemen or firemen in the actual emergency event.

We used an implementation of our emergent crowd system to reproduce a simple scenario of an urban emergency situation. The scenario takes place in a virtual city environment where people in the park are confronted with a dangerous gas leak. It includes simulation of pre event, emergency event and post-event behaviors where behavioral rules guide transitions between agents' autonomous behaviors in agreement with the changes of the environment. There are three different groups of agents involved – ordinary people, firemen and medics. According to their professions, agents act differently facing the emergency situation. Ordinary people in proximity of the threat panic and try to flee, however, as the gas is affecting them, some are unable to move and ask for help. If they are too long affected by the gas, they feel adverse effects, eventually leading to death. Medics find such people and provide them with aid. Finally, firemen approach the gas leak and act to neutralizing it. Figure 14.27 shows the panic situation.

14.6 Conclusions

In this chapter, we have described some models that aim at simulating crowds of Virtual Humans. At first, we were interested in defining the required aspects in order to model crowds in different applications. These aspects describe the data and methods used by different approaches to model human crowds: the *crowd structure, crowd information, crowd behaviors* and *crowd control*. Depending on the detail of information presented as well as the behaviors dealt with, the groups of agents can adopt programmed, interactive or autonomous behaviors that we have called programmed, guided and autonomous groups, respectively.

Possible applications were mentioned and discussed in Section 14.5. Some of them deal with a programmed behavior where the goal was to define the behavior of groups as easily as one single agent. Other applications describe the aspect of interaction with virtual agents in order to guide crowds. In addition, autonomous crowds can be built combining more detailed information as well as some complex behaviors.

The results and case studies presented some examples of the crowd application classified in Section 14.2.6. For instance, the crowd in the football stadium and in the virtual city applied behaviors which were completely programmed, and can be used to produce films. The behaviors and actions were easily programmed and we were not interested in the numerical results. On the other hand, the emergency situation case study (Section 14.5.4) describes an example of a *crowd motion simulation* where we are interested in evaluating the numerical results in order to propose improvements in environments design as well as solve problems of a large flow of people. The virtual *crowds integrated in a CVE* (Section 14.5.2) improved the sense of virtual people's presence as well as provided some interaction between agents and participants. Finally, the simulations involving reactive behaviors in the theater and also during the political demonstration described examples of *behavioral simulations* and interaction between agents.

15

Rendering of Skin and Clothes

Neeharika Adabala

This chapter presents techniques to create realistic images of the geometric representations of Virtual Humans. We concentrate on the rendering of skin and clothes, as these constitute the main visible parts of the Virtual Human. We focus on the techniques of rendering that improve the realism of the Virtual Human. The main aspects that are covered include texturing and illumination models. We also cover the techniques that account for the effect of the lighting in the environment on the appearance of the Virtual Human.

15.1 Introduction

The previous chapters have presented techniques to create the geometric representation of Virtual Humans and methods of animating them. In this chapter we cover the techniques to render these models and generate images from them. Rendering is important, as it is rendering that finally brings all the previously described models into a form that is perceived by the end user. The realism of appearance of the Virtual Human is dictated by the rendering scheme that is adopted.

This chapter focuses on two main aspects: rendering of skin and rendering of clothes. The other important problem when rendering Virtual Humans is rendering of hair. This requires special techniques that have already been covered in Chapter 8.

The main goal of any rendering approach whether for skin or clothes is realism. The term 'realism' has come to be associated with different meanings in computer graphics. In the context of computer-generated static images, it is possible to distinguish three types of realism by Ferwerda (2003):

- *Photo realism*: Image produces the same visual *response* as the scene.
- *Physical realism*: Image provides the same visual *simulation* as the scene.
- *Functional realism*: Image provides the same visual *information* as the scene.

Photo-realistic techniques employ heuristic techniques to achieve the realistic appearance desired, while physically realistic techniques simulate the actual physical phenomena of

---

Handbook of Virtual Humans Edited by N. Magnenat-Thalmann and D. Thalmann
© 2004 John Wiley & Sons, Ltd ISBN: 0-470-02316-3

light transport to achieve a realistic appearance. In functional realism only the information is important, for example, if a virtual character is angry, the skin is shown to be red, it is not considered whether the texture of 'redness' displayed is in fact a possible coloration of the skin. In this chapter we focus on photo and physical realism.

Apart from realism the other considerations when developing rendering techniques are computational and memory requirements. Typically there is a trade-off between computing on the fly and pre-computing to store partial results in memory for later use. The latter approaches tend to be faster than the former but require more memory.

This chapter is organized into two main sections, Section 15.2 on rendering of skin and Section 15.3 on rendering of clothes. In each section, we cover the techniques by starting from the straightforward technique of texturing from photographs and go on to physics-based simulations for the appearance of material that result in greater realism. We continue by presenting techniques that address the problems of capturing the influence of the environment on the appearance of the skin and clothing respectively, and techniques that capture specific features relevant to skin or clothing alone. We conclude each section by mentioning some directions for further research.

15.2   Rendering of Skin

Skin forms an essential part of the Virtual Humans that is visible and its appearance has to be captured effectively to create the desired realism of the Virtual Humans.

The skin exhibits various characteristics; different techniques have evolved that focus on capturing one or more of these features. In this section, we describe the techniques in the context of the key feature that they capture as follows:

- *Color and micro-geometry*: Skin forms the outer surface of the body and it exhibits variation in color and micro-geometry. Techniques that capture these aspects are covered in Section 15.2.1 on texturing.
- *Illumination model*: Light interacts not only with the surface of the skin but also penetrates the surface and exhibits sub-surface scattering. Techniques that capture this aspect are covered in Section 15.2.2 on physics-based approaches.
- *Interaction with the environment*: Distribution of lights in the environment results in varied appearance of the skin. Techniques that capture this aspect are covered in Section 15.2.3 on interaction with the environment.
- *Temporal features*: Skin exhibits characteristic changes of appearance such as wrinkling/folding and changing of color such as blushing and pallor. Techniques that capture these aspects are covered in Section 15.2.4 on temporal phenomena.

15.2.1   Texturing

These techniques consider skin as a surface and try to capture its surface properties. Skin exhibits gradual variations in color depending on the region of the body, for example, the color of skin in the palm is different from the back of the hand, the color on the inside of the arm is different from the outer arm. Such variations in color are best captured from photographs, and therefore use of photographs to generate textures of skin for the Virtual Humans is a well-established practice to achieve realism.

15.2.1.1   Texturing from photographs

The technique for generating textures from photographs for use on Virtual Humans was described in Chapter 2. All such techniques rely on the merging of photographs obtained from more than one view to generate an image that can be used to texture the geometry of the Virtual Human geometry. However, one limitation of photographs is that they are just images and they cannot capture the micro-geometry of the skin. Thus the subtle skin appearance that results from the micro-geometry of skin is absent when photographs are used directly as textures. Also, photographs are acquired under specific lighting conditions and it is a problem to isolate the actual appearance of the skin from the features that appear on the skin in a photograph due to the specific lighting conditions. An overview of approaches that attempt to separate the illumination features from actual appearance is presented in Section 15.2.3.

15.2.1.2   Micro-geometry from images

One approach to capturing the light interaction with the micro-geometry of the skin is to use a number of photographs of the skin under various lighting conditions to generate a Bi-directional Texture Function (BTF) of the skin that can be used for texturing. However, the skin on various parts of the body (knuckle, face, palm) differs significantly, and it has subject parameters (age/gender/health) discussed in Cula and Dana (2002). Also, skin is non-planar, non-rigid and not fixed, making it difficult to take measurements and acquire the large number of images that are needed to generate skin BTFs.

15.2.1.3   Micro-geometry by synthesis

One approach to the problem of requiring a large number of calibrated photographs model the BTF, is to synthesize the skin texture based on observation of the structure of the skin. Ishii et al. (1993) adopt this approach. In their work, they represent the skin as a three-level hierarchy of polygonalization using Voronoi division and define the micro-geometry of the skin in the form of furrows and ridges along these polygonalized regions. They combine this micro-geometry with an illumination model based on a multi-layer skin model that is described in the following subsection to achieve a realistic appearance of skin.

15.2.1.4   Constrained texture mapping

The wide difference in the appearance of skin on various regions of the body makes it essential to use texture-mapping techniques that associate the correct texture color with the corresponding three-dimensional feature of the model. Therefore, apart from techniques that generate the texture of the skin, there are also techniques that address the issue of performing a constrained-based texture mapping. In the work of Kalra and Magnenat-Thalmann (1993) and Litwinowicz and Lance (1994) the features in the image are associated with the features in the geometry of interactive selection and a suitable technique is developed to compute the texture coordinates in other regions of the geometry. This mapping is maintained as the geometry changes shape by warping the texture image.

In another approach by Bruno (2001), an attempt is made to map features that occur in the texture on the geometry defined by parameterized polygonal meshes, as against triangular meshes.

15.2.2   Illumination Models

When we consider skin as a surface, then texturing and capturing the coloration and micro-geometry complete the modeling of the skin. But skin is a material and light incident on it penetrates the surface and there is much more to the appearance of skin than just its coloration. We get the feeling of softness and health from the appearance of skin. It is precisely this aspect that has been studied extensively by dermatologists, and they can make inferences about the health of a person based on the appearance of the skin due to optical properties exhibited by the skin.

Techniques that treat skin as a material fall into two main categories: those that try to capture its reflective behavior and those that model both the reflective behavior and the subsurface scattering behavior.

15.2.2.1   Skin optics

In medical/dermatological studies, van Gemert et al. (1989) have made the following observations about the skin. The absorption characteristics of skin are defined in terms of melanin and hemoglobin and absorption is proportional to the volume fractions of melanosomes and blood. There is also a small contribution to the absorption from the remaining constituents of the skin. The dermal scattering is described in terms of the relative contributions of Mie and Rayleigh scattering due to collagen fibers. The epidermis scattering that is affected by keratin fibers, is similar to that of the dermis and is sufficiently thin not to be critical, thus dermal scattering alone can be used to describe the skin scattering. The above properties are typical of neonatal skin. The adult skin optics is quite variable in the scattering properties, the degree of melanin pigmentation, and the amount and distribution of blood profusion.

15.2.2.2   Reflectance spectrum

The reflectance properties of skin can be measured experimentally. The light reflected from a surface depends on the direction, the intensity and the spectrum of the light falling on the surface. In medical studies, typically laser or infrared light interaction has been studied extensively. However, there is a need to measure the reflective properties of skin in the visual spectrum in order for the observations to be useful to the computer graphics community. Angelopoulou (1999, 2001; Angelopoulou et al. 2001) has carried out one such extensive study.

Detailed measurements have been done on the reflectance behavior of in vivo human skin. They have shown that there is significant difference between in vivo human skin and non in vivo human skin. This is mainly due to the presence of blood in the in vivo human skin. Apart from being translated into Bi-directional Reflectance Distribution Function (BRDF) usable in graphics, these studies give useful insights as to why data from medical studies is not directly useful and highlight the importance of considering in vivo human skin samples. The studies have also demonstrated that the effect of the presence of blood in the skin on its reflectance properties decreases with increased pigmentation of the skin. This result of the studies conforms to observations.

15.2.2.3   Measuring BRDF

The technique for measuring the BRDF for human skin from photographs is presented in Marschner et al. (1999). This technique is much faster than techniques that use the gonioreflectometers to measure the BRDF and cost significantly less.

The BRDFs obtained by such measurements are the reflectance properties of skin at a specific location, for example, the forehead. There is a need to augment it to include spatial variations observed on the skin of humans. In Marschner et al. (2000), spatial variation of the skin BRDF is achieved by modulating the diffused reflectance according to the measurements taken from the subjects' faces. These measurements of special variance of reflectance are called albedo maps and are created from photographs.

All the techniques described so far capture the light interaction with the skin at the surface, now we go on to describe techniques where the light penetration into the surface is considered.

15.2.2.4 Sub-surface scattering

The work of Hanrahan and Krueger (1993) presents a model for sub-surface scattering in layered surfaces in terms of one-dimensional liner transport theory. They develop a sub-surface reflection and transmission formulation where the appearance of the natural surface can be simulated by inserting measured parameters. When they applied the model to the human skin, they represented the human skin as two layers with almost homogeneous properties. They used various texture maps to control parameters such as concentration of blood and melanin in the dermis and epidermis respectively. The technique of simulating light interaction as an addition of multiple occurrences of scattering rather than using the equation of transfer is described in the work of Pharr and Harahan (2000).

In the work of Ishii et al. (1993) they add the sub-surface scattering model to their model of synthesized micro-geometry of skin surface. They consider the horny layers of the skin to be essentially parallel. At each layer the light interaction is modeled by either reflecting upward, transmitting downward to the next boundary or scattering within the layer. Scattered light is either directed downward or upward, and possible interactions at layer boundaries of this scattered light repeat. Four factors, namely, reflection, transmission, scatter light transmission up and scatter light transmission down, are used to combine the effect of the various light interactions. The moisture content of the horny layer dictates the values of the refractive indices, absorption coefficients and scatter coefficients of the various layers.

Jensen et al. (2001) introduce a simple model for sub-surface light transport for translucent materials. It combines the exact solution for single scattering from Hanrahan and Krueger (1993) with a dipole diffusion approximation for multiple scattering. An important feature of the model is that it provides the ability to validate the results by comparing them with values measured with a suitable measurement set-up. The skin is highly scattering (it has a typical albedo of 0.95) and is very close to anisotropic (as the typical cosine of scattering angle is 0.85). These properties make it a highly scattering medium, making the dipole approximation of the multiple scattering crucial for effective capture of the realistic appearance of skin. This work has been extended for rapid rendering by using a hierarchical scheme in Jensen and Buhler (2002). A two-pass rendering technique that decouples computation of irradiance at the surface from the evaluation of the scattering component is used to achieve the speed-up.

The work of Stam (2001) describes an illumination model for skin that considers it as an anisotropic scattering layer bounded by two rough surfaces. A BRDF and a Bi-directional Transmittance Distribution Function (BTDF) are used to represent the optical properties of the skin. A discrete-ordinate solution of the radiative transfer equation is computed and lower order splines are fitted into the solution to enable building of an analytical shader usable by animators.

15.2.3   Interaction with the Environment

In this section we give an overview of techniques that enable the environment lighting to be reflected in the appearance of the skin.

15.2.3.1   Inverse illumination

As pointed out in the section on texturing, one of the main problems of texturing from photographs is the presence of the illumination under which the photograph was acquired. In the work by Marschner (1998), the process of inverse lighting was proposed to separate the illumination details from a photograph. The technique involves initially creating a set of basic images given a 3-D model, basic light positions and camera position. In the next stage when a photograph acquired under particular lighting conditions is presented, a least-square solution method determines the linear combination of these basic images that match the illumination in the photograph. The coefficients in the linear combination are the lighting solution. Regularization techniques such as generalized SVD can be used to accelerate convergence to a solution.

The inverse lighting is then used to create a rendering of the 3-D model from which the solution was determined. This rendering lacks detail compared to the original photograph. Another rendering of the 3-D model is done under the desired lighting. The ratios of pixel values of the two renderings are computed and these values are used to multiply the pixels in the original photograph to obtain the detailed image under the new lighting conditions.

15.2.3.2   Reflectance field for face

Debevec et al. (2000) present a technique for acquiring the reflectance field of a human face and use these measurements to render a face under new lighting conditions and from a new viewpoint. The reflectance field provides a way of quantitatively expressing the relation between reflected flux, leaving a point in a particular direction, given the incident flux in another direction. In this approach, the generality of a full BRDF is sacrificed and instead a model of specular and diffuse reflectance is used to extrapolate the appearance to novel viewpoints. However, under certain constraints on the possible re-lighting conditions, their technique implicitly has the ability to include the effects due to indirect illumination and subsurface scattering. Thus, they are able to consider subtle effects such as the effect of reflectance of color from clothes on the appearance of the person's skin. Complex lighting in an environment is modeled to re-illuminate a face by creating light maps.

They use shift, and scale the acquired reflectance model for rendering at changed viewpoints. The technique involves separating the specular and diffused components and transforming them based on the new viewpoint before combining them again.

15.2.4   Temporal Features

Apart from the spatial variation in appearance that is captured by standard texturing techniques, and the details of light interaction with skin that are captured by illumination models, the skin shows unique characteristics in the form of temporal variation in appearance. Such features that have been modeled include: color variations in skin due to vascular expressions and changes caused by the appearance and disappearance of wrinkles as the skin deforms. Techniques that capture these variations consider the skin as a living deformable part of the human body.

15.2.4.1   Vascular expression

In the work of Kalra and Magnenat-Thalmann (1994), the dynamic variation of the coloration of skin including effects like blushing and pallor are modeled. The rendering scheme is extended to enable time-dependent variation of color of selected portions of the face. They synchronize the emotional expressions due to muscular actions with the vascular expressions by using two signals, one for intensity of spatial changes and the other for color. The concept of Minimum Perceptible Color Action (MPCA), analogous to Minimum Perceptible Action (MPA) (Kalra et al. 1991), is introduced to parameterize the model for skin color change due to vascular activity. Texture mapping is used for rendering; they manipulate the visual characteristics of the image to be mapped onto the model to reflect the effects of dilations and contraction of facial capillaries. An image mask is used to incorporate the MPCAs. A shape inside the mask is used to define the region to be affected when the mask is applied on the textured image, and a suitable heuristic shading function is defined on this region to simulate phenomena like blushing and pallor.

15.2.4.2   Wrinkle rendering

The work by Wu et al. (1997, 1999) describes a technique for simulation and rendering of wrinkling of skin. Synthetic micro and macro structure patterns of the skin are combined with real photographs to obtain the detailed appearance of skin surface (Figure 15.1). The microstructure is generated using a technique similar to Ishii et al. (1993).

The potential wrinkle lines are separated into: the expressive wrinkles that traverse the muscle fibers which are active during the facial animation and the age wrinkles that come into existence due to repeated skin deformations over time. Macro furrow lines are introduced

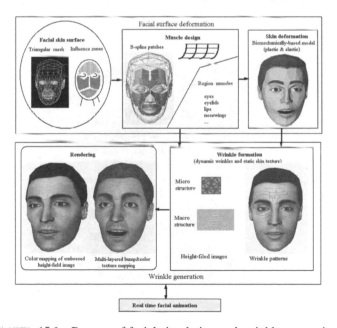

Figure 15.1   Process of facial simulation and wrinkle generation

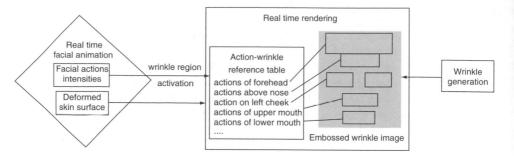

Figure 15.2   Wrinkle generation with real-time system

into the synthesized texture based on these wrinkle lines. Thus an important contribution of the technique is the ability to animate the wrinkles. Figure 15.2 gives the schematics of the real-time rendering of wrinkles.

Bump mapping is used to incorporate the illumination details. Different skin surface details and their deformations are stored in a series of texture images. These texture images include color, displacement and bump maps. Multi-layered texturing is used for rendering the skin.

15.2.5   Summary of Skin Rendering Techniques

In this section we have given an overview of the rendering techniques and here we give a brief comparison of the techniques in the context of the realism they can achieve, their memory requirements and computational requirements in Table 15.1.

Notice that no single technique is complete in addressing all the features that should be captured while rendering skin at this stage. It may be possible to obtain good results by combining two or more techniques in such a way that we achieve the benefits of each individual technique.

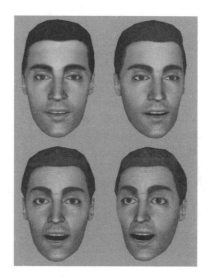

Figure 15.3   Demonstration of visualization of aging with realistic rendering of wrinkles

Table 15.1 Comparison of skin rendering techniques

	Technique	Photo realism	Physical realism	Memory requirement	Computational requirement
Texturing	Photographs Synthesis (Ishii et al. 1993) BTF (Cula and Dana 2002)	Limited / Medium / Medium	– / – / –	Low / Low / High	Low / Medium / Low
BRDF	From images (Marschner et al. 1999) From measurements	– / –	Medium / Medium	High / High	Low / Low
Sub-surface scattering	ID-linear transport (Hanrahan and Krueger 1993) Multiple layers (Ishii et al. 1993) Dipole approximation (Jensen et al. 2001) Discrete ordinate solution (Stam 2001)	– / – / – / –	High / High / High / High	Low / Low / Low / Low	High / High / Medium / High
Effect of environment	Inverse lighting (Marschner 1998) Reflectance field (Debevec et al. 2000)	– / –	High / High	Medium / High	High / Medium
Temporal features	Vascular expressions (Kalra and Magnenat-Thalmann 1994) Wrinkle simulation (Wu et al. 1999)	High / High	– / –	Low / Medium	Medium / Medium

15.3 Rendering of Clothes

Realistic physics-based dynamics of clothing using physical parameters described in Chapter 9 enables the creation of virtual clothing that moves as if made of cotton, silk, Lycra, etc. However, very often we can identify the material of the cloth from its appearance alone without perceiving the dynamics. This is because of the unique way in which light interacts with the clothes made of various materials. In this section, we focus on rendering techniques that attempt to capture this uniqueness of appearance.

A straightforward approach to capturing the appearance is to render the color variation by using texture mapping but this alone is not sufficient. The characteristic appearance of clothes of various materials is due to different reasons, including:

- material of fibers – silk, cotton, wool, synthetic, etc.;
- type of fibers – tightly spun, loosely spun, etc.;
- type of binding between fibers – knitting, weaving, etc.

To capture these properties of the cloth, techniques should have the ability to:

- model thread illumination;
- represent knit/weave milli-geometry;
- model light interaction or illumination.

Existing rendering techniques that capture these features in order to create a realistic appearance are described in Section 15.3.1 to 15.3.1.

The other aspects that have to be captured to generate realistic appearance of clothing include:

- macro-geometric details – rendering of wrinkles and folds;
- consistent transition of appearance based on distance of viewing;
- interaction with environment.

Section 15.3.5 gives an overview of techniques that address these aspects of rendering clothes.

15.3.1 Modeling Color Variation from Images

15.3.1.1   Color texture of micro/milli geometric details from a photograph

A straightforward approach to creating the realistic appearance of cloth would be to texture the cloth geometry with images of the cloth to generate the desired micro/milli geometric details. However, very often the illumination under which the photograph of the cloth was taken creates artifacts. This is illustrated in Figure 15.4 that shows a bumpy appearance that is created by the tiled texture containing illumination; the underlying geometry is actually flat in this case.

15.3.1.2   Color texture and bump map

The main limitation in the above technique is that when we try to capture the micro/milli geometric details in the photograph, we also capture the shadowing effects due to light incident on the material. Another approach would be to only capture the color variation in texture without the micro/milli geometric details and use it in conjunction with bump mapping. This is illustrated in Figure 15.5. However, it is noticeable that there is an inconsistency in appearance, in the figure the cloth has the appearance of being very smooth from a distance but the zoomed-in view of it appears rough. Also it is not possible to include well-structured subpixel details of complex binding patterns with bump mapping. However, this technique is easy to implement and very often used to create realistic renderings of roughly woven clothes.

Techniques that address the issue of smooth transition of appearance with various distances of viewing are described in Section 15.3.5.

15.3.2 Illumination Models

The above inconsistency can be handled by using a suitable illumination model while rendering the cloth when at a distance. The illumination models basically define the Bi-directional

Figure 15.4   Artifact due to illumination

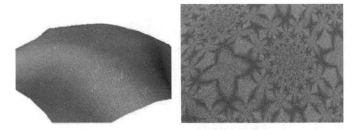

Figure 15.5 Rendering of cloth with color texture and bump mapping (b) gives a zoomed in view of (a)

Reflectance Distribution Function (BRDF). Various techniques of defining and representing the BRDF exist and many of these techniques are surveyed in the work of Schlick (1994). Here we describe some of the techniques that have been applied to define the BRDFs of textiles.

15.3.2.1 Shading model for cloth

Yasuda et al. (1992) consider the microstructure of the textile. The models represents fiber features such as a fiber's cross-sectional shape or weave. By measuring the reflected light intensity from actual cloth of several typical materials, they verified that their model could express the properties of several kinds of cloths. They defined suitable parameters in the model to enable tuning to get achieve desired appearance.

15.3.2.2 Micro/milli geometry BRDF

Westin et al. (1992) define a BRDF based on the microstructure of the surface on which the light is incident. The method is applicable to roughness scales that are large with respect to the wavelength of light and small with respect to the spatial density at which the BRDF is sampled across the surface, which is typically the case with textiles.

Their work includes three main components: a technique to represent BRDF, a technique to estimate the coefficients for the representations and the method of using scattering at one scale to generate the BRDF on a larger scale. It is the last result that is most relevant to the rendering of clothes, in their approach they integrate light interaction over the milli-geometry to obtain the desired appearance of the material when viewed from a distance. Their classic rendering of the nylon cushion demonstrates the effectiveness of their approach.

15.3.2.3 Microfacet-based BRDF

Another approach to defining BRDFs makes use of a distribution of mirrors. It assumes that the surface consists of a large number of small flat 'micromirror' facets, each of which reflects light only in the specular direction (Cook and Torrance 1981). By computing the number of visible microfacets at the appropriate orientation to specularly reflect light from the source to the viewer, one can determine the BRDF. The main advantage of this approach is the power of the technique to represent complex BRDF. A proper choice of the distribution of microfacets can easily model the appearance of velvet and satin, as demonstrated in the results presented in (Ashikhmin et al. 2000).

15.3.3   Representation of Milli-Geometry

While use of a suitable illumination model in the form of a well-modeled BRDF gives the desired appearance of cloth at a distance, the problem of representing the micro/milli geometric details of the cloth in the form of its detailed knit/weave patterns has to be addressed in order to be able to correctly render it at closer view points. Some of the techniques that address this issue are presented in this section.

15.3.3.1   Three-dimensional textures

One of the approaches when a surface exhibits geometric details is to actually create a geometric representation for it and render this geometry using suitable approaches. This can be thought of as three-dimensional textures. Typical examples of 3-D textures are the work of Kajiya and Kay (1989) for fur (see Chapter 8) and Perlin (1989). The 3-D texture approach is especially suited for rendering woolen clothes where the thickness of the material is significant.

Lumislice proposed by Xu et al. (2001) is an approach that can be applied to generate realistic images of free-form knitwear. They create the volume of the wool that forms the clothes by sweeping a cross-section of the wool that they called 'Lumislice' along the knit path. They render the knitwear by modeling the light penetration through this sweep volume.

The knit pattern that is needed to generate the knitwear is created as a combination of stitches as described in the work of Zhong et al. (2000) or by using the standards used the knitting industry like the WKT-data format as mentioned in the work of Meissner and Eberhardt (1998).

Drago and Chiba (2002) present a method of modeling knit and woven fabrics using procedural textures.

15.3.3.2   Bi-directional Texture Function (BTF)

One major limitation of 3-D texture approaches is the time required to render them, as these approaches have to rely on some form of ray casting along the volume occupied by the texture. We recall that volume textures are required in order to capture the light interaction with the geometric details present on the surface of the material. One approach to over-come the problems arising due to volume textures is to directly capture the appearance that results from the light interaction. By this technique one can avoid the ray casting required at the rendering phase. This is the method used by BTF that was proposed in the work of Dana et al. (1999) and can be viewed as an image-based approach for rendering the micro-geometry. The BTF can also be regarded as a six-dimensional function that captures the spatial variation of the BRDF.

The work of Dischler (1998), a technique of performing virtual ray tracing to generate the BTFs, is described. This is significant as it removes the limitation of having to obtain the physical object, having the desired micro-geometric details in order to generate a BTF.

Rendering using BTF is not straightforward and requires a large number of images to be correctly registered and indexed based on the direction of light and viewing. This makes it memory-intensive and tedious.

15.3.3.3   Polynomial texture Mapping (PTM)

The work of Malzbender et al. (2001) has been applied to capture light interaction with micro-geometry in the restricted case of the light interaction being diffused and isotropic. The polynomial texture mapping approach represents the color value at each pixel as a polynomial that is evaluated based on the directions of light incidence. The technique can generate the appearance of micro-geometric detail on the surface of textiles. The PTM can be perceived as a view-independent BTF.

15.3.3.4 Detailed geometry with 2-D surfaces

Daubert et al. (2001) developed an efficient technique for rendering coarsely woven or knitted fabric that takes into account the view-dependent effects such as small displacements causing occlusion and shadows as well as illumination effects. In their technique the based geometry of knits and weaves is modeled using implicit surfaces with skeletons of Bézier curves. They generate a triangle mesh from this representation using marching cubes. Sample points are generated on this mesh where the illumination and light interaction are defined in detail.

While representation of patterns for knit fabrics has been developed in the techniques previously described, the representation of weave patterns has not been developed for computer graphics. While some of the techniques address rendering of weave patterns other than the most common linen binding, there still of a technique that can handle is a lack complex weave patterns. In the next section we describe a technique that enables the generation of rich woven texture and also combines it with methods to render the micro-geometric details and corresponding BRDFs.

15.3.4 Rendering with Micro/Milli Geometric Detail and BRDF for Woven Clothes

This section presents an approach that accounts both for the milli-geometry as well as the illumination model of woven clothes. This is achieved by breaking up the problem of visualizing clothes into:

- representing the weave pattern;
- modeling the microstructure of the threads that make the cloth;
- modeling the light interaction with the cloth:
  - reflection behavior;
  - shadowing behavior between the threads in the weave pattern.

The outline of the algorithm is presented in Figure 15.6.

The approach works in real-time, therefore multi-texturing is used in the algorithm. Each of the modules, namely, the Micro-geometry shader, the BRDF Generator and the Horizon Map Generator results in a texture and the final rendering of the cloth is done by compositing these textures.

15.3.4.1 WIF interpreter

Woven fabrics exhibit well-defined structures, therefore, it is possible to use a procedural or grammar-based technique to represent the weave pattern. In CAD of textile there is a well-established technique for representing the weave pattern as a WIF format (Nielsen et al. 1997). This is a specification that provides the information required for weaving a fabric in the textile looms. The WIF includes information from which a grammar can be derived to indicate how warp and weft threads are interwoven. Since the WIF format was designed for manufacturing purposes rather than for visualization, it is not directly applicable to computer graphics. The WIF contains the threading information that defines which warp

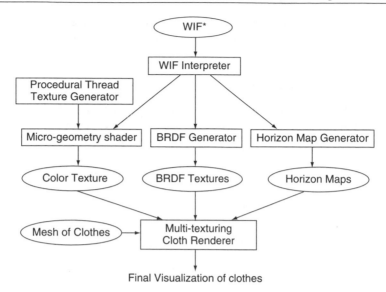

Final Visualization of clothes

*WIF = Weave Information File

Figure 15.6   Outline of algorithm

thread goes through the heddle into which shaft. It also contains a lift plan that represents the combination of shafts raised for the creation of each weft. The weave pattern can be obtained by combining the threading and the lift plan information.

The WIF format is parsed and the weave pattern is derived from it. The weave pattern is represented as a two-dimensional matrix, where the rows and the columns can be thought to index the weft and warp threads respectively. Each entry in the matrix indicates the visibility of the weft or warp thread at that point. The number of weft and warp threads present in the weave pattern determines the dimension of the matrix.

The WIF format also contains color information for each thread that can be directly combined with the pattern matrix to generate the color scheme for the weave pattern. Since the weave pattern matrix indicates which thread is seen at each point on one face of the cloth, the texture for the other side of the cloth is easily obtained by complementing the matrix. Figure 15.7 shows a color scheme of a complex weave pattern generated from a WIF format.

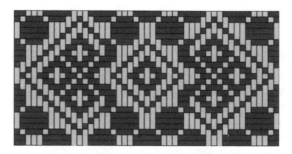

Figure 15.7   Example color scheme of a weave pattern

15.3.4.2 Micro-geometry shader

The woven fabrics are made up of interwoven twisted fibers. At the usual viewing distance the twisted nature of the thread facets is perceivable. The visibility is caused by the presence of dark shaded lines that follow the twist of the fibers of the thread. In some cases these lines are seen prominently while in other cases they are less prominent. It is possible to discern whether the threads are tightly or loosely twisted from these shaded lines. The shading present on the thread facet tends to remain approximately the same under various lighting conditions. This is due to the presence of a deep fine grove between the twists of the fiber into which the light never reaches. This feature is unlike the other illumination aspects of the macro-geometry of clothes in the form of shadowing between the threads that show variation with position of light. Also unlike wool where the fibers occupy a significant volume, the threads that are woven into a cloth are finer and are limited to almost a two-dimensional surface.

The above observations enable separation of the micro- and macro-geometry details present in the woven clothes. The almost two-dimensional nature of the cloth surface is exploited by modeling the facet of thread visible on the surface of a cloth as a two-dimensional procedural texture. The procedural texture has parameters to capture the tightness of the twist and thickness of the thread. Figure 15.8 shows examples of the thread shading textures that are generated procedurally.

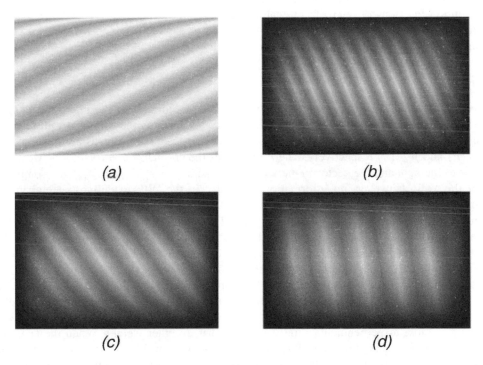

(a)   (b)

(c)   (d)

Figure 15.8 Output of procedural texture (a) Very loosely twisted thread without shading. (b) More tightly twisted thread, noise is added to simulate the presence of fibers about the thread. (c) Thicker fibers twisted into thread. (d) Tightly twisted thread

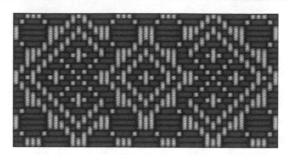

Figure 15.9 Example of color texture generated for the color scheme component in the tiled texture of cloth from photograph

These thread textures can be used along with the weave pattern to generate a color texture of a weave pattern that has the appearance of being woven from twisted fibers. An example of such a texture is shown in Figure 15.9.

15.3.4.3 BRDF generator

The BRDF generator makes use of the WIF information to define a BRDF. The micro-facet-based BRDF modeling (Ashikhmin et al. 2000) is flexible and can be used to model complex reflection behavior. In this approach the design of suitable probability distribution functions of micro-facet enables modeling of various types of textures. A generalization of the formulation for satin (Ashikhmin et al. 2000), given below, is used to represent the probability distribution of the micro-facets:

$$p(\vec{h}) = f_{warp} \times p_{warp}(\vec{h}) + f_{weft} \times p_{weft}(\vec{h}) \tag{15.1}$$

where $p(\vec{h})$ represents the probability distribution of the normals of the micro-facet, f_{warp} and f_{weft} are respectively the fractions of the surface occupied by the warp and weft threads. The probability distributions of facets on individual warp and weft threads are given by the $p_{warp}(\vec{h})$ and $p_{weft}(\vec{h})$ respectively. The $\vec{h}$ represents the normalized half-vector between the vector to the light and the vector to the viewer. The parameters f_{warp} and f_{weft} are computed from the WIF. However, no information is present in the WIF to define the probability distributions of the micro-facets on individual threads in the warp and weft directions, namely, the functions for $p_{warp}(\vec{h})$ and $p_{weft}(\vec{h})$. They are defined by a cylindrical Gaussian with $\sigma_y = \infty$ similar to the one described by (Ashikhmin et al. 2000) for this purpose. The width of the thread is used to choose the σ_x of the cylindrical Gaussian.

The clothes can appear more biased to the color of the warps or wefts depending on the angle of viewing. This view dependence of the appearance of the cloth can be incorporated into the BRDF when the colors that are woven together contrast with the help of Fresnel's co-efficient. The co-efficient is computed as a weighted sum as follows: when the angle of viewing is close to perpendicular, the warp color has a higher weight. When the angle of viewing is at grazing angles, the weft color has a higher weight. Thus, the cosine of the angle between viewing direction and the normal to the surface is used to compute the weight.

The cube map approach (Kautz and McCool 1999) enable real-time rendering of the BRDF. The above BRDF is defined for the whole cloth rather than for individual thread segments, therefore, some details such as, shadowing of threads on each other are not captured by it. These details are captured in the horizon maps that are described in the next section.

15.3.4.4 Horizon map generator

Horizon maps store shadows cast by small surface perturbations on the surface. There are two main kinds of shadows that are present in the woven cloth: shadow due to restricted access of light between the threads of the weave pattern, and shadow due to threads of weave casting shadow on neighboring threads.

The micro-geometry shader captures the first type of shadow, while the horizon maps capture the second type. In the case of fabrics in outdoor daylight scenes, this feature is relatively less important as there is a large amount of light incident on the fabric from all directions resulting in the absence of shadowing among threads. However, in the case of artificial lighting in indoor scenes, the fabrics tend to look significantly different under lighting and this is partially due to the shadows cast by the threads on each other.

The height of a facet of thread above the cloth surface is dependent on the length of the facet on which it occurs. However, the height is limited to a maximum level dictated by the tightness of the weave. This height in turn defines the shadow that it can cast on the neighboring thread facets. The WIF information in the form of the weave pattern matrix is used to compute the length of the facet at each location within the weave. This information is then translated into a height field that is further used to compute the horizon maps. The directions of the light are discretized and a shadow map for each of the directions is generated. This approach is less accurate than the techniques proposed by Heidrich et al. (2000) and Sloan and Cohen (2000), however, it gives reasonable results for real-time constraints.

The algorithm runs in real-time on a PC with a Pentium 4 processor (2 GHz), with an nVIDIA graphics card. Example images of jackets created from various WIF weave patterns are given in Figure 15.10. Use of the WIF-based method enables easy generation of many complex and interesting weave patterns. This provides the graphics community with the ability to generate a variety of clothes with designs created in weaves. The jacket on the right is textured by the weave pattern presented in Figure 15.8.

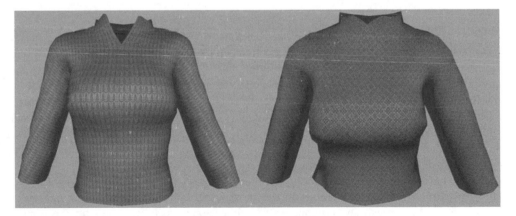

Figure 15.10 Versatility of the approach for generation of various weaves. The jacket on the right is textured by the weave pattern presented in Figure 15.8

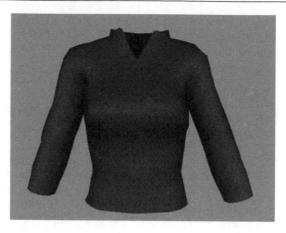

Figure 15.11 Directional dependence of the appearance of cloth when contrasting colored threads are woven together

Figure 15.11 illustrates the ability of the technique to handle directional dependence of the appearance of cloth when two very contrasting colored threads are woven together. The cloth appears blue in the perpendicular view direction while it appears red at grazing angles.

Zoom-in views on the cloth at various levels of detail are shown in Figure 15.12. The technique results in a very realistic appearance of the cloth even at close distances. The presence of shadows enhances the feeling of thickness of the cloth.

15.3.5 Macro-geometry and Interaction with the Environment

In this section, we cover the other aspects that have to be captured to generate the realistic appearance of clothing including: macro-geometric details – rendering of wrinkles and folds, capturing consistent transition of appearance based on distance of viewing, and interaction with environment.

15.3.5.1 Macro-geometric details – rendering of wrinkles and folds

The shape of meshes representing clothes is often complex, as clothes exhibit openings/holes, (sleeves, openings for the head to pass through, cuts that separate parts of the clothes that may be held together by buttons, etc.), folds and wrinkles. In fact, wrinkles are often added to low-resolution mesh representation of clothes to enhance realism as mentioned in Chapter 9.

Such complex meshes of clothes require suitable shading algorithms in order to appear realistic as they exhibit extensive self-shadowing because of the holes and folds. While standard global illumination models can be used to capture the effects of self-shadowing, such techniques are time-consuming and not suitable for rendering with polygon-based rendering.

Stewart (1999) presents a method that estimates the parts of the surrounding environment that are visible from sample points on the mesh. The technique involves taking several planar slices of the mesh and computing two-dimensional visibility cones for the vertices in each slice. These are stored at the closest vertex in the mesh and combined to form a visibility cone. This visibility cone is used to determine the incident primary irradiance at

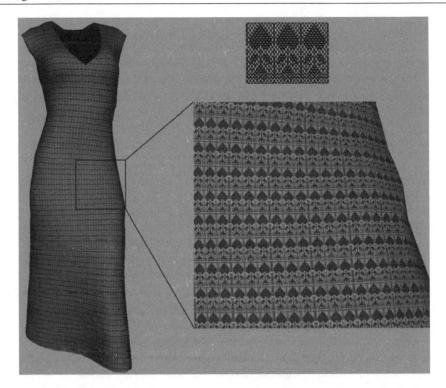

Figure 15.12 Illustration of ability to zoom in on detail. The image on the top right gives the weave pattern used to texture the dress

the mesh point. This computation is straightforward for a point light source, however, a contour integral is needed in the case of diffused illumination from area light sources. A local shading technique is used to determine the appearance of the surface, in (Stewart 1999) the local shading technique defined by Stewart and Langer (1997) is used.

Ganster et al. (2002) overcome the complex computations required in (Stewart 1999) when area lights are present by considering binary visibility maps. They discretize the hemispherical region on the folded surface and define a visibility map on it. They achieve real-time shading of the folded surface by this approach.

15.3.5.2 Capturing consistent transition of appearance based on distance of viewing

Virtual characters are viewed at various distances and therefore have to be rendered at various levels of detail. The clothes which exhibit micro/milli geometry have to be consistently rendered at various distances in order not to create a break in the perception due to an abnormal sharp transition in the appearance at different levels of detail. Thus, one has to achieve a smooth transition from the detailed representation of the surface of the cloth that is created by using displacement and bump maps to the representation of the cloth at a distance that uses the BRDF.

Becker and Max (1993) develop a technique of redistributing the normals in the bump map based on the viewing direction in a way that is consistent with the displacement map.

Heidrich et al. (2000) precompute the visibility of a surface defined by a height field and use it to define the illumination of the micro-geometry from various viewing directions.

15.3.5.3 Interaction with the environment

When a virtual character is present in an environment, the rendered image is convincing only if there is consistency in illumination of the character and the rest of the scene. However, it is not always feasible to use time-consuming global illumination techniques for rendering. In such cases, the technique of using environment maps to compute the lighting has gained importance. In these approaches images called environment maps of the surroundings are used to represent the incident illumination at a point. They were initially developed for the creation of appearance of reflective surfaces in scan line rendering approaches (Blinn and Newell 1976). However, now they are used extensively both with specular and diffused illumination models.

Cabral et al. (1999) incorporated the influence of the surrounding environment into the illumination model by generating a radiance environment map. This map pre-integrates a BRDF with a lighting environment. A reflection space Image-Based Rendering (IBR) is used to create the correct appearance of the object from various viewpoints. The reflection space IBR also correlates to the BRDF and the environment, this is achieved by warping the environment so that it models the BRDF well. Each point in the environment map is generated by a integration of the image of the environment and the BRDF.

Ramamoorthi and Hanrahan (2001) describe an efficient representation of environment maps. In (Ramamoorthi and Hanrahan 2002), they describe the technique of generating environment maps using spherical harmonics and develop an algorithm for fast pre-filtering.

Latta and Kolb (2002) develop a homomorphic factorization technique that allows for inclusion of the environment map into the BRDF factorization enabling real-time visualization with lighting resulting from the environment.

In this section, we have only briefly outlined some of the existing work in the area of influence of environment on the illumination model, in order to make the reader aware of the need for these techniques. These approaches have an application in the context of rendering any type of surface/object in a scene including clothes.

15.4   Conclusion

We have summarized several approaches to render clothes. The wide variation in the type of clothes from fine to roughly woven and knitted fabrics makes it impossible to develop a single rendering approach that can be applied to render all clothes. In the case of knit fabrics and rough fabrics created from thick fibers, the emphasis is on capturing the fluffy nature of the yarn and the details of the surface that result from the self-shadowing at the milli-geometric level. In the case of finely woven fabrics, the emphasis is more on the capture of the non-homogeneous nature of the material that results in a unique illumination model depending on the weave. The technique of spatially varying BRDF holds much promise of capturing these features.

Another aspect that has been ignored is modeling of light transmittance through the cloth material. Methods to model the non-homogeneous transmittance of light through the clothing are still to be developed.

16

Standards for Virtual Humans

Stéphane Garchery, Ronan Boulic, Tolga Capin, Prem Kalra

In recent years two coordinated standardization efforts focusing on Virtual Humans have emerged to improve animation interchange (H-Anim) and streaming (MPEG4-FBA). The present chapter surveys their major characteristics, starting with an overview of the H-Anim conventions followed by a discussion of its potential for animation re-use, and moving to the specialized area of MPEG-4 Face and Body Animation (FBA) for streaming applications.

16.1 Introduction

The ubiquity of Virtual Humans in various applications demands standardization. This chapter presents the standards for Virtual Humans. The standardization helps towards reusability of animation. MPEG-4 has proposed standards for both body and face animation. In this chapter we briefly outline the features of these standards. The standard for body animation is based on H-Anim, a specification scheme that is detailed first.

16.2 The H-Anim Specification Scheme

The standardization of the skeleton is the initial impulse that launched the H-Anim effort. This was motivated by the need to increase animation design productivity through the re-use of H-Anim compliant animations on any H-Anim compliant skeletons. In the next section, we focus on the H-Anim skeleton conventions and discuss the animation re-use potential based on an animation taxonomy. We describe a simple and versatile technique to handle spine mapping when an animation has to be converted between two H-Anim compliant skeletons with differing numbers of vertebrae.

16.2.1 The Need for a Standard Human Skeleton

Animating Virtual Humans is a challenging task; so many joints interact with one another to obtain even the simplest gesture that it requires great skills to achieve believable motions.

Handbook of Virtual Humans Edited by N. Magnenat-Thalmann and D. Thalmann
© 2004 John Wiley & Sons, Ltd ISBN: 0-470-02316-3

Thus animation production costs are high. Even motion capture techniques impose some additional work to adapt the motion to the production context (Menache 2000). Reducing costs by allowing the re-use of high quality motions for a wide range of characters is an animator's dream. However, when it comes to acquiring motion for Virtual Humans, the problem of highly differing models in resolution and choice of joint axis arises, thus triggering numerous conversion problems. The H-Anim impulse comes from the need to exploit *interoperable Virtual Humans*. Its motto is '*model once, animate anywhere.*' In the following sections we recall the major elements of the standard proposal, we discuss their limitations and suggest some re-use techniques depending on the type of motion.

16.2.2   H-Anim Skeleton Convention

Modeling and animating a Virtual Human are complex due to the high number of human joints. A wide range of models has been proposed for individual joints and some specific regions such as the shoulder complex, the foot, and above all, the spine. For a given skeleton approximation, almost every proprietary model has adopted a different convention for the local joint frames and, for those relying on this formalism, a different Euler angles sequence. The H-Anim standardization effort proposes a radical approach by imposing the same default orientation on all the joints and by accepting all the skeletons as topologically compliant with the standard topology (Appendix B). This feature allows the possibility to retain one or more joint sub-sets to meet performance requirements.

Although initially designed for animating Virtual Humans on the Web (Babski 2000) with VRML97, it is now adopted for general purpose applications like the anatomic deformations studied by Aubel (2002). In this later case it has been necessary to establish the correspondence between anatomy and H-Anim minimal design of joint mobility because animators and motion control techniques often rely on anatomic axis for the intuitive definition of postures and natural limits. See also (Baerlocher and Boulic 2001) for more details on anatomic joint representations and (Aubel 2002) for its correspondence with H-Anim.

Put briefly, the H-Anim standard defines a humanoid skeleton as a Node Hierarchy with JOINT nodes defining the internal skeleton (Figure 16.1). SEGMENT nodes define the geometry and can only be children nodes of JOINT nodes. SITE nodes define points of interest and can only be children nodes of SEGMENT nodes. Here follows a brief description of these components.

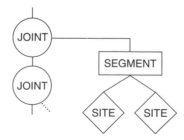

Figure 16.1   Topologic relationships between the JOINT, SEGMENT and SITE node types

16.2.2.1 JOINT

A joint has a name, a center of rotation, and a rotation relative to its parent joint. Joints also define a local frame in which upper and lower rotational limits can be applied (according to a decomposition of the joint rotation into Euler angles along the fixed axis x, y and z). Such a definition can be too crude for the fine control of anatomically-based models (Aubel 2002). However, in most interaction contexts, motion playback does not need to bother about enforcing tricky joint limits, so this feature is generally ignored.

16.2.2.2 SEGMENT

The SEGMENT nodes define the external envelope of the humanoid. The shape of a segment is typically defined by a polygonal mesh. This node also includes mass, center of mass, moments of inertia, and if necessary an array of *displacers*. A *displacer* entity specifies how the geometry of a segment can be locally deformed (assuming a polygonal mesh for the geometry). It stores references to vertices, along with displacement vectors and is useful for morph targets and muscle actions. Its typical application is facial deformation (Babski 2000).

16.2.2.3 SITE

These specify a location and orientation of a point relative to a Segment. They are especially useful for attaching accessories (glasses, hats, etc.) and as end effector locations (i.e. handles) for inverse kinematics solvers.

16.2.2.4 HUMANOID

The HUMANOID entity ties all the pieces together by storing arrays of reference to Joint, Segment, and Site (displacers are stored in the Segments). It also defines a name, version number and set of viewpoints, plus user info.

16.2.3 Benefits and Limitations of the Standard Skeleton

The expected benefit of the standard skeleton is the direct re-use of animation sequences on any compliant models, and the higher productivity of compliant motion engines. However, re-using animation data is more complex than the simple playback of joint trajectories from one H-Anim skeleton to another one. Let us examine cases of increasing complexity:

- *the two humanoids have the same skeleton*, i.e. the same number of joints and the same segment lengths (the trivial case). This is the only condition for an immediate re-use (i.e. no additional processing).
- *only the total size and/or mass changes while preserving the skeleton proportions*: the length scaling factor has to be applied to the global translation too, if any. For significant scaling factors, the whole motion dynamics changes as first shown in (Raibert and Hodgins 1991; Hodgins and Pollard 1997) A retargeting stage may be necessary (see Chapter 5).

Table 16.1 Animation classification with respect to spatial constraints and re-use potential

Animation type		Re-use potential for a different skeleton
Task-driven animation for interaction with the external world through precisely defined effectors' position and/or orientation constraints (hands, feet, center of mass, gaze, etc.)		*very limited* due to new location of end effectors
Expressive animation through gestures and body language, often motion-captured.	(1) involving self-contact such as hand-to-head postures, coordinated movements (e.g. applauding)	*small* due to new trajectories of end effectors with respect to one another
	(2) no interaction between body parts (dance, part of the 'body language', etc.)	*high* (for similarly sized skeletons) as the flow of motion is not significantly altered

- *the skeletons differ in number of joints and segment proportions*: there is less chance for the original motion's purpose to be retained due to the motion-intrinsic spatial constraints. Table 16.1 classifies animations into three categories according to their potential for direct re-use (the term *effector* denotes some body part that has a functional role in the movement like feet realizing steps or hands manipulating some elements).

16.2.4 Enforcing Motion Re-use

16.2.4.1 What to check for?

To summarize, we can split the motion re-use problem into three sub-problems:

1. *The scaling problem*: Are the ratios of total size and/or total mass important? This problem has to be treated if the motion involves the full body at high speeds.
2. *The mapping problem*: Does the target skeleton have a different set of Joints as the original one? This is the only problem to solve for low a dynamics expressive motions without self-contact and interaction with the environment.
3. *The constraint enforcement problem*: Should the final motion enforce some environment-related constraints (task-driven animation) or body relative constraints (expressive animation with self-contacts)?

Chapter 5 reviews the wide spectrum of existing motion retargeting techniques. In the following paragraph we concentrate on spine mapping as it is the region most likely to have different resolutions within the H-Anim compliant skeleton population. Thus, it is a critical point for any motion generator module or for the motion retargeting in general (e.g. in Figure 16.2 the right-most character has a reduced set of vertebrae while the other one has the complete set).

16.2.4.2 Case study: spine mapping

Due to the high number of vertebrae, an animation is rarely defined or captured at the fine level of each spine joint. The same stands for procedural animation as walking. Instead, higher-level information such as pelvis, torso and head orientations (Boulic et al. 1990;

Figure 16.2 Two H-Anim compliant characters

Molet et al. 1999) or user-friendly concepts (Monheit and Badler 1991), are exploited as the input to a spine mapping technique.

In the motion capture technique proposed in (Molet et al. 1999), three orientation matrices based on magnetic sensors measurements (head, thorax, spine base) are distributed on a constant set of eight vertebral joints. The principle is the following. For each joint of a region, it proceeds in four stages. First, as the rotation within each spine region remains small, it was deemed reasonable to decompose the desired orientation matrix into an Euler angles sequence along the three major spine movements (rolling sideward, torsion around a vertical axis and tilting forward). Second, a pre-defined fraction of each Euler angle is assigned to the joint. Third, the joint rotation matrix is computed from the concatenation of the Euler angles transformations. Fourth, the resulting transformation is removed from the desired orientation matrix. The accumulation of small errors is compensated for by attributing the whole remaining rotation to the last joint of the region

A less precise but more versatile approach has been retained for our H-Anim walking engine. Our spine mapping module distributes the relative orientation of the torso with respect to the pelvis (Boulic et al. 1990) on the thoracic and the lumbar regions of the spine while a constant head orientation constraint controls the cervical region. In the initial stage, when associated to an H-Anim humanoid, the walk engine checks which joints are present in the three regions: lumbar, thoracic and cervical. The relative orientation is decomposed into Euler angles producing the three basic spine movements: a forward-backward tilt (lateral horizontal axis), lateral roll (frontal horizontal axis) and torsion (vertical axis). The Euler angle values are then distributed on the available spine joints according to biomechanically inspired region-dependent coefficients (White and Penjabi 1990) (Table 16.2). The expressions of the coefficients are given in Figure 16.3 as functions of the number of available joints per region (it can be a composite region as for the tilt and roll angles). For each H-Anim joint, once the three Euler angles are determined, the corresponding rotations are concatenated to form the joint transformation. Although inducing a small orientation error, this approach is efficient and sufficient to obtain qualitatively the desired spine orientations (Figure 16.4 shows various spine configurations for an amplified walking movement).

Table 16.2 Expressions of the coefficients C_i for a spine region containing n joints, indexed by i, varying from 1 (pelvis side) to n (skull side)

Equal distribution:	Linear increasing:	Linear decreasing:
$C_i = \dfrac{1}{n}$	$C_i = i \cdot \left(\dfrac{2}{n \cdot (n+1)} \right)$	$C_i = (n+1-i) \cdot \left(\dfrac{2}{n \cdot (n+1)} \right)$

rotation angles		Forward-backward tilt	Lateral roll	Vertical torsion
H-Anim joints				
skullbase vc1 vc2 vc3 vc4 vc5 vc6 vc7	**(skull)** **cervical region**	linearly increasing	linearly increasing	linearly increasing
vt1 vt2 vt3 vt4 vt5 vt6 vt7 vt8 vt9 vt10 vt11 vt12	**thoracic region**			linearly increasing
v11 v12 v13 v14 v15	**lumbar region** **(pelvis)**	linearly decreasing	equally distributed	null

Figure 16.3 Types of rotation distribution (for tilt, roll and torsion) over the three spine regions

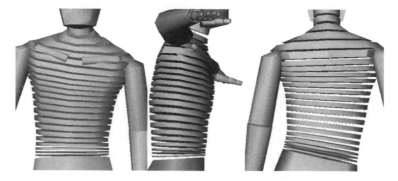

Figure 16.4 Three orthogonal projections (front, side and back) of various instants of a walking cycle (note the orientation of the pelvis and the vertebrae 'slices')

We now examine how the H-Anim standard has been exploited for the MPEG-4 Face and Body Animation standards.

16.3 The MPEG-4 FBA Standard

MPEG-4 is an object-based multimedia compression standard (specification of MPEG-4 standard). MPEG-4 allows for independent encoding of different audio-visual objects (AVO) in the scene. The visual objects may have natural or synthetic content, including arbitrary shape video objects, special synthetic objects such as human face and body, and generic 2-D/3-D objects composed of primitives like rectangles, spheres, or indexed face sets, which define an object surface by means of vertices and surface patches (Ostermann 1998). MPEG-4 specifies a compressed binary representation of animated synthetic audio-visual objects. It is important to note that MPEG-4 only specifies the decoding of compliant bit streams in an MPEG-4 terminal. The encoders have a large degree of freedom to generate MPEG-4 compliant bit streams.

Personal communication is one of the main applications of the MPEG-4 standard. To expand the personal communication capabilities of the MPEG-4 standard, a special visual object was identified targeting the efficient representation of real persons and synthetic characters, the FBA (Face and Body Animation) object. The FBA object is useful for a wide range of potential applications, enabling direct or indirect personal communications, in contexts such as e-commerce, games, virtual teleconferencing, virtual kiosks and call centers.

MPEG-4 FBA provides tools for model-based coding of video sequences containing human faces and bodies. Instead of representing the faces and bodies as coded 2-D raster images, the FBA object uses a 3-D synthetic model, which can be defined and animated by specific FBA parameters. These parameters are typically extracted or synthetically generated, coded and transmitted. Besides representing real human faces and bodies, FBA is also able to represent completely synthetic faces and bodies where no real target exists.

The FBA object encompasses 2-D and 3-D models that can look realistic as well as cartoon-like. FBA defines two sets of parameters to define the geometry and animation of the face and body:

- *Definition parameters*: These parameters specify the geometrical shape definition of the FBA model by means of FDPs (Face Definition Parameters) and BDPs (Body Definition Parameters). These parameters allow the decoder to create an FBA model with specified shape and texture.
- *Animation parameters*: These parameters define the animation of the face and body by means of FAPs (Face Animation Parameters) and BAPs (Body Animation Parameters). FDPs and BDPs are typically transmitted only once, while the FAPs and BAPs are transmitted for each frame. MPEG-4 defines 68 FAPs and 186 BAPs to define the state of the FBA object in one frame during animation. Each FAP/BAP has pre-defined semantics, and defines one degree of freedom. Additionally, 110 parameters are provided in the form of extension animation parameters.

There is no constraint on the complexity of the models: they can be realistic representations of real persons, as well as very simple cartoon-like models. To achieve this goal, MPEG-4 defines a large set of parameters to animate realistic FBA models in real time; applications can select subsets of these parameters to animate less complex models. The MPEG-4 FBA specification defines the syntax of the bitstream and the decoders' behavior. The way of generating the models (e.g. 3-D interactive modeling programs, vision-based modeling, template-based modeling) is not specified by the standard; this means that the encoders choose their method depending on the application. Furthermore, the encoder may also choose not to send the model, relying on the model available at the decoder. The standard defines a scalable scheme for coding FBA objects, and the encoder can choose the adequate coding parameters to achieve a selected bit rate and model quality.

The specification of the FBA object is distributed into two separate but related parts of the MPEG-4 standard: Systems (Part 1) and Visual (Part 2). The Systems part specifies the representation and coding of the geometry and the method to deform the surface of face and body, i.e. FDP and BDP parameters. The Systems part also defines the integration of FBA BIFS nodes[1] with other audiovisual objects in the same scene. The Visual part specifies the coding of the animation of these models, i.e. FAP and BAP parameters.

16.3.1   MPEG-4 Body Animation Standard

16.3.1.1   Skeleton representation

The MPEG-4 Body representation was defined simultaneously with Web3-D Humanoid Animation 1.0 specification (H-Anim); therefore, it is based on the same model to represent a standard humanoid body. The major difference comes from the rotation representation: while any H_ANIM joint accepts an arbitrary rotation transformation, the MPEG-4 specification restricts the Body Animation Parameters (BAP) to the anatomically pertinent Euler angles (from one to three Euler angles, on a joint-by-joint basis).

The FBA specification uses the BDP parameters to define body shapes and optionally information about how to animate it. Since BDPs are used to configure the body model, they are typically sent only once per session. Some applications may transmit BDPs many times during a session, particularly in broadcast scenarios or for character morphing. BDPs are encoded using the Binary Format for Scene BIFS (MPEG4). BDP data can be used in different levels. Three cases in terms of the implementation of an MPEG-4 body animation system can be identified:

- *No BDP data (only BAP data)*: Since no BDP data is sent, the local model at the receiver is animated with the received BAP data without performing any model adaptation.
- *Feature points*: A set of feature points are represented by their 3-D coordinates, and are sent to the receiver to calibrate the resident model. These feature points are represented as a set of *Web-3-D H-Anim* JOINT nodes arranged to form a hierarchy as defined in the H-Anim standard. This calibration model does not contain any Segment nodes.
- *BodyDefTables (BAT) and new 3-D model*: A complete H-Anim body model, that contains the JOINT nodes and SEGMENT nodes attached to them, is sent to the receiver to replace its resident model. The receiver is required to create a local model that has the correct joint positions and surfaces attached to them. Optionally, the model may contain skin deformation data for higher-quality body models. The next section will give an overview of skin representation.

---

[1] BIFS is the acronym for Binary Format for Scenes.

16.3.1.2 Skin representation

MPEG defines two alternatives for body skin deformation:

- *H-Anim Displacer Nodes*: As the MPEG-4 FBA bodies are represented using the H-Anim 1.0 standard, they may contain H-Anim Displacer nodes as part of the model (see 16.2.2.2).
- *BodyDefTables*: The BodyDefTable node is an extension of the FaceDefTable node. Note that each FaceDefTable is indexed by a single FAP. This means that either each vertex is controlled by only one FAP (i.e., each vertex appears in only one FaceDefTable), or each vertex may be controlled by more than one FAP (i.e., a vertex may appear in more than one FaceDefTable). In the latter case, the final displacement of the vertex is calculated by adding the displacements produced by different tables, with equal weights. In body animation, however, multiple BAPs typically affect the same vertex without equal coefficients (for example, the upper arm vertices may be deformed, based on elbow and shoulder BAPs). For these cases it is not sufficient to add the displacements from different tables. Therefore, the BodyDefTables use multiple BAPs to control vertices. A BodyDefTable contains 'key deformations', each key consisting of a combination of selected BAPs (see Table 16.3).

Note that each entry in the BodyDefTable corresponds to a combination of BAPs. If the current body posture is not one of these BAP combinations, the vertex deformations have to be interpolated based on these BAP combinations. A linear interpolation technique solves this problem with a low computational overhead. This technique works by representing the current BAP combination as a point in n-dimensional space. A weighted average between this point and key BAP combinations around it is calculated, weights being calculated as distances in n-dimensional space.

16.3.1.3 Body Animation in MPEG-4

BAPs manipulate independent degrees of freedom in the skeleton model of the body to produce animation of body parts. Similar to the face, the remote manipulation of a body model in a terminal with BAPs can accomplish lifelike visual scenes of the body in real-time without sending pictorial and video details of the body every frame.

The BAPs, if correctly interpreted, will produce reasonably similar high-level results in terms of body posture and animation on different body models, also without the need to

Table 16.3 BodyDefTable content

BAPs				Vertices			
BAP_1	BAP_2	$\cdots$	BAP_k	$Vertex_1$	$Vertex_2$	$\cdots$	$vertex_N$
0	0	·	0	0	0	·	0
0	0	·	100	D_{11}	D_{21}	·	D_{N1}
0	100	·	0	D_{21}	D_{22}	·	D_{N2}

initialize or calibrate the model. There are a total of 186 pre-defined BAPs in the BAP set, with an additional set of 110 user-defined extension BAPs. Each pre-defined BAP corresponds to a degree of freedom in a joint connecting two body parts. These joints include toe, ankle, knee, hip, spine (vc1-vc7, vt1-vt12, vl1-vl5), shoulder, clavicle, elbow, wrist, and the hand fingers (see H-Anim hierarchy in Appendix B). Extension BAPs are provided to animate additional features than the standard ones in connection with body deformation tables, e.g. for cloth animation.

The BAPs are categorized into groups with respect to their effect on the body posture. Using this grouping scheme has a number of advantages. First, it allows us to adjust the complexity of the animation by choosing a subset of BAPs. For example, the total number of BAPs in the spine is 72, but significantly simpler models can be used by choosing only Spine1 group. Second, assuming that not all the motions contain all the BAPs, only the active BAPs can be transmitted to decrease required bit rate significantly. This is accomplished by using a mask transmitted with the active BAP groups in a frame as discussed in the next section.

16.3.1.4   Coding of MPEG-4 body animation

Similar to other MPEG standards, the MPEG-4 standard does not specify the FBA encoding method, but only the FBA bitstream syntax and semantics, together with the corresponding decoding rules. The goal of using FBA compression is to reduce the bitrate necessary to represent a certain amount of animation data with a certain pre-defined quality or to achieve the best quality for that data with the available amount of resources (bitrate). BAPs are coded at a certain frame rate, indicated to the receiver, which can be changed during the session. Moreover, one or more time instants can be skipped when encoding at a certain frame rate. Since not all the BAPs are used all the frames, an FBA masking scheme is used to select the relevant BAPs, for each frame. BAP masking is done using a two-level mask hierarchy. The first level indicates, for each BAP group (Table 16.4), one of the following options (2 bits):

1. No BAPs are coded for the corresponding group.
2. A mask is given indicating which BAPs in the corresponding group are coded. BAPs not selected by the group mask retain their previous value, if any value has been previously set (no interpolation is allowed).
3. All BAPs in the group are coded.

For each group, if the mask for that group refers to the second option, a second mask indicates which BAPs in that group are represented in the bitstream, where a '1' indicates that the corresponding animation parameter is present in the bitstream.

BAPs can be coded as a sequence of frames, each one corresponding to a certain time instant, or as a sequence of FBA Object Plane Groups, each one composed by a sequence of 16 FBA frames, also called segments. Depending on the chosen mode, BAPs are coded using a *frame-based coding* mode or a *DCT-based coding* mode. Compared to the frame-based mode, the DCT-based mode can give, in some conditions, higher coding efficiency at the cost of a higher delay.

Table 16.4 BAP groups

Group	Number of BAPs
1. Pelvis	3
2. Left leg1	4
3. Right leg1	4
4. Left leg2	6
5. Right leg2	6
6. Left arm1	5
7. Right arm1	5
8. Left arm2	7
9. Right arm2	7
10. Spine1	12
11. Spine2	15
12. Spine3	18
13. Spine4	18
14. Spine5	12
15. Left hand1	16
16. Right hand1	16
17. Left hand2	13
18. Right hand2	13
19. Global positioning	6
20. Extension BAPs1	22
21. Extension BAPs2	22
22. Extension BAPs3	22
23. Extension BAPs4	22
24. Extension BAPs5	22

16.3.2 MPEG-4 Face Animation Standard

Faces with animation capabilities have many applications. MPEG-4 enables integration of face animation with multimedia communications and presentations and allows face animation over low bit rate communication channels, for point-to-point as well as multi-point connections with low delay. In many applications face acts as conversational agent, the integration of face animation and text-to-speech synthesizer are of special interest. MPEG-4 also defines an application program interface for text-to-speech (TTS) synthesizer.

The minimum set of face parameters needed to drive a synthetic talking face is quite small. All these parameters can be encoded into a very low bitrate signal for transmission over ordinary phone lines using either voice/data modem or data modem with digital audio compression. The application for this technology includes video conferencing, model-based coding, networked interactive games, tele-video marketing, enhanced public address in noisy environments, entertainment, speech recognition, and enhanced computer/human interaction.

16.3.2.1   Specification and animation of faces

MPEG-4 specifies a face model in its neutral state, a number of feature points on this neutral face as reference points, and a set of facial animation parameters (FAPs), each corresponding to a particular facial action deforming a face model in its neutral state. Deforming a neutral face model according to some specified FAP values at each time instant generates a facial animation sequence. The value for a particular FAP indicates the magnitude of the corresponding action, e.g., a big versus a small smile or deformation of a mouth corner. For an MPEG-4 terminal to interpret the FAP values using its face model, it has to have pre-defined model specific animation rules to produce the facial action corresponding to each FAP. The terminal can either use its own animation rules or download a face model and the associated face animation tables (FAT) to have a customized animation behavior. Since the FAPs are required to animate faces of different sizes and proportions, the FAP values are defined in face animation parameter units (FAPU). The FAPU are computed from spatial distances between major facial features on the model in its neutral state.

Conceptually the Face Body Animation (FBA) object consists of a collection of nodes in a scene graph that is animated by the FBA object bitstream. The shape, texture and expressions of the face are generally controlled by the bitstream containing instances of Facial Definition Parameter (FDP) sets and/or Facial Animation Parameter (FAP) sets. Upon construction, the FBA object contains a generic face with a neutral expression. This face can already be rendered. It can also receive the FAPs from the bitstream. If FDPs are received, they are used to transform the generic face into a particular face determined by its shape and (optionally) texture. Also, a complete face model can be downloaded via the FDP set as a scene graph for insertion in the face node.

As follows, we give details on the definition of a neutral face, facial animation parameter units, facial definition parameters, facial animation parameters, facial animation tables, and interpolation tables.

16.3.2.2   Neutral face

As the face neutral state is the start of each deformation/animation, it is very important to define neutral state of a face. This neutral state has the following properties (see Figure 16.5):

- gaze is in direction of the Z axis;
- all the face muscles are relaxed;
- eyelids are tangent to the iris;
- the pupil is one-third of the diameter of the iris;
- lips are in contact; the line of the lips is horizontal and at the same height of lip corners;
- the mouth is closed and the upper teeth touch the lower ones;
- the tongue is flat, horizontal with the tip of tongue touching the boundary between upper and lower teeth.

16.3.2.3   Facial animation parameter units

To define face animation parameters (FAPs) for arbitrary face models, MPEG-4 defines facial animation parameter units (FAPUs) that enable facial animation parameters applicable to any face model. These FAPUs are defined as fractions of distances between key facial

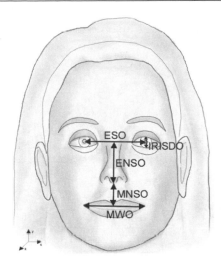

Figure 16.5 Facial Animation Parameter Units (FAPU) and their definition

features (see Figure 16.5). These features, such as eye separation, are defined on a face
model that is in the neutral state with the properties as described above. The FAPUs allow
interpretation of the FAPs on any facial model in a consistent way. The corresponding
measurements are shown in Table 16.5. The notation `3.1. y` in column 4 represents the
y coordinate of the feature point 3.1 (the feature definition points are described later and
shown in Figure 16.6).

16.3.2.4   Facial definition parameter set

MPEG-4 specifies 84 feature points on the neutral face (see Figure 16.6). The main purpose
of these feature points is to provide spatial references for defining FAPs. Some feature points
such as the ones along the hairline are not affected by FAPs. However, they are required
when defining the shape of a proprietary face model using feature points. Feature points
are arranged in groups like cheeks, eyes, and mouth. The location of these feature points

Table 16.5 Facial Animation Parameter Units (FAPU) and their definition

IRISD0	Iris diameter (by definition it is equal to the distance between upper and lower eyelid) in neutral face	IRISD = IRISD0/1024	`3.1.y-3.3.y =` `3.2.y-3.4.y`
ES0	Eye separation	ES = ES0/1024	`3.5.x-3.6.x`
ENS0	Eye – nose separation	ENS = ENS0/1024	`3.5.y-9.15.y`
MNS0	Mouth – nose separation	MNS = MNS0/1024	`9.15.y-2.2.y`
MW0	Mouth width	MW = MW0/1024	`8.3.x-8.4.x`
AU	Angle Unit	10^{-5} rad	

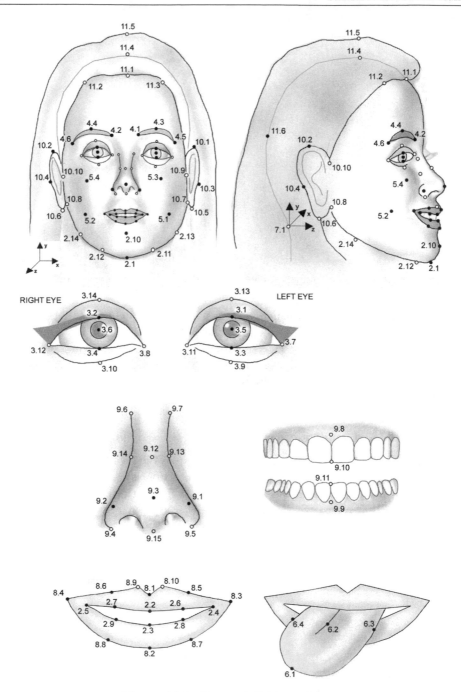

Figure 16.6 Feature definition point set

has to be known for any MPEG-4 compliant face model. The feature points on the model should be located according to Figure 16.6. It may be noted that the circled points with black fill are used for animation (or FAPs) and the ones without fill are the points not used for animation. The FDPs are used to customize the proprietary face model of the decoder to a particular face or to download a face model along with the information about how to animate it (Kshirsagar et al. 2000). Thus, the FDP node may contain:

- position of feature points, this allows morphing or customization of the proprietary face model. This may, however, have a 3-D mesh and texture for a generic head.
- a specific face model along with its corresponding feature points. This is meant to animate the specific head.

The FDPs are normally transmitted once per session, followed by a stream of compressed FAPs. However, if the decoder does not receive the FDPs, the use of FAPUs ensures that it can still interpret the FAP stream. This enables minimal operation in broadcast or teleconferencing applications. The FDP set is specified in Binary Format for Scenes (BIFS) syntax (MPEG-4 Document 1999).

16.3.2.5 Facial animation parameter set

The FAPs are based on the study of minimal facial actions and are closely related to muscle actions. They represent a complete set of basic facial actions, and therefore allow the representation of most natural facial expressions. Exaggerated values permit the definition of actions that are normally not possible for humans, but could be desirable for cartoon-like characters.

The 68 parameters are categorized into 10 groups related to the various parts of the face (see Table 16.6). FAPs represent a complete set of basic facial actions including head motion, tongue, eyes, and mouth control. Appendix C presents a complete description of all FAP.

There are also two high level parameters *visemes* and *expressions* in the FAP set. A viseme is a visual counterpart of a phoneme. The standard set has 14 static visemes that are clearly distinguishable. However, additional visemes can be included.

Table 16.6 FAP groups

Group	Number of FAPs
1 viseme and expression	2
2 jaw, chin, inner lowerlip, cornerlips, midlip	16
3 eyeballs, pupils, eyelids	12
4 eyebrow	8
5 cheeks	4
6 tongue	5
7 head rotation	3
8 outer lip position	10
9 nose	4
10 ears	4

The data structure of viseme has several fields: viseme_select1, viseme_select2, viseme_blend and viseme_def. The above structure allows blending of two visemes. This blending can be achieved using interpolation:

$$\text{Final\_viseme} = (\text{viseme\_select1}) \times (\text{viseme\_blend}/63) + (\text{viseme\_select2}) \times (1 - \text{viseme\_blend}/63)$$

The expression parameter (FAP 2) allows definition of high-level facial expressions. The facial expression parameter has a textual description (see Table 16.7). There are six primary facial expressions defined as indicated in Table 16.7 and shown in Figure 16.7. Use of the expression parameter provides an efficient way of animating faces.

The expression data structure is composed of a set of values:

$$\text{expression\_select1, expression\_intensity1, expression\_select2,}$$
$$\text{expression\_intensity2, init\_face and expression\_def.}$$

The resulting expression from two given expression FAPs is a superimposition of the two expressions weighted by the respective intensities :

$$\text{Final\_expression} = \text{expression\_select1} \times (\text{expression\_intensity1}/63) + \text{expression\_select2} \times (\text{expression\_intensity2}/63)$$

The output of the decoding process is a sequence of facial animation parameters. They are input to a display process that uses the parameters to animate a face object. Appendix C provide a full description of each FAP.

16.3.2.6 Facial animation tables

The Face Animation Tables (FATs) (also called FaceDefTable) define how a model is spatially deformed as a function of the amplitude of the FAPs. Each facial model is

Table 16.7 Textual description of the six basic facial expressions

No.	Name	Textual description
1	Joy	The eyebrows are relaxed. The mouth is open and the mouth corners pulled back toward the ears.
2	Sadness	The inner eyebrows are bent upward. The eyes are slightly closed. The mouth is relaxed.
3	Anger	The inner eyebrows are pulled downward and together. The eyes are wide open. The lips are pressed against each other or opened to expose the teeth.
4	Fear	The eyebrows are raised and pulled together. The inner eyebrows are bent upward. The eyes are tense and alert.
5	Disgust	The eyebrows and eyelids are relaxed. The upper lip is raised and curled, often asymmetrically.
6	Surprise	The eyebrows are raised. The upper eyelids are wide open, the lower relaxed. The jaw is opened.

Figure 16.7 The six primary facial expressions

represented by a set of vertices and associated information about the triangles joining them. This information is called 'IndexedFaceSet' in a geometric representation. A model can be composed of more than one IndexedFaceSets depending upon the textures and topology. For each IndexedFaceSet and for each FAP, the FAT defines which vertices are deformed and how.

We can consider two different cases of FAP:

- If a FAP causes a transformation like rotation, translation or scale, a Transform node can describe this animation.
- If a FAP, such as *open jaw*, causes flexible deformation of the facial mesh, the FAT defines the displacements of the IndexedFaceSet vertices. These displacements are based on a piece-wise linear motion trajectories (see Figure 16.8).

Syntactically, the FAT contains different fields. The *intervalBorder* field specifies the interval borders for the piece-wise linear approximation in an increasing order. The *coordIndex* field contains a list of vertices that are affected by the current deformation. The *Coordinate* field defines the intensity and the direction of the displacement for each of the vertex mentioned in the *coordIndex* field. Thus, there must be exactly *(num(intervalBorder) − 1)* num(coordIndex)* values in the *Coordinate* field.

Figure 16.8 Piecewise linear approximation of vertex trajectory

During animation, when the animation engine interprets a set of FAPs for current frame, it affects one or more IndexedFaceSet of the face model. The animation engine piece-wise linearly approximates the motion trajectory of each vertex of the affected IndexedFaceSet as shown in Figure 16.8.

FAT-based animation in Chapter 6 demonstrates an example of an implementation.

16.3.2.7 FAP interpolation tables

The encoder may allow the decoder to extrapolate the values of some FAPs from the transmitted FAPs. However, without providing the interpolation method, unpredictable results of FAPs may be derived at the decoder side. Alternatively, the decoder can specify the interpolation rules using FAP interpolation tables (FIT) (MPEG-4 Document 1997). A FIT allows a smaller set of FAPs to be sent for a facial animation. This small set can then be used to determine the values of other FAPs, using an interpolation function. For example, the top inner lip FAPs can be sent and then used for determining the top outer lip FAPs. The inner lip FAPs would be mapped to the outer lip FAPs using an interpolation function that is specified in the FIT. The FIT contains two major parts: an FAP interpolation graph and an interpolation function table. The proposed multivariable rational polynomial interpolation function can represent (or approximate) any type of interpolations, both linear and nonlinear.

Some simple examples where the use of FIT can be useful to reduce the bit rate for transmitting FAPs:

- Precise specification of the extrapolation of FAPs from their counter-parts on the other side of the face. If desired, this mechanism allows even for unsymmetrical face animation.
- Extrapolation of outer lip FAPs from inner lip FAPs.
- Extrapolation of eyebrow motion from FAP 34 (raise right middle eyebrow). This can be done with linear polynomials.
- Definition of facial expression (FAP 1 and 2) using low-level FAPs instead of using the pre-defined expression.

In order to specify the FITs for the examples, linear polynomials are usually sufficient. If it is desired to simulate the varying elasticity of skin for large FAP amplitudes, non-linear mappings might be useful. Following the example, we might want the inner and outer eyebrows to follow the middle eyebrow first roughly linearly, and then to a lesser extend. This gives eyebrows with increasing curvature as the FAP amplitude increases.

16.3.2.8 Summary

MPEG-4 defines a comprehensive set of parameters, which enable animation of human faces and bodies. The definition of parameters allows animation of a model over low bit rate communication channels, from point to point as well as multi-point connections (Garchery and Magnenat-Thalmann 2001). In the longer term, the MPEG-4 Animation Framework eXtension (AFX) standardization group aims at defining a collection of interoperable tool categories that can collaborate to produce a re-usable architecture for interactive animated contents (MPEG-4 Animation Framework eXtension 2001).

16.4   What's Next?

We have described two standards easing the exchange of body and face animations. This is a necessary starting point but the needs are far greater if we want to build systems including a large number of Virtual Humans involved in complex behavioral interactions. Does the present standards' definition allows the characterization of a real-world population including handicapped persons, children and elderly people? How could we specify a minimal behavioral level for achieving everyday live activities? A realistic model of these activities requires standardizing perception (visual, auditory), mobility potential and the ability to interpret cultural codes (languages, signs, dress codes, body language). Such an effort is multi-disciplinary as the know-how is split into independent research fields such as Knowledge Engineering, Social Simulation, Ergonomics, and Virtual Human Animation. Recently, some European projects from the ESPRIT and IST programs have explored various XML-based approaches to ease the rapid incorporation of lifelike agents into online applications or virtual worlds (Arafa et al. 2002; Kshirsagar et al. 2002) (Virtual Human Markup Language) (through CML for Character Markup Language, AML for Avatar Markup Language, VHML for Virtual Human Markup Language group).

Federating all efforts towards a flexible standard will leverage precious isolated know-how, and data bases, into a powerful interoperable model. This cross-disciplinary endeavor is the sole path for success as no research field alone encompasses all the concepts required to define a lifelike Virtual Human. Finding the right balance between each field's centers of interest is a difficult exercise but it is the price to pay to obtain a tool where the whole is more than the sum of the parts.

Appendix A

Damped Least Square Pseudo-Inverse $J^{+\lambda}$

The singular values decomposition of the Jacobian J, of dimension mxn, is (Press et al. 1992):

$$J = \sum_{i=1}^{r} \sigma_i u_i v_i^T \qquad r \leq m$$

where r is the rank of J, Jacobien, σ_i are the singular values (strictly positive), $\{u_i\}$ and $\{v_i\}$ are the basis respectively spanning the image space of J and the complementary space of N(J). The damped least square pseudo-inverse, for a given damping factor λ is then:

$$J^{+\lambda} = \sum_{i=1}^{r} \frac{\sigma_i}{\sigma_i^2 + \lambda^2} v_i u_i^T$$

When λ is zero, one obtains the standard expression of the pseudo-inverse J^+ which contains $1/\sigma_i$ terms tending to infinity when the corresponding singular values are small (neighborhood of a singularity). Conversely, when λ is strictly positive, the damping term continuously tends towards zero in the same context.

Source Maciejewski (1990).

Handbook of Virtual Humans Edited by N. Magnenat-Thalmann and D. Thalmann
© 2004 John Wiley & Sons, Ltd   ISBN: 0-470-02316-3

Appendix B

H-Anim Joint and Segment Topology

This is the complete set of joints considered in the H-Anim standard. It contains all the major body joints, including all the vertebral joints (Ressler). For the sake of simplicity, the foot topology includes only one joint for all the toes (the toes are combined into the forefoot segment). The H-Anim standard accepts any partial hierarchy respecting the topology described below; this allows us to define some simplified hierarchies better adapted to the application needs and the platform performances. Some *levels of articulation* have been suggested but they are not standardized (H-Anim 1.1). Additional non-standard joints cannot be inserted in the standard topology; they are only allowed as appendages. Figure B.1 shows the default posture and the HUMANOID coordinate system located at the ground level, between the feet (the bottom of the feet is at $Y = 0$). All joint nodes and sites nodes have the same orientation in the default posture. The root of the hierarchy is called the HumanoidRoot joint node; it is free to move with respect to the HUMANOID coordinate system. The whole topology is listed with a syntax indicating the segment attached to each joint, as follows:

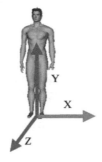

Figure B.1 Default posture and HUMANOID frame

Handbook of Virtual Humans Edited by N. Magnenat-Thalmann and D. Thalmann
© 2004 John Wiley & Sons, Ltd   ISBN: 0-470-02316-3

```
joint_name : segment_name
HumanoidRoot : sacrum
  sacroiliac : pelvis
  | l_hip : l_thigh
  |   l_knee : l_calf
  |    l_ankle : l_hindfoot
  |     l_subtalar : l_midproximal
  |      l_midtarsal : l_middistal
  |       l_metatarsal : l_forefoot
  |
  | r_hip : r_thigh
  |   r_knee : r_calf
  |    r_ankle : r_hindfoot
  |     r_subtalar : r_midproximal
  |      r_midtarsal : r_middistal
  |       r_metatarsal : r_forefoot
  |
  v15 : 15
  v14 : 14
   v13 : 13
   v12 : 12
    v11 : 11
     vt12 : t12
     vt11 : t11
      vt10 : t10
      vt9 : t9
      vt8 : t8
       vt7 : t7
       vt6 : t6
        vt5 : t5
        vt4 : t4
         vt3 : t3
         vt2 : t2
          vt1 : t1
          vc7 : c7
          | vc6 : c6
          |  vc5 : c5
          |   vc4 : c4
          |    vc3 : c3
          |     vc2 : c2
          |      vc1 : c1
          |       skullbase : skull
          |       l_eyelid_joint : l_eyelid
          |       r_eyelid_joint : r_eyelid
          |       l_eyeball_joint : l_eyeball
          |       r_eyeball_joint : r_eyeball
```

```
                    |       l_eyebrow_joint : l_eyebrow
                    |       r_eyebrow_joint : r_eyebrow
                    |       temporomandibular : jaw
                    |
                    l_sternoclavicular : l_clavicle
                    | l_acromioclavicular : l_scapula
                    |  l_shoulder : l_upperarm
                    |   l_elbow : l_forearm
                    |    l_wrist : l_hand (**)
                    |
                    r_sternoclavicular : r_clavicle
                     r_acromioclavicular : r_scapula
                      r_shoulder : r_upperarm
                       r_elbow : r_forearm
                        r_wrist : r_hand (**)

          l_wrist : l_hand (** continuing, same for right
                  hand with r_prefix))
          l_thumb1 : l_thumb_metacarpal
           l_thumb2 : l_thumb_proximal
            l_thumb3 : l_thumb_distal
          l_index0 : l_index_metacarpal
           l_index1 : l_index_proximal
            l_index2 : l_index_middle
             l_index3 : l_index_distal
          l_middle0 : l_middle_metacarpal
           l_middle1 : l_middle_proximal
            l_middle2 : l_middle_middle
             l_middle3 : l_middle_distal
          l_ring0 : l_ring_metacarpal
           l_ring1 : l_ring_proximal
            l_ring2 : l_ring_middle
             l_ring3 : l_ring_distal
          l_pinky0 : l_pinky_metacarpal
           l_pinky1 : l_pinky_proximal
            l_pinky2 : l_pinky_middle
          l_pinky3 : l_pinky_distal
```

Source (Web31)01)

Appendix C

Facial Animation Parameter Set

For each FAP, the list in Table C.1 contains the name, a short description, definition of the measurement units, definition of the direction of movement for positive values and FDP corresponding. FAPs act on FDP feature points in the indicated subgroups.

Table C.1   Facial Animation Parameter set

FAP no	FAP name	FAP description	FAP units	Pos FAP motion	Group	FDP subgrp num
1	viseme	A value determining the viseme for this frame (e.g. pbm, fv, th . . .)	na	na	1	na
2	expression	A value determining the facial expression	na	na	1	na
3	open_jaw	Vertical jaw displacement	MNS	down	2	1
4	lower_t_midlip	Vertical top middle inner lip displacement	MNS	down	2	2
5	raise_b_midlip	Vertical bottom middle inner lip displacement	MNS	up	2	3
6	stretch_l_cornerlip	Horizontal displacement of left inner lip corner	MW	left	2	4
7	stretch_r_cornerlip	Horizontal displacement of right inner lip corner	MW	right	2	5
8	lower_t_lip_lm	Vertical displacement of midpoint between left corner and middle of top inner lip	MNS	down	2	6
9	lower_t_lip_rm	Vertical displacement of midpoint between right corner and middle of top inner lip	MNS	down	2	7

Handbook of Virtual Humans Edited by N. Magnenat-Thalmann and D. Thalmann
© 2004 John Wiley & Sons, Ltd   ISBN: 0-470-02316-3

Table C.1 Continued

FAP no	FAP name	FAP description	FAP units	Pos FAP motion	Group	FDP subgrp num
10	raise_b_lip_lm	Vertical displacement of midpoint between left corner and middle of bottom inner lip	MNS	up	2	8
11	raise_b_lip_rm	Vertical displacement of midpoint between right corner and middle of bottom inner lip	MNS	up	2	9
12	raise_l_cornerlip	Vertical displacement of left inner lip corner	MNS	up	2	4
13	raise_r_cornerlip	Vertical displacement of right inner lip corner	MNS	up	2	5
14	thrust_jaw	Depth displacement of jaw	MNS	forward	2	1
15	shift_jaw	Side to side displacement of jaw	MNS	right	2	1
16	push_b_lip	Depth displacement of bottom middle lip	MNS	forward	2	3
17	push_t_lip	Depth displacement of top middle lip	MNS	forward	2	2
18	depress_chin	Upward and compressing movement of the chin (as in sadness)	MNS	up	2	10
19	close_t_l_eyelid	Vertical displacement of top left eyelid	ENS	down	3	1
20	close_t_r_eyelid	Vertical displacement of top right eyelid	ENS	down	3	2
21	close_b_l_eyelid	Vertical displacement of bottom left eyelid	ENS	up	3	3
22	close_b_r_eyelid	Vertical displacement of bottom right eyelid	ENS	up	3	4
23	yaw_l_eyeball	Horizontal orientation of left eyeball	deg	right	3	na
24	yaw_r_eyeball	Horizontal orientation of right eyeball	deg	right	3	na
25	pitch_l_eyeball	Vertical orientation of left eyeball	deg	down	3	na
26	pitch_r_eyeball	Vertical orientation of right eyeball	deg	down	3	na
27	thrust_l_eyeball	Depth displacement of left eyeball	ENS	forward	3	na
28	thrust_r_eyeball	Depth displacement of right eyeball	ENS	forward	3	na
29	dilate_l_pupil	Diameter of left pupil	ES	na	3	5

Table C.1 Continued

FAP no	FAP name	FAP description	FAP units	Pos FAP motion	Group	FDP subgrp num
30	dilate_r_pupil	Diameter of right pupil	ES	na	3	6
31	raise_l_i_eyebrow	Vertical displacement of left inner eyebrow	ENS	up	4	1
32	raise_r_i_eyebrow	Vertical displacement of right inner eyebrow	ENS	up	4	2
33	raise_l_m_eyebrow	Vertical displacement of left middle eyebrow	ENS	up	4	3
34	raise_r_m_eyebrow	Vertical displacement of right middle eyebrow	ENS	up	4	4
35	raise_l_o_eyebrow	Vertical displacement of left outer eyebrow	ENS	up	4	5
36	raise_r_o_eyebrow	Vertical displacement of right outer eyebrow	ENS	up	4	6
37	squeeze_l_eyebrow	Horizontal displacement of left eyebrow	ES	right	4	1
38	squeeze_r_eyebrow	Horizontal displacement of right eyebrow	ES	left	4	2
39	puff_l_cheek	Maximum horizontal displacement of left cheek	ES	left	5	1
40	puff_r_cheek	Maximum horizontal displacement of right cheek	ES	right	5	2
41	lift_l_cheek	Vertical displacement of left cheek	ENS	up	5	1
42	lift_r_cheek	Vertical displacement of right cheek	ENS	up	5	2
43	shift_tongue_tip	Horizontal displacement of tongue tip	MW	right	6	1
44	raise_tongue_tip	Vertical displacement of tongue tip	MW	up	6	1
45	thrust_tongue_tip	Depth displacement of tongue tip	MW	forward	6	1
46	raise_tongue	Vertical displacement of tongue	MW	up	6	2
47	tongue_roll	Rolling of the tongue into U shape	deg	concave upward	6	3
48	head_pitch	Head pitch angle from top of spine	deg	up	7	na
49	head_roll	Head roll angle from top of spine	deg	right	7	na
50	head_yaw	Head yaw angle from top of spine	deg	right	7	na

Table C.1   Continued

FAP no	FAP name	FAP description	FAP units	Pos FAP motion	Group	FDP subgrp num
51	lower_t_midlip_o	Vertical top middle outer lip displacement	MNS	down	8	1
52	raise_b_midlip_o	Vertical bottom middle outer lip displacement	MNS	up	8	2
53	stretch_l_cornerlip_o	Horizontal displacement of left outer lip corner	MW	left	8	3
54	stretch_r_cornerlip_o	Horizontal displacement of right outer lip corner	MW	right	8	4
55	lower_t_lip_lm_o	Vertical displacement of midpoint between left corner and middle of top outer lip	MNS	down	8	5
56	lower_t_lip_rm_o	Vertical displacement of midpoint between right corner and middle of top outer lip	MNS	down	8	6
57	raise_b_lip_lm_o	Vertical displacement of midpoint between left corner and middle of bottom outer lip	MNS	up	8	7
58	raise_b_lip_rm_o	Vertical displacement of midpoint between right corner and middle of bottom outer lip	MNS	up	8	8
59	raise_l_cornerlip_o	Vertical displacement of left outer lip corner	MNS	up	8	3
60	raise_r_cornerlip_o	Vertical displacement of right outer lip corner	MNS	up	8	4
61	stretch_l_nose	Horizontal displacement of left side of nose	ENS	left	9	1
62	stretch_r_nose	Horizontal displacement of right side of nose	ENS	right	9	2
63	raise_nose	Vertical displacement of nose tip	ENS	up	9	3
64	bend_nose	Horizontal displacement of nose tip	ENS	right	9	3
65	raise_l_ear	Vertical displacement of left ear	ENS	up	10	1
66	raise_r_ear	Vertical displacement of right ear	ENS	up	10	2
67	pull_l_ear	Horizontal displacement of left ear	ENS	left	10	3
68	pull_r_ear	Horizontal displacement of right	ENS	right	10	4

References

Web Addresses

AntZ movie, homepage, http://www.pdi.com/feature/antz.htm

BonesPro, a plug-in to 3-D Studio MaxTM, http://www.digimation.com/

Catia V5 Product from IBM (www-3.ibm.com/solutions/engineering/escatia.nsf/Public/know).

CAVELib™ toolkit from VRCO (http://www.vrco.org)

Character Studio 3 (2001) homepage, http://www.discreet.com/products/cs

dVise™ from Division (www.division.com)

ESPRIT IV 3 years project started in October 1997, http://ligwww.epfl.ch/~thalmann/Erena.html

Exodus, the evacuation model for the safety industry, homepage, http://fseg.gre.ac.uk/exodus/

Fast Light Toolkit (www.12.org).

Genesis3-D Engine (http://www.Genesis3-D.com)

H-Anim 1.1, www.hanim.org, (2003) Suggested body dimensions and levels of articulation, web page http://h-anim.org/Specifications/H-Anim1.1/appendices.html#appendixa

Humanoid Animation Working Group, www.hanim.org

KARMA (2003), Performance Game Dynamics, http://www.mathengine.com/ karma_f.html

LithTech Engine (http://www.lithtech.com)

Motivate product information, Motion Factory, http://www.motion-factory.com (acquired by http://www.softimage.com under name Softimage|RTK).

MPEG-4 Animation Framework eXtension (AFX) VM 3.0, Document ISO/IEC JTC1/SC29/WG11 N4020, edited by M. Bourges-Sévenier (iVAST), March 2001, Singapore.

MPEG-4 Document ISO/IEC 14496–1:1999.

MPEG-4 Document ISO/IEC JTC1/SC29/WG11 MPEG97/M2599, August 1997.

MRToolkit from University of Alberta, (www.cs.ualberta.ca/~graphics/MRToolkit.html)

NetImmerse Engine (http://www.ndl.com)

OpenMASK (www.irisa.fr/siames/OpenMASK)

Python. http://www.python.org.

Handbook of Virtual Humans Edited by N. Magnenat-Thalmann and D. Thalmann
© 2004 John Wiley & Sons, Ltd   ISBN: 0-470-02316-3

QuakeIII Engine (http://www.quake.com)

Renderware Engine (http://www.renderware.com)

SGI, OpenGL Optimizer(TM) Programmer's Guide: An Open API for Large-Model Visualization http://www.sgi.com/software/optimizer/

Simulex, evacuation modeling software, product information, http://www.ies4d.com/products/4DPerformanceAssessmentTools/simulex/simulex.htm

Specification of MPEG-4 standard, Moving Picture Experts Group, http://www.cselt.it/ mpeg

STEPS, Simulation of Transient Evacuation and Pedestrian movements, http://www.fusion2.mottmac.com/html/06/06_01.cfm

The Humanoid Animation Group (H-Anim), http://www.h-anim.org/

Unreal Engine (http://unreal.epicgames.com)

Vega™ from MultiGen-Paradigm (http://www.paradigmsim.com/products/runtime/vega/)

VICON Motion Systems http://www.vicon.com

VirTools (http://www.virtools.com)

Virtual Human Markup Language group: www.vhml.org

Virtual Reality Modeling Language (VRML) – 39L (www.39l.org).

Virtual Story Telling (http://wheelie.tees.ac.uk/ users/ f.charles/ virtualstorytelling/)

Visible Human Project, National Library of Medicine. http://www.nlm.nih.giv/research/visible/, 1995

web:mpeg4 Moving picture Expert Group (2001) Specification of MPEG-4 Standard. Editor Rob Koenen. http://mpeg.telecomitalialab.com/standards/mpeg-4/mpeg-4.htm.

Web3-D Consortium Incorporated, Humanoid Animation Working Group, H-Anim (2001) specification document http://www.h-anim.org/Specifications/H-Anim2001/, edited by Matt Beitler (2001).

WorldToolkit™ from Sense8 (www.sense8.com)

(http::3DS MaxTM) http://www.discreet.com/products/3dsmax/

(http::AIML) http://www.alicebot.org

(http::Ananova) http://news.bbc.co.uk/1/hi/entertainment/606855.stm

(http::Browzwear) http://www.browzwear.com/

(http::CAHRISMA)http://www.miralab.unige.ch/3research/research_project.cfm? projectid= CAHRISMA

(http::Cardlab) http://www.hec.afrl.af.mil/cardlab/applications/multivariate.html, Computerized Anthropometric Research and Design Laboratory

(http::Cyberware) http://www.cyberware.com/

(http::finalfantasy) http://www.finalfantasy-spiritwithin.com/

(http::gamasutra) http://www.gamasutra.com

(http::HAnimFeature) http://h-anim.org/Specifications/H-Anim1.1/appendices.html# appendixc.

(http::JUST) http://vrlab.epfl.ch/Projects/just.html

(http::LifePlus) http://www.miralab.unige.ch/subpages/lifeplus/HTML/intranet.htm

(http::LordoftheRings) http://www.lordoftherings.net/

(http::metrics) Oxford Metrics. (2000) Real-Time Vicon8 Rt. http://www.metrics.co.uk/ animation/ realtime/realtimeframe.html

(http::Motivate) http://www.motion-factory.com

(http::MyVirtualModel) Welcome to My Virtual Model(TM), http://www.landsend.com/

(http::NeMo) http://www.nemosoftware.com

(http::NORDSTROM) NORDSTROM, http://www.nordstrom.com

(http::STAR) http://vrlab.epfl.ch/Projects/star.html

(http::tammy) http://www.cyberware.com/wb-vrml/tammy/tammy.wrz

(http::Techmath) http://www.hs.tecmath.com/

(http::TerraCotta) http://www.miralab.unige.ch/3research/research_project.cfm? projectid= The% 20Xian%20Terra%2-DCotta%20Army

(http::TIMIT) http://www.ldc.upenn.edu/Catalog/LDC93S1.html

(http::titanic) http://www.titanicmovie.com/

(http::tombraider) http://www.tombraider.com

Addleman S (1997) Whole-Body 3-D Scanner and Scan Data Report. In *Three Dimensional Image Capture*, pp. 2–5.

Aggarwal JK, Cai Q (1999) Human Motion Analysis: A Review. *Computer Vision and Image Understanding*, vol. 73(3), pp. 428–440.

Aha DW, Kibler D, Albert MK (1990) Instance-based Learning Algorithms. Draft submission to *Machine Learning*.

Akimoto T, Suenaga Y, Wallace RS (1993) Automatic Creation of 3-D Facial Models. In *IEEE Computer Graphics & Applications*,

Alexa M, Mueller W (2000) Representing Animations by Principal Components. In *Proc. of Eurographics'00*, Interlaken, *Computer Graphics Forum*, vol. 19(3). pp.

Allen B, Curless B, Popović Z (2002) Articulated Body Deformation from Range Scan Data. *Proceedings SIGGRAPH 2002*, pp. 612–619, Addison-Wesley.

Allen JF (1995) *Natural Language Understanding*. 2nd edition. Benjamin/Cummings.

Amaya K, Bruderlin A, Calvert T (1996) Emotion from Motion. In *Proc. Graphics Interface 1996*, 22–24 May, Toronto, Ontario, Canadian Human-Computer Communications Society, pp. 222–229.

Anderson JD (1991) *Fundamentals of Aerodynamics*. McGraw-Hill, Inc.

André E, Klesen M, Gebhard P, Allen S, Rist T (1999) Integrating models of personality and emotions into lifelike characters, In Paiva A., Martinho C (eds). In *Proceedings of the Workshop on Affect in Interactions: Towards a New Generation of Interfaces in Conjunction with the 3rd i3 Annual Conference*, Siena, Italy, October 1999, pp. 136–149.

Andrews G (1991) Concurrent Programming Principles, The Benjamin Cummings Publishing Company Inc.

Angelopoulou E (1999) *The Reflectance Spectrum of Human Skin*. University of Pennsylvania Technical Report MS-CIS-99-29 (Tech Rep), December.

Angelopoulou E (2001) Understanding the Color of Human Skin. In *Proceedings of the SPIE Conference on Human Vision and Electronic Imaging VI (SPIE) 2001*. SPIE, vol. 4299. SPIE Press, May, pp. 243–251.

Angelopoulou E, Molana R, Daniilidis K (2001) *Multispectral Skin Color Modeling*. University of Pennsylvania Technical Report MS-CIS-01-22 (Tech Rep), June.

Anjyo K, Usami Y, Kurihara T (1992) A Simple Method for Extracting the Natural Beauty of Hair. *Computer Graphics (Proceedings of SIGGRAPH 92)*, vol. 26(2), pp. 111–120.

Aono M (1990) A Wrinkle Propagation Model for Cloth. In *Computer Graphics International Proc.*, Springer-Verlag.

Aono M, Breen DE, Wosny MJ (1990) Fitting a Woven Cloth Model to a Curved Surface. *Computer-Aided Design*, vol. 26(4), pp. 278–292.

Arafa Y, Kamyab K, Mamdani E, Kshirsagar S, Magnenat-Thalmann N, Guye-Vuillème A, Thalmann D (2002) Two Approaches to Scripting Character Animation. In *Proc. of Workshop 'Embodied conversational agents – let's specify and evaluate them!'*

Arbib MA, Lee HB (1993) Anuran Visuomotor Coordination for Detour Behavior: From Retina to Motor Schemas. In Meyer JA, Roitblat HL, Wilson SW (eds) *From Animals to Animats II*. MIT Press, pp. 42–51.

Ardissono L, Boella G, Lesmo L (1998) An Agent Architecture for NL Dialog Modeling. In *Proc. Second Workshop on Human-Computer Conversation*.

Argyle M (1988) *Bodily Communication*. Methuen & Co.

Arkin RA (1990) Integrating Behavioral, Perceptual and World Knowledge in Reactive Navigation. In Maes P (ed.), *Designing Autonomous Agents*. MIT Press, pp. 105–122.

Arnaud R, Jones M (1999) Innovative Software Architecture for Real-Time Image Generation. *Interservice/Industry Training Systems and Equipment Conference (I/ITSC) Conference* Ontario, Florida (www.intrinsic.com).

Arsal LM, Talkin D (1998). 3-D Face Point Trajectory Synthesis Using an Automatically Derived Visual Phoneme Similarity Matrix. In *Proceedings AVSP'98*. ACM Press.

Ascension (1994) The Flock of Birds Installation and Operation Guide. In *Ascension Technology Corporation*. POB 527 Burlington, Vermont.

Ashikhmin M, Premoze S, Shirley P (2000) A Microfacet Based BRDF Generator. In *Proceedings of SIGGRAPH 2000*. pp. 183–189.

Aubel A (2002) Anatomically-Based Human Body Deformations. PhD thesis, Swiss Federal Institute of Technology, Lausanne.

Aubel A, Boulic R, Thalmann D (2000) Real-time Display of Virtual Humans: Level of Details and Impostes, *IEEE Transactions on Circuits and Systems for Video Technology*, Special Issue on 3-D video Technology, 10(2).

Aydin Y, Nakajima M (1999a) Balance Control and Mass Centre Adjustment of Articulated Figures in Interactive Environments. *The Visual Computer*, pp. 113–123.

Aydin Y, Nakajima M (1999b) Database Guided Computer Animation of Human Grasping Using Forward and Inverse Kinematics. *Computers & Graphics*, vol. 23(1), pp. 145–154.

Ayoub M, Gidcumb C, Reeder M, Beshir M, Hafez H, Aghazadeh F, Bethea N (1981) *Development of an Atlas of Strength and Establishment of an Appropriate Model Structure*. Technical Report. Texas Tech University.

Ayoub M, Mital A (1987) *Manual Materials Handling*. Taylor & Francis.

Azuola F, Badler N, Ho P, Kakadiaris I, Metaxas D, Ting B (1994) Building Anthropometry-Based Virtual Human Model. In *Proc. IMAGE VII Conf*. Tuscon, AZ.

Babski C (2000) Virtual Humanoid on the Web. PhD thesis. Swiss Federal Institute of Technology, Lausanne.

Badler N (1997a) Real-time Virtual Humans. *In Proc. Pacific Graphics*. IEEE Computer Society Press.

Badler N (1997b) Virtual Humans for Animation, Ergonomics, and Simulation. In *IEEE Workshop on Non-Rigid and Articulated Motion*. Puerto Rico.

Badler N, Bindiganavale R, Bourne J, Palmer M, Shi J, Schuler W (1998) A Parameterized Action Representation for Virtual Human Agents. In *Workshop on Embodied Conversational Characters*.

Badler N, Manoochehri KH, Walters G (1987) Articulated Figure Positioning by Multiple Constraints. *IEEE Computer Graphics & Applications*, vol. 7(6), pp. 28–38.

Badler NI, Phillips CB, Webber BL (1993) *Simulating Humans*. Oxford University Press.

Badler NI, Phillips CB, Webber BL (1999) *Simulating Humans: Computer Graphics, Animation, and Control*. University of Pennsylvania, Oxford University Press, March.

Badler NI, Smoliar SW (1979) Digital Representations of Human Movement. *Computing Surveys*, vol. 11(1), pp. 19–38.

Baerends G (1976) The Functional Organization of Behavior. *Animal Behavior*, vol. 24, pp. 726–735.

Baerlocher P (2001) Inverse Kinematics Techniques for the Interactive Posture Control of Articulated Figures, DSc thesis 2393, Swiss Federal Institute of Technology, EPFL.

Baerlocher P, Boulic R (1998) Task Priority Formulations for the Kinematic Control of Highly Redundant Articulated Structures. In *IEEE IROS'98*, pp. 323–329.

Baerlocher P, Boulic R (2000) Kinematic Control of the Mass Properties of Redundant Articulated Bodies. In *Proceedings of IEEE Conference ICRA 2000*. San Francisco, CA, pp 2557–2562.

Baerlocher P, Boulic R (2001) Parametrization and Range of Motion of the Ball and Socket Joint. *Deformable Avatars*. Kluwer Academic Publishers, pp. 180–190.

Baerlocher P, Boulic R (2003) An Inverse Kinematic Architecture Enforcing an Arbitrary Number of Strict Priority Levels, submitted for publication.

Bajaj CL, Ihm I (1996) Smoothing Polyhedra Using Implicit Algebraic Splines. *Computer Graphics (SIGGRAPH'92 proceedings)*. Addison-Wesley, vol. 26(2), pp. 79–88.

Balcisoy S, Torre R, Ponder M, Fua P, Thalmann D, Augmented Reality for Real and Virtual Humans. In *Symposium on Virtual Reality Software Technology Proc. CGI 2000*. IEEE Computer Society Press.

Ball G, Breese J (1998) Emotion and Personality in a Conversational Character. In *Workshop on Embodied Conversational Characters*. Oct. 12–15, 1998, Tahoe City, CA, pp. 83–84, 119–121.

Baraff D (1996) Linear-Time Dynamics Using Lagrange Multipliers. In *Proceedings of SIGGRAPH'96*. ACM Press, pp. 137–146.

Baraff D, Witkin A (1998) Large Steps in Cloth Simulation. *Computer Graphics (SIGGRAPH'98 Proceedings)*. Addison-Wesley, 32, pp. 106–117.

Bar-Shalom Y, Li X (1993) *Estimation and Tracking: Principles, Techniques, and Software*. Artech House.

Bates J (1994) The Role of Emotion in Believable Agents. *Communications of the ACM*, vol. 37(7), 122–125.

Baudel T, Beaudoin-Lafon M (1992) *CHARADE: Remote Control of Objects Using Free-Hand Gesture*. Rapport de recherche, Université de Paris Sud.

Bécheiraz P, Thalmann D (1996) A Model of Nonverbal Communication and Interpersonal Relationship between Virtual Actors. In *Computer Animation'96*. IEEE Computer Society Press.

Bechmann D, Dubreuil N (1993) Animation Through Space and Time Based on a Space Deformation Model. *The Journal of Visualization and Computer Animation*, vol. 4, pp. 165–184.

Beck B, Key Strategic Issues in Online Apparel Retailing – The Need for an Online Fitting Solution, http://www.techexchange.com/thelibrary/online_fit.html.

Becker BG, Max NL (1993) Smooth Transitions Between Bump Rendering Algorithms, *Computer Graphics (SIGGRAPH'93 Proceedings)*. ACM Press. vol. 27, pp. 183–190.

Benesch H (1995) *Atlas de la Psychologie*. Encyclopédies d'Aujourd'hui.

Berger PL, Luckmann T (1966) *The Social Construction of Reality: A Treatise in the Sociology of Knowledge*. Anchor Books.

Berta J (1999) Integrating VR and CAD. *IEEE Computer Graphics and Applications*, pp. 14–19.

Berthoz A (2002) *The Brain's Sense of Movement*, Harvard University Press.

Beskow J (1995) Rule-Based Visual Speech Synthesis. In *Proceedings of Eurospeech 95*. (September 1995), ACM SIGGRAPH/Addison-Wesley.

Bierbaum A, Just C, Hartling P, Meinert K, Baker A, Cruz-Neira C, VR Juggler: A Virtual Platform for Virtual Reality Application Development, *Proceedings of IEEE Virtual Reality 2001 Conference* (www.vrjuggler.org).

Bindiganavale R, Badler N (1998) Motion Abstraction and Mapping with Spatial Constraints, *Proceedings of CAPTECH'98, Lecture Notes in Artificial Intelligence 1537*. Springer, pp. 70–82.

Bindiganavale R, Schuler W, Allbeck J, Badler N, Joshi A, Palmer M (2000) Dynamically Altering Agent Behaviors Using Natural Language Instructions, *Proceedings of the 4th Autonomous Agents Conference*, Barcelona, Spain, June, pp. 293–300.

Bishop CM (1995) Radial Basis Function. In *Neural Networks for Pattern Recognition*. Oxford University Press.

Bittar E, Tsingos N, Gascuel M-P (1995) Automatic Reconstruction of Unstructured 3-D Data: Combining Medial Axis and Implicit Surfaces. In Seidel H-P, Willis PJ (eds), *Computer Graphics Forum*, vol. 14, Eurographics Association, pp. 457–468.

Blacharski PA, Somerset JH (1975) A Three Dimensional Study of the Kinematics of the Human Knee *J. Biomechanics*, Pergamon Press, vol. 8, pp. 375–384.

Blakeley FM (1980) *CYBERMAN*. Chryslter Corporation, Detriot, Michigan, June.

Blanz V, Vetter T (1999) A Morphable Model for the Synthesis of 3-D Faces. In *Computer Graphics (Proc. SIGGRAPH'99)*. ACM Press, pp. 187–194.

Blinn JF (1982) A Generalization of Algebraic Surface Drawing. *ACM Transactions on Graphics*, vol. 1(3), pp. 235–256.

Blinn JF, Newell ME (1976) Texture and Reflection in Computer Generated Images. In *Communication of ACM*, vol. 19, pp. 542–546.

Bloomenthal J (1993) *Hand Crafted*, Siggraph Course Notes 25.

Bloomenthal J, Shoemake K (1991) Convolution Surfaces. In *SIGGRAPH 91*, pp. 251–256.

Blumberg B, Todd P, Maes P (1996) No Bad Dogs: Ethological Lessons for Learning in Hamsterdam. In *Proceedings of the 4th International Conference on the Simulation of Adaptive Behavior*.

Bohm K, Broll W, Sokolewicz M (1994) Dynamic Gesture Recognition Using Neural Networks: A Fundament for Advanced Interaction Construction, paper presented at SPIE Conference Electronic Imaging Science and Technology, California. Zentrum für Graphische Datenverarbeitung, Darmstadt.

Boman M, Verhagen H (1998) Social Intelligence as Norm Adaptation. In Dautenhahn and Edmonds (eds) *Proc Workshop on Socially Situated Intelligence*, 5th International Conference on Simulation of Adaptive Behavior.

Bonney MC, Case K, Hughes BJ, Schofield NA, Williams RW (1972) Computer Aided Workplace Design Using SAMMIE. *Proc. Ergonomics Research Society, Annual Conference*, Cardiff.

Bordeux C, Boulic R, Thalmann D (1999) An Efficient and Flexible Perception Pipeline for Autonomous Agents. In Brunet P, Scopigno R (eds) *Computer Graphics Forum* (Eurographics'99). The Eurographics Association and Blackwell Publishers, vol. 18(3), pp. 23–30.

Bottaci L (1995) A Direct Manipulation Interface for a User Enhanceable Crowd Simulator. *Journal of Intelligent Systems*, vol. 5(2–4), pp. 249–272.

Boulic R, Becheiraz P, Emering L, Thalmann D (1997) Integration of Motion Control Techniques for Virtual Human and Avatar Real-Time Animation. In *Proc. VRST'97*. ACM Press, pp. 111–118.

Boulic R, Huang Z, Thalmann D (1997) A Comparison of Design Strategies for 3-D Human motions. In *Human Comfort and Security of Information Systems*.

Boulic R, Mas R, Thalmann D (1994) Inverse Kinetics for Center of Mass Position Control and Posture Optimization, in Race Workshop on Combined Real and Synthetic Image Processing for Broadcast and Video Production (Monalisa Project), Hamburg, Springer-Verlag.

Boulic R, Mas R, Thalmann D (1996) A Robust Approach for the Center of Mass Position Control with Inverse Kinetics. *Journal of Computers and Graphics*, vol. 20(5), pp. 693–701.

Boulic R, Mas R, Thalmann D (1997) Complex Character Positioning Based on a Compatible Flow Model of Multiple Supports. *IEEE Transactions on Visualization and Computer Graphics*, vol. 3(3), pp. 245–261.

Boulic R, Thalmann D (1992) Combined Direct and Inverse Kinematics for the Correction of Pre-defined Motions. *Computer Graphics Forum*, vol. 2(4), pp. 189–202.

Boulic R, Thalmann D, Magnenat-Thalmann N (1990) A Global Human Walking Model with Real Time Kinematic Personification. *The Visual Computer*, vol. 6(6), December 1990.

Bouvier E, Cohen E, Najman L (1997) From Crowd Simulation to Airbag Deployment: Particle Systems, a New Paradigm of Simulation. *Journal of Electrical Imaging*, vol. 6(1), pp. 94–107.

Bouvier E, Guilloteau P (1996) Crowd Simulation in Immersive Space Management. In *Proc. Eurographics Workshop on Virtual Environments and Scientific Visualization'96*. Springer-Verlag, pp. 104–110.

Brand M (1999) Voice Puppetry. In *Proc. SIGGRAPH 99 Computer Graphics Proceedings*, Annual Conference Series, pp. 21–28.

Brand M, Hertzmann A (2000) Style Machines. In *Proc. of SIGGRAPH'00*, New Orleans, USA, and Technical Report TR-2000-14 MERL.

Bratman ME (1987) *Intentions, Plans, and Practical Reason*. Harvard University Press.

Breen DE, House DH, Wozny MJ (1994) Predicting the Drape of Woven Cloth Using Interacting Particles. In *Computer Graphics (SIGGRAPH'94 Proceedings)*. Addison-Wesley, pp. 365–372.

Bregler C, Covell M, Slaney M (1997) Video Rewrite: Driving Visual Speech with Audio. In *Proceedings of SIGGRAPH'97* (August 1997), Computer Graphics Proceedings, ACM SIGGRAPH/Addison-Wesley, pp. 353–360.

Bregler C, Malik J (1998) Tracking People with Twists and Exponential Maps. In *Conference on Computer Vision and Pattern Recognition*, Santa Barbara, CA.

Bridson R, Fedkiv R, Anderson J (2002) Robust Treatment of Collisions, Contact and Friction for Cloth Animation. *Computer Graphics (SIGGRAPH'02 Proceedings)*, Addison-Wesley.

Brogan D, Hodgins J (1997) Group Behaviors for Systems with Significant Dynamics. *Autonomous Robots*, vol. 4, pp. 137–153.

Bruderlin A (1999) A Method to Generate Wet and Broken-Up Animal Fur. *Pacific Graphics'99*. Seoul, Korea.

Brunelli R, Poggio T (1992) Face Recognition through Geometrical Features. In S Margherita Ligure (ed.), *ECCV'92*. Springer-Verlag, pp. 792–800.

Bruno L (2001) Constrained Texture Mapping. In *Proceedings of SIGGRAPH 2001*. Los Angeles, pp. 417–424.

Burnsides D, Boehmer M, Robinette K (2001) Landmark Detection and Identification in the CAESAR Project. In *Proc. 3DIM (3rd International Conference on 3-D Digital Image and Modeling)*, pp. 393–398.

Burt PJ, Andelson EH (1983) A Multiresolution Spline with Application to Image Mosaics. *ACM Transactions on Graphics*. ACM Press, 2(4), pp. 217–236.

Cabral B, Max N, Springmeyer R (1987), Bidirectional Reflection Functions from Surface Bump Maps. *Computer Graphics* (SIGGRAPH'87 Proceedings), vol. 21, pp. 273–281

Cabral B, Olano M, Nemec P (1999) Reflection Space Image Based Rendering. In *Proceedings of SIGGRAPH 2000*, pp. 165–170.

Caicedo A, Thalmann D (2000) Virtual Humanoids: Let Them Be Autonomous without Losing Control. In *The Fourth International Conference on Computer Graphics and Artificial Intelligence*.

Calvert TW, Patla A (1982) Aspects of the Kinematic Simulation of Human Movement. *IEEE Computer Graphics and Applications*, vol. 2(9), pp. 41–50.

Cani-Gascuel MP (1998) Layered Deformable Models with Implicit Surfaces. *Graphics Interface'98*, Vancouver, Canada.

Cani-Gascuel MP, Desbrun M (1997) Animation of Deformable Models Using Implicit Surfaces. *IEEE Transactions on Visualization and Computer Graphics*, vol. 3(1), pp.

Carignan M,. Yang Y, Magnenat-Thalmann N, Thalmann D (1992) Dressing Animated Synthetic Actors with Complex Deformable Clothes. *Computer Graphics (SIGGRAPH'92 proceedings)*, Addison-Wesley, vol. 26(2), pp. 99–104.

Carley KM, Newell C (1994) The Nature of the Social Agent. *Journal of Mathematical Sociology*, vol. 19(4), pp. 221–262.

Carlson DA, Hodgins J (1997) Simulation Levels of Detail for Real-time Animation. In *Proc. Graphics Interface'97*, pp 1–8.

Carolis BD, Carofiglio V, Pelachaud C (2002) From Discourse Plans to Believable Behavior Generation. In *Proceedings of Second International Natural Language Generation Conference*. ACM Press, pp. 65–72.

Carrere C, Istook C, Little T, Hong H, Plumlee T (2000) *Automated Garment Development from Body Scan Data*. Annual Report, NTC Project I00–S15.

Cassell J, (2000) More than Just Another Pretty Face: Embodied Conversational Interface Agents. *Communications of the ACM*, vol. 43(4), pp. 70–78.

Cassell J, Pelachaud C, Badler N, Steedman M, Achorn B, Bechet T, Douville B, Prevost S, Stone M (1994) Animated Conversation: Rule-Based Generation of Facial Expression, Gesture and Spoken Intonation for Multiple. In Glassner A. (ed.), In *Proceedings of SIGGRAPH'94*. ACM Press, pp. 413–420.

Cassell J, Thorisson K (1999) The Power of a Nod and a Glance: Envelope vs. Emotional Feedback in Animated Conversational Agents. *Applied Artificial Intelligence*, vol. 13(3), pp. 519–538.

Cassell J, Vilhjálmsson H, Bickmore T (2001) BEAT: the Behavior Expression Animation Toolkit. *Proceedings of SIGGRAPH'01*. ACM Press, pp. 477–486.

Cassell J, Vilhjálmsson H, Chang K, Bickmore T, Campbell L, Yan H (1999) Requirements for an Architecture for Embodied Conversational Characters. *Computer Animation and Simulation'99* (Eurographics Series). Springer Verlag, pp. 109–120.

Catmull E (1974) Subdivision Algorithm for the Display of Curved Surfaces, PhD thesis, University of Utah.

Catmull E, Clark J (1978) Recursively Generated B-spline Surfaces on Arbitrary Topological Meshes. *Computer Aided Design*, vol. 10(6), pp. 350–355.

Cavazza M, Charles F, Mead SJ (2001) Characters in Search of an Author: Ai-Based Virtual Storytelling. In Springer (ed.), *Virtual Storytelling: Using Virtual Reality Technologies for Storytelling*. International Conference ICVS.

Chadwick J, Haumann D, Parent R (1989) Layered Construction for Deformable Animated Characters. *Computer Graphics (SIGGRAPH '89 Proceedings)*, pp. 243–252.

Chaffin DB, Andersson GBJ, Martin BJ (1999) *Occupational Biomechanics*. 3rd edn, John Wiley & Sons, Ltd.

Cham TJ, Rehg JM (1999) A Multiple Hypothesis Approach to Figure Tracking. In *Conference on Computer Vision and Pattern Recognition*, vol 2, Ft. Collins, CO.

Channon AD, Damper RI (1998) *The Evolutionary Emergence of Socially Intelligent Agents*, Technical Report, University of Zürich, Zürich.

Chen D, Zeltzer D (1992) Pump it Up: Computer Animation of a Biomechanically Based Model of Muscle using the Finite Element Method. *Computer Graphics (SIGGRAPH'92 Proceedings)*, pp. 89–98.

Chen L-H, Saeyor S, Dohi H, Ishizuka M (1999) A System of 3-D Hair Style Synthesis Based on the Wisp Model. *The Visual Computer*, vol. 15(4), pp. 159–170.

Choi KJ, Ko HS (2000) Online Motion Retargeting. *Journal of Visualization and Computer Animation*, vol. 11(5), pp. 223–235.

Choi KJ, Ko HS (2002) Stable but Responsive Cloth. *Computer Graphics (SIGGRAPH'02 Proceedings)*. Addison Wesley.

Choo K, Fleet DJ (2001) People Tracking Using Hybrid Monte Carlo Filtering. In *International Conference on Computer Vision*, Vancouver, Canada.

Churcher GE, Atwell ES, Souter C (1997) *Dialogue Management Systems: A Survey and Overview*. Technical Report, University of Leeds.

Cohen JD, Lin MC, Manocha D, Ponamgi MK (1995) I-COLLIDE: An Interactive and Exact Collision Detection System for Large-Scale Environments. *Symp. of Interactive 3-D Graphics Proc.*, pp. 189–196.

Cohen MM, Massaro DW (1993), Modeling Co-articulation in Synthetic Visual Speech. In M-Thalmann N, Thalmann D (eds), *Models and Techniques in Computer Animation*. Springer-Verlag, pp. 139–156.

Cole R, Mariani J, Uszkoreit H, Varile G B., Zaenen A, Zampolli A, Zue V (1997) Survey of the State of the Art in Human Language Technology. In *Studies in Natural Language Processing*, Cambridge University Press.

Collier JR, Collier BJ, O'Toole G, Sargand SM (1991) Drape Prediction by Means of Finite-Element Analysis. *Journal of the Textile Institute*, vol. 82 (1), pp. 96–107.

Conte R, Castelfranchi C, Dignum F (1999) Autonomous Norm Acceptance. In Müller J, Singh MP, Rao AS (eds). *Proceedings of the 5th International Workshop on Intelligent*

Agents V: Agent Theories, Architectures, and Languages (ATAL-98). Springer-Verlag, vol. 1555, pp. 99–112.

Cook RL, Torrance KE (1981) A Reflectance Model for Computer Graphics. In *Proceedings of SIGGRAPH 1981, Computer Graphics*, vol. 15(3), pp. 307–316.

Cook RL, Torrance KE (1982) A Reflectance Model for Computer Graphics. *ACM Transactions on Graphics*, vol. 1(1), pp. 7–24.

Cootes TF Taylor CJ (1996) Locating Objects of Varying Shape Using Statistical Feature Detectors. In *European Conference on Computer Vision*, Cambridge, England

Coquillart S (1990) Extended Free-form Deformation: A Sculpturing Tool for 3-D Geometric Modeling. *Computer Graphics (SIGGRAPH '90 Proceedings)*, vol. 24(4), pp. 187–196.

Cordier F, Magnenat-Thalmann N (2002) Real-Time Simulation of Fully Dressed Virtual Humans. *Eurographics Proceedings*. Blackwell Publishers.

Cordier F, Magnenat-Thalmann N, (2002) Real-Time Animation of Dressed Virtual Humans. *Eurographics 2002*, Saarbrucken, Germany.

Cordier F, Seo H, Magnenat-Thalmann N (2002) Made-to-Measure Technologies for Online Clothing Store. *IEEE CG&A*, special issue on Web Graphics, pp. 38–48.

Cracknell J, Cairns AY, Gregor P, Ramsayand C, Ricketts IW (1994) Gesture Recognition: An Assessment of the Performance of Recurrent Neural Networks Versus Competing. *Applications of Neural Networks to Signal Processing (Digest No. 1994/248)*. IEEE.

Cremer J, Kearney J, Papelis Y (1995) HCSM: Framework for Behavior and Scenario Control in Virtual Environments. *ACM Transactions on Modeling and Computer Simulation* vol. 5(3), pp. 242–267.

Csuri C, Hakathorn R, Parent R (1979) Towards an Interactive High Visual Complexity Animation System. In *Computer Graphics*.

Cula OG, Dana KJ (2002) Image-based Skin Analysis, In *Proceedings of Texture 2002: The 2nd International Workshop on Texture Analysis and Synthesis*, pp. 35–41.

Curinga S, Lavagetto F, Vignoli F (1996) Lip Movements Synthesis Using Time Delay Neural Networks, *Proc. EUSIPCO 96*, Sep. 1996.

Cutkosky M (1989) On Grasp Choice, Grasp Models, and the Design of Hands for Manufacturing Tasks. *IEEE Transactions on Robotics and Automation*, vol. 5(3), pp. 269–279.

Daams BJ (1994) *Human Force Exertion in User-Product Interaction.* Delft University.

Daanen H, Talory SE, Brunsman MA, Nurre JH (1997) Absolute Accuracy of the Cyberware WB4 Whole Body Scanner. In *Three-Dimensional Image Capture*, pp. 6–12.

Daanen HAM, Van de Water GJ (1998) *Whole Body Scanners.* Elsevier, pp. 111–120.

Daldegan A, Magnenat-Thalmann N (1993) Creating Virtual Fur and Hair Styles for Synthetic Actors, in Magnenat-Thalmann N, Thalmann D. (eds) *Communicating with Virtual Worlds*. Springer-Verlag.

Daldegan A, Magnenat-Thalmann N, Kurihara T, Thalmann D (1993) An Integrated System for Modeling, Animating and Rendering Hair. *Computer Graphics Forum (Eurographics'93)*, vol. 12(3), pp. 211–221.

Dale R, Hovy E, Rosner D, Stock O (eds) (1992) Aspects of Automated Natural Language Generation, vol. 587. *Lecture Notes in Artificial Intelligence*. Springer-Verlag.

Dana KJ, van Ginneken B, Nayar SK, Koenderink JJ (1999) 'Reflectance and Texture of Real World Surfaces'. *ACM Transactions on Graphics*, vol. 18(1), pp. 1–34.

Danielson DA (1973) Human Skin as an Elastic Membrane. *J Biomechanics*, vol. 6, pp. 539–546.

Daubert K, Lensch HPA, Heindrich W, Seidel H-P (2001) Efficient Cloth Modeling and Rendering. In *Eurographics Workshop on Rendering 2001*, pp. 63–70.

Dautenhahn K (1998) The Art of Designing Socially Intelligent Agents. Special Issue *Socially Intelligent Agents. Applied Artificial Intelligence Journal*, vol. 12, pp. 573–617.

Davis JW, Bobick AF (1997) The Representation and Recognition of Action Using Temporal Templates. In *Conference on Computer Vision and Pattern Recognition*.

Davis JW, Bobick A (1998) A Robust Human-Silhouette Extraction Technique for Interactive Virtual Environments. In M. Thalmann N, Thalmann D (eds) Lecture Notes in Artificial Intelligence, No. 1537, 'Modeling and Motion Capture Techniques for Virtual Environments', International Workshop CAPTECH '98, Geneva, Switzerland. Springer, pp. 12–25.

Davis L, Borovikov E, Cutler R, Harwood D, Horprasert T (1999) Multi-perspective analysis of human action. In *Third International Workshop on Cooperative Distributed Vision*.

Davison AJ, Deutscher J, Reid ID (2001) Markerless Motion Capture of Complex Full-Body Movement for Character Animation. In *Eurographics Workshop on Computer Animation and Simulation*. Springer-Verlag LNCS.

Debevec P, Hawkins T, Tchou C, Duiker H-P, Sarokin W, Sagar M (2000) Acquiring the Reflectance Field of a Human Face. In *Proceedings of SIGGRAPH 2000*, pp. 145–156.

Debreuil N, Bechmann D (1996) Facial Animation, Computer Animation. *IEEE Computer Society*, pp. 98–109.

DeCarlo D, Metaxas M (1996) The Integration of Optical Flow and Deformable Models with Applications in Human Face Shape and Motion Estimation, Proc. CVPR'96, IEEE Computer Society Press, pp.231–23.

DeCarlo D, Metaxas D, Stone M (1998) An Anthropometric Face Model Using Variational Techniques. *Proceedings SIGGRAPH'98*. Addison-Wesley, pp. 67–74.

De Gelas J. (2000) ATI Back in Action: Radeon http://www.aceshardware.com/Spades/read.php? article_id=5000178.

Dekker L (2000) 3-D Human Body Modeling from Range Data, PhD thesis, University College London.

Dekker L, Douros I, Buxton BF, Treleaven P (1999) Building Symbolic Information for 3-D Human Body Modeling from Range Data, *Proceedings of the Second International Conference on 3-D Digital Imaging and Modeling*. IEEE Computer Society, pp. 388–397.

Delamarre Q, Faugeras O (2001) 3-D Articulated Models and Multiview Tracking with Physical Forces. *Computer Vision and Image Understanding*, vol 81, pp. 328–357.

Delaney M (2000) *Freeze Frame: Eadweard Muybridge's Photography of Motion*. Technical Report. National Museum of American History

DeLeon V, Berry R (2000) Bringing VR to the Desktop: Are You Game? *IEEE Multimedia*, April–June, pp. 68–72.

Delp SL, Loan JP (2000) A Computational Framework for Simulating and Analyzing Human and Animal Movement. *IEEE Computing in Science & Engineering*, vol. 2(5), pp. 46–55.

Delp SL, Loan JP, Hoy MG, Zajac FE, Topp EL, Rosen JM (1990) An Interactive Graphics Based Model of the Lower Extremity to Study Orthopaedics Surgical Procedures. *IEEE Transactions on Biomechanical Engineering*, vol. 37, pp. 757–767.

Deng XQ (1988) A Finite Element Analysis of Surgery of the Human Facial Tissue, PhD thesis, Columbia University, New York.

DeRose T, Kass M, Truong T (1998) Subdivision Surfaces in Character Animation. In *Computer Graphics (Proc. SIGGRAPH)*, pp. 85–94.

Desbrun M, Schröder P, Barr A (1999) Interactive Animation of Structured Deformable Objects. *Proceedings of Graphics Interface.*

Deutscher J, Blake A, Reid I (2000) Articulated Body Motion Capture by Annealed Particle Filtering. In *Conference on Computer Vision and Pattern Recognition.* Hilton Head Island, SC.

De Vito JA (1967) A Linguistic Analysis of Spoken and Written Language. *Central States Speech Journal*, pp. 81–85.

Digman JM (1990) Personality Structure: Emergence of the Five Factor Model. *Annual Review of Psychology*, vol. 41, pp. 417–440.

Dischler J-M (1998) Efficiently Rendering Macrogeometric Surface Structures Using Bi-Directional Texture Functions. In *Eurographics Workshop on Rendering*, pp. 169–180.

Dischler J-M (1999) A general model of animated shape perturbation. *Graphics Interface'99* June, pp. 140–147.

Dong F, Clapworthy G, Krokos M, Yao J (2002) An Anatomy-Based Approach to Human Muscle Modeling and Deformation. *IEEE Transactions on Visualization and Computer Graphics*, vol. 8(2), pp. 154–170.

Donnart JY, Meyer JA (1996) Learning Reactive and Planning Rules in a Motivationally Autonomous Robot, *IEEE Transactions on Systems, Man, and Cybernetics – Part B: Cybernetics.* vol. 26(3), pp. 381–395.

Dooley M (1982) Anthropometric Modeling Programs: A Survey. *IEEE Computer Graphics and Applications.* IEEE Computer Society, vol. 2(9), pp. 7–25.

Douglass BP (1999) *Doing Hard Time: Developing Real-Time Systems with UML, Objects, Frameworks, and Patterns.* Addison-Wesley.

Douros I, Dekker L, Buxton B (1999) An Improved Algorithm for Reconstruction of the Surface of the Human Body from 3-D Scanner Data Using Local B-Spline Patches. In *ICCV Workshop on Modeling People.* Corfu, Greece

Dow E, Semwal S (1993) A Framework for Modeling the Human Muscle and Bones Shapes, In Tang Z (ed.) *New Advances in Computer Aided Design & Computer Graphics.* International Academic Publishers, pp. 110–113.

Drago F, Chiba N (2002) Procedural Simulation of Interwoven Structures. In *Advances in Modeling, Animation and Rendering*, pp. 123–138.

Drogou LA, Ferber J (1994) Multi-Agent Simulation as a Tool for Studying Emergent Processes in Societies. In: Gilbert N, Doran J (eds), *Proceedings of Simulating Societies: The Computer Simulation of Social Phenomena.* North-Holland.

Drummond T, Cipolla R (2001) Real-time Tracking of Highly Articulated Structures in the Presence of Noisy Measurements. In *International Conference on Computer Vision*, Vancouver, Canada.

D'Souza DF, Wills AC (1998) *Objects, Components and Frameworks with UML.* Addison-Wesley.

Dubreuil N, Bechmann D (1996) Facial Animation, Proc. Computer Animation'96 IEEE CS Press.

Eberhardt B, Etzmuss O, Hauth M (2000) Implicit-Explicit Schemes for Fast Animation with Particles Systems. *Proceedings of the Eurographics Workshop on Computer Animation and Simulation*, pp. 137–151.

Eberhardt B, Weber A,. Strasser W (1996) A Fast, Flexible, Particle-System Model for Cloth Draping. *Computer Graphics in Textiles and Apparel (IEEE Computer Graphics and Applications)*, pp. 52–59.

Ebert DS, Musgrave FK, Peachey D, Perlin K, Worley S (1998) *Texturing and Modeling.* Academic Press.

Egges J, Nijholt A, Akker (2001) Dialogs with BDP Agents in Virtual Environments. In *Proceedings Second IJCAI Workshop on Knowledge and Reasoning in Practical Dialogue Systems*, August 2001.

Eischen JW, Deng S, Clapp TG (1996) Finite-Element Modeling and Control of Flexible Fabric Parts. *Computer Graphics in Textiles and Apparel* (IEEE Computer Graphics and Applications), pp. 71–80.

Eisert P, Girod B (1998) Analyzing Facial Expressions for Virtual Conferencing. *IEEE, Computer Graphics and Applications*, vol. 18(5), pp. 70–78.

Ekman P (1982) *Emotion in the Human Face.* Cambridge University Press.

Ekman P, Frisen WV (1978) *Facial Action Coding System, Investigator's Guide Part II.* Consulting Psychologists Press Inc.

Elman JL (1990) Finding Structure in Time. *Cognitive Science*, vol. 14, pp. 179–211.

El-Nasr MS, Ioerger TR, Yen J (1999) PETEEI: A PET with Evolving Emotional Intelligence. *Autonomous Agents'99.*

Emering L (1999) Human Action Modeling and Recognition for Virtual Environments. PhD thesis, Swiss Federal Institute of Technology, EPFL-DI-LIG.

Emering L, Boulic R, Thalmann D (1999) Conferring Human Action Recognition Skills to Life-like Agents. *Applied Artificial Intelligence Journal*, Special Issue on 'Animated Interface Agents: Making Them Intelligent, vol. 13(4-5), pp. 539–565.

Engin AE, Tuemer ST (1989) Three-Dimensional Kinematic Modeling of Human Shoulder Complex – Part I: Physical Model and Determination of Joint Sinus Cones. *Journal of Biomechanical Engineering*, vol. 111, pp. 107–112.

Enmett A (1985) Digital Portfolio: Tony de Peltrie. *Computer Graphics World*, vol. 8(10), pp. 72–77.

Essa IA, Pentland AP (1997) Coding, Analysis, Interpretation and Recognition of Facial Expressions. *IEEE Transactions on Pattern Analysis and Machine Intelligence*, vol. 19(7), pp. 757–763.

Evans SM (1976) *User's Guide for the Program of Combiman.* Report AMRLTR-76-117, University of Dayton, Ohio.

Faigin G (1990) *The Artist's Complete Guide to Facial Expression.* Watson Guptill Publications.

Faloutsos P, Van de Panne M, Terzopoulos D (2001) Composable Controllers for Physics-Based Character Animation. *Proceedings of ACM SIGGRAPH 2001*, Los Angeles.

Farenc N, Boulic R, Thalmann D (1999) An Informed Environment Dedicated to the Simulation of Virtual Humans in Urban Context. In *Proc. Eurographics'99.* Blackwell, pp. 309–318.

Fayad ME, Johnson RE (eds) (1999) *Domain-Specific Application Frameworks: Frameworks Experienced by Industry.* John Wiley & Sons.

Fayad ME, Schmidt DC (eds) (1999), Building Application Frameworks: Object-Oriented Foundations of Framework Design. John Wiley & Sons.

Fayad ME, Schmidt DC. Johnson RE (eds) (1999) *Implementing Application Frameworks: Object Oriented Frameworks at Work.* John Wiley & Sons.

Featherstone R (1986) *Robot Dynamics Algorithms.* Kluwer Academic Publishers.

Featherstone R (1987) *Robot Dynamics Algorithms.* Kluwer Academic Publishers.

Fels, Hinton G (1998) Glove-Talk II: A Neural Network Interface which Maps Gestures to Parallel Formant Speech Synthesizer Controls. *IEEE Transactions on Neural Networks*, vol. 9, January.

Ferwerda, JA (2003) Three Varieties of Realism in Computer Graphics. *Proceedings SPIE Human Vision and Electronic Imaging 2003*, in press.

Fetter WA (1982) A Progression of Human Figures Simulated by Computer Graphics. *IEEE Computer Graphics and Applications*, vol. 2(9), pp. 9–13.

Forsey D (1991) A Surface Model for Skeleton-Based Character animation. *Proceedings of the 2nd Eurographics Workshop on Animation and Simulation*, pp. 155–170.

Franklin S, Graesser A (1996) Is it an Agent, or Just a Program?: A Taxonomy for Autonomous Agents. *Proceedings of the Third International Workshop on Agent Theories, Architectures, and Languages*. Springer Verlag.

Freund E, Rossmann J (1999) Projective Virtual Reality: Bridging the Gap between Virtual Reality and Robotics. *IEEE Transactions on Robotics and Automation*, vol. 15(3), pp. 475–485.

Friesen EWV (1978) *Facial Action Coding System: A Technique for the Measurement of Facial Movement*. Consulting Psychologists Press.

Frisken S, Perry R (2001) A Computationally Efficient Framework for Modeling Soft Body Impact. *Siggraph'01 Conference Abstracts*. ACM Press.

Frisken S, Perry R, Rockwood A, Jones T (2000) Adaptively Sampled Distance Fields: A General Representation of Shape for Computer Graphics. *Proc. Siggraph'00*, pp. 249–254.

Fua P (1993) A Parallel Stereo Algorithm that Produces Dense Depth Maps and Preserves Image Features. In *Machine Vision and Applications*, 6(1):35–49, Winter.

Fua P (1997) From Multiple Stereo Views to Multiple 3-D Surfaces. *International Journal of Computer Vision*, vol. 24(1), pp. 19–35.

Fua P (1998) Face Models from Uncalibrated Video Sequences. In *Proc. CAPTECH'98*, pp. 215–228.

Fua P (1999) Human Modeling from Video Sequence. *Geomatics Info Magazine*, vol. 13(7), pp 63–65.

Fua P (2000) Regularized Bundle-Adjustment to Model Heads from Image Sequences without Calibration Data. *International Journal of Computer Vision*, vol. 38(2), pp. 153–171.

Fua P, Miccio C (1999) Animated Heads from Ordinary Images: A Least Squares Approach. *Computer Vision and Image Understanding*, vol. 75(3), pp. 247–259.

Fujimura K, Toriya H, Yamagushi K, Kunii TL (1983) Octree Algorithms for Solid Modeling. *Computer Graphics, Theory and Applications (InterGraphics'83 Proceedings)*. Springer-Verlag, pp. 96–110.

Funge J, Tu X, Terzopoulos D (1999) Cognitive Modeling: Knowledge, Reasoning and Planning for Intelligent Characters. In *Proceedings of SIGGRAPH'99*. Los Angeles, pp. 29–38.

Gan L (1991) A Finite Element Analysis of the Draping of Fabrics. In *Proc. of the 6th Int. Conf. on Finite Element Methods*, Australia, pp. 402–414.

Gan L (1995) A Study of Fabric Deformation using Non-Linear Finite Elements, *Textile Research Journal*, vol. 65(11), pp. 660–668.

Ganster B, Klein R, Sattler M, Sarlette R (2002) Realtime Shading of Folded Surfaces. In *Advances in Modeling, Animation and Rendering*. Springer-Verlag, July, pp. 201–213.

Garchery S, Magnenat-Thalmann N (2001) Designing MPEG-4 Facial Animation Tables for Web Applications. *Multimedia Modeling 2001*. Amsterdam, pp. 39–59.

Garcia C, Zikos G, Tziritas G (2000) Wavelet Packet Analysis for Face Recognition. *Journal Image and Vision Computing*, vol 18(4), pp. 289–297.

Garg A, Chaffin DB (1975) A Biomechanical Computerized Simulation of Human Strength. *AIIE Transactions*, pp. 1–15.

Gascuel JD, Cani MP, Desbrun M, Leroy E, Mirgon C (1996) Smoothed Particles: A New Paradigm for Animating Highly Deformable Bodies. In *6th Eurographics Workshop on Animation and Simulation'96*.

Gascuel MP (1993) An Implicit Formulation for Precise Contact Modeling between Flexible Solids. *Computer Graphics (SIGGRAPH '93 Proceedings)*, pp. 313–320.

Gascuel MP, Verroust A, Puech C (1991) A Modeling System for Complex Deformable Bodies Suited to Animation and Collision Processing. *The Journal of Visualization and Computer Animation*, vol. 2, pp. 82–91.

Gavrila DM (1999) The Visual Analysis of Human Movement: A Survey. *Computer Vision and Image Understanding*, vol. 73(1), pp.

Gavrila DM, Davis L (1996) 3-D Model-Based Tracking of Humans in Action: A Multi-View Approach. In *Conference on Computer Vision and Pattern Recognition*. San Francisco, CA.

Gilbert EG, Foo CP (1990) Computing the Distance Between General Convex Objects in 3-D Space. *IEEE Transactions on Robotics and Automation*, vol. 6(1), pp. 53–61.

Gilbert N (1996) Simulation: an emergent perspective http://www.soc.surrey.ac.uk/research/simsoc/tutorial.html.

Girard M, Maciejewski AA (1985) Computational Modeling for the Computer Animation of Legged Figures. In *Proc. of SIGGRAPH'85, Computer Graphics*, vol. 19, pp. 263–270.

Giroux S (1996) Open Reflective Agents. In Wooldridge M, Muller JP, Tambe M (eds), *Intelligent Agents* Vol. II, *Agent Theories, Architectures, and Languages*. Springer-Verlag, LNAI (1037) Edition, pp. 315–330.

Gleicher M (1998) Retargeting Motion to New Characters. In *Proc. of SIGGRAPH'98*. ACM Press, pp. 33–42.

Gleicher M (2001) Comparing Constraint-based Motion Editing Methods. *Graphical Models*. Academic Press, vol. 63, pp. 107–134.

Gleicher M, Litwinowicz P (1998) Constraint-based Motion Adaptation. *The Journal of Visualization and Computer Animation*, vol. 9, pp. 65–94.

Goff BL, Benoit C (1996) A Text-to-Audiovisual-Speech Synthesizer for French. In *Proceedings ICSLP 96* (Philadelphia, PA, 1996), vol. 4, pp. 2163–2166.

Golam A, Kok CW (2000) Dynamic Time Warp Based Framespace Interpolation for Motion Editing. In *Proc. of Graphics Interface'00*, Montreal, pp. 45–52.

Goldman DB (1997) Fake Fur Rendering. In *Proceedings of SIGGRAPH'97*, pp. 127–134.

Gottschalk S, Lin MC, Manocha D (1996) OBB-Tree: A Hierarchical Structure for Rapid Interference Detection. *Computer Graphics (SIGGRAPH'96 Proceedings)*. Addison-Wesley, pp. 171–180.

Gourret JP, Magnenat-Thalmann N, Thalmann D (1989) Simulation of Object and Human Skin Deformations in a Grasping Task, *Computer Graphics (SIGGRAPH'89 Proceedings)*, pp. 21–30.

Graf H, Cosatto E, Ezzat T (2000) Face Analysis for the Synthesis of Photo-Realistic Talking Heads, *Fourth IEEE International Conference on Automatic Face and Gesture Recognition*.

Grandstrom B (1999) Multi-Modal Speech Synthesis with Applications. Chollet G, Di Benedetto M, Esposito A, Marinaro M, (eds) *Proceedings of the 3rd International School on Neural Nets*, June 1999.

Granieri J, Becket W, Reich B, Crabtree J, Badler N (1995) Behavioral Control for Real-Time Simulated Human Agents. *Symposium on Interactive 3-D Graphics*, pp. 173–180.

Grosso M, Quach R, Otani E, Zhao J, Wei S, Ho P, Lu J, Badler NI (1989) *Anthropometry for Computer Graphics Human Figures*, Technical Report MS-CIS-89–71, Department of Computer and Information Science, University of Pennsylvania.

Grzezczuk R, Terzopoulos D, Hinton G (1998) Neuroanimator: Fast Neural Network Emulation and Control of Physics-Based Models. *Computer Graphics (SIGGRAPH'98 Proceedings)*. Addison-Wesley, pp. 9–20.

Gu J, Chang T, Gopalsamy S, and Shen H (1998) A 3-D Reconstruction System for Human Body Modeling. In *Modeling and Motion Capture Techniques for Virtual Environments, Proc. CAPTECH'98*. Springer, LNAI LNCS Press, pp. 229–241.

Guenter B (1992) A System for Simulating Human Facial Expression. In *State of the Art in Computer Animation*, pp. 191–202.

Guenter B, Grimm C, Wood D, Malvar H, Pighin F (1998) Making Faces. *SIGGRAPH'98*, pp. 55–67.

Guo S, Robergé J (1996) A High-level Control Mechanism for Human Locomotion Based on Parametric Frame Space Interpolation. In *Proc. of EGCAS'96, 7th Eurographics Workshop on Computer Animation and Simulation*. Springer-Verlag, pp. 95–107.

Guye-Vuillème A, Thalmann D (2000) A High-Level Architecture for Believable Social Agents. *Virtual Reality*, vol. 1(5), pp. 95–106.

Hadap S, Bangerter E, Volino P, Magnenat-Thalmann N (1999) Animating Wrinkles on Clothes. *IEEE Visualization'99 Conference Proceedings*.

Hadap S, Magnenat-Thalmann N (2000) Interactive Hair Styler based on Fluid Flow. *Eurographics Workshop on Computer Animation and Simulation '2000*.

Hadap S, Magnenat-Thalmann N (2001) Modeling Dynamic Hair as a Continuum. *Computer Graphics Forum*, vol. 20(3), Eurographics 2001 Proceedings, Manchester, United Kingdom, pp. 329–338.

Halstead M, Kaas M, DeRose T (1993) Efficient, Fair Interpolation, using Catmull-Clark Surfaces. *Computer Graphics (SIGGRAPH'93 Proceedings)*. Addison-Wesley, pp. 35–44.

Hanafusa H, Yoshikawa T, Nakamura Y (1981) Analysis and Control of Articulated Robot with Redundancy. *IFAC, 8th Triennal World Congress*, vol. 4, pp. 1927–1932.

Hand C (1997) A Survey of 3-D Interaction Techniques. *Computer Graphics Forum*, vol.16(5), pp. 269–281.

Hand C, Sexton I, Mullan M (1994) A Linguistic Approach to the Recognition of Hand Gesture. *Designing Future Interaction Conference*. De Monfort University, Leicester, UK.

Hanrahan P, Krueger W (1993) Reflection from Layered Surfaces Due to Subsurface Scattering. In *Proceedings of SIGGRAPH 1993*, August, pp. 165–174.

Hareesh PV *et al.* (2000) Evacuation Simulation: Visualisation Using Virtual Humans in a Distributed Multi-User Immersive VR System. In *Proc. VSMM'00*. ACM Press.

Hauth M, Etzmuss O (2001) A High Performance Solver for the Animation of Deformable Objects using Advanced Numerical Methods. In *Eurographics 2001 Proceedings*.

Heidrich W, Daubert K, Kautz J Seidel H-P (2000) Illuminating Micro Geometry Based on Precomputed Visibility. In *Proceedings of SIGGRAPH 2000*, ACM Press, pp. 455–161.

Helbing D, Farkas I, Vicsek T (2000) Simulating Dynamical Features of Escape Panic. *Nature* vol. 407, pp. 487–490.

Held M, Klosowski JT, Mitchell JSB (1995) Evaluation of Collision Detection Methods for Virtual Reality Fly-Throughs. In *Proceedings of the 7th Canadian Conference on Computational Geometry*.

Herbelin B, Riquier F, Vexo F, Thalmann D (2002) Virtual Reality in Cognitive Behavioral Therapy: A Study on Social Anxiety Disorder. In *Proc. VSMM 2002*, Seoul, Korea.

Herbison-Evans D (1986) *Animation of the Human Figure*. Technical Report CS-86-50, University of Waterloo Computer Science Department, November.

Herda L, Fua P, Plänkers R, Boulic R, Thalmann D (2001) Using Skeleton-Based Tracking to Increase the Reliability of Optical Motion Capture. *Human Movement Science Journal*, vol. 20(3), pp. 313–341.

Hill DR, Pearce A, Wyvill B (1988) Animating Speech: An Automated Approach Using Speech Synthesized by Rule. *The Visual Computer*, vol. 3, Springer-Verlag, pp. 277–289.

Hilton A, Beresford D, Gentils T, Smith R, Sun W (1999) Virtual People: Capturing Human Models to Populate Virtual Worlds. In *Computer Animation*, Geneva, Switzerland.

Hirota G, Fisher S, State A, Lee C, Fuchs H (2001) An Implicit Finite Element Method for Elastic Solids in Contact. *In Proceedings of Computer Animation'01*, Seoul.

Hodgins J, Brogan D (1994) Robot Herds: Group Behaviors for Systems with Significant Dynamics. In *Proc. Artificial Life IV*, pp. 319–324.

Hodgins J, Georgia Tech. Animation Lab. website, Simulating Human Motion/ Evaluation, http://www.cc.gatech.edu/gvu/animation/Areas/humanMotion/humanMotion.html

Hodgins J, Wooten WL, Brogan DC, O'Brien JF (1995) Animating Human Athletics. In *Proc. of Siggraph 95*, pp. 71–78.

Hodgins JK, Pollard NS (1997) Adapting Simulated Behaviors for New Characters. In *Proc. of SIGGRAPH'97*, Los Angeles, pp. 153–162.

Hogg D (1983) Model-Based Vision: A Program to See a Walking Person. *Image and Vision Computing*, vol. 1(1), pp. 5–20.

Hosoi M, Ishijima S, Kojima A (1996) Dynamical Model of a Pedestrian in a Crowd. In *Proc. IEEE International Workshop on Robot and Human Communication*.

Houle J, Poulin P (2001) Simplification and Real-time Smooth Transitions of Articulated Meshes. In *Proc. of Graphics Interface'01*, Canada.

Huang Z, Boulic R, Magnenat-Thalmann N, Thalmann D (1995) A Multi-Sensor Approach for Grasping and 3-D Interaction. In *Proceedings of Computer Graphics International*, Leeds.

Hubbard PM (1996) Approximating Polyhedra with Spheres for Time-Critical Collision Detection, *ACM Trans. on Graphics*, vol. 15(3) pp. 179–210.

Huston RL (1990) *Multibody Dynamics*, Butterworth-Heinemann.

International Center of Photography (1984) *Encyclopedia of Photography*. Crown.

Intrator N, Reisfeld D, Yeshurun Y (1996) Face Recognition using a Hybrid Supervised/Unsupervised Neural Network. In *Pattern Recognition Letters*, vol. 17, pp. 67–76.

Ip HS, and Yin L (1996) Constructing a 3-D Individual Head Model from Two Orthogonal Views. In *The Visual Computer*, Springer-Verlag, vol. 12, pp. 254–266.

Isard M, Blake A (1998) CONDENSATION – Conditional Density Propagation for Visual Tracking. *International Journal of Computer Vision*, vol. 29(1), pp. 5–28.

Ishii T, Yasuda T, Yokoi S, Toriwaki J (1993) A Generation Model for Human Skin Texture. In *Proceedings of CGI'93*, pp. 139–150.

Jager W, Popping R, van de Sande H (2001) Clustering and Fighting in Two-party Crowds: Simulating the Approach-avoidance Conflict. *Journal of Artificial Societies and Social Simulation* vol. 4(3), pp.

Jensen HW, Buhler J (2002) A Rapid Hierarchical Rendering Technique for Translucent Materials. In *Proceedings of SIGGRAPH 2002*, ACM Press, pp. 576–581.

Jensen HW, Marschner SR, Levoy M, Hanrahan P (2001) A Practical Model for Subsurface Light Transport. In *Proceedings of SIGGRAPH 2001*, ACM Press, pp. 511–518.

Johanson G (1973) Visual Perception of Biological Motion and a Model for its Analysis. *Perception and Psychophysics*, vol. 14, pp. 201–211.

Johnson R (1997) Frameworks = Patterns + Components. *Communications of the ACM*, vol. 40(10), October.

Johnson W, Rickel J (1997) Steve: An Animated Pedagogical Agent for Procedural Training in Virtual Environments. In *SIGART Bulletin*, ACM Press, vol. 8(1–4), pp. 16–21.

Jollife IT (1986) *Principal Component Analysis*. Springer Verlag.

Jordan MI (1986) Attractor Dynamics and Parallelism in a Connectionist Sequential Machine. In *Proceedings of the Eighth Annual Conference of Cognitive Science Society*, Erlbaum, pp. 531–546.

Ju X, Siebert JP (2001a) Conforming Generic Animatable Models to 3-D Scanned Data. In *Proc. 6th Numerisation 3-D/Scanning 2001 Congress*, Paris, France.

Ju X, Siebert JP (2001b) Individualising Human Animation Models. In *Eurographics Short Presentations*, Manchester, UK

Ju X, Werghi N, Siebert JP (2000) Automatic Segmentation of 3-D Human Body Scans. In *Proc. IASTED Int. Conf. on Computer Graphics and Imaging 2000 (CGIM 2000)*, Las Vegas.

Just C, Bierbaum A, Hartling P, Mcinert K, Cruz-Neira C, Baker A, (2001) VjControl: An Advanced Configuration Management Tool for VR Juggler Applications. In *Proceedings of IEEE Virtual Reality 2001 Conference*.

Kadous W. (1996) *Machine Recognition of Auslan Signs Using Powergloves: Toward Large-Lexicon Recognition of Sign Language*. Rapport technique, University of New South Wales.

Kagarlis M (2004) *Navigating an Agent*. International Patent Application, Publication No. WO 2004/023347 A2.

Kähler K, Haber J, Seidel HP (2001) Geometry-based Muscle Modeling for Facial Animation. In *Proceedings Graphics Interface 2001*, pp. 37–46.

Kajiya J, Kay T (1989) Rendering Fur with Three Dimensional Textures. In *Proceedings of SIGGRAPH 1989*, ACM Press, vol. 23(4), pp. 271–280.

Kakadiaris I, Metaxas D (1995) 3-D Human Body Model Acquisition from Multiple Views. In *International Conference on Computer Vision*.

Kakadiaris I, Metaxas D (1996) Model Based Estimation of 3-D Human Motion with Occlusion Based on Active Multi-Viewpoint Selection. In *Conference on Computer Vision and Pattern Recognition*, San Francisco, CA.

Kallmann M (2001) Object Interaction in Real-Time Virtual Environments, DSc Thesis 2347, Swiss Federal Institute of Technology – EPFL.

Kallmann M, Thalmann D (1998) Modeling Objects for Interaction Tasks. In *Proc. Eurographics Workshop on Animation and Simulation, Springer*

Kallmann M, Thalmann D (1999) A Behavioral Interface to Simulate Agent-Object Interactions in Real-Time. In *Proc. Computer Animation 99*. IEEE Computer Society Press, pp. 138–146.

Kallmann M, Thalmann D (2002) Modeling Behaviors of Interactive Objects for Real Time Virtual Environments, *Journal of Visual Languages and Computing*, vol.13(2), pp.

Kallmann M, Monzani J, Caicedo A, Thalmann D (2000) ACE: A Platform for the Real Time Simulation of Virtual Human Agents. In *EGCAS '2000 – 11th Eurographics Workshop on Animation and Simulation*, Interlaken, Switzerland.

Kalra D, Barr AH (1992) Modeling with Time and Events in Computer Animation. In *Proc. Eurographics'92*. Blackwell, pp. 45–58.

Kalra P Magnenat-Thalmann N (1994) Modeling of Vascular Expressions in Facial Animation, In *Computer Animation 1994*, pp. 50–58.

Kalra P, Magnenat-Thalmann N (1993) Simulation of Facial Skin using Texture Mapping and Coloration. In *Proceedings of ICCG'93, Bombay, India, in Graphics, Design and Visualization*, pp. 247–256.

Kalra P, Magnenat-Thalmann N, Moccozet L, Sannier G, Aubel A, Thalmann D (1988) Real-Time Animation of Realistic Virtual Humans, *IEEE Computer Graphics and Applications*, vol. 18(5), pp. 42–56.

Kalra P, Mangili A, Magnenat-Thalmann N, Thalmann D (1991) SMILE: A Multi-layered Facial Animation System *Proc. IFIP WG 5.10, Tokyo, Japan*, pp. 189–198.

Kalra P, Mangili A, Magnenat-Thalmann N, Thalmann D (1992) Simulation of Muscle Actions using Rational Free Form Deformations. In *Proc Eurographics'92, Computer Graphics Forum*, Blackwells, vol. 2(3), pp. 59–69.

Kang YM, Cho HG, (2000) Bilayered Approximate Integration for Rapid and Plausible Animation of Virtual Cloth with Realistic Wrinkles. In *Computer Animation 2000 proceedings*, IEEE Computer Society, pp. 203–211.

Kang YM, Choi JH, Cho HG, Lee DH, Park CJ (2000) Real-Time Animation Technique for Flexible and Thin Objects. In *WSCG '2000 Proceedings*, pp. 322–329.

Kautz J, McCool M (1999) Interactive Rendering with Arbitrary BRDFs using Separable Approximations. In *Eurographics Workshop on Rendering 1999*, pp. 281–292.

Kelso J, Arsenault LE, Satterfield SG, Kriz RD (2002) DIVERSE: A Framework for Building Extensible and Reconfigurable Device Independent Virtual Environments. In *Proceedings of IEEE Virtual Reality 2002 Conference* (www.diverse.vt.edu).

Kijanka B (2002) Gas-powered Games, Dungeon Siege, GameDeveloper. *CMP Media*, September, pp. 42–49.

King SA, Parent RE (2002) Lip Synchronization for Song. *Computer Animation*, Geneva, pp. 233–239.

Kingsley EC, Schofield NA Case K (1981) SAMMIE – A Computer Aid for Man-Machine Modeling. *Computer Graphics* vol. 15(3), pp. 163–169.

Klein CA, Huang CH (1983) Review of Pseudo-Inverse Control for Use with Kinematically Redundant Manipulators. *IEEE Trans. on SMC*, vol. 13(3), pp.

Klosowski JT, Held M, Mitchell JSB (1997) Efficient Collision Detection Using Bounding Volume Hierarchies of k-dops. In *IEEE Transactions on Visualization and Computer Graphics*, vol. 4(1), pp.

Klüpfel H, Meyer-König M, Wahle J, Schreckenberg M (2000) Microscopic Simulation of Evacuation Processes on Passenger Ships. In Bandini S, Worsch T (eds) *Theoretical and Practical Issues on Cellular Automata*. Springer, pp. 63–71.

Ko H, Badler NI (1996) Animating Human Locomotion with Inverse Dynamics. *IEEE Comput Graph Appl*, vol. 16, pp. 50–59.

Koch RM, Gross MH, Carl FR, Von Buren DF, Fankhauser G, Parish YI (1996) Simulation Facial Surgery Using Finite Element Models. In *Proc. of SIGGRAPH'96, Computer Graphics*, ACM Press, pp. 421–428.

Koda T, Maes P (1996) Agents with Faces: The Effects of Personification of Agents. In *Proceedings of Human-Computer Interaction*, pp. 239–245, London, UK.

Koga Y, Kondo K, Kuffner J, Latombe JC (1994) Planning Motions with Intentions. *Computer Graphics, Proc. SIGGRAPH '94*, vol. 28, pp. 395–408.

Komatsu K (1988) Human Skin Model Capable of Natural Shape Variation. *The Visual Computer*, vol. 3, pp. 265–271.

Komura T, Shinagawa Y, Kunii T (1999) Calculation and Visualization of the Dynamic Ability of the Human Body. *Journal of Visualisation and Computer Animation*, vol. 10, pp. 57–78.

Komura T, Shinagawa Y, Kunii TL (2000) Creating and Retargeting Motion by the Musculoskeltal Human Body Model. *The Visual Computer*, vol. 16, pp. 254–270.

Kong W, Nakajima M (1999) Visible Volume Buffer for Efficient Hair Expression and Shadow Generation. In *Proceedings of Computer Animation'99, IEEE Computer Society*. IEEE Press.

Korein JU (1985) *A Geometric Investigation of Reach*, The MIT Press.

Kovar L, Gleicher M, Pighin F (2002) Motion Graphs. In *Proc. of SIGGRAPH '2002*, Austin.

Krishnamurthy V, Levoy M (1996) Fitting Smooth Surfaces to Dense Polygon Meshes. *Computer Graphics (SIGGRAPH'96 Proceedings)*, pp. 313–324.

Kroemer KHE, Kroemer HJ, Kroemer-Elbert (1990) Engineering Physiology. In *Bases of Human Factors/Ergonomics*. 2nd edn, Van Nostrand Reinhold.

Kry PG, James DL, Pai DK (2002) EigenSkin: Real Time Large Deformation Character Skinning in Graphics Hardware. In *ACM SIGGRAPH Symposium on Computer Animation*, pp. 153–159.

Kshirsagar S, Escher M, Sannier G, Magnenat-Thalmann N (1999) Multimodal Animation System Based on the MPEG-4 Standard. In *Proceedings Multimedia Modeling'99, Ottawa, Canada, October 1999*, World Scientific Publishing, pp. 215–232.

Kshirsagar S, Garchery S, Magnenat-Thalmann N (2000) Feature Point Based Mesh deformation Applied to MPEG-4 Facial Animation. In *Post Proceedings Deform, 2000*, Geneva, Switzerland, Nov. 29–20, Kluwer Academic Publishers, pp. 23–34.

Kshirsagar S, Guye-Vuilleme A, Kamyab K, Magnenat-Thalmann, N, Thalmann D., Mamdani, E (2002) Avatar Markup language. In *Proceedings of 8th Eurographics Workshop on Virtual Environments*, ACM Press, pp. 169–177.

Kshirsagar S, Magnenat-Thalmann N (2000) Lip Synchronization Using Linear Predictive Analysis. In *Proceedings of IEEE International Conference on Multimedia and Expo*, New York, August 2000.

Kshirsagar S, Magnenat-Thalmann N (2002) A Multilayer Personality Model. In *Proceedings of 2nd International Symposium on Smart Graphics*, June 2002, pp. 107–115.

Kshirsagar S, Molet T, Magnenat-Thalmann N (2001) Principal Components of Expressive Speech Animation. In *Proceedings Computer Graphics International 2001*, IEEE Computer Society, July, pp. 38–44.

Kuratate T, Yehia H, Bateson EV (1998) Kinematics-Based Synthesis of Realistic Talking Faces, *Proceedings AVSP'98*, pp. 185–190.

Kurihara T, Anjyo K, Thalmann D (1993). Hair Animation with Collision Detection. In *Models and Techniques in Computer Animation*. Springer-Verlag, pp. 128–138.

Kurihara T, Arai K (1991) A Transformation Method for Modeling and Animation of the Human Face from Photographs. In *Proc. Computer Animation'91*, Geneva, pp. 45–57.

Lafleur B, Magnenat-Thalmann N, Thalmann D (1991) Cloth Animation with Self-Collision Detection. In *IFIP Conference on Modeling in Computer Graphics Proceedings*. Springer-Verlag, pp. 179–197.

Lamarche F Donikian S (2001) The Orchestration of Behaviors using Resources and Priority Levels. In *EG Computer Animation and Simulation Workshop*.

Lamouret A, Van de Panne M (1996) Motion Synthesis by Example. In *Proc. of the Eurographics Workshop on Computer Animation and Simulation, EGCAS'96*, Poitier.

Lande C, Francini G (1998) An MPEG-4 Facial Animation System Driven by Sythetic Speech. In *Proceedings Multimedia Modeling, IEEE Computer Society*, pp. 203–212.

Lander J (1998) Skin Them Bones. *Games Developer*, pp 11–16.

Lanir Y (1987) Skin Mechanics. In Skalak R (ed.), *Handbook of Bioengineering*. McGraw-Hill Book Company.

Larrabee WF (1986) A Finite Element Method of Skin Deformation: I, Biomechanics of Skin and Soft Tissues. *Laryngoscop*, vol. 96, pp. 399–419.

Larsson S, Traum D (2000) Information State and Dialogue Management in the TRINDI Dialogue Move Engine Toolkit. In *Gothenburg Papers in Computational Linguistics*, April 2000.

Lasseter J (1987) Principles of Traditional Animation Applied to 3-D Computer Animation. *Computer Graphics, (SIGGRAPH 87)*, vol. 21(4), pp. 35–44.

Latombe JC (1991) *Robot Motion Planning*. Kluwer Academic Publishers.

Latta L. Kolb A (2002) Homomorphic Factorization of BRDF-Based Lighting Computation. In *Proceedings of SIGGRAPH 2002*, ACM Press, pp. 509–516.

Laumond JP (1998) *Robot Motion Planning and Control*. Lecture Notes in Control and Information Sciences 229, Springer.

Lavagetto F, Pockaj R (1999) The Facial Animation Engine: Towards a High-Level Interface for the Design of MPEG-4 Compliant Animated Faces. In *IEEE Trans. on Circuits and Systems for Video Technology*, vol. 9(2), pp.

Lazlo J, Van de Panne M, Fiume E (1996) Limit Cycle Control and its Application to the Animation of Balancing and Walking. In *Proc. of SIGGRAPH'96*, pp. 155–162.

LeBlanc A, Kalra P, Magnenat-Thalmann N. Thalmann D. (1991) Sculpting with the 'Ball & Mouse' Metaphor. In *Proc. Graphics Interface'91, Calgary, Canada*. Morgan Kaufmann Publishers, pp. 152–159.

LeBlanc A, Turner R, Thalmann D (1991) Rendering Hair Using Pixel Blending and Shadow Buffer. *Journal of Visualization and Computer Animation*, vol. 2, pp. 92–97.

LeBon G (1895) *Psychologie des Foules*. Alcan.

Leclercq A, Akkouche S, Galin E (2001) Mixing Triangle Meshes and Implicit Surfaces in Character Animation. In *Animation and Simulation'01 (12th Eurographics Workshop Proceedings)*, Manchester, pp. 37–47.

Lee Xu Y (1995) *Online, Interactive Learning of Gestures for Human/Robot Interfaces*. Rapport technique, Carnegie Mellon University.

Lee HK, Kim JH (1999) An HMM-Based Threshold Model Approach for Gesture Recognition. In *IEEE Transactions on Pattern Analysis and Machine Intelligence*, vol. 21(18), pp.

Lee J, Chai J, Reitsma PSA, Hodgins J, Pollard NS (2002) Interactive Control of Avatars Animated with Human Motion Data. In *Proc. of SIGGRAPH 2002*, Austin, TX.

Lee J, Shin SY (1999) A Hierarchical Approach to Interactive Motion Editing for Human-Like Figures. In *Proc. of SIGGRAPH'99*, Los Angeles.

Lee PLY (1993) Modeling Articulated Figure Motion with Physically- and Physiologically-based Constraints, PhD dissertation in Mechanical Engineering and Applied Mechanics, University of Pennsylvania.

Lee W, Magnenat-Thalmann N (2000) Fast Head Modeling for Animation. *Journal of Image and Vision Computing*, vol. 18(4), pp. 355–364.

Lee WS, Kalra P, Magenat Thalmann N (1997) Model Based Face Reconstruction for Animation. In *Proc. Multimedia Modeling (MMM)'97*, Singapore, pp. 323–338.

Lee WS, Magnenat-Thalmann N (1998) Head Modeling from Pictures and Morphing in 3-D with Image Metamorphosis Based on Triangulation. In *Proc. Captech98 (Modeling and Motion Capture Techniques for Virtual Environments)*. Springer LNAI LNCS Press, pp. 254–267.

Lee Y, Lee S (2002) Geometric Snakes for Triangular Meshes, Computer Graphics Forum. *Eurographics 2002*, vol. 21(3), pp.

Lee Y, Terzopoulos D, and Waters K (1995) Realistic Modeling for Facial Animation. In *Computer Graphics (Proc. SIGGRAPH)*, pp. 55–62.

Leung TK, Burl MC, Perona P (1995) Finding Faces in Cluttered Scenes using Random Labelled Graph Matching. *Computer Vision*

Levinson L (1996) Connecting Planning and Acting: Towards an Architecture for Object-Specific Reasoning, PhD thesis, University of Pennsylvania.

Lewis J-P (1989) Algorithms for Solid Noise Synthesis. In *Computer Graphics (Proceedings of SIGGRAPH 89)*, vol. 23(3), pp. 263–270.

Lewis JP, Cordner M, Fong N (2000) Pose Space Deformations: A Unified Approach to Shape Interpolation and Skeleton-Driven Deformation. In *Proceedings SIGGRAPH 2000*, Addison-Wesley, pp. 165–172.

Liégeois A (1977) Automatic Supervisory Control of the Configuration and Behavior of Multibody Mechanisms. In *IEEE Transaction on Systems, Man and Cybernetics*, vol. SMC-7 (12), pp. 868–871.

Lin M, Gottschalk S (1998) Collision Detection between Geometric Models: A Survey. In *Proceedings of IMA Conference on Mathematics of Surfaces*.

Ling L, Damodaran M, Gay RKL (1996) Aerodynamic Force Models for Animating Cloth Motion in an Air Flow, *The Visual Computer*, vol. 12, pp. 84–104.

Litwinowicz P, Lance W (1994) Animating Images with Drawings. In *Proceedings of SIGGRAPH 1994*, pp. 409–412.

Liu CK, Popovi Z (2002) Synthesis of Complex Dynamic Character Motion for Simple Animation. In *Proc. of SIGGRAPH'02*, Austin, TX.

Liu JD, Ko MT, Chang RC (1996) Collision Avoidance in Cloth Animation. *The Visual Computer*, vol. 12(5), pp. 234–243.

Liu Z, Gortler SJ, Cohen M (1994) Hierarchical Spacetime Control. In *Proc. of SIGGRAPH'94*, ACM Press, pp. 35–42.

Livingston MA, State A (1997) Magnetic Tracker Calibration for Improved Augmented Reality Registration. *Presence*, vol. 6(5), pp. 532–546.

Lofqvist A (1990) Speech as Audible Gestures. In Hardcastle WJ, Marchal A (eds), *Speech Production and Speech Modeling*. Kluwer Academic Publishers, pp. 289–322.

Lorenz K (1981) *Foundations of Ethology*. Simon and Schuster.

Lutz M (1996) *Programming Python*, O'Reilly. (see also: www.python.org).

Maciejewski AA (1990) Dealing with the Ill-Conditioned Equations of Motion for Articulated Figures. In *IEEE CGA*, vol. 10(3), pp. 63–71.

Maciejewski AA, Klein CA (1985) Obstacle Avoidance for Kinematically Redundant Manipulators in Dynamically Varying Environments. *The International Journal of Robotics Research*, vol. 4(3), pp. 109–117.

Maciel P, Shirley P (1995) Visual Navigation of Large Environments Using Textured Clusters. In *1995 Symposium on Interactive 3-D Graphics*, pp. 95–102.

Mac Kenna M, Zeltzer D (1996) Dynamic Simulation of a Complex Human Figure Model with Low Level Behavior Control. *Presence*, vol. 5(4), pp. 431–456.

Maes P (1989) How to Do the Right Thing. *Connection Science Journal*, vol. 1, pp. 291–323.

Maes P (1991) A bottom-up mechanism for behavior selection in an artificial creature. In Meyer JA, Wilson SW (eds), *From Animals to Animats: Proceedings of the First International Conference on Simulation of Adaptive Behavior*. MIT Press/Bradford Books.

Maes P, Darrell T, Blumberg B, Pentland A (1995) The ALIVE System: Full-body Interaction with Autonomous Agents. In *Proc. Computer Animation'95*. Geneva, Switzerland, IEEE Computer Society Press, Los Alamitos, California, pp. 11–18 (cf. also 'http://www-white.media.mit.edu/vismod/demos/smartroom').

Magnenat-Thalmann N, Kshirsagar S (2000) Communicating with Autonomous Virtual Humans. In *Proceedings of the Seventeenth TWENTE Workshop on Language Technolgy*, Enschede, Universiteit Twente, October 2000, pp. 1–8.

Magnenat-Thalmann N, Laperriere R, Thalmann D (1988) Joint-Dependent Local Deformations for Hand Animation and Object Grasping. In *Proceedings of Graphics Interface'88*, pp. 26–33.

Magnenat-Thalmann N, Papagiannakis G, Ponder M, Molet T, Kshirsagar S, Cordier F, Thalmann D (2002) LIFEPLUS: Revival of Life in Ancient Pompeii. In *Proc. VSMM (Virtual Systems and Multimedia)*.

Magnenat-Thalmann N, Primeau NE, Thalmann D (1988) Abstract Muscle Actions Procedures for Human Face Animation. *Visual Computer*, vol. 3(5), pp. 290–297.

Magnenat-Thalmann N, Thalmann D (1987) The Direction of Synthetic Actors in the Film *Rendez-vous à Montreal*. In *IEEE Computer Graphics and Applications*, IEEE Computer Society Press, vol. 7(12), pp. 9–19.

Magnenat-Thalmann N, Thalmann D (eds) (1996) *Interactive Computer Animation*. Prentice Hall.

Magnenat-Thalmann N, Volino P, Cordier F (2002) Avenues of Research in Dynamic Clothing. In *Computer Animation 2000 Proceedings*, IEEE Computer Society, pp. 193–202.

Malzbender T, Gelb D, Wolters H (2001) Polynomial Texture Maps. In *Proceedings of SIGGRAPH 2001*, pp. 519–528.

Marcel S, Bernier O. (2000) Hand Gesture Recognition using Input-Output Hidden Markov Models. *Automatic Face and Gesture Recognition Conference*, Grenoble. CNET France Telecom.

Marey EJ (1994) *Le mouvement*. Editions Jaqueline Chambon, Reedition of Editions Masson.

Marschner SR (1998) Inverse Rendering for Computer Graphics, PhD thesis, Cornell University.

Marschner SR, Guenter B, Raghupathy S (2000) Modeling and Rendering for Realistic Facial Animation. In *11th Eurographics Rendering Workshop*, pp. 231–242.

Marschner SR, Westin SH, Lafortune EPF, Torrance KE, Greenberg DP (1999) Image-based BRDF Measurement Including Human Skin. In *10th Eurographics Rendering Workshop*, pp. 139–152.

Mas R, Thalmann D, (1994) A Hand Control and Automatic Grasping System for Synthetic Actors, Proc. Eurographics'94, pp.167–177

Massaro D, Beskow J, Cohen M, Fry C, Rodriquez T (1999) Picture My Voice: Audio to Visual Speech Synthesis Using Artificial Neural Networks. In *Proceedings of Audio-Visual Speech Processing 1999*, pp. 185–190.

Maurel W, Thalmann D (2000) Human Upper Limb Modeling including Scapulo-Thoracic Constraint and Joint Sinus Cones. In *Computers & Graphics*, Pergamon Press, vol. 24(2), pp. 203–218.

Maya, Alias/Wavefront, (2001) *Maya User Manual*, 2001.

McAllister DV, Rodman RD, Bitzer DL, Freeman AS (1997) Lip Synchronization for Animation. In *Proc. SIGGRAPH'97*, Los Angeles, CA.

McCrae RR., John OP (1992) An Introduction to the Five-Factor Model and its Applications. Special Issue: The Five-Factor Model: Issues and Applications. *Journal of Personality* vol. 60, pp. 175–215.

McPhail C (1991) *The Myth of Madding Crowd*. Aldine de Gruyter.

McPhail C, Powers WT, Tucker CW (1992) Simulating Individual and Collective Actions in Temporary Gatherings. *Social Science Computer Review*, vol. 10(1), pp. 1–28.

Meissner M, Eberhardt B (1998) The Art of Knitted Fabrics: Realistic and Physically Based Modeling of Knitted Fabrics. *Computer Graphics Forum*, vol. 17(3), pp. 355–362.

Menache A (2000) *Understanding Motion Capture for Computer Animation and Video Games*. Morgan Kaufmann

Meunier P, Yin S (2000) Performance of a 2-D Image-Based Anthropometric Measurement and Clothing Sizing System. *Applied Ergonomics*, vol. 31(5), pp. 445–451.

Meyer JA, Doncieux S, Filliat D Guillot A. Evolutionary Approaches to Neural Control of Rolling, Walking, Swimming and Flying Animats or Robots. In Duro RJ,Santos J, Graña M (eds), *Biologically Inspired Robot Behavior Engineering*. Springer Verlag.

Millar RJ, Hanna JRP, Kealy SM (1999) A Review of Behavioral Animation. *Computer & Graphics*, vol. 23, pp. 127–143.

Miller GSP (1988) From Wire-Frames to Furry Animals. *Graphics Interface'88*, pp. 138–145.

Mirtich B (1996) Impulse-Based Dynamic Simulation of Rigid Body Systems. PhD thesis, University of California, Berkeley.

Mirtich B (1998) V-CLIP: Fast and Robust Polyhedral Collision Detection. In *ACM Transactions on Graphics*.

Moccozet L (1996) Hand Modeling and Animation for Virtual Humans, PhD thesis, University of Geneva.

Moccozet L Magnenat-Thalmann N (1997) Dirichlet Free-Form Deformations and their Application to Hand Simulation. In *Proc. Computer Animation'97*, IEEE Computer Society Press, pp. 93–102.

Moeslund TB, Granum E (2001) A Survey of Computer Vision-Based Human Motion Capture. *Computer Vision and Image Understanding*, vol. 81(3), pp.

Molet T, Aubel A, Çapin T, Carion S, Lee E, Magnenat Thalmann N, Noser H, Pandzic I, Sannier G, Thalmann D (1999) Anyone for Tennis? *Presence*, vol. 8(2), pp. 140–156

Molet T, Boulic R, Thalmann D (1999) Human Motion Capture Driven by Orientation Measurements, *Presence*, vol. 8(2), pp. 187–203.

Molina-Tanco L, Hilton A (2000) Realistic Synthesis of Novel Human Movements from a Database of Motion Capture Examples. In *Proc. of IEEE Workshop on Human Motion, HUMO '2000.*

Molnar P, Starke J (2001) Control of Distributed Autonomous Robotic Systems Using Principles of Pattern Formation in Nature and Pedestrian Behavior. In *IEEE Trans. Syst. Man Cyb. B* vol. 31(3), pp. 433–436.

Moltenbrey K (1999) All the Right Moves. *Computer Graphics Word*, vol. 22, pp.

Monaghan JJ (1992) Smoothed Particle Hydrodynamics. *Annual Review of Astronomy and Astrophysics*, vol. 30, pp. 543–574.

Monheit G, Badler N (1991) A Kinematic Model of the Human Spine and Torso. *IEEE CGA*, pp. 29–31.

Monzani JS, Baerlocher P, Boulic R, Thalmann D (2000) Using an Intermediate Skeleton and Inverse Kinematics for Motion Retargeting. In *Proc. Eurographics 2000*, Interlaken.

Monzani JS, Caicedo A, Thalmann D (2001) Integrating Behavioral Animation Techniques. In *Proceeding Eurographics*, Manchester, vol. 20, issue 3.

Morishima S (1998) Real-Time Talking Head Driven by Voice and its Application to Communication and Entertainment. In *Proc. AVSP 98, International Conference on Auditory-Visual Speech Processing.*

Morris D, Rehg J (1998) Singularity Analysis for Articulated Object Tracking. In *Conference on Computer Vision and Pattern Recognition*, pp. 289–296.

Morris JP (1995) An Overview of the Method of Smoothed Particle Hydrodynamics. In *AGTM Preprints.*

Multon F, France L, Cani-Gascuel MP, Debunne G (1999) Computer Animation of Human Walking: A Survey, *Journal of Visualizaion and Computer Animation*, vol. 10, pp. 39–54.

Musse SR (2000) Human Crowd Modeling with Various Levels of Behavior Control. PhD thesis, EPFL, Lausanne.

Musse SR, Thalmann D (2001) Hierarchical Model for Real Time Simulation of Virtual Human Crowds. In *IEEE Trans. on Visualization & Computer Graphics*, vol. 7(2), pp. 152–164.

Muybridge E (1955) *The Human Figure in Motion.* Dover Publications.

Nagel B, Wingbermühle J, Weik S, Liedtke CE (1998) Automated Modelling of Real Human Faces for 3-D Animation, Proceedings ICPR, Brisbane Australia.

Nahas M, Hutric H, Rioux M, Domey J (1990) Facial Image Synthesis Using Skin Texture Recording. *Visual Computer*, vol. 6(6), pp. 337–343.

Nahas M, Huitric H, Saintourens M (1988) Animation of a B-spline Figure. *The Visual Computer*, vol. 3(5), pp. 272–276.

Nakamura Y, Hanafusa H (1986) Inverse Kinematic Solutions with Singularity Robustness for Robot Manipulator Control. *Journal of Dynamic Systems, Meas., and Control*, vol. 108, pp. 163–171.

NASA Reference Publication 1024 (1978) *The Anthropometry Source Book*, vols I and II.

NASA-STD-3000, *NASA Man-Systems Integration Manual.*

Nebel JC (1999) Keyframe Interpolation with Self-Collision Avoidance, Proc. Eurographics Workshop on Animation and Simulation, Milan.

Nedel L, Thalmann D (1998) Real-TimeMuscle Deformations Using Mass-Spring Systems. In *Proc. CGI'98*, IEEE Computer Society Press.

Neyret F, (1998) Modeling, Animating, and Rendering Complex Scenes Using Volumetric Textures. In *IEEE Transactions on Visualization and Computer Graphics*, vol. 4(1), pp. 55–70.

Ng-Thow-Hing V (2000) Anatomically-Based Models for Physical and Geometric Reconstruction of Humans and Other Animals, PhD thesis, Department of Computer Science, University of Toronto.

Nielsen R, Keates R, Sinkler R, Breckenridge S, Cartwright D, Eisenstein J, Kloosterman M, Myhre M (1997) *Weaving Information File Version 1.1*. http://www.mhsoft.com/wif/wif.html.

Noh J, Neumann U (1998) *A Survey of Facial Modeling and Animation Techniques*. USC Technical Report.

Nolfi S Floriano D (2000) *Evolutionary Robotics: The Biology, Intelligence, and Technology of Self-Organizing Machines*.

Norgan NG (1994) Anthropometry and Physical Performance. In Ulijaszek SJ, Mascie-Taylor CGN (eds), *Anthropometry: The Individual and the Population*. Cambridge University Press, pp. 141–159.

Noser H, Renault O, Thalmann D, Magnenat Thalmann N (1995) Navigation for Digital Actors Based on Synthetic Vision, Memory and Learning. In *Computers and Graphics*. Pergamon Press, vol. 19.

Nurre J (1997) Locating Landmarks on Human Body Scan Data. In *International Conference Recent Advances in 3-D Digital Imaging and Modeling*, IEEE Computer Society Press, pp. 289–295.

O'Brien J, BodenHeimer RE, Brostow GJ, Hodgins JK (2000) Automatic Joint Parameter Estimation from Magnetic Motion Capture Data. In *Proc. of Graphics Interface '2000*, Montreal, pp. 53–60.

Oesker M, Hecht H, Jung B (2000) Psychological Evidence for Unconscious Processing of Detail in Real-Time Animation of Multiple Characters. *J. Visual. Comput. Animat.*, vol. 11, pp. 105–112.

Okada Y, Shinpo K, Tanaka Y, Thalmann D (1999) Virtual Input Devices based on motion Capture and Collision Detection. In *Proceedings of Computer Animation*, Geneva.

Okazaki S, Matsushita S (1993) A Study of Simulation Model for Pedestrian Movement with Evacuation and Queuing. In *Proc. International Conference on Engineering for Crowd Safety*.

Olives J-L, Mottonen R, Kulju J, Sams M (1999) Audio-visual Speech Synthesis for Finnish. In *Proceedings Audio-Visual Speech Processing*.

O'Rourke J, Badler NI (1980) Model-Based Image Analysis of Human Motion Using Constraint Propagation. *IEEE Transactions on Pattern Analysis and Machine Intelligence*, vol. 2(6), pp. 522–536.

Ortony A, Clore GL, Collins A (1988) *The Cognitive Structure of Emotions*. Cambridge University Press.

Ostermann J (1998) Animation of Synthetic Faces in MPEG-4. *Computer Animation*, pp. 49–51, Philadelphia, Pennsylvania, June 8–10.

Owen M, Galea ER, Lawrence PJ, Filippidis L (1998) The Numerical Simulation of Aircraft Evacuation and its Application to Aircraft Design and Certification. *The Aeronautical Journal*, vol. 102(1016), pp. 301–312.

Palmer IJ, Grimsdale RL (1995) Collision Detection for Animation using Sphere-Trees. *Computer Graphics Forum*, vol. 14, pp. 105–116.

Pandy MG (1990) An Analytical Framework for Quantifying Muscular Action During Human Movement. In Winter JM, Woo SL-Y (eds), *Multiple Muscle Systems: Biomechanics and Movement Organization*. Springer Verlag.

Pandya AK, Maida JC, Aldridge AM, Hasson SM, Woodford BJ (1992) *The Validation of a Human Force Model to Predict Dynamic Forces Resulting from Multi-Joint Motions*. Technical Report 3206 NASA, Houston, Texas.

Panne M, Fiume E (1993) Sensor-Actuator Networks. *Proceedings of ACM SIGGRAPH'93*, pp. 335–342.

Panton RL (1995) *Incompressible Flow*. John Wiley & Sons, Ltd., 2nd edn.

Panzarasa P, Norman T, Jennings N (1999) Modeling Sociality in the BDI Framework. In *1st Asia-Pacific Conf. on Intelligent Agent Technology*, pp. 202–206.

Papagiannakis G., L'Hoste G., Foni A., Magnenat-Thalmann N. (2001) Real-Time Photo Realistic Simulation of Complex Heritage Edifices. In *Proceedings of VSMM 2001 (Virtual Systems and Multimedia)*, October.

Papaginanakis G, Schertenleib S, Arevalo-poizat M, Magnenant-Thalmann N, Thalmann DMixing (2004) Virtual and real Scenes in the Site of Ancient Pompeii. *Computer Animation and Virtual Worlds*, (to appear).

Parent R (2002) *Computer Animation, Algorithms and Techniques*. Morgan Kaufmann Publishers.

Parke F (1972a) Computer Generated Animation of Faces. Master's thesis, University of Utah, Salt Lake City.

Parke FI (1972b) Computer Generated Animation of Faces. In *Proc. ACM annual conference*.

Parke FI (1974) A Parametric Model for Human Faces, PhD thesis, University of Utah, Salt Lake City, Utah.

Parke FI (1982) Parameterized Models for Facial Animation. *IEEE Computer Graphics and Applications*, vol. 2(9) pp. 61–68.

Parke FI (1989) Parameterized Models for Facial Animation Revisited. In *ACM SIGGRAPH Facial Animation Tutorial Notes*, pp. 53–56.

Parke FI (1991) Techniques of Facial Animation. In Magnenat-Thalmann N, Thalmann D (eds), *New Trends in Animation and Visualization*. John Wiley and Sons, pp. 229–241.

Parke FI, Waters K (1996) *Computer Facial Animation*. AK Peters Ltd.

Patel M (1992) Making Faces: The Facial Animation, Construction, and Editing System, PhD thesis, University of Bath.

Patterson EC, Litwinowicz PC, Greene N (1991) Facial Animation by Spatial Mapping. In *Proc. Computer Animation'91*, Geneva, pp. 31–44.

Pelachaud C (1991) *Communication and Coarticulation in Facial Animation*. University of Pennsylvania.

Pelachaud C, Magno-Caldognetto E, Zmarich C, Cosi P (2001) An Approach to an Italian Talking Head. In *Proceedings Eurospeech 2001* (Aalborg, Danemark), pp. 3–76.

Pelachaud C, van Overveld C, Seah C (1994) Modeling and Animating the Human Tongue during Speech Production. In *Proc. Computer Animation*, pp. 40–49.

Penn A, Turner A, (2001) Space Syntax Based Agent Simulation. In Schreckenberg M, Sharma SD (eds) *Pedestrian and Evacuation Dynamics*. Springer-Verlag.

Perlin K (1985) An Image Synthesizer. *Computer Graphics (Proceedings of SIGGRAPH'85)* vol. 19(3), pp. 287–296.

Perlin K (1989) Hypertexture. In *Proceedings of SIGGARPH'89*, pp. 253–262.

Perlin K, Goldberg A (1996) Improv: A System for Scripting Interactive Actors in Virtual Worlds. In *Proceedings of SIGGRAPH'96*, pp. 205–216.

Perlin K, Hoffert EM (1989) Hypertexture. In *Computer Graphics (Proceedings of SIGGRAPH'89)*, vol. 23(3) pp. 253–262.

Perng WL, Wu Y, Ouhyoung M (1998) Image Talk: A Real Time Synthetic Talking Head Using One Single Image with Chinese Text-to-Speech Capability. In *Proccedings Pacific Graphics*, pp. 140–149.

Pharr M, Hanrahan P (2000) Monte Carlo Evaluation of Non-Linear Scattering Equations for Subsurface Reflection. In *Proceedings of SIGGRAPH 2000*, pp. 75–84.

Philips CB, Zhao J, Badler NI (1990) Interactive Real-Time Articulated Figure Manipulation Using Multiple Kinematic Constraints. *Computer Graphics*, vol. 24(2), pp. 245–250.

Phillips CB, Badler N (1991) Interactive Behaviors for Bipedal Articulated Figures. *Computer Graphics*, vol. 25(4), pp. 359–362.

Picard R (1998) *Affective Computing*, The MIT Press.

Pieper S, Rosen J, Zeltzer D (1992) Interactive Graphics for Plastic Surgery: A Task Level Analysis and Implementation. *Computer Graphics, Special Issue: ACM SIGGRAPH, 1992 Symposium on Interactive 3-D Graphics*, pp. 127–134.

Pixar (1998) Meet Geri: The New Face of Animation. In *Computer Graphics World*, vol. 21(2)

Plänkers R, Fua P (2001) Articulated Soft Objects for Video-based Body Modeling. In *International Conference on Computer Vision*, Vancouver, Canada, pp. 394–401.

Plänkers R, Fua P (2003) Articulated Soft Objects for Multi-View Shape and Motion Capture. *Transaction on Pattern Analysis and Machine Intelligence*.

Platt S, Badler N (1981) Animating Facial Expression. *Computer Graphics*, vol. 15(3), pp. 245–252.

Platt J, Barr A (1988) Constraint Methods for Flexible Models. *Computer Graphics (SIGGRAPH'88 Proceedings)*, pp. 279–288.

Poggi I, Pelachaud C, De Rosis F (2000) Eye Communication in a Conversational 3-D Synthetic Agent *AI Communications*, vol. 13(3), pp. 169–182.

Pollard NS (1999) Simple Machines for Scaling Human Motion. In *Proc. of Eurographics Workshop on Computer Animation and Simulation, EGCAS'99*, Springer Verlag, pp. 3–12.

Ponder M, Herbelin B, Molet T, Schertenlieb S, Ulicny B, Papagiannakis G, Magnenat-Thalmann N, Thalmann D (2003) Immersive VR Decision Training: Telling Interactive Stories Featuring Advanced Virtual Human Simulation Technologies. In *Proc. 9th Eurographics Workshop on Virtual Environments*.

Popović Z, Witkin A (1999) Physically Based Motion Transformation. In *Proc. of SIGGRAPH'99*, Los Angeles.

Porcher-Nedel L (1998) Anatomic Modeling of Human Bodies using Physically-Based Muscle Simulation, PhD thesis, EPFL, Lausanne.

Poter TE, Willmert KD (1975) Three-Dimensional Human Display Model. *Computer Graphics*, vol. 9(1), pp. 102–110.

Poulin P, Fournier A (1990) A Model for Anisotropic Reflection. In *Computer Graphics (SIGGRAPH'90 Proceedings)*, vol. 24, pp. 273–282.

Powers WT (1973) *The Control of Perception*. Aldine.

Pratt DR, Pratt SM, Barham PT, Barker RE, Waldrop MS, Ehlert JF, Chrislip CA (1997) Humans in Large-Scale, Networked Virtual Environments. *Presence*, vol. 6(3), MIT Press, pp. 547–564.

Press W, Teukolsky S, Vetterling WT, Flannery BP (1992a) Singular Value Decomposition. In *Solution of Linear Algebraic Equation from Numerical Recipes in C*, 2nd edition, Cambridge University Press, pp. 59–70.

Press WH, Flannery BP, Teukolsky SA, Vetterling WT (1986) *Numerical Recipes: the Art of Scientific Computing*. Cambridge University Press.

Press WH, Flannery BP, Teukolsky SA, Vetterling WT (1988) Numerical Recipes in C: *The Art of Scientific Computing*. Cambridge University Press.

Press WH, Vetterling WT, Teukolsky SA, Flannery BP (1992b) *Numerical Recipes in C*. 2nd edition, Cambridge University Press.

Proesmans M Van Gool L (1997) Reading Between the Lines: A Method for Extracting Dynamic 3-D with Texture. In *Proceedings of VRST*, pp. 95–102.

Provot X (1995) Deformation Constraints in a Mass-Spring Model to Describe Rigid Cloth Behavior. *Graphics Interface'95 Proceedings*. Quebec, Canada, pp. 147–154.

Rabiner LR, Schafer RW (1978) *Digital Processing of Speech Signal*. Prentice Hall.

Raibert MH, Hodgins JK (1991) Animation of Dynamic Legged Locomotion. In *Proc. SIGGRAPH'91, Computer Graphics*, vol. 25, pp. 349–358.

Ramamoorthi R, Hanrahan P (2001) An Efficient Representation for Irradiance Environment Maps, Proceedings of SIGGRAPH 2001, ACM Press, pp.497–500

Ramamoorthi R, Hanrahan P (2002) Frequency Space Environment Map Rendering. In *Proceedings of SIGGRAPH 2002*, ACM Press, pp. 517–526.

Rao AS, Georgeff MP (1991) Modeling Rational Agents within a BDI-Architecture. In Allen J, Fikes R, Sandewall E (eds), *In Proceedings of the 2nd International Conference on Principles of Knowledge Representation and Reasoning*. Morgan Kaufmann publishers Inc. pp. 473–484.

Reeves WT (1983) Particle Systems: A Technique for Modeling a Class of Fuzzy Objects. *ACM Transactions on Graphics*, vol. 2(2), pp. 91–108.

Reeves WT, Salesin DH, Cook RL (1987) Rendering Anti-Aliased Shadows with Depth Maps. *Computer Graphics (Proceedings of SIGGRAPH'87)*, vol. 21(4), pp. 283–291.

Reinders MJT, Beek PJL, Sankur B, Lubbe JCA (1995) Facial Feature Localization and Adaptation of a Generic Face Model for Model-Based Coding. In *Signal Processing: Image Communication* vol. 7, pp. 57–74, Elsevier.

Reinders MJT, Koch RWC, Gerbrands JJ (1996) Locating Facial Features in Image Sequences using Neural Networks. In *Automatic Face and Gesture Recognition*, pp. 230–235.

Reiter E, Dale R (1997) Building Applied Natural Language Generation Systems. *Natural Language Engineering*, vol. 3, pp. 57–87.

Renault O, Magnenat-Thalmann N, Thalmann D, (1990) A Vision-Based Approach to Behavioral Animation, Journal of Visualization and Computer Animation, Vol.1, No.1, pp.18–21

Ressler S, Tutorial on Human Joints with their Type, the Number of Degrees of Freedom and Some Suggestions for the Min-Max Values of Angles. website http://ovrt.nist.gov/projects/vrml/h-anim/landmarkInfo.html

Reynolds CW (1987) Flocks, Herds, and Schools: A Distributed Behavioral Model. In *Computer Graphics (SIGGRAPH'87 Conference Proceedings)*, vol. 21(4), pp. 25–34.

Rickel J, Johnson WL (1997) Integrating Pedagogical Capabilities in a Virtual Environment Agent. In *Proceedings of the First International Conference on Autonomous Agents*.

Rijpkema H, Michael G (1991) Computer Animation of Knowledge-Based Human Grasping. In *Proceedings of ACM SIGGRAPH'91*, vol. 25(4), pp. 339–348.

Roach P (1983) *Further Phonology: Symbols and Syllables*. Cambridge University Press.

Robbins C (1999) Computer Simulation of Crowd Behavior and Evacuation. *ECMI Newsletter*, No. 25, March 1999. http://www.it.lut.fi/fac/mat/EcmiNL/ecmi25/ node5.html

Roberts T (1995) *Understanding Balance: The Mechanics of Posture and Locomotion*. Chapman & Hall.

Rose CF III, Sloan PP, Cohen M (2001) Artist-Directed Inverse Kinematics Using Radial Basis Function Interpolation. In *Eurographics '2001, Computer Graphics Forum*, vol. 20(3), Blackwell Publishers.

Rosenblatt JK, Payton D (1989) A Fine-Grained Alternative to the Subsumption Architecture for Mobile Robot Control. In *Proceedings of the IEEE/INNS International Joint Conference on Neural Networks*. IEEE, p. 65.

Rosenbloom PS, Laird JE, Newell A (1993) *The Soar Papers: Research on Artificial Intelligence*. MIT Press.

Rosenblum R, Carlson W, Tripp E (1991) Simulating the Structure and Dynamics of Human Hair: Modeling, Rendering and Animation. *Journal of Visualzation and Computer Animation*, vol. 2, pp. 141–148.

Rousseau D, Hayes-Roth B (1998) A Social-Psychological Model for Synthetic Actors. In *Proceedings of the Second International Conference on Autonomous Agents*. New York. ACM Press, pp. 165–172.

Sabin M (1986) *Recursive Subdivision: The Mathematics of Surfaces*. Clarendon Press, pp. 269–282.

Sadek MD, Bretier P, Panaget F (1997) ARTIMIS: Natural Dialogue Meets Rational Agency. In Pollack ME. (ed.), In *Proceedings of the 15th International Joint Conference on Artificial Intelligence*, Morgan Kaufmann Publishers, pp. 1030–1035.

Sagawa, Ohki M, Saziyama T, Oohira E (1996) Pattern Recognition and Synthesis for a Sign Language Translation System. *Journal of Visual Languages and Computing*, vol. 7, pp. 109–127.

Saito H, Kanade T (1999) Shape Reconstruction in Projective Grid Space from Large Number of Images. In *Conference on Computer Vision and Pattern Recognition*, Ft. Collins, CO.

Saiwaki N, Komatsu T, Nishida S (1999) Automatic Generation of Moving Crowds in the Virtual Environments. In *Proc. AMCP'98, LNCS 1554*, Springer-Verlag.

Sakagushi Y, Minoh M, Ikeda K (1991) A Dynamically Deformable Model of Dress. *Trans. Society of Electronics, Information and Communications*, pp. 25–32.

Sannier G., Balcisoy S., N. Magnenat-Thalmann, D. Thalmann, (1999) VHD: A System for Directing Real-Time Virtual Actors. *The Visual Computer*, Springer, vol. 15(7/8), pp. 320–329.

Schaufler G (1997) Nailboards: A Rendering Primitive for Image Caching in Dynamic Scenes. In *Proc. of 8th Eurographics Workshop'97 on Rendering*, St Etienne, France, pp. 151–162.

Schaufler G, Stürzlinger W (1996) A Three Dimensional Image Cache for Virtual Reality. In *Proc. Eurographics'96*, pp. C-227–C-234.

Scheepers F, Parent RE, Carlson WE, May SF (1997) Anatomy-Based Modeling of the Human Musculature. In *Computer Graphics (SIGGRAPH'97 Proceedings)*, pp 163–172.

Schlick C (1994) A Survey of Shading and Reflectance Models for Computer Graphics. *Computer Graphics Forum*, vol. 3(2), pp. 121 132.

Schweingruber D (1995) A Computer Simulation of a Sociological Experiment. *Social Science Computer Review*, vol. 13(3), pp. 351–359.

SDFAST User Manual, 1990.

Sederberg T, Parry S (1986) Free-From Deformation of Solid Geometric Models. In *Computer Graphics (SIGGRAPH'86 Proceedings)*, pp. 151–160.

Sengers P (1997) Socially Intelligent Agent-Building. In *Proceedings of AAAI-97 Workshop on Socially Intelligent Agents*. Menlo Park CA.

Seo H, Cordier F, Philippon L, Magnenat-Thalmann N (2000) Interactive Modeling of MPEG-4 Deformable Human Body Models. In *Proc. Deform'2000, Workshop on Virtual Humans by IFIP Working Group 5.10 (Computer Graphics and Virtual Worlds)*, Kluwer Academic Publishers, pp. 120–131.

Sevin E, Kallmann M, Thalmann D (2001) Towards Real Time Virtual Human Life Simulations, Submitted to *Computer Graphics International Symposium 2001*.

Shah JJ, Mäntylä M (1995) *Parametric and Feature-Based CAD/CAM*. John Wiley & Sons, Ltd.

Shahrokni A, Vacchetti L, Lepetit V, Fua P, (2002) Polyhedral Object Detection and Pose Estimation for Augmented Reality Applications. In *Proceedings of Computer Animation 2002*, Geneva, Switzerland

Shan Y, Liu Z, and Zhang Z (2001) Model-Based Bundle Adjustment with Application to Face Modeling. In *International Conference of Computer Vision*, Vancouver, Canada.

Shen J, Chauvineau E, Thalmann D (1996) Fast Realistic Human Body Deformations for Animation and VR Applications. In *Proc. Computer Graphics International'96*, pp. 166–173.

Shih Ni-J, Wei-Der S (1996) Gesture Modeling for Architectural Design. *Computers & Graphics*, Pergamon, vol. 20(6), pp. 849–862.

Shin HJ, Lee J, Shin SY, Gleicher M (2001) Computer Puppetry: An Importance-Based Approach, *ACM Transaction on Graphics*, vol. 20(2), pp. 67–94.

Sichman JS (1995) Du Raisonnement Social chez les Agents. PhD thesis, Institut National Polytechnique de Grenoble.

Siciliano B, Slotine JJ (1991) A General Framework for Managing Multiple Tasks in Highly Redundant Robotic Systems. In *Proc. of ICAR'91*, vol. 2, pp. 1211–1215.

Sidenbladh H, Black MJ, Sigal L (2002) Implicit Probabilistic Models of Human Motion for Synthesis and Tracking. In *European Conference on Computer Vision*, Copenhagen, Denmark.

Sims K (1991) Artificial Evolution for Computer Graphics. In *Proceedings of ACM SIGGRAPH'91*, vol. 25(4), pp. 319–328.

Singh K, Kokkevis E (2000) Skinning Characters Using Surface-Oriented Free-Form Deformations. In *Proc. of Graphics Interface 2000*, pp. 35–42.

Sloan P, Rose C, Cohen M (2001) Shape by Example. *2001 Symposium on Interactive 3-D Graphics*.

Sloan P-P, Cohen MF (2000) Interactive Horizon Mapping. In *Eurographics Workshop on Rendering 2000*.

Smelser N (1962) *Theory of Collective Behavior*. Routledge & Kegan Paul.

Sminchisescu C, Triggs B (2001) Covariance Scaled Sampling for Monocular 3-D Body Tracking. In *Conference on Computer Vision and Pattern Recognition*, Hawaii.

Smith R (2000–2003) *Open Dynamics Engine*, http://q12.org/ode.

Snyder J, Lengyel J (1998) Visibility Sorting and Compositing without Splitting for Image Layer Decompositions. In *SIGGRAPH'98 Proceedings*, pp. 219–229.

Sommer R (1979) *Personal Space*. Prentice Hall.

Stam J (2001) An Illumination Model for a Skin Layer Bounded by Rough Surfaces. In *Proceedings of the 12th Eurographics Workshop on Rendering 2001*, pp. 39–52.

Starck J, Hilton A (2002) Reconstruction of Animated Models from Images Using Constrained Deformable Surfaces. In *Conference on Discrete Geometry for Computer Imagery*, Bordeaux, France, Springer-Verlag, pp. 382–391.

Starner T (1995) Visual Recognition of American Sign Language using Hidden Markov Models. Master's thesis, MIT Media Lab, July 1995.

Stewart JA (1999) Computing Visibility from Folded Surfaces. *Computers and Graphics*, vol. 23(5), pp. 693–702.

Stewart JA Langer MS (1997) Towards Accurate Recovery of Shape from Shading under Diffuse Lighting. In *IEEE Transactions on Pattern Analysis and Machine Intelligence*, vol. 19(9), pp. 1020–1025.

Still GK (2000) Crowd Dynamics. PhD thesis, Warwick University.

Stone M (1991) Toward a Model of Three-Dimensional Tongue Movement, *Journal of Phonetics*, vol. 19, pp. 309–320.

Sullivan S, Sandford L, Ponce J (1994) Using Geometric Distance Fits for 3-D Object Modeling and Recognition. *IEEE Transactions on Pattern Analysis and Machine Intelligence*, vol. 16(12), pp. 1183–1196.

Sun W, Hilton A, Smith R, Illingworth J (1999) Building Layered Animation Models of Captured Data. In *Eurographics Workshop on Computer Animation and Simulation*, Milan, Italy.

Szyperski, C (1997) *Component Software: Beyond Object-Oriented Programming*. Addison-Wesley.

Tak S, Song OY, Ko HS (2000) Motion Balance Filtering. In *Proc. of Eurographics '2000, Computer Graphics Forum*, vol. 19(3), Blackwell publishers.

Takahashi T, Shiizuka H (1992) Refuge Behavior Simulation by Network Model. *Memoirs of Kougakuin University*, no. 73, pp. 213–220, October 1992.

Tamura M, Masuko T, Kobayashi T, Tokuda K (1998) Visual Speech Synthesis Based on Parameter Generation from HMM: Speech Driven and Text-and-Speech Driven Approaches. In *Proc. AVSP'98*, International Conference on Auditory-Visual Speech Processing.

Tecchia F, Chrysanthou Y (2000) Real-Time Rendering of Densely Populated Urban Environments. In *Proc. Eurographics Rendering Workshop*.

Terzopoulos D, Fleischer K (1988) Modeling Inelastic Deformation: Viscoelasticity, Plasticity, Fracture. *Computer Graphics (SIGGRAPH'88 proceedings)*, Addison-Wesley, vol. 22, pp. 269–278.

Terzopoulos D, Platt JC, Barr H (1987) Elastically Deformable Models. *Computer Graphics (SIGGRAPH'97 Proceedings)*. Addison-Wesley, vol. 21, pp. 205–214.

Terzopoulos D, Waters K (1990) Physically-Based Facial Modeling, Analysis, and Animation. *Journal of Visualization and Computer Animation*, vol. 1(4), pp. 73–80.

Teven D (1999) Virtools' NeMo. *Game Developer Magazine*, September.

Thalmann D (1995) Virtual Sensors: A Key Tool for the Artificial Life of Virtual Actors. *In Proc. Pacific Graphics'95*, Seoul, Korea, pp. 22–40.

Thalmann D, Musse SR, Kallmann M (2000) From Individual Human Agents to Crowds. *INFORMATIK / INFORMATIQUE 1*.

Thalmann D, Shen J, Chauvineau E (1996) Fast Realistic Human Body Deformations for Animation and VR Applications. *Computer Graphics International'96*, Pohang, Korea.

Thompson PA, Marchant EW (1995) A Computer-Model for the Evacuation of Large Building Population. *Fire Safety Journal*, vol. 24(2), pp. 131–148.

Thórisson KR (1997) Gandalf: An Embodied Humanoid Capable of Real-Time Multimodal Dialogue with People. In *First ACM Conf. on Autonomous Agents'97*, Los Angeles – Marina Del Rey, pp. 536–537.

Tinbergen N (1951) *The Study of Instinct*. Oxford University Press.

Tolani D, Badler N, (1996) Real Time Human Arm Inverse Kinematics, Presence, Vol.5, No.4, pp.393–401.

Tolani D, Goswami A, Badler N (2000) Real-Time Inverse Kinematics Techniques for Anthropomorphic Arms. *Graphical Models*, vol. 62, pp. 353–388.

Torborg J, Kajiya J (1996) Talisman: Commodity Real-time 3-D Graphics for the PC. In *SIGGRAPH'96 Proceedings*, pp. 353–363.

Traum DR (1996) Conversational Agency: The TRAINS-93 Dialogue Manager. In *Proceedings of the Twente Workshop on Language Technology: Dialogue Management in Natural Language Systems (TWLT 11)*, pp. 1–11.

Trefftz H, Burdea G (2000) *3-D Tracking Calibration of a Polhemus Long Ranger Used with the Baron Barco Workbench*. Technical Report CAIP-TR-243, CAIP, Rutgers University

Tromp J, Snowdon D (1997) Virtual Body Language: Providing Appropriate User Interfaces in Collaborative Virtual Environments. In *Proc. Symposium on Virtual Reality Software and Technology 1997 (VRST'97)*, September 15–17 1997, Swiss Federal Institute of Technology (EPFL), Lausanne, Switzerland.

Tu X, Terzopoulos D (1994) Artificial Fishes: Physics, Locomotion, Perception, Behavior, In *Computer Graphics*, vol. 28.

Tucker CW, Schweingruber D, McPhail C (1999) Simulating Arcs and Rings in Temporary Gatherings. *International Journal of Human-Computer Systems*, vol. 50, pp. 581–588.

Turner R, Thalmann D (1993) The Elastic Surface Layer Model for Animated Character Construction. In *Proc. Computer Graphics International'93*, Lausanne, Switzerland, Springer-Verlag, pp. 399–412.

Tyrrell T (1992) Defining the Action Selection Problem. In *Proc. of the Fourteenth Annual Conf. of the Cognitive Society*. Lawrence Erlbaum Associates.

Tyrrell T (1993) The Use of Hierarchies for Action Selection. *Journal of Adaptive Behavior*, vol. 1(4), pp. 387–420.

Ulicny, B, Thalmann, D, (2001) Crowd Simulation for Interactive Virtual Environments and VR Training Systems. *In Proc. Eurographics Workshop on Animation and Simulation'01*, Springer-Verlag, pp. 163–170.

Ulicny B, Thalmann D, (2002) Towards Interactive Real-Time Crowd Behavior Simulation, Computer Graphics Forum Vol.21(4), pp.767-775

Vaananen, Bohm K (1992) Gesture Driven Interaction as a Human Factor in Virtual Environments: An Approach with Neural Networks. In *Virtual Reality Systems*, Zentrum für Graphische Datenverarbeitung, Darmstadt, pp. 93–106.

Vacchetti L, Lepetit V, Papagiannakis G, Ponder M, Fua P, Magnenat-Thalmann N, Thalmann D (2003) Stable Real-Time Interaction Between Virtual Humans and Real Scenes. In *Proc. International Conference on 3-D Digital Imaging and Modeling*, Banff, Alberta, Canada.

van Gelder A (1998) Approximate Simulation of Elastic Membranes. *Journal of Graphics Tools*, vol. 3(2), pp. 21–42.

van Gelder A, Wilhelms J (1997) An Interactive Fur Modeling Technique. *Graphics Interface'97*, pp. 181–188.

van Gemert MJC, Jacques SL, Sterenborg HJCM, Star WM (1989) Skin Optics. *IEEE Trans Biomed Eng*, vol. 36, pp. 1146–1154.

Varner D, Scott DR, Micheletti J, Aicella G (1998) UMSC Small Unit Leader Non-Lethal Trainer. In *Proc. ITEC'98*.

Verroust A, Lazarus F (1999) Extracting Skeletal Curves from 3-D Scattered Data. In *Shape Modeling International*. Aizu Wakamatsu.

Viaud ML, Yahia H (1992) Facial Animation with Wrinkles. In Forsey D, Hegron G (eds), *Proceedings of the Third Eurographics Workshop on Animation and Simulation*.

Vlachos A, Peters J, Boyd C, Mitchell JL (2001) Curved PN Triangles. *ACM Symposium on Interactive 3-D Graphics*.

Volino M, Courchesne M, Magnenat-Thalmann N (1995) Versatile and Efficient Techniques for Simulating Cloth and Other Deformable Objects. In *Computer Graphics (SIGGRAPH'95 proceedings)*. Addison-Wesley, pp. 137–144.

Volino P, Magnenat-Thalmann N (1994) Efficient Self-Collision Detection on Smoothly Discretised Surface Animation Using Geometrical Shape Regularity. In *Computer Graphics Forum (Eurographics'94 proceedings)*. Blackwell Publishers, vol. 13(3), pp. 155–166.

Volino P, Magnenat-Thalmann N (1997) Developing Simulation Techniques for an Interactive Clothing System. In *Virtual Systems and Multimedia (VSMM'97 Proceedings)*. Geneva, Switzerland, pp. 109–118.

Volino P, Magnenat-Thalmann N (1998) The SPHERIGON: A Simple Polygon Patch for Smoothing Quickly your Polygonal Meshes. *Computer Animation'98 Proceedings*.

Volino P, Magnenat-Thalmann N (1999) Fast Geometrical Wrinkles on Animated Surfaces. *WSCG'99 Proceedings*.

Volino P, Magnenat-Thalmann N (2000a) Accurate Collision Response on Polygonal Meshes. *Computer Animation 2000 Proceedings*.

Volino P, Magnenat-Thalmann N (2000b) Implementing Fast Cloth Simulation with Collision Response. *Computer Graphics International 2000*, pp. 257–266.

Volino P, Magnenat-Thalmann N (2001) Comparing Efficiency of Integration Methods for Cloth Simulation. *Computer Graphics International 2001*.

Wachter S, Nagel H-H (1999) Tracking Persons in Monocular Image Sequences. *Computer Vision and Image Understanding*, vol. 73(3), pp. 174–192.

Wagner M (2000) 3-D E-Commerce: Fact or Fiction? In *Proc. 6th International Conference on Virtual Systems and MultiMedia (vsmm)*, Ohmsha Press, pp. 634–642.

Wahlster W (ed.) (2000) *Verbmobil: Foundations of Speech-to-Speech Translation*. Springer.

Waters K, Levergood, T (1995) Decface: A System for Synthetic Face Applications. *Multimedia Tools and Applications*, vol. 1, pp. 349–366.

Waite CT (1989) The Facial Action Control Editor, FACE: A Parametric Facial Expression Editor for Computer Generated Animation. Master's thesis, MIT.

Wang CLY, Forsey DR (1994) Langwidere: A New Facial Animation System. In *Proceedings of Computer Animation*, pp. 59–68.

Wang X, Verriest J (1998) A Geometric Algorithm to Predict the Arm Reach Posture for Computer-aided Ergonomic Evaluation. *The Journal of Visualization and Computer Animation*, vol. 9, pp. 33–47.

Ward GJ (1992) Measuring and Modeling Anisotropic Reflection. *Computer Graphics (SIGGRAPH'92 proceedings)*. Addison-Wesley, vol. 26, pp. 265–272.

Watanabe Y, Suenaga Y (1989) Drawing Human Hair Using Wisp Model. In *Proceedings of Computer Graphics International'89*. Springer-Verlag, pp. 691–700.

Watanabe Y, Suenaga Y (1992) A Trigonal Prism-based Method for Hair Image Generation. *IEEE Computer Graphics & Applications*, vol. 12(1), pp. 47–53.

Waters K (1987) A Muscle Model for Animating Three-Dimensional Facial Expression. In Stone MC (ed.), *Computer Graphics (SIGGRAPH Proceedings, 1987)*, vol. 21, pp. 17–24.

Waters K, Levergood TM (1995) DECface: A System for Synthetic Face Applications, Multimedia Tools Appl. Vol.1, No.4, 349-336.

Watt A, Watt M (1992) *Advanced Animation and Rendering Techniques*. Addison-Wesley, ACM Press.

Webb RC, Gigante MA (1992) Using Dynamic Bounding Volume Hierarchies to Improve Efficiency of Rigid Body Simulations. *Communicating with Virtual Worlds, (CGI'92 Proceedings)*, pp. 825–841.

Weber D (2000) Run Time Skin Deformation http://www.imonk.com/jason/bones/weberj.doc

Weil J (1986) The Synthesis of Cloth Objects. In *Proc. SIGGRAPH'86, Computer Graphics*, vol. 24, pp. 243–252.

Weimer H, Warren J (1999) Subdivision Schemes for Fluid Flow. In *Proceedings of SIGGRAPH'99*, pp. 111–120.

Weizenbaum J (1996) ELIZA: A Computer Program for the Study of Natural Language Communication between Man and Machine. *Communications of the ACM*, vol. 9(1), pp. 36–45.

Wejchert J, Haumann D (1991) Animation Aerodynamics. In *Computer Graphics (Proceedings of SIGGRAPH'91)*, vol. 25(4), pp. 19–22.

Wernecke J (1994) *The Inventor Mentor: Programming Object-Oriented 3-D Graphics with Open Inventor Rel. 2*. Addison-Wesley.

Werner HM, Magnenat-Thalmann N, Thalmann D (1993) User Interface for Fashion Design. In *Graphics, Design and Visualization (ICCG'93 Proceedings)*, pp. 165–172.

Westin S, Arvo JR, Torrance KE (1992) Predicting Reflectance Functions from Complex Surfaces. In *Proceedings of SIGGRAPH 1992*, pp. 255–264.

White AA, Penjabi MM (1990) *Clinical Biomechanics of the Spine*, 2nd edition, J.B. Lippincott Company.

Whitney D (1969) Resolved Motion Rate Control of Manipulators and Human Prostheses. In *IEEE Trans. on Man-Machine Systems*, vol. MMS-10(2), pp. 47–53.

Wiley DJ, Hahn JK (1997) Interpolation Synthesis of Articulated Figure Motion. *IEEE CGA*, vol. 17(6)

Wilhelms J (1997) Animals with Anatomy. *IEEE Computer Graphics and Applications*, vol 17(3), pp. 22–30.

Wilhelms J, van Gelder A (1997) Anatomically Based Modeling. *Computer Graphics (Proc. of SIGGRAPH'97)*, pp. 173–180.

Williams JR (1995) A Simulation Environment to Support Training for Large Scale Command and Control Task. PhD thesis, University of Leeds.

Williams L (1990) Performance Driven Facial Animation. *Proc. SIGGRAPH'90, Computer Graphics*, vol. 24(3), pp. 235–242.

Witkin A, Kass M (1988) Spacetime Constraints. *Proc. SIGGRAPH'88, Computer Graphics*, vol. 22(4), pp. 159–168.

Wooldridge M (2000) *Reasoning about Rational Agents*. MIT Press.

Wooldridge M, Jennings NR (1994) Agent Theories, Architectures, and Languages: A Survey. In Wooldridge M, Jennings NR (eds), *Proc. ECAI Workshop on Agent Theories, Architectures and Languages*, Amsterdam, pp. 1–32.

Wooldridge M, Jennings NR (1995) Intelligent Agents: Theory and Practice. *Knowledge Engineering Review*, vol. 10(2), pp.

Wren C, Azarbayejani A, Darrell T, Pentland A (1995) Pfinder: Real-Time Tracking of the Human Body. In *Photonics East, SPIE*, vol. 2615.

Wren C, Pentland A (1999) Understanding Purposeful Human Motion. In *ICCV Workshop on Modeling People*, Corfu, Greece.

Wu Y (1998) Skin Deformation and Aging with Wrinkles. PhD thesis, University of Geneva.

Wu Y, Kalra P, Magnenat-Thalmann N (1997) Physically-based Wrinkle Simulation and Skin Rendering. In *EGCAS'97*, Budapest, Hungary.

Wu Y, Kalra P, Moccozet L, Magnenat-Thalmann N (1999) Simulating Wrinkles and Skin Aging. *The Visual Computer*, vol. 15(4), pp. 183–198.

Wu Y, Magnenat-Thalmann N, Thalmann D (1994) A Plastic-Visco-Elastic Model for Wrinkles in Facial Animation and Skin Aging. *Proc. 2nd Pacific Conference on Computer Graphics and Applications*, Pacific Graphics.

Wyvill B, Guy A, Galin E (1998) The Blob Tree. *Journal of Implicit Surfaces*, vol. 3.

Wyvill G, McPheeters C, Wyvill B (1986) Data Structure for Soft Objects. *The Visual Computer*, vol. 2(4), pp. 227–234.

Xu Y, Chen Y, Lin S, Zhong H, Wu E, Guo B Shum H (2001) Photorealistic Rendering of Knitwear Using the Lumislice. In *Proceedings of SIGGRAPH 2001*, pp. 391–398.

Yamaguchi K, Kunii TL, Fujimura K (1984) Octree Related Data Structures and Algorithms. *IEEE Computer Graphics and Applications*, pp. 53–59.

Yamamoto E, Nakamura S, Shikano K (1998) Lip Movement Synthesis from Speech Based on Hidden Markov Models. *Speech Communication*, Elsevier Science, vol. (26)1–2, pp. 105–115.

Yan XD, Xu Z, Yang J, Wang T (1999) The Cluster Hair Model. *Journal of Graphics Models and Image Processing*, Academic Press.

Yang Y, Magnenat-Thalmann N (1993) An Improved Algorithm for Collision Detection in Cloth Animation with Human Body. *Computer Graphics and Applications (Pacific Graphics'93 Proceedings)*, vol. 1, pp. 237–251.

Yasuda T, Yokoi S, Toriwaki J, Inagaki K (1992) A Shading Model for Cloth Objects. *IEEE Computer Graphics and Applications*, vol. 12(6), pp. 15–24.

Yoshimito S (1992) Ballerinas Generated by a Personal Computer. *The Journal of Visualization and Computer Animation*, vol. 3, pp 85–90.

Zajac F (1989) Muscle and Tendon: Properties, Models, Scaling and Application to Biomechanics and Motor Control. In *CRC Critical Reviews in Biomedical Engineering*, CRC Press, vol. 17, pp. 359–411.

Zckler M, Stalling D, Hege H-C (1996) Interactive Visualization of 3-D-Vector Fields Using Illuminated Streamlines. In *Proceedings IEEE Visualization'96*, pp. 107–114.

Zhao J, Badler N (1994) Inverse Kinematics Positioning using Nonlinear Programming for Highly Articulated Figures. *ACM Transactions on Graphics*, vol. 13(4), pp. 313–336.

Zheng JY (1994) Acquiring 3-d Models from Sequences of Contour, IEEE Transactions on Pattern Analysis and Machine Intelligence, IEEE Computer Society Press, 16(2), pp. 163–178

Zhong H, Xu Y, Guo B Shum H (2000) Realistic and Efficient Rendering of Free-Form Knitwear. *Journal of Visualization and Computer Animation*, Special Issue on Cloth Simulation.

Zhu QH, Chen Y, Kaufmann A (1998) Real-time Biomechanically-based Muscle Volume Deformation using FEM. *Computer Graphics Forum (Eurographics'98 Proceedings)*, pp. 275–284.

Ziemke T (1998) Adaptive Behavior in Autonomous Agents. *Presence*, vol. 7(6), pp. 564–587.

Zorin D, Schröder P, Sweldens W (1996) Interpolating Subdivision for Meshes with Arbitrary Topology. *Computer Graphics (SIGGRAPH'96 Proceedings)*, Addison-Wesley, pp. 189–192.

Index

2
2-D feature points, 38
2-D patterns, 227

3
3-D feature points, 39
3-D reconstruction, 55, 60, 87
3-D scattered data, 56
3-D textures, 364

A
Abstract Muscle Action, 126
ACE, 271–274, 286, 317
action lines, 101, 151–153
action response, 287, 289
Action Units, 122, 242
activity space, 288, 289, 302
actor-object interactions, 304, 307, 308,
    321, 322
agent-object interactions, 23
agents, 1, 2, 22, 23, 235, 252, 253,
    260–264, 266–269, 271–273, 277–281,
    286, 299, 304, 309, 312, 324, 329,
    332–338, 347, 349–352, 391
Agents' Common Environment, 271
AMA, 126
Ananova, 9
anatomic skeleton, 56
anatomical landmarks, 77
anatomical modeling, 66
animation
    behavioral, 21, 99, 260–286, 304,
        312, 329
    facial, 6, 22, 46, 47, 49–51, 119, 122,
        123, 126, 129, 130, 133, 136, 137,
        230–245, 247, 249, 250, 252, 253,
        258, 259, 359, 360, 384, 385, 387,
        388, 390
    hair, 165, 168, 169, 178, 189, 190
    key-frame, 18, 232
    performance-driven, 129
    skeletal, 18
    task, 7
anisotropic, 165, 204, 210, 357
ANN, 265
Anthropometric Body Modeling, 75–98
anthropometry, 75–78, 81, 82, 85
anti-aliasing, 23, 162, 167
articulated figures, 7, 103, 104, 106–108
articulated skeleton, 53, 54, 56, 67, 68
articulated structure, 53, 58, 60, 64, 66,
    106, 109, 140, 142, 145, 148, 306, 338
Artificial Intelligence, 19, 25, 232, 265
Artificial Life, 2, 19, 265, 289
Artificial Neural Network, 265
Augmented Reality, 8, 15, 16
automatic reach and grasp, 7
autonomous
    agents, 1, 23, 261, 267, 278, 304
    behavior, 253, 276, 332, 338, 349, 351
    crowds, 324, 333, 335, 349, 352
    Virtual Humans, 2, 21, 24, 231, 252, 253
autonomy, 252, 253, 261, 262, 278, 286,
    324, 333, 334

B
BAP, 379–383
barycentric coordinates, 41, 94, 221
BDI, 254, 278, 279
believability, 2, 9, 21, 99, 100, 111, 113,
    117, 244, 302
Bézier patches, 141, 156, 201
Bi-directional Reflectance Distribution
    Function, 356
Bi-directional Texture Function 355
biomechanics, 151, 154, 159, 160
bisecting plane, 143, 346
bitstream, 380, 382, 384
Body Animation Parameters, 379, 380
BodyDefTables, 380, 381
boids, 330
bounding volume, 212–215, 224, 263, 297

Handbook of Virtual Humans Edited by N. Magnenat-Thalmann and D. Thalmann
© 2004 John Wiley & Sons, Ltd   ISBN: 0-470-02316-3

BRDF, 356–358, 361, 363–366, 368, 371, 372
B-spline, 128, 137, 141, 144, 147, 151, 154, 156, 157, 339, 340
BTF, 355, 361, 364, 365
Buford, 4
bump mapping, 223, 224, 360, 362, 363

C
Candidate Action Set, 297, 298
Canny edge detector, 36
Cartesian, 24, 103–107, 109, 113, 188, 293, 294, 298
CAS, 297, 298
Catmull-Rom spline, 128
cellular automata, 326, 329
center of mass, 82, 106, 117, 118, 154, 294, 307, 375, 376
clump, 163, 167, 170, 177, 178
cluster, 161–163, 167–169
co-articulation, 137, 230, 231, 234, 236, 238, 239, 242, 243, 251–253
Cognitive Modeling Language, 267
collaborative virtual environments, 332
collision avoidance, 164, 169, 171, 263, 264, 308, 314, 323, 332, 346
collision detection, 7, 94, 136, 140, 179, 192, 193, 201, 204, 212–216, 224, 227, 301, 322,
collision filter, 263
collision response, 201, 212, 216–220
collision-free path, 263, 306
Combiman, 3
compression, 197, 294, 379, 382, 383
Computer Tomography, 129
computer vision, 53, 111, 231, 240, 291, 327
computer-generated movies, 16, 230
Conjugate Gradient method, 210
constrained texture mapping, 355
continuity equation, 180, 188
continuum, 169, 178–183, 185, 187, 189, 199–201, 207, 327
contour, 3, 28, 47, 85, 88, 94, 137, 142, 143, 144, 147, 151, 157, 159, 220, 340, 371
covariance matrix, 246, 247

Critter system, 148
crowd
  classification of, 330
  emergent, 324, 335–337, 351
  evacuation, 325, 327
  management, 327
  simulation, 323–352
  visualization, 324, 338, 339, 341, 343, 345
curvature, 196, 200, 201, 203, 206, 215, 220, 221, 390
Cyberman, 3

D
damping factor, 105, 116
database access, 262, 264
decimation, 339
deformation
  body, 20, 99, 102, 140, 142, 144–146, 148, 150, 152, 154, 156, 158–160, 382
  cloth, 196, 228
  facial, 119–139
  global, 57
  local, 57, 65, 129, 130, 141, 201, 224
  multi-layered, 140, 144
  skin, 84, 88, 89, 124, 127, 129, 137, 140–144, 359, 380, 381
degrees of freedoms, 182
Delaunay triangles, 41, 42
depth first search (DFS), 92
DFFD, 32, 33, 39, 149
dining philosopher's problem, 314
Dirichlet Free-Form Deformations, 33
discretization, 111, 185, 199–203, 207, 209
displacement map, 94, 145, 371
DOF, 182, 183, 294, 298
DOGMA, 128
Dozo, 6
draping, 193, 195, 198, 199, 204, 207, 211, 213, 227, 228
Dream Flight, 5

E
eigenvalue, 94, 218, 247
eigenvector, 94, 247
electro-magnetic sensors, 46
emblem, 244

end effector, 104, 105, 109, 114–117, 294, 297, 298, 375, 376
environment maps, 372
equation of state, 181
ergonomics, 85, 100, 103, 391
Euclidean, 28, 68, 95
Euler angles, 67, 374, 375, 377, 380
Euler method, 208, 209, 225
Eulerian method, 185
example-based techniques, 84
exponential maps, 64, 65, 67
expression blending, 230, 231, 234, 239, 243, 250, 252
expressions
  emotional, 359
  facial, 6, 9, 13, 20, 22, 24, 47, 50, 119, 122–124, 126, 128, 231, 234–236, 243, 244, 250, 252, 253, 255–258, 261, 267, 271, 387–389
  vascular, 358, 359, 361
eye gaze, 231, 244, 267

F
fabric, 22, 192–195, 197, 198, 202, 205, 206, 222, 223, 224, 227, 364, 365, 367, 369, 372,
Face and Body Animation, 373, 379
Face Animation Parameter, 47, 123, 379
face cloning, 26–51, 58
face motion capture, 24, 26–51
FaceDefTable, 381, 388
Facial Action Coding System, 122
Facial Animation Markup Language, 235
Facial Animation Table, 123, 129
facial communication, 230, 231, 232, 234, 236, 238, 240, 242, 244, 246, 248, 250, 252, 253, 254, 255, 256, 257, 258, 259
Facial Definition Parameter, 384
facial deformation, *see* deformation
facial expressions, *see* expressions
facial modeling, 27, 29, 31, 34, 37, 39, 41, 43, 45, 83, 119, 231, 233
facial skeleton, 121
FACS, 122, 124–126, 129, 137, 138, 232, 234, 239
FACS+, 122

FAML, 235, 236
FAP, 47, 49, 50, 122, 123, 133, 135, 136, 138, 232, 234–236, 239, 242–244, 248, 250–252, 259, 379–381, 384, 385, 387–390
FAPU, 123, 384, 385, 387
FAT, 123, 133, 135, 136, 384, 388–390
FBA, 373, 379–385, 387, 389
FDP, 129, 133, 379, 380, 384, 387
feature detection, 33–35, 38, 90
feature points, 28, 31–34, 38–42, 45, 47–49, 51, 58, 59, 77, 78, 90–93, 130–133, 239, 245, 380, 384, 385, 387
feature based, 27, 29, 31, 33, 35, 37, 39, 41–43, 45
FEM, 128, 129, 138, 147, 153, 154, 159
FFD, 126, 127, 130, 142, 148, 149
FFM, 253, 256–258
finite element, 22, 102, 119, 128, 137, 147, 153, 154, 157–159, 201, 202, 204, 207, 210
finite state machine, 254, 269, 305, 313, 336, 337
FIT, 390
Five Factor Model, 253, 256
flocking systems, 330, 332, 333
fluid dynamics, 178–1800, 185–187
fluid flow equation, 171
Fourier Transform, 239
free-form deformation, 120, 339
friction, 179, 181, 188–190. 197, 198, 212, 216, 217, 220
FSM, 337, 338
functional realism, 353, 354

G
Gamasutra, 261
Gandalf, 289
garment design, 193, 207, 226, 227
garment prototyping, 228
garment simulation, 85, 192, 193, 198, 201, 202, 213, 224, 226
Gaussian, 34, 36, 37, 68, 95, 144, 156, 368
Gaussian Radial Basis Functions, 95
genetic algorithm, 279, 306
geometric vision, 262, 263

Geri's Game, 7, 128
gesture recognition, 24, 287–292, 294, 296, 298, 300, 302
Gouraud shading, 167, 220
grammar based, 291, 365
Graphical State Machine, 313
grasping, 105, 153, 288, 293, 299, 304, 306, 308
grid-based, 187

H
hair modeling, 161, 163, 168, 169
hair rendering, 23, 161, 162, 165, 167–169, 173
hair simulation, 161–191
Hamming window, 189, 241
H-Anim, 57, 58, 77, 78, 112, 373–382
Hidden Markov Model, 111, 239, 291
hierarchical decision structure, 265
HMM, 111, 239–291, 291
horizon maps, 366, 369,
humanoid, 58, 92, 288, 298, 374, 375, 377, 380
hypertexture, 163, 166
hysteresis, 197, 198

I
ideal flow elements, 170, 171, 175
image-based
    anthropometric measurement, 80
    approach, 60, 364
    motion capture 74
    rendering 372
impact space, 288
implicit surface, 54, 56, 68, 70, 127, 145–149, 155–157
impostor, 339–345
IndexedFaceSet, 133, 135, 389, 390
Instance Based Learning, 290
Intelligent Virtual Agent, 271–273, 276, 286
interaction features, 307, 308, 309, 310
interpolation
    linear, 127, 144, 150, 234, 381
    polynomial, 208, 390
    shape, 123

inverse kinematics, 21, 63, 99, 100, 101, 104, 105, 107, 109, 110, 111, 117, 160, 261, 271, 306, 307, 311, 312, 315–317, 319, 322, 375
inverse lighting, 358, 361
iso-surface, 147, 155
IVA, 271–273, 276

J
Jack, 7, 81, 82, 110
Jacobian, 68, 70, 106, 109, 114, 116
JLD, 141
joint
    angles, 20, 21, 53, 63, 71, 104, 105, 141, 144, 149, 294, 299
    interpolators, 96
    limits, 75, 82, 103, 109, 110, 111, 375
    parameters, 91, 92, 96, 104
Joint-dependent Local Deformation, 141

K
Kalman filter, 60, 65, 66
Kawabata Evaluation System for Fabric, 197
key-framing, 21, 62, 105, 119
key-shapes, 144, 145, 159, 160

L
Lagrange equation, 193, 200, 201
Laplace equation, 170
laser scanner, 27, 28, 30, 31, 42, 43, 55, 56, 60, 144
learning, 8, 59, 65, 86, 224, 265, 278, 289, 290, 291, 322, 351
least squares estimator, 69
LEMAN system, 155, 157
level of detail, 89, 107, 142, 339
Linear Predictive Coding, 239
locomotion, 61, 62, 64, 105, 266, 269, 283, 285
LU decomposition, 95, 173, 174

M
macro-geometric details, 362, 370
Magnetic Resonance Imaging, 129
manipulation space, 287, 288, 322
manipulators, 244, 310, 311

mass-spring systems, 159, 203, 210
mechanical joint, 100, 102, 103
mechanical properties, 22, 101, 120, 192,
    193, 195, 197, 202, 226
Mel-frequency Cepstral, 239
mesh deformation, 49, 94, 123, 130,
    223, 233
mesh modeling, 49
mesh smoothing, 220
mesh traversal, 131, 132
metaballs, 54, 67–69, 146, 149,
    150, 157
micro/milli geometric details, 362, 364
micro-geometry, 354, 355, 357, 364–367,
    369, 372
microstructure, 204, 359, 363, 365
Midpoint method, 208, 209, 210
Minimum Perceptible Action, 359
Minimum Perceptible Color
    Action, 359
momentum equation, 181, 188, 189
monocular, 65
mood, 2, 244, 253, 256–259,
    276, 279
morphing, 17, 144, 380, 387
motion analysis, 6, 61, 62
motion estimation, 52–54, 67, 69
motion planning, 99, 110, 306, 323
motion retargeting, 105, 113, 118,
    261, 376
MPA, 122, 138, 232, 234, 359
MPCA, 359
MPEG-4 standard, 47, 379, 380, 382
multi-agent system, 2, 279, 326
Multi-Body System, 100, 101, 103
multi-camera, 50, 60, 66
multi-modal, 8, 66
multi-ocular, 64, 65
Multiple Priority Levels Inverse
    Kinematics, 99, 100
multi-resolution technique, 39, 40
muscle
    linear, 121
    pseudo, 119
    sphincter, 121
musculo-skeletal system, 100, 101, 102

N
Neural Network, 239, 265, 291
neutral face, 384, 385
Newton-Raphson method, 109
Newton-Raphson steps, 154
non-verbal communication, 24, 267
non-verbal interaction, 267
null space, 109, 114
NURBS, 137

O
object specific reasoning, 304
OCC model, 256
opacity factor, 166
optical flow, 64
optical trackers, 46
optimization, 54, 66, 68–71, 82, 89, 90, 92,
    93, 105, 109, 110, 114, 116–118, 213,
    224, 267, 332, 338
orthogonal basis, 94, 96
orthographic camera, 341, 342, 345
OSR, 304

P
PAR, 268, 276
parameterization schemes, 119, 120,
    233, 234
Parameterized Action Representation, 268
parametric models, 4, 55
particle systems, 22, 161, 162, 165, 168,
    193, 199, 200, 202, 207, 210, 211, 218,
    224, 330–332
PaT-Net, 267, 268, 276
pattern-matching, 254, 264
perception, 2, 3, 20–22, 24, 25, 61, 118,
    228, 262–265, 272, 282, 286, 327, 329,
    330, 371, 391
performance driven facial animation, 46, 49
phoneme, 51, 232, 234, 238–242, 244, 246,
    248, 250, 251, 253, 387
Phong shading, 220, 221
Photo realism, 353
photo-cloning, 32
photogrammetry, 55
physical realism, 137, 353, 354
physics-based modeling, 60

physics-based spring system, 53
pixel blending, 167
plaster, 17, 28, 29
Poisson coefficient, 195–197
Polhemus, 56, 62
polyhedral models, 52
polylines, 167
polynomial texture mapping, 364
posture recognition, 289, 291
Principal Component Analysis, 50, 51, 59,
   84, 94, 111, 245, 246, 250
Projective Virtual Reality, 287
pseudo-inverse, 109, 110, 114–116
PTM, 364, 365
Punctuators, 244
Python, 271, 272, 274, 281, 314

Q

quadric surfaces, 60
quasi-static models, 195
quaternions, 67, 111, 183, 184

R

range data, 28, 30, 31, 41, 42, 45, 145
Rational Free Form Deformation 127
ray tracing, 163, 167, 364
RBF, 144
real-time animation, 7, 129, 130, 132, 225,
   226, 235, 245, 303
regularization, 29, 115, 358
Regulators, 244
rendering
   of clothes, 353, 354, 361, 363, 365, 367,
      369, 371
   of skin, 353–360, 362, 364, 366, 368,
      370, 372
   wrinkle, 222, 359
RFFD, 127, 128
Rigidity modulus, 195, 197, 198
Runge-Kutta methods, 208

S

Sammie, 4
scalp, 23, 161, 162, 169, 170, 172, 173,
   175–178, 183, 184
scattering, 354, 356–358, 361, 363

Sculptor, 28
segmentation, 34, 57, 65, 251, 343
self-collision, 23, 162, 198, 214, 215, 307
self-shadowing, 165, 168, 220, 224, 370, 372
shadow buffers, 167
shape extraction, 33, 34, 37, 38
silhouette, 30, 38, 57, 58, 59, 60, 65, 69,
   70, 71, 289
simulation
   acoustic, 11
   cloth, 192–229
   hair, 161–191
   mechanical, 22, 157, 192, 193, 198–203,
      205, 207, 209, 212, 216, 217, 220,
      224, 227
Singular Value Decomposition, 109
skeletal, 3, 18, 56, 89, 91, 93, 94, 96, 100,
   101, 102, 103, 142, 144, 145, 147, 151,
   153, 155, 159
skeleton fitting, 90–94
skeleton-driven deformation, 88, 91, 93
skin deformation, *see* deformation
skin fitting, 90
skin refinement, 94
skinning, 58, 141–145, 147, 148, 159
Smart Object Modeler, 310
smoothed particle hydrodynamics, 179, 185
SNHC, 123
soft objects, 54, 67, 69
SOMOD, 310–314, 317
space-time constraints, 107
spherical joint, 103, 183, 184
spine mapping, 373, 376, 377
Stereoscopy, 28
stick figure, 5, 52, 53
stiffness dynamics, 164, 178, 179, 180, 182,
   183, 188
stiffness matrix, 129, 153
stress-strain relationship, 129, 153
Stripe generator, 28
subdivision surface, 128, 145, 204, 220, 339
surface distance, 130–132
synchronization, 230–232, 238, 239, 259,
   261, 267, 272, 303, 313–315, 323
synthetic actors, 7, 277
Synthetic Natural Hybrid Coding 123
synthetic vision, 262, 263

T

Task inspection algorithm, 275
telepresence, 3
template matching, 33, 289, 291
template model, 83–85, 88–94
texel, 166, 342, 343, 345
text-to-speech, 9, 238, 342, 383
texture mapping, 32, 39, 59, 222, 340, 355, 359, 361, 364
texture refreshment, 342, 345
texturing, 224, 353–356, 358, 360, 361, 365, 366
The Abyss, 7
the Juggler, 5
Tin Toy, 6, 125, 128
tongue, 121, 136, 137, 384, 387
Tony de Peltrie, 6
torque, 20, 102, 103, 106, 107, 109, 118, 185
tracking, 33, 46, 47, 51, 53, 54, 60, 62–66, 71, 105, 239, 245, 274, 289, 294, 301
tri-phones, 240

V

vascular expressions, 358, 359, 361
Vicon, 11, 47, 63, 245
ViCrowd, 324, 330, 332–334, 347, 349
video conferencing, 383
video games, 1, 9, 18, 103, 105, 142, 260, 262, 268, 269
video stream, 29, 288
video-based motion capture, 61, 64
video-based shape, 54, 60
video-based systems, 60
Virtual Assistants, 9
virtual characters, 7, 8, 17, 18, 22, 66, 107, 118, 119, 140, 194, 202, 204, 224, 225, 226, 228, 230, 329, 371

Virtual Environments, 1–3, 9, 23, 26, 58, 80, 85, 266, 277, 278, 303, 304, 324, 332, 335
Virtual Heritage, 11
Virtual Human Society, 2
Virtual mannequins, 8, 13
Virtual Presenter, 1, 8, 9
Virtual Reality, 1, 12, 14, 15, 28, 42, 287,
Virtual Storytelling, 268, 286
Virtual Try-On, 84
Virtual Worlds, 2, 7, 18, 19, 24, 192, 193, 229, 261
Virtuality, 287–289, 299, 301
visco-elastic, 120, 125, 200, 204
visemes, 46, 50, 136, 232, 234, 238, 239, 240, 242, 243, 250, 259, 387, 388
visibility, 8, 24, 62, 103, 167, 223, 343, 344, 345, 366, 367, 370, 371, 372
Visible Human Database, 147
volume buffer, 167
volumetric textures, 161–163, 164, 166, 168, 176, 177
vortex, 170, 171
vorticity, 170
VRML, 32, 42, 135, 305, 314, 374

W

weave pattern, 364–366, 368, 369, 371
WIF format, 365, 366
wireframe, 17, 52
wisp, 163
wrinkle, 36, 120, 128, 129, 136, 137, 198, 201, 211, 220, 222–224, 358–362, 370

Y

Young modulus, 195–198, 209

Z

Z-buffer, 166, 167, 262, 345